# DEFYING HITLER

# DEFYING HITLER

THE GERMANS WHO RESISTED NAZI RULE

## GORDON THOMAS
## and GREG LEWIS

CALIBER

CALIBER

An imprint of Penguin Random House LLC
penguinrandomhouse.com

Copyright © 2019 by Gordon Thomas and Greg Lewis

LIBRARY OF CONGRESS CATALOGING-IN-PUBLICATION DATA
Names: Thomas, Gordon, 1933–2017 author. | Lewis, Greg, 1968– author.
Title: Defying Hitler : the Germans who resisted Nazi rule / Gordon Thomas
   and Greg Lewis.
Description: New York : Dutton, [2019] | Includes bibliographical references.
Identifiers: LCCN 2018021073 | ISBN 9780451489043 (hardcover) |
   ISBN 9780451489050 (ebook)
Subjects: LCSH: Anti-Nazi movement—Germany. | Germany—Politics and
   government—1933–1945.
Classification: LCC DD256.3 .T47 2019 | DDC 943.086—dc23
LC record available at https://lccn.loc.gov/2018021073

Printed in the United States of America
10   9   8   7   6   5   4   3   2   1

BOOK DESIGN BY TIFFANY ESTREICHER

*For all those who fight fascism*

*There are times when madness reigns*
*And then it is the best who hang.*

—ALBRECHT HAUSHOFER

# CONTENTS

# KEY PEOPLE

## THE HARNACK/SCHULZE-BOYSEN GROUP

**Arvid Harnack.** Senior official at the German Ministry of Economics who gave Nazi secrets to the Americans and the Russians.

**Mildred Fish-Harnack.** American-born academic who helped her husband, Arvid, create a major antifascist underground in Berlin.

**Harro Schulze-Boysen.** A Luftwaffe intelligence officer who was supported by Hermann Göring but was secretly spying on Nazi plans to invade the Soviet Union.

**Libertas Schulze-Boysen.** Used her society and film-industry connections to build up a file on Nazi atrocities on the Eastern Front.

**Greta Lorke.** A distinguished academic and friend of Mildred Fish-Harnack. Recruited writers, filmmakers, and poets to create poster campaigns against the regime.

**Adam Kuckhoff.** Greta's husband and a longtime political activist against the Nazis.

**John Sieg.** Michigan-born former journalist who worked on the German railways and helped unite working-class and academic resisters in Berlin.

## THE BAUM GROUP

**Herbert Baum.** An electrician by trade, he was an inspiring leader who planned acts of sabotage against the regime.

**Marianne Cohn.** Led the Baum group with her husband, Herbert, creating anti-Nazi propaganda that she spread across Germany.

**Heinz Birnbaum.** A devoted follower of Baum's, he used his work as a factory foreman to plan sabotage.

**Sala Kochmann (née Rosenbaum).** Funny and spirited, joined Cohn as one of the key female leaders of the Baum group.

**Martin Kochmann.** Baum's childhood friend who was forced to go on the run in Nazi Germany.

**Suzanne Wesse.** Catholic member of the Baum group who spoke a number of languages and recruited resisters among forced laborers.

**Charlotte Paech.** Nurse whose worked to help fellow Jews and members of the Baum group put her on a Gestapo wanted list.

## THE GERMAN MILITARY

**Hans Oster.** A senior figure in the Abwehr, Germany's military counter-intelligence department, whose hatred of the Nazis made him one of the regime's most consistent opponents.

**Hans von Dohnanyi.** A lawyer and Abwehr officer who created a file of Hitler's crimes and worked with Oster to rescue Jews.

**Admiral Wilhelm Canaris.** The Abwehr spy chief who played a dangerous game, appearing loyal to Hitler while allowing Oster to create an anti-Nazi clique inside the organization.

**Pastor Dietrich Bonhoeffer.** A leading German theologian, and Dohnanyi's brother-in-law, he was brought into the Abwehr as it sought to make peace with the Allies.

**General Ludwig Beck.** A former chief of staff of the German armed forces who would become a key member of the resistance.

**Major Friedrich Heinz.** An uncompromising officer who, having fallen out with the Nazis, agreed to Oster's suggestion that he assassinate Hitler.

**Josef Müller.** A broad-shouldered, cunning lawyer who became an Abwehr agent, relaying peace messages to the British via the Vatican.

**Colonel Henning von Tresckow.** Decorated for bravery during World War I, Tresckow loathed the Nazis and was a driving force behind wartime efforts to kill Hitler.

**Colonel Claus von Stauffenberg.** War hero and devoted Christian who volunteered to kill Hitler.

## THE STUDENTS

**Hans Scholl.** A medical student who served on the Russian Front. Turned against Nazism to form the White Rose resistance group in Munich.

**Sophie Scholl.** Inspired by her father's liberal ideas, Sophie supported her brother Hans's resistance and became a key figure in the White Rose.

**Alexander Schmorell.** Student and soldier who refused to swear the army's oath of allegiance to Hitler and joined with the Scholls' resistance.

**Christoph Probst.** Young father who hated Nazi crimes against Jews and the sick. Joined the White Rose.

**Willi Graf.** Devoted Catholic who was recruited to the White Rose by Probst. Had witnessed atrocities in Poland and the Soviet Union.

**Traute Lafrenz.** Encouraged her boyfriend, Hans Scholl, to organize resistance in Munich and then inspired a "northern" White Rose in her native Hamburg.

## THE LONERS

**Fritz Kolbe.** Unassuming diplomat who would become one of the United States' most efficient spies in the Third Reich.

**Kurt Gerstein.** SS officer ordered to supply concentration camps with poison gas, he became a key witness to the Holocaust.

**Georg Elser.** Cabinetmaker whose burning resentment of the Nazis led him to make an attempt on Hitler's life.

## NON-GERMANS

**William E. Dodd.** Chicago academic who became US ambassador to Germany. His support for those with antifascist sympathies brought him into conflict with the Nazis.

**Martha Dodd.** The ambassador's daughter, whose parties became a breeding ground for anti-Nazi sentiment. A close friend of Mildred Fish-Harnack.

**Donald Heath.** First secretary at the US embassy whose real task was to spy on Germany's economic capability. Arvid Harnack became his key agent.

**Allen Dulles.** Monitored the German resistance from Switzerland for the US Office of Strategic Services. Ran Fritz Kolbe as an agent and delivered his intelligence to the United States.

**Alexander Korotkov.** Bold Soviet agent who became a senior spy in Berlin—and obtained information about the Nazi invasion of Soviet Union.

## THE HUNTERS

**Walter Schellenberg.** Wily German spy chief whose rivalry with the Abwehr would have grave consequences for the resistance.

**Manfred Roeder.** Military prosecutor whose ruthlessness and cunning made him the ideal investigator to put in pursuit of "enemies of the state."

**Robert Mohr.** Experienced detective who joined the Gestapo in 1938 and led the hunt for the men and women of the White Rose.

**Franz Sonderegger.** SS officer and dogged detective who became convinced that the Abwehr was hiding an anti-Hitler conspiracy.

**Walter Huppenkothen.** Ruthless SS colonel who helped track down the July 20 bomb plotters, pursuing his victims right up to the war's end.

# BRIEF GLOSSARY

**Abwehr.** German military intelligence.

**ARPLAN (Arbeitsgemeinschaft zum Studium der sowjetischen Planwirtschaft).** Economic group set up by Arvid Harnack to study the Soviet Union.

**BDM (Bund Deutscher Mädel).** Nazis' League of German Girls organization.

**d.j.1.11.** A boys' club whose nonconformist nature attracted Hans Scholl.

**Gestapo (Geheime Staatspolizei).** Nazi Secret State Police.

**GRU.** Soviet military intelligence.

**HJ (Hitler Jugend).** Hitler Youth organization for boys.

**KJVD (Kommunistischer Jugendverband Deutschlands).** Communist Youth League of Germany.

**KPD (Kommunistische Partei Deutschlands).** German Communist Party, outlawed by the Nazis.

**NKVD.** Soviet secret police.

**OSS (Office of Strategic Services).** US intelligence department, forerunner of the CIA.

**RAD (Reichsarbeitsdienst).** Nazi National Labor Service.

**RKG (Reichskriegsgericht).** The Reich Court-Martial, the most senior military court in Germany.

**SA (Sturmabteilung).** Storm Detachment, the brownshirts, part of the Nazi Party's private army.

**SD (Sicherheitsdienst).** Security Service, the intelligence branch of the SS.

**Sonderkommission 20 Juli.** Unit created to track down members of the July 20 bomb plot.

**SS (Schutzstaffel).** Hitler's personal bodyguard, later developed into the Nazi Party's own army.

**T4.** Nazi program to terminate the lives of those with mental illness.

# DEFYING HITLER

# Introduction

O N THURSDAY, APRIL 20, 1939, the people of Berlin awoke to the sound of military units arriving for the grand birthday parade of the chancellor and Führer of the Greater German Reich, Adolf Hitler. The sounds and sights gladdened the hearts of many. Even the sun shone brightly, providing glorious "Führerwetter," as Joseph Goebbels, the propaganda minister, had dubbed it. A public holiday had been declared and the entire city urged to line the route leading to the review stand in Wilhelmstrasse and give a collective Sieg Heil salute as the Führer passed in his seven-liter black Mercedes.

Fifty thousand troops—one thousand for each birthday year—would march past the review stand, followed by columns of tanks, armored cars, and motorcycle sidecar units. The parade would take four hours to pass.

Swastikas were draped from balconies and windows, and shops and office buildings displayed photographs and busts of Hitler. Combined with a flood of propaganda and praise for the individual at the heart of the state, the message seemed clear. Germany was Hitler, and Hitler, Germany.

The strongman of Europe had annexed Austria, with the Anschluss bringing the country of his birth inside the new German Reich, and had executed his will to tear the Treaty of Versailles to shreds. Germany had rearmed and faced down Britain and France, two of the powers that had defeated it a generation before. At home, he had promised and shown a way out of the economic depression.

In the United States, shocked by Hitler's dominance, *Time* magazine made him its "Man of the Year" for 1938. "To those who watched the closing events of the year," it noted, "it seemed more than probable that the Man of 1938 may make 1939 a year to be remembered."

A defeated nation, a nation that had been made to feel ashamed for its part in the Great War, a nation trampled down by poverty and unemployment, was now for many a great nation again.

Some people, yes, were being put in concentration camps: Marxists and socialists who talked Germany down; Jews, who had been blamed for the war and for the economic collapse. But these were "defeatists," "the enemy within," the Nazi propaganda proclaimed. All "good" Germans, real Germans, must show their pride in the Fatherland, and that must mean supporting Hitler.

Didn't it?

HITLER'S BIRTHDAY APPEARED to be a day of double celebration for the tall, handsome Luftwaffe officer Harro Schulze-Boysen. As he watched the Heinkel bombers and Messerschmitt fighter aircraft cross the city skyline in tight formation, colleagues congratulated him on his promotion to lieutenant.[1] He had been told that he would soon be taking on a new role in the air force intelligence division, scanning foreign press reports and writing briefings for one of the most powerful figures in the Third Reich, Hermann Göring, who had come to see himself as something of a mentor to the young aristocrat.

But Schulze-Boysen was in fact a daring, sometimes reckless anti-Nazi. Aided by his wife, Libertas, he planned not only to reveal some of the regime's most heinous crimes, but also to turn over its military secrets to the enemy. As war consumed the world, he would become one of the most significant spies at the heart of the Reich.

ARVID HARNACK WATCHED the spectacle of the birthday parade from outside the Economics Ministry, where he worked. He had met Schulze-Boysen and, terrified by his bravado, had distanced himself from him. But soon their paths would cross again.

Serious and fiercely intelligent, Harnack was a highflier, one of the nation's greatest academic minds, who had studied in England and the United States. At the ministry, he was the perfect Nazi, working to ensure that Germany had the economic power Hitler would need to carry out his will—at home and abroad.

But in reality, Harnack was at the center of a growing opposition movement to Hitler, and was already sharing some of the Reich's most confidential secrets with both Washington and Moscow.

As he watched an SS man carrying a staff on which stood a gilded eagle clutching a swastika in its talons, he wondered what his wife, Mildred, would make of all this. She was American but loved Germany. She had recently visited England and Denmark, and seen what the foreign press was reporting about the Nazis. She despaired when young students she had taught at the University of Berlin told her that Hitler was saving Germany from the Jews.

That Thursday, busy passing Harnack's secrets to America's only spy in Germany, Mildred had not wanted to be anywhere near the parade.

Later, Harnack would tell her that the sheer length of time it took the troops to goose-step pass was a reminder of how Hitler appeared to be taking Germany and its people nearer to war.

AS A DISPLAY of military might, the parade was like nothing the foreign dignitaries and members of the international press had ever seen. But it obscured one thing: that there were people in the uniforms of the Third Reich who not only had plotted to overthrow Hitler but also hoped to assassinate him.

Lieutenant-Colonel Hans Oster, a talkative, open, and honest man who had served bravely in the Great War, despised Hitler and his "politicization" of all aspects of German society; among friends, he would insist on only referring to the Führer dismissively as "Emil." His senior role in German military counterintelligence, the Abwehr, allowed him to discover the real truth behind the torture of political dissidents, Jews, and religious figures, and of the concentration camps. Oster, a pastor's son, believed Hitler intended to drive Germany's Jews to destruction and felt a growing responsibility before God for their rescue.[2]

His friend Hans von Dohnanyi—a studious-looking man with dark hair swept to one side and thin metal-rimmed glasses—was collecting a Chronicle of Shame, a legal file of Hitler's crimes to be used in a prosecution of the Führer following a coup.

Oster was intent not only on resisting the Nazi regime, but also on removing Hitler. By that spring morning in 1939, he had already planned one coup and was now planning another. For Oster there would be no trial of Adolf Hitler. He planned to kill him.

DOHNANYI WAS A close friend of the Harnacks and brother-in-law to theologian Dietrich Bonhoeffer. Through such links the academic, military, civil service, and religious dissenters found themselves connected.

Pastor Bonhoeffer had spoken out against Hitler from the start and was now banned from speaking in Berlin. He had returned to Germany two days before Hitler's birthday, having been on a visit to England, and like many agonized over how to avoid compulsory military service in the war that he was certain was coming.

Back in Berlin, Dohnanyi told him more about the camps, detailed information that many outside of dedicated antifascist circles would struggle to obtain: Ex-prisoners were forbidden to speak of their experiences in the camps. Only some dared describe the ill-treatment they had seen: the rapes and murders, the starvation of prisoners. Dohnanyi, Oster, and Bonhoeffer had learned the truth, and it horrified them.

In London, Bonhoeffer had been with two churchmen—a Dutchman and an Englishman—who had both said they would help him in any way they could. Both hated the Nazis and had spoken out against the persecution of Jews.

Bonhoeffer knew that when war came he would need these friends abroad if he was to help find a way toward peace.

LIKE BONHOEFFER, KURT Gerstein had been repulsed by Hitler's creation of a German Reich Church: Christians loyal to the National Socialists, who encouraged youngsters away from church groups and into the Hitler Youth.

That Thursday he was shown an article by the "German Christians" that celebrated "with jubilation" the Führer's birthday. "In him God has given the German people a real miracle worker," the Nazi Christian publication declared.[3]

Gerstein's determination to expose the crimes of the Nazis would take him into the dark uniform of the Waffen-SS and the even darker heart of Hitler's Holocaust. It was a journey of such moral complexity that a human spirit would struggle to survive.

Many in their opposition to Hitler wished to bear witness in some fashion—Dohnanyi through his Chronicle of Shame, Libertas Schulze-Boysen in her record of atrocities in the East—but Gerstein's mission would lead him on a twisted path of complicity and collusion, which still shocks and confuses today.

DIPLOMAT FRITZ KOLBE read reports about the parade on cables from the Foreign Ministry. Sitting in his office at the German consulate in Cape Town,

Kolbe noted that many of his colleagues wished they were in Berlin to see it, and their Hitler salutes were delivered with a little more energy that day. Kolbe never returned the greeting, but his countrymen did not really challenge him. They saw him as a strange little man, obsessed with walking and chess, and knew he was going through a messy separation from his second wife.

Short, bald, and approaching forty, Kolbe wondered what part he might have in a coming war. If conflict came, he was certain South Africa would go with other members of the Commonwealth and side with Britain. Where would that leave him? In Berlin, with the Nazis he loathed?

As he worried about his future, he never imagined that within a few years he would become the United States' most successful spy in Germany.

A FEW MONTHS earlier, in order to mark his birthday, Hitler had opened the new Reich Chancellery, a huge building running from Wilhelmstrasse and along the length of Voss Strasse.

Behind its yellow stucco and gray stone front, its vast rooms included Hitler's study, with its thirty-foot-high ceiling, and a marble gallery that was twice the size of the famed Hall of Mirrors at Versailles. Visitors, boasted Hitler, would get a "taste of the power and grandeur of the German Reich!"[4]

Some four thousand workmen labored day and night for one year to complete the enormous project, and many wanted to find a place in the street nearby for the parade. Many of the factories in the city lay silent that day so workers and their families could enjoy the celebration. Those operated by Jewish workers stayed running.

Over the last few years Germany's Jews had been removed from various professions, forcing Jewish teachers, musicians, lawyers, and doctors to work in hard manual-labor jobs for the Reich: on road-making projects, as rubbish-disposal men, and in sewage plants. They were kept separate from Gentiles and had to survive on fewer rations.

But in areas like working-class Neukölln, Jews and Gentiles found common ground in their hatred of the Nazis. Many congregated around electrician Herbert Baum and his wife, Marianne, who were developing a flair for the dramatic, creating their own antifascist propaganda to counter that of Goebbels. They had already humiliated the "poison dwarf" once and planned to do so again.

The Baums and their Jewish friends intended to fight back.

\* \* \*

IT WAS NOT only Berlin that rang with the choreographed bluster of Hitler's birthday celebrations. Flags flew throughout the country, and the Nazi-controlled press recorded the day of deification in special editions.

As elsewhere, official buildings and many homes in the southern city of Ulm were bedecked with swastikas, garlands, and busts of the Führer. The city on the Danube was proud of its special place in German history, having been a final resting place for medieval German kings and emperors.

In a large second-floor apartment in Olgastrasse, across the rooftops from the steeple of Ulm Minster, lived the family of Robert and Magdalena Scholl. There were no flags flying from their windows that April day. Herr Scholl, who had turned forty-eight a week before Hitler's fiftieth, was a man of deep conviction and strongly held liberal beliefs. Fiercely independent-minded, he "translated" the Nazi propaganda on the radio for his family and told them war was coming. He had maintained his friendships with Jewish friends and associates in Ulm when others shunned them.

Scholl had brought up his five surviving children in his image. Hans, the elder boy, was the dominant character among them, but Sophie matched him in spirit. As they learned about the treatment of Jews across Germany, the words of one friend struck them deeply: "They are crucifying Christ a second time, as a people!"

For the Scholls, opposition to Hitler was a moral imperative, a simple question of right versus wrong. No matter what the consequences. In the horrors that Hitler would create in the coming years, the family would pay a terrible price for its desire for a better Germany.

AS THE DARK Mercedes passed through the crowds, the Führer stood with his right arm outstretched in salute. His face was as impassive to the people's adulation as it would later be to their suffering. His eyes remained fixed, the faces passing in a blur, featureless; he looked at them only as a single force by which he would achieve his ambitions.

Names did not matter in the compliant mass. The state need not concern itself with those who followed, or with that large proportion who granted it their passive consent. There were many who had not greeted Hitler's coming to power with jubilation but who had shrugged and said it would all just "blow over." When it did not, they found their nation had changed, but they went on with their lives and their work.

It was the individuals who did not conform who needed to be identified. Those who resisted, opposed, refused, and stood up to be counted in the darkest of times, even though they were painfully vulnerable in a state overrun by paranoia, fear, and terror. The ones who, in Dietrich Bonhoeffer's words, felt, "Silence in the face of evil is evil itself: God will not hold us guiltless. Not to speak is to speak. Not to act is to act." They could not be granted the anonymity of the crowd.

These were the men and women whom the state sought to identify, then to wipe from its memory.

Through the telling of the story of their lives, this book seeks to overturn a popular myth: that the German people followed Hitler as if as one mass, mesmerized like the children of Hamelin by the Pied Piper.

These are the ones who through a love of Germany committed treason against it, rejecting the shackles of a warped, corrupt, and evil state.

They stood up in the knowledge that almost all dissent would be punished by death.

They gave their lives with one thing foremost in their minds: that through their actions they might redeem the honor of their nation.

# 1

## Meetings in Madison

THE LITTLE GROUP huddled together, clapped their gloved hands, and pulled their winter hats down over their ears. Smoke rose from the fire where the pork chops sizzled. There was an argument about cooking them slowly, not allowing them to burn; then more laughter, which echoed along the frozen shore of Lake Mendota.

Some of the boys vied for the attention of the newcomer, a twenty-five-year-old with wispy blond hair and keen gray-green eyes. A little shy, she was exceptionally bright, dreamed of being a writer, and could argue long and hard her strong feminist ideals. Her name was Greta Lorke, and they were all a little fascinated with her; and having worked so hard to get to the United States, she was intrigued by them, too.

The daughter of a metalworker and a seamstress, Lorke had grown up in a tenement house in the eastern German industrial town of Frankfurt an der Oder, where her parents, Georg and Martha, rented out rooms to make ends meet. The couple made many sacrifices to ensure she had the best education, and she thanked them for the work ethic, Catholic conscience, and sense of justice that they had gifted her. An American friend had suggested she come to the United States, discover life in America, and extend her theories of economics. She had saved hard, and when she arrived in America, she was bowled over by it: Whereas German universities were staffed by stuffy, old-fashioned men, in Madison many of the academics were young and eager to treat students as equals. For Lorke, seeing a professor sit on the floor of their student house, sipping coffee and asking them their opinions on economic theory, was a dizzying revelation.

It was no surprise that, despite memories of the Great War, she had found a warm welcome in Madison, Wisconsin. Many students were from nearby Milwaukee, where three out of four people were of German descent, and there was a fascination with Europe, an interest in how it was healing after the battles of the previous decade. Lorke told her new friends that she had lived in Berlin and seen up close the horrors of poverty. While studying economics at the University of Berlin, she had worked in an orphanage in the working-class area of Neukölln. The children she worked with were disfigured by rickets, disease, and hunger. Seeing such poverty had a massive effect on Lorke. Lorke felt that the "old order" of not just Germany but most of Europe—the monarchs, aristocrats, and church leaders—had failed the people. That system did not work, and she looked for something that might replace it. It was 1927, and the world had readjusted after the war. It was time for the people to have their say.

The group stopped chatting to greet two new friends, who were skating on the frozen lake. Both were tall, and even though they wore bulky winter clothing, Lorke could see that they made a handsome couple. She recognized immediately the man's strong German accent, but it was the woman who interested her the most, and they quickly began to talk.

BORN IN 1902, three months before Lorke, Mildred Fish-Harnack had grown up close to a district of Milwaukee that housed the city's large German community. Although not of German extraction herself, she had always felt close to German culture. The youngest daughter of William and Georgina Fish, she did not have a particularly happy home life. Her parents were hopelessly mismatched. William tried and failed in business, preferred his horses and dog to his children, and was devoted to Wild West stories. Georgina was the family rock. A convert to Christian Science, she told her children never to be afraid and instilled in them a strong sense of confidence and a commitment to the truth. After the Fishes separated, William struggled to cope alone, and in 1918, he was found dead in a barn where he had been sleeping during a blizzard.

Georgina moved her family to Washington, where she took a job as a stenographer. Mildred spent her teenage years immersed in poetry and playing sports, at which she excelled. She dreamed of being a journalist and in 1921 enrolled at the university in Madison, where as well as studying she worked as a drama and film critic for the *Wisconsin State Journal* and joined a group of poets and radicals on the *Wisconsin Literary Magazine*. The magazine was satirical, liberal, and highbrow, and it sold on newsstands as far away as New York. Working for it made Mildred feel like a writer. After her graduation in 1925 she stayed on at the university to work as an English teacher. One day, a German student walked into her classroom by mistake and was bowled over by her poise and appearance. He felt an instant kinship. "I felt as if Mildred was a member of my family," he later recalled.[1]

The visitor's name was Arvid Harnack. A year older than Mildred, he was the eldest child of a family of theologians and history professors in Darmstadt, the capital of the Grand Duchy of Hesse. Like Mildred, Harnack was blond, blue-eyed, and tall. He was also hardworking, self-confident, and arrogant. Already a doctor of law with a fiercely bright brain for economic theory, he had arrived in Madison as a student paid for by the Rockefeller Foundation—a scholarship given to only four students in the whole of the United States.

Standing in Mildred's classroom, he apologized for his poor English and she for her German: They agreed to meet and practice each other's languages. Romance blossomed over canoe rides and picnics during which they talked about their love of poetry and literature, of Goethe and Whitman. In reflective moments they talked of their fathers. Like Mildred, Harnack had lost his father when he was a teenager. Otto Harnack, who suffered severe depression, had drowned himself in a river.

The couple's courtship was brief and intense, with Mildred aware that one day Harnack planned to return to Germany and work for the Ministry of Labor. Georgina Fish approved of Mildred's German boyfriend, and in August 1926, Mildred and Harnack were married. A free spirit, ahead of her time, she hyphenated her surname to Fish-Harnack.

GRETA LORKE HAD none of the self-confidence that Harnack's privileged background had instilled in him, and she was acutely conscious of their differences in "class," but she felt no such inhibition toward Mildred Fish-Harnack and a strong friendship quickly developed.

Energized by both women's interest in economics and progressive politics, Harnack introduced them to John R. Commons, a distinguished professor and renowned labor historian whose proposals became a rallying call for trade union leaders. Commons invited them all to be regulars at his exclusive weekly party at the campus, known as the "Friday Niters Club," where discussions took place on liberal ideas about social and economic policy. His invitation was an acknowledgment of the three students' intellectual standing. Commons and his students debated liberal and progressive ideas around state unemployment insurance, a minimum wage, and income tax, and many would go on to be key personnel in Franklin Roosevelt's New Deal administration.[2] Harnack said in the meetings that those who owned the means of production continued to make money during war, depression, or hyperinflation. Working people needed more power.

During Harnack's two and a half years in the United States, Commons became a mentor to the German, who wrote a study of the pre-Marxist working class in North America, which was later published in Germany.[3] Inspired by Commons, Harnack met and interviewed workers who had been imprisoned after a coal strike in Colorado.[4]

The open atmosphere at Commons's meetings was such that Lorke, the daughter of a metalworker, felt empowered to share her thoughts. She praised America but, noting the way white students separated themselves from black students, said that the United States also needed reform.

After the meetings, the three students would sit and read the German newspapers, which Harnack's family could afford to send to the United States, and they would discuss the future for Germany. They had not yet seen the Nazis coming, but the seeds of the Harnacks' and Lorke's opposition to Hitler were sown during those dreamy nights in Wisconsin.

IN SEPTEMBER 1928, when Arvid Harnack's fellowship in economics ended and he had to return home to Germany, his wife stayed on in the United States and taught at a women's college in Baltimore. But her intention was always to follow her husband, and the following summer she was able to take up an academic fellowship in Germany to study for a doctorate in American literature in Jena, a liberal-minded city in the hilly landscape of eastern Germany that had become a center for education and research. For Fish-Harnack, with her love of German literature and philosophy, it was the place where Schiller and Hegel had taught.

She had chosen Jena because it was where Harnack's family lived, and on arrival, Fish-Harnack was introduced to his mother, Clara, and his five siblings, including the youngest, Falk, who was then just sixteen. They all got on immediately, with Clara charmed by Fish-Harnack's knowledge of Greek and Goethe, and her always-improving German.

Mildred Fish-Harnack had married into German academic royalty. Harnack's paternal grandfather had been a professor and university rector, while his mother's father had been so distinguished in the field of agricultural chemistry that he had a university named after him. Clara Harnack, who was fluent in several languages, worked as an art teacher and had turned one of the four rooms in the family's apartment into a studio. She was a committed socialist and pacifist who cared little for what other people in her social class said about her. Otto—her late husband—had been a professor of literary history and aesthetics, who had written books on Goethe and Schiller. Arvid Harnack had been brought up in an environment that Greta Lorke later described as "kulturdurchtränkt"—saturated with culture—and that had only intensified after his father's death. Otto had been the youngest of four professorial brothers, and on his death, his oldest brother, Adolf, had taken on the role of mentoring Arvid and his siblings. They had moved to Berlin to be with him and found him to be a major and dominating influence. This influence would extend to many others in his sphere who would eventually oppose the Nazis.

Although soft-spoken and witty, Adolf von Harnack was a disciplined, exacting, and intellectually towering figure. He was also exceptionally well connected socially, being a regular guest at state dinners and court functions. He had been raised to nobility—symbolized by the "von" in his name—by Kaiser Wilhelm and was a pillar of the Bildungselite, that class of academics and civil servants that drew deep respect from the German people. A preeminent theologian—the Harnacks were Lutherans—and church historian, he was a professor and subsequently rector of the University of Berlin. He inspired Harnack and would do the same for his wife. When they met, he took her to his study and they discussed her career and her upcoming doctorate. When she confessed that she was a little anxious about the lectures in philosophy and economics she would be attending alongside her major studies in North American literature, he told her that difficulties are in the world so one might "overcome them." Within a few days Professor Harnack was introducing her to his powerful friends at the Kaiser Wilhelm Society and at an official dinner between the ministers for state and culture.

Although he was a pillar of the German establishment, Adolf von Harnack's influence would not necessarily be a conservative one, or one that inspired conformity or blind nationalism. He was very much his own man. He had been a key figure in the German pacifist movement during the Great War and had warned against an aggressive expansionist foreign policy. Despite being a prewar member of the Kaiser's inner circle, he had eventually turned against the monarch in favor of supporting the Weimar Republic. He had even helped draft the elements of the republic's constitution that dealt with the church and education. He believed scholars should intervene in politics, offering a guiding hand, and this philosophy permeated throughout his extended family, which included the Bonhoeffers and Delbrücks, who were also destined to become involved in the resistance to Hitler.

Adolf von Harnack's home on Kunz-Buntschuh-Strasse in the affluent western Berlin suburb of Grunewald, which includes the forest that gives it its name, was a place where Karl Bonhoeffer, the University of Berlin's leading psychiatrist and neurologist, and Hans Delbrück, Adolf's brother-in-law and a leading military historian, met and debated. They were free-thinking men, opposed to Germany's anti-Semitism, with a circle of friends that included Adolf Grimme, the Social Democratic minister of culture. Their children, including Arvid and Falk, Klaus and Dietrich Bonhoeffer, and Justus Delbrück, were all in awe of this older generation, and would be deeply influenced by it. It was influence of a kind that, during the coming years of fascism in Germany, would profoundly affect all of their lives.

GRETA LORKE ARRIVED back in Germany in October 1929, a few days before the Wall Street Crash sent its shock waves across the world and the German economy collapsed. Germany had relied heavily on American capital for its growth during the 1920s, and that money was now being withdrawn. Rampant inflation and mass unemployment led to poverty and hardship for millions. The German mark was destroyed and with it people's savings.

Taking a series of jobs in order to get by, Lorke set her heart on returning to a first love, the theater, which was thriving in Berlin as political and social ideals were explored by ambitious and radical dramatists such as Bertolt Brecht and Adam Kuckhoff at the Staatstheater. During the summer of 1930 she went to a drama festival in Hamburg and met Kuckhoff. A moody but attractive figure fifteen years Lorke's senior, Kuckhoff immediately pursued the younger, independent-minded woman. She, in turn, was attracted by his confidence and the sense of danger he emitted: Kuckhoff had only recently been sacked as editor of an influential political and cultural magazine, *Die Tat*, having been accused by the owner of taking it too far to the political left.

Kuckhoff and Lorke took a romantic boat trip around the harbor at Hamburg, from where she had caught the boat for America. He listened to her stories from Madison, took her to dinner and then to his bed in his hotel room. Only when she returned to Berlin did she discover he was married.

EVEN BEFORE THE Nazis had come to power, their influence among the student population was growing. In 1931, at Giessen, one of the places Mildred Fish-Harnack went to work for a semester, a third of the student body supported the Nazis. Germany's young people—raised against the ghastly backdrop of the Great War—knew they faced the darkness of unemployment and economic misery, and they were looking for somebody who could offer them hope. Foreshadowing what was to come, some students sought to oppose and attack members of the faculty who espoused leftist views.

Arvid Harnack joined a student group that took the opposite view and sought to promote socialism and pacifism in the young. Following in the footsteps of his American mentor, Commons, and his uncle Adolf, he created a discussion group that would meet weekly to discuss philosophy, economics, literature, and sociology. Harnack's leadership of such groups of thinkers would be given greater meaning when the Nazis grew stronger.

In 1930, Mildred Fish-Harnack won a fellowship to continue her studies and to teach English and American literature at the University of Berlin, whose faculty included Albert Einstein. As Lorke had discovered, the city was alive with culture and ideas, with thriving experimental theater productions, and museums and avant-garde galleries. It was, Harnack's cousin Klaus Bonhoeffer claimed, "perhaps intellectually the liveliest city in the world."[5] Despite the hardships faced by many, the middle classes still sought out the places to be seen: the Tiergarten; the old royal hunting park, which provided a setting for Sunday walks; and the restaurants and shops of Friedrichstrasse.

Fish-Harnack mixed mainly with Harnack's family and friends, but always slightly homesick, she also met friends among the American students at the Amerika-Institut, joined day trips and picnics organized by the American Student Association, and participated in forums held by the American Church. These attracted people from across the political spectrum in attempts to bridge gaps between sections of society. Forums might include pro-Nazi as well as pro-Communist speakers, or those from the business world or journalism. In her teaching, Fish-Harnack discussed with students the ideas of freedom and democracy in American literature, but on her journeys home the numbers of beggars and rough sleepers were growing, and the Harnacks heard stories about tent cities on the outskirts of Berlin. She wrote to her brother that "times are very bad here and growing continually worse."[6]

The Harnacks knew instinctively what the Nazis stood for. In October 1930, Fish-Harnack wrote to her mother about the "disturbing" rise in supporters for Hitler. "The group calls itself the National Socialists although it has nothing to do with socialism and the name itself is a lie," she said. "It thinks itself highly moral and like the Ku Klux Klan makes a campaign of hatred against the Jews."[7]

The Nationalsozialistische Deutsche Arbeiterpartei, NSDAP—the National Socialist German Workers' Party—had been formed in 1919, but for much of the 1920s it had been an insignificant party on the fringe of German politics. Quickly becoming known simply as the Nazi Party, it preached an extreme message of anti-Semitism and the superiority of the "Nordic Aryan race," called for the destruction of the Treaty of Versailles, and wanted the democratic Weimar Republic swept away in a social revolution. This message was a popular one: Versailles had imposed on Germany large war payments to Britain and France and the moral guilt of the sole responsibility for the war, and in many German minds, Versailles and Weimar were linked—the republic feeling something like the bastard child of the victorious Allies. The Nazis' paramilitary squads provided opportunities for disaffected soldiers and wayward youths to take their anger to the streets.

The cabinet of the Weimar government, led by Heinrich Brüning of the Center Party, was struggling to deal with the spiraling cost of the by-now six million unemployed and the collapse of the economy. People were terrified that the country might fall apart if someone did not take control: In 1931, there had been such financial panic that all of Germany's banks had closed for three weeks. It was a time when desperate people searched for a savior, someone with solutions to the terrible problems caused by the Great Depression.

For their answers, the Harnacks—like many other intellectuals—looked not to the Nazis but to the Soviet Union. From a distance—largely sealed off from the rest of Europe—Moscow appeared to have some of those answers, and the Harnacks were determined to find out more. Fish-Harnack's

German students were telling her that their families were struggling to afford food, and unemployment had quadrupled since the Wall Street Crash; Fish-Harnack believed that Russia was the "only country which tries to give all of her citizens work and food and to treat them equally."[8] She and Harnack discussed his doctoral work on the American working class, and wondered how a planned economy might help people in Germany. They had no feeling for Stalin, but were idealists, searching for hope.[9]

While Harnack was in Marburg, finishing postdoctoral research that would enable him to take up a university professorship, he met a history lecturer, Egmont Zechlin, who would become his close friend. Zechlin and Harnack agreed Germany's place lay somewhere between a capitalist West and a socialist East, with Harnack telling him he believed Germany could "partner" the Soviet Union in its Communist future.

In Berlin, Fish-Harnack set about studying Russian as well as American history, and going to the cinema to see films by Eisenstein and Dovzhenko. She discovered that the Soviet Union had taken a radical stance on women's issues, simplifying divorce, legalizing abortion, and legislating for equal rights and equal pay for women. One of her students was arrested for leading a Communist demonstration and was expelled from the university. Desperate and starving, he took his own life. When she witnessed a fight between a group of Nazis and a starving crowd shouting Communist slogans, she was horrified to see the police weigh in on the fascist side. She walked home with the jobless workers' cries of "Do not shoot, policemen, we are your brothers!" ringing in her ears. Mildred told friends she was worried for the young who saw no future ahead of them.

The Harnacks had concerns about their own futures, too. Mildred was not paid a salary by the university, instead receiving money for each of the students she attracted to her classes, and the European bonds into which they had plowed their savings from their lives in America were no longer paying interest due to the Depression. In addition, Harnack feared that a rising number of unemployed graduates would make it harder for him to obtain university work, especially outside Berlin. He decided to move back to the capital and seek work as a lawyer.

In the fall of 1931 Harnack returned to Berlin, and the couple moved into a small home in a new brightly colored housing estate in the suburb of Zehlendorf. Here they jogged in the nearby pine forest before breakfast, discussing economics and philosophy and Harnack's new plan to bring together a group of writers and scholars to report on Soviet economic planning. Always committed and dedicated to his work, he quickly set up the group, which became known as ARPLAN (Arbeitsgemeinschaft zum Studium der sowjetischen Planwirtschaft). It met once a month, and felt similar to Commons's meetings back in Wisconsin. At the first meeting in January 1932 were University of Berlin professor Adolf Grabowski, a former member of the Reichstag; economist Richard Oehring, who had spent time in the Soviet Union; Sergei Bessonov, an economist assigned to the Russian trade mission; and Alexander Hirschfeld, the first secretary in the Soviet embassy.

At the time, Russian and German industry were working in harmony, with weapons being manufactured for Germany in Kharkov and Moscow to help Germany circumnavigate the arms restriction placed on it by the Treaty of Versailles. Many German workers were employed in the Russian factories. But despite this cooperation, a spirit of suspicion and competitiveness still existed between the two nations. Stalin wanted to know more about the technological advances in the German chemical, iron, steel, electrical, and aviation industries, and much of that demand for information fell on the trade mission in Berlin to which Sergei Bessonov belonged. The Soviets saw organizations like ARPLAN as an opportunity to recruit economists, engineers, and scientists who either wanted to go to Russia to work or would provide Moscow with Germany's technical secrets. Bessonov, one of Russia's leading economists, had been charged with looking out for suitable candidates. Highly educated, cultured, and a good conversationalist, he was to become good friends with Arvid Harnack.

In May 1932, Mildred lost her job. The university was in financial difficulty, and there was growing prejudice against foreign and female workers as so many German men were out of work. Her students organized a petition calling on the university to keep her on, but Mildred had angered the new head of the American department, who was an ardent Nazi, and he enthusiastically oversaw her departure.

The couple's neighbors in Zehlendorf, too, were now keen supporters of the growing Nazi movement, and they were sometimes quick with comments about the American leftist in their midst. So that summer the Harnacks decided to move, finding rooms in a partitioned apartment on Hasenheide, on the edge of the working-class district of Neukölln, where Lorke had worked while a student. Though the space was small, the couple had room for their books and a desk each. From where she sat reading, Fish-Harnack could look out over a view of steep green roofs and wide avenues. They made time to walk together, passing the white stone beauty of the steeple of the St. Johannes Basilika in a nearby square and strolling along the bank of the River Spree.

But while they wrote, read, and studied, they were also aware of the situation worsening around them. They saw a rally of starving workers trail past the former Kaiser's palace, the marchers begging for a change in the country's economy, and Mildred wrote home to claim the unrest was turning into a "casual civil war." But despite the chaos on the streets and in the government, the Harnacks were still convinced that the Germans would not turn to Hitler. The Nazis were opportunists, Harnack felt, exploiting the difficult times of the moment but offering no long-term solution. Sergei Bessonov, of the Russian trade mission, suggested that Harnack and more than twenty other members of his ARPLAN group take a look at what was happening in Russia, and in August 1932 the group paid 500 marks a head to make the trip. For economists, the opportunity to work out why the Soviet Union appeared to be the only major world nation that was not suffering a depression was too good to miss.

Soviet economic success, though, was a facade, enabled by tight restrictions on the domestic press and on foreign correspondents. At the time the ARPLAN group traveled through Ukraine to Kharkov, a terrible famine was killing the peasantry of the area. Throughout the 1920s the Soviet government had organized a system by which grain would be requisitioned by the state and distributed throughout urban areas. When demand increased and low rainfall affected three annual harvests in a row, the rural grain-producing areas of Ukraine and the Kuban area of southern Russia were left with insufficient reserves to sustain themselves. Between four and a half million and six million people were starving to death.[10]

The ARPLAN group saw the crowds of peasants at the railway stations as they passed through but naively wondered if this abject poverty was a legacy of the past, the cruel tsarist Russia that Stalin was trying to transform. Their guides were not going to inform them that the hungry and weary crowds were actually a terrible consequence of the five-year plans they admired so much. Mildred Fish-Harnack, who could not travel with the group, instead made her own visit to Leningrad and Moscow, where she spoke to women workers and found that their rights had been improved, as she had been told. However, she saw that Russia was a land whose "cultural level" was far below the United States and Europe, and felt that while "immense improvement has taken place since 1917, there is very much more still to be done."[11]

But neither of the Harnacks were disillusioned by their trip. Arvid Harnack returned to his desk in Hasenheide to work day and night on a report detailing what the ARPLAN members had seen, and gave a series of talks on Marxism, sometimes at their home but often in a restaurant near the Alexanderplatz, the bustling railway station around which many beggars in rags now sat and appealed for a few coins. The talks soon developed into a handbook on the Soviet Union, its cultural and political makeup and its system of state planning. With both a doctorate in law from the University of Hamburg and a scholarship from the London School of Economics, Harnack had clear ideas of his own about the way governments should run their economies, and having lived through the stock market crash, he had seen that there were problems with the capitalist system.

Fish-Harnack returned to Berlin full of renewed hope and excited to be taking up a new job at a night school for adults that had been set up in 1927 to offer affordable classes for people from all economic backgrounds. Mildred was the only woman on the staff of the Berlin Abendgymnasium (BAG), but she enjoyed the company of her fellow teachers and the pupils. She saw in the adult learners a desire not only to better themselves but to help Germany, too. Her students enjoyed the novelty of being taught by an American, and enthusiastically tried to join her when she broke into "Oh My Darling, Clementine" and "John Brown's Body." She was keen to remove any barriers between teacher and student, socializing with them after class and taking walks with them in the Tiergarten. Mildred wrote home to tell her mother she had the work that she wanted and "glorious prospects."

But the Harnacks had failed to see that a rise in support for the German Communist Party had helped drive nationalists and conservatives into the arms of the Nazis. The day after Mildred wrote home to say, "Life is good," President Paul von Hindenburg appointed Adolf Hitler the new chancellor of Germany.

# 2

## Enemies of the People

ITLER IS REICH Chancellor," noted Joseph Goebbels, in his diary. "Just like a fairytale."[1] As fairy tales went, it would be a dark one. But Goebbels, always one to recognize his own importance, could see that his expertise as head of the party's propaganda unit and election campaign chief had played a significant role in helping to drag the Nazis from the political fringes.

Less than five years earlier, in elections for the Reichstag, the Nazis had won just twelve seats, polling only 2.6 percent of the vote.[2] The Communists had won fifty-four seats. In the elections of 1930, with consensus government feeling the heat of economic collapse, the number of Communists in the Reichstag rose to seventy-seven, but Nazi support had grown even faster, securing them 107 members of the new parliament. Hitler had attracted more than six million votes, and his popularity was rising. The Great Depression was moving people to the extremes of politics, and the old conservative and industrial class saw him as the only challenger to the Communists, who threatened their wealth and power. Hitler played on their fears. He courted bankers, businessmen, and politicians, telling them he alone could stop the rise of the German left.

In the presidential election of March 1932, Hitler stood for president against the Communist Ernst Thälmann, army officer Theodor Duesterberg, and the incumbent, Paul von Hindenburg. He received 30 percent of the votes, but there was no outright winner. In a second election, held a month later, Hindenburg recovered his support to win 53 percent—more than nineteen million votes. Hitler got more than thirteen million, and Thälmann had been well beaten into third. There were rumors that the Nazis had planned a coup if Hitler received the most votes, and in response, for a short time, two of its organizations were banned: the brown-shirted Sturmabteilung (SA), which had been the paramilitary wing of the party since 1921, and the at-this-time much smaller Schutz-staffel (SS), an elite group of Aryan-blooded bodyguards for Hitler. Both the SA and SS had been at the center of many street fights and violent assaults.

On May 29, 1932, Hindenburg—with the support of Hitler—asked for Brüning to resign as chancellor. He was replaced by Franz von Papen, and a new election was set for July. Street violence over the next few weeks reached new levels, with more than one hundred left dead. When the people went to the polls, the Nazis received nearly fourteen million votes—37 percent of all the votes cast. It was now, for the first time, the largest party in the Reichstag, although it did not have outright power. Papen refused to hand over the chancellorship to Hitler, the Reichstag was again dissolved, and a new election was called for November.

But the new election did nothing to break the political stalemate. In fact, the Nazis' vote went down by two million and the Communists did well. Hindenburg sacked Papen and appointed his adviser, General Kurt von Schleicher, as chancellor. Keen to cement his own power and to defeat any forces of the left, Schleicher told Hitler he would support him in return for a place in his cabinet. Schleicher himself had little support in the Reichstag. Papen met Hitler in secret on January 4, 1933, to discuss the formation of a broad nationalist coalition government. Papen promised the support of wealthy businessmen and industrialists in return for positions of power for his friends. They agreed to exclude Jews, Communists, and Social Democrats from politics. Hitler would be chancellor. Hindenburg agreed to the plan, and Schleicher resigned as chancellor on January 27. On January 30, 1933, Adolf Hitler became the chancellor of Germany.

By seven o'clock that evening—to complete his fairy tale—Goebbels improvised a torchlight procession of SS and SA men through the center of Berlin, with a stirring commentary broadcast over the radio. The march lasted until after midnight, with Goebbels excitedly claiming that a million men had taken part. The British military attaché claimed it was as few as 15,000.[3]

Arvid Harnack watched the march from outside the chancellery and caught a glimpse of Hitler as he leaned forward to acknowledge the adoration of the crowd. Harnack later told friends, "This is not a comedy that is being prepared but a great tragedy, not only for Germany but also for mankind."[4] Mildred Fish-Harnack told a Jewish colleague, who planned to leave Germany soon after, that people had to decide what they would do now that Hitler was in power. Her friend knew from the start that Mildred intended to resist the Nazis. But how?

GRETA LORKE HAD tried to escape the agonies of an affair with a married man, taking a job teaching English to the children of a lawyer friend in Switzerland and later traveling to England.

But Adam Kuckhoff did not forget her, and sitting on the steps of the British Museum, she read not only the international newspapers with the latest news from Germany but also Kuckhoff's insistent and pleading letters urging her to join him in Berlin. "It is because I love you that I cannot give up having you at my side in the political struggle," he told her.[5] Wanting to be near him and to be with Germany at a time of need, she returned home and, now thirty, enrolled in a course of study for a sociology doctorate in Berlin. Meeting up with Kuckhoff again, she also became close to his circle of friends, radical writers and playwrights who challenged the status quo and were sure to come into conflict with the Nazis.

Chief among this group were John Sieg and Günther Weisenborn. Michigan-born John Sieg was the son of a German Catholic family that had immigrated to Detroit, where he had been born in 1903. After the death of his father in 1912, Sieg moved to Germany and lived with his grandfather and became a German citizen in 1920. Keen to become a journalist—and working under the name Johann—he started writing for Adam Kuckhoff's political and literary monthly, *Die Tat*, and later for the prestigious liberal daily *Berliner Tageblatt* and the arts section of the German Communist Party newspaper, *Die Rote Fahne*, the largest of the fifty Communist newspapers in pre-Hitler Germany. A committed Communist, like many Germans on the left, he traced his political ideology to Marx but was suspicious of Stalin. Blond, energetic, and handsome, Sieg was married to a Polish secretary named Sophie Wloszczynski, who was small like him and blessed with a sharp mind. Like the Harnacks, and Kuckhoff and Lorke, the Siegs would put their fight against Hitler at the heart of their lives together.

Weisenborn had already had a major theatrical hit. *U-Boat S-4*, which told the imagined tale of six American sailors trapped in a submarine off the coast of New Jersey, had been loved by audiences but hated by the Nazis and the nationalist press, which attacked it as pacifist propaganda. A smiling young man with a toothy grin and a nose for mischief, Weisenborn was a friend of Brecht's. But unlike Brecht, who was already planning to leave Germany, Weisenborn had opted to stay and confront the Nazis head-on.

On March 16, he premiered a new play at the Künstler Theater in Rank-estrasse, *Warum lacht Frau Balsam?* (*Why Is Mrs. Balsam Laughing?*), which was written with the Berlin dadaist Richard Hülsenbeck. Halfway through the performance a group of SS men stormed the stage, demanding to see the authors. The play was closed down immediately.

As Nazi power increased, Greta Lorke's new friends would be danger-ous to know.

ALTHOUGH CHANCELLOR OF Germany, Hitler was still without a majority in the Reichstag. Calling fresh elections for March 5, he worked on a plan to finally defeat the Communists.

The Reichstag building, in which all this political wrangling had taken place, had been built at a cost of 87 million gold marks almost thirty years earlier. Constructed of sandstone blocks, with tall towers on each corner and a glass dome in its center, it was unpopular with Berliners, who called it the "biggest round cheese in Europe."[6] On the evening of February 27, a man was seen on one of the building's balconies carrying a burning torch. As he went from room to room, lighting fires, the police and fire brigade were called, and the arsonist—clad in only shoes and trousers despite the icy-cold evening—was apprehended as he came out of the building. His papers identified him as a Dutch Communist named Marinus van der Lubbe, and with a deranged look he told police he was acting alone, but the rumor swirled around the city that the Nazis had used van der Lubbe in a plan to discredit the Communists.

Sefton Delmer, of the *Daily Express*, was on hand when Hitler arrived to see the Reichstag burning, and his article for his readers back in England left them in no doubt about what had happened. "More probably, the fire was started by the Nazis, who used the incident as a pretext to outlaw po-litical opposition and impose dictatorship," he wrote.[7] The fire certainly played perfectly into the Nazis' hands.[8] On seeing the smoke-filled lobby to the building, Hitler stated: "This is a God-given signal! If this fire, as I be-lieve, turns out to be the handiwork of Communists then there is nothing that shall stop us now crushing out this murderous pest with an iron fist."

Hitler then turned to Delmer, who was following him through the build-ing: "You are witnessing the beginning of a great new epoch in German history," he stated. "This fire is the beginning."[9]

Against a backdrop of the ashes of the oak-paneled rooms and the bro-ken glass of the dome, the Nazis began a violent campaign against all po-litical opposition. By July, at least eleven thousand members of the KPD—the German Communist Party—had been arrested, beaten, or killed. The SA and SS attacked Social Democratic members of the Reichstag, too. Göring told the press that the Communists planned political assassinations, at-tacks on other public buildings, and the murder of the families of public figures—although he produced no evidence of these plots.[10] Hitler told a cabinet meeting the day after the fire that the "psychologically correct mo-ment for the showdown" with the KPD had come and that they should not be hindered by "judicial considerations."[11] In these acts of terror, the Nazis were protected by Hindenburg's decision to invoke an emergency article of the constitution that ended the Weimar Republic's guarantee of civil liber-ties, allowed for imprisonment without trial, and severely restricted the right of assembly. The dangers of having any connection at all with Com-munism had now greatly increased.

As a member of the KPD, John Sieg was among the first rounded up and taken to the Sicherheitsdienst (SD) detention center at Hede-mannstrasse, where, after having his fingers broken, he was made to strip naked and run a gauntlet of whips. Some died under the onslaught, but Sieg survived and was moved to Plötzensee prison, where the cells would become the place of nightmares for so many resisters. Sieg was released in June because Theodor Haubach, a former colleague on *Die Rote Fahne*, had excellent police contacts and made the files on the newspaper's staff mem-bers disappear. On his release an SA group leader who admired Sieg's writ-ing asked him to work for the Nazi press, but he refused. His commitment to the anti-Nazi cause was solid, but it left him unemployed and unemploy-able. He and Sophie got by on her wage from her job as a secretary to a Jewish lawyer.

Another friend of Kuckhoff's and Lorke's was the actor Hans Otto, who was also Kuckhoff's brother-in-law and a favorite actor of Brecht's. He feared for his many Jewish friends in the theater world and was shocked to see political prisoners being crammed onto a train by the Nazis. Through-out the summer of 1933 he worked to create networks of survivors of the crackdown on left-wing activists. He reasoned that for the opposition to Hitler to remain a coherent force it would need some sort of organization, which could be turned into an effective network when the arrests and beatings died down.

On November 13, 1933, he met with his friend and fellow actor Gerhard Hinze at a café near the Tiergarten. But the SA had been tipped off. The actors were dragged into a truck and taken to a restaurant outside of the city. There, as dance music played in the background, they were flogged, beaten, and kicked in the stomach as their tormentors demanded to know the names of their underground circle. They said nothing, and by the time they were delivered to the Gestapo, Otto's face was so swollen he could not speak. Hinze survived, but thirty-three-year-old Otto died in custody and his body was thrown into the street. His wife was told he committed suicide and discouraged from asking questions.

Many in the theater world were afraid to attend his funeral, although Adam Kuckhoff made sure he was there.

As the mourners lowered the actor's battered body into his grave, Gestapo agents stood menacingly nearby, the collars of their long coats up. Even at this very early stage of Nazi reign, its opponents knew all too well where dissent would take them.

DESPITE THE INTIMIDATION and the arrests of opposition politicians and activists, the continuing street violence, and the fact that in some polling stations SA men tried to intimidate voters as they marked their ballot papers, the Nazis again failed to win an absolute majority in the March 1933 elections—polling just over 43 percent nationally. Hitler only achieved power with the support of the nationalist and anti-Weimar Deutschnationale Volkspartei, the DNVP. Communist deputies, who had gained almost five million votes, were barred from the Reichstag.

A few weeks later, broadening his support to include the Center Party—of which Papen, his vice-chancellor, was a leading member—Hitler rushed through the Enabling Act. This granted Hitler four years of power as a dictator and allowed the government to alter the constitution as it saw fit. The Communists had again been barred, and only the Social Democratic deputies, in the face of much harassment, voted against the act.

The Weimar constitution was dead. Hitler, at forty-four, had seized power from under the noses of the German people, and his vision for the Nazis could now become a reality for the whole of Germany.

The very darkest elements of that vision were already being enacted. About a fortnight after the March 1933 election, Heinrich Himmler, who had been elected to the Reichstag in 1930, announced that a special camp had been set up to house political prisoners. Situated in Bavaria, twelve miles northwest of Munich on the Amper River, it would be called Dachau.

Two other camps were also to be created that year, in different parts of the country: Buchenwald in central Germany and Sachsenhausen in the north. These would form the nucleus of Nazi Germany's concentration camp system.

ON MAY 10, 1933, encouraged by the new propaganda minister, Goebbels, groups of people stormed libraries and bookshops and seized works by Jews, Communists, and other writers whom the Nazis considered unacceptable. The books were piled high in the street and burned, as supporters of the destruction gave the Nazi salute. Among the first books in the flames were works by the nineteenth-century poet Heinrich Heine, who had written: "That was only a prelude: Where books are burnt, in the end people are also burnt."[12] Bertolt Brecht's works burned, as did those of Günther Weisenborn.

The book-burning dramatically demonstrated to the Harnacks how writing and ideas were now considered a danger to the Nazi state. They knew that if these ideas were deemed against the state, then the people who expressed them must be, too. The way that many university faculties gave in to the outrage suggested a wider capitulation of much of the German intellectual class. Fish-Harnack was dumbfounded by the fact that many of her former university colleagues had supported the book-burning, which had been led by the National Socialist German Student Association. And now the adult education school at which Mildred worked, the BAG, came under fire. Large numbers of staff were dismissed, and a special cell of the Nazi student association was brought in to oversee the students' education. The ideals of the liberal-minded founders of the school were wiped out. Ideological pressure to conform increased across society, but in particular on teachers and civil servants, who were encouraged to join the Nazi Party, and huge numbers did. By May 1933 the party had two and a half million members, 1.6 million of whom had joined since Hitler became chancellor. "Opportunism intermingled with genuine idealism," as one historian has put it.[13]

In conversations with his cousin Klaus Bonhoeffer, a leading lawyer, Harnack discussed the way in which the Nazis were creating their own judicial system inside the existing state: Special Courts, which dealt exclusively with political crimes, and the People's Court for allegations of treason. Even as tyrants, they would present a facade of justice. But those accused of crimes against the state would have no defense or character witnesses, there would be no press scrutiny of proceedings or a public gallery, and even the defense lawyers were jaundiced and prejudiced against those they purported to represent. Trials in which the punishment was death could be heard in less than a day.

After the Reichstag fire the Nazis brought in a law that allowed "enemies of the people" to be held in protective custody (Schutzhaft) without a charge being brought. In coming months the definition of who constituted an "enemy" was expanded to include not only all political opponents but also religious dissidents and Jews. People in the industrial working class were particular targets, with many cases being brought for criticisms of the economic and social policies of the regime.[14]

To support Schutzhaft, laws were introduced that saw the creation of a nationwide political police force, the Geheime Staatspolizei, or Gestapo, which officially came into being two months after the Reichstag fire. As head of the Gestapo, Himmler answered to Hitler alone.[15] His officers developed a centralized card-index system that allowed them to create an entry for every individual arrested. The most dangerous individuals were categorized A1, and a red mark was added to their card. These were the "enemies of the state." The A2s were marked with blue and were to be arrested in the event of a war. The A3s were a large and varied group who were deemed "politically dangerous." Special departments would deal with religious bodies, Freemasons, and Jews. The Gestapo relied on a network of informants to create a myth of omnipresence: Anyone speaking out against the regime faced denunciation from neighbors, friends, even family. All kinds of what might have been considered everyday activities—from telling anti-Nazi jokes or criticizing the government over a drink, to listening to foreign radio stations—had been declared criminal offenses. Those who had a score to settle could easily drop a note at a Gestapo office.

As the Nazis imprisoned and tortured their political enemies, the Harnacks wondered if it was time to take stock, to take a step back into the shadows. Perhaps, even, to appear compliant. Arvid Harnack disbanded ARPLAN and burned its membership lists. His book on the Soviet Union, which was ready to go to press, was abandoned and the printing plates destroyed. He gave up on returning to academia and managed to get a job as a lawyer for Lufthansa, thanks to Klaus Bonhoeffer, who was in charge of the company's legal department. During the evening he prepared for civil service examinations.

Mildred Fish-Harnack took the first step at the BAG. Intent on keeping her job and her influence as a bulwark to Nazism at the school, she joined the National Socialist teachers organization. She also, after much deliberation, took the distasteful step of agreeing to sign off her official letters with "Heil Hitler," as was now expected. This bought her time, and her social activities continued. Mildred was secretary of the city chapter of the Daughters of the American Revolution, treasurer of the American Church, and a leading member of Berlin's American Women's Club. To her and Arvid Harnack, America seemed to be the great hope now. Inspired by Franklin D. Roosevelt and the New Deal and by their memories of the hopes and dreams shared with Commons in Wisconsin, they wondered how they could reach out to the United States and encourage its people to take an interest in what was happening in Germany.

Then a train chugging into Lehrter Bahnhof in central Berlin seemed to bring with it new hope.

# 3

# The American Embassy

IT HAD BEEN an uncomfortably warm June day when the call had come through to William E. Dodd's office. The ringing had broken his concentration, and as he reached forward a little grumpily, the material of his shirt—damp with sweat—peeled away from the back of his leather chair.

Dodd was sixty-four, trim, and a little below average height. His blue-gray eyes and serious expression hid a dry, lively wit. Although he was busy with his duties as head of the history department at the University of Chicago, he wanted to devote his time to completing the first book in a planned four-volume history of the Old South. But he had been a keen supporter of Roosevelt during his presidential campaign and had written to him a number of times since he had taken office with advice on diplomatic and economic matters, so he knew the voice on the other end of the line immediately.

After brief pleasantries the president said: "I want to know if you will render the government a distinct service. I want you to go to Germany as ambassador. I want an American liberal in Germany as a standing example."[1]

The German-speaking academic, who had earned his PhD at the University of Leipzig at the turn of the century, thanked the president for the offer and asked for time to think it over.[2] Roosevelt said, "Of course," but gave him only two hours. After discussion with his wife, Mattie, Dodd agreed to take the position, imagining there would be ample time at the Berlin embassy to devote to writing. The couple then persuaded their son, Bill, a twenty-eight-year-old history teacher, and daughter, Martha, a college dropout and now assistant literary editor of the *Chicago Tribune*, to come with them. The challenges of Germany would be great, but living there would be exciting, Dodd told them.

By the time they stepped down onto the busy platform at the Lehrter

Bahnhof on July 13, 1933, they were exhausted. On arrival at Hamburg earlier that day, they had had an argument with customs over the paperwork for the family Chevrolet, and Dodd had been lectured by an embassy official all the way down the track about how to be a diplomat in the new Germany. Mattie and Martha had escaped to the peace of a neighboring carriage, surrounded by their cases and the flowers given to them at the Hamburg docks. Bill had sorted out the papers for the car and was driving it to Berlin. The family was about to undergo quite a culture shock: from a quiet home in Chicago to the heart of a brutal, corrupt, and cruel totalitarian state. They would never recover.

Mildred Fish-Harnack had been chosen by the American Women's Club to go to the station to meet the new ambassador. Eager to find out what sort of man he was, she watched him step down from the train and sized him up. After polite greetings, she realized that they would get on well, but it was with his daughter that she knew a close friendship would blossom. Blonde, blue-eyed, always smiling, Martha was twenty-four—six years younger than Mildred—and full of life. They quickly chatted about shared interests, discussing favorite books and authors and their own love of writing. "It's a hindrance to be lonely and isolated in one's work," Mildred said. "Ideas stimulate ideas, and the love of writing is contagious." Martha, she sensed, had a real desire to understand the world. "Therefore our interests touch." Martha Dodd, for her own part, was drawn to Mildred immediately. "She was slow to speak and express opinions; she listened quietly, her large gray blue eyes serious . . . weighing, evaluating, trying to understand."[3] Very soon the pair were editing a book column in an English-language newspaper together, and Mildred was advising Martha on the short stories she was writing.

Martha was flirtatious and charming, with a driving need to have the same attention from everyone that she got from her doting father. She set about conquering Berlin. She and her brother quickly found themselves at the center of a hard-drinking group of young people who loved to party, dance, and talk. The American embassy at Tiergartenstrasse 27a became an important hub for discussion about life in Germany.[4] Mildred talked about the new ambassador with Harnack, who was delighted to know that Dodd was such a keen supporter of Roosevelt. He was also flattered to learn that Professor Dodd knew the distinguished Harnack name and liked to be in the company of respected academics. Dodd was delighted when Mildred offered to help him type up his manuscript on the Old South, and he invited the American Women's Club to hold events at the embassy. The women's club and its links with the embassy now helped the American expatriates stay in better touch with their own culture as the society in Germany hardened.

Fish-Harnack carefully briefed Dodd on the Nazis' control of the German cultural life. The dead hand of censorship, after a temporary absence during the twenties, was back, and its grip on Berlin tighter than anything known under the Kaiser. With the departure of so many stage and movie directors, writers, and actors to the United States and England, the Berlin theater lost its edge and its audience. The greatest theatrical success was *Krach um Jolanthe*, a barnyard farce in which the heroine is a sow. Hitler, who had seen the production several times, called it "epoch-making," and the film version was given an award for its "outstandingly cultural" contribution.[5] But if the daring and vigor of pre-Nazi cinema and theater had been stifled, the public would not read about it in the press. Nazi control of newspapers was rigorous. In 1928 Berlin had 147 independent daily and weekly newspapers. By the spring of 1933, it had none.[6] Many of the journalists and writers who spoke out disappeared into concentration camps.

AT FIRST, MANY pillars of the Nazi establishment were drawn to the American embassy, keen to be seen at some of the most exclusive parties in town and to meet the ambassador's daughter, the "femme fatale" who had quickly become a talking point in society circles. Intoxicated by what she saw as the power and glamour of the Nazi hierarchy, Martha Dodd began a series of friendships and affairs that angered many at the embassy. Her dance with Fritz von Papen Jr., the vice-chancellor's son, at an embassy ball made the newspapers. Great War flying ace Ernst Udet took her for a flight in his private plane, a prelude to a brief love affair, while Reichsmarschall Hermann Göring invited her falcon-hunting on his country estate.

Then, most ominously, she met and began an affair with a brutal Gestapo chief named Rudolf Diels, a man with a face with deep dueling scars and an air of malevolence that "created a nervousness and tension that no other man possibly could, even when people did not know his identity."[7] Despite being feared by most and dubbed the "Prince of Darkness," Diels proved deeply attractive to many women and enthusiastically wooed Dodd. Their lovers' trysts and walks through the Tiergarten were a source of embarrassment to her father, but they were also eventually to open her eyes to the true nature of the Nazi state. Perhaps to impress his new American girlfriend, Diels told her about his world of tapped telephones and secret surveillance. "There began to appear before my romantic eyes . . . a vast and complicated network of espionage, terror, sadism and hate, from which no-one, official or private, could escape," she said.[8] Her friend Sylvia Crane remarked: "Martha was not a political theoretician . . . She just liked sleeping with attractive men, and that's how she learned about politics and history."[9]

The failed relationship with Diels—and a tour through a country town in which she witnessed a family of Jews assaulted in the street—brought her in line with her father's gathering thoughts on the Nazis. Dodd had wasted no time in realizing that the Germany he had known and loved as a young man had changed. Only two weeks after he had arrived, he had confided to his diary his anger at the Nazis' attitude to the Jews: "Such treatment can only bring evil to the government which practises such terrible cruelty."[10] Hoping to find at least "some decent people around Hitler," he had quickly become disillusioned. "It is so humiliating to me to shake hands with known and confessed murderers," he wrote, and knowing that many in the US saw the New Deal as a form of Marxism and admired Hitler from afar, he nevertheless set himself up as an early opponent of isolationism.

On August 30, 1934, he wrote to Secretary of State Cordell Hull: "With Germany united as it has never been before, there is feverish arming and drilling of 1,500,000 men, all of whom are taught every day that continental Europe must be subordinated to them. I think we must abandon our so-called isolation."[11]

A KEY MOMENT in Dodd's understanding of the brutality of the Hitler regime came at the end of June 1934.

By that spring, Hitler's grip on power seemed secure. He had silenced opposition and forced even the political parties that had joined with him to disband. A new law against the formation of parties ensured that Nazi Germany was a one-party state in what was, in effect, a constant state of emergency.

Hitler now began to see enemies inside his organization. The leader of the SA, Ernst Röhm, was a brutish former German army captain who had been one of the first to join the Nazi Party. A ruthlessly ambitious man,

Röhm began to talk about a "second revolution" in which his storm troopers received greater rewards for the work they had done for the party. Himmler sensed an opportunity to remove Röhm and told Hitler that the SA leader was planning a coup. Hitler was ready to believe him, as he now found the SA's reputation as street brawlers to be a hindrance to his alliances with conservative army generals and business leaders—two groups who had access to and influence over President Hindenburg.

On June 30, 1934, Hitler acted, using Himmler's SS—which was still technically part of the SA—to turn on the storm troopers. Hitler personally traveled to Bavaria to witness Röhm's arrest. Röhm was shot two days later, in a round of bloodletting that would become known as the Night of the Long Knives. Using the cover of an operation against a coup, Hitler disposed of not only SA leaders but also people with whom he had a score to settle, including the former chancellor General von Schleicher, who was shot at home along with his wife by a six-man SS execution squad. Estimates on the numbers killed vary from about eighty-five to around four hundred; the killings gathered their own momentum.

The very earliest opponents of Hitlerism in the German establishment were also caught up in the massacre.

A group of conspirators, sometimes referred to as the "Young Conservatives," had been wondering how the Hitler government could be overthrown. They were led by Edgar J. Jung, a Munich lawyer and a speechwriter for Papen, and Herbert von Bose, a former intelligence officer in the Imperial German Army and now Papen's forty-year-old press officer. Although anti-Communist and unsure about the effectiveness of democracy, they desperately wanted to bring about the fall of the Nazi regime, finding Hitler personally detestable.

The pair planned to use Papen's and Hindenburg's influence to put forward eighty non-Nazi candidates for the next Reichstag elections to weaken Hitler. They felt they had to act quickly before Nazi power was completely consolidated. On June 17, 1934, at the University of Marburg, Papen delivered a speech—written by Jung—that pleaded for religious freedom and the restoration of right and justice, and warned against the excesses of a totalitarian state. Hitler banned publication of its text, but copies were circulated. Jung and Bose believed it would help create an atmosphere of political tension that would allow them to prompt President Hindenburg to declare a state of national emergency. The coup that followed would have allowed the

Nazi government to be stripped of executive power, with the German army, the Reichswehr, disarming the SA and the SS. President Hindenburg would then take over himself, although in practice the eighty-six-year-old would leave the running of the government to Papen's aides and the generals. Hitler and Göring would be allowed to join a Reich directorate that was to consist of Papen, former chancellor Heinrich Brüning, conservative politician Carl Friedrich Goerdeler, and General Werner Freiherr von Fritsch. The plotters knew that, with the support the Nazis had, they could not remove Hitler in one sweep: Bringing him into the directorate would calm his supporters; he would be removed from any access to power later on.

The Marburg speech could have been enough to ignite the fuse, but Papen hesitated to take the next step. The conspirators needed him to rush to Hindenburg's estate in East Prussia, where the elderly president was by now desperately ill, and convince him of the necessity of mobilizing the Reichswehr against the SA and the Nazi Party.

On the morning of June 30, on the day Papen had finally intended to see Hindenburg, an SS squad and Gestapo officers occupied the vice-chancellery. Hindenburg's son had revealed the plot, and word had passed to Himmler.

Bose was directed into his office and told he was to be interrogated. As he sat down, he was shot in the back ten times. Albert Speer said that he later passed the room and saw a large pool of Bose's dried blood on the floor.

Jung had already been arrested in connection with the Marburg speech a few days before. He was found dead in a ditch near Oranienburg on July 1.

Papen escaped death. Hitler feared the killing of the vice-chancellor would cause him diplomatic embarrassment. Instead Papen was put under house arrest, where—persuaded by his own personal ambitions—he soon came to terms with the idea of working with Hitler again. He would go on to be Hitler's ambassador to Austria and later Turkey.

Bose and Jung had put their trust and hopes in the wrong man. They were dead, among the first anti-Hitler conspirators to pay the highest price for failure. But they were the vanguard of conservative resistance, which would form the army and civil service conspiracies to come.

PUBLIC REACTION TO the crackdown on German Communists and the murders of the Night of the Long Knives was muted.

Supporters of former center and conservative parties feared Communism and workers' rights, so they broadly supported the banning of the

German Communist Party as well as the persecution of Social Democrats and trade unionists. In the early months the Nazi press carried detailed reports on its measures against the left as they sensed public support, although after 1933 terror against left-wing dissidents would be less frequently reported.

As for Röhm—who was homosexual—Goebbels had ensured he and the other leaders of the SA were depicted as "sexually depraved" troublemakers. When, the day after the killings, the propaganda minister claimed in a radio broadcast that the Nazi government had acted to stop a coup by Röhm and Schleicher, there was widespread approval for Hitler's "decisive" action. Germany was desperate for a period of stability, and to many, Hitler's actions showed that he was committed to decency and law and order. In one of his last public statements before his death, Hindenburg praised Hitler for his "gallant personal intervention," which had "rescued the German people from great danger."[12]

That spirit allowed Hitler, a former First World War corporal, to beguile the army, too. Days after Hindenburg died in August 1934, he made himself head of state and took the accompanying title, the supreme commander of the armed forces. Everyone in uniform was made to swear an oath of allegiance to him personally: "I swear by God this holy oath: I will render unconditional obedience to the Führer of the German Reich and people, Adolf Hitler, the Supreme Commander of the Armed Forces, and will be ready, as a brave soldier, to stake my life at any time to this oath."

Conspiracy against the Nazis, for men of honor in uniform, would mean not only the personal betrayal of Hitler but also, by extension, betrayal of the Fatherland itself.

IN THE US embassy, Dodd watched it all in horror, agreeing with an assessment in the *Times* of London that a kind of "medievalism" had returned to Germany. A colleague of Mildred Fish-Harnack's called to see him and said that Hitler "has aroused a savagery and barbarism which he thought had long since disappeared."

Looking solemnly at the American, the university professor added: "Poor Germany, she cannot recover in decades to come."[13]

The man was hoping to leave Germany by getting a professorship abroad. His colleague Fish-Harnack had no such thoughts for the time being. The government might be one you did not like, but it would pass; for now you gathered friends around you and sought to cling to the ideals and beliefs that sustained you.

EVERY SATURDAY MILDRED Fish-Harnack would light candles and put out fresh flowers in their apartment at Hasenheide before collecting an order of food from a nearby restaurant. When the Harnacks' guests arrived, there would be thin bread slices with butter and fine liverwurst and cheeses, tomato slices, cookies, and a dish of fruit awaiting them.

Arvid Harnack was snobbish in his recruitment of opponents to the regime, favoring intellectuals over manual laborers. Once sure of the allegiances of his company, he would talk on Marxism and the importance of economics. The group would study the forbidden texts of Marx and the French economist Charles Gide. Even when Mildred Fish-Harnack led a talk on Rudyard Kipling's *Kim*, it was to spark discussion about colonialism. Eager for intellectual stimulation, Harnack was again building a discussion group in the image of his evenings at Madison, Wisconsin. There were publishers and editors such as Samuel Fischer, Ernst Rowohlt (who had published Ernest Hemingway and William Faulkner in Germany), and Max Tau; novelist Max Mohr; Adam Kuckhoff and Greta Lorke, who were then living in a room on a lake in the western suburb of Pichelswerder; journalist Margret Boveri; and a number of Mildred's students.

Boveri was a sharp-thinking correspondent from the *Berliner Tageblatt*, for whom Mildred had begun writing reminiscences of her childhood in Wisconsin and articles on writers such as Walt Whitman. A graduate in history and political science from Munich and Berlin, Boveri intently studied Arvid Harnack's political thinking, and found him to be not a starry-eyed Communist utopian but rather an educated, principled economic realist. He admired America, she noted, suggesting that his ideas about capitalism and planned economies were "by no means orthodox Marxist ones." For Boveri, Mildred Fish-Harnack "embodied . . . the very prototype of the American puritan." She was "high thinking and plain living," believing "in progress and in human improvement." Mildred, she said, was "dedicated to reform and to action," and was ambitious for her ideas. She was "certainly not" a Stalinist—"it just would not have been her way."[14]

Martha Dodd also became a regular at the gatherings, and was invited to literary lectures that Mildred gave at the home of Klaus Bonhoeffer. The initial subject that brought this group together was books and publishing. Dodd was eager to get Rowohlt to publish one of her stories in a magazine, while Mildred had started writing for *Die Dame* magazine, which was edited by another regular, Ludwig Reindl. New books were always the topic for lively discussion. But these were also people who were like-minded politically: not all Communists, by any means, but worried by and opposed to Nazism. Discussion about what could be done to stymie the Nazis was never far from the center of the debate. Harnack's nephew by marriage, Wolfgang Havemann, who attended some of the meetings, remembered: "Our work . . . from the beginning was literary; it ended politically. And the more it become political, the more it became conspiratorial."[15] One Jewish friend said she felt she could "hardly breathe" as the Harnacks and the other guests casually called Hitler and Himmler "utter fools."[16]

With determination, the Harnacks spread their net wide in a search for people who might want to join their crusade against Hitler. Havemann said: "Both the Harnacks were, if I may say it, Menschenjäger—people who hunt for other people. Mildred looked for people who were clean, ethical, noble . . . she looked for the worthwhile core in humans and she found it."[17]

But there were also those who "hunted for people" for perhaps more sinister reasons.

One evening, at a fashionable nightclub called Ciro's, a tall, good-looking man with short light-brown hair approached Martha Dodd and asked her to dance. His smile and humor were disarming. "I am with the Soviet embassy," he told her as they moved in each other's arms. "Are you afraid?"

"Of course not, why should I be afraid?"

The man's name was Boris Winogradov, and he was well-known among diplomats and journalists in Berlin.[18] His charm was such that even the most conservative American newspapermen liked and enjoyed his company, even though he was a dedicated Communist.[19] Whereas Diels had been brooding and menacing, Winogradov was warm and funny with smiling blue-green eyes. He had been tasked by Moscow with befriending the circle of leftists that had formed around the former writers of *Die Tat*, Adam Kuckhoff in particular, and the hard-partying Dodd seemed to provide a perfect way into the group.

Neither he nor Dodd spoke the other's language, but they conversed in broken German, and even though Winogradov was hiding a wife and child at home in Moscow, they fell in love. Martha Dodd was invited to the Soviet Union for a tour. She came back to report to her friends that she saw no

signs of discrimination in Moscow—against Jews or any other minority—
and that the people seemed to have a higher living standard than the Germans. Mildred and Arvid Harnack, who were still regular visitors to the
American embassy, were among those who saw the way the visit to the
Soviet Union had impressed Dodd and turned her head.

While the Soviets circled this group of Berlin intellectuals and economists, the Harnacks continued to look to the United States for support. Arvid Harnack was keen to use his wife's friendship with Martha Dodd to
extend their network of contacts and build closer bridges with Washington.
When Martha Dodd asked Fish-Harnack to put together a guest list for a
party honoring the visiting American novelist Thomas Wolfe, Harnack suggested Greta Lorke become involved. Lorke's circle of friends extended beyond the academics and senior civil servants whom the Harnacks knew.

The embassy tea became a meeting of the groups that circled around
the Harnacks and Kuckhoff. Kuckhoff brought along John Sieg, who made
sure the views of many working-class Berliners were represented over the
cocktails and canapés. Some German workers, he told them, had initially
been enthused by the Nazis because of the employment created in public
works programs, but that support was now dissipating because they were
no longer able to use union power to argue for better wages. There were
many industrial workers' cells of former trade unionists, socialists, and
Communists, and of working people who simply hated the Nazis, he said,
and he described the trips he and others had made across the border to
Prague, where many who had fled the Nazis were now in exile. He and a
friend had set up a printing operation, based in a builder's hut in Rudow, a
suburb of Berlin, but using machines hidden in apartments across the city.
They were printing news sheets for distribution in factories, but Sieg was
keen to do more than write about the regime that he hated.

Boveri, Rowohlt, and Reindl clustered around Donald S. Klopfer, of
Random House, whose sensational win at a court in the United States had
enabled him to publish James Joyce's *Ulysses*.[20] It was a major source of conversation in Berlin, where all literary activities were now regulated by Goebbels's Reichskulturkammer (the RKK) "to unite all creative persons in a
cultural uniformity of the mind." Goebbels wished to be the patron of
"good" Nazi art, and so all of Germany's writers, critics, theater directors,
radio producers, librarians, and book publishers had to join the RKK. Fish-
Harnack had survived the squeeze on the industry, writing about Faulkner

in the journal *Die Literatur* and the *Berliner Tageblatt*, and working on a translation of Irving Stone's biographical novel of Vincent van Gogh, *Lust for Life*.[21] But her access to getting her own thoughts into magazines had been closed off. Editors, now personally responsible to the state for the views of their contributors, would take no chances. They were more than content for their magazines and books to be safe and a little dull if it meant they kept their jobs and stayed out of jail. To make ends meet, Fish-Harnack worked as a freelance reader for the Berlin publishing scene, seeking out British and American books that might be suitable for translation. The Nazis' restrictions on subject matter and permissible authors made it a thankless task.

Chief among the Nazis' forbidden material was anything created by Jewish writers. The Harnacks followed developments against the Jewish population, and one of their best friends, Max Tau, a Jewish writer and editor, had been at the embassy tea party. Until now, Nazi anti-Semitism had seemed to manifest itself in wildly offensive press articles, the burning of books by Jewish authors, and the boycotting of Jewish businesses and shops. But a summer of anti-Jewish violence ahead would end with the introduction of the highly restrictive Nuremberg Laws, stripping Jewish people of their German citizenship and barring marriage and extramarital sexual relations between Jews and Germans. The general public, for the most part, passively accepted the discrimination, more intent on following their daily lives, but the socialist underground identified the track being taken by the Nazis. "The Nazis have indeed brought off a deepening of the gap between the people and the Jews," wrote one illegal newspaper. "The feeling that the Jews are another race today is a general one."[22]

This acceptance of anti-Semitism and the widespread sense that German Jews were no longer German angered the Harnacks and their friends. They wondered what would happen next. The civil servants in the Reich Chancellery were creating laws amid an atmosphere of chaos inside the regime, with many already arguing for the Führer to go further. Hitler continued to ponder his answer to the "Jewish question," but he had never hidden his racial hatred.

And Greta Lorke soon set about showing the full extent of his racial theories to the English-speaking world. Hitler's *Mein Kampf* had so far only been published abroad in abridged form, but a Berlin-based Irish writer, Dr. James Murphy, was now considering a new translation and he asked Lorke to help. After a lot of consideration, she realized that people in Britain and the United States were so far unaware of the full content of Hitler's racist ideology. Her translation work with Murphy would reveal it all.

The West would have no more reason to say they could not have known about the sickness in the Führer's mind.

WHILE TO THE Harnacks and others, the average German could be dismissed as a Mitläufer—one who just followed along—to the man and woman in the street Hitler appeared to be presiding over an economic miracle and the complete restoration of the nation's pride.

Hitler's anger at the restrictions imposed by the Treaty of Versailles reflected that of many of the German people. The treaty had stripped Germany of land, wealth, and pride, and Hitler was determined to restore all three.

Erhard Milch, founder of Deutsche Luft Hansa, the civilian airline that in January 1934 became known simply as Lufthansa, believed his business could be used as a means of secretly rebuilding the German air force, which was forbidden under the terms of the treaty. Göring appointed Milch state secretary of the Air Ministry in 1933 and together they set about creating the Luftwaffe.[23] By the time its formation was officially announced in March 1935, it already had eleven thousand men and 1,800 aircraft. Soon after, the Nazis reintroduced conscription—another infringement of the treaty.[24]

On March 7, 1936, Hitler sent his armies into the Rhineland, which had been declared a demilitarized zone after the First World War. There was no meaningful reaction from the international community, which lacked the will and unity to intervene. Hitler's confidence, which had been growing since he had taken the bold step of leaving the League of Nations in 1933, received another boost. These successes, thanks largely to the nation's propaganda machine, became very much associated with Hitler's standing as national leader. These were his successes. It became possible for even people who dismissed National Socialism as an ideology to support and admire the Führer. He stood for the achievements of the regime.[25] The public reaction to his success in the Rhineland outstripped anything that had gone before. Hitler was tearing up Versailles and restoring sovereignty over German territory. Some had feared he was risking war, but when threat of that dissipated, there was euphoria. The 140,000 cheering supporters who attended the Nuremberg rally that year heard him tell them: "It's a miracle of our times that you have found me . . . among so many millions! And that I have found you, that is Germany's good fortune!"

Mildred Fish-Harnack witnessed some of this euphoria when one night, as she walked back from the Berlin Abendgymnasium, she was suddenly surrounded by uniformed SS men outside the UFA Filmpalast on Tauentzienstrasse. She and her pupil Emil Kortmann, who was walking with her, were bunched into a crowd positioned to flank the double doors at the entrance to the building. Both had no idea what was happening until the doors opened and Hitler strode out, Goebbels at his side. Hitler posed and saluted the crowd, who shouted "Heil!" as he climbed into his car and was driven off with his SS escort.

Mildred and Kortmann looked at each other in shock—having never seen the object of their loathing in the flesh before—and then it gradually dawned on them that a huge excitement seemed to be pulsing through all those around them. One older woman cried out: "What an historic moment!"

Mildred and her friend walked on in the direction of Zoo Station, their minds filled with the realization that the antifascist movement had an awful lot to do.[26]

THE FRUSTRATIONS OF the history academic at Tiergartenstrasse 27a, whom Roosevelt had sent to Berlin to be a liberal voice, were growing. Ambassador Dodd felt he had sent warning after warning to Washington, while at the same time losing face in Germany. He had simply become unable to continue shaking the hands of the murderers in the regime and was becoming more and more isolated.

After the Rhineland occupation, he wrote a letter only for the eyes of Secretary Hull, in which he let go of his frustrations: "With armies increasing in size and efficiency every day; with thousands of airplanes ready on a moment's notice to drop bombs and spread poison gas over great cities; and with all other countries, little and great, arming as never before, one cannot feel safe anywhere. What mistakes and blunders since 1917, and especially during the past twelve months—and no democratic peoples do anything, economic or moral penalties, to halt the process!"[27]

# 4

## The Battle for German Youth

IN THE LONG term, the Nazis knew, they needed to ensure the obedience of German youth, and they dedicated a great deal of energy to winning them over.

After strict investigations into their racial background, boys and girls as young as ten were eligible to join groups such as the Jungvolk and the Jungmädel before transferring to the Hitler Jugend (HJ), the Hitler Youth, and Bund Deutscher Mädel (BDM), the League of German Girls, at fourteen. At eighteen, the boys would become fully fledged members of the SA, which had been reorganized, not disbanded, after the Night of the Long Knives. The girls were to be prepared for motherhood and domestic tasks.

The young were told that their responsibilities and loyalties were to the state and not to their parents, and when Hitler said, "You are flesh of our flesh, blood of our blood, and your young minds are driven by the same spirit that possesses me," many young people felt that they really mattered to the nation. They greeted each other on the way to school with "Heil Hitler!"; their local Hitler Youth leader, or Blockwart—a Nazi official watching over an apartment block—would chat to them about National Socialism and who believed in it. Teachers—who now taught with a framed picture of Adolf Hitler watching over them—were warned: "Should a remark against the Hitler Youth be uttered in the heat of the moment the trust between pupils and teaching staff will be damaged and not easily restored. But the more effort a teacher makes to enter into the spirit and code of the Hitler Youth, the greater will be his success." The state was sowing the seed of warped loyalty that would eventually see some children betraying teachers and even their own parents for not supporting the Nazis staunchly enough.

Hitler talked about Germany's "magnificent youngsters," and most children and teenagers did not appear to find these youth organizations restrictive. They went hiking and camping, sang songs and waved flags, and they felt they were part of something.

The Scholl family lived in Ulm, a city on the Danube that had long been connected with powerful leaders. It had been declared an Imperial City, a Reichsstadt, by Frederick Barbarossa in 1181 and had been the site of a Königspfalz, a resting place, for medieval German kings and emperors. But Germany's defeat in the Great War and its consequences had hit the city hard. Local industry had been geared to armaments and exports, both of which had been restricted by the Treaty of Versailles, and the Weimar Republic's commitment to paying reparations to the victors made it unpopular. Soon after the Nazis came to power, the Rathaus was decorated with a large banner that proclaimed "Adolf Hitler für Deutschland."

Inge Scholl, the eldest of the five children, said: "We heard much oratory about the Fatherland, comradeship, unity of the Volk, and love of country. This was impressive, and we listened closely when we heard such talk in school and on the street."[1] It seemed to the young that politics—and therefore Hitler—was about making Germany stronger and wealthier, and it was difficult not to want to be a part of it.

A year younger than his sister Inge, Hans Scholl was fourteen at the time the Nazis came to power; his younger sisters, Elisabeth and Sophie, were thirteen and eleven, and his younger brother, Werner, was ten. Hans enthusiastically joined the Hitler Youth and rose to be a Fähnleinführer—a squad leader. His sister Sophie was later excited to join the BDM. It was perhaps a surprising start on the road to adolescence for the two people who were to become the most famous of the civilian resisters to Hitler, but they found the wearing of uniforms and the torch-lit processions intoxicating. As a squad leader, Hans was in charge of 150 boys. He would leave his home for meetings or country marches, dressed in his brown shirt, black shorts, and knee-length gray socks, with a swastika on his armband and a ceremonial dagger on his hip. On it were inscribed the words "Blood and Honor." Sophie was in the brown coat and white blouse of the BDM, having joined with most of her classmates. Their sisters and young brother also joined the Nazi youth groups. All loved the uniforms and the chance to camp out, although Sophie was worried about one aspect of the BDM immediately: Her friend Luise Nathan was not allowed to join, as she was Jewish.

Their father, Robert, had tried to encourage his children to grow in their own way, but he hated the Nazis and had angry confrontations with his elder son. "The Nazis are wolves, wild beasts," he told the teenager. "They misuse the German people terribly."[2] Hans argued back, and for some time they barely spoke at all. To the teenagers, their father seemed out of touch with the feelings of the time.

Robert Scholl was a man of deep principle. A pacifist and medical orderly during the First World War, he had met his wife, Magdalena, in a military hospital where she had been a nursing sister. They had married in 1916 and had brought up five children in the traumatic political and economic years that followed the war. A forward-thinking man who succeeded in bringing the railway to the town of Forchtenberg, where he was mayor in the 1920s, he encouraged his children to think for themselves and not follow anyone else's lead.

Books were important in his home, and the children effortlessly moved from the fairy tales of the Brothers Grimm to the poetry of Goethe and Schiller, which they would recite to each other at home. Sophie loved the outdoors and nature, going for long walks, swimming in a local lake, and climbing high trees. She looked up to Hans, who was tall, athletic, and handsome. Charming but also sullen and outspoken, Hans vied with his father for the role of family leader, as teenage boys often do.

Robert Scholl had been voted out of mayoral office in Forchtenberg in 1930, as the small provincial village felt the turbulence of the difficult economic and political times and his liberal views became less popular. Resourceful and intelligent, Robert Scholl found work as a tax consultant in Ulm, and it was here the family would call home during the years of the Nazi regime.

He had instilled in his children liberal, unselfish, analytical attitudes that were the antithesis of Nazism. He hoped that as they came of age these values would shine through.

ULM MIGHT HAVE suffered its economic hardships, but the Bavarian air was still clear and the surrounding countryside fruitful, the orchards rich and green, and the slopes and hillsides carpeted with vines. The Scholls' life was decidedly middle-class and comfortable. Other youngsters had grown up in poverty.

The economic nightmare that had engulfed Germany was felt most keenly in poor industrial areas such as Neukölln in Berlin, where Greta Lorke had seen the deprived children in the orphanage in which she had worked. In the years after the war there had been no safety net to catch the crippled soldiers, young women driven to prostitution, and starving pensioners who gathered there in cheap apartment blocks and squats. Even a brief period of relative prosperity for Germany—before the Wall Street Crash—passed Neukölln by. Beggars crammed into the doorways of dark, forbidding tenement blocks, pleaded for a few coins, and watched the garbage blow in the street.

It was a hot spot for radical politics, where the poor and the working class demanded revolution from the right and the left. The SA clubs and bars were popular, but many others looked to Communism.

Herbert Baum lived there. Born just before the First World War in Posen, he had moved with his family to Berlin after the town had been handed to Poland as part of the war reparations demanded in 1919. He took immediately to life in the busy capital and, aged thirteen, became friends with Martin Kochmann, who attended the same school and also loved drama, reading, and science.

The area, and everyone they knew, was loyal to the Social Democratic Party. They were working people, and Communism and socialism spoke for them. During the 1920s a third of the German electorate supported either the Communist Party or the Social Democrats, and political engagement among the youth in the years after the war was very much the norm. Baum and Kochmann joined youth groups that spoke up for social justice and against poverty; they were also regular members of the many Jewish youth groups still flourishing in Germany at the time. Their friends were Jews and non-Jews, with their parents stressing that assimilation into all aspects of German life and culture was vitally important.[3] There were political meetings and discussions, but also Boy Scout–like adventures, with the youngsters meeting under the bridge at the Alexanderplatz train station, "the Alex." Kochmann's girlfriend, Sala Rosenbaum, and Marianne Cohn, whom Baum was sweet on, joined them.[4] Rosenbaum was well loved, with a bright smile and a sharp wit. She was the sort of friend you went to when you had troubles. Cohn was outgoing, bossy, and funny; she found Baum's seriousness about Marx and Lenin very amusing. They were all young idealists, believing in a fairer society, reading Thomas Mann and Émile Zola, and hiding from the pimps, thieves, and prostitutes who worked the area around the Alex.

When the Great Depression struck Germany, the group chatted less about idealism and more about the real problems facing their families and their communities. They talked about anti-Semitism and Zionism—some, but not all, believed that a Jewish state had to be created in a land known as the British protectorate of Palestine—and about economics and poor wages. In 1931, as the Nazis maneuvered hard to obtain power, Baum joined the Kommunistischer Jugendverband Deutschlands (KJVD), the Communist Youth League of Germany, believing like many German Jews that Communism was the answer to Germany's political crisis. The German Communist Party had positioned itself as the key anti-Nazi movement, and the Nazis preached the removal of "foreign" (Jewish) influence from Germany. When Adolf Hitler took power, there were approximately 500,000 Jews living in Germany—some 160,000 of them having their homes in Berlin. By and large they considered themselves as German as they were Jewish.[5] To the Nazis all Jews were foreigners, even those born in Berlin. Communist and leftist organizations were the natural home for Jews or those who opposed Hitler.

On April 1, 1933, Nazi brownshirts stood in front of Jewish shops and stopped customers from entering. Some held placards stating "Don't buy from Jews." Later thirteen-year-old Heinz Birnbaum went around to the flat in Friedrichshain shared by Baum and Marianne Cohn, who were both now twenty-one, to discuss what he had seen—people being dragged away as they tried to enter Jewish shops—and what they should do now that Hitler was in power.

Only a little younger than Hans Scholl in Ulm, Birnbaum was seeing the flipside of the Nazi "miracle."

Baum told him: "Jews have to stay in Germany and fight together with all other German anti-fascists to topple Hitler."[6] Baum showed him a series of antifascist pamphlets that he had been writing, and Birnbaum said he wanted to help. Birnbaum, like so many others, instinctively took to the inspirational Baum. He was easy to like and filled with enthusiasm. As another friend remembered: "We all tried to outdo ourselves when he participated."[7]

The young people met in rooms in large buildings owned by the Jewish community in the area around Oranienburger Strasse. They talked about how to survive inside Hitler's Reich and what they might do to help those opposing it. The regime was still young and might be fragile. Protest could make all the difference. Small groups—cells—of resistance would be developed in different streets and regions. Anyone who hated the regime was welcome, no matter what their religion or political philosophy. No one was ever to tell outsiders the names of members or where they met. The country was dangerous, even for teenagers—which many of these were—and security was an important concern. Baum was warm and fair-minded; he did not bring his Communism to these meetings, knowing all did not share his views. He attended as a committed antifascist. Twenty when Hitler came to power, he was older than many of the others and was happy to nurture and guide them. The youngsters beamed with pride when Baum congratulated them on something they had said or an idea they had contributed. They felt a great sense of solidarity, preached a love for their fellow human beings, and were vehemently antiwar.[8] Baum—a dark-haired man with prominent ears and a steadfast gaze—seemed to be the natural leader.

Baum was now working as an electrician for a private contractor and taking night classes to follow his dream of becoming an engineer. It was a dream he knew would be made more difficult by the Nazis, as they were closing down the work opportunities available to Jews. Cohn had trained as a kindergarten teacher and was working in a Jewish school. Their teenage romance had developed into a deep love. They sometimes joked it was because they were born only a day apart, she on February 9, 1912, and he the day after. When they had some savings, they planned to get married.

First, though, they had all those anti-Nazi leaflets in their new flat, and they planned to do something with them.

HERBERT BAUM AND his girlfriend, Marianne Cohn, were fearless. Working with Martin Kochmann and Sala Rosenbaum, Herbert Ansbach, Heinz Birnbaum, and Werner Steinbrink—a non-Jewish friend—they took their antifascist leaflets into the street and handed them out to passersby. Both Cohn and Rosenbaum were as respected as Baum himself, and women were to play as key a role in the group as the men.

Meeting in each other's flats, they would have impassioned chats and debates on politics and philosophy of the kind that would be familiar to students from any age or nation—only these were firmly in a dissident subculture, denied access to the theater, concerts, and many of the books that they loved.

Sometimes they would just sit on the floor and listen to Rosenbaum read; she had a beautiful, clear reading voice. She would recite Heinrich Heine to them, political poems from a century earlier that satirized the political torpor of the German people and ridiculed the greed of the ruling class.

These cultural chats would often turn up new simple slogans that they would apply to leaflets urging their countrymen to "Be a good citizen—think for yourself!" or "Love your country, think for yourself—a good German is not afraid to say 'no.'"[9] Simple words, but running completely contrary to totalitarianism.

Each time they went out with the leaflets, they took fresh risks. Opponents of the new regime were being beaten, arrested, and imprisoned for much less than what they were now doing. Baum came up with a new idea for the distribution of leaflets and asked his friends to collect the large vegetable cans of the type used in restaurants. He cleaned and emptied these and placed a small explosive charge in the bottom half. He covered that with a round metal plate and stuffed the leaflets in on top. A rudimentary timer using a clock was placed on the side of the can.

Baum took the first of his leaflet bombs into the crowded State Library on Unter den Linden, and timed it to go off after he had made his escape. When the device went off, it littered the room with flyers. Baum watched from a safe distance as a Gestapo car pulled up and agents rushed to seal off the building. Everyone inside was questioned, but no one had seen anything.

Buoyed by his success, Baum staged an even more daring escapade, smuggling a friend with a leaflet bomb into the Funkturm building ahead of an important radio show whose main guest was Nazi propaganda minister Joseph Goebbels. Baum had a friend place the "bomb" in a flower box behind the podium. It went off and showered five hundred pieces of paper, which urged people to listen to Radio Moscow, onto Goebbels and the audience. It was a spectacular prank, and one Goebbels did not forget.

The third of Baum's leaflet bomb actions took place at the Alexanderplatz on July 11, 1934, and involved seven of his closest friends. It was a busy summer's day and the station was crowded—perfect, as far as Baum was concerned. The group planted eight of the devices on the roof of the station, setting the timers for an hour ahead. All went off, showering leaflets on the people below. Some snatched them up and took them home, reading in the safety of their kitchens: "The workers and peasants shall overcome fascism and rejoice!"

Some friends were frightened by Baum's daring, but he was charismatic and courageous—few said no when he asked them to help. And every few weeks he seemed to have a fresh idea.

On August 1, 1934, Berlin's antifascists planned an "antiwar day" to mark the twentieth anniversary of the outbreak of the Great War. Baum and his friends took children's lettering-stamp sets and wrote out short antifascist slogans on small pieces of paper. This time they would put on a show in the street, he told them.

They separated and met up again on a busy avenue in Kreuzberg, one of the most crowded boroughs in the capital. Home to many newspapers and small industries, the area was buzzing with workers on their break. Baum and his friends placed their cans on the ground and lit fuses. Almost instantly, they began to spew different colored smoke, which caught the attention of shoppers and passersby. Then others rode through on bicycles, throwing leaflets in the air: "Against Fascist War Preparation!"

The elation was short-lived. A week later Martin Kochmann was arrested by the Gestapo in a swoop on known leftists. During interrogation the police asked Kochmann about a Jewish friend he had named Bubi, but Kochmann pleaded ignorance of anyone by that name. Bubi was one of the code names used by Baum.

When Kochmann was released, the group discussed how dangerous the leaflet campaign had become—particularly in light of the Nazis' "legal" crackdown on Jewish people—and it was decided to call a halt for a while. Instead, their focus shifted to a biweekly antifascist newspaper, *Junge Garde Süd-Ost*, which was reproduced on a duplicating machine owned by a non-Jewish friend, Gerhard Prauge, and distributed around the southeast region of the city. The daring Prauge also joined the local Hitler Youth to report back information to be used in the publication.

Then, early in 1935, Nazi newspapers planned a civil defense exercise that would test the Berlin population's reactions in an air raid. The city would be blacked out from dusk until dawn. Baum, Steinbrink, and Ansbach set about creating a special poster for the occasion—reading in large letters, "Today rehearsal, tomorrow dreadful reality!"[10] Using the blackout as cover, they then plastered hundreds of these posters around the city.

Improvements in radio sets meant that many homes could now tune to Radio Moscow, the BBC, and other foreign stations. This form of dissent could be hard for the Gestapo to detect and—even when the news from the foreign broadcasters was not disseminated—it led to a general undermining of confidence in the German news media. A "broadcasting crime"—listening to a foreign station—was an imprisonable offense; during wartime it would become a capital one. Baum used the information from broadcasts in his articles and leaflets. In practice the danger was not in listening to the radio; it was in the production—buying stencils and typewriters—and the distribution of the leaflets. Baum's were some of tens of thousands of leaflets distributed around Germany during the first three years of the regime, although this volume fell as the dissenters found themselves in jail or conscripted into uniform.[11]

These early acts of resistance by Herbert Baum and his Jewish friends were simple acts of political defiance that in a democracy would seem largely inconsequential; in Nazi Germany, however, these were courageous deeds, symbolic of the fact that many Jews in Berlin would resist this warped state's representation of the Jewish people as a scapegoat for all that had gone wrong for Germany.

In Ulm, the young Scholls had begun to see through the nationalistic fervor to the anti-Semitism that underpinned everything the Nazis believed.

AT THE HEART of the Nazis' ultraconservative vision was a utopian concept of Volksgemeinschaft—national community—in which all sources of friction and unease had been removed, all abnormality expunged, to create the "ideal order."[12] For the Nazis, you were either "with us or against us." There could be no opposition, ridicule, or debate. The regime demanded conformity. It dictated how people greeted each other, what they thought, and how children were taught. Those who made these apparently small adaptations to their behavior and ignored the misfortunes of the outsiders could become good national comrades, Volksgenossen. The apparatus of state would not affect them.

As Jews, Baum and his friends did not have the option of becoming Volksgenossen, even if they denied their Communist feelings. But had they been able to deny their growing sense of revulsion, the Scholls—as a middle-class Aryan family—could have fit in perfectly.

But amid the most powerful manifestation of the Volksgenossen, Hans Scholl developed his doubts.

In September 1936, the annual Party Day rally was held at the Zeppelin

Field at Nuremberg. The vast field was awash with regimented groups in the uniforms of various Nazi organizations—fifty thousand people all marching in step, praising Hitler. Hundreds of thousands more watched from the concrete grandstand, which was so big it was lined with thirty-four evenly spaced towers.

This year the young people took center stage, as 1936 had been designated the "Year of the German Jungvolk." It was a decade since the creation of the Hitler Youth and therefore the children born in 1926 were now ten and eligible to join.

The field was enclosed and decorated with tens of thousands of flags, and there were more among the parades that passed through. Hitler saluted the young banner carriers as the "guarantors of our future." The flag of the Hitler Youth contingent from Ulm was carried by the tall and handsome figure of Hans Scholl. This was a great honor, but in reality, Hans's enthusiasm was already on the wane.

As the sun shone down on the parade and the area echoed with the sound of Hitler's voice booming through the loudspeaker system, a change was taking place in Hans. He was suddenly realizing that the lines of fluttering swastikas, the repetitive cries of "Sieg Heil!" by a seemingly brainwashed crowd, and the sense of shared delirium were beginning to repulse him. There were no individuals, only boorish talk of uniforms and Volk, and of the perfidy of Jews. Standing in a tented village on the edge of the city, where the HJ groups were staying, he began to feel completely out of place. The racially obsessed songs of his drunken brown-shirted comrades, the lines of merchandise stalls selling Hitler photographs and swastika flags, the endless roll calls and marching, seemed at odds with his tender and poetry-loving upbringing. He slowly realized that he did not want to be blindly obedient—he wanted to be like his dad, believing in freedom and the goodness of people. The nonconformist side of the father was coming out in the son.

On his return to Ulm, his sisters noticed a change in Hans, but he could not confide his doubts at first. Then he got into a fight with a senior member of the local Hitler Youth and was stripped of his role as a troop leader. He took the demotion as a relief. He had never been anti-Semitic and now realized just how much the songs they had sung about spilling Jewish blood had disturbed him.

Less extroverted than her brother, Sophie had never enjoyed the drama of the Nazi youth movements. Hating the Nazis' ideas for girls—that they should eschew work and studies and only prepare for marriage and motherhood—she resolved to take a teenage stand. She decided that she did not even want to look like a traditional hausfrau and wore her hair in a short, boyish bob—a style that earned her the nickname Baubamädle, tomboy, from her schoolmates.[13]

Since she preferred to spend her time reading or writing in her own journal, the indoctrination had never had any impact upon her. Unsettled by the rising anti-Semitism, she had already displeased a BDM leader by openly reading the banned German Jewish writer Heinrich Heine. "Whoever does not know Heine, does not know German literature," she told the startled teenager loftily. The Nazis' anti-Jewish Nuremberg Laws had had a far-reaching effect on Sophie's Jewish classmates: They could no longer go to the swimming baths, movie theaters, or parks. Sophie tried to maintain her friendships with them and invited them home for tea.

One day she was on a BDM field trip with her sister Inge, and she quickly grew bored at the relentless marching and singing. Dragging Inge off for a walk through the woods on their own, they smelled camp smoke and found, in a secluded spot, a tent around which sat a group of boys. The youngsters were of an age that meant they should have been serving in the Hitler Youth, but they were not in uniform. For a moment the teenagers looked at each other curiously, even suspiciously. Then, as youngsters do, they began to talk. Sophie was intrigued by the boys' apparent rebellion and asked what they were doing. One of the boys stared at the girls' BDM uniform and suddenly cast his eyes down. Sophie realized he was Jewish and in fear that these two young Nazis would report him and his friends to their BDM leader.

It was a moment of clarity for Sophie. She did not feel at home in the BDM but had joined because all her schoolfriends had. But here now were people of her own age who were not conforming. Perhaps, yes, some had been forced to be outsiders by the Nazis' racial laws, but maybe there were others who rebelled through choice. Over the coming months she began to see more clearly that the friends who congregated at the Scholls' home all appeared to feel disillusioned with the political situation in Germany. It made her realize that although she felt a sense of alienation from the growing conformity around her, she might not be completely alone.

*  *  *

AS THE NAZIS' hatred for Germany's Jewish population became further enshrined in state law, Herbert Baum and his friends increased their plans for rebellion. Baum had resumed his leaflet campaign. The acts against the Jews, the warmongering attitude of the Nazis, had to be faced down. Why should the Jews be made to feel like they did not have the right to work, to be Germans, to be humans? As one of his comrades, Inge Gongula, noted: "The idea was . . . that we are Jews and they'll kill us anyway, so do something against them before we get killed."[14]

Working with his core team—Marianne Cohn, Martin Kochmann, Sala Rosenbaum, and Herbert Ansbach—Baum posted flyers around Berlin, on the walls of train stations and police stations, and even inside S-Bahn trains. The team organized sports groups, which covered for antifascist meetings, and gave leaflets to friends in factories to be left on machinery at the end of shifts. The friends would take turns listening to foreign radio stations and share what was being said about Germany in Britain, France, and the Soviet Union.

While Baum's anger toward the regime was political, it was also now personal: He had had to abandon his dream of becoming an engineer after he was thrown out of his night-school course. The authorities decided the quota of Jewish students had been exceeded.

His friend Werner Steinbrink started going out with Lisa Attenberger, who, like Steinbrink himself, was not Jewish. Attenberger had built up her own small group among fellow workers and customers of the branch of Woolworth's at which she was a sales clerk. Attenberger brought Ansbach and others into her group and, in early 1936, came up with what seemed like a radical idea to help them distribute their leaflets much farther afield than Berlin. They formed a car rental company that could cover a courier system for their material. While some cars would be genuinely used by renters, others would carry suitcases filled with leaflets and newspapers. The idea could have seen Baum's words distributed across Germany, but bad luck struck right at the outset.

Having volunteered to do the first run herself, Attenberger was stopped and questioned by a suspicious Gestapo agent in her native city of Kiel. On discovering the material in the car, he took her to his local headquarters and tortured her. Attenberger gave the Gestapo the address of the rented room in Neukölln that she had been using as a base and the names of some of her friends, including Ansbach, who was arrested soon afterwards. Ansbach was sentenced to two and a half years in prison for being involved with an illegal newspaper. Steinbrink was picked up, too, but was released for lack of evidence.

IN 1937, HANS Scholl met Ernst Reden, a dark, brooding, and handsome man who reminded Sophie of Rainer Maria Rilke, a poet with whom they were all obsessed. Trading on his resemblance to Rilke, Reden wrote poetry and prided himself on his image as a bohemian outsider, reciting work by banned Jewish writers and sharing his thoughts on philosophy, which he had studied at college.

Reden had come to Ulm from Cologne as part of his compulsory military service—which he hated. Wearing his disillusionment with society as a badge of honor, Reden introduced Hans Scholl to an organization called the German Boys Club of November 1—known by its lowercase German initials d.j.1.11.

The group had been founded on November 1, 1929, by a band of liberal intellectuals who broadly supported the Weimar Republic and rejected nationalism and militarism. Groups met across Germany and worked hard to foster a sense of internationalism: They camped using a style of tent that was popular in Lapland, and they sang Cossack and Balkan songs; they enjoyed the culture that they wanted to, not that which was prescribed by Hitler. Members also enjoyed childish but subversive humor. "What is an Aryan?" one would call while sitting at the campfire. "Blond like Hitler!" the others would call back. "Tall like Goebbels!" (Goebbels was short enough to have been given the nickname "Giftzwerg"—poison dwarf—by some.) "And slender like Göring!"[15]

Hans Scholl took his group—including his younger brother, Werner—on a three-week camping trip, even traveling outside Germany to Copenhagen and Stockholm. They sang songs and chatted; it was an outlet for teenage energies, away from the uptightness of the Hitler Jugend, but no one among them saw it as outright resistance to the Nazi state.

However, even such apparently gentle rebellion put them at serious odds with the regime. These d.j. groups, as they became known, were not sanctioned by the government. Their very existence was an act of defiance. Members took to calling each other by nicknames to protect their identities. They invented passwords and developed ways of knotting a scarf that would identify themselves to each other. The very style of their name, written in lowercase letters, was a modernist touch inspired by the Bauhaus movement in art and architecture, which the Nazis despised.

That summer Hans—who was now preparing to go to the university—and Inge went into Munich to see an exhibit at the new Haus der Deutschen Kunst, the House of German Art. As they walked around, they were unmoved by the new representations of the idealized Nazi German families and the painting of the peasant engrossed in a Nazi newspaper. Afterwards, they walked the few blocks to the exhibition of the Entartete Kunst—the degenerate art—which had been compiled by Goebbels to show the pieces that the new Germany rejected because they were considered Bolshevik, Jewish, or modernist. The exhibition included works by Marc Chagall, Jean Metzinger, and Wassily Kandinsky, and was held on the second floor of the former Institute of Archaeology. The paintings were deliberately badly hung or unframed, and they had been given new labels, such as "Peasants depicted in the Yiddish manner," "An Insult to German Womanhood," and "Nature as seen by sick minds." Despite this, the Scholls found the works inspiring, an antidote to the ideologically driven works of the Nazi exhibition. The pair took away much to discuss about the way German art and culture had become a homogeneous mass of soulless propaganda. Inge took her thoughts back to the new reading group she had joined with Sophie. Hans took his back to the d.j. group. In fact, the exhibition of degenerate art might have been a rare miscalculation by Goebbels: As it toured, it became the most popular exhibition staged under the Third Reich, with more than two million people coming to view it.

THAT SUMMER PROVED a watershed in the short life of Sophie Scholl. One day on one of her regular visits to the home of a friend, she met a young man in uniform, four years her senior.

While the friend played songs from her enviable collection of 78 rpm records, the man introduced himself as Fritz Hartnagel, graduate of the elite training school for officers at Potsdam. Sophie was immediately taken with him, and in their conversations they agreed that the army was still a proud non-Nazi organization. They argued about a lot of other things—which left Hartnagel much impressed and a little shocked by her strong and sometimes nonconformist beliefs—but they agreed to keep in touch.

\*   \*   \*

ON SEPTEMBER 22, 1937, Hans turned nineteen. He had passed the abitur, the examination that qualified him for admission to the university, but he first had to complete six months in the Reichsarbeitsdienst (RAD), the National Labor Service, working on the construction of an autobahn that would run through the Swabian countryside, and then serve in the military for two years.

In 1935, Hitler had removed the last military restriction placed on Germany in the Treaty of Versailles when he reinstated compulsory military training. Hans signed up for a cavalry unit, which was stationed at a spa town called Bad Cannstatt, only about fifty miles from Ulm. Hans loved horses, and he got to ride and work with them. In the evenings he read and wrote letters to his old friends in the d.j.

That was a mistake. In a national crackdown on non-Nazi-sanctioned youth organizations, the Gestapo went after the d.j.1.11. Hans Scholl was already on their list of suspects—with local Ulm Hitler Youth leadership well aware of his membership in the d.j.1.11—and Gestapo men arrived at his barracks to arrest him for membership in an illegal organization.

As Hans was rushed to a cell at the Gestapo headquarters in Stuttgart, another plain-clothed police squad arrived at the Scholl home in Ulm and, as Robert Scholl protested, placed Inge, Sophie, and Werner under arrest. Regaining her composure in an instant and playing the part of the near-invisible German hausfrau, Magdalena Scholl wandered around the house with her shopping basket under her arm, casually dropping anything she thought might be incriminating into it. She then walked to the front door and said to the Gestapo: "The gentlemen will excuse me—I have to hurry to the baker's."

The three youngsters were taken by open truck to Gestapo headquarters in Stuttgart and placed in separate cells. None had any idea what was going on, but fortunately their ordeal was not to last for long. Sophie was released later that day, but Inge and Werner—who was also a member of d.j.1.11—were kept in custody for a week before being released, the Gestapo believing they had been sufficiently intimidated to knock any sense of rebellion out of them.

Hans Scholl was taken to a cell in Düsseldorf, where he learned that membership in the d.j. was not the only charge against him. A few days earlier, concerned about the young poet Reden's recklessness, Scholl had reported a rumor to the Hitler Youth leadership that Reden had been expelled from the HJ in Cologne for same-sex activity—a crime punishable by a prison sentence. Now, the Gestapo told him, a teenager had claimed he had been in a brief homosexual relationship with Scholl when they were both in the Hitler Youth. Scholl admitted they were "close" but said he was the victim of "mud-slinging" from people arrested for membership in the d.j. Over weeks of questioning, Scholl himself refused to talk about the group or name people in it.

Scholl appeared before the Special Court in Stuttgart on June 2, 1938, after months of worry about his future. The teenager with whom Scholl was alleged to have had a relationship played it down, said it was very mild in its nature and nonsexual. Scholl told the court his d.j. group was not opposed to National Socialism, and a cavalry officer from Scholl's unit gave his soldier a glowing testimonial. The court put Scholl's "failings" down to "youthful exuberance," and he was acquitted on all charges and allowed to leave the court without a stain on his character.[16]

Throughout the months waiting for the trial, Scholl had suffered a humiliating time in the barracks. In Ulm, too, there had been questions. Word spread quickly around the small city about the three youngsters from the same family who had been whisked away by the Gestapo, and the rumors about Hans, who was well-known, were ripe for gossip. Sophie was constantly asked by classmates: "What on earth have you people been up to?"[17]

One evening early in the ordeal, Robert Scholl had been walking along the river with his daughter Elisabeth, who was a year older than Sophie but had not been arrested, when his anger suddenly turned again to Hitler: "If those bastards harm my children in any way, I'll go to Berlin and shoot him!"[18]

The family had come through it, but its opposition to the regime had been galvanized. By nature they favored an individualistic and free-spirited approach to life; to live in an oppressive society obsessed with conformity was far too stifling. Individuals needed air to breathe and a way to stand out.

# 5

## The Moscow Connection

THE REICH MINISTRY of Economics was in the heart of the Nazi government district of Berlin and close to the embassy of the Soviet Union. Its location on a walk between the Reich Chancellery and Moscow's men in Berlin would be highly symbolic of the next few years of Arvid Harnack's life.

Having passed a rigorous entry examination in the spring of 1935, Arvid Harnack had been appointed to the Economics Ministry and told that he would be handling some of the most sensitive economic data in the Reich. As with all new employees, the ministry sent him on an indoctrination course to a National Socialist camp. He went along with it, as he had to, but his intention was clear: to gather what information he could from his new job and use it against the regime.

His past friendships with Russians were known, but senior thinkers in his position were expected to have had contacts abroad. His new employers reckoned his extensive knowledge of the Soviet Union would be, in fact, a most valuable asset to the Nazi ministry. He was, after all, an expert on the Soviet Union and its economy, and a member of one of Germany's finest academic families. Even in the paranoid atmosphere of the Nazi state, the general sense was that someone of his class and background could not be anything other than a loyal citizen.

Harnack had grown frustrated with the Americans. He had passed information on to Dodd about life for Jews, academics, and political activists in Germany, but although the ambassador was a sympathetic ally, he received little support from Washington. What many influential figures in the United States wanted Dodd to do was look after America's business interests, help negotiate on loans unpaid by German businesses, and avoid any conflict or argument that would interfere with trade.

So when Harnack was contacted by an agent of the Soviet Union, he listened to what he had to say. The contact came through two old friends from ARPLAN, the economic discussion group that Harnack had set up but disbanded when the Nazis came to power. Sergei Bessonov, Arvid's old friend at the Soviet embassy, had told Moscow about Harnack's new role, and an NKVD spymaster instructed embassy official and NKVD officer Alexander Hirschfeld to make contact.

They met on August 8, 1935, and talked for three hours. There was no problem with Harnack's access to information; however, he insisted he would not simply be Moscow's man in Berlin. Harnack was certain in his mind he would not become a Russian spy; he was an antifascist German Communist: He would act not through commitment to Stalin but through commitment against Hitler. Hirschfeld, worried that other activities might compromise his new source of intelligence, tried to persuade him otherwise, but Harnack refused. He would not break off contact with any of his Communist friends and in fact, within months, traveled to Paris alone to seek friends in the French Communist Party. For Arvid Harnack, it was important that he was not a spy or traitor; he was actively—albeit secretly—agitating for change in his country.[1] Moscow assigned Harnack a code name—Balt—and a control officer, an NKVD intelligence officer in Berlin named Alexander Belkin. For Harnack, and his friends, the die was cast.

FOLLOWING HIS MEETING with Hirschfeld, Arvid Harnack immediately began to supply information to Moscow. He would be as rigorous and in-dustrious in his secret work as he always had been in his studies.

He copied notes and documents on German currency holdings, the state of the economy, highly confidential summaries of Germany's invest-ments abroad, and details on the nation's foreign debt. Moscow was par-ticularly pleased when he provided them with information on Germany's secret trade agreements with Poland, the Baltic states, and Persia.

But as he collected information, Harnack also passed it to others who opposed Hitler, such as John Sieg, who spread the word through contacts in Germany's factories and friends elsewhere in the civil service. The object was to show the discrepancies between what the regime said and what it did. All those who opposed war—and did not believe Hitler when he said he did not want war—were especially interested in what Harnack passed on with regard to Germany's continuing rearmament. This sharing of information also provided a source of morale: Those who hated the regime got a boost from knowing there were others out there—and who knew how many—who were prepared to criticize and share worries about what was happening.

However, the Nazi Party's grip on the civil service continued to tighten. Careerists, or anyone who wanted to keep their job, knew there was only one way to establish their loyalty and that was to join the party. Few now hesitated, even if their heart was not in it. Arvid Harnack had particular reasons for not wanting his own loyalty questioned, so he, too, joined the party. Friends wondered what had changed, and became even more confused when he joined the conservative Deutscher Klub, formerly the Herrenklub, which met in an elegant building near the Reichstag. Once the hallowed meeting place of aristocrats, industrialists, and financiers, it was now very much a special place for senior figures in the regime—and therefore an ideal place for Harnack to cultivate new sources of information and to overhear pieces of gossip. It was also frequented by men who would become key members of the German military and diplomatic resistance circles, such as General Ludwig Beck and the diplomat Ulrich von Hassell.[2]

Mildred Fish-Harnack shared her husband's intelligence with her countryfolk at the embassy, using her friendship with Martha Dodd as a reason for her frequent visits. Fearful that the building had been rigged with listening devices by the Gestapo, the two women would disappear to the toilet together during parties and receptions. The first time Fish-Harnack had insisted on it, Dodd had laughed, but her friend explained that she felt bathrooms were more difficult to bug as they were more sparsely furnished than other rooms. When the details of what Fish-Harnack wanted to tell her became clear, Dodd started to understand the need for care, and she began to have "sleepless nights" over whether she had been overheard. The notes Dodd took were included in embassy cables.[3] Her father regularly added his own opinions, writing for the attention of General Douglas MacArthur, the US Army chief of staff: "In my judgement, the German authorities are preparing for a great continental struggle. There is ample evidence. It is only a question of time."[4]

Martha Dodd would also visit the Harnack home, where another element of the resistance was developing: the printing of information, available from foreign news services but kept out of the German press by Goebbels. Together they typed up news from the Spanish Civil War, foreign opinion of the Nazi regime and Hitler's policies, and information about the labor movements in other countries. Fish-Harnack and Greta Lorke translated parts of speeches by Roosevelt and Winston Churchill, who was then a lonely voice in the British Parliament speaking against the appeasement of Hitler. These leaflets were disguised as romances or harmless pamphlets, and given innocuous titles such as *Elektrowärme im Haushalt* (*Home Heating by Electricity*) so they could be carried and read secretly.

THE DILEMMA FOR many during the years since Hitler had come to power had been whether to leave Germany. By 1936 many of the Harnacks' friends had gone. Some had left but then returned, drawn by thoughts of home and a need to be a part of the nation as it went through what they saw as its darkest hours.

Others, who saw what Hitler intended and feared the dark path ahead, felt they could not stay. The Harnacks helped Jewish writer and publisher Max Tau escape to Norway. But it was not just Jews who were leaving.

Rudolf and Franziska Heberle were old friends of the Harnacks. Rudolf had been a Rockefeller scholar like Harnack, and had met Mildred around the same time. The "campus beauty," he had called her, with a "bold and noble profile." All three had lain in the woods in Wisconsin and read poetry together. Lyrical, sunlit days that seemed now like another lifetime. In 1935, Fish-Harnack had become godmother to the Heberles' daughter, Antje. They felt the choice of a dedicated anti-Nazi was a good omen for Antje's life ahead.

But now Rudolf Heberle, a leading sociologist, had been denounced by one of his students, who had told the Gestapo that he was teaching Marxism. Not only was his job in danger, but his life was, too.

A job offer from Louisiana State University gave the Heberles a chance of freedom, and Rudolf told Harnack he planned to take it. He was shocked by the way Harnack turned on him when he said he was moving to the United States. Harnack was angry, not because he felt Heberle was deserting Germany, but because he was leaving his duties to the resistance. It was a scandal, Harnack told him, that he had got himself into a position where he had to leave.[5] He should have been able to hide his opinions from his students, as Harnack was able to do every minute of every day at the Economics Ministry. Arvid Harnack, Heberle felt, was unstoppable in his opposition to Hitler.

The old friends shook hands and said good-bye.

* * *

MILDRED FISH-HARNACK ALSO began to waver. Her writing often turned to home and to her childhood in Wisconsin. From a distance, America had become a sentimental vision of her youth: her mother singing "Sweet land of liberty" and the band in the park playing "The Star-Spangled Banner." She had not seen her mother since 1930, and now word reached her that Georgina was gravely ill. She had to find a way to return, and in January 1937 she arrived in New York on board the *Manhattan*. Her return caused a period of great confusion for her old friends, such as Clara Leiser, with whom she stayed. Although sure Fish-Harnack was not a committed follower of Hitler, Leiser removed every item of anti-Nazi literature from her home. But during her visit Fish-Harnack was reticent and noncommittal; she had become so used to hiding her true feelings in new or unfamiliar company that her guard firmly remained up. She was remote and self-conscious, an aloofness that Leiser took for a kind of arrogance and condescension of the kind "long exercised by Europeans toward America and Americans." Another old schoolfriend noted that, even in New York, Mildred appeared to be looking over her shoulder, not just cautiously but as if she were extremely frightened.[6]

Leiser held a party in Fish-Harnack's honor. Many of her friends from Wisconsin were there, but she again remained tight-lipped and restrained. Leiser explained to one that Fish-Harnack was afraid that even here anything she said about Hitler could cause trouble for her or her husband in Germany. One curious friend asked Mildred about her trip to Russia and was told: "We don't talk about that."[7]

Ambassador Dodd had recommended Fish-Harnack to a number of friends in American universities, and she was able to carry out a short lecture tour, describing the reception in Europe of a number of American writers, including Jack London and Thomas Wolfe, whom she had met in Berlin. The tour even took her to Madison, where her family urged her to leave Germany. Her niece Jane found that she simply would not talk about anything to do with their life in Berlin. "I hold Arvid's head in my hands," Mildred told her.

Was she being paranoid, or were her concerns justified? Germans living in the United States were undoubtedly interested in meeting and hearing from an American who knew their country so well. They were keen to see how she viewed and presented Germany in her lectures. Fish-Harnack knew that among them were members and supporters of the German American Bund, whose role was to promote a favorable view of Hitler's state. Based in Manhattan, on East 85th Street, the bund had established local groups across the United States and even had a training camp in Wisconsin. Bund rallies and meeting places were daubed with Nazi insignia, and members greeted each other with their right arms extended in the Hitlergruss. They preached against Roosevelt, Communism, and trade unions, and were fiercely anti-Semitic. They would have found the Harnacks' true feelings abhorrent had they sensed what they were, and through their links to Berlin—their leaders had visited Hitler in the Reich Chancellery in 1936—would have ensured their concerns reached the Gestapo.[8]

Before leaving the United States, Fish-Harnack did find a quiet moment to open up a little to Jane. Inviting her niece to Berlin for the summer, and delighted when she accepted the invitation, Mildred suggested she read *Das Kapital* before she came. It would give them something to talk about when they were assured of privacy.

MILDRED FISH-HARNACK RETURNED to Germany knowing that her place was with her husband. But her friend Ambassador William Dodd was now certain that he had had enough of Nazi Germany and was longing to leave.

After four years in the post, Dodd had ceased to function. He had withdrawn from meaningful public roles—having always refused to attend Nazi rallies—and had been isolated by the German authorities, who saw him as an intractable opponent. Dodd believed he was upholding American values, as instructed, but there was disquiet among the diplomatic corps. William C. Bullitt, who had moved from Russia to Paris during Dodd's tenure, wrote to Roosevelt: "Dodd has many admirable and likeable qualities, but he is almost ideally ill-equipped for his present job. He hates the Nazis too much to be able to do anything with them or get anything out of them. We need in Berlin someone who can at least be civil to the Nazis and speaks German perfectly."[9]

When Dodd became aware of criticism against him, he wanted to resign, but he feared that to do so would be a "confession of failure." He felt under a great deal of stress and chastised himself for not being able to render his country service.

His agony worsened when he became involved in the case of a Jewish

American citizen named Helmut Hirsch, who had been accused of trying to bomb two Nazi buildings in Nuremberg, and charged with conspiracy to commit high treason and possession of explosives with criminal intent, despite the fact that he had no explosives at the time of his arrest. Dodd requested a meeting with Foreign Minister Joachim von Ribbentrop to plead Hirsch's case and ensure that he received a legitimate trial. After the meeting, Dodd had returned to his office and cabled the State Department to state that Ribbentrop said Hirsch must be executed. Dodd then sent a personal appeal to Hitler, but it was ignored. On June 4, 1937, Hirsch was executed by decapitation. In his daily log Dodd recorded: "Poor Hirsch had his head chopped off this morning at sunrise."[10] He added the following day: "What is to come of all this one cannot say: German domination of all Europe or another war?"[11] The embassy doctor, who had been treating Dodd for stress, concluded the death of Hirsch had led to "unbearable tension in the ambassador."[12]

William Dodd's health had been suffering since he had arrived in Berlin. In the summer of 1937 he requested leave in the United States and sought out a specialist in Baltimore. On hearing of Dodd's headaches, which lasted for days, and the bouts of digestive problems that caused him to be unable to eat, the doctor advised complete rest and suggested he resign his post in Berlin. Dodd met with Roosevelt that August, and the president asked him to stay on in his post for a few more months. He also said Dodd should lecture in the United States and "speak the truth about things" in Germany.[13] That gave Dodd some heart, until he heard that Prentiss Gilbert, the chargé d'affaires at his embassy, had attended the Nazi Party rally in Nuremberg in his absence. Dodd, who had consistently turned down invitations to Nazi rallies as a way of signaling his—and America's—distaste of Hitler's policies, felt undermined and humiliated by a member of his own staff. Dodd complained in a confidential letter to Secretary Hull and was shocked to see his complaint leaked to the *New York Herald Tribune*. On seeing Dodd's words of criticism of the Nazis in the press, the German ambassador to America complained to Hull, although he stopped short of demanding Dodd's removal.

Dodd continued to find sympathy from the president himself, though, and met again with him, this time at Roosevelt's home in Hyde Park. Afterwards, Dodd confided in his diary that the president was anxious about foreign affairs, worrying about whether the United States, Britain, France, and Russia could cooperate and closely watching the conflict between Japan and China.

Dodd listened and advised where he could, and then asked the president if he could stay in the post in Berlin until March 1, 1938. He did not want the German "extremists" to think they had got their way in having him replaced. Roosevelt nodded, and Dodd sailed for Germany that October feeling he could leave the toughest of assignments with his head held high. The president, though, gave in to pressure from the State Department and the German Foreign Office. On November 23, 1937, an order from Hull came through to Dodd: He had to leave Berlin by December 15, or Christmas at the latest. By the end of the year the Dodds had left Germany. He told friends before he left that the nations of the world were "farther apart than ever."[14]

ONE OF THOSE keen for Ambassador Dodd to stay in Germany had been his own daughter, Martha, now a willing informer for the Soviet embassy. She had reported that she had access to confidential correspondence between her father, the State Department, and Roosevelt. The Soviets asked her to provide short summaries of her father's reports, especially anything on Germany, Japan, and Poland. Like Arvid Harnack, she was told to sever her links with other antifascists and to report only to Moscow. Unlike Arvid Harnack, she obeyed.

Mildred Fish-Harnack and Martha Dodd met for the last time in a busy restaurant where at a corner table they could talk without being heard above the din. They chatted about books, Arvid, Martha's "men," and the future—like all parting friends. They would write, of course, and there would be much to say. Fish-Harnack's conversation was dominated by her work. How the resistance was growing more effective. How there would be a new Germany built on the foundations of what they were doing.

Germany was a dark place, with uniformed thugs on the street and buildings and park benches marked for non-Jews only, but Mildred Fish-Harnack could see beyond this. Outside, she suddenly pulled Martha Dodd close and kissed her.

She turned on her heel and moved off down the street. Dodd stood and watched her go. Tall, distinguished, confident.

Then she was gone.

*      *      *

THE DODDS HAD played a most unusual role in the Harnacks' life, with the couple finding themselves in the middle between the United States and the Soviet Union. Bizarrely, the Harnacks now saw their contacts with both nations severed.

William Dodd had been the most genuinely sympathetic ear that the Harnacks had found in a foreign nation. He instinctively despised the Nazis and had a sharp enough understanding of both European history and current affairs to see where the Nazis were taking Germany. Through him, information and opinions had been relayed directly back to Washington. Martha Dodd had supported the flow of intelligence to both her father and the Russians.[15] Harnack had also been providing information to his own Moscow contact, Alexander Hirschfeld.

But in the summer of 1938, Hirschfeld suddenly disappeared.

Throughout the 1930s Stalin had faced opposition on a number of fronts inside the Soviet Union. Many veteran Bolsheviks felt his was a dictatorship, a temporary emergency measure left over from the revolution and the civil war. There were calls for more democratic control and a crackdown on corruption. Stalin acted ruthlessly. Purges began to "cleanse" the party of opposition, first with members being expelled but later jailed and executed. Then, in December 1934, when an ally of the Soviet leader—Sergey Kirov—was murdered in Leningrad, Stalin used his death as an excuse for what became known as the Great Purge. Hundreds of thousands of people were arrested, with many facing the firing squad; the murders accelerated into a seemingly industrial scale during 1937 and 1938. Stalin claimed to have uncovered a huge cadre of fascist spies who would have been a deadly fifth column during any upcoming war.

The first consequence of the Great Purge for the Soviets' Berlin embassy was the abrupt recall to Moscow of Sergei Bessonov, Arvid's friend from the ARPLAN days, and all those linked to the NKVD. In Moscow, they faced trial for supposedly being part of an anti-Stalin plot. Bessonov "confessed" to being in league with Stalin's exiled opponent Trotsky, and was jailed for fifteen years. Alexander Hirschfeld—Harnack's contact—simply disappeared. The Soviet Union's foreign intelligence team in the embassy at Berlin had been decimated.[16]

Harnack now got a sense of Stalin's cruelty for the first time and spoke out "vehemently" to friends about what the Soviet dictator was doing.[17] But he remained committed to cooperating with anyone who could help rid his country of Hitler and the Nazis. He continued to work at the heart of Hitler's burgeoning military economy and could see the way the entire state was being built up for war, but he now had no one with whom to share this information.

However, destined for Berlin was a man who would become not only Harnack's friend but also his new intelligence contact. A professional spy, he was not coming from Moscow but was making his way by boat from the United States.

The Americans had decided to send their first spy into Berlin. Donald Heath was being posted to Germany to obtain economic, not military, data: The penny had not yet dropped in Washington that heavy war clouds were gathering over Europe.

# 6

## Hans Oster

DARKNESS WAS ALREADY falling that late afternoon in November 5, 1937, when the staff cars and their escorts brought the heads of Germany's military to the Reich Chancellery for a meeting with Hitler.

As the officers hurried inside, they expected little more than a routine discussion on the allocation of steel supplies to the armed forces, as per the agenda laid out on the invitation; the only moment of drama might be another heated exchange between Admiral Raeder and Göring over the navy chief's perception that the Luftwaffe was getting the larger slice of Reich funds.[1] However, as soon as Hitler spoke, they realized the meeting would have a more ominous purpose. No minutes would be taken, but one man, Colonel Friedrich Hossbach, made notes, as he knew his mentor, General Ludwig Beck, would want to know what was being said. For two hours Hitler spoke about the need to create Lebensraum, German "living space." The incorporation of Austria and Czechoslovakia, he said, would improve the security of Germany's borders, and when the moment arrived to attack the Czechs, there would need to be a "lightning fast" offensive. "For the solution of the German question all that remains is the way of force," he said.[2]

When Hitler stopped talking, there was some shock among those present. Hossbach noted that the discussion that followed "at times took a very sharp tone."[3] Field Marshal Werner von Blomberg, Hitler's minister for war, and General Werner Freiherr von Fritsch, the commander in chief of the army, warned Hitler against the risks of a war with Britain and France. Hitler was angry and left Berlin for Berchtesgaden. Both sides—the conservative generals and the egomaniacal tyrant—were now completely disillusioned with the other. Within weeks, though, Blomberg and Fritsch were gone.

Blomberg had been in a relationship with Erna Gruhn, a woman with "a past" who did not meet the strict requirements of the German officer corps. But he loved her, wanted to marry her, and asked his friend Göring for advice. Göring urged that the union should go ahead, and on January 12, 1938, Blomberg and Gruhn were married. By the time they returned from their honeymoon, Göring said a police file had come to light that appeared to show the new bride had once worked as a prostitute and posed for lewd photographs. Two weeks after his wedding day, Blomberg met Hitler to resign from his post in shame.

Fritsch, who would have been a candidate as Blomberg's successor, also suddenly appeared in a police file. A man arrived at the Reich Chancellery and accused Fritsch of being a homosexual. The charge was false and the witness hired, but the damage done was enough to see Fritsch, who disliked Hitler, dismissed from his post, too. Hitler appointed himself commander in chief of the armed forces and made Göring a field marshal. The most powerful opponents of his plan as outlined in November had been silenced.

Hans von Dohnanyi, at the Ministry of Justice, had vigorously defended Fritsch. A close friend of Arvid Harnack's for many years—they had worked together at the Institute for Foreign Policy as young men—Dohnanyi was one of those German intellectuals who had been greatly influenced by Harnack's uncle Adolf. He had grown up listening to Sunday afternoon political discussions at Adolf von Harnack's home and was instinctively anti-Nazi. He saw the grubby fingerprints of a Nazi smear campaign all over the Fritsch case and helped uncovered the fact that the witness—a known blackmailer—had mistaken Fritsch for another officer. Himmler and his deputy, Reinhard Heydrich, it seemed, had known this but feared a humiliation for the Gestapo. After Fritsch had been removed, he was found innocent and given a meaningless honorary position in the army. But Dohnanyi's work had brought him to the attention of Hans Oster at the Abwehr, who like Dohnanyi was sometimes dangerously outspoken about the Nazis, and Oster now drew him into his circle of resisters.

ALTHOUGH HITLER DESPISED the army's officer corps and the generals who had "betrayed him" as a soldier in World War I, he loved and admired the military way of life, and he had spent his first years in power courting the military. Army leaders were generally pleased by the ruthless purge of the SA in the Night of the Long Knives in 1934, as they saw the paramilitary organization as rebellious, ill-disciplined, and a threat to their own power. The general staff began to see Hitler as their man, and his determination to rip up so many of the military restrictions placed on Germany by the Treaty of Versailles flattered them further. The reintroduction of conscription in March 1935 and the remilitarization of the Rhineland the following year helped restore the army, in many senior officers' eyes, back to its rightful, central position in German society.

However, the generals' complacency had weakened them, and they had failed to identify the Nazification of their own service. Few had voiced disapproval when Hitler changed the oath of allegiance sworn by the army to one pledged not to "people and country" but to "the Führer of the German Reich and people, Adolf Hitler," but it should not only have worried them; it should have highlighted the fact that a new generation was coming, not one brought up in the pre–First World War monarchist tradition of the German army, but one that looked directly to the Führer. These young, newly conscripted officers had been schooled in the ideological tutoring of the Hitler Youth: They were heavily influenced by the Nazis' obsession with the twin "evils" of Judaism and Bolshevism, a conviction that had existed in the middle and upper classes of European society since the Russian Revolution, which Hitler exploited to develop a complete ideology. In addition, most generals failed to see that the true beneficiary of the Night of the Long Knives had been not the army but Himmler, who had control of the concentration camp system through the SS and was extending his powers throughout the police system of the Reich.

However, as word spread from the November meeting, there were murmurings of concern and anger. There was a great deal of fear among the general staff that Hitler's ambitions might draw Germany into another war with Britain and France—and memories of the last one were painful and raw.

DETAILS OF THE November 5 meeting had quickly reached the shabby apartment house near the Ministry of War that housed the Abwehr, the military intelligence department founded after the First World War to gather and assess intelligence material for the military and the government.

This building of dark passages, concealed doors, and tiny closet-like offices was nicknamed the Fuchsbau, the fox's den, by visitors who knew that as well as having officers from all branches of the military on its books, the Abwehr ran agents and informers in all departments of the government and civil service.

Since 1935, the Abwehr had been headed by the chief fox, Admiral Wilhelm Canaris, a man with an insatiable curiosity, a sharp political mind, and a wide range of contacts abroad. Canaris had been handpicked by naval intelligence during the First World War after escaping a South Pacific island where his cruiser had been scuttled and making his way back to Europe on a fake Chilean passport. After a period in Spain as an intelligence officer, he had taken command of a U-boat in the Mediterranean. Canaris was staunchly anti-Communist, fiercely nationalistic, but disdainful of the Nazis. He saw the SS as a rabble.

The Fritsch affair had a deep effect on fifty-one-year-old Canaris, who feared the way the military had lost its independence and grew concerned that every senior position in the state was being taken over by a Nazi. However, he found himself in a personal moral quandary: His interpretation of duty and honor prevented him from outright opposition to Hitler, and he knew that if he resigned, he, too, would be replaced by a Nazi. To circumvent his own principles, he decided to close off the Abwehr from SS influence and allow those around him to build up an anti-Nazi clique inside military intelligence.

Key to the clique was Canaris's right-hand man, Hans Oster. Although only a few years apart in age, they made a strange pair. Canaris was white-haired and soft-spoken, unmilitary in his bearing, and only a little over five feet tall. Oster was tall, elegant, outgoing, with an eye for beautiful women, and was a man steeped in the military and monarchist traditions of pre–First World War Germany. He had chosen to stay in the army in the 1920s when it had been diminished by the Treaty of Versailles, but had been forced to resign in 1932 following an affair with a fellow officer's wife. His sharp mind had immediately brought him to the attention of the Abwehr.

Oster would visit the admiral in his office, where Canaris sat behind the desk on which he kept small brass statues of the three wise monkeys. These reminded him of the cardinal virtues of the spy: "See all, hear all, say nothing." Although Canaris chose to remain above Oster's anti-Hitler schemes, he liked to know his friend was working on something.

And he always was. A devout Christian, Oster felt a growing hatred toward the Nazis rooted in a profound sense of justice. He loathed the treatment of the Jews from the beginning and, unlike many others, had quickly seen through the Nazis' brand of nationalism and prejudice. He had resented the murder of Schleicher and the Nazi campaign against the Christian churches, quickly realizing that Nazism was not his brand of prewar nationalism but a revolution "of the gutter."

Oster had read a decree issued by Hitler after the removal of Fritsch with alarm. "From henceforth," Hitler said, "I exercise personally the immediate command over the whole armed forces." In the coming days Hitler removed sixteen generals from their posts and transferred more than forty to other duties.[4] Hitler had outwitted the general staff. As a body, they were no longer a check on his ambitions; the army—having already sworn personal allegiance to the Führer—had become a private Nazi apparatus, subordinate to the Nazi state and, in particular, the will of its leader. The *Völkischer Beobachter* reported excitedly on the "fusion between the Wehrmacht and the Party."[5] The Fritsch smear campaign intensified Oster's hatred of the SS and Gestapo; from now on he would be the most committed opponent of the regime: That tendency toward danger and irresponsibility that had seen him almost lose his career over a love affair would now be channeled into secret rebellion against his head of state.

Few others in the German military would match Oster's zeal, and his network of contacts spread throughout the military, political, and diplomatic sections of German society. They included Hans Bernd Gisevius, a very tall, stiff Prussian who had joined the Gestapo believing he was doing work for the state but had found it to be, to his mind, a criminal enterprise. "Tell me, please," he once asked a colleague, "am I in a police office, or in a robber's cave?"[6] Alarmed at what he had learned about the concentration camps, he copied reams of documents and brought them with him to the Abwehr and to Hans von Dohnanyi. Together Gisevius and Dohnanyi collected documentary proof of Nazi crimes, which Dohnanyi—at great risk—would keep in a filing cabinet in the corner of his office at the Ministry of Justice. Dohnanyi's wife, Christine, would later reveal that his growing file contained everything "from murder and attempted murder in the concentration camps . . . to common-or-garden foreign exchange rackets run by Gauleiters and distasteful goings-on in the higher reaches of the Hitler Youth and SA."[7] Dohnanyi dubbed his file the "Chronicle of Shame."[8]

Oster's contacts tried to take care not to draw attention to themselves.

Aware that, owing to interdepartmental rivalry, both the Gestapo and SD (the intelligence branch of the SS) were spying on them, Oster's friends avoided airing their anti-Hitler views in Bendlerstrasse. Instead they chatted on walks in the Tiergarten or at private dinner parties, and used codes to refer to different personalities: For instance, Oster was Uncle Whitsun and Hitler was Emil.[9] Oster was tireless in his efforts to bring together a network of anti-Nazis, and as 1938 went on, he became more and more convinced that Hitler should be not only removed but assassinated.

THE FEAR OF war was being discussed in different bourgeois circles of the Reich, and one of the people to whom Oster reached out was Carl Goerdeler, the former mayor of Leipzig.

Goerdeler, a puritanical but highly persuasive man in his midfifties, had grown up in the conservative home of a Prussian district judge. Described by some as possessing an "almost ineradicable optimism," Goerdeler accepted a post as Reich commissioner of prices at the beginning of the regime.[10] The role's responsibility was to help tackle inflation, but Goerdeler believed he could also use his power to change from within the elements of the regime with which he disagreed. In November 1936, against his wishes, the Nazis removed a bronze statue of the German composer Felix Mendelssohn, who was Jewish, which had stood outside the Gewandhaus concert hall in Leipzig for more than forty years. Goerdeler, who was in Finland on business at the time, had previously declared that if the statue went, then so would he. True to his word, on his return Goerdeler resigned as mayor and went to work as an economic adviser to the electrical company Bosch, whose chairman, Dr. Robert Bosch, was a pacifist and no supporter of the Nazis.

Goerdeler offered Oster a range of contacts in the army and senior diplomatic and non-Nazi political circles. His like-minded friends included Ludwig Beck, Ulrich von Hassell, who was dismissed as German ambassador to Rome at the time of the Fritsch crisis, and Major General Friedrich Olbricht; all three would become key opponents of the regime. Goerdeler also drew support from a group of former trade union leaders, including Social Democrat Wilhelm Leuschner, Christian Socialist Jakob Kaiser, and the conservative white-collar union leader Max Habermann. Together they plotted ways in which the labor movement could oppose Hitler.

Like Harnack and Hassell, Goerdeler had contacts abroad. His job with Bosch allowed him to travel extensively outside Germany, and in June 1937 he went to London to stress the strength and scope of discontent with Hitler's policies. He told officials at the British Foreign Office that all issues could be resolved between the two nations "when the right men were in control in Germany."[11]

AUSTRIA HAD BEEN created out of the dismemberment of the Habsburg Empire at the end of the First World War. Overwhelmingly German-speaking, many Austrians—like many Germans—dreamed of Anschluss (union) with Germany. Austrian-born Hitler had always seen it as a primary aim in his desire to bring all German-speaking people together in a Greater Germany. He had been working to undermine the Austrian government from the very beginning, and for some time Austrian Nazis had been eroding the country's independence from the inside. Hitler had demanded a fresh plebiscite on union. When Austrian chancellor Kurt von Schuschnigg, whose predecessor, Dollfuss, had been killed by Austrian Nazis, appealed to Britain for help, he received a telegram from Lord Halifax, who had recently become British foreign secretary, stating that Britain was "unable to guarantee protection." A fox-hunting aristocrat with a lisp and a prosthetic left hand, Halifax was a determined proponent of appeasement in Europe. He and Prime Minister Neville Chamberlain were keen to avoid another war, wishing to protect the British Empire—which had been hugely weakened by the First World War and might not survive another—and privately accepting that some of the restrictions imposed on Germany at Versailles would need adjustment.

Following the Halifax telegram, Schuschnigg resigned and Nazi mobs rampaged through Austrian cities, occupying government buildings. In a radio appeal, Schuschnigg urged Austria not to yield to Hitler's force. Under the pretext of helping to restore unity to the deeply divided Austrian society, Hitler ordered the Wehrmacht to cross the border. No shots were fired.

On the afternoon of March 12, 1938, Hitler crossed a narrow bridge that marked the Austrian border at his birthplace, Braunau am Inn, in a cavalcade of open-topped gray Mercedes cars. He had fulfilled his dream of uniting Germany and Austria. As Hitler traveled through the Austrian countryside on his way to Vienna, church bells rang and people lined the streets to wave.

Within days, laws had been drawn up to make Austria a German province and the Austrian army had been made to swear the oath to Hitler. Austria's Jews quickly became the targets of abuse and violence, with Nazi thugs beating and robbing them in the streets without fear that the law would step in. Thousands converged on the train stations looking for a way out, and the Czech authorities turned back crowds at the border. Many Viennese Jews committed suicide.

In Germany, where the peal of the celebratory church bells was reported in the press but the violence was not, the people celebrated Hitler's Austrian "miracle," which had been achieved "without bloodshed."

Shortly afterwards, Goerdeler made his second visit to London, this time at the behest of Oster. He told London that plans were now in place for a coup against Hitler, and he urged Britain to stand firm against Hitler. For Goerdeler and Oster, Austria marked a dangerous "foreign" escalation of Nazi aggression, and they knew where it would turn next. In fact, even as he celebrated in Vienna, Hitler's thoughts turned to Czechoslovakia, whose border defenses had been greatly weakened by Austria's incorporation into Germany.

Czechoslovakia was an independent state created at Versailles in 1919, and three and a half million German-speakers lived in a border region known as the Sudetenland. Hitler wanted the region brought into his Greater Germany. Hitler's ally in the Sudetenland was Konrad Henlein, a former gymnastics instructor who now headed the Sudetendeutsche Partei (SDP), the Sudeten German Party, which received money from Hitler to cause as many problems for the Czech government as it could. Hitler told him privately to make demands that Prague would be unable to meet, and Henlein, a streetwise bruiser of a politician who recognized his moment in history had come, performed with élan. He demanded that Sudeten Germans should have legal autonomy in the state with complete freedom to profess adherence to German ideology. Henlein knew that Prague could never agree to such demands, as it would open the door to similar calls from other ethnic minorities and effectively signal the end of the Czech state.

The rabble-rousing Henlein also encouraged riots in the guise of demonstrations against Czech "oppression," and Hitler began to talk about protecting his fellow Germans in the Sudetenland. On May 21, the Czechs mobilized their armies, believing an invasion was imminent. France vowed to protect the Czechs, and Lord Halifax warned Hitler that "once war should start in Central Europe it was quite impossible to say where it might not end."

But privately the British government was worried that its own warnings to Hitler might provoke war. Halifax told his staff that Britain must not go to war and warned the French that they could not count on British support in the event of war with Germany.[12]

In Berlin, Hitler was wise to Britain's fears and told military commanders that Czechoslovakia would be "wiped off the map."[13] A deadline was set for October 1—four months hence. Afterwards, Hitler took a number of senior army commanders aside, including Beck and Colonel-General Walther von Brauchitsch, the new commander in chief of the army, and told them that after he had dealt with the East, he would give them "four years for preparations, and then we will deal with the West."[14] The words left them staggered: Hitler actively wanted another war with Britain and France. No one knew how to respond.

When Oster heard about the meeting, he wondered whether the anxiety of his colleagues might be turned into determination to take action against Hitler. Oster believed Hitler was wrong, and that the British and the French would stand up for Czechoslovakia.

He was certain that he had just four months to stop a major European war.

GENERAL LUDWIG BECK, as chief of the general staff, was in charge of the office preparing Germany for war. It was a job for which Beck was eminently capable. A decorated war hero from the First World War, he was clever, well-read, an expert on international relations, and the author of one of the army's key manuals of tactics. He was well liked, fair, and charming.

He and Oster got on well. Both liked horse-riding, could discuss literature and military history, and were religious, and Beck took a keen interest in the Abwehr. For Oster, persuading Beck to support a conspiracy could be the difference between success and failure. He already knew that the general found the Nazis vulgar and that he had been shocked by Hitler's aggressive foreign policy. Oster had seen a memorandum written by Beck after the November 5, 1937, meeting in which Beck had argued that foreign trade would be a better way to grow Germany economically than the belligerent hunt for Lebensraum. Beck also preached that Germany should not underestimate Britain and France.

However, Oster had also seen his reactions to the Fritsch affair. When General Franz Halder had told Beck that he should tell the general staff the truth about the way Fritsch was being smeared, Beck told him that "mutiny and revolution are words that have no place in a German officer's vocabulary." Having heard that Beck had banned members of the general staff from discussing the issue, Oster feared that Beck was at best tentative, at worst hostile to conspiracy.

In fact, Beck was agonizing in his own mind over how to persuade Hitler against any aggression toward Czechoslovakia. He had tried to gain the support of his superior, Brauchitsch, but he was intimidated by Hitler. However, at a dinner at the Esplanade in Berlin, Beck managed to persuade a large proportion of the general staff that a battle with the Czechs in the East would leave Germany vulnerable to attack from the French in the West.

On hearing the content of the speech, Oster recognized that Beck—the man charged with planning the invasion that he so opposed—seemed a certain ally after all. He began to spend long mornings in Beck's office, where the chief of staff analyzed the personal oath that he had sworn to Hitler. The circumstances appeared to be changing to a point where he felt that the oath could be compromised. "The soldier's duty to obey ends when his knowledge, his conscience, and his sense of responsibility forbid him to carry out a certain order," he said.[15] But Beck still favored persuasion over a coup. Back in his office Oster decided he needed to know what the British were thinking.

TWICE IN THE summer of 1938, Erich Kordt traveled to London for Oster. Kordt—a small, bespectacled, owlish man—had been a diplomat with the German Foreign Office under Joachim von Ribbentrop since 1934. Although relatively junior, he was considered essential by the limited and lazy Ribbentrop, and so had access to high-level conferences and state visits, and freedom to travel widely. Kordt's contacts in London had been expanded through his brother, Theo, who was chargé d'affaires at the German embassy in London.

One of the brothers' closest English friends was the historian Philip Conwell-Evans, who had been a lecturer at Königsberg University and had the ear of Sir Robert Vansittart, the British Foreign Office's chief expert on Germany.

Kordt told him he represented a senior general—Oster had given him a message from Beck—who said that a firm declaration of support for the

Czechs by the British would place him in a position to incite the German army to active revolt against the regime should Hitler go to war with Czechoslovakia.

Conwell-Evans's response was cautious. He told him that a British diplomat was now in Prague to arbitrate between the Czech government and the Sudeten Germans, and that the British believed a solution would soon be found. But Kordt warned that the Sudeten Germans had been told to accept nothing from Prague, no matter how generous the offer.

Conwell-Evans took the information to the Foreign Office, where it was considered. However, the historian was a major figure in the Anglo-German Fellowship, an organization mainly consisting of international businessmen who were seen as being pro-Nazi, as they wanted to maintain good commercial links to Germany. Conwell-Evans's views were adjudged to be prejudiced, and the fellowship's close links with the ardent Nazi Ribbentrop only served to weaken this intelligence further. Perhaps, the Foreign Office concluded, it was all a trick.

KORDT HAD BEEN able to report back only that the message had been delivered. But whatever the British believed, Beck became convinced that if Hitler went ahead with his plan to invade Czechoslovakia, then the generals would refuse to lead their men. This, he hoped, could lead to the coup that Oster championed.

Beck persuaded Brauchitsch to call an extraordinary meeting of Hitler's generals at Bendlerstrasse in which Beck read from his new assessment of the consequences of an invasion of Czechoslovakia: that it would provoke Britain and France to a war, which would eventually bring in the Soviet Union and the United States. In such a war, he said, Britain and France would no longer be satisfied with the restoration of Czech territory; it would be a "life-and-death war with Germany."[16]

The consensus in the room was that the mood of the German people and the army was against war, but a noncommittal Brauchitsch still held back from calling for the "generals' strike" that Beck had suggested. He refused to read a speech that Beck had drafted calling for collective protest against Hitler.

All the same, Beck optimistically told Erich Kordt afterwards that if Hitler tried to force his way into Czechoslovakia, "a revolt would take place."[17]

When Hitler was given Beck's assessment of an attack on Czechoslovakia and told about the meeting, he fumed: "Is it right that I should have to drag the generals into war? I do not require that my generals understand my orders; only that they obey them."[18]

He had already decided that the "defeatist" Beck had to go.

EWALD VON KLEIST-SCHMENZIN, a forty-eight-year-old lawyer, landowner, and monarchist, had been one of the earliest opponents of Hitler, having been arrested twice in 1933. A close friend of both Canaris and Oster, he had come to Abwehr headquarters to offer his help.

Like Beck, Oster believed that the most direct way to stop the Czech invasion was a bold statement from the British. Using Abwehr connections and false paperwork, he had Kleist-Schmenzin flown on a Junkers Ju52 to London, where, under a false name, he checked into the luxurious Park Lane Hotel overlooking Hyde Park. Before leaving, Kleist-Schmenzin had been sent by Oster to meet Beck. "Bring me certain proof that England will fight if Czechoslovakia is attacked and I will make an end of the regime," Beck had told the emissary.

"But what proof?" Kleist-Schmenzin had asked.

"An open pledge to assist Czechoslovakia in the event of war."

Through the efforts of his friend Ian Colvin, a British journalist who belonged to the same Berlin private members club as Kleist-Schmenzin, the German was able to meet with Vansittart and tell him that war was now an "absolute certainty" unless Britain spoke out. If Britain and France did not show real resolution, the Sudetenland and then Czechoslovakia would follow Austria. Hitler, he said, was convinced that Britain and France would never take action over Czechoslovakia, but a major speech by a leading British statesman could change that view and would tap into the German public's uncertainty and concerns. The speech should "appeal to this element in Germany, emphasizing the horrors of war and the inevitable general catastrophe to which it would lead."[19] Kleist-Schmenzin appealed to Vantissart to make Chamberlain listen, because by making this trip he was placing a noose around his neck.

Kleist-Schmenzin also secured a meeting with Winston Churchill, who was then a backbench MP who had fallen out with the Conservative leadership. The two men talked as Churchill drove wildly around the grounds of his Chartwell country estate. With Churchill, Kleist-Schmenzin was pushing at an open door, as Churchill had been speaking out about Hitler's rearmament and threats to peace for some time. The question was, could he make anyone listen? He promised he would try.

Kleist-Schmenzin knew that Churchill was an outsider and that the predominant feeling in Britain remained the need to appease Hitler. Back at Abwehr headquarters Kleist-Schmenzin was despondent when he briefed Canaris and Oster on his trip to London. "I have found nobody in London who wishes to take this opportunity to wage a preventive war," he said. "I have the impression that they wish to avoid a war at almost any cost this year. Yet they may slip into it without wishing to."[20]

ONE OF THE problems for the British was that it was difficult for them to assess if there was a difference between Hitler's nationalism and that which motivated the conservative, monarchist emissaries.

People like Kleist-Schmenzin and Goerdeler were products of a pre–First World War Germany. Although they were anti-Nazi, they were Wilhelmine imperialists who themselves believed some revision to the Versailles boundaries was justified. Goerdeler actually felt the Anschluss with Austria, the cession of the Sudeten region, and the revision of the border with Poland were acceptable if achieved peacefully. This made the British suspicious, and many in London argued that the emissaries were tools of the general staff in Berlin, seeking some sort of advantage for Germany. They did not understand that these men were deeply religious, and their morality had been deeply offended by the lawlessness of Nazi Germany and its inhumanity to so many of its citizens.

Churchill recognized the warnings, as they fit with his worldview, and he wrote to Halifax that a German invasion of Czechoslovakia would result in a war that "would be fought to the bitter end."

In Chamberlain's view the men were traitors, trying to engage the commitment of a foreign power to help them achieve their own ambitions of taking over their country. The prime minister vowed that only he himself could negotiate with Hitler and halt the march to war.

TO UNDERMINE BECK, Hitler invited group commanders and chiefs of staff to his private home in the Bavarian Alps, the Berghof, for lunch. From the giant picture windows of the Führer's mountain retreat, the generals could look down on Salzburg in Austria, which a few months earlier had been an independent state and now, thanks to the Führer's cunning, was a state of Germany, just like Bavaria.

For those who did not get the message, Hitler gave a rambling speech about his desire to smash Czechoslovakia. As he ended, he looked around the room and said that he knew his soldiers would not let him down and he hoped his generals would not either.

Following the meeting, Brauchitsch was ordered to communicate to Beck that the generals were convinced of the need for war. Beck went to his superior's office and tendered his resignation: Realizing he could not stop the Führer, he was determined not to carry responsibility for what was ahead. He asked Brauchitsch if he would resign as well and was told: "I am a soldier; it is my duty to obey."

Hitler appealed to the aristocratic Beck's honor and asked him not to make his resignation public, as the international situation was so tense and such news could weaken his nation. Beck agreed and only told his immediate staff that he was leaving. For the conspirators Oster and Gisevius, this was a missed opportunity to communicate the fears of the army general staff to the public: The people did not even hear that the chief of the general staff had resigned over Hitler's foreign policy.

Oster realized that, even with their concerns, the generals would not stand up to Hitler unless the British made it plain that a Czech invasion would lead to war. He had also seen that reasoned arguments like Beck's made no impact on Hitler.

Removing Hitler seemed to be the only way forward, and he quickly found that this could still be an option. The man who was replacing Beck, General of Artillery Franz Halder, called Oster to his office and asked about the coup plans. Halder had been deeply upset by the Nazis' treatment of Fritsch, but he was a cautious, noncommittal man, and he asked who the civilian administrators were who might be part of a post-Hitler government. Halder was unimpressed by the mention of Goerdeler, but he was interested in Dr. Hjalmar Schacht, a former Nazi minister of economics who had resigned over a disagreement with Göring, but remained—for the time being—president of the Reichsbank.

Oster arranged for the two men to meet at Schacht's apartment. Halder, who was humorless, impatient, and unused to making small talk, asked the economist immediately if he would take over if Hitler's push to war "made a violent overthrow of his regime unavoidable." Schacht said he would, and Halder nodded.

The next night Halder summoned Gisevius to his apartment to find out what the police thought of the proposed coup. The general answered the door and hurried the former Gestapo man in himself, having given his servants the night off. Gisevius, who was close to Arthur Nebe, of the Kripo, the criminal police, found that Halder's hatred of Hitler appeared to be strong. He called the Führer a madman and a criminal for the events of the Night of the Long Knives and the "countless murders" in the concentration camps.

However, Gisevius was concerned by Halder's apparent hesitancy over the coup. He seemed to favor waiting for the Czech invasion to go ahead and, if the British and French intervened, launching the coup then. Even so, he felt Hitler should meet with an "accident" or air attack that could be attributed to the British, and would not appear to the German public to be a coup by the army.

Halder had no reservations about Gisevius. He contacted Oster to say he was so impressed with the man that he wanted the two of them to prepare an outline of all police measures to be taken in the event of a coup.

Oster then met with infantry general Erwin von Witzleben, who commanded the army in Berlin. A no-nonsense, uncomplicated man who had commanded Oster during the 1920s and was fond of him, Witzleben listened intently to the details of the coup. His only question was with regard to a rumor he had heard that Hitler had a secret agreement with Britain and France in which they allowed him to take certain territories as long as he supported them against Bolshevism. Was the rumor true? Witzleben asked. No, there was no agreement, Oster told him. Hitler was misleading his generals and driving Germany toward war. Witzleben placed himself at the conspirators' disposal.

Gisevius met with Wolf-Heinrich Graf von Helldorf, the president of the city's police and a former member of the SA. Gisevius had known Helldorf for some time and had been gently preparing him for the possibility of a coup. Helldorf's loyalties were not entirely clear, and Gisevius was careful not to tell him names of coconspirators. All the same he said he was with them.

Lieutenant-General Carl Heinrich von Stülpnagel, a deputy to Brauchitsch, began to draw up plans for the coup, onto which Gisevius put a detail after being driven around Berlin in plainclothes in a private car by two friends of Oster. The army would be able to target SS barracks, Nazi Party offices, and the Reich Chancellery without interference from the police. There would be a military state of siege for a few days until the army handed power to the civilians under Schacht.

Halder said Hitler had promised to give him three days' warning before military action would be taken against the Czechs and twenty-four hours' warning before the final order. The coup d'état would take place in the narrow window between the final order and the first exchange of shots.

The only disagreement among the conspirators was what to do with Hitler. Himmler could be removed without causing public alarm, as "people believed him capable of any crime," but Hitler remained popular. Hans von Dohnanyi, who had been preparing a legal file to support a prosecution of Hitler in court, approached his father-in-law, Professor Karl Bonhoeffer, one of Germany's most distinguished neurologists, with his file on Hitler's actions and illnesses. Dohnanyi wanted Hitler to be declared insane and sent to an institution for an indefinite period. The professor said, "From this it would seem very likely that the man is not quite sane," but refused to issue a medical report until he could examine Hitler.[21]

Gisevius was clear that Hitler had to die: A Hitler in jail would be dangerous to the coup. "Rebels could not afford the moral luxury of giving their main enemy even the smallest opening by which to escape and possibly launch a counter-attack," he argued.

IN THE HIGHEST echelons of government in London the concern throughout the summer had been how to support France in its commitment to the Czechs without provoking a war with Germany.

In the Cabinet Room at 10 Downing Street, on August 30, Lord Halifax told his colleagues gravely that the "only deterrent" to Hitler would be an announcement that if Germany invaded Czechoslovakia, Britain would declare war. But they should be uneasy about making a threat they would not follow up on, he added. The same went for Churchill's call for a "joint note to Berlin from a number of Powers."[22] Such a note was bound to force the signatories into having to face difficult questions about what they would do if Hitler invaded.

Halifax then said that he had received messages from some "moderate Germans," but he treated these with "reserve." He did not believe that "the internal regime of one country was destroyed as the result of action taken by some other countries."²³ Significantly, he then added that even after a war, the same Czech state might not be reconstituted in the same way, such were the claims for change from the country's dissident German, Hungarian, and Polish minorities. To the rest of the British cabinet this appeared to mean that even if they went to war over Czechoslovakia, they would not save it.

Only Duff Cooper—the aristocratic first lord of the Admiralty—argued that Britain should be clear that it was prepared to use force, and the meeting closed with backing for Halifax's suggestion that it should "keep Germany guessing as to our intentions."²⁴

The British public, the ministers felt, were very much supportive of appeasement, although "if we were right up against war public opinion might well change suddenly." There were fears of "disunity in the country," and the official press statement about the meeting acknowledged only that there was a discussion of the international situation.²⁵

Chamberlain, who was keen not to alarm the public, left the meeting and traveled north to Scotland on holiday.

OSTER'S EFFORTS TO get Britain to draw a line in the sand had so far failed.²⁶ But he felt he had one more throw of the dice. Early in September he asked Theo Kordt, Erich's brother on the staff of the German embassy in London, to meet Lord Halifax.

Slipping into Number 10 by a rear garden gate, Kordt said he was there to put "conscience before loyalty."²⁷ He told Halifax that Hitler was poised to attack Czechoslovakia within a few weeks and that "the political and military circles I am speaking for strongly object to that policy." If the British would make a "clear and unmistakable" statement supporting the Czechs, then the German army leaders were "prepared to act against Hitler's policy."

At last, the appeals from Oster's emissaries appeared to be getting through to the British foreign secretary. "War would become impossible to prevent if Hitler used violence against the Czechs," Halifax said.

Over the following days Halifax thought about little else. He drafted a speech with a warning for Hitler, then put it aside, before deciding to write a private warning to Hitler, seeking to dissuade him from making any ultimatum that might lead to war. A struggle that begun with an attack on Czechoslovakia would be "disastrous to all concerned—victors and vanquished alike," he warned. If France became involved, then it would be "inevitable" that "Great Britain could not stand aside."²⁸ These were desperately dangerous times, Halifax knew, and he agonized over whether his warning would actually end up committing Britain to the war it so sought to avoid.

Chamberlain did not like the message but consented to it being sent. It was wired to the Berlin embassy and forwarded to the British ambassador to Germany, Sir Nevile Henderson, who was in Nuremberg as a guest at the Nazi Party rally. He choked on Halifax's words and said passing this message to Hitler now would be "ill-timed and disastrous in its effect." It would "drive Herr Hitler straight off the deep end."

A nervous Chamberlain, on being assured by Henderson that Hitler already knew where Britain stood on the Czech question, ordered Halifax to recall the message. The warning was not delivered to Hitler.

A few days later Hitler stood before thousands of spectators at the Zeppelin Field, the party faithful hanging on his every word. Behind him two enormous braziers burned brightly as he claimed the Czechs had tried to "annihilate" the Sudeten Germans, and Britain and France had supported them. "If these tortured creatures can find no justice and no help, they will get both from us," he cried. The uproar of excitement on the rally field was mirrored in the Sudetenland by riots. The Czechs responded by declaring martial law, which in Germany seemed like further oppression of the ethnic Germans.

Events continued to dance to Hitler's tune—and it was a war march. On September 14, Hitler issued mobilization orders to his generals, and there was a sense of panic in the corridors of power in Berlin. Many planning for war who had to maintain an outward display of loyalty were now doubly anxious: As war came closer, so did the fact that they would have to risk everything and launch the coup.

With the Nuremberg rally at an end, Hitler traveled from his hotel in Munich to the home of his friend Martin Bormann in Pullach, a pretty village in a river valley where many of the Nazi elite took holidays.

As the Führer relaxed, he saw a car belonging to Ribbentrop come into the private estate. The foreign minister had a message from Chamberlain. Hitler took it, read it, and said: "Ich bin vom Himmel gefallen!"—"I am flabbergasted!"[29]

# 7

## Munich

FOR ONCE, IT was Chamberlain who had wrong-footed Hitler. The message was an announcement that he was flying to Germany the following day to find a "peaceful solution" to the Czech problem.

Chamberlain's decision was met with great approval in London, where the public feared a devastating new war in which bombers destroyed cities from the air. A crowd gathered at Downing Street to wave him off as he traveled to Heston Airport to take his first major flight in an airplane—he had flown once before, but only for a few moments. The six-hundred-mile flight to southern Germany would take more than three hours, and the world had seen nothing like this before: face-to-face shuttle diplomacy to save Europe from war.

Chamberlain had already decided that he would support a plebiscite in the Sudetenland. The expected win for the ethnic Germans would then get the international community out of a diplomatic hole: "It would be difficult for the democratic countries to go to war to prevent the Sudeten Germans from saying what form of Government they wanted to have," Chamberlain stated. Duff Cooper had told the British cabinet that the "choice was not between war and a plebiscite, but between war now and war later," but he endorsed Chamberlain's mission for peace.[1]

In Berlin, Hans Oster and the other conspirators wondered what Chamberlain thought he could achieve. They knew Hitler's mind; knew that when he sensed weakness in an enemy, he would push further and further; knew that war could only be averted with his removal.

Oster also knew that if Chamberlain did not stand up to Hitler, then Halder—the chief of the general staff of the army—would not take part in the coup, and his plans were sunk.

*   *   *

THE SIXTY-NINE-YEAR-OLD CHAMBERLAIN was in many ways a typical upper-class Englishman: the product of a remote father and an unhappy period at boarding school. He was both painfully shy and keen to prove himself. He was stern, appearing to be without emotion or sympathy. Accustomed to dominating his fellow man, he could be sneering and aloof.[2] Tall, gaunt, and usually carefully dressed in a winged collar and swallow-tailed coat, he had earned the nicknamed "the Coroner" from some parliamentary backbenchers, and he would now be dealing with a man for whom death, trickery, and threats were a way of maintaining and expanding his power.

Chamberlain arrived in Berchtesgaden from Munich by train on the afternoon of September 15, 1938, was greeted with an SS honor guard from the Leibstandarte Adolf Hitler, and then driven into the mountains for the meeting at the Berghof. As Chamberlain stepped from the car, Hitler stood halfway up a flight of steps to meet him. The Führer was bareheaded but wearing his khaki-colored coat with its swastika armlet. The Iron Cross was on his chest. Chamberlain noted his "disagreeable" expression, his "black patent-leather" shoes, and decided he looked "entirely undistinguished"— just like the "house painter he once was."[3] Hitler greeted Chamberlain unenthusiastically and brought him inside, where a round table had been laid out for tea. Chamberlain—the stiff, proper English gentleman—was directed to a seat at which he was overlooked by a large Italian painting of a nude woman. When he tried to make small talk through the interpreter, Hitler said little. Chamberlain mistook sullenness for shyness.

Discussions took place in a small room upstairs in which there was just a table, three chairs, and a sofa. The interpreter was the only other person present. Chamberlain spoke no German, and Hitler no English. The Englishman wanted to have a general conversation and discuss the Sudetenland later, but Hitler disagreed. He demanded the return to the Reich of the Sudeten Germans and said he would "face any danger and even the risk of war for this end." He said he wanted not just the people but any territory "where there was a majority for Germany."

"Would Britain agree to the secession of these areas," Hitler asked, "or would she not?"[4]

Chamberlain, feeling his face-to-face meeting had brought him to the nub of the issue, went home to confer with his cabinet. A joint press statement revealed that a further meeting would take place in a "few days."

In Downing Street, he outlined his meeting to the cabinet and said that in his assessment, Hitler's objectives were "strictly limited."[5] He reported that he had told him "on principle" he "had nothing to say against the separation of the Sudeten Germans from the rest of Czechoslovakia."[6] The majority of the cabinet supported Chamberlain, but the voices of dissent were growing. This time there were more nods of approval when Duff Cooper spoke out, saying the primary interest of Britain had to be preventing "any single power dominating Europe." Leaning forward, the old Etonian with the neat mustache and swept-back dark hair said he found it difficult to believe that the "self-determination of the Sudeten Germans was Hitler's last aim." He saw "no chance of peace in Europe so long as there is a Nazi regime in Germany."

The Lord Privy Seal, Earl De La Warr, did not disagree with a plebiscite but said to hold one based on German threats would be "unfair to the Czechs and dishonourable to ourselves." Lord Halifax, on whom the true nature of Hitler's promises was slowly dawning, said the British were being blackmailed by the Germans.

But Chamberlain had effectively opened the door to Hitler for a solution by self-determination. All he had in return so far was a promise by Hitler to postpone a military solution for a few days. Britain now consulted and obtained the agreement of the French, and only then did they consult the Czechs, who were told they must surrender parts of their country or face the Wehrmacht alone.

The Czech president, Edvard Beneš, a veteran politician and skilled diplomat, asked his chief of military intelligence how long his forces would hold out against the Germans without help.

"About three weeks," was the reply.

With Poland and Hungary also threatening to act for their citizens in Czechoslovakia, Beneš felt he had little choice. He hoped, he said, that if the Czechs accepted the plan and Hitler attacked anyway, then the British and French would come to his people's aid.

IN BERLIN, THE conspirators felt that as there had been no agreement between Hitler and Chamberlain at the Berghof, then they had to go ahead with the final preparations for their coup.

Meeting at Oster's home on the Bayerische Strasse south of the Kurfürstendamm in Wilmersdorf, they discussed the arrest of Hitler, and the Abwehr colonel introduced them to a short, stocky man in his late thirties who had a very different bearing from the middle- and upper-class men gathered around the room.

Major Friedrich Wilhelm Heinz had been a teenage soldier during the First World War and a member of various right-wing groups in the deeply troubled years that followed it. A commander in the feared Stahlhelm, Bund der Frontsoldaten (Steel Helmet, League of Front Soldiers), he had been suspected of many political murders but had fallen out with the Nazis and had only narrowly avoided being killed with his close friend Gregor Strasser during the purge of 1934. An agitator with an axe to grind, Heinz had been taken in by Oster and provided the protection of the Abwehr. He would now lead the armed escort that would accompany Witzleben into the Reich Chancellery to arrest Hitler. Heinz had already chosen and assembled the thirty soldiers to take part, and had brought them together on the pretext of a special training course. The men were being held in various private apartments around Berlin, while Abwehr Major Helmut Groscurth—a parson's son and an old-style Christian nationalist like Oster who loathed the Nazis—had procured weapons and explosives.

Oster explained that there were between twelve and fifteen members of the Leibstandarte Adolf Hitler on duty at the Reich Chancellery at any one time. There was a guard at the main entrance on Wilhelmstrasse and at various points inside. Heinz said they all could be overwhelmed as long as his raiders had the element of surprise.

Listening to Heinz, the resisters acknowledged that the arrest might entail bloodshed but stressed the words of Ludwig Beck, who was not present: "Assassination is still murder." Carl Goerdeler told Oster: "This [new] nation must not begin by flouting the Fifth Commandment." All agreed that if Hitler ordered the attack on Czechoslovakia, he would be arrested and detained for trial.

As the others left, Heinz and Franz Maria Liedig, a Kriegsmarine lieutenant-commander attached to the Abwehr, stayed behind. Now speaking frankly, both stressed to Oster that Hitler must not be arrested: He had to be killed. "A Hitler alive is stronger than all of our divisions," Heinz said.[7]

Oster nodded and looked at the door through which his coconspirators had just left. He was aware that he was entering a conspiracy within a conspiracy, taking a route that most of his friends had expressly forbidden. But he also felt that Heinz was right. For Oster, National Socialism had become "an ideology of such sinister immorality that traditional values and loyalties no longer applied."[8]

They decided that whether or not Hitler's guards at the Reich Chancellery opened fire, Heinz would—and in the confusion Hitler would be killed.

Heinz was no idealist for freedom and democracy. He was a violent and unapologetic fascist. But, for mainly personal reasons, he was the man now most likely to kill Adolf Hitler and stop a war.

HITLER HAD OFFERED to fly to England for the second meeting, although he accepted that might cause anti-German demonstrations and worsen the situation. Instead he shortened Chamberlain's flight by meeting in the lower Rhine resort of Bad Godesberg.

Hitler waited on the west bank of the Rhine on the terrace of the Rheinhotel Dreesen, a favorite of his. It was owned by a longtime Nazi supporter, and it was from this hotel that Hitler had launched his Night of the Long Knives. Chamberlain's hotel was on the other side of the river. Owned by the businessman behind Eau de Cologne, it offered guests fifteen different samples of the product in its sumptuous rooms. But the reception for Chamberlain was far from sweet.

At the Dreesen, Hitler led Chamberlain into a large room with a very long table topped with green baize. Hitler sat at the head of the table and Chamberlain sat on his right. There was silence, and then Hitler made a gesture that the Englishman and the translator interpreted as "Your move."

Chamberlain told him that the Anglo-French plan for a cessation of territory occupied by a majority of Sudeten Germans had been accepted by Prague, to which Hitler replied: "I am very sorry, but all that is no longer of use." Czechoslovakia was an "artificial structure," Hitler said. The Polish and Hungarian claims to Czech land must be settled, too, and all non-German-speaking Czechs had to move out of areas occupied by Germans. The German army would move in, and a plebiscite could follow in which only the German-speakers would vote.

Hitler took Chamberlain downstairs to where maps had already been laid out on a table, and he showed him where the "language boundary" should be. His armies were ready to move at a "moment's notice," Hitler said.

Chamberlain returned to London, shocked and disappointed. He had put his political career on the line and had brought Hitler exactly what he had said he wanted at the Berghof. Hitler's change of mind put him under further pressure. British public opinion was likely to change if he made further concessions to the German leader. While there was fear of war, there had already been large demonstrations in Whitehall with marchers carrying "Stand by the Czechs" banners.

On his flight home Chamberlain's plane followed the Thames, and he imagined a German bomber taking the same course. The thought made his blood run cold. Back in Downing Street, he asked his cabinet whether Hitler's new demands "justified us in going to war" and said he felt Britain had no choice but to let Germany occupy the Sudetenland.[9] All around the table listened gravely to his words, knowing that to give Hitler what he wanted would effectively place the rest of Czechoslovakia at Hitler's mercy.

Lord Halifax, the foreign secretary who had agonized over betraying Chamberlain, felt he could no longer support appeasement, saying Hitler has "given us nothing." He added: "So long as Nazism lasted, peace would be uncertain."[10]

But while Halifax said he did not feel that it would be right to put pressure on the Czechs to accept, the cabinet found itself again fudging the issue: agreeing not to say what Britain would do if Prague rejected Hitler's demands. They feared the prospect of encouraging the Czechs to fight, as they did not feel Britain could help defend them.

All the same, they agreed the Czechs could yield no more. They consulted the French government, which agreed, saying that Hitler proposed to "destroy Czechoslovakia and dominate Europe."[11] Chamberlain composed a letter to be hand-delivered by Sir Horace Wilson, a senior civil servant, to Hitler, who was now back—within reach of the anti-Nazi conspirators—in Berlin.

Wilson, Sir Nevile Henderson, and Sir Ivone Kirkpatrick—part of Henderson's staff at the Berlin embassy—were ushered into Hitler's office in the Reich Chancellery at five in the afternoon on September 26. The letter was read out by Hitler's translator with the Führer making angry interjections throughout. When Hitler heard that his demands were "wholly unacceptable" to the Czechs, he pushed back his chair and walked to the door. Then he turned and came back.

Chamberlain had asked for a "settlement of negotiation" based on a meeting between representatives of the German and Czech governments. Hitler said a Czech leader could visit Germany as long as he realized that the territory should be handed over before October 1.

Afterwards, Kirkpatrick noted that Hitler seemed "bent on having his little war."[12]

HITLER WENT STRAIGHT from the reading of the letter to the packed auditorium of the Sportpalast on Potsdamerstrasse where he addressed SS, SA, and other Nazi Party members.

In an hour-long speech he spat out the name of the Czech president more than thirty times and dismissed the Czech nation as a "Bolshevik canal" into Europe. It was for Beneš to choose between war and peace, Hitler said, and he must "make his choice!"

As Hitler slumped into his chair, Goebbels—who stage-managed the events at the Sportpalast—screamed into the microphone: "One thing is sure: 1918 will never be repeated!"

Hitler leaped back to his feet, pounded the lectern in front of him, and shouted: "Ja!"[13]

Hitler, the American journalist William Shirer noted, appeared to have "completely lost control of himself," and there was an unease about the possibility of war around Berlin.[14]

To rally the people around its armed forces, Hitler ordered a motorized division on its way to the Czech frontier to be diverted through the center of the city at dusk when everyone was leaving work for home. Horse-drawn cannons, trucks, tanks, and soldiers paraded down Wilhelmstrasse in a long column, but there were no flowers thrown and no cheers. Some people ducked into the subway to avoid having to acknowledge the parade; others just looked on in silence. They appeared not to see a proud display of might, as Hitler had intended, but a reminder of the horrors of 1918. These were hard sentiments to express in such a tightly controlled police state. Shirer said: "It has been the most striking demonstration against war I've ever seen. They [the German people] are dead set against war."[15]

Hitler stood on the balcony to review the parade, but there were no shouts of support and no hands raised in the Hitler salute. The contrast with the handpicked crowd inside the Sportpalast was stark. Whatever the public's feeling toward the Sudeten Germans, only a small proportion thought them worth going to war over.

Knowing that he had staked his prestige on seizing the Sudetenland within days, Hitler skulked back inside and let the rest of the column march by unreviewed.

GISEVIUS DISCUSSED THE reaction of the people with Oster. He had never seen soldiers treated so badly in Berlin. People had turned away, even raised their fists.

The conspirators realized that if Hitler went to war now and they acted quickly, they could actually succeed—and have significant support from the population.

Oster reacted to Hitler's obstructiveness and fresh demands at Bad Godesberg with enthusiasm. To him they had constituted real proof that Hitler wanted war, no matter what.

Hitler's order to attack must be only days away. Erich Kordt had checked whether new security measures had been brought in at the Reich Chancellery. They had not. Oster said Heinz and his men were now waiting at a single location near Wilhelmstrasse, where they had been fully briefed.

Berlin was ready, but what would London now do?

THE POSITION BEFORE Chamberlain's cabinet was stark.

To appease Hitler, the Czechs would have to withdraw behind the red lines that Hitler had drawn through their country or be invaded.

Sir Horace Wilson telephoned London from Berlin to say that Hitler appeared to only want the Czechs to accept this one demand. Wilson told Chamberlain that Hitler had told the crowd at the Sportpalast: "I have no further interest in the Czech state . . . We want no Czechs!"[16]

Chamberlain asked his cabinet if he should advise the Czechs to accept their fate. Duff Cooper said the British government would in effect be asking the Czechs to surrender and he "could not be associated with it." Halifax said: "We could not press the Czechoslovakian Government to do what we believed to be wrong."

With a sigh, Chamberlain acceded to a cabinet decision that if France went to war in aid of Czechoslovakia, then Britain would support the French.

Closing the meeting, he announced that he had authorized the mobilization of the Royal Navy.

Chamberlain sat alone as everyone left, feeling his efforts to maintain peace had come to nothing. The other members of the cabinet wandered out slowly, speaking in hushed tones.

Only Duff Cooper moved quickly. He rushed to put a call through to the press section of the Admiralty to make sure the mobilization of the fleet was in the morning newspapers.

ON SEPTEMBER 28, Berlin's corridors of power buzzed with the news that Britain and France had taken measures toward mobilization. Oster was in his office among the maze of corridors in the Abwehr office. The Western powers seemed to be making a stand—an intervention that would allow Oster to launch the coup. He prepared to order Heinz and his men to move.

But this would be a day for diplomats. At the Reich Chancellery, as Hitler brooded and wondered if the British and French were bluffing, his aides handed him a letter from the US embassy. It was signed by Roosevelt and called for a conference of "all the nations directly interested" to be held at a neutral location in Europe. In the meantime, Chamberlain contacted the Italians and asked them to support the idea of the conference. Mussolini, unclear on Hitler's plans, said he would, and the Italian ambassador to Germany rushed to the Reich Chancellery, where he backed the proposal made in Roosevelt's letter.

Hitler thought long and hard, and then agreed to a conference as long as Mussolini attended in person. Invitations were drawn up immediately and sent to London and Paris. The conference would take place the next day in Munich.

The intervention by Mussolini broke the tension in the Reich Chancellery. Hitler returned in silence to his office. He had initially reacted to Il Duce's support for a conference with anger, but now he saw that it gave him a way to save face and buy time. To him it was obvious that Britain and France would do anything to avoid war and that he would go to Munich and press home his advantage.

He had been unnerved by the sight of the people in Berlin, silent and grave as the soldiers had gone by, and by the news that Britain had mobilized its fleet—the Royal Navy still engendering a sense of awe in Europe.

His military plan for the invasion of Czechoslovakia had been dependent on a surprise attack. That element of surprise had been lost over recent weeks. It suited Hitler to wait it out and strike later.

Word of the peace conference spread quickly through the conspirators.

When Oster's telephone rang, he listened to the news and replaced the receiver in silence. It was completely unexpected. The rug had been pulled from beneath his feet.

In Munich, Hitler and Chamberlain agreed that German soldiers would occupy the Sudetenland on October 10. Plebiscites would be held later.

The government in Prague had lost a key fortified frontier and any real sense that the international community would protect it. Duff Cooper resigned from the cabinet and told the House of Commons: "We have taken away the defences of Czechoslovakia in the same breath as we have guaranteed them, as though you were to deal a man a mortal blow and at the same time insure his life."

Churchill said Britain had suffered a "total and unmitigated defeat" and that "silent, mournful, abandoned, broken" Czechoslovakia "recedes into the darkness."

"This is only the first sip—the first foretaste of a bitter cup which will be proffered to us year by year—unless by a supreme recovery of our moral health and martial vigour, we rise again and take our stand for freedom," he stated.

Chamberlain, who had returned to Britain waving the agreement from Hitler and declaring it "peace for our time," awaited the parliamentary vote. The resolution was to approve the policy of "His Majesty's Government by which war was averted in the recent crisis and [the House] supports their efforts to secure a lasting peace." Approval for the Munich Agreement was carried 366 votes to 144. It had an even easier passage through the French parliament.

The Czechs had made all the sacrifices.

THE DAY AFTER the Munich Agreement was signed, Hitler's forces entered the Sudetenland. The German people rejoiced in another bloodless victory, and the conspirators felt unable to act.

Halder and many others would not now support a coup, and the troops would not revolt at the hour of Hitler's greatest triumph. To act now, as Hitler had not only "rescued" the Sudeten Germans but also maintained the peace, would have made the conspirators the new "stab-in-the-back" villains of the German people. Without military or public support, the coup would not succeed.

The conspirators had pinned their plans on two elements that were beyond their control: British and French support, and Hitler's declaration of war. They had come close but were now despondent. They had, though, delicately developed the first organized unit of violent resistance to Hitler, and some of the spirit would remain. Heinz, who had been tasked to kill Hitler, would be one of history's "nearly men." He and his men had been armed and stationed at army headquarters before the decision had been made to stand down.

In Berlin, Oster and Gisevius brought their files on the coup to Witzleben's home and began to toss them on the roaring fire in the grand fireplace in his living room. As the documents burned, the conspirators sat and had a drink, not to celebrate Hitler's triumph but to commiserate "on the calamity that had befallen Europe."

Gisevius said: "Chamberlain has saved Hitler."[17]

FROM HIS HOTEL room in the Hotel Adlon, close to the Brandenburg Gate, American journalist William Shirer watched a team of men dismantling an antiaircraft gun that had been placed on the roof of the IG Farben headquarters directly across the Unter den Linden.

Perhaps now there would not be war after all.

A few blocks away, another American had a more informed perspective. His knowledge was based on intelligence from the heart of German economic planning: from Arvid Harnack himself. Donald Heath knew that Munich had not stopped war, only postponed it.

# 8

## America's Spy

LOCKED IN HIS cabin on the trans-Atlantic liner, Donald Heath had avoided the cold chill of the deck and immersed himself in the stack of paperwork that had been thrust on him when he had left the United States.

Heath was a career foreign service officer, with a great deal of other experience besides. With a sociable wife, Louise, Heath could play the part of the perfect diplomat, but he was also a former newspaperman who had served as an army lieutenant during the First World War. A short, handsome extrovert, Heath was a skilled listener and collector of information. He spoke excellent German and was a shrewd judge of people: an excellent choice for America's spy in Berlin.

Officially, Heath had been assigned as first secretary to William Dodd's replacement as ambassador, Hugh Wilson. Wilson was one of the old-fashioned diplomats whom Dodd despised. To him, the foreign service was a "pretty good club," and he intended to make sure he made no waves with his new hosts. A committed isolationist, he told Germany's foreign minister, Joachim von Ribbentrop, that if war in Europe came, he would do all he could to keep Roosevelt out of it.

The Nazis were pleased with the new appointment—a troublesome, if ineffective liberal had been replaced with someone who dismissed the American press as "Jewish-controlled" and believed Hitler had "pulled his people from moral and economic despair."[1]

But as Wilson sought to build bridges with the Nazi regime and German businesses, Heath would be doing something quite different. The forty-three-year-old had been personally chosen for the mission by one of the most powerful men in the United States, Treasury Secretary Henry Morgenthau, who had expressed a desperate need for good economic intelligence from Germany. The role in many ways reflected Washington's view at the time: That there was felt to be a primary need for economic intelligence, rather than confirmation of the persecution of the Jews or the conditions in concentration camps, revealed that the Americans had not yet woken up to the crimes against humanity that the Nazis had built into their political structure.

Morgenthau's desire for an economic spy in Berlin caused problems with the accountants. Cost-cutting at the State Department dictated that while the first secretary would be nominally attached to the department, he would be primarily employed by the office of the Coordinator of Information (COI), the forerunner of the intelligence agency the Office of Strategic Services. There would be additional pay and a special entertainment allowance to help gain contacts and mix in the right circles.

Morgenthau had high hopes for his new spy, but the Kansas-born Heath knew he had his work cut out for him. Even before he left, he was made aware of a cable from the chargé d'affaires quoting an article in the *Völkischer Beobachter* that warned Germans "against treasonable acts involving the delivery of economic information to foreigners." Traitors would be executed.

THE PAPERWORK THAT Heath spent the voyage from New York to Hamburg reading reflected his dual role as first secretary and spy. It included his State Department brief alongside additional requests from Morgenthau. The treasury secretary wanted details on the holdings, position, and operation of the German Treasury and the Reichsbank, and assessments of the German economy, its levels of debt, and the value of its gold reserves.

Finding good sources of information would be difficult, but thanks to the reports of Dodd's connections in Berlin, he could see he had a head start. The notes the file contained on Arvid Harnack seemed to suggest the German at the Economics Ministry might be able to provide Heath with much of the information he needed. Harnack worked on balance of payments and issues surrounding foreign exchange, and played a key advisory role in decisions on German policy on international trade. On a daily basis he consulted and met with civil servants working on desks at the Foreign Office relating to various countries, and so had a perfect grasp of the international situation and knowledge of trading and diplomatic relationships, and contracts. He knew about Germany's economic capacity, its reserves and production data. Heath saw immediately that there were few people more knowledgeable about the state of the German economy.

Heath knew that he had to take care in the way he approached Harnack. He did not know how Harnack would react to a stranger, and despite Dodd's relationship with Harnack and Harnack's American wife, Heath could not be sure he was not a Nazi double agent. He also knew that by approaching Harnack, he could be putting the German's life in great danger.

Once in Berlin, Heath, his wife, and their two sons set about settling into their new home, while he warned Washington that he would need to be cautious in approaching potential contacts, so they would need to be patient. Circumstances "beyond his control" might get in the way of his getting the highly confidential information demanded.

In the spring of 1938 he approached Harnack, who immediately wanted to help but was concerned about security. How could he be sure that Heath's embassy reports were not being intercepted by the Nazis? Heath said he would look after his informant, disguising his identity in correspondence with Washington. Heath seemed to be a man who knew what he was doing, and Harnack was reassured. He said he could keep the United States informed about Germany's economic capacity, production, and foreign trade.

Heath was elated. He contacted the US Treasury Department to say that the "circumstances" that might stand in the way of his getting information had been removed: He had a "confidential source," a "high official of the Economics Ministry" on his side.

The source got even better when Harnack was promoted to a role that allowed him to meet openly with representatives of foreign countries. The Harnacks visited the Heaths' home for evening meals, and Louise Heath became Mildred Fish-Harnack's guest at the American Women's Club. The two couples spent weekends together and even enjoyed skiing holidays. Once back in the office, Heath would cable Washington with reports on the German armaments boom, details of wage levels, and the foreign trade balances of major German companies, such as IG Farben.

Fish-Harnack's niece Jane, who had visited her in Berlin, had stayed in Germany after meeting a friend of Harnack's named Otto Donner. The two started a romance and married in 1938.

Donner worked in the Research Office for Military Economics but shared the antifascist politics of his friends the Harnacks and Max

Delbrück. Harnack knew Donner would be another great contact for Heath, and he introduced the two men. Washington could barely believe the quantity and quality of intelligence it was receiving. Heath's name was talked of in glowing terms. Such was the volume of material being passed that Heath and the Harnacks agreed on a new way to pass it on. Mildred became tutor to Heath's son, Donald Heath Jr., and he would be used to carry messages between the two men.

In his messages home, Heath pulled no punches either about the lengths his sources had to go to avoid detection in Nazi Germany or about their left-wing politics. He told Morgenthau in a confidential memo that it was a "practical necessity" for them to be members of the Nazi Party as they wished to "advance" their positions in government. They felt the Nazi movement was too strong for there to be a "possibility of combating it from without," so they had to seek promotion to gain more influence and "modify the government." He described the resisters as "young liberals" and told the treasury secretary "the majority of this group are inclined to be moderately Socialist in their views."[2] He added: "What they object to [in Nazism] is the restriction on personal liberty, freedom of thought and the present policy of military aggression, instead of international cooperation, which they feel will eventually lead to a European war."[3]

IN 1939, WHEN Arvid Harnack learned that the Ministry of Economics planned to send him to Washington to negotiate a contract with US trade officials to provide the Reich with copper and aluminum supplies, he asked Donald Heath to arrange for him to meet State Department officials so that he could urge them to be aware of Hitler's continuing ambitions and ask them to support the German opposition.

Heath told his chiefs that Harnack was "a well-placed and balanced member of the regime." He said the German antifascists were disillusioned with Britain and France, as they felt "a firm stand" against Hitler at Munich would have made him afraid to go to war and "the check on his prestige would have been sufficient to bring down his regime." He added: "Their one hope is President Roosevelt, in whose democratic ideals and ability they have a very considerable belief."[4]

Heath succeeded in getting Harnack a short, secret meeting with Treasury Department officials, but the German was asked almost no questions and his answers were brushed aside. Back in Berlin, Harnack lamented to his wife that even after Austria and Czechoslovakia, the Americans could not see the danger. They had seemed more suspicious of him than Hitler.

Lawyer and diplomat Adam von Trott zu Solz knew Harnack through their mutual friend, the historian Egmont Zechlin. Trott encountered the same suspicion when he visited Britain and the United States that summer. Forced to acknowledge to an old friend from Oxford University that some of the conservative members of the resistance would expect Germany to keep the Sudetenland if peace were agreed, he was written off. Even his old friend decided he was "really on the side of the Nazis," and Trott was tailed by FBI agents the whole while he was in America.[5]

When a young American diplomat put together a policy paper for Roosevelt, he warned against the "siren songs" of the German opposition "who held out the hope of overthrowing Hitler and setting up a government of 'reasonable men.'"[6]

All the same, Donald Heath continued to meet Harnack and report back what he was told. Their meetings were carefully arranged, with both men arriving separately in the parkland of the Tiergarten or Spreewald, a wood to the east of Berlin. More regularly, information was passed via Donald Jr. when he came to Fish-Harnack for lessons in English and American literature. Twice a week the boy would go to the Harnack apartment with his schoolbag filled with books from the reading list Mildred had given him. When the day's lessons were over, Donald returned home with a package inside the bag to give to his father. It contained documents that Arvid believed could be of interest to the United States. They were sent in the next diplomatic bag to Washington.

Sometimes the young boy was present when his father and Harnack met. He would be warned not to tell the family's German domestic staff where they had been or with whom they had talked. The caution was well-advised: One day Heath came home to find the family cook photographing the pages of his wife's diary with a Leica camera. She was dismissed immediately.

The risk seemed worthwhile when Heath was informed that his reports now reached the desk of Sumner Welles, the undersecretary of state and the key architect of Roosevelt's foreign policy. One note included a message direct from Harnack asking Roosevelt to use his influence abroad: "[The] President, in the desire to bring the world back to sanity, must endeavour to exert an influence not only on the governing circles in Great Britain but also on Germany as well."[7]

On one of their walks through the Grunewald, Harnack stopped and told Heath he was worried about Mildred. Knowing full-scale war was coming, he asked the American if he could persuade her to leave and go to America. Back in the city, Harnack went to a travel agent and booked an open ticket for her on an American ship. He gave it to her, saying she could use it anytime. She thanked him, kissed him, but said she planned to stay.

DESPITE HIS SOMETIMES difficult financial position, Harnack never asked Heath for money. His work had one aim: the removal of Hitler and a better future for the whole of Germany; personal gain did not interest him.

Harnack refused to be America's man any more than he had been the Soviets'. He was working for Germany: his Germany. That meant that although Heath would have disapproved, he continued with much of his other antifascist work.

His younger brother, Falk, managed to get him a powerful Blaupunkt shortwave radio, on which he and his wife listened to foreign news. Greta Lorke, who was by now married to Adam Kuckhoff, was also another source of information. While by night she offered Jews planning to leave Germany free lessons in the English language, by day she worked as a translator of international texts, including newspapers and periodicals from Italy.

Information from Falk's radio and Lorke's notes on Mussolini's fascist policies—including his racial policies against the Jews—now found its way into small newsletters that Harnack prepared for friends and contacts. If Heath had found out about Harnack's "propaganda," he would have been angry: He staunchly but perhaps unrealistically believed you "don't mix political activism with intelligence work."[8]

HARNACK KNEW THROUGH Heath that the Americans were treading carefully around Hitler, that while the antifascists' message might find support in the German exile and Jewish communities of New York and California, it could easily be drowned out by the isolationist rhetoric that was bound to demand Roosevelt put American considerations first in the event of a European war.

But Harnack felt all he could do for the time being was share information with the foreign powers who might hold Hitler in check. His appeal to America had fallen on deaf ears. He knew of some but not all of the other attempts to appeal to Britain and France. He hoped Dohnanyi and the others might eventually find a way to remove Hitler.

And he remained upbeat in his reports to Heath.

One Heath observation summed up how the opposition had felt and would continue to feel. They were waiting, he told Morgenthau, for a "favourable internal or external event" that would bring about the regime's "downfall."[9]

# 9

## Kristallnacht

WHILE THE WORLD had watched the Czech crisis and then breathed a sigh of relief as war seemed to be averted, life for Germany's Jews had become dangerous in the extreme.

At the end of May 1938, a one-thousand-strong mob had roamed Berlin, smashing Jewish-owned shops. The police followed them, taking the shop owners into "protective custody." A couple of weeks later shops in the Kurfürstendamm, the large street in the commercial heart of the city, were targeted, as well as shops in other cities across Germany. The mobs were acting out the hatred of their Nazi leaders, and were an extension of the government policy to force Jews to leave Germany, but Hitler was displeased. Mob action demeaned Germany in the eyes of the international community, and did nothing to help him resolve the "Jewish question."

In the minds of key Nazi leaders, war, expansion, and the eradication of European Jewry had now become part of the same battle. Heinrich Himmler told SS leaders they must be prepared for "ten years" of "ideological struggle" against the "entire Jewry, freemasonry, Marxism, and churches of the world" so that Germany and Italy would not be "annihilated." He added: "In Germany the Jew cannot hold out. This is a question of years. We will drive them out more and more with an unprecedented ruthlessness . . ."[1] Hitler agreed that it might take ten years to remove all the Jews from Germany; Goebbels felt that was far too long. What was needed was an extended, nationwide pogrom of the kind suggested to him by Adolf Eichmann, of the SD's "Jewish Desk," but an uprising of that kind needed a spark.[2]

In October 1938, Hitler expelled seventeen thousand Polish Jews living in Germany, forcing them to return to Poland. Most had to leave their homes without notice, and many had no current passport. When they were refused entry into Poland by border guards, there was chaos. Twelve thousand men, women, and children were stranded, unwanted by Poland and hated by the Nazis. The temperatures were freezing; they had no shelter and very little food.

The parents of German-born Herschel Grynszpan were among those caught in this trap, and they wrote to their son in France, describing their desperate situation.

Grynszpan became obsessed with the idea of protest and revenge, and on November 7, he bought a revolver and went to the German embassy in Paris, where he lived. He wanted to kill the ambassador, but he was unavailable, so instead Grynszpan was shown into the office of a third secretary, Ernst vom Rath. With a cry that he was avenging his family, Grynszpan shot Rath in the chest. He was later arrested by French police, who found a postcard addressed to his parents in his pocket. It read: "My dear parents, I could not do otherwise, may God forgive me, the heart bleeds when I hear of your tragedy and that of the 12,000 Jews. I must protest so that the whole world hears my protest, and that I will do. Forgive me."[3]

The news of the Grynszpan attack reached Germany that same day—just as Nazi leaders were meeting to commemorate the Munich beer hall putsch, Hitler's failed coup in Bavaria in 1923. Goebbels immediately saw the shooting as an opportunity to increase anti-Semitic activity and used the media to present it as part of a worldwide Jewish conspiracy. The newspapers called for retaliation, and although the Nazis would later portray what was to come as a spontaneous outburst of popular anti-Semitism, a secret plan of action against Jewish people, businesses, and synagogues was quickly put in place. The police were told the trouble was coming but that they were not to take any action to obstruct it.

On the night of November 9, the SS went into action. Shops and homes were looted and burned. More than a thousand synagogues were destroyed. Four hundred German Jews were killed, and many thousands more were arrested. The debris that littered the streets the morning after gave the night its name: Kristallnacht, the Night of the Broken Glass. The night would usher in a raft of new anti-Jewish laws: Within weeks Jews were excluded from all German economic life, Jewish pupils were expelled from school, and Jewish businesses were closed.

There were those among the German people who supported the thugs in the street. There were those who looked the other way, out of a sense of apathy or fear. There were others who turned away and cried. And there were those for whom that night only increased their determination to change the path their nation was taking.

ON KRISTALLNACHT IN Ulm, as in towns and cities across the Reich, the synagogue burned. A unit from the local SA arrived at the fifty-five-year-old building at Weinhof and torched it. The fire brigade only doused the flames when they realized that nearby non-Jewish buildings were in danger of burning, too. A few days later the city administration ordered that the ruins of the synagogue be demolished, and that the local Jewish population—fifty-six of whom had been sent to Dachau during the outrage—foot the bill for the work.[4] The regional newspaper, the *National Socialist Courier*, described the violence as "just vengeance" but was shocked and bewildered to report that some in the area were "sentimental" and not all were in favor of the destruction. "I have heard of a few people whimpering and complaining about operations against the Jews in the past few days," wrote a columnist. "Such simpletons are beneath contempt."[5]

The Scholls would have been one of those families that the writer in the *Courier* would have held in contempt. Over the past few years the children had listened to their father's anger about the treatment of the Jews and the creation of the concentration camps; they had seen their friends and teachers persecuted. "All of us felt that we had to stand together to shield what we believed in and cherished," Inge Scholl wrote later. "What began among us as doubts and misgivings about the Nazis had turned into indignation and outrage."[6]

But they were at the heart of a state in which they had become the outsiders. Even the street on which they lived—once called Olgastrasse—had been renamed. The sign on the corner now said "Adolf Hitler Ring."

Soon after, the Scholls moved to a seven-room apartment on the fifth floor of a building in Münsterplatz, the affluent square outside the cathedral. The lampposts around the wide square were draped with huge swastikas.

KRISTALLNACHT PERSUADED SOPHIE Scholl that to fight on the side of the Nazis would be evil. She told male friends who were in military service that if there was a war, they should not kill anyone. She hated even the conformity of her school uniform and wore a small flower behind her ear just to be different.

And now she was in danger of losing her close confidant Hans again. He had completed his compulsory military service and was looking forward to studying medicine. He set his sights on a course at Ludwig Maximilian University of Munich.

Sophie was in awe. It was her dream to go there, too, and she had already started studying for her Abitur, the certificate that would get her to Munich. Sophie still looked up to her older brother, but now he respected his seventeen-year-old sister, too. They shared conversations on morality, conscience, and belief, all issues that made them think about Nazism.

The spirit of their father was extending through the family, too. Sophie's younger brother, Werner, had had enough of Nazi indoctrination, and one night he told an openmouthed squad leader that he was resigning from the Hitler Youth. Werner turned on his heel and walked out, his conscience suddenly feeling clearer. For his moment of rebellion he would be denied the chance of going to the university and would instead be drafted straight into the army.

Unperturbed, late one night, he went further, scaling a statue outside the courthouse in Ulm and wrapping a swastika blindfold over the stone lady holding the scales of justice.

It was an act of which the young followers of Herbert Baum in Berlin would have been proud.


HERBERT BAUM HAD always urged his fellow German Jews to stay in Germany and resist. After Kristallnacht, he changed his mind.

He had already helped his friend Herbert Ansbach escape. Ansbach, who had been arrested when the rental car company being used to distribute anti-Nazi propaganda was uncovered by the Gestapo, had been released from Brandenburg prison, but his health was failing. Although he was only in his midtwenties, the hardship of life in jail had seen him develop a heart condition. On being told the Gestapo was poised to arrest him again, he escaped to Czechoslovakia just before Kristallnacht.

One of Baum's friends, Siegbert "Sigi" Rotholz, had been at the Weissensee Jewish cemetery when the violence began. A confirmed antifascist who found Baum's friendship inspiring, Rotholz was a furniture upholsterer who struggled to find enough money to help his parents and siblings, all of whom lived in a small apartment on Rombergstrasse. Despite the danger, instead of heading straight home, Rotholz hurried to a telephone booth and told all his Jewish friends to leave their homes quickly and find Gentile friends with whom to spend the night. The homes of Jews were all potential targets.

Baum told his friends: "It is now clear that we are too exposed as Jews and limited in what we can do," he told them. "You should all try to emigrate."[7]

He, though, remained determined to stay.

ABWEHR COLONEL HANS Oster and lawyer Hans von Dohnanyi had followed the increasing anti-Semitic activity inside German society with growing concern. Kristallnacht further convinced them their plotting had to continue. Their fellow conspirator Helmut Groscurth confided to his diary, "We must be ashamed even to be German," and diplomat Ulrich von Hassell, who would soon act as an envoy to the British for the conspirators, wrote of the "despicable persecution of the Jews."

During the September 1938 coup attempt, Oster had gained power inside the Abwehr when Canaris had promoted him to his second-in-command, a way of showing the colonel that he approved of his actions. Oster had brought Dohnanyi into the Abwehr in a full-time post as an adviser on foreign and military policy, allowing him to add reports from foreign newspapers and agents to his file and giving him an office next door to his own. The dedicated antimilitarist Dohnanyi looked uncomfortable in his uniform and with the rank of captain he had been given, but he knew Oster gave him his best hopes of working against the regime, and he began to recruit or introduce his friends into the conspiracy, including lawyer Justus Delbrück and the Protestant pastor and theologian Dietrich Bonhoeffer.

Bonhoeffer was Dohnanyi's brother-in-law. Much more than a friend, he provided spiritual guidance for the serious, bespectacled lawyer as he contemplated the evil that had befallen their country. Like Dohnanyi, he was close friends with the Harnacks and had given a eulogy at the funeral of Arvid's inspirational uncle, Adolf von Harnack, in 1930, and they all regularly met at the Bonhoeffer family home on Marienburger Allee, a large cream house with white shutters and a red-tiled roof, where the family kept a study in which Bonhoeffer could write.

A well-known theologian and academic, Bonhoeffer was a long-standing opponent of the Nazis who had been taken off the air mid–radio broadcast just two days after Hitler came to power. Broadcasting at the Potsdamer-strasse radio station, Bonhoeffer had spoken of how a leader who became idolized could easily become a Verführer—a mis-leader. The microphones had been switched off, most probably by a frightened radio station manager rather than directly by the Nazis, halfway through the speech. Bonhoeffer later reproduced the text as an article in a politically conservative newspaper. He had been both delighted and inspired by his ninety-one-year-old grandmother, who had marched past a cordon of brown-shirted thugs to enter a Jewish shop.

Government power had not been enough for the Nazis. Hitler wanted control over all aspects of society and developed a policy of Gleichschaltung—coordination—in which Nazi influence was extended to schools, youth groups, sports clubs, and churches.[8] The German Protestant church was divided into twenty-eight separate regional churches, each with slightly different doctrines. It had no strong single leader to bring together its forty million worshippers, or to stand up to Hitler. Hitler wanted it unified into a Reich church—which he could control—under a Reich bishop, and made sure his choice for the role, Ludwig Müller, a fifty-year-old former naval chaplain and ardent Nazi, was elected to the role. Across the country Nazi youth and church leaders developed the organization of the "German Christians," who put dedication to National Socialism and Hitler at the heart of the Reichskirche. Martin Niemöller, the pastor of Dahlem in Berlin, led a breakaway group that gained huge support and became known as the Bekennende Kirche, the Confessing Church. Hitler's attempt to unite the church for his own ends failed, and it became no more than an irritation to him.

Like many others from this group of resisters—including his cousin Arvid Harnack and brother Klaus—Bonhoeffer had traveled outside Germany, to Mexico, Cuba, and the United States, where he taught a fellowship at New York City's Union Theological Seminary. Bonhoeffer found the seeds of the civil rights movement, which he witnessed at the African American Abyssinian Baptist Church, both inspiring and instructive. He wondered how such resistance might work in his own country.

When he was offered a parish post in Berlin in the autumn of 1933, Bonhoeffer instead decided to leave Germany again and take an appointment overseeing two German-speaking churches in London. But even while in England, Bonhoeffer stayed in contact with Niemöller, and he spread the word about what was happening in Germany. He became close friends with the bishop of Chichester, George Bell, who had been in Germany at the height of the controversy over the "German Christian" movement and had later spoken out over the treatment of the Jews.

Born in 1883, Bell was more than twenty years older than Bonhoeffer, and he became an inspiration and a mentor. Bell was a literary man with a great interest in internationalism and justice. While dean of Canterbury Cathedral, he had commissioned T. S. Eliot to write his celebrated play *Murder in the Cathedral* about the murder of Thomas à Becket and had invited Gandhi to the cathedral during a visit to Britain in 1931. Bonhoeffer told Bell that the issue at the heart of the German church would become a "question of the existence of Christianity in Europe."[9] Bell had already developed a reputation as "bishop to refugees" for his work with those fleeing Nazi Germany, and had confronted diplomat and future ambassador to the United Kingdom Joachim von Ribbentrop during one of his visits to England on Nazi persecution of churchmen.[10] As a member of the House of Lords, Bell would be a key ally for Bonhoeffer in the coming years.[11]

After two years in England, Bonhoeffer returned to Germany. The Confessing Church had been declared illegal and Niemöller had been arrested in the summer of 1937 and sent to a concentration camp.

For many Germans in the mid- and late 1930s, the concentration camps were an extension of the prison system, for criminals and people who wanted to make trouble for the nation. A children's prayer, "Lieber Gott, mach mich fromm, dass ich in den Himmel komm" ("Dear God, make me good, so I can go to Heaven"), became "Lieber Gott, mach mich stumm, dass ich nicht in Dachau kumm" ("Dear God, make me dumb, so that I don't to Dachau come"), but of course the children had little idea of what life was really like in a camp. Ex-prisoners were forbidden to speak of their time in the camps, and only those prepared to risk a return to the camp would tell others about the ill-treatment they had seen and experienced.

Because of Dohnanyi's growing Chronicle of Shame file, Bonhoeffer was one of those who had some idea. Dohnanyi would bring the file to the Bonhoeffer home and tell him all about the conditions Jews and enemies of the state were being kept in; about the rapes and murders, the starvation of prisoners. Dohnanyi's evidence horrified Bonhoeffer, but he knew he had to tackle the often deeply held Lutheran view that the Jews were "cursed" for the way they had rejected and killed Christ. Bonhoeffer himself had taken some time to come to terms with his own view on this, finally settling on the clear idea that the church owed a duty to "all the desolate and deserted" from wherever they came.

In 1937, Dohnanyi had helped get Bonhoeffer's friend Franz Hildebrandt, whose mother was Jewish, out of Plötzensee prison, into Switzerland and eventually to London, where he was now working with Bishop George Bell helping other refugees like himself. It had been painful to say good-bye to someone he had known for more than ten years—and enjoyed lively theological arguments with every day—but Bonhoeffer feared that Hildebrandt had become targeted by the Nazis and would soon become a victim of the Gestapo.

Banned from ministering in church, Bonhoeffer was traveling between his underground seminaries in Köslin and Gross-Schlönwitz in Pomerania on the Baltic coast when the horror of Kristallnacht occurred. On hearing of the events across the country—and of the destruction of the synagogue in Köslin—Bonhoeffer took to his Bible for inspiration.

Verses jumped out at him. From Romans: "They are Israelites, and to them belong the adoption, the glory, the covenants, the giving of the law, the worship, and the promises. To them belong the patriarchs, and from their race, according to the flesh, is the Christ who is God over all."

The Jews were God's people, and Jesus came from them. The evil done to the Jews was done to God and His people.

He read Psalm 74. The second half of verse 8 made him frown: "They burn all of God's houses in the land."

For Bonhoeffer, this was a revelation. God was speaking to him. This was about the here and now. He took a pencil, and next to the line from the psalm, he wrote the figures of the date of Kristallnacht: "9.11.38."

MANY OF BERLIN'S Jews were now desperate to find a country they could move their families to. Some bought telephone books from the United States, the Netherlands, even South America, and searched for people with their surname. They would then write to them, suggest they might be related, and appeal to them to host them when they went into exile. Only a few responses to these desperate appeals would come back.

Georg Prager, who ran a company supplying fabrics to wholesalers, had been among those looking for relatives abroad who might take in his family.

Prager did not want to leave Germany—it was his home, and the medal he had received for his service during the Great War had pride of place on the sideboard—but he was frightened for his wife, Jenny, and their daughters, Marianne and Ilse, who were sixteen and twelve. "It will be bad for us," he had told Jenny when Hitler came to power, but even he had not known how bad.

The violence of Kristallnacht had brought the hatred right into the open. Now it was plain to see that synagogues could be burned to the ground and Jews could be murdered in the street, and nothing would be done about it. "What next?" he asked his wife as they looked from the window in the third floor of the tenement building on Belforter Strasse. The family was already having to sell off many of its possessions to survive.

Leaving was not easy. The Nazis would not let Jews take money out of the country, and there were endless forms to fill out. On top of that, there were few Western countries willing to take large numbers of Jews. In June 1938 the liner *St. Louis*, carrying 930 Jewish refugees, had been turned away from Cuba and the United States. Some passengers had killed themselves as the liner headed back across the Atlantic toward Germany; the rest were only saved when Belgium, Holland, Britain, and France agreed to share them. The United States required an immigrant to have a sponsor in America who could support them if they became destitute.

Georg Prager did not speak English, so a friend helped him write to people with the same name in America, found in a telephone directory lent him by a fellow Jew. "I think we might be related . . ." went the letter, before explaining the situation in Germany and the help they needed. It was a begging letter: humiliating to write but very necessary. Nothing came back and, desperate, Prager decided he would have to separate the family in order to keep his youngest child safe.

Writing to a cousin in London, he asked him to take Ilse in. The cousin agreed and became a sponsor for the young girl as part of the Kindertransport program, which the British government had agreed to: Jewish children would be allowed into Britain as long as someone in the Jewish community could support them.

On May 20, 1939, Marianne helped her sister pack her clothes into a small suitcase, making sure there was room for her treasured roller skates, and gave her a small diary to write in. It would be as if they were having a conversation.[12] The following morning Ilse was one of hundreds of children at the railway station, all with identity tags pinned to their chests. Ilse recognized some from school.

Marianne's eyes filled with tears as she watched her little sister board the train, and she prayed that Ilse would be safe in England. Everyone cried; her father cried the hardest.

Turning away, Marianne wanted to seek solace in her friends. For the past couple of years—banned from theaters and forbidden to buy newspapers—she had sought stimulation in the group of young antifascists who sat around discussing politics and books forbidden by the Nazis. Their leader was a fascinating man named Herbert Baum.

"Marianne always had to prove that she was never afraid," Ilse recalled later.[13]

# 10

## A Summer Ends in War

THE SUMMER THAT would end with the world plunged into war
began with bright sunshine and blue skies over Western Europe.
Sophie Scholl prepared to take a vacation with her boyfriend,
Fritz Hartnagel. Mildred Fish-Harnack spent glorious days with her books,
sitting among the sunbathing crowds at the inland beach at Wannsee. But
if life went on, there was a dreadful undercurrent to it all. Dietrich Bonhoeffer felt it keenly, and agonized over his and Germany's future. Now
aged thirty-three, the pastor was becoming eligible for compulsory military service, during which he knew he would have to swear the personal
oath to Adolf Hitler. Bonhoeffer told his friends that he viewed the oath
as both corrupting and sacrilegious and as "perhaps the worst thing of
all," but in truth, there was something worse: He might also find himself
in a war for the Nazis, which he would find "conscientiously impossible
to join."[1]

Because after the Sudetenland and the Munich conference, Hitler had
the confidence to push his aggressive, expansionist foreign ambitions
much further.

THE WORLD HAD predicted it but done too little to prevent it. On March
15, 1939, Hitler moved his forces into the rest of Czechoslovakia. German
tanks and trucks headed toward Prague with only the mist and snow to
slow them down.

Hitler knew the Sudetenland occupation had given him a chance to occupy the whole of Czechoslovakia. Consumed by both racism and egoma-
nia, he had always had an intense personal dislike of the Czechs but also
yearned for the opportunity of a triumphant entry into the historic city of
Prague.

Before the Munich Agreement, he had confided to Goebbels that he would concede to Britain and France, wait a short time, and take the rest of Czechoslovakia later.[2] The Czech regions of Bohemia and Moravia were industrial heartlands, rich in raw materials, which would be valuable in a coming war—as would the Czech government's large reserves of gold and foreign currency.

Hitler blustered and threatened, and fearing the sight of Stuka dive-bombers over Prague, the new Czech state president, Dr. Emil Hácha, told his armies not to resist occupation. Again German tanks and troops marched forward, unopposed. As he headed to Prague, Hitler—with a dubious, prejudiced sense of history—told his personal staff that the "union of Czechia with the Reich" had been striven for for centuries, and this was the "happiest day of my life." He spent one night in Prague to celebrate, but the streets were deserted and the snow fell hard. His feelings of euphoria fell flat. He left the next morning, leaving his troops to run what had been Central Europe's last democracy.

Hitler's reception was warmer in Berlin. Goebbels organized a tunnel of light on the Unter den Linden, with huge searchlights crossing in the sky, and a firework display that lit up the sky as his leader accepted the cheers of the crowd from the balcony of the Reich Chancellery. How different it was from a few months earlier when the people thought the crisis over the Sudetenland would mean war. Of course, much of the crowd were the party faithful, organized by Goebbels, and many Germans were not persuaded by Hitler's actions. "Was that necessary?" many people asked, and they wondered what right Germany truly had to Czechoslovakia. Most northern Germans had no connection—personal, spiritual, or political—to the Czech lands.[3]

William Shirer wrote: "It is almost banal to record his breaking another solemn treaty. But since I was personally present at Munich, I cannot help recalling how Chamberlain said it not only had saved the peace but had really saved Czechoslovakia."[4] The Western powers quibbled over their obligations to the Czech state, and as the French put it when they were told Hácha had told his forces not to resist, "Well, Czechoslovakia wasn't invaded, was she?"[5]

But Poland was now in the Führer's sights. Hitler was determined to turn it into a German satellite state, an ally and buffer against the Soviet Union. Its very existence as an independent country was a frustration, its having been ceded by the Treaty of Versailles both the port of Danzig and a corridor of land that allowed it access to the sea—land that cut German East Prussia off from the rest of the Fatherland. Ribbentrop had proposed a nonaggression pact in which Poland would return Danzig to Germany, but Warsaw had resisted.

Munich indicated to Hitler that Britain and France were reluctant to argue with German claims in Central and Eastern Europe. With bravado and trust in Providence, Hitler was prepared to gamble all. But this time Britain and France had guaranteed to protect the Poles. Neville Chamberlain for once was very clear as to where Britain stood. "In the event of any action which clearly threatened Polish independence, and which the Polish government accordingly considered it vital to resist with their national forces, His Majesty's Government would feel themselves bound at once to lend the Polish Government all support in their power," he told the House of Commons on March 31, 1939.[6]

When Hitler saw that threats against Poland had not worked and that this time the British were clear that they would fight against him, he flew into a rage, slamming his fist on the marble-topped table of his study in the Reich Chancellery. Staring Ribbentrop in the eye, he shouted: "I'll brew them a devil's potion!"

He ordered Colonel-General von Brauchitsch to draw up a plan for the invasion of Poland. Known as Fall Weiss (Case White), it was delivered to the Führer's study having been prepared in extra-large type so that he could read it without spectacles. Hitler then added his own preface to the plan, stating that should Poland "adopt a threatening attitude towards Germany," the aim would be to "destroy Polish military strength" and return Danzig to the Reich. Fall Weiss was issued to the army with instructions that units should be ready to carry out the invasion any time after September 1. The chief of the general staff, Halder, who a year earlier had supported Oster's coup plans, now enthusiastically backed the "instinctively sure policy of the Führer" and predicted a rapid victory over the Poles.

Hitler heard Halder's words with a smile. This time there would be no hesitation from his generals. They would smash Poland quickly, hopefully limiting the war to a single campaign, but if Stalin or Chamberlain interfered, then so be it.

However, perhaps there was a way to keep the Soviet Union out of the battle over Poland.

Stalin had felt sidelined by the British and French when they had cut him out of the Munich peace talks, and Poland had further angered him by moving into the Czech province of Teschen at the same time as Hitler had taken the Sudetenland. Deeply concerned by the West's failure to stand up to Hitler, Stalin offered to make an alliance with Britain and France in which they would all agree to come to the aid of any Central European country threatened by an aggressor. Chamberlain feared antagonizing Hitler and hated Communism, but he did not wish to turn down the Soviet dictator, so he played for time.

Once again, Hitler sensed hesitation. He believed his successes so far were down to his iron will, and to the fact that he had refused to be hemmed in by Britain and France. He summoned his foreign minister, Ribbentrop, and outlined the most outlandish proposal: a pact between Nazi Germany and the Communist Soviet Union. Ribbentrop's staff had already been intimating to the Russians that there "was a possibility of improving Soviet-German relations."[7] Ribbentrop and Soviet diplomats began work on an agreement that would allow Hitler to wage his war against Poland and, if necessary, Britain and France without Soviet interference, and would give Stalin the opportunity to seize the Baltic states and sections of eastern Poland, unopposed by Hitler. Importantly for Stalin—who knew that one day it was inevitable that the Soviet Union and Germany would fight over the right to dominate Europe—the agreement would also mean that he would be left alone to rebuild his armies after the purges and that Germany could be weakened by a war in the West.

The world first learned about the pact at 11:30 a.m. on August 21 when an announcement was made by the German Foreign Ministry. Two days later Ribbentrop flew to Moscow to sign the deal. For the German people there was immense relief: The fear of being drawn into a war with the mighty Soviet Union had been a terrifying prospect. Stalin toasted Hitler with Ribbentrop.

Meanwhile, at the Berghof, Hitler's home at Berchtesgaden in the Bavarian Alps, the Führer clenched his fist and banged the table—this time not in anger, but in triumph. "I've got them!" he shouted to his aides. "I've got them!"[8]

His promise to Stalin could be broken at any time, when he was ready. But for the time being, it allowed him the freedom to press on with his plans for Poland. Even now, he believed Britain and France would shrink from war when the time came.

IN MARCH, SHORTLY after Hitler's armies rolled into Prague, Dietrich Bonhoeffer told Bishop Bell in a letter that if he took a public stand, his actions "would be regarded by the regime as typical of the hostility of our church toward the state." He was afraid he might put in danger other members of the Confessing Church who might not even agree with him on his military duties.[9]

Visiting England that same month, he sought out Bell's advice face-to-face, and early in April was introduced to a Dutchman named Willem Visser 't Hooft, the thirty-eight-year-old secretary-general of the Geneva-based World Council of Churches. Hitler's Reichskirche had recently published a declaration stating that the "Christian faith is the unbridge-able religious opposition to Judaism," and Visser 't Hooft had urged a response that denied the idea that race, national identity, or ethnic background had anything to do with Christian faith. "The Gospel of Jesus Christ is the fulfilment of the Jewish hope," the organization stated in response to the Reichskirche's declaration. "The Christian church rejoices in the maintenance of community with those of the Jewish race who have accepted the Gospel."

Bonhoeffer and Visser 't Hooft had heard a lot about each other but had never met. Within a short time, Visser 't Hooft remembered later, they were chatting like old friends. War was coming, probably later that year, Bonhoeffer told him, and "had not the time now come to refuse to serve a government that was heading straight for war and breaking all the commandments?"[10] Visser 't Hooft said he had been visiting friends in Tübingen and Stuttgart at the time of Kristallnacht and had been shocked to see the synagogues in flames, and that if Bonhoeffer ever needed him he should come to Switzerland.

On his return to Germany, Bonhoeffer received notice that he must report for his compulsory military service, but it seemed Bell and Visser 't Hooft had helped him make up his mind. He decided to take up invitations from New York to serve as a pastor to German refugees and to teach at the Union Theological Seminary. But he made the trip with a heavy heart: He did not want to leave Germany at this time of crisis and, within days of arriving in the United States, told astonished friends he wanted to return to Germany as soon as he could.

His friends told him to remain in America, that he was in danger, but he felt the tug of home. Sitting in the peace of the Union seminary, looking out over Broadway and 121st Street, he could not stop thinking about his homeland. "Nearly two weeks have passed without any news of what is happening over there," he confided to his private journal. "It is almost unbearable."

It was June in New York and hot in the subway, but Bonhoeffer would make his way to Times Square and stare up at the newsreel, or smoke a cigarette and read a newspaper in Central Park. All the while he thought of his brethren at home, and when a friend described his fear about the rise of anti-Semitism in the United States, Bonhoeffer saw that his place was in his own troubled homeland. He thought of Dohnanyi and the others, bearing witness to the hatred, and he realized he must be there with them. He had known it from the moment he left.

After less than a month in New York, Bonhoeffer boarded a ship heading for Europe. It would turn out to be the last scheduled steamer to cross the Atlantic before the outbreak of war.

He had received a twelve-month deferral on his military service, but friends were sad to see him return, feeling he was sure to put himself in greater danger with the regime as war approached. But as Bonhoeffer wrote in his journal: "We cannot escape our destiny."

ON AUGUST 23, 1939, the day Ribbentrop flew to Moscow to sign the deal with the Soviet Union, the British ambassador to Germany, Sir Nevile Henderson, went to Munich and drove up to the Berghof. It was a last-ditch attempt to stop war. Hitler told him the British had encouraged the Poles to be obstinate and aggressive. When Henderson left, Hitler ordered the army to begin the final preparations for invasion.

On his return to Berlin, Henderson found that London had ordered the British embassy to burn all secret papers. Embassy staff worked through the night, some carrying bundles of documents to a bonfire while wearing their pajamas. Over the next few days staff would throw themselves enthusiastically into the task of drinking the stocks of champagne in the cellars.

On August 25, Hitler came to the capital and met again with Henderson. The Führer was angry when Henderson told him Britain wanted him to not only desist in his aggression toward Poland but also withdraw from Czechoslovakia. That night Britain and Poland signed a formal pact. Hitler was shocked, but when Göring asked Hitler whether an attack on Poland was necessary, the Führer told him: "In my life I've always gone for broke."[11] For Hitler that was answer enough.

LATE IN THE afternoon of August 31, 1939, with the outbreak of war just hours away, the conspirator Hans Bernd Gisevius went to Abwehr headquarters to see Oster. The atmosphere was charged; all knew that Germany was about to declare war on Poland. He was spotted by Admiral Canaris, who took him aside. "This means the end of Germany," Canaris told him.

AS DURING THE Munich crisis, Mussolini again offered to mediate, but this time Hitler rejected the offer. He was ready for war. The battleship *Schleswig-Holstein* was off to Danzig, ready to rain down shells on Polish positions near the mouth of the Vistula. A million and a half German troops were amassed near the border, with General Heinz Guderian determined to push his Panzer force into Poland at a mind-spinning pace.

And for months the Goebbels-controlled press and radio had been streaming seemingly endless anti-Polish propaganda about the aggressive stance of the government in Warsaw and the plight of Poland's ethnic Germans. The pièce de résistance came in the grotesque form of a fake Polish attack carried out by a handpicked group of SS men on a German customs post and radio station in the border town of Gleiwitz. The Germans stormed into the radio studio, firing shots into the air and pretending to be Polish soldiers launching an attack on Germany. One grabbed the microphone and gave a speech in poorly delivered Polish, which ended with the words "Long live Poland!" Meanwhile, outside, his comrades pulled the drugged bodies of concentration camp prisoners from a truck and scattered them around the building. The prisoners were then machine-gunned and left as the apparent casualties of a brief gun battle.

German radio broadcast news of the Polish "attack." At 4:45 a.m. the German tanks rolled.

BRITAIN AND FRANCE ordered the general mobilization of their troops and at first issued ultimatums to Hitler without clear deadlines for the removal of German troops from Poland.

When Chamberlain appeared before the House of Commons, the mood was hostile. He realized his government would fall if he did not take a firmer line with Hitler.

On September 2, the oppressive summer heat in London broke with the lashing rain of a heavy thunderstorm. Chamberlain summoned the French ambassador to Downing Street, and they agreed just before midnight on the words of their two countries' new ultimatums to Hitler.

These were issued first thing the next morning. In Berlin, Hitler was completely taken aback and turned on Ribbentrop, who had been ambassador to Britain a couple of years previously and had repeatedly assured him that Britain would never go to war over Poland. "What now?" Hitler asked him.

The deadline for a response was 11 a.m. None came. The summer was over.

AS THE WORLD had stumbled toward war, Sophie Scholl had been coming of age through her deepening romance with Fritz Hartnagel.

They had spent a fortnight together in northern Germany, with the sun blazing down on them as they took boat trips and walks. Hartnagel's officer's pay allowed them to enjoy good meals and visits to art galleries, and they laughed and swam in the North Sea.

But in quiet moments they wondered where events would take them, and Hartnagel in particular—for he was a young man, a soldier, and the war was about young men and soldiers, wasn't it? It was they who fought.

While Sophie worried, Hartnagel held her face in his hands and said their time together made him ready to face his work again. When Hitler ordered mobilization, Hartnagel was recalled from his leave early.

With typical independence of mind, Sophie stayed on for a short time in Worpswede, near Bremen, and took walks alone along the North Sea coast. The landscape was dark and peaceful, the air clean and pure. The wind in her short hair made her feel free.

But she was no longer any freer than the whole of Germany. Suspicion was everywhere and was growing with the threat of war. One night she returned to the youth hostel to find that another guest had looked through her books, found banned literature, and reported her to the manager. A row broke out and Sophie became very frightened, but the manager persuaded the snoop not to go to the police; she did it not to protect Sophie but to save her hostel from embarrassment.

On the eve of war, the incident felt like a warning.

By the time Sophie returned to Ulm to begin her final year at school, the war that they dreaded had begun. Sophie wrote to Hartnagel: "I just can't believe that people's lives are now under constant threat. I'll never understand it, and I find it terrible. Don't go telling me it's for the sake of the Fatherland."[12]

NEWS FROM POLAND was reported excitedly on German radio. The bombing raids on Warsaw. The army groups invading from Prussia in the north and Slovakia in the south who would soon meet at Lodz in the center of Poland. The brave Stuka dive-bomber pilots who paved the way for Blitzkrieg—the lightning war that saw the leading Panzers reach the outskirts of the capital on September 8, having covered 140 miles in only eight days. The unpreparedness of Western leaders and the counteroffensive from Britain and France that did not come: British forces landed in France but did not clash with the Germans until December; French armies were geared to defensive strategies and did nothing.

On September 17, the Red Army crossed the Polish border to the east, as Stalin and Hitler had secretly agreed. Poland was doomed. Warsaw held out bravely for eighteen days of continuous bombing but finally surrendered on September 27. Those Poles who could fight on joined the underground or escaped west, many eventually joining the Royal Air Force. Some carried fistfuls of Polish earth in their pockets.

Unreported went the killings of civilians and Jews. Confidential German army documents revealed that more than 16,000 civilians were executed in Poland that September, and 65,000 met the same fate by the end of the year.[13] There were large-scale massacres in gravel pits near Mniszek and the woods near Karlshof. For many soldiers and ethnic German militia units, the bearded Jews of the East, who removed their hats on greeting and were nervously eager to be respectful and liked after lifetimes of persecution, conformed neatly to the racist stereotypical evasive and ingratiating Jew of the Nazis' vicious propaganda.

In Germany, victory in Poland without major interference from Britain and France seemed like another victory for Hitler. Some Germans now began to dream that peace might be possible—after all, the "dispute" over Poland was concluded, the problem removed. The Allies, who had pledged to defend Poland, had failed. They could now walk away, without war. That, in fact, was Hitler's gamble.

After a visit to Poland at the end of the campaign, he stood before the Reichstag, which assembled in the Kroll Opera House, to justify his actions but also to offer peace. "Why should there be war in the West? To restore Poland? The Poland of the Treaty of Versailles shall never rise again." The structure of the Polish state was for Russia and Germany to decide, not the West. God, he said, might find a proper path "so that not only the German Volk but all of Europe may rejoice in the new happiness of peace."

Rumors spread through Germany that this offer of peace had been accepted, and people said they heard an early-morning report on the radio say that the British government had fallen and there would be an armistice. Journalist William Shirer in Berlin wrote colorfully that on hearing the rumor, "fat old women in the vegetable markets . . . tossed their cabbages in the air, wrecked their own stands, and made for the nearest pub to toast the peace with schnapps."[14] Goebbels went on the radio to condemn the "peace-loving rumour mongers" and the "fishwives' gossip."[15]

William Russell, a clerk at the American embassy, watched a gloom descend on Berlin when the city realized there would be no peace. "The faces which had been alight with joy all day were secret and hurt," he wrote. "Berlin was completely blacked out. Just like every other night. But in the heart of the people it was blacker still."[16]

In Ulm, Sophie Scholl—who spent a great deal of time thinking about the meaning of her dreams—described the latest in a letter to her boyfriend in the Wehrmacht. It felt like a dark glimpse into the future of many of those whose destiny was to oppose Nazism now that it finally had brought war down upon the world.

"I dreamt I sat in a prison cell," she wrote, with a "heavy iron ring around my neck."[17]

Britain and France had declared war on Germany, but as yet, they had made no move against Hitler's borders. Belgium and the Netherlands remained neutral. Hitler's plan remained to "bring the French and British to the battlefield and to rout them," but many of his generals felt Germany should maintain a defensive position, consolidate its successes, and let the war go "to sleep." Brauchitsch and Halder urged caution, while others—specifically General Georg Thomas, chief of the armaments office, and General von Stülpnagel, quartermaster general—were vociferous in their objections, talking of the "insanity of the attack" on Poland.[18]

Over walks in the Tiergarten and meals in discreet restaurants, Hans Oster outlined to friends how he saw the situation. The German people did not want full-scale war with Britain and France, he said. War had been declared, but no damage had yet been done in the West. Peace was still achievable.

Oster knew that many senior officers in the German army had been seduced by Hitler's successes and that arguments that Germany was not prepared for war were no longer believed by many officers who might earlier have opposed Hitler's aggressive foreign policy. Many of those whom he and Beck had recruited to the September 1938 plot had been transferred, promoted, or seduced by Hitler's successes, or simply had lost interest in being involved.

But Oster still enjoyed the support of a core group who believed plans to undermine and remove Hitler must continue. Witzleben continued to recruit anti-Hitler officers to his command; Erich Kordt and another diplomat, Ernst von Weizsäcker, sought to recruit in Germany's foreign service; and that small cabal at the heart of the Abwehr continued around Oster himself. If Germany and Britain could reach a negotiated settlement, Oster told friends, peace might still be restored. Could he and other conspirators, such as Beck, remove Hitler and replace him with a government determined to keep the peace?

Oster shared his friends' concerns and sense that they had been let down by Chamberlain's appeasement of Hitler at Munich. Like them he had been left demoralized and unsure what to do next. But the period of stasis following the defeat of Poland offered a fresh opportunity—as long as he could find new ways of communicating with the British now that war had been declared. Without some British recognition and support for the opposition, a coup would again be impossible.

One day an idea came to him and he visited Canaris's office to run it past his chief. The German resistance's ideas must be conveyed to the Western powers through a neutral and respected head of state, Oster said, and with a dramatic pause he suggested Pope Pius XII.

Canaris digested the idea while looking fondly at the model of one of his former ships, the light cruiser *Dresden*, which he kept in his office. After a long pause he stood and walked in silence to the small balcony that looked out over the Landwehr Canal. Always thinking of several angles at once and fascinated at the thought of opening up a channel to the Vatican,

Canaris at last said he liked the idea. He told Oster he had known Pius when he was papal nuncio to Germany, and they had often ridden together in the Tiergarten. But he was intrigued: How did Oster think such an approach should be made?

Oster and Dohnanyi set about finding the right emissary and discovered a Munich lawyer named Josef Müller. He was clever, cunning, and well-known in the Vatican for the work he had done keeping church property out of the hands of the Nazis. Müller was invited to Berlin for a secret meeting with Oster. "We know far more about you than you do about us," Oster the spymaster said, preparing to extort Müller's allegiance.[19]

Müller shrugged. He was not one to be bullied. Far from being a typical city lawyer, Müller was a physically strong farmer's son who rejoiced in the nickname "Ochsensepp"—"Joe the Ox." Forty-one years old and a devout Catholic, he hated the Nazis and was proud of it.

Oster relaxed. "The central directorate of German military intelligence, where you now are, is also the central directorate of the German military opposition," Oster told him grandly. "We are led by General Beck."[20]

Oster said he knew about Müller's excellent church connections and that he was friends with Cardinal von Faulhaber, the archbishop of Munich-Freising, a churchman who had complained about the Nazis' treatment of the Jews. After Kristallnacht, Cardinal von Faulhaber had sent a truck and driver to the chief rabbi of Munich to help him save the sacred relics from the ruins of the synagogue.

Those church connections were now one of the most valuable assets to the resistance, Oster said. General Beck requested Müller "in the name of decent Germany . . . to re-establish contact with the present Pope" to ask him to act as a go-between with the British government and to explain that German officers were planning to overthrow Hitler to prevent an attack on the West."[21]

Müller told him he had already made several trips to the Vatican, carrying sensitive documents from the German Catholic Church, which had suspected its mail was being read by the Gestapo. Without hesitation, he agreed to help Oster.[22]

Oster said he would bring him into the Abwehr so that it would be easier for him to travel. It also served Oster's plan to keep his conspirators close and within the organization. Müller was given the rank of lieutenant of the Reserve Army, with his own office at Abwehrstelle Munich. Canaris told those who asked that Müller was keeping an eye on the Italians—it was excellent cover, as many senior Nazis mistrusted Mussolini's government. The operation would be designated X after Müller's code name for the trips to Rome.

Müller made his first trip to Rome at the end of September 1939 and with the help of a friend met with Father Robert Leiber, a German Jesuit who was the pope's confidential assistant, and explained the nature of his mission. Leiber said he would consult with the pope, and when Müller returned to the Vatican a few weeks later, Leiber told him that, while the pope would not meet him personally, he would convey Müller's messages to the British. Leiber said the pope had told him: "The German opposition must be heard in Britain."

Pius XII understood diplomacy. He had been cardinal secretary of state for nine years prior to his elevation. Despite being fond of the German nation, the pope was disturbed by Hitler's invasion of Poland. As well as allowing Leiber to meet with Müller, he urged another German, Monsignor Ludwig Kaas, to seek out the British ambassador at the Vatican, Sir Francis D'Arcy Osborne, and explain the situation. Kaas, the former leader of Germany's Center Party, which had helped Hitler pass the Enabling Act that had provided the constitutional foundation for Hitler's dictatorship in 1933, was skeptical, but did as he was asked.

Over the coming months Müller would make a number of trips to Rome, where he would make a telephone call from the small Abwehr office to Leiber and state simply: "I am here." Leiber would then suggest a meeting time, and on arrival at the Vatican, Müller would be ushered inside Leiber's personal quarters at the Gregorian University and be asked to answer a query or provide a clarification for the British. As time passed and Müller became concerned about following the same routine, they switched the meeting place to a small Jesuit church on the outskirts of Rome.

Each time Müller left, the pope would request a visit from Osborne and then give him an oral briefing on what had been said. Osborne would then write a report, which would be put into the diplomatic pouch for the Foreign Office.

The pope told Osborne that the messenger said that the German opposition to Hitler existed in strength and that what they wanted from Britain was an assurance that when Hitler was dead they would not be forced to accept a draconian peace settlement like Versailles.

The conspirators were buoyed to hear that their messages were getting through.

As well as Oster's Operation X, there were other attempts by anti-Hitler factions to appeal to Britain to keep the war from escalating.

The Foreign Ministry included a number of senior men who despised Hitler and wished to avoid war. These included the Kordt brothers; Ulrich von Hassell, a former ambassador to Italy; and Ernst von Weiszäcker, a former Imperial Navy commander and now state secretary. All knew each other well, and Hassell—who had lost his job in Rome during the Fritsch affair—was a friend of Goerdeler's and Ludwig Beck's.

Beck told Hassell that he had been to Poland and "found his worst suspicions surpassed." The SS had "taken 1,500 Jews, including many women and children, and shuttled them back and forth in open freight cars until they were all dead." Peasants were forced to dig graves for the Jews and were then themselves murdered.[23]

In February 1940, Hassell visited Arosa in Switzerland, where his son was in a sanatorium. The visit provided a cloak for a meeting with James Lonsdale-Bryans, a British adventurer who had offered himself as a mediator for Lord Halifax. Although suspicious of Hassell, Halifax supported the meeting because such talks "can do no harm, and may do a lot of good."

Hassell found Lonsdale-Bryans to be a literary man, an anti-Communist, and a conservative—in short, a man after his own heart. Lonsdale-Bryans assured him that he was a personal emissary for Halifax and that Hassell's name would not be revealed to anyone else. "I am not in a position to name the men backing me," Hassell told him as they sat in the diplomat's room in the Hotel Isla. "I can only assure you that a statement from Halifax would get to the right people."

Hassell was seeking a statement from Britain that an "eventual regime change in Germany would not be exploited by the other side" but would be used as a "means of arriving at a lasting peace."[24] Hassell told Lonsdale-Bryans to stress to Halifax that the agreement could only be reached before the opening of military operations in the West.

This "mad" war, Hassell went on, had to be stopped quickly or Europe was in danger of complete destruction or "Bolshevization."

When Lonsdale-Bryans reported back, the British considered what was said and noted that it tallied with the messages from "Mr. X" in Rome. But they did not feel they could give the written assurance that Hassell required. In the meantime, Hitler invaded Denmark and Norway. When Lonsdale-Bryans and Hassell met again, the German diplomat got the impression that Halifax had "no real faith in the possibility of attaining peace" through regime change in Germany.

After conversations with Oster, Weiszäcker sent Theo Kordt to Bern in neutral Switzerland to meet his old friend, the pro-German historian Philip Conwell-Evans. He told Conwell-Evans that "the removal of Hitler would mean the deaths of thousands instead of millions."[25] The Englishman told him that London was losing patience and demanding an assurance that Poland be evacuated of German forces as soon as Hitler was overthrown. Kordt discussed this with Beck, who said they could only make that assurance if there was no longer a threat from the Soviet Union—which in the meantime had invaded Finland.

Kordt told Beck that he and his brother, Erich, had done "all that was humanly possible to convince our friends [in England]" of the "absolute reliability" of the opposition to Hitler.

To Conwell-Evans, Theo Kordt said he would continue to strive for peace even after Hitler moved westward. He did not want to be a German, he said, who, like Samson in the Bible, tore down the pillars of the palace and buried everything in the ruins.

# 11

## Crossing the Rubicon

O N THE MORNING that Britain had declared war, Erich Kordt sat with his Foreign Office colleague Ernst von Weizsäcker in his office on Wilhelmstrasse. Every few minutes the door had opened and an aide had popped in with a news update. The Foreign Ministry had been buzzing. Sir Nevile Henderson had delivered Chamberlain's official demand and it had been rebuffed.

In silence, Kordt had taken off his reading glasses and gone to the window. In the streets, the newsboys were shouting the headlines from the specially printed extra editions of the German newspapers. "British ultimatum turned down . . . England declares a state of war with Germany!"

At noon the loudspeakers on the Wilhelmplatz had begun to blast the news. People stood in the sunshine and listened. Shocked. They had not believed that Britain and France would say enough is enough.

Weizsäcker stared into space and wondered aloud: "Is there no way to prevent this war?"

Erich Kordt was thirty-five, a convinced Anglophile. He had studied at Oxford University. Although he worked closely for Ribbentrop, he hated him, and knew that he had been a driving force behind Hitler's reckless foreign policy.

He turned and looked at Weizsäcker, and realized that the other man had spoken without having or expecting an answer. But the words stuck with Kordt, and he began to look around for some way to stop Hitler.

DESPITE HIS EARLY hopes Hans Oster had soon realized that a conspiracy on the scale that he had built up a year earlier was no longer feasible. Friedrich Heinz had stepped forward once again, and was prepared to lead Hitler's arrest squad, but the wider will of the generals was simply not there.

The always-wavering Franz Halder, who had replaced Beck as chief of the general staff in 1938, typified the response of many. Although pleased by his new role in Germany's military successes, he still detested the domestic terrorism of the Nazis and disapproved of their political interference in the army. But when Oster took a risk and challenged him to help, he said he was torn between doing what might be right for Germany and the oath he had sworn to Hitler. Like most of his class he was steeped in a culture that stressed not only duty but also a strict obedience to authority. "A breach of my oath to the Führer is not justified," he told Oster.

But the Abwehr colonel continued to lobby him, pointing out that he carried a loaded gun into his meetings with Hitler, so why didn't he use it? Gisevius was dismissive: "He simply lacked the will."[1]

Halder knew his moral responsibility, and he knew his military duty, but he ended up satisfying neither. This agony of conscience affected him more than most. Halder went on in his role knowing he should have done something and slowly heading into a nervous collapse, which for Oster represented the wider disintegration of his conspiracy. When Oster looked around his army contacts, this time he realized they were too few, too weak, and too disorganized to act, and Hitler's pact with Stalin, which appeared to have transformed the vast armies of the Soviet Union into an ally, made them fear war far less than before.

A coup, with the army taking over Berlin, was once again abandoned.

Instead, Oster went back to the radical measure that he alone among senior staff had so far dared to contemplate: assassination.

ONE DAY, WHILE out walking with Erich Kordt, he told him about Halder and the fact that he had abandoned thoughts of an army coup. With a sigh, he added: "We have no one who will throw a bomb to free our generals from their scruples." Then he stopped, turned to the thirty-five-year diplomat, and said gravely: "I've come to ask you to do it."

Kordt's blood ran cold. Oster had seen it; Kordt had not: He was the man to kill Hitler. The Reich Chancellery was next door to the Foreign Ministry, and Kordt was a regular visitor. He knew the vast building well and could get through the marble hall and into the vast anteroom outside Hitler's quarters without raising suspicion. He was both highly regarded by Ribbentrop and a familiar face to the Führer, and was no longer even subject to the chancellery's identity checks. Although he could not get into

Hitler's private office, he was often present when Hitler came out to speak to his adjutants.

Kordt would be, of course, condemning himself to death by the actions he was considering. But his conscience told him he must do it. His mind went back to Weizsäcker's words on September 3: "Is there no way to prevent this war?"

The former Oxford University student swallowed hard. He had no military experience and the thought of killing terrified him. But could he in all consciousness absolve himself of the responsibility to save countless lives?

He told Oster it must be a simple plan. Oster agreed: A gun? No, Kordt said at last, a bomb. He would strap it to his body and detonate it when he was standing close to the Führer.

The latest date to be considered by Hitler for his Western Offensive was November 12.

"All I need is a bomb," Kordt told Oster, the palms of his hands sweating despite the chill in the Berlin air.

"You will have the bomb by November 11," Oster said.

ERICH KORDT BEGAN to make more frequent visits to the Reich Chancellery to take messages personally to Hitler's adjutants. He wanted the officers and guards to continue to be used to seeing him around so they would not ask awkward questions later.

Oster called one of his inner circle of Abwehr conspirators, Colonel Erwin Lahousen, the head of the Austrian service, to his office. Dohnanyi and Heinz were already there.

Lahousen was a tall, charming man, with a keen sense of humor, but there was nothing amusing in the conversation that was about to take place.

Oster told him that he needed a special explosive and detonator as an assassination was to be attempted on Hitler. The bomb would be worn and possibly thrown at Hitler from close range. It would need to be small enough to conceal beneath clothing, and in the event of a failure to detonate, it must not be traceable back to them. Lahousen said all such material was held by a technical section and could not be removed without permission from its head and for a specific reason. However, he said he would think of a way. After making inquiries, he told Oster there were explosives kept at the embassy in Sweden for possible sabotage attacks in that country and that he might be able to get access to them without raising suspicion and without a record being kept of their delivery to Berlin.

"Does the admiral know about this?" Lahousen asked.

"No, the Old Man's nerves are shot as it is."[2]

Oster knew that the preparations for war were getting on top of Canaris and that the admiral would never allow Abwehr explosives to be used in a plot against Hitler. They would unbalance the tightrope on which he was walking.

Oster told Lahousen he had until the beginning of November to get the bomb. Lahousen nodded solemnly. Trying to obtain the explosives was a far greater challenge than Oster realized, and it would put Lahousen in great danger, but he would try.

However, the plans of the conspirators were about to be shattered by the actions of a single man, a lone wolf who planned to do exactly as Oster hoped to do: kill Hitler.

GEORG ELSER WAS a thirty-six-year-old cabinetmaker from Württemberg. Small in stature, he had grown up at the family lumber mill, where he and his four siblings had suffered the nightly violence of an angry and aggressive father. Seeing the injustice meted out to his brothers and sisters, and always remembering those beatings from someone who was meant to love him, had left Elser with a hatred of bullies and a profound sense of justice.

Through the economic depression he had worked as a carpenter—and gained a reputation as a perfectionist—but spent a great deal of time unemployed. He supported the Communists, not for ideological reasons—he had no interest in that—but because they seemed to be for the working man. When Hitler came to power and his neighbors appeared to fall into step without questioning the new Nazi creed, Elser would not. He would leave the room when Hitler came on the radio, and when told by a colleague to raise his arm in the Hitler salute when a Nazi parade went by, he replied: "Kiss my arse!"[3] Local officials threatened him because of his views, but he refused to change.

He became surlier and more withdrawn. The family business failed and they all fell out. Elser lost contact with his parents. He started an affair with a married woman and had a child by another woman whom he did not love. He felt trapped, seeing so many of his own problems from his childhood, and his hatred of Hitler grew. During the Munich crisis he saw Hitler as a bullying father on a grand scale, and the ecstatic response of many of his countrymen to the Führer's diplomatic "masterstroke" made him feel even more isolated. Feeling alone, without hope himself, and without any connection to any anti-Nazi groups, he slowly developed a fixation on assassinating Hitler. It occupied his every daily thought as he walked through town and saw the swastikas draped from lampposts and the Rathaus, and it kept him awake at night.

Coldly and methodically, he drew up a plan. He gave himself a year to cautiously collect what he needed without raising suspicion, and even took a job in a quarry for a few months so that he could obtain the right explosives. Something in his sullen, obsessive personality equipped him to be a lone-wolf killer; he confided in no one, never came close to giving himself away.

He had settled on the date and place of the assassination from the outset. November 8, 1939, would see the annual commemorative ceremony of Hitler's putsch of 1923, at which Hitler would address the "Old Fighters" at the Bürgerbräukeller on Rosenheimer Strasse in Munich. A popular restaurant, it was also a place of pilgrimage for dedicated Nazis who wanted to see where it all began. There was little security ahead of the event, and Elser began visiting as a regular customer to work out where to place his bomb.

In the weeks before the ceremony was to take place, he took to eating at the restaurant at 9 p.m. and then sneaking into the gallery of the function room, where he would hide in a storeroom until the bar closed and the staff went home. He had until 7:30 a.m. to work before sneaking out a back door when the first staff arrived. He spent several evenings removing a wooden panel from one of the stone-and-cement pillars holding up the roof of the beer cellar. It was here he would create a recess for the bomb in the stonework. Ever the perfectionist, he transformed the panel into a secret door that covered his work but was easy for him to gain access to over the coming nights. He worked slowly, afraid that the slightest noise might give him away.

By day he worked on the bomb mechanism at his rented accommodation in the city. He adapted the movement of two Westminster clocks to fashion a timer—and a backup timer as a fail-safe—which would allow him to set the bomb days in advance and be well away from Munich before it exploded. On the night of November 2—after more than thirty nights at work in the cellar—he installed the bomb and encased it in a wooden box lined with cork to muffle the sound of the ticking. The bomb was set for 9:20 on the evening of Wednesday, November 8. Hitler was due to speak between 8:30 p.m. and 10 p.m.

On that day Hitler flew down to Munich, but because fog was expected, he instructed his staff that he would return to Berlin by special train. The train was due to leave at 9:31 p.m. and the Führer was told he would need to start speaking half an hour earlier than planned and complete his speech by 9:10 p.m. in order to get to the station. Hitler spoke, ranting against the English and their "broken promises," while only a few feet away Elser's bomb ticked down the last few minutes toward its detonation.

Hitler left the cellar at 9:07 p.m. to the cheers and cries of "Sieg Heil!" from the three thousand faithful who were packed into the cellar and seated at long wooden tables. Most followed him out, waving him on his way, but a core of drinkers remained, raising beer jugs and singing party songs.

At 9:20 p.m., exactly as he had planned it, Georg Elser's bomb went off. It smashed the pillar in which it had been planted, brought down the gallery above, and filled the room with smoke and falling masonry. The dais and lectern where Hitler had been standing were crushed by the collapsed roof. Eight of the "Old Fighters" in the room died either instantly or later in the hospital; more than sixty were injured.

Georg Elser had originally planned to be well away—even out of Germany—by the time the bomb went off, but his keenness to ensure everything went well had brought him back to the beer cellar the night before the explosion to make sure the bomb was still ticking.

On the evening of the speech he arrived at the border of the town of Konstanz, hoping to sneak across the border fence. Challenged by two German border guards, he was taken to their guard post and asked to empty his pockets. He placed a pair of pliers, a postcard of the Bürgerbräukeller marked with an X, a fuse, and sketches of a bomb on the table. Elser had kept the items as trophies to prove to the Swiss and to history that he was the man who had killed Adolf Hitler.

When the guards heard the news about the explosion, the Gestapo was called and Elser was brought back to Munich. The criminal police had sifted through the wreckage of the cellar and found the remnants of the bomb. The X on the postcard in Elser's pocket marked the pillar in which the bomb had been concealed, and staff remembered him as a regular customer. After several days' questioning, which involved him being beaten, whipped, and kicked, Elser was sent to Sachsenhausen, but both Hitler and Himmler refused to believe that he was working alone as he had claimed.

In Berlin, many of Oster's conspirators had been listening to the radio broadcast of Hitler's speech and had gone to bed unaware of the assassination attempt. The telephones started ringing before midnight. There were rumors first that it was a foreign plot and then that it had come from the inside. Many of the conspirators began to think that it was one of their colleagues.

Then an event on the Dutch border seemed to make everything clear.

HIMMLER WAS CONVINCED the bomb attack was the work of British intelligence and had been briefed over the previous weeks about an operation led by Walter Schellenberg, a major in the SS and Reinhard Heydrich's chief of counterintelligence.

Before abandoning his army coup, Hans Oster had heard rumors that Heydrich had launched a campaign to root out traitors in the army. The rumors were true. Schellenberg was on the conspirators' trail.

He had set up a most remarkable operation in which his men had been meeting with two British agents, Major Richard Stevens, who was based in the Hague, and Captain Sigismund Payne Best. Schellenberg and his men had convinced the British that they were speaking on behalf of an anti-Nazi group of German military leaders who wanted to negotiate with London. Schellenberg hoped that if they could be convincing enough, then the British might provide them with information to help him uncover the real anti-Nazi "traitors."

Schellenberg had been playing the long game, but in light of the bomb, Himmler decided on immediate revenge. Schellenberg was to kidnap and arrest the two British agents.

The day after the bomb in Munich, Stevens and Best drove to meet Schellenberg—whom they knew as "Major Schaemmel"—at a café on the Dutch side of the border on the outskirts of the town of Venlo. They were accompanied by a Dutch officer, Lieutenant Dirk Klop. As they pulled into the parking lot, another car rushed at them and skidded to a halt, their bumpers touching. Four men jumped out with machine guns, firing over their heads and dragging them out of their car. "Our number is up, Best," Stevens said as the two British agents were handcuffed.[4]

Suddenly shots rang out. Klop had crept out of the car on the Germans' blind side and was running toward the road, firing as he ran. His bullets slammed into the German car's windshield, and Schellenberg's men returned fire. Klop was struck and crumpled on the shoulder of the road.

The Germans thrust their guns into the two Englishmen's backs and frog-marched them the few yards across the border.[5]

Across Germany, the Elser attack provided the Nazis with a further excuse to persecute those they hated. More than seventy known leftists were arrested in Düsseldorf, and forty monarchists were taken into custody across Bavaria.

In Buchenwald, groups of Jews were taken from their huts and shot in the name of senseless revenge. How many were killed was not recorded.[6]

BOTH THE ELSER attack and the Venlo incident played into the Nazis' hands and dashed the hopes of the genuine conspirators inside the Reich.

Hitler saw his survival not in terms of needing to catch a train but as Providence. "I had the most extraordinary feeling, and I don't myself know how or why," he said. "But I felt compelled to leave the cellar just as quickly as I could."[7] The Nazi-controlled press expanded on the myth of the Führer's invincibility: "Miraculous Escape for the Führer—Chamberlain's fervent hopes are not fulfilled," claimed the *Völkischer Beobachter*.[8] The attack on Hitler—and the rumored links to British spies—increased German public support for the war with Britain.

Georg Elser had been the kind of assassin whom Hitler most feared. "There will never be anyone in the future with as much authority as I have," he had said on the eve of the outbreak of war. "My continued existence is therefore a major factor of value. I can, however, be removed at any time by some criminal or idiot."[9]

Hitler would not have imagined there were apparently loyal men in walking distance of the Reich Chancellery who were plotting his murder—or that Elser appeared to have put a stop to their plans and saved his life again, but that is, in effect, what he did. Elser's plot made it too dangerous for Lahousen to get the explosives. He dared not ask the Abwehr's Swedish office, as such requests were being monitored by the Gestapo. It would also have been impossible to smuggle Kordt into an Abwehr training course to learn how to use them.

In any case, security around the Führer was massively increased, and, ironically, Lahousen was charged with ensuring that the head of the Abwehr's technical section tightened up its issuing of explosive devices.

Despite all that Oster had done to galvanize the resistance, the conspiracy once again faded away. Kordt was furious, seeing it as another failure of the army to tackle Hitler. "Along comes a civilian, such as myself, who is prepared to run the kind of risk that our gallant Prussian generals should themselves have run long ago, and these bloody professional heroes . . . are not even in a position to supply an uncompromising diplomat with something as simple as a small bomb," he said.[10]

In some ways, Oster was relieved the plan had collapsed. He had begun to regret asking Kordt to take on the huge task of murdering a man. Oster feared that the diplomat would not have the courage to turn suicide-assassin. At the last moment the significance of what he was doing might well overcome him—and discovery would have brought them all down. It would take a soldier to kill Hitler, Oster believed.

In any case, the Abwehr man confided to Hans von Dohnanyi, what was the point of killing Hitler but allowing Göring, Goebbels, Himmler, and Heydrich to survive? Assassination without coup d'état would leave the ruthless regime in place to crush the resistance.

FOR OSTER, VENLO also had another demoralizing consequence.

As Schellenberg had tricked the British by pretending to be a member of the German resistance, Oster's peace messages through the Vatican now looked even more suspicious to London. The British knew that the messages were coming from high up in the Abwehr, as had those a year earlier. They had been suspicious then, and now, with war on, they were naturally more inclined to be disbelieving.

Venlo had been a trick, and who was to say the other approaches were not, too? They appeared to be classic counterintelligence ploys. Which Canaris was the British to believe was the real one: the man they assumed might have had a hand in the Venlo incident or the one who might be involved in the overtures of peace?

In addition, the feelings and reports of the British ambassador at the Vatican, Sir Francis D'Arcy Osborne, to Lord Halifax had been influenced

by Monsignor Ludwig Kaas, who felt their peace negotiations were prema-
ture. Kaas "strongly resents this endeavour to involve the Vatican in dubious and nebulous intrigue," Osborne noted in his diary.[11] The pope, in his
briefings to Osborne, said his communication was "purely for information" and he "did not wish in the slightest degree to endorse it or to recom-
mend it." When Osborne asked the pope if he could guarantee the good
faith of the generals, the pope said he could not, although he begged the
British to be careful with the information or the "lives of the unnamed
German generals would be forfeit." The pope told Osborne he continued to
act as messenger as there "might be conceivably one chance in a million of
its serving the purpose of sparing lives."[12]

While the British recognized that the pope had no way to vouch for the
generals, his uncertainty heightened their unease. Some in the Foreign Office in London began to discuss whether the messages through the Vatican
were part of a conspiracy led by Kaas himself. His political history suggested a tie to the Nazis. They also learned that the Gestapo had a spy inside the Vatican Secretariat of State and that his name began with *K*.
Although this was not Kaas, and Osborne assured London that Kaas was
anti-Nazi, suspicion was heightened and continued to stick.[13] When Kaas
told Osborne that the conspirators said Hitler would use "every form of
horror, microbes, gas" in the coming offensive in the West, London's intelligence services wondered whether this was not Nazi disinformation designed to affect morale in Britain and France.

In February 1940, the pope passed on four pages of typescript from the
German resisters, outlining how they saw Germany after the coup. There
was a strong possibility of a civil war with the SS and Nazi supporters on one
side and anti-Nazis on the other, so a military dictatorship might be necessary for a short time, but then there would be a "conservative," "moderate,"
"decentralized," "democratic" government overseeing a federal Germany—
which would include Austria.

The British saw this as a Germany defined by the Munich Agreement,
but they were not completely put off by that. Chamberlain and Halifax
were prepared to return to appeasement if it meant discussion with moder-
ates rather than with Hitler—and indeed were agreeable to a plebiscite in
Austria, allowing Austrians to decide for themselves whether they wished
to remain a part of Germany.

However, even without Hitler, the military might of Germany would remain dominant, and how long would it stay peaceful? As Osborne told the pope: "Even if the government [of Germany] was changed, I don't see how we could make peace as long as the German military machine remained intact."[14]

In the end the British were left with two overwhelming feelings. First, suspicion. After everything that had happened over the past few years—the remilitarization, the Munich lies, and broken treaties—London could not take a chance on the conspirators.

And second, frustration, because what irritated them most was the fact that for two years now they had been listening to talk by the generals of their getting rid of Hitler. When at another meeting the pope took Osborne aside and said the Germans had again confirmed their wish to change their government, his response summed up British feelings: "If they want a change of government, why don't they get on with it?"[15]

HANS OSTER NOW felt almost as isolated as Georg Elser had been. It seemed to him that he alone was being driven to the point of distraction by a desire for peace.

And knowing that the chances of stopping war with Britain and France were now small and only getting smaller, he took action that would cause him the most intense personal pain.

If he himself could not galvanize support for a coup, and if the British could do nothing to help, then the only possible way forward was to damage Hitler's reputation with the public and the army. That meant disrupting the German war effort by helping to inflict defeats on its armed forces. For a serving officer who had been in the army for more than thirty years, and whose pastor father had taught him the importance of human life, the decision was an agonizing one.

It was also a lonely one. He could not share it with others. Even those who wanted Hitler brought down could not imagine betraying the nation's armed forces in the process.

On the night of November 7, 1939, Hans Oster was driven through Berlin by his friend Franz Maria Liedig. As they drove, the two men barely spoke: Liedig sensed that Oster did not want to talk. He just stared out of the window, his eyes unseeing; he was lost in his thoughts, and Liedig could see that he was deeply troubled by them.

At last, as if speaking to himself, Oster said: "It is much easier to take a pistol and gun someone down, far simpler to charge into a burst of machine-gun fire for the sake of the cause, than to do what I have in mind."

Liedig pulled up at their destination and turned to his friend. Oster leaned toward him. "Please stay friends with me even when I am dead," he said. "Be the friend who knows how things were with me and what moved me to do things which other people may never understand or would certainly never have done themselves."[16]

They had pulled up outside an apartment block where the Dutch military attaché to Berlin, Colonel Gijsbertus Sas, lived. Oster and Sas had been good friends for several years. Oster's face was grave as he disappeared inside the building.

On his return to the car, his demeanor had not changed. If anything, he seemed more troubled. He told Liedig he had "crossed the Rubicon."

Sighing deeply, he added: "There is no way back for me."

Oster's handsome face was gray—the look of the soldier who had betrayed his own countrymen.

Liedig turned to his friend and asked him what he meant. Oster could not speak.

The Abwehr man had told Sas the complete German invasion plan for the Netherlands, Belgium, and France. Hitler, he had said, planned to send tanks and infantry through the Ardennes Forest into southeastern Belgium and northern Luxembourg—a strategy that Britain and France had not considered. Oster had even given Sas the proposed date: November 12, 1939. This was not only high treason; he was taking actions that would put German lives at risk.

Over the coming months that invasion date changed many times as Hitler postponed his attack, but Oster kept Sas informed of every amendment, repeating to Sas everything he learned in his morning conferences in Canaris's office. Oster, of course, did not have the whole picture, and the postponements made his intelligence look shaky. The Dutch were skeptical to start with and lost faith in their informant—although Sas, who saw the agony in Oster's face, did not.

On May 9, 1940, the two men went for dinner and Oster said the date for the German thrust west had been set for the following day. Afterwards, Oster called at army headquarters before returning to the taxicab where

Sas was waiting. "My dear friend, now it is really all over," he said. "The swine has gone off to the western front. Now it is definitely over. I hope that we shall meet again after this war."

The invasion of France and the Low Countries was on. As he had done before, Sas informed his superiors of the information he had received from Oster. The same information—again from Oster—had been delivered via the pope, who had received the latest message from Josef "the Ox" Müller on his final trip to the Vatican on May 1. While the pope had taken it seriously, warning the papal nuncios in Brussels and the Hague, and the Belgian and Dutch governments and the Italian crown prince, Umberto, whose wife was Belgian, the intelligence was considered tainted at best—lies, at worst—because of its source and was largely disregarded.[17]

Sas said his government believed the information to be a clever German intelligence bluff. The Dutch secret service intelligence chief rang Sas, and the sarcasm in his voice was thick in the code that he used.

"I've received such bad news from you about your wife's operation," the chief said. "So sorry to hear about it. Have you consulted all the doctors?"

"Yes," Sas snapped back, being careful not to cross the line into clear, as the phone was monitored by the Germans, "and I can't see why you're bothering me in the circumstances. I've spoken to all the doctors. It's set for daybreak tomorrow."[18]

Sas slammed the phone down.

Neither the Netherlands nor Belgium mobilized their armed forces for fear of provoking the Germans. Within six weeks Western Europe was conquered, Hitler's troops had taken Paris, and Germany was within striking distance of the English coast.

When a senior Dutch officer later criticized Oster for being a "miserable fellow" who had achieved nothing, Sas rounded on him angrily, saying he had never met so bold or courageous a character.[19]

Oster and Müller only narrowly survived an investigation by Lieutenant-Colonel Joachim Rohleder, a dogged counterespionage officer inside the Abwehr itself. Rohleder read the transcripts of Abwehr intercepts of Sas's telephone calls and of telegrams sent by the Belgian ambassador to the Vatican, and realized a "traitor" had revealed the plans for the Western Offensive. He took his suspicions to Canaris, who, much to Rohleder's anger, swept them under the carpet.[20]

However, Canaris sought to distance himself from Oster and told him that resolute opponents of the regime had dwindled to such an extent they could be counted on the fingers of one hand.

He ordered Oster and Dohnanyi to destroy any files relating to their peace overtures or coup attempts. Dohnanyi—who considered himself an "ardent civilian" to whom military life was "alien"—argued with Oster over the admiral's order, and secretly decided to keep his files. He felt in the wake of any coup success, the generals would take the credit; his files would "prove that we civilians had done something too."[21] Dohnanyi's files were deposited in a safe-deposit box in the Prussian State Bank. It was a decision that would have far-reaching consequences for them all.

Many of Oster's conspirators, almost certainly at the instigation of Canaris, were now dispersed. Heinz took a military command. Gisevius was posted to Zurich for the Abwehr, where he would later become a messenger between the resistance and the Americans, and Liedig was posted abroad, too. The success in France had changed Canaris's view, and for the time being, he wanted no more part of the resistance. Only Oster remained.

Oster had believed France would prove to be Hitler's first military setback and made a bet with two colleagues. When Paris fell, he was forced to take them for a luxurious meal at the Berlin Cavalry-Guards Club. All around him there was celebration: Paris has fallen! Nineteen-eighteen revenged!

With dark humor Oster bought his friends oysters and champagne, but the meal did not taste good.

# 12

## The Luftwaffe Officer

ARVID HARNACK WAS alone when the man called. Mildred was taking a break in the country to celebrate her thirty-eighth birthday and to escape the RAF air raids, which had begun on Berlin the previous month. Work had kept Harnack in the city, and he was sitting in a chair reading when the doorbell rang at their fifth-floor apartment in Woyrschstrasse, a trendy street south of the Tiergarten.

The visitor was unexpected and a stranger. Tall and very thin, he spoke German but with a Russian accent. It was September 1940 and the Soviets were still allies, still had an embassy in Berlin, but Harnack had had no contact with anyone from Moscow for two years.

Taking off his hat to reveal smooth, slicked-back hair, the man said he was a comrade of Harnack's old friend Alexander Hirschfeld, the embassy official who had been part of the ARPLAN economic group eight years earlier. Harnack was suspicious: The man could well be a Gestapo plant.

Cautiously, giving nothing away, Harnack invited the man in, but neither sat. The visitor studied the paintings on the wall and the lines of books on the shelves, and said his name was Alexander Erdberg and that he worked for the Soviet embassy. Moscow was keen to renew its relationship, Erdberg said boldly.

Sensing Harnack's suspicion, Erdberg invited the German to the embassy so that he could prove he was who he said he was. Harnack took up the offer and was convinced.

In fact, thirty-one-year-old Erdberg was a Soviet agent whose real name was Alexander Korotkov. He was a close associate of Lavrenty Beria, Stalin's head of intelligence, and his boldness and confidence were something of a trademark. Thanks to them, he had so far enjoyed a charmed career. As a nineteen-year-old keen to join the OGPU (the forerunner of the NKVD), he had sidled up to an intelligence official at a soccer match and made friends. The man had got him a job as an elevator operator in the OGPU's headquarters, the Lubyanka, a seemingly unpromising position but one from which Korotkov had been able to make the acquaintance of a number of important officers. Having taught himself German, he got a job in the foreign intelligence service and had been with the trade mission in Berlin during Stalin's brutal purges. Recalled to Moscow when so many of his colleagues had been arrested, he escaped execution by appealing directly to Beria himself. He had now returned to Berlin, officially as third secretary to the embassy, but in reality with a daunting mission: to create a Soviet spy network inside Berlin.

Harnack told Korotkov that he was not interested in money or becoming a puppet for Moscow, but he did feel sympathy for the "ideals" of the Soviet Union. Korotkov sharply observed that the German was more interested in his own "antifascist conspiracy" than being a source for Soviet intelligence, and therefore he would be a difficult agent to control.

But when Harnack agreed to work with him, Korotkov quickly realized he had struck gold: The first thing Harnack told him was that Hitler planned to break his agreement with Stalin and invade the Soviet Union.

Korotkov's intelligence reports began arriving on Beria's desk, quoting his source Harnack under his new Soviet code name, Korsikanets (Corsican). These reports immediately expanded on Hitler's plans to go east, using the occupation of Romania as a stepping-stone to continue into "western European Russia" and to turn the rest of the Soviet Union into a Vichy-style pro-Nazi state.

If Korotkov was expecting warm praise and a medal for this massive intelligence coup, he was disappointed. The intelligence he had gathered from Harnack ran counter to everything Stalin—and many others in Moscow—currently believed. The Hitler-Stalin pact appeared strong; Stalin was convinced that Hitler still needed to invade Britain, and that there was no rational reason for the Führer to start a war on a second front. It made no military sense.

When Stalin asked Beria for his opinion, the intelligence chief chose to back his master's view rather than argue for his agent.

KOROTKOV WOULD HAVE to do more and took Harnack into his confidence. Harnack realized that his economic reports were not enough to jolt

Stalin into understanding what Hitler was planning. Inviting Adam Kuck-hoff and Greta Lorke to his home, he asked for their views. Lorke immedi-ately came up with an idea. A short time ago she and Kuckhoff had attended a party at the home of a cinema executive named Herbert Engelsing, an anti-Nazi who wanted to give Kuckhoff some work writing dialogue for the light comedies and romances that his company specialized in.

Engelsing's wife, Ingeborg, was a Mischling (a half-Jew under Hitler's laws), but she enjoyed the protection of Göring, who wanted her contin-ued friendship so that he could stay close to one of the couple's most famous actresses. Ingeborg Engelsing was well aware of the Kuckhoffs' opposition to the Nazis and had been keen to introduce them to a dash-ing young couple who had commanded a great deal of attention at the party.

The man was an important figure at the Air Ministry, she said, but his views would be of interest.

Lorke told Harnack that she remembered the man's name. It was Harro Schulze-Boysen.

TALL AND FAIR, with blue eyes and chiseled features, Harro Schulze-Boysen was the perfect Nordic Aryan physical specimen, with the family pedigree to go with it.

The great-nephew of Admiral Alfred von Tirpitz, his father, Com-mander Erich Schulze, had been chief of staff to the German naval com-mander in Belgium during the First World War. His mother, Marie-Luise Boysen, was from a family of distinguished lawyers and was a central fig-ure in the most exclusive society circles in Kiel.

Schulze-Boysen both reveled in his family's past and rejected it. Hand-some and good-humored, he had a tendency to see himself as a romantic hero, but he had rebelled at an early age against his family's upper-middle-class snobbery. While studying law at Freiburg University, he had joined a republican group whose aims had been to attack the values of German bourgeois society. Later, while studying in Berlin in 1930, he joined a more radical organization called the National Revolutionaries, which opposed all the mainstream political parties then vying for power in the Weimar Re-public. Clad always in a black sweater, Schulze-Boysen was every bit the typical revolutionary student, hanging around surrealists and opposing everything.

When the National Revolutionaries launched a magazine, *Der Gegner* (*The Opponent*), it aimed to bring together all the discontented in Germany, but its main opponent was National Socialism. Schulze-Boysen became its editor, working with the support of his close friend Henry Erlanger, a Jew. Schulze-Boysen's editorials were increasingly hostile to Nazism, and the magazine was quickly banned after Hitler came to power. All the same, Schulze-Boysen planned to join the Nazis' May Day parade while carrying a *Der Gegner* banner—a provocation in keeping with the streak of recklessness that ran through him.

But Schulze-Boysen was betrayed, and on learning of the May Day plot, Himmler sent an SS unit to trash the magazine's office at Schellingstrasse and arrest Harro and Henry. They were brought to the unit's headquarters, stripped naked, and made to run the gauntlet between two lines of SS men, all armed with lead-tipped whips. Three times Schulze-Boysen was forced to run through the hail of blows, but he refused to let the violent bullies defeat him. At the end of the third run he suddenly turned and ran back through. Reaching the end again, he was on the verge of passing out but instead stood straight, clicked his heels, and shouted: "Reporting for duty! Order carried out plus one for luck!" The SS men smiled grimly; the show of bravado had impressed them. "Man, you really belong with us," one said.[1]

Then they turned to Erlanger, who fell on the third run. Shouting anti-Semitic insults, the SS thugs beat him to death. With a seriously damaged kidney and the top of his ear sliced off by a whiplash, Schulze-Boysen could do nothing to help his friend. He was thrown into a cell.

Schulze-Boysen's mother argued successfully for his release and brought him to the family home. It would be a year before he was well enough to return to Berlin. As he recovered, he brooded and reflected on what he was sure were Hitler's plans for Germany. "I have the vague but definite feeling that, in the long run, we are heading for a European catastrophe of gigantic proportions," he confided to his parents.[2] His mother pleaded with him to stop challenging the Nazis, but Schulze-Boysen still winced with pain at the thought of the swastika one of the SS men had carved into his leg with a knife and at the thought of his friend's cruel death. He told another friend: "I have put my revenge on ice."[3] But from that day his commitment to avenge Erlanger was irrevocable.

* * *

THE IDEA OF hiding in plain sight appealed to Schulze-Boysen's swashbuckling side, and he began to consider a life in uniform. His family connections—and the fact that he was a keen sailor—seemed to make the navy an obvious choice. But after some thought he opted for the air force instead, beginning a yearlong observers' course before his astonishing skill for languages—he could speak French, English, Swedish, Norwegian, Danish, and Dutch—was picked up by his superiors and they found him a role as an interpreter in the rapidly expanding Luftwaffe.

While sailing on the Wannsee in the summer of 1935, he met a young aristocrat named Libertas Haas-Heye, who was blonde, beautiful, and brimming with confidence. Known to her friends as Libs, she shared Schulze-Boysen's wild sense of romance and—despite her being an enthusiastic Nazi—they fell in love. Libertas was the granddaughter of a prince of the aristocracy, Philipp zu Eulenburg und Hertefeld. Privately educated by a tutor into her teens, she had been sent to a finishing school in Switzerland and a college in England. She returned to Germany to resume living in her family's Schloss Liebenberg, a castle surrounded by manicured gardens and a library filled with thirty thousand books. In the evenings she played the grand piano in the music room after a day riding one of the stallions in the stables. Her elegance, horse-riding, and musical talents combined to encourage more than one suitor to come calling. She merely flirted with them all. She had been the center of attention her whole life: Even when her parents separated, they remained in bitter competition for her love.

In 1933 she had joined the Nazi Party's youth movement, attracted by its keep-fit programs. The political lectures she had to attend made no impression on her; the castle library had all the information she needed. Nevertheless, the attraction of Berlin drew her to the city, and she moved into one of her grandfather's houses. Within a week she had been hired by the Hollywood film studio Metro-Goldwyn-Mayer as its Berlin publicist.

Although Libertas dreamed of life as a film star or poet, her connections with the dark side of the Nazi state were close. Her father had run an art school at Prinz-Albrecht-Strasse in Berlin, where Himmler had now established the headquarters of the Gestapo. The family's Liebenberg country estate counted Göring as a neighbor. He loved to visit and hear Libertas's mother, Countess Thora, play sentimental songs on the piano. When Schulze-Boysen and Libertas married in the castle chapel at Liebenberg the year after they met, Göring was a witness at the wedding. His wedding gift to Harro Schulze-Boysen had been a job at the Reich Air Ministry, housed in a new building that stretched 250 meters along Wilhelmstrasse. With its two thousand rooms, stair banisters of aircraft aluminum, and foyer lighting modeled on antiaircraft searchlights, it was the largest office building in Berlin, and Schulze-Boysen now found himself at its heart.

The ministry's press office, where Schulze-Boysen worked hard writing for various Luftwaffe publications, was part of the Luftwaffe general staff and liaised closely with the section charged with keeping a watch on foreign air forces. His superiors talked highly of him and he was promoted to lieutenant. His articles criticized Bolshevism and praised Hitler. On the surface he was now the perfect Nazi from a classic German military family, but his antifascist opinions had not changed, only hardened.

THE REPORTS THAT had passed across Harro Schulze-Boysen's desk at the Air Ministry during 1938 convinced him of one thing: that Hitler's aggressive international foreign policy was leading Germany into a European war. That October he wrote to his parents: "I now say that in 1940/41 at the latest, but probably even next spring, there will be world war in Europe with class warfare as its sequel. I state unequivocally that Austria and Czechoslovakia were the 'first battles' in this new war." While he cloaked his outward opinions under the veil of a Nazi follower, he now had a small private group with whom he could share his inner thoughts.

He had persuaded his wife, Libertas, against Nazism and introduced her to some old friends, a group of bohemian dissidents who looked to him as their leader. Libertas noted that Kurt Schumacher was as blond and handsome as her husband. The two had been friends since Harro's time on *Der Gegner*. A talented sculptor from Stuttgart, Schumacher had been a leading exponent of abstract art until his work was banned by the Nazis. The son of a trade unionist, Schumacher was anti-state and anti-bourgeois but was not a member of the Communist Party. Neither was his wife, Elisabeth Hohenemser, a happy and sociable woman with wavy blonde hair.

Half-Jewish, she had managed to keep her work as a poster artist and photographer. Her money supported the couple now that Schumacher had little work.

Another friend, Walter Küchenmeister, was a committed Communist. A First World War veteran, he had edited a left-wing newspaper during the late 1920s. When the Nazis came to power and cracked down on known Communists, they sought out Küchenmeister and put him in one of their first concentration camps, at Sonnenburg. There he developed tuberculosis and stomach ulcers, and by the time he was eventually released, he was unfit to work. He was nursed back to health by his devoted lover, Dr. Elfriede Paul, another old friend of the Schumachers'. A shy, birdlike woman with round spectacles, Paul had a busy practice in the fashionable suburb of Wilmersdorf.

Libertas Schulze-Boysen brought two others into the group: her cousin Gisela von Pöllnitz and her friend Günther Weisenborn. Pöllnitz was an ambassador's daughter who had started a career with the United Press, the American press agency in Berlin, and longed to do something decisive against Hitler. Her poor health, though, was a constant concern to her friends.[4] Weisenborn, the journalist turned playwright who knew Kuckhoff and Lorke, got to know Libertas through his work in film. Having tried to get around a ban on his work by writing under various pseudonyms, Weisenborn had immigrated to the United States for a year but was now back in Germany. He had resumed his friendships with Kuckhoff and John Sieg, and had fallen for Libertas. Within a short time, and with the knowledge of Harro—the Schulze-Boysens enjoyed an open marriage— Weisenborn became Libertas's lover.

These friends met in each other's homes and talked about what could be done against the Nazis. They looked to Harro Schulze-Boysen, with his respected military position and astonishing access to state secrets, for inspiration. "If you are anti, must you not actually do something against it?" Kurt Schumacher asked his friends one day. All nodded slowly.

LIKE SO MANY on the antifascist European left in the 1930s, the Schulze-Boysen group had looked at the civil war in Spain as a harbinger of what was to come.

Hitler committed to sending troops, arms, and munitions to support General Franco, whose coup against the Popular Front government had widened into an all-out civil war, which already looked to many like a rehearsal for a wider European conflict.

Inside the Air Ministry, Göring had set up "Special Staff W," a department charged with directing men and supplies to Spain. Information on this German support for Franco would not only aid the antifascist struggle—now joined by leftists and idealists from around world, including Germany, as part of the International Brigades—but also be of value to Stalin. With Britain and France championing a noninterventionist policy, aid for the Republican Army facing Franco came mainly from Moscow.[5]

Quickly and carefully, Schulze-Boysen began to compile all he could about the work of Special Staff W: details of air and sea transports to Spain, the numbers of men deployed and how many officers accompanied them, and the German Abwehr's operations behind the lines in Spain. His group typed up reports, and Gisela von Pöllnitz volunteered to post the envelope through the mailbox of the Soviet trade delegation at Lietzenburger Strasse 11. The Gestapo had the address under observation, followed her to her office at the United Press, and put her under arrest.

On hearing the news, the group panicked. Küchenmeister left for Cologne to prepare to escape over the Dutch border, while Weisenborn and Schulze-Boysen made plans to follow him or head for Luxembourg. When Pöllnitz refused to reveal what was in the envelope, the Gestapo let her go, although they did investigate her friends. Schulze-Boysen's home in Berlin was searched, but nothing was found, and when questioned, his superiors described the wonderful work he was doing at the Air Ministry.

AFTER THEIR SCARE with Pöllnitz's arrest, the Schulze-Boysen gang quickly went back to work again. Now meeting at Schulze-Boysen's home, they worked together on a news sheet called *Der Vortrupp* (*The Advance Guard*), while Schumacher and Küchenmeister wrote antifascist leaflets, which would be copied on a duplicator or typed up in a rented room in Waitzstrasse, off the bustling Kurfürstendamm.

Sometimes members of the group walked through the streets leaving leaflets in bus shelters and telephone booths; other times random names and addresses were taken from the telephone directory and the propaganda leaflets were posted to their homes.

Despite an effort to keep the group secure, there was a human desire to share their work with others, to feel less isolated in their opposition to the regime. Telling others was a huge risk, but slowly they took it and drew more people in, finding support from people from various walks of life, such as Oda Schottmüller, a well-known dancer and sculptor, and Dr. Hugo Buschmann, a wealthy cement merchant.

Libertas Schulze-Boysen was, by now, a key element in her husband's group. Apart from their official jobs, they devoted their time to resistance. They lived well—eating out every night—and remained deeply in love. For Schulze-Boysen, Libertas was his "closest companion and confederate." Realizing that his group depended on him, he told his wife that if anything happened to him she would need to be especially strong, in order to carry on with their efforts.

The beautiful, spoiled aristocrat and the handsome military man were unusual "leftists" and were almost certainly never Soviet Communists. They lived in the upper-class Altenburger Allee in the West End, "enemy territory" to any dyed-in-the-wool German Communist, but found their best allies in their fight against Hitler on the Communist side. As Schulze-Boysen's mother put it, "the most active, uncompromising, and courageous resistance fighters were in [the Communist] ranks."[6] For Schulze-Boysen, Germany's future appeared locked between either a dictatorship of the right or the left, and "the Fascist dictatorship gives the Marxist new arguments." The Communists who fought back and faced concentration camps and death were "the martyrs," he said, and he never forgot his pledge to avenge Henry Erlanger.

Schulze-Boysen's group now met only twice a month, but they were altogether lighter affairs than those officiated over by the Harnacks. There would be a literary element, with Libertas and Küchenmeister reciting poetry, but there would also be music and dancing, food and gossip. Libertas was the heart and soul of these evenings, breathlessly sharing bits of news and insisting everyone sing when she played the accordion. Political discussion would not be built around an agenda but would mix in through the night: the natural energy of old friends talking and arguing. Sometimes as many as forty people would join the parties—which also included picnics on the Liebenberg estate and sailing on the Wannsee. New friends included Walter Husemann, a toolmaker and trade unionist who had served time in Buchenwald, and his wife, Marta Wolter, star of the 1932 film *Kuhle Wampe*, a Depression-themed drama written by Bertolt Brecht. Like Weisenborn, both knew John Sieg, the working-class, American-born journalist who linked the Harnacks and Kuckhoffs to groups of antifascists in industry and on the railways.

A young dentist named Helmut Himpel and his fiancée, Maria Terwiel, joined the group, too. Like many, they had personal as well as political reasons for loathing the Nazis. As a Jew, Terwiel had been banned from practicing law and marrying Himpel. Himpel hit back by forging ration cards and travel documents for Terwiel and other Jews. Two Communists, Heinrich Scheel and Hans Coppi, who as a teenager in the early years of the Nazi regime had already been in prison for preparing antifascist leaflets, completed the core element of the network.

And the resistance work continued. Dr. Paul's waiting room in Wilmers-dorf provided an additional space for copying leaflets, with articles denouncing the Spanish Civil War. The leaflets were put in plain envelopes, and Dr. Paul—who traveled regularly making house calls to patients—would post them from mailboxes all over the city.

AT THE AIR Ministry, Göring was delighted with his protégé's work. The personnel reports the Reichsmarschall received about young Schulze-Boysen—highlighting his skills at reading foreign-language reports and putting together succinct but in-depth summaries of the state of other nations' air forces—seemed to confirm that his faith had been well placed. Göring, who enjoyed the attention of the aristocracy, still went shooting on the estate owned by Libertas's family, and was persuaded that Schulze-Boysen's brushes with the left were youthful indiscretions. "That's yesterday's news," Göring had said when one Luftwaffe officer had nervously raised the issue of Schulze-Boysen's early career in anti-Nazi journalism. "Let it go."[7]

Of course, Schulze-Boysen was copying the material that passed his desk and taking it home. Being courted by Nazi power and simultaneously betraying it greatly appealed to Schulze-Boysen's sense of adventure.

And having Göring's support was vital. The Gestapo remained

suspicious of Schulze-Boysen following the Pöllnitz arrest but knew they had to step carefully.

Then they thought they might have reason to suspect him again.

AT THE HEIGHT of Schulze-Boysen's undercover work copying and sharing Nazi secrets about military operations in Spain, one of his key contacts, a newspaper photographer named Werner Dissel, was arrested by the Gestapo. Dissel had helped Schulze-Boysen obtain information about the deployment of two Panzer companies but had been arrested for spreading "Communistic demoralization." Some at the Gestapo still suspected that Schulze-Boysen was not all he appeared to be, and knowing of his friendship with Dissel, they suggested the Luftwaffe officer should meet him in his cell.

Schulze-Boysen immediately sensed that something was wrong and knew enough about Gestapo methods to suspect that the room in which they met would be bugged, the Gestapo hoping that the two men would say something that would incriminate them both.

Their trap set, the police left the two men alone and Schulze-Boysen calmly offered Dissel a packet of cigarettes. Written on the packet was a short note telling Dissel that the Gestapo knew nothing and he should give nothing away. Schulze-Boysen shared an innocuous conversation with Dissel before rising to leave. His parting look told the other man to keep strong.[8]

THE WEATHER HAD been hot and humid in Berlin when the city had awakened on August 23, 1939, to the news that the government had signed the pact with the Soviet Union.

At work Schulze-Boysen had listened to colleagues' assessment of the agreement: Not only would there be a newly opened back door for the import of food and raw materials from the Soviet Union, but there also would be no way Britain's Royal Navy could strangle the Reich as it had done during the Great War—and Stalin was going to allow Germany to deal with the troublesome Poles. Older veterans told friends there would be no repetition of the winter of 1917, when turnips had been the staple diet.

But that night, Schulze-Boysen told his friends that Germany and the Soviet Union were fundamentally different and that the Nonaggression Pact was a "Not-Yet-Aggression Pact."[9]

A few days later while sailing on the lake at Wannsee with Günther Weisenborn, his friend and his wife's lover, Schulze-Boysen said: "Tomorrow night we move against Poland." Weisenborn stopped what he was doing, watching Schulze-Boysen steer the boat, a strong wind blowing through his blond hair. "So far Hitler's had room to maneuver," the Luftwaffe man went on, "but now he will start to box himself in. Now the real world history will be made, but not by him alone. We're all going to play our little part, everyone around us and we ourselves. It will be the biggest war in world history, but Hitler won't survive it."[10]

Weisenborn, a man of words, had nothing to say by way of a reply. His eyes settled on the darkening trees along the edge of the lake, and he wondered where the next few years would take them.

ON THE EVENING of September 1, Schulze-Boysen went to the home of film producer Herbert Engelsing to celebrate their joint birthdays. Schulze-Boysen was turning thirty, a landmark that he felt fell appropriately on the day Germany had gone to war: He saw his life as somehow inextricably linked to the conflict ahead.

The Schulze-Boysens, as was normal, led the festivities. Libertas had brought her accordion, and together they sang songs they had heard from Great War veterans in their families: "La Marseillaise" and "It's a Long Way to Tipperary."

Schulze-Boysen lurched from wild excitement to deep melancholy as the night went on. His blue eyes hard and piercing, he told friends that Hitler was leading them into avoidable catastrophe, that perhaps they could not be sure of the Russians, and that he was sure the United States was the only hope for victory against the Nazis.

Then he was on his feet, dancing and belting out at the top of his lungs the Polish national anthem: "Poland is not yet lost, as long as we still live . . ."

Terrified, Frau Engelsing walked around the house to check no one was listening.

When she went back inside, Harro Schulze-Boysen was taking turns dancing with the women one by one. Despite his drunkenness he was elegant, swift, slender.

But eventually the dancing stopped. As dawn broke, they were all silent.

* * *

SCHULZE-BOYSEN'S GROUP HAD courted danger in a way that Harnack never had. In fact, five years earlier, the two men's paths had crossed briefly.

Harnack's friend Rudolf Heberle had known Harro Schulze-Boysen since they had shared a long correspondence during the latter's days editing *Der Gegner*. Heberle's wife, Franziska, was a distant relative of Harro's. The circles around the conspirators in Berlin were tight, but Heberle learned about his old acquaintance's work with his group and planned to bring him together with Arvid Harnack. The fit seemed perfect.

One evening in 1935, Heberle and Schulze-Boysen had arrived at the Harnacks' home and they talked. As Heberle had suspected, they agreed entirely on ideas, but their personalities were very different. Harnack was cautious, careful in what he said; Schulze-Boysen was eager, enthusiastic, with a flamboyance at odds with the other man. They shook hands, and Schulze-Boysen left. Harnack sighed and turned to Heberle. "Tell your cousin that I appreciated meeting with him," he said. "I was very interested but I don't want to see him again because it's too dangerous."[11]

Now, though, Germany was at war, and Korotkov was building up a dossier to persuade Stalin that Hitler was really his enemy. Harnack knew he had to reconsider. Greta Lorke was right. He had to put aside his security fears and reach out to Schulze-Boysen.

Harnack was committed to making the United States and the Soviet Union see that they had to stand up to Hitler before it was too late. The kind of intelligence Schulze-Boysen would provide from his job at the Air Ministry could well be critical.

IN OCTOBER 1940, within a couple of weeks of having Korotkov arrive at his door, Arvid Harnack called the first meeting at which he, Adam Kuckhoff, and Harro Schulze-Boysen were all present.

Harnack and Schulze-Boysen each shared with the other the secret orders reaching their desks. Luftwaffe documents Schulze-Boysen copied contained demands for more airfields, more pilots, more aircraft, more surveillance flights, more aviation fuel. Arvid's paperwork dealt with the economic consequences of the fighting for Germany.

They discussed the kind of information they needed to continue, how it would be collected, and how it would be passed to Alexander Korotkov. Schulze-Boysen said he would work with anyone who would bring down the Nazis.

Harnack met Korotkov and told him that he and Schulze-Boysen were now in regular contact.

Delighted, Korotkov reported directly to Lavrenty Beria, the head of all Soviet intelligence gathering, that he had his Berlin spy ring.

# 13

## God's Witness

I N SEPTEMBER 1940, a thirty-year-old man from a distinguished legal family applied to join the Waffen-SS, an organization consisting of the combat units of the SS, members of Hitler's bodyguard, and the Totenkopfverbände, the Death's Head units responsible for guarding the concentration camps.[1]

Kurt Gerstein's application revealed that he wished to be a part of Heinrich Himmler's vision for a comprehensive state-protection corps, the military backbone of Himmler's state police. Gerstein knew that recruits faced ideological and military training as political soldiers, and swore an oath under the motto "Loyalty is my Honour." That loyalty was to the Nazi movement.

But Gerstein had something remarkable in mind, and his actions against the Nazi state are perhaps the most morally complicated of all resisters, taking him into the darkest areas of humanity's depravity. In the coming years Gerstein would speak out against the Holocaust—but would also be a part of it.

KURT GERSTEIN WAS a tall, slim man with a serious face and dark, penetrating eyes. He had been born in Münster in 1905 into a deeply conservative and nationalist household. Most of the Gerstein family had been in the service of the judiciary, and his father, Ludwig, sat on the bench in Saarbrücken, Halberstadt, and then, when Gerstein was sixteen, in Neuruppin to the north of Berlin.

Ludwig Gerstein was a strict disciplinarian who stressed obedience and hard work, and this went against the young Kurt's tendency to rebel. At school he gained a reputation for truancy and for writing criticisms of his Latin homework on the blackboard. He was regularly punished by his teachers but did not seem to care what they thought of him.

At home, he did not relate well to his six brothers and sisters, and became a solitary child. His brother Karl described him as being the "most difficult" of his siblings. "He had always gone very much his own way, so that he was not exactly easy to approach," Karl said.[2] Gerstein spent most of his time either alone or with the family's devoutly Catholic maid, Regina.[3]

After the First World War, in which they had lost their eldest son, Ludwig and Clara Gerstein became—in Kurt's eyes—even colder and more remote than he had felt them to be before. Judge Gerstein defended the austerity at home with a dismissive wave of the hand and the saying "We have lost the war and we have become poor."

But something of his upbringing did strike a chord with Gerstein: the distinctive flavor of German Protestantism. And as religious fervor took a stronger hold, the pranks seemed to stop and the rebellion turned into a deep desire to defend the church.

Despite a poor start at school, he did well enough to be accepted at the University of Marburg in 1925 and—most probably to please his father—became a member of the Teutonia, a highly nationalistic student association. He found the fraternity members to be rather frivolous and did not take part in any of its rituals. By that time his faith had become the most important aspect of his life. He joined the German Association of Christian Students, the Evangelical Youth Movement, and, most influential of all, the Federation of German Bible Circles—the Bund Deutscher Bibelkreise, known to all as the BK.

But he did not just attend. He spoke and wrote about his thoughts and faith. For him, God was a God of wrath, and through devotion he felt he developed "a personal bond with Christ." But he struggled to lose an adolescent fear that sex was "an unclean secret" and began to agonize over concepts of purity and human guilt. The more badly behaved the young people seemed to be around him, the more he studied his Bible. If he spent a night in a tavern, his studies would become even more obsessive as he tried to cleanse himself of sin.

After three semesters at Marburg he switched to technical universities in Aachen and then Berlin, and graduated as a mining engineer in 1931. By this time he was well-known in the BK, traveling around Germany to conduct meetings. Wherever he went, young people gathered around him and followed him like a leader.

When Hitler came to power in 1933, Gerstein at first saw no conflict with his faith and in May he joined the Nazi Party and soon after the SA. When a friend, Pastor Kurt Rehling of Hagen, cautioned him against joining, Gerstein had told him that if there was a danger from the Nazis, then, "How else do you think you can help except from inside?"[4] This cryptic response would shine a half-light onto the workings of Gerstein's mind.

Gerstein watched closely the events of the summer of 1933—when Hitler made his bid to take over the German Protestant church, the move that so incensed pastors such as Dietrich Bonhoeffer—and began to see that the Hitler Youth planned to "lure the new generation away" from Christian groups. For Gerstein and others this was "Nazified Christianity." He saw the pro-Nazi element—the "German Christians"—holding Nazi-style meetings in Cologne in which it was argued that Hitler was there "by God's grace," and told a friend: "We may be obliged to give up the visible Church to others for them to stage their parades in, for their 'mass mission,' and to build for ourselves the true Church, the invisible Church."[5]

Baldur von Schirach, the leader of the Hitler Youth, and others were in talks with Christian groups to merge them into the Hitler Youth. Late in 1933 the merger went through, with Reich Bishop Müller announcing that the eight hundred thousand members of the Protestant youth movement had spontaneously joined the Hitler Youth. Two days after the announcement, Gerstein sent angry telegrams to Schirach and Müller, calling the merger a "stab in the back." "Church is dying at Bishop's hands," he cabled Müller starkly.

This was the beginning of Gerstein crossing swords with Nazi leaders in correspondence and later in print.

His anger also turned to elements of foreign policy. Although still a confirmed nationalist, in July 1934 he condemned the assassination of Austrian chancellor Engelbert Dollfuss—in a failed putsch by Austrian SS men—saying it was an "abominable act of murder from beginning to end." In a letter to friends in the BK, which would have got him arrested if it had been turned in to the authorities, he railed against the Nazis' "continuous chain of crimes," and added: "We will have nothing to do with such an act, nor with the methods of those who committed it."[6]

Gerstein supported the continuing development of the Confessing Church and its opposition to Müller. He saw it as his life's work now to speak out. "Bearing witness is becoming for me a necessity," he told a friend, "from which I am less and less able to escape."[7] Again the words were hinting at the part he wished to play in anti-Nazi history, although he could have no concept of where this dark path would lead him.

His outspoken views were becoming well-known to the Nazis, and a member of the Hitler Youth infiltrated one of his Bible groups and reported back on what Gerstein was telling students: "The remarks that this young man permitted himself came close to insolence . . . [He was] encouraging the candidates for the HitlerJugend who were present to leave the HJ, to come back into the church organisations, and to urge their comrades to do the same."[8]

Then, in February 1935, Gerstein—who had been described by one schoolfriend as "impulsive" and a "passionate idealist"—took his anger into the open when the Hitler Youth organized a production of an anti-Christian play in Hagen. Gerstein went along to *Wittekind*, by Edmund Kiss, knowing he would be offended. He sat in the front row, between people in HJ uniform, and halfway through stood up and shouted, "This is unheard of! We shall not allow our faith to be publicly mocked without protest!"[9]

The Hitler Youth members, who must have been waiting for the protest, dragged him outside and beat him up. He was left with a black eye and a bleeding mouth, and without several teeth.

But the beating did not put him off. He continued to combine his life of Bible study with his work as a mining engineer, and in 1935 he passed an examination to become a Bergassessor—a junior inspector of mines. That summer he organized a holiday camp for young Christians but found it subject to a search by Gestapo agents. The raid was entirely in keeping with the Nazi political police's view of any other group over which the party did not have control, and Gerstein was incensed. The letter of complaint he wrote to the Gestapo headquarters in Dortmund was again a dangerous provocation of a brutal, paranoid state. Their measures, he told them, "provoke nothing but bitterness."[10]

Everywhere Gerstein went, he carried a briefcase with tracts and pamphlets that he had written and had printed at his own expense. All argued for the preservation of church autonomy in direct conflict with Nazi policy. At a meeting in Strasbourg he made friends with Protestant leaders from France, who asked about the damage to his jaw and then heard about his beating in Hagen. "Please God you will never have to suffer what we are undergoing in Germany," he told them.[11] His fiancée, Elfriede Bensch, a pastor's daughter, supported him in his work but did not travel with him.

The authorities watched him closely, and then, while organizing the first congress of the German Miners' Association in his new hometown of Saarbrücken, he went too far. On window posters for the event he joked about "Compartment for travellers accompanied by mad dogs . . . Compartment for travellers with contagious diseases." To all who read it, these were unsubtle references to the Nazi officials who took the best seats on local trains.

An official at the Ministry of Mines where Gerstein was based saw the posters before they were sent out and reported them to the Gestapo. Gerstein was arrested and his house was searched. Hidden in a cupboard, the Gestapo found a series of letters and leaflets that Gerstein was preparing to send to lawyers and judges to inform them of the "battle" being waged against the church. They included banned pamphlets from the Confessing Church.

Elfriede contacted the leaders of the Confessing Church, including Pastor Niemöller, to tell them about her fiancé's arrest, and they petitioned for his release. Gerstein spent six weeks in prison, was expelled from the Nazi Party, and was dismissed from his job. He was also banned from public speaking anywhere in the Reich.

Nothing Gerstein had done so far had brought his father any pride— and now there was only shame. Judge Gerstein and Kurt's brother Fritz pressured him to apologize and to beg to be readmitted into the Nazi Party. Fritz wrote a letter of appeal to the Supreme Court of the Nazi Party in Munich and made Gerstein sign it. "I feel intimately bound up with this movement and passionately desire to serve it and the work of Adolf Hitler with my life, with all my strength, with all I possess," it stated.[12] Gerstein told Elfriede that in his defense to the Nazi Party "my family has driven me almost to the point of lying and I am very unhappy about it."[13]

Gerstein and Elfriede Bensch were married on August 31, 1937, and— unable to find employment because of the Nazi blacklisting—Gerstein toyed with studying first theology and then medicine, eventually enrolling at the university in Tübingen. His main energy he threw back into writing and distributing pamphlets, spending long weeks on the road, defending the Confessing Church against the "German Christians," and lecturing on moral problems faced by the male youth of Germany. Again, Gerstein was calling on the young to turn their backs on National Socialist organizations in favor of Christian ones.

Then a joint investigation by the Berlin and Stuttgart departments of the Gestapo claimed to have uncovered a plot to restore the monarchy to Germany. A monarchist politician named Reinhold Wulle—who had been General von Schleicher's deputy—had led the discussions over drinks and cigars, and among those present had been Gerstein. Gerstein had probably done little other than listen, exchange a few ideas in letters, and fail to report the others for their "treasonous" discussions.

Gerstein was imprisoned in the jail on Büchsenstrasse in Stuttgart, where he found a previous prisoner had scratched, "Pray, Mother of God will help you," into the metal frame of the bed. This brought him comfort for a few days until the guards came and transferred him to Welzheim, a small concentration camp in the forests to the east of Stuttgart.

Now officially branded a Häftling—an enemy of the state—Gerstein got his first glimpse of life in the camps: guards with dogs biting at the heels of inmates; cold, hunger, lice, beatings; a world in which there seemed to be no one to protect or look out for you, no one to stop the cruelty. Gerstein became depressed, ill, and suicidal. The camp doctor "diagnosed a heart disorder which he hopes is only nervous in character."[14]

But Gerstein also got lucky. A Gestapo man named Ernst Zerrer had led his interrogations. A devoted Protestant, he had read Gerstein's work and even shown it to his son. Although recognizing that Gerstein was an "implacable opponent" of National Socialism, he felt he deserved only a short term in jail. Welzheim was part of the concentration camp network but only a minor camp that did not compare with what Gerstein would see later, and the Gestapo had some influence. After only six and a half weeks Zerrer got Gerstein released, and he returned to Elfriede.

At only thirty-three years of age Gerstein was in poor health and lived in fear that even when his medical studies at Tübingen were complete, he would be unemployable because of his politics. To aid his son's recuperation, his father helped fund a much-belated honeymoon for the couple.

On an Italian steamer in the Mediterranean, Gerstein agonized over his future. In Germany, members of the Confessing Church were being rounded up and jailed. Niemöller was in a concentration camp and nothing had been heard of him. Gerstein himself had got lucky. But for how long would his luck continue? Like others who resisted the Nazis, he now began to wonder whether to make a life outside Germany. He thought of Switzerland, France, or perhaps even the United States, and then in the seclusion of his cabin he wrote to his uncle Robert Pommer, who had immigrated to America many years earlier and was now a wealthy grain merchant in Missouri. Planning to send the letter through an intermediary in Strasbourg, Gerstein felt he could afford to paint an honest picture of life in Hitler's Germany:

"The totalitarian spirit of National Socialism sets out to gain possession of a man's whole being, body and soul, and to dominate him entirely," he wrote. "The height of perfection for the boys and girls of Germany is held to be that by day and night they should think of no-one but Adolf Hitler and of nothing but Germany. Any higher relationship, with God for example, is regarded as being in the highest degree obnoxious . . . It is a question of whether the German people and German youth are to continue to hear God spoken of in a manner that merits serious attention, or whether they are to believe in nothing but a blood-stained flag, and the sacred places and emblems of a cult—in blood, soil and race . . . The situation in Germany is now such that the supreme values of Justice and Faith in God can only be maintained at the cost of struggle and suffering."

Gerstein went on to describe his incarcerations at the hands of the Nazis—"a very painful experience which I still cannot describe in detail"—and his fear of being arrested again. "In view of the remorselessness with which National Socialism has perused its aims, we see very hard times ahead."

Back in Germany, despite his fear that Hitler was now "free to do whatever he likes," Gerstein had to support his father's efforts to get him back in the party, although after Kristallnacht, he dared to express his concerns to his father. Pretending to still believe in Nazism, he told his father that "these latest happenings have hit me hard."[15] This was the first time he had expressed in writing any concern for the plight of the Jews.

His father's efforts to get him reinstated into the party gained some success, and in June 1939 his exclusion was commuted to a provisional membership, which allowed him to work in private industry.[16] He got a job in a potassium mine in Thuringia, but found that the Nazi bosses had a file on him. He was continually rebuked and spied on, and when war broke out, he tried to join the army. Because he was in a reserved occupation, deemed essential to the war effort, his application was turned down.

So Gerstein made a decision. He would conform, turn into the perfect Nazi. He moved to a different branch of the mining company and told people he was trying to make up for his past. He helped the local Hitler Youth, organized collections of scrap metal, and delivered it personally by handcart. When the local senior Nazi official, the Gauleiter, heard about his efforts, he presented Gerstein with a certificate of good citizenship. Importantly, Gerstein cut all links with the church and his religious writing. It appeared a complete conversion to Nazism, and the local officials were delighted. As Gerstein was from a great German family, with an impeccably pure Aryan bloodline, they were only too eager to accept that he had "come to his senses."

But in his mind he had reached the conclusion that the Nazis would certainly destroy anyone they perceived as an enemy; the only way to change anything was from inside the Nazi structure of power and command.

In September 1940, Gerstein's employer was informed that he had volunteered for the Waffen-SS.[17] Gerstein told a close friend in the church that from now on, if he were to hear "strange things about me, don't think that I have changed."

Gerstein's remarkable infiltration of the Nazi state killing machine had begun. His intention to see what was happening from the inside was about to become personal, political, and sickeningly real.

THROUGH HIS CONNECTIONS in the Ministry of Justice, the police, and the Abwehr, Hans von Dohnanyi was already documenting some of the crimes at the heart of the "unchristian" Reich.

His Chronicle of Shame dossier was now swollen with reports from the brutal occupation of Poland. For the Nazis the violence of war and occupation was the perfect backdrop against which to play out its fanatical ideological crusade. Party leaders sent in to run the civil administration saw it as their duty to "Germanize" the new territories as speedily as possible. Poland's resources were to be plundered, its people treated as inferior human beings. The country, with its large Jewish population, would be an "experimental playground" for what was to come.[18] The Polish nobility, clergy, and intelligentsia would be wiped from the face of the earth.

In the first week of the invasion Heydrich grew angry at the numbers being tried by military courts—despite two hundred "official" executions a day—and demanded hanging and shooting without trial in a general "ground cleansing" of the country. The Einsatzgruppen—the special task forces who served as agents of death and terror—would be used without mercy, shooting hostages, people suspected of being "insurgents," and people dragged from their homes as a warning to others.

Dohnanyi collected everything in his file. Canaris had returned from a visit to Silesia, where he had confronted General Wilhelm Keitel about the killing of Polish clergy and nobles, and had been told it had "been decided by the Führer." There were individual reports, such as that of the massacre of Jews in a church, and intelligence that army officers were concerned about the effects of the killing on their men. Dohnanyi managed to obtain copies of film footage of some of the atrocities.

Dohnanyi constantly updated his friends Oster and Bonhoeffer. Bonhoeffer responded with a book—the last to be published in his lifetime—on the psalms of the Old Testament. In the context of Nazi racial and "Christian" theory, the book was explosive, underlining the importance of Jewish influence on Christianity and the church. In it he expanded on the theories that had come to him in his contemplations after Kristallnacht: that Christianity was linked to Judaism through Jesus the Jew. Bonhoeffer arranged printing without reference to the Nazi censor, the Board for the Regulation of Literature, which he knew would not permit its publication. In July 1940 the Gestapo raided a church conference while Bonhoeffer was on the stage, followed him into the street, and ordered him to report regularly to a local police station. It was a warning. Eventually the book would cause him to be banned from writing.

When Dohnanyi heard, he talked to Hans Oster about bringing Bonhoeffer into the Abwehr as a civilian employee. It would discourage the Gestapo and allow Bonhoeffer to avoid military service. His cover would be that he was intelligence gathering while going about pastoral business; the Abwehr used all sorts of people as agents. Although considered a nuisance over his religious beliefs and writings, Bonhoeffer had done nothing else to arouse suspicion and was happy to greet people with a "Heil Hitler!"— "We'll have to run risks for many different things, but this silly salute is not one of them!" he told an anti-Nazi friend.[19]

Bonhoeffer had long had an urge to do more. He had applied to be a battlefield chaplain but had been told positions were only open to those already on military service. Pondering on whether churchmen should be doing more in a time of great oppression, he wrote a "church confession of guilt" in 1940—although it was never published—in which he asked if the church had been "silent where she should have cried out." He wrote: "The church confesses that she has witnessed the lawless application of brutal force, the physical and spiritual suffering of countless innocent people, oppression, hatred and murder, and that she has not raised her voice on behalf of the victims and has not found a way to hasten to their aid. She is guilty of the deaths of the weakest and most defenceless brothers of Jesus Christ."[20] Perhaps Dohnanyi, with his own strong faith and his restlessness for greater forms of resistance, might help him find a path to take him forward.

The Abwehr based Bonhoeffer in Munich, where he quickly became friends with Joe "the Ox" Müller, the "Mr. X" who had been Oster's go-between with the Vatican. Dohnanyi had told Bonhoeffer all about the big lawyer's resistance activities, and they were of great interest to Bonhoeffer.

Müller found Bonhoeffer accommodation in the picturesque fourteenth-century Benedictine abbey at Ettal in the Bavarian Alps. The Dohnanyis enrolled their three children in the local school so they would be safe from air raids on Berlin and could spend time with Uncle Dietrich. The children being at the school gave Dohnanyi an extra reason for visiting Bonhoeffer, and in the seclusion of the abbey, new visitors arrived, including Carl Goerdeler and Müller's contact at the Vatican, Father Leiber. In Bonhoeffer's monk's cell, a plan was developing in which this time he would be the one reaching out to the Allies with plans for peace.

# 14

## Corsican Delivers

AS THE SECOND winter of the war hardened in Berlin, a story went round about one woman's good fortune. Running for a suburban train, she had been caught up at the back of a crowd on the platform and, cursing to herself, had watched her train's doors close with many of those who had unintentionally blocked her way now inside. She had to wait for another, but when it came, it was quickly held up on the track: The train she had missed had been blown to pieces by an RAF bomb.

The story and its popularity summed up a little of the way Berliners were beginning to feel. They were in a war now; there was no going back. The war and the RAF were the enemy. The city and the nation had to stick together. Trust to luck, muddle through. In Britain, they called this the "blitz spirit."

The raids were bad, of course. Thirty-one people had died one night. But they were not the huge raids they had feared. The British bombers were small and did not yet have the huge payloads they would carry later in the war.

There was no coffee, tea, chocolate, or fruit in the shops, and very little in the way of new clothing to buy; and people missed their children, but they were safe in the countryside, evacuated under the Kinderlandverschickung scheme, safe from the bombs; but the war appeared to be going well. Goebbels claimed the German army were masters of Europe, and the Luftwaffe had spent fifty-eight consecutive nights pounding London. Millions of Germans had tuned in to hear famous broadcaster Eugen Hadamovsky describe being on a bomber approaching along the Thames. "Beneath us, we saw the red blazing metropolis of England, the centre of plutocrats and slaveholders, the capital of 'World Enemy number one,'" he said, his voice rising. "We saw the fires of destruction. Clouds of smoke and pillars of fire looked like the flow of lava from a titanic volcano . . . London is wrapped in flames."[1] Listeners suffering their own nightly raids found it hard not to feel a disconcerting mix of sympathy and righteous revenge.

Arvid Harnack heard the broadcast and read the reports in the Nazi press, but he also saw what Goebbels did not want the people to see: the true numbers of casualties (thirty-one dead and ninety-one injured in one raid; thirty-three workers killed in a single incident when a British bomber crashed on a factory, the deaths caused by faulty flak shells); the fact that government buildings in Wilhelmstrasse had themselves been hit; and that Hitler—fearing the true extent of bombing that could eventually be delivered onto German cities—had ordered a massive public works program to build shelters and overhaul air-defense provisions.[2] Harnack was determined to share this information with others, especially through contacts in Germany's factories.

Although not a man known to have doubts, Harnack was troubled by what he sensed to be a new feeling in the German public. It was a kind of loyalty to the regime brought on by circumstance and little hope of any other way forward: a fear among a growing proportion of the population who were neither staunchly for nor against Hitler that, now the war had got this far, Germany must strive on. There was no turning back. Defeat would mean a fate far worse than Versailles and the economic and security horrors that followed.

For Harnack, the anti-Hitler opposition appeared to be fighting an impossible battle. But he knew he had no choice but to redouble his efforts, to continue to expand his network: Hitler was planning the most audacious move of the war, the invasion of the Soviet Union.

After several weeks of meetings, Harnack's Moscow contact had gone quiet. Korotkov had returned to Moscow to report on his network in Berlin and had not sent word. Harnack began to wonder if Stalin had ordered a fresh purge and Korotkov had fallen victim.

Then, shortly before Christmas 1940, Harnack found a note in his mailbox: "I am back in Berlin. Came to see you and didn't find you there. I'd be very pleased if you would visit me."[3]

According to an agreed code, the leaving of the note meant that the two should meet in exactly one week at 8 a.m. at a previously arranged telephone booth in Fasanenplatz.

In Moscow, when Korotkov had reported on his agent Corsican, he had been greeted with equal levels of suspicion and interest by Beria and his deputy director of intelligence, Pavel Sudoplatov. German Communists were always frustratingly independent, and the leaders of Korotkov's German network did not even appear to be party members. As bourgeois intellectuals and aristocrats, could they be trusted? Might they even be Abwehr spies? Some of the intelligence they could deliver appeared almost too good to be true. On the other hand the apparent cooperation of one of Germany's leading and best-placed economists, a renowned writer—Kuckhoff—and a senior Luftwaffe intelligence man—Schulze-Boysen—could not be ignored. They decided to make a series of demands of the new network.

Korotkov told Harnack that he needed detailed information on the planned invasion of the Soviet Union; a description of the opposition in Germany, including a picture of the conservative and military resistance; and wide-ranging intelligence on Germany's military and economic capability in the event of war in the East.

Harnack responded quickly. He described his network as numbering about sixty people, mainly writers and civil servants, but also including engineers and technical workers, and said that as they had developed into secure, smaller circles, he himself no longer personally knew all of them. Korotkov reported all to Moscow, adding that Corsican's American wife was a key member of his group, as were a number of her former students, including Karl Behrens, who was an engineer with the electrical company AEG.

Harnack also told him that the invasion plans were under way and that Schulze-Boysen's colleagues were analyzing large-scale aerial photos taken by the Luftwaffe along the Russian border with Poland. Hitler had ordered that the preparations were to be completed by May 15, 1941. The information had come from Schulze-Boysen.

Korotkov told Harnack that he wanted to meet Schulze-Boysen, whom he had code-named Starshina (Master-Sergeant).

Harnack was reluctant. Schulze-Boysen had been transferred from the Air Ministry to a special underground complex opened by Göring near Potsdam. He came into Berlin only twice a week, to teach young officers at the university's Institute of Foreign Affairs, and was usually in uniform. A meeting would be dangerous, but Korotkov—recognizing Schulze-Boysen as his most significant source—was insistent. He wanted to weigh for himself the attitude and personality of this mysterious Luftwaffe officer who knew Göring personally but was prepared to betray his country at such a critical time.

When Harnack sounded out Schulze-Boysen, he agreed to meet the Russian. Korotkov found him to be a man of action who seemed "fully prepared to tell me everything he knows."[4] A few weeks later Korotkov also met Kuckhoff.

In the meantime, Schulze-Boysen took on his most unusual recruit, the fortune-teller and psychic Annie Krauss.

KRAUSS WAS A round, matronly woman with staring eyes and a tendency to tell people their fortunes whether they wanted to hear them or not. She lived next to the Schulze-Boysens and had a thriving business in the Stahnsdorf quarter of Berlin. With so much uncertainty in the world, many people seemed to desire the services of a clairvoyant.

Libertas Schulze-Boysen was one of Krauss's devoted followers, and when the young woman told her about her hatred for the Nazis, Krauss said she would do anything to help. She had already worked with another friend of the Schulze-Boysens, a journalist named John Graudenz, to help a young Jewish woman escape abroad.

Now, as well as letting them use her living room to print flyers, Krauss also spread antiwar gossip. The Schulze-Boysens shared their news with her, and when later she claimed to have predicted the invasion of the Soviet Union, this was probably due to what she had been told by a physical presence in Luftwaffe uniform rather than by a spiritual guide she had met in a clairvoyant's trance.

Her greatest mission for Schulze-Boysen involved Colonel Erwin Gehrts, a department head of the Luftwaffe training unit. Gehrts, a former journalist, was an old friend of Schulze-Boysen's. He had been a keen supporter of the Social Democrats and was vehemently anti-Nazi. He was also, however, a staunch Catholic and would have no sympathy for espionage for the enemy, especially the Soviets. Schulze-Boysen knew Gehrts was handling the transfer of new pilots and crews to the East and wanted to get him to share the information.

Gehrts was recently divorced, and his love for a woman in his office was not being reciprocated. In his dark mood he confided in Schulze-Boysen that he had been consulting Nostradamus about the future as, although very religious, he also believed deeply in astrology. Schulze-Boysen said he knew someone he could talk to as a more personal spirit guide, and he introduced Gehrts to Annie Krauss.

Before the colonel went for his first consultation, Schulze-Boysen briefed her on what kind of questions to ask and how to steer the conversation toward his work, using his love for his coworker. The consummate actress, Krauss received Gehrts in her luxurious apartment and told him that her "advice" was governed by his professional duties; she could better help him if he could explain his work.

Once a week he came to her apartment and talked about his office pressures and how he was trying to deal with his problems. Soon he brought to her documents and reports. By now, Gehrts knew he was being duped in some way, but he saw himself as an unwitting informant and believed that what he was doing must be helping in the fight against the Nazis.

He did not ask any questions; he just listened to Annie Krauss's comforting predictions. He even went along when she asked him to leave some of the documents with her overnight as, she claimed with a reassuring look, if she could lay her hands on them, she would get clearer answers.

Once Gehrts had gone, the documents were photographed and passed to Schulze-Boysen.

THE FLOW OF information to Moscow now became a flood. Russian experts were being recruited to Göring's staff. Reconnaissance flights were taking place over Soviet territory. The Russian naval base at Kronstadt had been photographed and a bombing raid planned. Troop mobilizations to the Soviet border had been ordered, and details for the invasion of Ukraine—the Soviet Union's main industrial base—were being finalized. Harnack reported that only one active division remained in Belgium, suggesting an invasion of Britain had been further postponed.

In April, Schulze-Boysen revealed that the Luftwaffe's plan of action had been completed. He described the railroad junctions, power stations, and factories that would be key targets.

That same month Korotkov reported an anti-Soviet campaign had been launched in the Nazi press, claiming that Moscow had malevolent intentions toward Germany. Through his historian friend Egmont Zechlin, who knew many in the Germany high command, Corsican reported that the invasion could take place as early as the first day of May.

\*   \*   \*

IN EARLY JUNE, Korotkov reported to Moscow that Starshina—Schulze-Boysen—stated that bases in Poland were being equipped to receive large numbers of aircraft and that Corsican had a list of quartermasters who would keep the German army equipped as it pushed into Russia. The pair described in detail the pincer movement with which the Germans would advance in the north and south.

Amiak Kobulov, the NKVD station chief in Berlin, added his own note to Korotkov's report, saying it came "straight from the heart." A few days later another message arrived in Moscow that the German military was prepared: "The blow can be expected to fall at any moment."

Kobulov's words struck a note of desperation. Moscow's men in Berlin were convinced of the authenticity of the Corsican network and assured Harnack that all his messages were getting through.

What they did not tell him or Schulze-Boysen was that they were not being believed.

WHILE PASSING ALL this information to Moscow, Arvid Harnack continued to spy for the United States, too. Throughout the latter months of 1940 and the first half of 1941, he warned Donald Heath that Hitler intended to attack the Soviet Union. Heath passed the information on to Washington. Sumner Welles warned the Soviet ambassador to the United States, who called the German embassy and was told it was an American rumor designed to damage German-Soviet friendship.

Harnack also came clean to his American friend that he was working for the Soviets. Heath accepted his socialism but tried to argue him out of working for Moscow. Harnack said it was part of his struggle for Germany. As the two men walked in the Spreewald, the conversation became heated, as Heath demanded to know who Harnack's Moscow contact was, but their friendship was too strong to be broken and Harnack was too good a source for Heath to lose.

A few weeks later Heath's teenage son, who was still being tutored by Mildred Fish-Harnack, told his father about a trip he and his tutor had taken on the S-Bahn out to Potsdam. While walking in a park, she had told the thirteen-year-old: "A lady will join me and we will walk ahead. You fall behind." Shortly afterwards a handsome woman had arrived carrying a briefcase just like Mildred's. Young Donald stood back and thought perhaps they were exchanging documents.

Having listened to the story, Heath wondered if his son had seen either a member of Harnack's spy network or perhaps even his Russian contact.

Then, in May, a shock. Donald Heath was being withdrawn from Berlin and sent to Chile.

The decision seemed a nonsensical one. Heath had developed essential intelligence contacts in Germany, and there was nowhere more crucial to international affairs at that moment in time. His withdrawal left all this intelligence to the Russians.

DESPITE MOSCOW'S SUSPICION of his group, Korotkov continued to send couriers to meet Harnack and collect messages.

The courier was often unknown to Harnack and would approach with the question: "How do you get to the Woyrschstrasse?" Harnack's reply was that he lived there.

Meetings would take place at the Charlottenburger Strasse entrance to Tiergarten S-Bahn station, a café, or a prearranged spot in the park, and always before or after Harnack's working hours.

As the messages of war reached Moscow, the NKVD decided to hedge its bets. If Corsican was right, then they would need to be able to contact him after Korotkov had been forced to leave. They sent Berlin two portable radios capable of receiving and transmitting at a distance of six hundred miles.

One was hidden in the home of the Schulze-Boysens' friend Erika von Brockdorff, while Greta Lorke agreed to meet the Russian to take possession of the other and headed to the Thielplatz subway station. Korotkov arrived, smiling and relaxed, and suggested they walk to Breitenbachplatz. The street was full of SS men, and Lorke's anxiety was raised when he actually dropped the suitcase in which the transmitter was fitted.

Picking it up, he told her to hide it with her air raid kit so she could grab it when the alarm sounded. Lorke rushed home as quickly as she dared, handed the case to Kuckhoff, and grabbed their small son, Ule, for a hug. When Kuckhoff checked out the radio, he realized it had been damaged. After it was repaired, it was handed to twenty-six-year-old Hans Coppi, a lathe operator in a small engineering factory whom Harnack had designated the network's radio operator. Tall and lanky, with thick spectacles that made his dark eyes look larger than they were, Coppi was brave and committed, but he had absolutely no idea how to work a radio transmitter.

FOR STALIN THE messages coming from Korotkov in Berlin fell into a pattern described to him in advance by Adolf Hitler himself.

On New Year's Eve 1940, the Führer had ordered his Moscow embassy to deliver a confidential personal message to Stalin. Despite having already signed Directive 21—putting into effect the planning for Operation Barbarossa, the invasion of the Soviet Union—Hitler reassured him that there would be no war between their two countries.

There would be, however, "rumours of planned invasions." Hitler wrote: "I do not wish to dwell on the absurdity of such nonsense . . . [but] I predict that as our invasion of the [British] Isles draws closer, the intensity of such rumours will increase and fabricated documents will perhaps be added to them. I will be completely open with you. Some of these rumours are being circulated by appropriate German offices."

The true source, though, Hitler stated, was Britain and its allies. To complete the charade and with a dash of dark humor that must have made him smile grimly, the Führer added a suggestion that they meet at the "end of June," by which time he was secretly certain that the invasion would be under way.[5]

Stalin remained convinced that Hitler must subdue Britain before he turned on him. Hitler's note and an Abwehr deception using neutral diplomats to pass information to him about an invasion plan that was being used as a deception to fool Britain convinced him.

When Schulze-Boysen's warning that the blow was imminent arrived on his desk, he scribbled on it a note for his intelligence chief.

He wrote: "You can send your 'source' from the German air force staff to his much-fucked mother! This is not a 'source' but a disinformer. J. Stalin."[6]

FIVE DAYS AFTER Schulze-Boysen's final warning, at dawn on Sunday, June 22, 1941, Hitler launched Barbarossa, staking everything on his defeat of Stalin and pouring three million men into the battle.

Soviet military intelligence had been forbidden from giving any advance warning to forward units. Using the aerial reconnaissance information highlighted by Schulze-Boysen, the Luftwaffe wiped out more than 1,400 Soviet aircraft in a single day.

Over the next ten weeks, as the German army thrust into Russia at a speed of fifty miles a day, more than 850,000 Russian prisoners were taken.

OVER THE COMING months the war in the Soviet Union energized Harnack, Schulze-Boysen, Kuckhoff, and their friends. The invasion quickly became unpopular, felt like it might be a turning point for military fortunes, and was a supremely dangerous development for Germany, behind which they felt they could galvanize anti-Nazi public feeling.

Libertas Schulze-Boysen used her connections as the former MGM press agent to get a highly sensitive political role with the Reich's Kulturfilm office, from which Goebbels enjoyed complete control of the German film industry.

As well as recruiting Adam Kuckhoff as a scriptwriter and field producer whose assignments took him to Poland, Libertas developed her own career as a documentary maker. She asked for footage from Poland and Russia to be sent to her, and began to build up a dossier of Nazi crimes, similar to that of Hans von Dohnanyi's but consisting mainly of pieces of film and copies of prints that she made with a small Leica camera. She managed to get photographs going back as far as the Röhm massacre that recorded the torture and murder of Poles, Jews, and Soviet civilians. Soldiers who had taken photographs at the front were invited to Libertas's office, and using a mixture of flirtation and flattery, she coaxed out of them their stories and asked to copy their photographs. The names and addresses of those who had committed atrocities were carefully noted in her file. Because it was part of her work, Schulze-Boysen could in effect hide the dossier in plain sight in her office among the box files and film canisters.

Compiling the dossier became an obsession, but it was a harrowing experience. As she tried to cope, Libertas confided in Greta Lorke about what she was hearing. One soldier had a fascination with insects and could not hurt a beetle, but then "displayed a photo of himself with a tiny baby that he was about to hurl against a wall."[7]

Libs, as Lorke always called her, said she was surprised looking at the photographs from Poland and Russia at how many of the perpetrators were content to be photographed at the scene of the killings. "In my deepest heart, even though I've seen the reports and the photos, I can't believe that German people are capable of committing such horrible deeds," she told Lorke. "I know what Harro went through [in detention in 1933], Hans Otto, and Ossietzky, and countless others. But this murder of entire peoples! I can't take it anymore!"[8]

Schulze-Boysen shared the soldiers' testimonies with Kuckhoff and Sieg, who wrote a letter that purported to be from a soldier on the Eastern Front and described his anger and shock at seeing and hearing about atrocities committed. The letter was a slowly developing conversational piece that built toward an incident in which a fellow soldier had been made to execute a woman and her three children. "Why?" asked the letter writer. "It was an order," came the reply.

The man had made the children kneel in the snow, but the shooting had been delayed by the two-year-old girl, who had wanted to make her doll kneel, too, but could not get it to stand.

When the family was dead, the "insignificant doll" had become the "murderer's little obsession." He could not shake it out of his mind.

The letter was circulated throughout the armies in the East with the help of the sculptor Kurt Schumacher, who had been drafted and posted to Poznań.

As the group in Berlin listened with revulsion to Libertas's stories from Russia, it stepped up its leaflet campaign to try to combat the propaganda from Goebbels.

Psychotherapist John Rittmeister, who described himself as a "leftist pacifist," worked with twenty-year-old artist Cato Bontjes van Beek, Maria Terwiel, and others on a pamphlet decrying the "murders" that the Nazis had committed and stating: "Each one of us must do exactly the opposite of what this government demands." With a daring of which Harro Schulze-Boysen must have approved, they sent the publication not only to senior religious leaders and intellectuals they believed might be anti-Nazi, but also to Hitler's half brother, Alois, and to Roland Freisler, at the Ministry of Justice, who was soon to take over as the People's Court's senior judge.

In another news sheet, Schulze-Boysen himself wrote a piece that described the "unspeakable suffering" of the war's victims and predicted that, in Russia, "Hitler will go under just as Napoleon went under." With the help of John Sieg and Walter Husemann, this was distributed in factories across Berlin, and later in Hamburg, and was posted to senior churchmen, professors, and judges. A copy was placed on the desk of Joseph Goebbels, as he liked to critique even the enemy's propaganda to see what he might learn.

Kuckhoff would regularly walk from his smart apartment to Sieg's home in troubled Neukölln to work on their writing or to deliver leaflets. He carried them in a briefcase, the offending literature tucked inside the covers of a copy of Hans Christian Andersen's fairy tales.

Sieg, who had taken a job with the Reichsbahn, the state railways, in 1937, had worked his way up through a variety of positions. As a signalman, he had counted boxcars headed off to supply Hitler's armies and reported back on their numbers. He now worked in the railroad telegraph office at Tempelhof and found he could delay troop and supply trains without danger to himself. His information was relayed through Schulze-Boysen and others to Harnack.

And every night Arvid Harnack came home from the Economics Ministry and began writing messages for Hans Coppi, his radio operator, to send to Moscow.

KOROTKOV HAD ESCAPED Germany after the invasion, so Harnack's group could now only communicate with Moscow via Coppi's radio.

In the woods near his home in Tegel four days after the invasion, Hans Coppi sat down with a copy of a popular novel, *Der Kurier aus Spanien* (*The Courier from Spain*), and began to write out a message. The book had been chosen as the source for his coded messages. A radio operator in Moscow had been provided with the same 1939 edition.

Tuning to the correct frequency, Coppi successfully tapped out: "Eintausend Grüsse an alle Freunde." "A thousand greetings to all our friends."

Within a few moments a reply came back. The test message had been received and understood.

Coppi was Harnack's sole radio operator. The other transmitter provided by Korotkov was in storage.

Over the coming months Harnack would write the messages and Behrens would deliver them to Coppi. The young man, with his wife, Hilde, helping, would then encode them and find a location in a wood from which to transmit.

The gathering of the intelligence and Coppi's use of the radio was highly dangerous work—but it was all now a complete waste of time: Although he had operated the radio successfully, the novice Coppi had misunderstood the schedule of times and dates of transmission that were to follow the opening test message, and was transmitting when no one in Moscow was listening. Soviet handlers in Minsk, and later Stockholm and

London, tuned in on the correct date at the right time but heard only the static noise in the ether coming back to them.

After that first message, not one of Coppi's intelligence-packed reports from Berlin would be received, decoded, and acted upon in Moscow.

For the Soviets the radio silence was a mystery. They realized after Barbarossa just how accurate Harnack and Schulze-Boysen had been. They urgently need more from them or at least to find out what they were doing. An urgent meeting inside the Lubyanka speculated as to whether the Germans had been rounded up; an optimist suggested there might simply be something wrong with the radios. Either way, it was decided, they needed to find out what was happening: The source was too valuable to abandon.

Late in August the Soviet spy chiefs made a decision to make physical contact using a Brussels-based agent of the military intelligence service, the GRU. For the Moscow handlers it was all they could do, but it was an act that would have murderous consequences for those trying to work for them in the deadly atmosphere of wartime Berlin.

# 15

## Life Unworthy of Life

IN HITLER'S WARPED mind a caricatured image of the mentally ill threatened the purity of the German Volk. In his nightmares he saw patients "bedded on sand or sawdust because they continually befouled themselves," and he became fascinated with the idea of the elimination of the weak.[1]

Early in 1939 he called two senior Nazi civil servants to his office in Berlin. One of them was Hans Lammers, chief of the Reich Chancellery and one of Hitler's most trusted legal advisers. Lammers later recalled that Hitler "considered it to be proper that the 'life unworthy of life' of severely mentally ill persons be eliminated by actions [Eingriffe] that bring about death."[2]

That October Hitler ordered that certain registered doctors should have the authority to see that "patients considered incurable according to the best available human judgement [menschlichem Ermessen] of their state of health, can be granted a mercy death [Gnadentod].[3] The decree was written on Hitler's private stationery and would be issued straight to chosen physicians, bypassing the official state bureaucracy and the scrutiny of the public—both of whom it was felt might not be willing to accept such a policy.

There were about one million people in Germany in 1939 who came within the scope of the decree.[4]

To oversee the new program, a special section of the chancellery was created. The department was camouflaged under the title the Reich Work Group of Sanatoriums and Nursing Homes, or Reichsarbeitsgemeinschaft Heil- und Pflegeanstalten (RAG). The program would be referred to by the code name T4, taken from the Tiergartenstrasse 4 address of the chancellery itself.

Questionnaires were sent to psychiatric institutions, hospitals, and homes for chronic patients across the Reich, and one had to be filled in for every patient. It sought to identify people who, because of "specified diseases" such as schizophrenia, epilepsy, "senile diseases," and encephalitis, might be "not employable"; patients who had been institutionalized for at least five years; those who were criminally insane; and those "who are not German citizens, or are not of German or kindred blood."[5]

Doctors were not told the purpose of the forms and were given very little time to complete them. Tragically, some doctors exaggerated patients' conditions out of compassion as they feared the authorities were seeking to return sick people to work or military service.

The Nazis opened six main killing centers in converted mental hospitals and nursing homes surrounded by high walls. All were isolated buildings so that buses could be brought in without arousing suspicion and the screams of patients would not reach the outside world.

To begin with, the Nazis experimented with killing by injections of various combinations of morphine, scopolamine, curare, and prussic acid (cyanide), but this was found to kill too slowly, with the victim often requiring a second injection.[6] Under the guidance of Christian Wirth, a superintendent in the criminal investigation department of the Stuttgart Police, the program then took possession of a gas chamber, which was disguised as a shower room into which "water pipes" were inserted. The gas was pumped in through the pipes.

At the first demonstration of this early Nazi gas chamber, August Becker, an SS chemist, watched through a peephole as eighteen to twenty naked people were led inside. Very quickly they "toppled over or lay on the benches" without "scenes of commotion." The corpses were then incinerated in a crematory oven.

The macabre blueprint for T4 and the Holocaust had been established.

BETWEEN JANUARY 1940 and August 1941, more than seventy thousand people were murdered as part of the T4 program.

The family of each person received a falsified death certificate so that the authorities could cover up the truth. Common causes of death given were infectious diseases, pneumonia, and heart failure. Trainee doctors joining the scheme were advised on how to make up a reason for death that would be consistent with the patient's condition.[7]

Despite Hitler's wish to keep T4 from the public, it was a secret that was too large to keep. Working at the killing centers caused stress, and many workers ended up drinking in local bars and unburdening themselves on others. People who found themselves working in the kitchens or laundries told friends.

Pastor Paul Gerhard Braune of Berlin was among the first to speak out against the program. A formidable-looking man of Prussian military bearing, he wrote directly to Hitler at the Reich Chancellery about these "intolerable" measures. "Where is the limit to be?" he wrote. "Which is abnormal? Who is anti-social? Which are the hopeless cases? . . . Whom if not the helpless should the law protect?"[8]

Then a senior Catholic priest was to speak out—and as well as forcing Hitler to temporarily close down T4, he would inspire an even wider resistance against the Nazis.[9]

CLEMENS AUGUST GRAF von Galen was the bishop of Münster and one of the most outspoken churchmen in the country. Stern and unsmiling, he had turned against the Nazis early on. Then, over three Sundays in July and August 1941, he delivered sermons that shocked his congregation for the vehemence directed against Hitler's regime. Calling for the rule of law to be restored in Germany, he said: "Unless this call for justice is answered this German folk and Fatherland, despite the heroism of its soldiers and its famous victories, will perish from inner rot and foulness."[10] He then turned on the Nazi T4 policy of euthanasia: "If the principle that man is entitled to kill his unproductive fellow man is established and applied, then woe to all of us when we become aged and infirm . . . It does not bear thinking of, the depravity, the universal mistrust, which will spread even in the bosom of the family, if this terrible doctrine is tolerated, accepted and put into practice."[11]

The contents of Galen's sermons were quickly printed and distributed throughout the country. In Abwehr headquarters in Berlin, when one was shown to Hans Oster, he remarked: "He's a man of courage and conviction . . . There should be a handful of such people in all our churches, and at least two handfuls in the Wehrmacht! If there were, Germany would look quite different."[12]

Hitler took a different view. When the Gestapo brought him a copy, he demanded the bishop's immediate arrest. It was only wartime considerations that saved the aristocratic priest: Galen was hugely popular across a large part of Germany, having served in a number of parishes and been an adviser to Pope Pius XI (the previous pope) during the 1930s. "If anything is done against this bishop," the Führer was advised, "all of Münster will have to be written off for the war effort—and the whole of Westphalia, as well."[13]

One of the leaflets containing Galen's words was pushed through the door of the Scholls' home in a plain brown envelope, and it created a sensation among the family. The euthanasia program had been rumored but not confirmed—to hear it described by a priest was shocking. But more than that, no public figure had spoken like this since Hitler had come to power. People were terrified to criticize the regime in a public house, let alone from the pulpit of a cathedral. "At last," Hans Scholl said, "somebody has had the courage to speak out."

Scholl read and reread the Galen leaflets and hung on the words. "Woe to our German people, if the divine commandment 'Thou shalt not kill' . . . is not merely violated but the violation is tolerated and remains unpunished!"[14] "An obedience that enslaves souls—that is to say, penetrates to the innermost sanctuary of man's freedom where his conscience lives—is uttermost slavery."[15] The leaflet writer had added personal comments in the margins and at the bottom asked everyone who read it to make six copies and mail them to friends. Standing in his father's office with his sister Inge, the leaflet in his hand, Hans said, "One definitely ought to have a duplication machine of one's own."[16]

THE T4 LEAFLET showed Hans Scholl a way in which one might take action against the regime. On active service in France he had tended the wounds of fellow soldiers in a field hospital near Reims. Seeing their suffering, he grew angry at the sickness at the heart of the regime that they were fighting for. At home on leave, he wondered aloud to Sophie how long the "mass murder" would go on for.

Sophie told him that just because Germany was enjoying a series of breathtaking victories did not make what it was doing "right." Right and wrong, she concluded, have "nothing to do with politics and nationality."[17] Conflicted with the idea of being in love with an army officer, she pushed Fritz Hartnagel in a letter to say whether he had to carry out an order even if he considered it to be wrong. Later she told him that for her "justice takes precedence over all other attachments" and it was wrong for a person—whether they be French or German—to defend their own nation "just because it's 'his.'"[18]

Having graduated as a kindergarten teacher in March 1941 and been accepted on a course to study biology and philosophy at Munich's Ludwig Maximilian University, Sophie had been "bursting" with excitement at the thought of being near Hans, whose medical unit alternated periods on active service with months of course work.

Unfortunately, the authorities did not think her time in the kindergarten course was sufficient work for the state and she was instructed to do more. Orders came to present herself at Krauchenwies labor camp—about fifty miles from her home—early the following month.

On the day she arrived, Hitler's forces attacked Greece and then Yugoslavia, where Hartnagel was now in action. The madness was expanding. Sophie's new base was a run-down manor house that would provide billets for eighty women, all under the age of twenty-five and nearly all committed National Socialists. To the stern-looking camp leader, each of the women was a "labor maid," a form of address to which Sophie responded under her breath: "My name is Sophie Scholl—remember that!"[19] Although she shared a room with ten others, Scholl did not mix well with the group, remaining aloof—an attitude that some took as shyness, others as middle-class snobbery. When not working in a variety of jobs on nearby farms, she walked alone in a nearby park, reading poetry, Thomas Mann, and the writings of Saint Augustine.

Sophie was on a break from the labor camp when German radio announced news of the attack on the Soviet Union. She had spent the day in the sunshine walking through the valley of the upper Danube with her sister Inge, but when she returned to the manor house, she found many of the labor maids listening intently to Hitler's proclamation, which Goebbels had German radio repeat throughout the day: "German people! At this moment a march is taking place that, as regards extent, compares with the greatest the world hitherto has seen . . . The German Eastern Front extends from East Prussia . . . to the shores of the Black Sea. The task of this front, therefore, no longer is the protection of single countries, but the safeguarding of Europe and thereby the salvation of us all."[20]

The reaction of the labor maids was mixed, reflecting that across Germany. Many Germans had never understood why there had been a treaty with the Soviets in the first place and, having been bombarded with anti-Soviet propaganda, felt they were now "fighting our real enemy."[21] For some, the war now made sense. There were others, though, who felt a terrible sense of shock, and Sophie was one of them. She understood the gravity of turning on Russia and told a friend she feared the war was now having its "full effect." Sometimes, she said, "I've felt that it's grossly unfair to have to live in an age so filled with momentous events."[22] She worried for Hans: "What does the immediate future hold for you, I wonder?" she wrote to him. "We live in interesting times."[23]

Hans Scholl took fresh steps to communicate his anger about the regime.

His sister Inge became friends with a serious but intelligent young man named Otto Aicher, who was known to all as Otl Aicher and became a regular guest at the family home in Ulm. He had taken the same action as Werner Scholl and resigned from the Hitler Youth and was therefore barred from attending the university. Instead, with Inge's help, he had thrown his energies into the production of a journal that he called *Windlicht—Storm Lantern*—featuring essays on art, literature, and culture.[24] While not outright attacking the Nazis, the journal displayed an intellectual freedom at odds with the regime, which aimed to give readers hope that there were still people who cared for culture beyond that prescribed by Hitler and Goebbels.

When Hans learned about *Windlicht*, he immediately wrote an article that compared Hitler to Napoleon and ended with the line "Remember what happened to Napoleon and have hope!"[25] Inge helped circulate the journal, and she had a copy with Hans's essay in her handbag when one day she was stopped and questioned by a Gestapo agent. Fortunately she was not searched.[26] In another essay Hans Scholl then turned his fire on the Christian churches, which he felt had been apathetic in the face of Nazi practices, in particular the policy of "euthanasia action" to kill the mentally ill, physically handicapped, and terminally sick.

"It's high time that Christians made up their minds to do something," he said. "What are we going to show in the way of resistance—as compared to the Communists, for instance—when all this terror is over? We will be standing empty-handed. We will have no answer when we are asked: 'what did you do about it?'"

ONE DAY AFTER university classes Hans Scholl traveled to the Munich suburb of Solln and knocked on the door of the home of Carl Muth.

Muth was a distinguished Catholic editor whom Aicher felt might be further inspiration for Scholl. Scholl carried a letter of introduction from Aicher. Over the next few weeks the men talked at length, about philosophy, literature, and Germany, and Hans brought Inge and Sophie to meet the seventy-four-year-old scholar as well. They discussed religion, and although the Scholls were Lutheran, they had a deep respect for the Catholic faith and looked through his library of banned books. To Muth these young people represented the "other" Germany that had not been corrupted by Nazism. Muth told them of his belief that freedom of thought, religion, and free speech must be defended, but in a nonviolent manner. There must be a "spiritual resistance" to National Socialism.

When Scholl asked Muth about reports of atrocities in the East, Muth sent him to meet an architect named Manfred Eickemeyer, who as well as having an office in Munich had a studio in Kraków. He had traveled a great deal through the occupied territories as he worked on a number of construction projects in Poland. He had seen Jewish men, women, and children lined up in front of pits on the sides of the road and explained to Hans what an Einsatzgruppen was. He described whole villages being rounded up, stripped of their valuables and clothes, before being led away. He said Russians and Poles were being forced into camps as slave labor, and young girls were being made to work in SS brothels. To Scholl, this treatment of people was an "abomination." "I could not imagine that after such methods of domination a peaceful reconstruction of Europe would be possible," he said.[27]

Through Muth, the young Scholls also met Theodor Haecker, a writer and thinker who had been silenced by the Nazis. Haecker was a sixty-three-year-old widower with penetrating blue eyes and bushy eyebrows, who always wore a bow tie. An exceptional scholar who had been a leading translator and interpreter of Kierkegaard, he had been under Redeverbot since 1935: banned from writing a word in any publication or speaking on a public platform.[28] Haecker expressed the powerful notion that Germany would one day be destroyed by God for what it was doing to the Jewish people. He shared with the Scholls his fear that "a time may come when Germans will have to wear a swastika on the left side of their clothing, a sign of the Antichrist. They are crucifying Christ a second time, as a people!"[29] Like the Scholls he saw the situation as right and wrong, and feared too few Germans realized that they were on the "wrong road and the wrong side."[30] Nazism, Haecker told them, was a religion opposed to Christianity and therefore should be opposed by every Christian. "An idea achieves its full value and significance only when it is converted into reality by action," he said.

Eickemeyer and Haecker not only inspired Hans Scholl, they also made him feel like doing nothing was no longer an option: "I could not remain indifferent to the fate of my people. I decided to assert my convictions in deeds, not merely in thoughts."[31]

BEFORE HE APPLIED to the Waffen-SS, two pictures had been put into Kurt Gerstein's mind, and they were both troubling him.

One was a story of atrocities having been committed in Poland, and the other was the story of the T4 euthanasia program. His friend Dr. Theophile Wurm, bishop of Württemberg, told him the "mentally afflicted" were being killed in special hospitals.

Soon after, Gerstein applied to join Hitler's killing unit, refusing to give his wife any other explanation other than "I have to." He then traveled to his friend Robert Weiss's home in Alsace and told him what he had heard.

"It's quite horrifying," Gerstein told him. "The poor devils are taken off like cattle to the slaughter-house, their eyes wide with terror, knowing perfectly well what's going to happen to them."[32]

Gerstein appeared anxious and uncertain, and then said he was joining the SS. Weiss did not know what to make of it.

As Gerstein left, he told Weiss: "Germany must not win this war."

IN FEBRUARY 1941, Kurt Gerstein attended a family funeral, walking behind a small procession carrying the ashes of Berta Ebeling into the tree-lined cemetery in Saarbrücken.

Berta had been the local pastor's daughter and sister to Karl Gerstein's wife. Kurt supported his brother Karl and his sister-in-law as they walked, but all the while he felt like he was keeping a terrible secret.

Berta had been taken ill with an unspecified illness and had been treated in the local hospital, until one day her family received a letter to say she had been transferred to a clinic in Hadamar, a small town in Hesse two hundred miles away. The move was a shock to the family and soon after came a more terrible one: Berta had died, apparently of "cerebral thrombosis."

Berta's ashes had been delivered to the family, together with a letter from the head of the clinic. "Her severe mental affliction caused her great suffering, and you must therefore accept her death as a merciful release," it stated. "Owing to the danger of an epidemic in the clinic, the police authorities have ordered the immediate cremation of the body."[33]

The family had shown Gerstein the letter before the funeral. He knew what it meant. Hadamar was one of the institutions that those who opposed the euthanasia program had heard all about. It was said that heavy smoke was visible over the crematorium there every day, and local children, without understanding the horror of what they were saying, taunted the buses arriving with new patients with the cry "Here come some more to be gassed!"[34]

With Berta's ashes interred in her grave, the group walked slowly back into the town. Kurt Gerstein was agitated, and suddenly turned on his brother. "Do you realise what they did to Berta?" he said. "Hadamar is a slaughter-house. The Nazis are clearing out all the mental hospitals in Germany by systematically exterminating the patients. Berta didn't die a natural death. She was murdered!"[35]

Karl shielded his wife and walked her away. What Kurt was saying was insulting rubbish—and on the very day of the funeral! He was listening too much to the British propaganda on the BBC.

As the couple walked off, Gerstein shouted after them: "I intend to know what's going on!"

Seeking out one of his spiritual leaders, Pastor Kurt Rehling, Gerstein told him: "Those people are so vicious that they must not and cannot win the war. They're so evil that they will bring down everyone who opposes them with themselves. The only course is to join them, to find out what their plans are and to modify them whenever possible. A person operating within the movement may be able to sidetrack orders or interpret them in his own way. That is why I've got to do what I've decided to do. I want to know who gives the orders and who carries them out; who sends people to concentration camps, who maltreats them and who kills them . . . And when the end comes I want to be one of those who will testify against them."[36]

Gerstein's mix of religious zeal, obsessive morality, and rebelliousness appeared to be coming together in the most remarkable way. And now it would be hidden under the cloak of ultimate Nazi conformity: the gleaming lightning flashes of the SS collar insignia.

On March 15, 1941—six months after he applied—Kurt Gerstein was accepted into the Waffen-SS and sent to Hamburg for training.

"I am on the trail of so many crimes," he told Rehling.[37]

# 16

## Dangerous to Know

THE SUN SHONE that day on August 22, 1941, when Marianne Prager and Heinz Joachim were married at the Neue Synagogue in Oranienburger Strasse. Marianne looked so happy, delighted to be free of the work overalls she wore most days at the Alfred Teves factory in Wittenau.[1] Her dress was a dazzling white with puffed sleeves; Joachim looked handsome in his suit.

After the ceremony everyone went to their rented furnished flat in Rykestrasse, where the guests sang a song particular to German Jewish weddings, serenading the couple as they sat together on a love seat.

Only the faces of Marianne's parents betrayed a sense of sadness. Their daughter was not yet twenty; they had sold most of their belongings to survive; and their other daughter, Ilse, was in England—they had not seen her for more than two years, since the day she had left Berlin on the Kindertransport. She would be fourteen now, changing all the time. But she was safe, they hoped—although the bombs that came from their own homeland rained down on the very country in which they had found her shelter. They wondered, was this really the time to be getting married?

Looking around the guests, they knew most were now working in the war industries—in factories as metalworkers, electricians, and skilled laborers. Most looked up to the older man who, with his determined look and slightly overserious conversation, seemed to inspire them, even in these desperate of times. The grim, monotonous work of Berlin's munitions factories was proving a rich recruiting ground for Herbert Baum.

IN THE NAZI drive to put skilled Jews to work, Herbert Baum—who had by now married his girlfriend, Marianne Cohn—was assigned to the electrical-motor division of the giant Siemens plant. He was among more than five hundred Jewish forced workers there, each paid a very low hourly wage for their ten-hour shift. Baum had been appointed their spokesperson, the only Jew allowed to talk to the German overseer. It was an ideal role for his clandestine activities as it enabled him to move between different departments, searching for new recruits to his band of resisters. Through an old friend, machinist Alfred Eisenstädter, and a new contact named Edith Fraenkel, he linked up with a small cell of antifascists, led by Heinz Joachim, the man whose wedding he was attending that August day.

Joachim had been a promising young jazz musician, studying the saxophone and clarinet at a private Jewish music school in Charlottenburg until it had been closed down in 1938. As a Mischling of "mixed blood"—his mother was Aryan, but his father was Jewish—he had fallen foul of Hitler's anti-Jewish laws and been forced to work at Siemens. Outside the production line Joachim cut a stylish figure. He dressed in a jacket and tie, long coat, and fedora, and always had a Benny Goodman or Artie Shaw tune on his lips—when he was sure there were no Nazis nearby to hear him. He was intelligent and had brought together a tight group who loathed Hitler and would do anything to oppose him. Like Baum's group, Joachim's cell comprised both men and women, Jews and Gentiles.

He had already heard about Baum through his sweetheart, Marianne Prager, who like him was obsessed with music and loved to entertain friends on the piano. After Kristallnacht she had told friends: "If they ever come for my books or my piano, they will have to take me first!"[2]

His group included his best friend, Lothar Salinger, who lived on Rosenthaler Strasse, where he had a small darkroom in which he developed his photographs—ideal for creating false papers. Salinger, like many of the others, especially the young, had not identified primarily as Jewish until the persecution began. "Hitler made me a Jew," he told a friend, "and I will remain one as long as anti-Semitism exists."[3] Salinger longed to be a journalist—another profession closed to Germany's Jews.

Together Baum and Joachim recruited others: Hildegard Loewy, a committed Zionist who had graduated from school with the highest marks in her year despite having suffered the childhood trauma of losing an arm in a tram accident, Herbert Meyer, Heinz Rotholz, Helmut Neumann, Ellen Compart, and Sigi Rotholz and his wife, Lotte, the nineteen-year-old daughter of a maggid, a Jewish preacher.[4] Some worked in other factories and helped expand the whispering campaign against Hitler: Compart worked in a division of IG Farben, while Neumann was a forklift operator at a Kodak factory in Köpenick. Neumann's father had been taken away without warning by the Gestapo, and he worked hard to distance his mother from his anti-Nazi activities.

Baum still had the support of toolmaker Heinz Birnbaum—who as a thirteen-year-old had helped him make placards when Hitler came to power in 1933—and also now Birnbaum's girlfriend, a non-Jewish woman named Irene Walther, who worked at the Siemens-Schuckertwerke, an aircraft-parts factory that spread across a two-hundred-acre site in the northwest of the city. Walther worked as a secretary at the factory and had been persuaded by Birnbaum to leave the BDM and join the antifascist resistance. She had fallen for Birnbaum, who was four years younger than her, when she had gone back to his flat on the Wilmersdorfer Strasse one night on the promise that he would cook her something on the little hot plate he kept in the corner of the room, and had found that he was unable to make even the simplest recipe.

The foreman at the Siemens-Schuckertwerke had started Birnbaum off on a machine but soon realized that as a trained toolmaker he would be of more use as a subforeman. Birnbaum was now able to move around the large single-story building at will, especially after five in the afternoon when only one non-Jewish supervisor was left on site. It was Birnbaum's job to take a blueprint from the foreman, set up the machines for the workers, and explain to them what they needed to do. He did his job, but with humor and a smile he also muttered to them about Lenin and Marx, about banned books, about how the workers should turn to Communism. When one girl—with whom he liked to flirt—told him, "Never mind Communism, let's kill Hitler!" he went away laughing to himself.[5]

But Birnbaum's visits to the machine desks also allowed him to do something else. Through his chats and jokes he worked out which of the workers might help him carry out small acts of sabotage, like pouring sugar into a machine's transmission to make it seize up or changing the measurements on a job to ensure it had to be done again. These things could only be done sparingly and not repeated by the same person, so Birnbaum took care to recruit as many helpers as he could.

Sometimes he thought about his mother and sister, who had escaped to London before the war. There was always a part of him that wondered if he should have gone, too. But Germany was as much his country as it was the Nazis': He would stay and fight for it.

BUT LIFE AND the fight for life was getting harder all the time.

Almost half of Germany's remaining Jews were now in Berlin.[6] Most lived in Judenhäuser, tenement buildings in the outlying regions of the city, away from the prying eyes of non-Jewish residents who might ask questions of the regime. They were no longer neighbors, integrated, just Germans. The Jews seemed to be dwindling in number, and too few discussed why.

Despite the tribulations and hardships, many of Berlin's Jews opened their doors to the Baum group, allowing them to hold their meetings at a variety of addresses to avoid suspicion falling on their own homes.[7]

Most of Baum's friends were in Judenhäuser. Forcibly removed from their own homes and forbidden from most rental property, they lived in these dilapidated blocks, often subletting rooms from friends or strangers. Each room had to be occupied by two Jews, and with so many sharing a bathroom, there was always a mad scramble in the morning: No one could afford to be late for work as they would then run the risk of deportation. If there was running water, some would sneak into the bathroom at five in the morning and return to bed for a quick nap afterwards. Anyone who dared spend too long in the bathroom was subject to an angry banging on the door by housemates.

The petty persecution, name-calling, abuse, restriction of rights, and harassment had developed into a life in what was in effect a Berlin ghetto. The German Jews had become "refugees within their own country."[8]

So, Marianne's parents had found it hard to lift their spirits on the day of their lovely daughter's wedding. They had gone from successful business people to tenement dwellers. All around them there was so much misery. Their own country had turned against them. Every day there was a fresh story, not only about deportations but also about friends taking their own lives.

By the autumn of 1941, two thousand Berlin Jews had committed suicide.

IN POLAND, FOLLOWING the German invasion, the Nazi authorities had brought in the mandatory wearing of Star of David badges by the Jews. The same rule had been established in Nazi-occupied land in the Soviet Union. The idea had started with Joseph Goebbels and Reinhard Heydrich, and harked back to the Middle Ages; nothing like it had been seen in Western Europe since before the French Revolution.[9]

On September 1, 1941, Heydrich decreed that all Jews over six years of age across the Reich must wear the star on their chests. This, of course, applied in Berlin and across Germany itself. The design of the badge varied across the German-occupied nations. In Germany it consisted of a simple yellow star, outlined in black, with the word "Jude" written in Hebraic style in its center. The badge not only stigmatized and humiliated the wearer; it also helped the authorities segregate them and control their movements.

Baum had a tailor in a Jewish tenement work on the idea of a removable jacket pocket. These were attached to friends' jackets and anyone who wanted to be able to hide. The wearer could even pull off the star to visit Aryans-only shops and cinemas before popping it back on quickly if they came to a police checkpoint. It was extremely dangerous—being caught would result in immediate deportation—but it was an act that gave the wearer a sense of great pride and power.

Then, that October, the full-scale transport of Berlin Jews to Auschwitz began. Twenty-five trains left the city over the following ten weeks. The need to hide became a desperate one. Across Berlin, several thousand Jews went "underground" to avoid detection and deportation. They became known as the "U-boats." Few could survive without the help of their non-Jewish neighbors, and it has been estimated that on average seven non-Jewish Germans were involved in each collaboration required to keep one Jewish person safe.[10]

Many who had received a notice of deportation came to the Baum group for help. Baum found that the rising number of foreign workers in Berlin's factories could help him obtain more passes that could be bought and forged for use by Jews in hiding.

Baum's friend Suzanne Wesse became a key figure in the plan. Wesse was the French Catholic wife of engineer Richard Wesse, a Mischling under Hitler's racial laws, who also worked with the group. She had had a privileged upbringing, thanks to her father's highly successful Calais curtain factory, and had attended schools in England, Spain, and Germany.

Having worked as a translator in Berlin since 1935, she was Baum's liaison between the foreign workers at Siemens and other factories in the region, passing them information from abroad that was not in the Nazi press and sharing news about what was going on in different factories. Baum and his friends wrote articles for illegal newspapers urging Germans to show "solidarity" with foreign workers, as growing solidarity could be "fatal to Hitler's fascism." Some of Baum's non-Jewish friends were also required to provide rooms for foreign workers, and this provided another way to share news and maintain a sense that there were many people opposing Hitler's Germany.

With their new contacts from abroad, Baum and Wesse arranged the purchase of French, Belgian, and Dutch identity cards and passes that Berlin Jews could use to try to "pass" as Aryans—or, more likely, to live "underground." Those with passes were forced to abandon their homes and stay with Aryan friends. A Jewish cobbler named Max Kronbosch crafted hollow removable soles for Jewish people trying to escape so that they could hide money and other valuables from the Gestapo.

Baum, who, at almost thirty, was about ten years older than most of his followers, tried to bolster the morale of everyone he met. Hitler had underestimated Britain and had taken on more than he should have with the Soviet Union. The antifascist struggle was the right one, he told them, because it was the fight for peace and was against mass murder. These discussions quickly developed into a new round of pamphlets, which mocked the Nazi leadership and called on Berliners to revolt. Those who stood by, one pamphlet said, could not escape blame: "Guilty is the Hitler regime, its disciples and everyone who does not work in the antifascist resistance, and does not declare in word and deed their dissent."

Baum probably had a hand in writing a more sarcastic and satirical pamphlet, *Der Ausweg* (*The Way Out*), which was distributed at the same time. Among other things, it suggested that Deputy Führer Rudolf Hess had fled to England, as Hitler and Göring were mad and had tried to kill him. A second edition of *Der Ausweg* followed quickly in December 1941 and included letters written by soldiers on the Eastern Front. "I am ashamed to be German," one wrote after witnessing the execution of Russian prisoners. "Peace with Hitler—never!" wrote another. "These enemies of humanity must be put on trial . . . Refuse orders, shoot Nazi officers, have no mercy!"[11]

Dozens of people were involved in the production of the newspapers, which were typed by Irene Walther and Suzanne Wesse, who obtained some of the materials needed from the offices she visited in her job as a translator.

The campaign cost money, too. Werner Steinbrink, one of Baum's closest friends, who had edited the newspaper *Junge Garde Süd-Ost* with him, collected and stored funds. Intelligent, resourceful, and handsome, with blond hair swept slickly back, Steinbrink had been drafted into the Wehrmacht but had avoided frontline service, as his skills were needed at the Kaiser Wilhelm Institute, where he worked as a chemical technician. With his former girlfriend Lisa Attenberger in jail, he had met and fallen in love with Hilde Jadamowitz, who was also dedicated to the resistance and helped him manage the group's funds.

Their friend Hans Mannaberg, another non-Jew, helped them out with his printing skills. Mannaberg's father ran a large printing business in the Kreuzberg district, and for years Hans had been involved in printing anti-Nazi material. He had already paid a heavy price, serving four months in jail in 1935 before being picked up a second time by the Gestapo. In the early years of the war he was released from Sachsenhausen, where eighteen months in the large camp north of Berlin had done nothing to break his spirit. While he had been in Sachsenhausen, it had been filling with Jews from across northern Germany. He was more determined than ever for the German public to understand the horrors that were unfolding in the concentration camp system, although he also took extra care not to be seen with his resistance friends. All believed, largely incorrect, that the Gestapo maintained a level of surveillance on some prisoners released from the camps.

Ink for the pamphlets was provided by George Vötter, an experienced typesetter, and his wife, Charlotte, who had organized discussion groups about the Nazis for several years. The pamphlets were all run off by Baum and Heinz Joachim on the duplicating machine in the basement of Baum's apartment block.

The Vötters and Steinbrink organized groups to create mailing lists for the pamphlets. Names and addresses were taken at random from the Berlin telephone directory, and friends in the military provided some addresses for soldiers' families. Everyone in the group took turns writing on envelopes so that nobody's handwriting might be identified, and they went in pairs when the time came to post the material. One kept lookout, while the other went to the mailbox. One of the group, Hans Fruck, who worked at Siemens with Baum, drove around Berlin on a motorbike, using different mailboxes.

THE NAZI ACTIONS against the Jews brought many into the expanding hubs of the Harnack and Schulze-Boysen groups.

The musician Maria Terwiel recruited the young and politically conservative Catholic Helmut Roloff, a pianist and property landlord who was motivated to take a stand after one of his Jewish tenants put her head in her gas oven rather than face deportation. Roloff helped Terwiel type and copy dozens of Galen's anti-Hitler sermons.

Terwiel and her fiancé, Helmut Himpel, Roloff, and a friend of the Schulze-Boysens', John Graudenz, forged ration cards and identity cards to help the "U-boats." Graudenz, a craggy-faced journalist who had worked for the *New York Times* bureau in Berlin, also wrote leaflets condemning the Nazis' anti-Jewish laws. He had left journalism after Hitler's restrictions on the press made it impossible to carry out his work in an honest and unrestricted way.

Harnack's radio operator, Hans Coppi, and his wife, Hilde, hid Jewish people in their home. Hilde, the twenty-three-year-old daughter of a Mitte shopkeeper, worked as a senior clerk at the Reich Insurance Institute for Clerical Workers, where she used office stationery to create false documents. Fearless and determined, she also agreed to accompany Jewish families as they moved between safe houses in the city.

HERBERT BAUM ALSO teamed up with Robert Uhrig, a thirty-eight-year-old Berlin toolmaker who controlled a large factory-based resistance network of his own. Uhrig, who was originally from Leipzig, was in contact with small groups of workers carrying out small acts of sabotage at factories in a number of cities, including Hamburg and Essen. He concentrated on infiltrating saboteurs—mostly non-Jews—into armaments factories.

Uhrig was obsessed with security and worked hard to keep his resistance cells safe. He maintained contact with Baum only through his old friend Hilde Jadamowitz. On meeting the Baum group, Uhrig was particularly concerned by a new member, Joachim Franke, who had been brought in by a friend of typesetter George Vötter.

Franke's apartment quickly became known for his wild parties, where he openly boasted about his work to oppose Hitler.

Where Baum was adventurous and stubborn, Uhrig was cautious. Immediately sensing that Franke was a security risk, he distanced himself from Baum's group.

But Baum kept Franke close. It was a loyalty that would cost many lives.

WITH FALSE PAPERS it was still possible for some Jews to leave Berlin. Herbert Baum made contact with Erich Elkan, a Jewish Berlin lawyer, who was living under various disguises. He had already helped arrange the paperwork and escape from Germany of 180 Jewish children, including 60 from the same orphanage. Elkan had contacts in the Luftwaffe, including Bernt Engelmann, who, despite being an air force officer, was a committed anti-Nazi and was based in France. Three of Baum's friends, on the verge of detection for leafleting in a factory, had fled Germany and managed to get to Paris. Elkan asked Engelmann to visit them in the hotel where they were hiding and give them passes and instructions that would get them through France and across the border into Spain at Hendaye. The friends were suspicious of Engelmann at first, but he won them over and they saw that he was truly of the same mind as them. They told him that when he was back in Berlin, he and Elkan should link up with "the Baum."[12]

Soon after, it was Baum's friend Alfred Eisenstädter's turn to leave. Amazingly, he would leave legally, as an American visa that he had applied for in 1934 came through after more than six years. As he prepared to leave, the group held a farewell gathering. Many who had been at the wedding of Heinz Joachim and Marianne Prager were there, too. Eisenstädter smiled as he watched the couples talking: love still flourishing among all this. Baum and Cohn had recently married, as had those other childhood sweethearts, Sala Rosenbaum and Martin Kochmann.

The little flat was filled with chatter, memories, and stories, but behind it all Eisenstädter sensed a sadness: Everyone had the terrible feeling that those who did not get out would not survive.

"Good for you," Baum said, without a hint of bitterness, as he clapped his friend on the back. "You're getting out!"[13]

Eisenstädter knew that Baum would probably not leave even if he pressed a valid visa into his hand, and that made him feel a little ashamed.

As he looked around the room at his friends, he felt a cold shiver run over him. Something told him that he would never see them again.

# 17

## Operation 7

ABWEHR LAWYER HANS von Dohnanyi watched the roundups of Berlin's Jews with growing revulsion.

On walks with Hans Oster in the Tiergarten he discussed the latest reports from the camps, many of which he was copying for his secret record of Nazi crimes. Dohnanyi knew that several times in the past Oster had helped Jews by employing them as Abwehr agents or informers in the belief that no one would suspect military intelligence of employing a Jew. He now confessed that for some time he had been trying to work out how he could protect a lawyer friend of his named Friedrich Arnold, a Jew who had converted to Christianity. Arnold had appealed to Dohnanyi and Dietrich Bonhoeffer for help for himself and others who were in fear of deportation.

And an idea had formed in the two men's minds, which they wanted to share with Oster. It was based not just on Oster's recruitment of Jewish people into the organization but on Bonhoeffer's own extensive trips abroad over the past few months.

OSTER HAD NEVER given up on his efforts to send messages to Britain, and Bonhoeffer had become his new chosen emissary. Through Dohnanyi he had organized a series of trips for Bonhoeffer, who, as a nonmilitary man and a respected Christian, Oster believed would be given a fair, respectful hearing by the British.

While the approaches to the British before the war broke out had been far from successful—although the difficulties had been many—Oster realized that London had little idea that a core group of conspirators remained alive, in positions of some power, and still committed despite the war.

Bonhoeffer's friend Willem Visser 't Hooft, the Dutch theologian he had last seen in London shortly before war broke out, was based in Geneva and had told him to contact him if he needed to. Dohnanyi helped Bonhoeffer get the necessary German travel papers, and Bonhoeffer himself secured the sponsorship in Switzerland of Protestant theologian Professor Karl Barth, who had lost his job at the University of Bonn after refusing to swear an oath to Hitler.[1] He named Barth as his sponsor to distance himself from Visser 't Hooft, as he had other hopes for his meeting with the Dutchman. Barth was shocked to find Bonhoeffer was working for German military intelligence, and Bonhoeffer chose not to explain the true nature of his work, saying only that it was "top secret" and asking him to trust him. "At a time in which so much must be based simply on personal trust, everything is finished when mistrust emerges," he told him.[2]

Visser 't Hooft was delighted to see Bonhoeffer again. The German pastor looked no different than when he had seen him in London: the same smart gray three-piece suit with silver pocket watch tucked into the waist, the same swish of fine gray hair combed tightly across the high dome of his head. But his personality had hardened. Bonhoeffer briefed him on life in Germany, the continuing persecution of the Jews, the arrests of Christian churchmen, and the T4 euthanasia program of which Dohnanyi was collecting evidence.

Visser 't Hooft said he would contact Bishop George Bell immediately, and Bonhoeffer shook his hand gratefully. He knew that Bell, with his seat in the House of Lords, would have access to the most powerful people in Britain, perhaps even the prime minister, Winston Churchill.

A FEW MONTHS later Bonhoeffer returned to Zurich, this time with a memorandum for the British to be passed on by Visser 't Hooft. He told the Dutchman that British indifference to the German resistance might discourage them from removing Hitler and that the conspirators had to know that the Allies recognized they were distinct from the Nazis.

Bonhoeffer read a section aloud to his friend: "The question must be faced whether a German government which makes a complete break with Hitler and all he stands for, can hope to get such terms of peace that it has some chance to survive. It is clear that the answering of this question is a matter of urgency, since the attitude of opposition groups in Germany depends upon the answer given."

Visser 't Hooft asked Bonhoeffer what he prayed for, and the German pastor looked grave. "If you want to know the truth," he said, "I pray for the defeat of my nation. For I believe that is the only way to pay for all the suffering which my country has caused in the world."

By now, the reports of the atrocities in the Soviet Union were crossing Dohnanyi's desk and they were uppermost in Bonhoeffer's mind. But the invasion had hardened Allied hearts, too. When Bonhoeffer appealed to Britain, he must have realized that it could no longer make decisions alone. As one senior official in the German department of the Foreign Office later put it, if Stalin was to hear that Britain was negotiating in secret with German generals, "[he] might well have been tempted to see whether he could not again come to terms with Hitler."[3] And at this stage of the war, what could London do? It could not second-guess the political makeup of a postwar Germany and make promises it might not keep. There was no question of logistical support for the "resistance"—whatever it felt that constituted—and also the German army had access to its own supplies and could arm its own coup. Churchill was fighting a war of desperation and felt he could give no quarter to the Germans: In his public statements the Germans were Nazis, pure and simple.

However, in Chichester, when Bishop Bell received Dietrich Bonhoeffer's messages from Switzerland, he resolved to bring them to the attention of not only the British government but also—in a cautious way, so as to protect his source—the British public. "I am sure that there are very many in Germany, silenced now by the Gestapo and the machine gun, who long for deliverance from a godless Nazi rule, and for the coming of Christian order in which they and we can take our part," he told one meeting. "Is no trumpet call to come from England, to awaken them from despair?"[4]

At the height of the war, with Germany rampant, Bell's attempts to raise interest in "good" Germans earned him ridicule and sometimes abuse. "Get back to Germany where you belong!" a woman shouted at him one day at a parish meeting.[5]

AMONG THE INTELLECTUAL circles of the Prussian nobility a left-leaning group with a hatred of Nazism had developed around Helmuth James Graf von Moltke, who lived on the Kreisau country estate, where tenant farmers worked the land in a valley of undulating farmland in central Silesia in the eastern reaches of interwar Germany.[6] A great-grandnephew of a field marshal who was remembered as bringing the German army into the "modern age," Moltke had studied law but had declined an invitation to become a judge, as it would have meant joining the Nazi Party. Instead, he had set up a practice in international law in Berlin that helped people emigrate.

When back home on the estate, he invited like-minded intellectuals there to discuss Hitler's fascism, and their group became known as the Kreisau Circle. His closest confidants were his cousin Peter Graf Yorck von Wartenburg, who had also studied law and suffered a career setback when he refused to join the Nazi Party; London-born Fritz-Dietlof Graf von der Schulenburg, whose father had been the Kaiser's military attaché to Britain, and who had turned against the Nazis after the violence of the Röhm purge; and lawyer and diplomat Adam von Trott zu Solz, whose extensive travels before the war had included a spell at Oxford University. Trott had visited Britain and the United States before the war, to appeal for support for the German opposition to Hitler. He had met Lord Halifax and William Donovan, who would go on to create the US Office of Strategic Services (OSS). Although largely Protestant, the group also reached out to other Christians, including Jesuit priest Father Alfred Delp.

As liberal bourgeois intellectuals, they had struggled to see why Hitler had been so popular with the public during the early and mid-1930s and had assumed that it would not take long for the people to realize he would bring disaster upon Germany. Moltke did not believe that Germany could win the war and feared the survival of Europe was dependent on Germany's defeat. It was a terrible and painful conclusion for someone from such a proud German military family.

The group discussed at length what kind of Germany they could build after Hitler's downfall. Their government would be based on both Christian and socialist values, with all adults over twenty-one given the vote in local and provincial elections. Industry would be nationalized, and workers would have a say in the running of businesses. Even after the war began, they continued to believe they could rescue Germany from being an international pariah, so that it would become a leading member of a peaceful community of European nations, which would include Britain and the Soviet Union. Two guests of the meetings at the Kreisau estate also met with members of the Arvid Harnack group: Hans Peters, a former chair of the University of Berlin's ruling board, knew Schulze-Boysen, while economist Horst von Einsiedel knew Harnack himself.

Knowing that only the military could physically overthrow the Nazis, the Kreisau Circle felt it was their responsibility to have in place a plan that would see a Germany in crisis avoid repeating the ideological and political disaster of 1933. They knew that taking action called for deep ethical considerations, that the resistance could be accused of treason, but it must have one objective: the removal of the head of state. The resistance must cause the complete collapse of the Nazi political system; it was the only way to rebuild a society on secure and just principles. Despite their differences with Goerdeler, who they saw as a reactionary, he was still their favored candidate to be the new German chancellor.

Oster might have been plotting a coup for some time, but it was within the Goerdeler group and the Kreisau Circle that the seeds of the movement to carry out the most audacious coup attempt of the war were developing. That, though, was ahead.

First, Moltke had Abwehr business to attend to. Canaris had brought Moltke into his intelligence service early in the war as an adviser on international law, although the aristocrat—who was thirty-two when war broke out—refused to wear a military uniform and was always kept separate from the Oster group by the wily old admiral. Moltke traveled extensively in Poland and saw the results of the atrocities there. While aware of the dangers of a Hitler-led Germany from the beginning—he had warned friends in 1933 that "whoever votes for Hitler votes for war"—he was still shocked by the savagery of the regime. Moltke told his friend the American journalist Wallace Deuel, of the *Chicago Daily News*, late in 1940 that the hopes for those who opposed Hitler were slim and that Hitler "will compromise all Germans and make them responsible for the atrocities in the occupied territories and in Germany."[7]

Moltke was close friends with Dohnanyi, who shared with him some of the contents of his Chronicle of Shame, and he condemned the actions of the army, as well as the SS, stating: "[We have] no proper generals but military technicians, and the whole is a gigantic crime." On hearing of the mass roundups of Berlin Jews, he wrote to a friend: "What shall I say when I am asked: 'And what did you do during that time?'" In another letter, he said: "How can anyone know these things and walk around free?"[8]

Moltke asked Dohnanyi to use his legal skills to draft a report examining the oath of loyalty in a dictatorship and the legal and moral "right of resistance."[9]

In return, Dohnanyi had a request for him. In April 1942 he sent him a message telling him to prepare for a special trip abroad.

AFTER HIS MISSIONS to Switzerland, Dietrich Bonhoeffer was determined to continue to reach out to the Allies. Dohnanyi suggested linking up with the Kreisau Circle, which had developed strong links with a senior clergyman, Bishop Eivind Berggrav, who was an outspoken opponent of Norway's pro-Nazi government led by Vidkun Quisling. The opposition saw Berggrav as a powerful ally and, when they learned that Quisling planned to arrest him, decided to send Bonhoeffer and Moltke to Norway to assess the situation.

Both were provided with a complete cover story by the Abwehr for the trip. Bonhoeffer's official task was to attempt to smooth over the anger that Quisling had stirred up with the country's Protestant church and that was threatening to cause widespread protest in the occupied nation. The Norwegian church had been united in its opposition to the Nazis, with every bishop severing connections to the Norwegian government.

On April 10, 1942, Bonhoeffer and Dohnanyi took a train to Sassnitz, a picturesque town on Rügen Island on Germany's northern coast, where Dohnanyi introduced Bonhoeffer to Moltke before returning to Berlin.

The next day Bonhoeffer and Moltke were sitting at a table in a café when they saw the ferry appear out of the fog. They crossed the Baltic Sea to Malmö, took the long journey up the Swedish coast by train, and crossed into Norway. In Oslo, Bonhoeffer—on his "official" mission from the Abwehr—was allowed to talk with representatives of Bishop Berggrav, who had been placed under house arrest by Quisling. Instead of trying to smooth things over, he encouraged the Norwegian church to keep fighting, "even as far as martyrdom."[10] The two Abwehr emissaries then went to the Norwegian government and persuaded them to release Berggrav to help maintain order. Quisling agreed.

Through Bonhoeffer's brother Klaus, who as a lawyer for Lufthansa had an extensive range of contacts in the Norwegian business community, it was arranged for Moltke and Bonhoeffer to meet Norwegian industrialists to encourage contact with Crown Prince Olav, who was in exile in London, and to ask him to be a conduit for messages from the German resistance.

Back in Berlin, Bonhoeffer learned that Bishop Bell would be making an extended visit to neutral Sweden. There could be no better opportunity to provide an up-to-date, face-to-face report on the conspiracy to the British government.

Dohnanyi and Oster managed to arrange a special courier pass through the Foreign Ministry, and Bonhoeffer was able to catch a plane to Stockholm, arriving on May 31 and immediately heading to the Nordic Ecumenical Institute in Sigtuna to meet Bell. The pair had not met for three years, but despite all that had happened across Europe and the fact that Bell had had no advanced warning of Bonhoeffer's visit, they were quickly talking as old friends. Bonhoeffer persuaded Bell of the depth and scale of the conspiracy throughout the army and military intelligence, and took the risk of giving as many names as he could, including Goerdeler and Oster, and trade union leaders such as Wilhelm Leuschner and Max Habermann. He said he wanted London to be assured that these Germans recognized their nation's sins and did not wish to escape its need for repentance. He suggested a future German monarchy under Louis Ferdinand, a Prussian prince his brother had introduced to the conspiracy. The British should mention his name to the Americans, Bonhoeffer said, as the prince had met President Roosevelt before the war.

The British bishop thanked the German pastor warmly for his "spirit of fellowship and of Christian brotherliness" and hoped God would be with him in his work. But, having witnessed the understandable anti-German feeling across Britain, he warned that Churchill would be skeptical of the messages from Germany and that there were many in London who, after the failed attempts at appeasement before the war, would not trust any German.

Back in London, Bell met with British foreign minister Anthony Eden and said he was convinced of Bonhoeffer's integrity and that there had to be a clear distinction drawn between the Nazis and the "anti-Hitlerites" who stood up to defy them. The other Nazi-occupied countries of Europe had been promised liberation, but the anti-Nazi Germans had been refused the same promises by the Allies. He also spoke to Sir Stafford Cripps, a powerful member of Churchill's war cabinet, who had been impressed by Visser 't Hooft and reports he had brought from Bonhoeffer and Moltke's friend Adam von Trott.

Unfortunately, though, the British government decided that it was not "in the national interest for any reply whatever" to be sent to the conspirators. At this stage they would never negotiate with the German opposition for fear of antagonizing Stalin and certainly not without the consent of the United States government.

When Bell delivered a copy of his report to the American ambassador in London—with a promise that it would be passed to the State Department—he did not receive a message back.

WHILE PLANNING THE Oslo trip, Dohnanyi and Bonhoeffer had sought Moltke's advice on their plan to smuggle Jews out of Germany. Moltke's legal expertise on obtaining Swiss visas had been essential.

Back in Berlin, Dohnanyi developed the plan and a list of people to help, including Friedrich Arnold himself, a retired Jewish lawyer named Julius Fliess who had won a number of bravery medals during the First World War, and Fliess's wife and family. Fliess was an invalid and had already been threatened with deportation. Bonhoeffer also wanted to help Charlotte Friedenthal, a convert who had worked as secretary to the central offices of the Confessing Church.[11] There were seven names on the initial list, so Dohnanyi code-named the plan Unternehmen 7, or U7 (Operation 7).[12]

To hide the male refugees in the Abwehr, Dohnanyi used the same routine as when employing his brother-in-law Dietrich Bonhoeffer: By declaring the men "uk"—unabkömmlich, meaning that they were indispensable to the Abwehr—he ensured that they could not be conscripted for work or active service by any other branch of the military, and that for confidential operational reasons they were essential to the Abwehr's work. The additional bridge he had to cross was the removal of the Jews from deportation lists, which he achieved through police contacts.

Then, with Canaris's blessing—the admiral knew some of the people to be helped by U7—Dohnanyi developed a complete cover story for the operation. It was typically convoluted: The Jews had been "briefed" to explain to the Swiss that the stories of Nazi persecution were malicious rumor and Allied misinformation, and they would later seek to get to the United States and spread the same information there. This cover story Canaris shared with the Gestapo to make the operation appear legitimate. The cover was so convincing that some of the Jews at first refused to go. Dietrich Bonhoeffer took Friedenthal aside and persuaded her that this story was just a charade: When they got to Switzerland, they could behave and say what they wished, as if they had reneged on their "deal" with the Abwehr.

The next problem was getting permission from Switzerland to allow the people to enter. The Swiss were reluctant to take the refugees. Bonhoeffer said he could speak to Alphons Köchlin, the president of the Schweizer Kirchenbund, the Swiss Protestant Church organization, and ask him to sponsor the granting of Swiss entry visas. Dohnanyi decided another trip by Bonhoeffer would look suspicious, so he sent Wilhelm Schmidhuber, a dark-haired smooth talker with a reputation for giving lavish gifts, who had been working in a part-time capacity for the Abwehr in Munich for several years and had been the one who had suggested the use of Joseph Müller for the Vatican peace conversations. Well-known at border checkpoints and with a reputation for being involved in many different roles—including one as honorary Portuguese consul—Schmidhuber crossed easily into Switzerland and delivered a note from Bonhoeffer to Köchlin, who was pleased to help.

But by this time the seven escapees had almost doubled to thirteen.[13] Dohnanyi realized they would need money to survive in Switzerland and worked out a scheme to allow them to exchange their German currency and some personal items of value for Swiss francs from Abwehr accounts. The illegal payments to the refugees would be disguised as compensation for the confiscation of property and would be deposited in a Swiss bank by Schmidhuber. The refugees would then be able to access it and start a new life.

Dohnanyi's new conspiracy would take many months to organize and put into operation. If it failed, it would bring down himself, his friends, perhaps the whole organization.

# 18

## Tresckow

ON JUNE 6, 1941, Adolf Hitler had instructed his armies that when they moved into the Soviet Union they were to execute all Soviet military leaders who were captured. The so-called Commissar Order contravened military codes and shocked many still tied to concepts of military morality and honor. Even the anti-Bolshevik propaganda of the Nazi period had not prepared many senior officers for it. Hitler scoffed when he heard their complaints and said they must "overcome their scruples." But many could not. As the war unfolded in the East, they saw an erosion of morality that infected not only the SS but also their own troops.

At first, there was often confusion. Philipp von Boeselager was a twenty-five-year-old lieutenant attached to the staff of Army Group Center—one of three armies on the Eastern Front—and working as aide-de-camp to Field Marshal Günther von Kluge. Kluge and Field Marshal Fedor von Bock, commander of Army Group Center, had been among a number of commanders who had secretly agreed not to enforce the Commissar Order. Reading through a series of dispatches that he was then expected to summarize for Kluge, Boeselager found an entry from an SS lieutenant-general named Erich von dem Bach-Zelewski that referred to "special treatment for five Gypsies"—a term that Boeselager queried. At their next meeting, Kluge asked Bach-Zelewski what he meant by "special treatment."

Bach-Zelewski, a bull of a man who oversaw the work of the SS in the central Russian sector, looked shocked that the field marshal bothered to ask about the gypsies. "Those?" he sneered. "We shot them!"

"What do you mean, 'shot them'? After a trial before a military tribunal?"

"No, of course not," the SS man said impatiently. "All the Jews and Gypsies we pick up are liquidated—shot!"

When Kluge protested, Bach-Zelewski cut him short, saying it was "our mission" to liquidate "all the enemies of the Reich."[1]

Boeselager carried the words in his head for months. For Bach-Zelewski and others—for the Nazis—the killing of Jews and gypsies had become the "commonly shared war goal" of both the SS and the Wehrmacht. The state, the young officer reflected, was "riddled with vice and crime," and the army, "by remaining silent, was making itself the system's accomplice." Boeselager agonized over how to extricate himself from the horror. "I had not become an officer in order to shoot the head of state like a dog," he said, but as he looked around him, he saw more and more senior officers of Army Group Center whose loyalty had reached the breaking point.[2]

ON OCTOBER 20, 1941, Carl-Hans Graf von Hardenberg, a kindly father of five who had resigned his interwar roles in regional government when he refused to join the Nazi Party, was being flown to the headquarters of Army Group Center on the banks of the Berezina River. Having been called up as a reservist at the outbreak of war, Hardenberg was now personal adjutant to Bock. As the aircraft banked toward landing, the small city of Borisov was spread out before him and he saw huge crowds of people being herded through the streets toward massive ditches. As he watched, he saw the muzzle flashes of machine guns, the bodies dropping on top of each other. Hardenberg was witnessing a massacre.

Before the war, as many as one in five people living in Borisov had been Jewish.[3] For three centuries they had played an important role in the cultural and mercantile life of the city, becoming well-known as bakers and sweet makers, trading with towns along the river and in the regional capital, Minsk. They had faced pogroms by Polish troops after the First World War, but even that did not prepare them for what happened when the Nazis arrived and created a ghetto, which on October 20 the SS—comprising mainly Latvian troops—decided to "clear." Herding crowds at gunpoint to long ditches, the SS machine-gunned their victims until the ditches filled up. Even when dirt was thrown over the bodies, the blood leaked out. Lime and more dirt were thrown on top. Around seven thousand people were murdered in this way.[4]

Hardenberg was still in a state of shock when he reached Bock's headquarters. As he explained what he had seen to Colonel Rudolf-Christoph von Gersdorff, an Abwehr liaison officer with the army, and to Bock, he could not contain his anger. He tearfully begged Bock to end "the orgy of executions." Bock immediately tried to find out who was in charge of the massacre and have them punished, but the civilian commissioner, Wilhelm Kube, laughed in his face. Hitler had unleashed hell and the devils were acting on his orders.

Gersdorff took the highly unusual step of recording in the Army Group Center war diary that he had the "impression that there is almost universal detestation in the officer corps for these shootings of Jews, prisoners and commissars." He added: "These shootings are regarded as a stain on the honour of the German Army and in particular of the German officer corps."[5]

Also present when Hardenberg reported the horror he had witnessed was Bock's nephew, a committed, cultured, and energetic officer who would now form the nucleus of a new stage of active resistance to Hitler.

His name was Colonel Henning von Tresckow.

TRESCKOW WAS FORTY years old when the Germans launched their attack on the Soviet Union. A Prussian Protestant from a family distinguished by its military and political achievements, he had proved himself to be a remarkable soldier on the Western Front of the First World War when, while still a teenager, he won the first of three Iron Crosses.

Balding, with kind eyes and a determined expression, he was known to be patient with others but demanding of himself. Never the typical stiff Prussian military man, he recited poetry, enjoyed languages and travel, and was warm toward other nationalities. He had long despised the Nazis, angered by the illegality of the murders during the Röhm purge and hating the way Blomberg and Fritsch had been humiliated by Hitler. Unlike many military men, he had abhorred Hitler's invasion of Poland and was unpersuaded by its success, believing this act of aggression represented a moral defeat for Germany. In the invasion of Russia, Tresckow saw the army being dragged into a genocidal racial war for the Nazi Party, and his hatred turned to a conviction to do something about Hitler. Without action, he felt, "the German people will be burdened with a guilt the world will not forget in a hundred years."

As senior staff officer of Army Group Center, Tresckow read reports from across the sector. He read about the work of the Einsatzgruppen; about "energetic and ruthless" action taken on Hitler's orders against "Bolshevik agitators, guerrillas, saboteurs, and Jews"; and about the "special treatment" that Bach-Zelewski had described to Kluge.

As Oster had done in the Abwehr, Tresckow began to gather around him like-minded officers, including his cousin Fabian von Schlabrendorff, a young reserve lieutenant and lawyer whom he appointed as his own aide-de-camp, and former cavalryman Gersdorff, who became his intelligence officer.

Finally, keen to connect to the civilian opposition to the Nazis, Tresckow also brought in Lieutenant-Colonel Berndt von Kleist as his supply officer. Kleist, who had lost a leg during the First World War, was friends with Goerdeler.

On hearing details of the Borisov massacre, Tresckow was incensed and resolved to take drastic action. But Hitler's death would not be enough on its own: Plans had to be in place in Berlin to take control of the departments of state.

He sent Schlabrendorff to Berlin to meet with Oster and Dohnanyi, whom he knew. He learned that Oster was talking to Field Marshal von Witzleben about initiating an uprising inside the army in France. Oster asked Schlabrendorff what sort of support a coup would get from the army in the East, and Schlabrendorff explained that Tresckow was trying hard to bring his uncle, Bock, the commander of Army Group Center, on board. Tresckow also had asked Schlabrendorff to speak to the diplomat Ulrich von Hassell about his views on how the Allies would view a coup. Hassell told him a "respectable" Germany would have a good chance at negotiating an "acceptable peace." Hassell then secured the support of General von Falkenhausen, military commander in Belgium and northern France, and Brauchitsch, who had failed to support Beck in his conspiracy before the invasion of Czechoslovakia but who now—according to another conspirator, General Georg Thomas—saw that he must bear a "share of the responsibility" for the "beastliness." Unfortunately, no sooner had Brauchitsch indicated his support than Hitler removed him as commander in chief and placed himself in charge.

With military men in France, Berlin, and Russia now showing commitment to a coup, the civilian opposition was enlivened. Hassell, Trott, Yorck, and Moltke renewed their discussions of how they might form a government after the Nazis. Berlin meetings were held in private houses, with participants leaving their cars in neighboring streets to avoid suspicion. In Moltke's flat he hung a well-known poster from the time that warned "The enemy is listening in"—although his friends knew that he took it to mean the Gestapo rather than Allied agents as the poster intended. Moltke also organized some meetings with conspirators under the guise of a civil service committee ironically set up to work out the demands of the armed forces in the event of a German victory. In reality, Moltke's subcommittee discussed the legal framework that could hold Germany together when the Nazi regime collapsed. In January 1942, Hassell accompanied a small group of conspirators, including Oster, Dohnanyi, Goerdeler, and Beck, to meet Falkenhausen in Brussels and Witzleben in Paris. Over a series of discussions all agreed on the need for a coup, but there was concern that the troops in France and Belgium had not had sufficient frontline service to see through the action required. In the event of a civil war they might not stand up to the forces that the Nazis could throw against them. A few weeks later Witzleben was forced to retire due to ill health, and the conspiracy lost a key ally in France, while in Russia, Tresckow suffered a further setback when he failed to persuade his uncle, Bock, to support a coup. "I will not allow the Führer to be attacked!" he shouted at Tresckow. "I shall stand before the Führer and defend him against anyone who dares attack him!"

However, by late March 1942, the army resistance had developed into a ghost organization with Oster as Berlin chief of staff, Schlabrendorff as liaison officer between Berlin and Army Group Center, and Dohnanyi acting as a courier for messages between Oster and Tresckow. Beck's home became the conspirators' operational headquarters. As he had resigned his post before the war had begun, Beck always retained particular integrity in the eyes of the others—as Gisevius noted, he was "the only general with an unimpaired reputation, the only general who had voluntarily resigned."[6]

Oster concentrated on plans for the military takeover of Berlin using troops stationed to the east of the city and members of a newly formed Brandenburg Division, which was under the operational command of the man who had been poised to kill Hitler during the 1938 coup, Friedrich Heinz. Now a lieutenant-colonel, Heinz was prepared to use this highly trained special operations unit—set up on the orders of Canaris—as a coup d'état force.

MILITARY OPERATIONS IN Russia during the summer of 1942 left army leaders with little time to work on the coup, but Tresckow still labored to build and maintain alliances. He met with Kluge, Goerdeler, and Oster, who introduced him to Ludwig Beck, and he sent Schlabrendorff—a courtroom duelist with a lawyer's tenacious skill for argument—to negotiate with General Friedrich Olbricht, who was head of the General Army Office and a deputy to the commander of the Ersatzheer, the Home or Replacement Army.

Obtaining Olbricht's support was essential. He could mobilize groups of troops under the guise of sending recruits to various parts of the Reich. Having supported Oster before, Olbricht agreed to use units in Berlin, Cologne, Munich, and Vienna to support a coup, although Tresckow doubted his "resolve."

Tresckow knew he could not take any risks: Any attempt on Hitler's life must succeed. Failure could mean destruction of the conspiracy and would leave the regime on such high alert that no further attempt might ever be made. He had his men draw up a plan, exploring three possibilities for killing Hitler: shot by a lone assassin, bombed by a team, or killed by a commando-style raid.

Although he felt a gun to be more gentlemanly, he feared a pistol attack had a high chance of failure and grew to favor the use of a bomb, although he never fully resigned himself to the loss of innocent life it would cause. He was also troubled by the knowledge that the assassin would be denounced as a traitor. His reservations, however, were far outweighed by his fear of Germany's impending Götterdämmerung: "I wish I could show the German people a film, entitled 'Germany at the end of the war,'" he said sadly. "Perhaps then they would realize, with horror, what we're heading for."[7]

Tresckow and Schlabrendorff discussed the use of different explosives, but found the German timing mechanisms available to them made too much noise and might be discovered. Gersdorff, the Abwehr liaison man who acted as Tresckow's intelligence officer, suggested the use of British explosives, which had a silent chemical fuse and could be hidden without causing suspicion. He contacted Dohnanyi in Berlin and was told the

Abwehr could provide British plastic explosives, designed for destroying railway lines, which had been captured in RAF airdrops meant for the French resistance.

Tresckow's group in Army Group Center now numbered about thirty officers, who never met in large groups and usually reported to Tresckow in his bunker late at night over a game of chess. He felt that drawing any more people into the heart of the conspiracy would endanger security, and he anxiously felt that the fewer people who knew where these explosives had been delivered, the better. Therefore, Dohnanyi took the train to Smolensk and personally handed the explosives to Tresckow. Tests were carried out in fields near the Dnieper by Tresckow, Schlabrendorff, and Gersdorff. Tresckow was particularly keen to test the timers on the chemical fuses and to ascertain how much of the explosives would be needed depending on where the explosion would occur.

Tresckow also set about developing his own coup d'état force, similar to Heinz's Brandenburgs in Berlin. Having heard about a young cavalry officer named Georg von Boeselager from his brother Philipp, Tresckow invited him to accompany Kluge on a visit to headquarters. Kluge, who spent parts of the flight shooting at foxes from a window of the aircraft, did not inquire why Tresckow wanted to meet Boeselager so urgently.

Tresckow was impressed with Boeselager, who, as a holder of the Oak Leaves to the Knight's Cross, was one of the most highly decorated soldiers in the Wehrmacht, and they discussed the formation of a special cavalry unit that could be sent at a moment's notice to carry out special operations anywhere along the front. The idea was approved by Kluge, who left the details to the two officers.

In private, Tresckow revealed that the unit might be used not only in special operations against the enemy but also in a coup against Hitler. Over the next few hours Boeselager agreed his unit would be at the disposal of Tresckow's conspiracy. His brother Philipp would lead one of the unit's battalions.

Georg von Boeselager had never met Tresckow before the day he agreed to support him: an indication of the keen loyalty the mild-mannered but fiercely intelligent Tresckow inspired in all who served with him. If any expressed doubt about what they were doing, Tresckow would suppress them not with anger, but with a paternal hand on the shoulder. When the Allies decided at the Casablanca Conference to accept only Germany's unconditional surrender, Philipp von Boeselager wondered aloud if there were any point continuing with the assassination plans. "Every day we are assassinating nearly 16,000 additional victims," Tresckow told him. "We have no choice."[8]

A COUP WITHOUT a plan to hold Germany together in its aftermath would almost certainly result in chaos and civil war, so debate continued between old-fashioned conservative nationalists, such as Goerdeler, and the younger, socialist, and Christian members of the Kreisau Circle, particularly Moltke, Trott, and Yorck, who saw Germany not as a dominating power in Central and Eastern Europe but as a part of a federal Europe modeled in some ways on the United States of America.

On being told by Tresckow that he hoped to attempt a coup in the spring, Beck planned to bring together the two groups of political thinkers for the first time. The meeting was organized in great secrecy and with considerable effort by Fritz-Dietlof Graf von der Schulenburg with the help of Father Delp, who did not in the end attend. The attendees arrived at Yorck's Berlin home on January 8, 1943, at different times, leaving their cars several streets away. Some feared they were being watched by the Gestapo, and that only added to the tension inside the house.

The "young," as Ulrich von Hassell called the Kreisau Circle—Moltke, Yorck, Trott, Schulenburg, and Protestant theologian Eugen Gerstenmaier, who were all under forty—quickly found themselves in an argument with the "old": Beck, Goerdeler, Hassell, the right-wing former Prussian finance minister Johannes Popitz, and Dr. Jens Peter Jessen, a professor of political science who was advising on a new constitution for Germany. The "old" were mainly in their late fifties or early sixties, but the generation gap was not the only issue. The Kreisau Circle wanted the discussion to describe real change in a post-Hitler Germany, not a return to pre-WWI militarism but a democratic Germany in a European federation. When Goerdeler dismissed that discussion as being for another time, the "young" felt that was just his reactionary views coming through. There was agreement, though, that some kind of "semi-authoritarian" regime would be needed for a limited period after the coup and that the coup should take place as soon as possible. Beck asked Goerdeler to compile a formal list of ministers for the post-Nazi government.

When Beck reported to Oster, the Abwehr man felt more emboldened than ever. At long last he sensed that the tentacles of the conspiracy stretched from France in the West to the often disaffected armies in the East, and that the civilian political opposition was uniting with the army resistance.

Hitler's death would throw the regime into a paroxysm of shock: There would be fighting between the Wehrmacht and SS in Berlin, but the coup could succeed.

Then a relatively minor conspiracy threatened to come back to haunt Oster.

# 19

## Questions for the Abwehr

T HE CUSTOMS INVESTIGATION Bureau in Prague depended on tip-offs and information from banks and border controls, as well as detective work by its agents. Black marketeers thrived on war and occupation, and so the bureau and its chief, Johannes Wapenhensch, were kept busy.

When a note crossed his desk that a large sum of US dollars was to be offered for sale at a railway station in the city, Wapenhensch was doubtful. Dollars were the most sought-after currency, but the bureau had not confiscated any in quantity for some time. All the same, it was too good to overlook, and smuggling foreign currency was a grave crime in wartime; Wapenhensch sent two men to check it out.

They returned with a well-known black marketeer named David who worked as a chief clerk in a large firm handling large sums of money. Just as the tip-off had predicted, he was trying to sell $10,000 to a local man for a very high rate of exchange. Wapenhensch had the man put his briefcase on his desk, and the investigator sifted through it. As well as the money, there were two envelopes filled with precious stones. Both envelopes were marked with the names Schmidhuber and Ickrath. The black marketeer told Wapenhensch that these were two men who were officers of the Abwehr in Munich and that he had been trying to sell the stones for them. He regularly worked as a courier for them, David said, even taking money to Switzerland.

Wapenhensch found the story far-fetched—and feared it would take him in a direction he was unsure whether to follow—but the nature of his work meant that he pulled every thread to see where it would lead. He contacted the Munich office of the Abwehr, established that there were indeed two officers of that name, and formally requested they be brought to Prague for questioning.

Wilhelm Schmidhuber had been overseeing the payments for Hans von Dohnanyi's Operation 7, smuggling Jews to safety in Switzerland. Thirteen had by now crossed the border to safety. All had to be kept supplied with money from Schmidhuber. Heinz Ickrath was Schmidhuber's friend and colleague in Munich; together they had been carrying out some currency exchanges for their own gain and selling some of the precious stones that the Jewish refugees had exchanged for Swiss currency.

Once in Prague, Schmidhuber claimed the cash and jewels were part of a counterintelligence operation, and were being used as payment for a Czech woman who lived in Switzerland. She took the money in return for passing false information to—and receiving sound intelligence from—a British Secret Intelligence Service agent with whom she was sleeping. The black marketeer and the valuables must be released immediately so the Abwehr operation could continue, Schmidhuber told Wapenhensch. But the wily investigator was not easily intimidated and could sense when someone was covering for their own greed. The release of the money and jewels was impossible, he stated flatly—investigations would continue.

Rethinking strategy and eager to get out of the investigator's clutches, Schmidhuber adapted his story, confiding that he had begun to suspect that the black marketeer, David, was a double agent and was withdrawing money—perhaps payments from the British—from the same bank in Switzerland each time he visited there. Schmidhuber said that he and Wapenhensch could work together to uncover a British plot. It would be a major coup for them both. Wapenhensch, of course, recognized that if this was true it could be advantageous to him, and he agreed to give Schmidhuber a little time to make inquiries.

A few days later Schmidhuber returned to Prague and told Wapenhensch that he had been able to confirm that the bank account in Switzerland did belong to a British agent and that David was indeed taking payments from it. Schmidhuber hoped that this would leave him in the clear; that Wapenhensch would simply charge the unfortunate Czech black marketeer, lock him up, and let the Abwehr "deal" with the espionage inquiry.

Instead, Wapenhensch nodded, brought in David, and confronted him with Schmidhuber's accusation that he was a double agent.

David went pale. "My neck's at stake now," he said. "I'll tell the truth. But what Herr Schmidhuber has told you isn't true."[1]

David hurriedly told his version of events, pleading with Wapenhensch that he was telling the truth. He said he was part of a smuggling operation headed by Schmidhuber and Ickrath. He helped them transport currency, jewels, and paintings, generally buying in Slovakia and transporting items into Germany.

Making inquiries with colleagues in Bratislava, Wapenhensch discovered they had files on another man linked to the Abwehr who had had dealings with David. The man had been arrested for illegal currency dealings. Wapenhensch suspected he was uncovering a major smuggling operation, but the Abwehr angle worried him. It would be politically sensitive. Seeking advice, he was told to contact the Abwehr headquarters in Berlin. His inquiry was picked up not by Oster's section, but by an ardent Nazi named Herzlieb who mistrusted Oster and despised Hans von Dohnanyi. He immediately recognized Schmidhuber as a close friend of Dohnanyi's and a regular visitor to Oster's office. He encouraged the customs investigator to step up his inquiries.

Oster and Dohnanyi had no idea that danger was closing in on them.

JOHANNES WAPENHENSCH WAS an experienced customs investigator, but the military intelligence angle to his Schmidhuber case continued to gnaw at him.

Then he remembered that a former colleague, Karl Süss, was now working for the Abwehr in Munich. He would not only be able to advise him but also to help him arrest Schmidhuber and Ickrath. Wapenhensch quickly put through a call to Munich.

Captain Süss listened to his story with growing interest, but then explained that the two men both had Luftwaffe reservist ranks and he would need to be empowered by a military authority to make an arrest. Wapenhensch said he would travel to Munich to try to arrange the paperwork.

After Süss replaced the receiver, he immediately went to see Schmidhuber, Ickrath, and Josef "the Ox" Müller. Wapenhensch had picked the wrong man of whom to ask advice: Süss was a supporter of the men's anti-Nazi activities.

Müller contacted Berlin. It was now that Oster, Dohnanyi, and Canaris became aware of Wapenhensch's investigation. The news sent a chill through them all. Schmidhuber not only knew about Operation 7; he also knew about the Vatican peace conversations. He knew enough to see them all hang. A frantic discussion took place in which the three even discussed killing Schmidhuber to silence him, but Dohnanyi angrily dismissed the idea. He suggested transferring the compromised businessman to Italy and sending Ickrath away, too, while they worked to head off the inquiry. Canaris and Oster reluctantly agreed.

Schmidhuber checked into a small hotel in Merano, while Ickrath went into hiding in southern Austria, near the Wörthersee. Meanwhile, Süss and Müller cleared out Schmidhuber's safe and destroyed any incriminating material.

When Wapenhensch arrived in Munich, he kicked up a huge fuss and managed to get the Luftwaffe to draw up warrants for the two men's arrests for desertion. Wapenhensch insisted on traveling to Italy to be there when Schmidhuber was apprehended. Late in October 1942, the investigator was delighted to snap the handcuffs on the Abwehr adventurer and to bring him back to a Wehrmacht prison in Munich.

Schmidhuber was in a cell before Admiral Canaris and the others knew he had been arrested.

When he found out, the admiral contacted Wapenhensch and told him Süss must sit in on any interrogations—so as to protect the security of any information relating to Abwehr operations—and that questions must be kept to "military matters." Canaris tried to make him stop his investigations, but the customs officer held firm: "I refuse to discontinue my investigations," he said.[2] Canaris ordered Süss to be as obstructive as he dared.

When Wapenhensch began the interrogation, Süss tried to block questions about any other Abwehr officers, and Wapenhensch angrily told his old friend that he was risking his own neck.

Schmidhuber told his inquisitors that his currency deals were official Abwehr work carried out with the knowledge of Dohnanyi and Müller. Through the listening Süss, he was effectively threatening the Oster resistance group, warning them that unless they helped him he would reveal all about their work against the regime.

On hearing this, the conspirators made a desperate decision. Knowing there was little they could do to control Schmidhuber's admissions to the inquiry, they decided they had to destroy his credibility. They created a file purporting to show his procurement of foreign passports, his links to British intelligence, and a claim that he had been promised the role of high commissioner of Germany by the British.

When they handed over the faked file, it rocked the investigation, but rather than simply causing doubts, it persuaded Wapenhensch and the others that the case was too hot to handle.

Wapenhensch took the exact action that the conspirators had been hoping to avoid. In November 1942, he handed the inquiry into the Abwehr over to the Gestapo.

ADMIRAL CANARIS HAD never taken an active role in the resistance, but he continued to cover for Oster. Now the activities of his underlings threatened to bring down his whole organization. Gestapo and SD investigators had spent months trying to expose the inefficiency of the Abwehr, and in the Schmidhuber case they believed they had something that would show the department was not only failing but corrupt.

Canaris headed to Munich himself to find out directly from Müller what was going on. They met in a room in the Regina Palast Hotel, and the strongly built lawyer saw immediately how agitated the little admiral appeared to be by the investigation. He spent the first few minutes searching the room for hidden microphones and then draped his overcoat over the telephone. "What Oster and Dohnanyi are doing is treasonable," Canaris told him.

Müller shrugged, saying he did not care much for what Hitler considered treason. Anyway, Müller said, it did not matter why they were in this mess, but how they were going to get out of it.

Canaris told him they were all in for a rough ride. He had heard that an old suspicion had resurfaced. Back in 1940 Canaris had been able to scotch an investigation by one of his own men, Joachim Rohleder, who, on studying telegrams sent by the Belgian ambassador to the Vatican, had begun to suspect Müller of passing on German military secrets. The Gestapo had now reopened the case as part of a wider investigation into what it suspected were peace overtures being made via the Vatican. Another name that had been recently added to the file was Peter Graf Yorck von Wartenburg, of the Kreisau Circle, who also had links to the Abwehr and had recently been put under surveillance. If they got to Müller, they would get to Oster and Dohnanyi, and eventually to him.

Schmidhuber and Ickrath were now in cells in the Gestapo headquarters at Prinz-Albrecht-Strasse, Canaris added. And since they had smeared Schmidhuber as a British spy, he no longer had any reason to be faithful to his old friends.

In fact, his best hope of survival would be to tell the Gestapo everything.

# 20

## Rote Kapelle

ANATOLI GOUREVITCH SAW himself as a figure from a spy novel. With his self-consciously cool poses and his thinking man's pipe, he was mainly preoccupied with impressing and bedding women. A key figure in the Soviets' Western European spy network, based in Brussels, he had insisted on the code name Kent, a character in a prewar English spy novel.

Gourevitch's chief was a different man altogether. Leopold Trepper was a Polish-born Communist Jew who had built an import-export business—based initially on raincoats—which had become the perfect cover for his spy network. Until Barbarossa, he had sent messages to Moscow via the Soviet military attaché in Vichy France; since June 1941, he had used radios in Belgium and the Netherlands.

His very earliest messages had been intercepted and forwarded to the Funkabwehr, Radio Signals Security, which was based only a short walk from the Harnacks' apartment in Berlin. Over the coming months the team collected hundreds of messages, all in code and as yet indecipherable. Staff always named radio operators "pianists" and networks "kapelle," meaning "orchestra" or "chapel," and as the radio signals coming back seemed to be coming from Moscow, they dubbed this network Rote Kapelle, Red Orchestra. It was a name that would come to stick, even though Harnack and the others, and even their radio operator, Hans Coppi, had no idea they could be considered part of a much wider network.

On August 26, 1941, Anatoli Gourevitch was elated to receive a fascinating, thrilling, and obviously vitally important mission from Moscow. "Go to Berlin to Adam Kuckhoff or his wife in Wilhelmstrasse 18, tel. 83 62 61, second stairway to the left, upper storey," went the message, "and explain that you were sent by a friend of Arvid's and Harro's, that Arvid knew as Alexander Erdberg . . . Suggest to Kuckhoff that he arrange a meeting with Arvid and Harro."

The message told him to ask what was happening with the radio, get information on the whereabouts of group members, arrange future transmissions, and suggest the use of a courier to take messages to the Soviet trade mission in either Istanbul or Stockholm.

Finally, Moscow added: "If Kuckhoff cannot be found, contact the wife of Harro, Libertas Schulze-Boysen, at Altenburger Alle 19, tel. 99 58 47. Explain that you come from someone who met with Elisabeth [Schumacher] in Marquardt . . ."

Moscow had no idea that Coppi was transmitting on the wrong schedule. Its impatience with not having received any messages had forced it into a drastic step.

Gourevitch told Trepper he had been given a major mission and showed him the message. When the Pole saw the addresses and names in Moscow's message, he shook his head in shock at the foolhardy breaches of security. "It's not possible," he said. "They have gone crazy!"[1]

In their desperation to make contact with the group in Berlin, Moscow had given names, addresses, telephone numbers. It had taken an outrageous risk with the Berliners' lives.

Trepper's sixth sense told him there was trouble around the corner, but he went ahead and started to plan for the paperwork and travel documents that would get Gourevitch to Berlin.

ON OCTOBER 29, 1941, Libertas Schulze-Boysen answered the telephone at home and found herself talking to a man who spoke German with a heavy Russian accent. Without giving his name the man mentioned "meeting Elisabeth at the bathing resort." Libertas paused, seemed to get the reference, and agreed to meet him at the Zoo subway station.

Having met Gourevitch and told him all of the network were well, she agreed he could visit her husband at their apartment. Far from being concerned about the security lapse, Schulze-Boysen was delighted to greet the visitor, explaining that they had been anxious that their information was not getting through to Moscow as they had heard nothing back. Gourevitch then quickly took out his notebook as the Luftwaffe officer outlined all he knew about the German plans in the Caucasus and their strategy for attacking Moscow. Schulze-Boysen also gave the Russian the approximate location of Hitler's Wolf's Lair headquarters in East Prussia, details of German losses on Crete, the extent of Germany's chemical weapons program, and data on aircraft production. He spoke for four hours as the Russian filled his notebook.

Before he left, Gourevitch gave addresses to which to write in Brussels, Paris, Istanbul, and Stockholm, and took down a postal address suggested by Schulze-Boysen to where the Russians themselves could write. The issue with the radio remained unresolved, and Gourevitch said he would send all of Schulze-Boysen's information to Moscow on his return to Brussels.

Gourevitch was good to his word. He and his radio operator, Mikhail Makarov, spent seven nights encoding and sending the messages. All were intercepted by the Germans, and the Funkabwehr in Matthäikirchplatz passed them to their code breakers. Radio-detecting teams worked tirelessly to home in on the signal. The extensive content of the messages meant that Makarov had to stay on the air for five hours at a time. It was a suicidal schedule. The direction finders narrowed the search to Brussels and then to the streets of Etterbeek, where the signal-locating vans parked, listened, and then moved in.

At 2:30 a.m. on December 13, shadows moved in Rue des Atrébates and headed to the house with the number 101. There were thirty-five of them, all heavily armed, but their boots had been covered with layers of thick woolen socks and they barely made a sound.

Kicking down the door, they found one of Trepper's top agents, Sophie Posnanska, decoding messages. Her tired eyes suddenly filled with fear, and she began throwing paper into the fireplace but was grabbed and dragged outside. Her friend and courier, Rita Arnould, was arrested, too, but Trepper and Gourevitch were at another address, and Makarov escaped.

The contents of the building, including materials used for forging documents and all the equipment relating to the radio, were carefully packaged up and transported to investigators in Berlin.

DR. WILHELM VAUCK loved a mathematical puzzle. A schoolteacher in peacetime, he had been a reserve lieutenant in the army but had not looked forward to army life. The special secondment to Signals Security, though, suited him perfectly.

The brief appeared challenging but exhilarating: Assemble a team of mathematicians and languages experts, and crack the code found on messages seized during the Gestapo raid in Brussels.

Vauck quickly homed in on a half-burned sheet of paper that had been rescued from the fireplace. What remained of it showed columns of figures that Vauck believed had been part of the radio operator's encoding table. For six weeks he and his team worked on the numbers. They deduced that it was a checkerboard system based on a book key. From the frequency of the vowels it appeared the book was in French. The only word they managed to uncover was "Proctor," but for now that got them nowhere.

The Gestapo in Brussels interrogated Posnanska in Saint-Gilles, but she remained silent and later killed herself to avoid further torture. Arnould gave them some information that she possibly thought of little value: The agents often carried with them the same novels, which they seemed intent on keeping safe.

An officer from the signals team, Captain Carl von Wedel, traveled to Brussels and then Paris to search bookshops for copies of the books Arnould listed. Vauck told him it was essential he got them all and in their various French editions, and that he should search them for a character named Proctor.

Wedel tracked them all down except one, but none had any connection to the name Proctor. The missing book was a very rare novel by the author Guy de Téramond. *Le Miracle du Professeur Wolmar* had been a limited edition issued free to readers of a Parisian magazine in 1910. Wedel searched the bookshops of occupied Paris to find a copy. On May 17, 1942, he finally found one. Leafing through its pages, he found the name Proctor, and immediately contacted Vauck. They now had the book on which the messages between Moscow and Brussels were based.

THERE WAS STILL plenty for Vauck and his team to do. Every one of the book's 286 pages had to be searched each time to work out the passages that fit the 120 messages that had come from Makarov's set.

But with each success the team got quicker. By June they were deciphering two or three messages a day. Vauck stood over his encoders as the extent of the military secrets in the last few messages was revealed. He was not a spy, but he realized that the source had to be either a high-ranking German officer or someone with regular access to confidential documents. However, while it was top-level information, it was now—months later—largely of historic value, so he decided to switch the majority of his team to the task of deciphering the messages that had come the other way, from Moscow to Brussels.

On July 14, 1942, Vauck deciphered the August 26 message from Moscow to Kent, which had named "Arvid," Adam Kuckhoff, and the Schulze-Boysens. Just as Trepper had been, he was completely taken aback. Could Russia's secret service really be so stupid as to hand over these high-level agents in such a clumsy manner?

Wedel was required to make a report to the Gestapo. Within days the case had been handed over to the SD spymaster Walter Schellenberg, who quickly put fifty people under surveillance.

Telephones were tapped, letters opened, and suspects followed. The names of the people involved shocked even a man of Schellenberg's experience, but he decided to hold his nerve and see if the surveillance would expose an even wider network.

UNDER DIFFERENT CIRCUMSTANCES, Harro Schulze-Boysen, who spoke so many languages, might have been a candidate for Vauck's decipher team. While he had not been recruited, a friend of his was.

Corporal Horst Heilmann, of the Luftwaffe signals service, was a shy young man who had been one of Schulze-Boysen's students at the university. Having turned against Nazism, he had become a devoted admirer of the officer and tutor, passing him information as long as Harro promised it would not lead to the death of German soldiers.

Fluent in English, French, and Russian, he had been a natural choice for Vauck's team. He had not suspected for a moment that the Russian messages from Brussels would be traced back to Berlin and to anyone he knew.

At the end of August a gossiping friend on the team told him the "amazing content" of the August 26 message. "You'll never guess who it mentioned?" the man said. "Our old tutor—Schulze-Boysen!"

Heilmann went pale, then tried to hide his shock. Hurrying back to his desk, he dialed Schulze-Boysen's home number. The officer's maid answered and said he was away. Heilmann said he must call him as soon as possible and took the desperate risk of giving the office number.

At the end of the day Heilmann still had not heard from his friend and he went home. Later that night the phone on his desk began to ring.

Dr. Vauck was the only one of the team present.

"Hello?"

"Schulze-Boysen here. You wished to speak to me."

Vauck was dumbstruck. The key suspect in the spy ring was calling. It made no sense.

"I'm sorry," he stuttered. "I didn't quite hear."

"Schulze-Boysen. My maid has just given me your message. I was to call you as soon as possible. What can I do for you?"

Vauck thought he should stall, try to work out what was going on. Pretending to write the caller's name, he said: "Is that with a 'y' or an 'i'?"

"With a 'y,'" Schulze-Boysen said patiently. "Of course, I think I must have the wrong number. Do forgive me."

"Not at all."[2]

Without knowing of Heilmann's friendship with Schulze-Boysen, Vauck was left scratching his head.

VAUCK REPORTED THE strange telephone call from Schulze-Boysen, but it was the next day before it reached Schellenberg. There was an urgent discussion about what it meant and what was to be done.

Schellenberg decided the waiting game was over. The telephone call was more than a coincidence: Schulze-Boysen had obviously been warned by an acquaintance in the deciphering department. The SD man ordered Schulze-Boysen's immediate arrest and an urgent investigation into who had tipped him off.

HAVING HEARD NOTHING from Schulze-Boysen, Heilmann took another risk and called at his apartment. Libertas answered and he quickly showed her the decoded message.

Terrified but calm, she picked up the telephone and rang her husband's private line in the Potsdam command center. A man called Major Seliger answered. She had never heard of him before. He told her that her husband had left on official business and that she may not see him for a while.

Libertas pretended to be reassured and unconcerned. As soon as she put down the receiver, she told Heilmann that Harro must have been arrested and all her friends must be warned. Heilmann had no idea of the extent of the couple's anti-Nazi work, but he admired Harro and was deeply in love with Libertas.

Together they rushed around the flat taking illegal pamphlets, photocopied documents, and banned books from their hiding places and jamming them into a large suitcase.

Libertas called her assistant at the Kulturfilm unit, Alexander Spoerl, a tousle-haired young man who had helped her with her dossier of Nazi crimes. He began to tidy up incriminating documents in her office.

Libertas took the suitcase to the playwright Günther Weisenborn, who offered to keep it while she continued to alert the others. One of the network's radio sets was dumped in the River Spree, while Helmut Himpel, the dentist, took the other to Helmut Roloff's house.

Roloff put his hand nervously on Himpel's shoulder as the dentist left.

"We know one thing," he said quietly. "If that's found it's 'off with our heads.'"

"That's why it must not be found," Himpel said, and hurried off into the night.

LIKE SHADOWS, THE hunters pounced. The only way that members of the group knew a friend had been arrested was when they could no longer reach them on the telephone.

Heilmann was quickly identified as the man in the signals department who must have alerted Schulze-Boysen, and he was arrested at his parents' home in Hölderlinstrasse.

Libertas Schulze-Boysen hid at her friend Spoerl's house for a few days but, having warned everyone she could, decided to escape Berlin and head for the home of friends in the Moselle. But she was still under surveillance.

SS Second Lieutenant Johannes Strübing, a career policeman who had transferred to the SS in 1937, watched her leave Spoerl's home, followed her to see where she was going, and arrested her as she stepped onto the train at the Anhalter station. He was the same officer, he informed her proudly, who had arrested her husband.

Over the following days Strübing led teams to arrest Hans and Hilde Coppi, John Sieg, Kurt and Elisabeth Schumacher, Helmut Himpel and his fiancée Maria Terwiel, Helmut Roloff, Günther Weisenborn, and many more. Adam Kuckhoff was arrested in Prague, where he was at work on a film for the army.

His wife, Greta Lorke, was at home with her son, Ule, when the Gestapo arrived, and she asked them if she could leave him at the kindergarten on the ground floor of the building until her grandmother could collect him. The policeman followed her, and before he could stop her, she told the teacher she was being arrested.

The policeman pulled Lorke away and told the teacher: "Frau Kuckhoff is mentally ill. We are taking her to a hospital."

SINCE THE ATTACK on Pearl Harbor, Mildred Fish-Harnack, the American in Berlin, had concealed her growing stress from her fellow resisters, hiding the fear she suspected filled all their lives. The connections with the Dodds, the American spy Donald Heath, and the Russians had increased the tension in her voice and had left her weary and pale. Yet when a friend asked if she longed to go home to America, she would always say her place was at Harnack's side.

Harnack hated the effect their underground life was having on her: not eating and losing sleep, walking through the apartment in the small hours, listening at a black-curtained window as the police and fire engine sirens raced through the streets. He would lead her back to bed, and they would lie in the darkness. He did not say anything; there was little to say; there was no way out. They were in too deep.

It was on Mildred's urging that the Harnacks and two friends, Egmont and Anneliese Zechlin, traveled to the Kurische Nehrung, a sixty-mile spit of land on the coast of East Prussia, lying between a lake on one side and the Baltic Sea on the other, and rented a blue-shuttered fisherman's cottage. She knew that Harnack would want to talk to Zechlin about their friend Adam von Trott and his peace messages to Britain, but there would be time to walk, watch the birds on the windswept beach, and dream of better times. As required, Harnack had obtained a leave pass from the ministry and left a contact address with his office.

The two couples spent their first night walking through Priel, the men trailing behind, engrossed in conversation. Harnack looked northwest to the coast of neutral Sweden and wondered whether it was time to rent a boat and escape. Then dark clouds gathered over the sea, and the four of them rushed back to the cottage just as the thunder broke and rain lashed the tiled roof.

When Zechlin woke the next morning, he dressed and told his wife he was looking forward to a long walk with Arvid. It was then that he realized he could hear voices outside.

Stepping through the front door, he found Harnack at the gate talking to three men in long coats and hats. Seeing Zechlin, one of them flashed a badge and said: "We're from the police alien registration office. We've come to search the town." In Nazi Germany, such a thing was not unusual and Zechlin shrugged. Then he saw the wry look on Harnack's face—it seemed his friend knew exactly what was really happening. The man then added: "We have also been ordered to tell Oberregierungsrat Harnack that he is needed in his ministry."

Anneliese Zechlin appeared at her husband's side. "They could have just sent a wire!" she snapped.

The three men stepped inside the cottage and stood over the Harnacks as they packed.

Harnack saw the look of concern on his friend's face and said: "We're going with these gentlemen to Berlin." Then stepping closer, he murmured: "It's a shame what in Germany you . . ."

One of the men stepped between them, and Zechlin was forced to step back. Mildred was no longer packing for herself: One of them was doing it for her.

Harnack asked Zechlin to make coffee.

Mildred Fish-Harnack made the beds and was then led downstairs. She sat and put her hands over her face and sighed: "What a shame! Oh, what a shame!"

The men said it was time to go. Mildred stood, straightened the table-cloth, and placed a vase of flowers that she had picked the night before in the center of the table.

As the Harnacks left with a Gestapo man at their sides, one of the officers stepped forward and told the Zechlins: "I believe that you are too intelligent not to know what is going on here . . . I hereby inform you that you are to remain silent about everything you have seen and heard. Otherwise we'll have to arrest you."

Zechlin argued but was warned again. Outside, he kissed Mildred's hand and stood face-to-face with Harnack.

"Dear Egmont," Harnack said, "I thank you for everything."[3]

In ten years of close friendship, Harnack had never called him by his given name. The Harnacks stared ahead as they were driven off.

Standing in the cottage doorway, the Zechlins felt a blast of drifting sand across their faces, turned in silence, and went back inside.

OVER THE COMING months the Gestapo arrested more than 130 people in connection with the case. They brought the men to Prinz-Albrecht-Strasse and locked up the women in the police cells at Alexanderplatz.

Each prisoner was painstakingly photographed in profile and full face for the files. Some were in their uniforms; many, like Kurt Schumacher, whose statues had been smashed to pieces during his arrest at his studio, showed signs of bruising.

Gestapo arrest records showed that Hilde Coppi and nineteen-year-old Liane Berkowitz, who was part of John Rittmeister's circle of pamphleteers, were both pregnant at the time they were brought in. In the photograph taken when she was in custody, Berkowitz appears on the edge of tears.[4]

HARRO SCHULZE-BOYSEN'S QUESTIONING began with twelve blows from an axe handle. Harnack and Kuckhoff were beaten with rubber batons and whipped. As the days passed, believing any friends who had not been arrested would now have gone underground, the prisoners began to reveal names. The Gestapo encouraged prisoners to spread stories of torture from cell to cell to put greater fear into those waiting to be questioned.

A shorthand typist named Gertrud Breiter met Libertas Schulze-Boysen in an outer office and realized she might befriend the young aristocrat, who was scared, disorientated, and in shock. Whenever Schulze-Boysen came for interrogation, Breiter chatted with her, slowly becoming a confidante, a friendly face: A friendship developed in which Breiter seemed a shoulder to cry on. She even gave Schulze-Boysen hugs—but everything was being reported back to the Gestapo investigators. Over a number of meetings Schulze-Boysen spoke about her friends, confirming the names the Gestapo suspected. Breiter received 5,000 Reichsmarks, a medal, and a personal letter of commendation from Himmler for her work.[5] When Libertas discovered she had been tricked, she fell into a deep depression.

On October 11, one of John Sieg's resistance friends went to meet him outside Tempelhof train station where he worked. Sieg appeared late and with two men close behind him. Sieg gave his friend an intense stare of warning and walked straight past. The friend then watched Sieg bundled into a car.

Detroit-born Sieg had seen the inside of a Nazi prison before and had always told friends what he would do if he was arrested again. After four days at Gestapo headquarters, he hanged himself in his cell. His friend Herbert Grasse, who had run a printing operation, pulled free from a guard at Alexanderplatz and jumped to his death from a fifth-floor window. Many in the Neukölln resistance would owe their lives to the two men's acts of self-sacrifice.

Others tried to take their own lives. Walter Husemann grabbed his interrogator, Walter Habecker, and tried to drag him out of a window with him, but was beaten to the floor by guards. Mildred Fish-Harnack tried to swallow pins.

ON NOVEMBER 9, 1942, Moscow's messenger Anatoli Gourevitch was arrested in France and brought to a special isolation cell in Prinz-Albrecht-Strasse.

Lieutenant Strübing carefully assessed the rather vain dreamer and played to his vanity, describing how he had cunningly conned and tricked them as one of Moscow's top agents. Strübing said they had picked up most of the network but that Gourevitch was the man to fill in the blanks. Gourevitch described Trepper's network in Western Europe and his own trip to Berlin.

When he hesitated to say more, Strübing gently reminded him that they were holding his girlfriend and their child in custody.

Strübing laid an album of arrest photographs on the table between them, and Gourevitch picked out Harro and Libertas Schulze-Boysen as his contacts in Berlin.

It was now that the loose groups surrounding the Harnacks, Schulze-Boysens, and Kuckhoffs became formally identified as part of what the Gestapo termed the Rote Kapelle. It was not a name that the group had ever heard or used themselves. They never considered themselves Moscow's spies. They were anti-Nazi. Some were Communists and socialists, others were conservative—but they were working for the other Germany, the one that existed inside themselves.

They provided secrets for Moscow and for Washington: Their one desire was to rid Germany of the Nazis, by whatever means.

# 21

# Fire in Berlin

BY SPRING 1942, all the Jews Herbert Baum knew in Berlin had emigrated, were working as forced laborers, or were in concentration or death camps.

The Gauleiter of Berlin was Hitler's propaganda minister, Joseph Goebbels, whose anti-Semitism was matched only by his Führer's. During the past year, Goebbels had been wielding his power to destroy the Jews in the city. In his warped mind he felt a personal humiliation that his city was not yet Judenfrei. "This is a thing which is unbearable," he recorded in his diary. "The cause is that there are many Jewish people in armament . . . [I] will try to get all Jewish people not in the industry to be deported."

Over the coming months he would battle with Armaments Minister Albert Speer to gain Hitler's permission to remove the last Jews from the arms factories. Speer was holding on to them, not for moral reasons, to keep them from death in the East, but for practical ones, as they were doing useful work.

For now, Baum and his comrades remained in the factories, kept spreading dissent and carrying out acts of sabotage, and continued to circulate antifascist literature. Small notes were passed around the factory floor: "Work slow!" and "Down with the war!" All small acts that would make people feel they were not alone and even a small downturn in production might have an effect on the war effort.

They still wore the removable Star of David, too, unfastening it so they could break the eight o'clock curfew for Jews, to use a tram or a telephone booth, and to visit a fancy coffee shop.

Baum wanted to step up the action. Believing Hitler could be defeated in the Soviet Union as soon as the summer, he told friends, "We are going on the offensive."

That April, inspired by Joachim Franke, Werner Steinbrink, and Artur Illgen, who had painted "Hitler step down" across the outside of a factory in the small hours of the night, Baum sent out teams across Berlin to write the phrase "No to Hitler's suicidal politics! No! No! No!" on public buildings. "Use whatever paint, chalk, grease pencil you can get a hold of," they were told. "We want Berlin covered in one night!"[1]

Helmut Neumann, the group's joker, said that if the saboteurs were spotted, they should pretend to be lovers on a romantic tryst. Looking at the women, he said, "Anyone need to rehearse?"

Neumann, Ellen Compart, Lothar Salinger and his fiancée Ursula Ehrlich, Hella Hirsch, Felix Heymann, and Siegbert and Lotte Rotholz were among those who went out that night. Dressed in dark clothing, they worked in pairs, and all returned safely. The slogans caused a lot of people the trouble of removing them, but the group of friends argued about its effectiveness. "How much good did it do?" asked one who had not gone out that night. "Every show of defiance brings us a step closer," Ellen Compart answered.[2]

But if Baum truly wanted to go on "the offensive," the group needed more money. The costs of printing the leaflets had taken much of what they had, and the false identity papers they were still buying from foreign workers were setting them back 150 Reichsmarks at a time. Many of the group had now gone underground to avoid deportation and were having to be supported without ration cards.

After the failure of appeals for cash from wealthy Jews—in which they made the point that the Nazis would eventually take their money anyway—Baum came up with a radical, daring, and morally questionable plan. He decided on what he called "expropriation action" and brought together Birnbaum, Steinbrink, and another man, Richard Holzer, to work out the details.

On May 6, a wealthy Jewish family—the Freundlichs—who still lived in a large apartment in Lietzenburger Strasse, in Charlottenburg, were awoken at dawn by a sharp knocking at the door. Terrified, Rosetta Freundlich got out of bed, quickly wrapped a dressing gown around herself, and opened the door to find two men in coats, hats, and leather gloves standing in the hallway. Even as she opened the door they were pushing past her. One waved a piece of paper in her face and said loudly, "Gestapo!"

The two men demanded to see the identification cards of all who lived at the apartment: Freundlich, her daughter Margarete, and their lodgers. Everyone responded quickly, suddenly very much awake and frightened.

The men insisted on being told every item that was of value in the house, and one made a list. An oil painting, a typewriter, two cameras, an opera glass. "What's in that bag?" one of the men shouted. "Rugs," said Frau Freundlich. The man making the list looked inside and wrote down: "Fourteen small carpets."

"Nothing is to be removed!" the Gestapo man told Freundlich. "We will return tomorrow. Heil Hitler!"[3]

The family was left in shock. They were losing their valuables, but at least there was no mention of deportation. They lived in heightened fear for twenty-four hours.

But the two Gestapo men were Steinbrink and Birnbaum. They had traveled to Charlottenburg not in a Gestapo car but on the S-Bahn. Steinbrink's briefcase, in which he had kept his list and his fake Gestapo papers, had been given to him by Baum.

The following day, again at dawn, Steinbrink and Birnbaum returned, and this time Baum and Holzer came, too, although they waited outside.

Everything they had listed was removed from the Freundlich apartment. Rosetta Freundlich was too terrified to say anything or even to look out the window after them. If she had, she might have seen that the heavy bag of carpets only made it a short distance down the street, where some were quickly stashed in the home of Harry Cühn, a friend of Birnbaum's and the fiancé of Baum's friend Edith Fraenkel. Cühn helped her and his friends survive by buying and selling goods smuggled to Berlin from Paris on the black market.

The four thieves then took a taxi back to Baum's apartment building on Stralauer Strasse, where they stored the goods in the basement until they could be sold.

Despite her fear, Frau Freundlich contacted the police about her property and was told the men who had called at her home were not policemen.

Shortly afterwards, on May 13, the Berlin newspapers—including the *Völkischer Beobachter*—reported that "three bogus detectives" had carried out an "insolent swindle" in Charlottenburg. They had made off with 20,000 marks' worth of goods.

By the time the report reached the newspapers, the Herbert Baum group was on the verge of its most outrageous action: an attempt at sabotage in daylight in the center of Berlin.

It was to be the act of rebellion that would finally bring the young idealists down.

THE SIEMENS-SCHUCKERTWERKE WAS a vast factory with huge rooms lined with hundreds of machines. Built just before the First World War next to Lake Tegel in the northwest of Berlin, it had been a hub of activity since the war began. The Hohenzollern Canal ran alongside it, and heavy supplies were unloaded from barges throughout the day.

There were night shifts, too, orders and instructions echoing down the long corridors, and machine rooms filled with a deafening noise, even during the blackout. The guards on the Jews at night tended to be their own foremen, with Nazi staff preferring not to stay on duty in the small hours. There were sometimes opportunities for a longer break, an extra snack that someone smuggled in.

In Ellen Lewinsky's area of the factory, they only ever worked on one particular aircraft part. Although the work kept them from deportation, it was monotonous. Heinz Birnbaum was the subforeman, and he not only knew what he was doing, but he was kind and funny, too. Ellen also knew that he occasionally whispered to friends to do something to weaken a part or slowly foul up a machine.

It was on one night shift that Lewinsky caught him working on something new. It was small and she could not see what it was, and when the foreman came around, he put it to one side and covered it with a cloth. The next night she watched Birnbaum again, and sure enough, when he was not being watched, he took out the mystery object and began to work. On the third night she plucked up the courage to grab a word with him. "Are you making something for a friend?" she whispered.

Birnbaum looked at her. He knew she could be trusted, but he dared not say much. "Yeah, a friend," he said, and told her to go back to work.

When the shift was finished, Lewinsky was riding home on the U-Bahn, the underground train, when Birnbaum squeezed into the empty seat beside her. Even though there was no one else on board, he still spoke in low tones and leaned close to her ear. "You know that exhibition at the Lustgarten?" he said with a smile. "We're going to blow it up."[4]

* * *

THE EXHIBITION AT the Lustgarten was the brainchild of Joseph Goebbels.

Goebbels had put the struggle against the Soviet Union at the center of his propaganda work, and there were two strands to it. The first was an almost mystical celebration of the stoicism shown by German soldiers during the hell of their first freezing Russian winter. "Their eyes flicker with a strange light," his weekly newspaper, *Das Reich*, stated. "They have seen more than human eyes are wont to see. Their features have become harder and stonier. A smile on faces like this has the effect of a blessing."[5] The snow and ice, it added ridiculously, were "no longer so biting" since Hitler had taken over the supreme command of the army a few months earlier.

The second and perhaps most important strand to Goebbels's propaganda offensive against the Soviet Union was his dehumanization of the Russian people. In May 1942, Goebbels launched a major exhibition on the Lustgarten, the open parkland by the Protestant cathedral and the River Spree at the eastern end of the Unter den Linden. Housed in a specially constructed building, the exhibition was sarcastically titled *The Soviet Paradise* and through panels, dioramas, and exhibits presented the horror of life under the Bolsheviks. Bolshevism, as was usual with Goebbels, was linked to Judaism throughout: The "inventor of Marxism was the Jew Marx-Mordochai" declared one panel, and in one large image a Jew holding a gun stood over a dead Christian woman. It was a distortion designed to explain to Germans why the invasion of the Soviet Union had been necessary and to present the Jews as the dark evil to the East.

For the antifascists in Berlin, Goebbels's presentation of recent history, the idea that the Jews were the aggressor, and the claims that Hitler was forced into fighting the war to protect the world were too much to take. They resolved to do something about it.

Herbert Baum had discussed the idea of distributing leaflets to visitors to the exhibition, and Martin Kochmann and his wife, Sala Rosenbaum, Suzanne Wesse, Gerhard Meyer, Heinz Joachim, and Irene Walther all agreed to help. Then Joachim Franke took Baum and Werner Steinbrink to see the exhibition. On their way they saw that someone had pasted handbills all over the original exhibition posters in the streets, stating: "Nazi Paradise. War, Hunger, Lies, Gestapo. How much longer?" They admired the work and were fortified in the knowledge that others were not taken in by the

Nazi propaganda. They could not know it, but the handbills were the work of the Luftwaffe's Harro Schulze-Boysen and a few of his friends.

After the visit to the exhibition, Baum came back to his flat to meet again with the core of his group. There had been a change of plan, he told them: They would carry out an arson attack on the exhibition.

The group shifted uncomfortably in their chairs as they listened to Baum and exchanged nervous glances. This group of people was already taking extreme risks. Most were Jews, whose lives were worth nothing to the Nazis except, at that moment, the work they could do in the factories. The leafletting was dangerous—enough to get them killed if they slipped up—but arson would ensure the Gestapo would hunt them down.

Some looked to Kochmann—Baum's oldest school friend—and they could see he disagreed with the plan, but it was not in his nature to start an argument. He said nothing. Later, when the arguing stopped, he said he could see that the attack was an understandable continuation and escalation of their resistance work, but he did not want to take part in it.

Richard Holzer and Felix Heymann, though, spoke out vehemently against the plan. Neither lacked courage. Both had been committed antifascists for a decade; Holzer had taken part in the fake-Gestapo-agent operation, and Heymann had painted slogans across the city. But both felt that even if the operation was successful—indeed, especially if the operation was successful—it would lead to severe reprisals against the remaining Jews and suspected antifascists across Berlin. Both also said they did not want to take part.

The non-Jews in the group—Wesse, Walther, Steinbrink—backed Baum. They had all worried over how effective the pamphlets and leaflets had been, and whether that campaign had been worth the risk. Many had argued for some time that they needed to confront the Nazi state more directly. Now, as Baum had told them before, they could go on the offensive. They had already done enough in the eyes of the law to make them enemies of the state. What was the alternative—to stop and accept the Nazis?

If the plan worked, Baum told them, this time they would not be able to return to their jobs and their homes. Everyone who took part would be provided with a fake French passport and would escape Berlin.

Heinz Birnbaum, who since his early teenage years had helped Baum, had lived with Herbert and Marianne for a while. He loved and admired them both. His loyalty to Baum was unwavering.

Skilled with a lathe and with access to materials, he agreed to make a detonator with a firing pin for an explosive device. That is what Ellen Lewinksy had seen him working on secretly in a corner of the Siemens-Schuckertwerke and what he told her about now as they traveled home on the U-Bahn.

"I NEED HELP to get it out of Schuckert," Birnbaum told Lewinsky as the train clacked along the rails, their shoulders bucking together. "Will you help me?"

Lewinsky was just nineteen—Hitler had been in power for as long as she could remember. She had grown up in Blesen, a small town where her grandfather Siegfried had been a well-respected grain merchant. He had been traumatized by the events of Kristallnacht and had died soon afterwards. She had moved to Berlin to be with relatives and been put to work in the factory. Her boyfriend, Erich, whose father had been a top doctor and had won the Iron Cross for bravery during the First World War, had been banned from studying medicine because of his Jewishness.[6] Ellen Lewinsky hated Nazism and everything it stood for. The chance to do anything—no matter how small—to hurt the regime was something she jumped at.

The next night, as the shift ended, Birnbaum gave Lewinsky the detonator and she tucked it into her bra. As she walked out of the factory, she opened her coat as she did every night and the guard waved her through. The two conspirators met up again on the U-Bahn, and Lewinsky took out the detonator and passed it quickly to Birnbaum, who stuck it into his coat pocket. "Thanks," he said quietly. Then he asked if she could suggest any man he could trust on her shift. She named someone Birnbaum knew. The next day Birnbaum took the young man aside and asked him if he would help smuggle out some wire. "I want to mend this light in my apartment," Birnbaum told him. "Sure," said the man.

Birnbaum took him into a side room and had him take off the top half of his clothes. He wrapped the wire around the man's waist and over his shoulders, and then told him to put back on his shirt and jacket.

The guard again waved the workers through, and in the eerie light of an empty U-Bahn carriage, Birnbaum helped the man take off his clothes and spun him around, taking off the wire before the next stop.

* * *

JOACHIM FRANKE AND Werner Steinbrink had set to work on making the explosives. Steinbrink, a chemist working at the Kaiser Wilhelm Institute, had smuggled home gunpowder made of a mixture of saltpeter, sulfur, and charcoal. Later, using a manual borrowed from the city library, he and Franke added a solution of carbon disulfide and phosphorus. They believed that could make a series of small devices based on British incendiary bombs, with detonators made with cardboard and a flashlight battery.

On Sunday, May 17, the group was ready and congregated at Kochmann and Rosenbaum's flat at Gipsstrasse, a fifteen-minute walk from the Lustgarten. Although he had told Baum he would not take part, Richard Holzer came to the meeting, solely to try to persuade them to abandon the plan.

"Herbert, it's too dangerous," Holzer said. "Nothing good can come of it. All it will do is bring terrible reprisals against Jews and anti-fascists. Think about it—how will the Nazis respond to such an affront, especially if they find out that Jews were involved?"

Holzer and Baum had a massive row as the others—resigned and prepared for the action—looked on. In the end Baum told Holzer he was throwing him out of the group and asked him to leave. It was a painful moment. Holzer looked around the room at his friends. Angry and upset as he was, he prayed he would see them again.

After Holzer left, Baum told the others that Werner Steinbrink had visited the exhibition again and decided where to target the attack. He had picked a restaurant—the Speisehaus—as the place to leave the incendiaries. More of the group arrived, including Hans Mannaberg and Hilde Jadamowitz, who now learned for the first time that this was to be an arson attack rather than leafleting. They agreed to go anyway.

At that point an excited Joachim Franke arrived. The group still did not know what to make of him. He talked too much and seemed like an adventurer, but he had come up with the plan with Baum and Steinbrink, and he seemed committed to the cause. In the discussion that followed he was introduced to the group by name for the first time.

At four o'clock in the afternoon they left the apartment in small groups and met at the captured Soviet KV-2 self-propelled gun that stood at the entrance to the exhibition. Mannaberg purchased tickets, and the group joined the queue. Each of the Jews had removed their yellow stars, as Jews were forbidden from entering the exhibition. Steinbrink and Franke carried devices in their pockets. Passing safely through the concrete entrance to the exhibition hall, they were suddenly confronted with the fact that the place was filled with people. Goebbels claimed that a quarter of a million people had passed through its entrance gates the week before. Baum realized they would have to wait until the Sunday crowds died down. Afraid to hang around and worried their return later that day might make someone at the ticket booth suspicious, they agreed to postpone the attack until eight the following evening.

The next night Joachim Franke carried a number of the incendiary devices in a small briefcase and Steinbrink carried two small chemical devices in his jacket, one of which he handed to Baum as soon as they were inside. The others came as support and lookouts; some carried small wads of cotton soaked in phosphorus.

They passed between the panels and headed for the Speisehaus. When they got there, they found that it was closed. Franke and Steinbrink walked off in a hurry, looking for another target. The "farmhouse" was a small, grubby replica of a Soviet peasant's house. It was made to look dirty and primitive, no better than a pigsty. The two men slipped inside, and before Steinbrink knew what was happening, Franke broke the glass tubes on his incendiary bomb, allowing the flammable chemicals to begin to mingle. He dropped it down on the "farmer's" bed, but realized that he had also damaged one of the other devices in his briefcase—and the case started to burn. "It's on fire," Franke said. "Let's get out."

The whole group moved quickly back through the exhibition hall. Steinbrink took the detonator from his pocket and tossed it aside. Baum found that the device in his jacket had started to burn and his jacket pocket was smoldering. He took it out and chucked it into a drain.

Behind them the "farmhouse" had started to burn.

Outside Hilde Jadamowitz and Marianne Cohn walked off down the Unter den Linden together. Cohn looked back for her husband, but Herbert Baum was nowhere to be seen. Hans Mannaberg caught them in the street and urged them to get away. Mannaberg and Jadamowitz headed for a safe location, Steinbrink's mother's house, where Steinbrink himself arrived later.

Marianne Cohn waited at a safe distance, searching for her husband. Standing much closer was Joachim Franke. Instead of leaving the scene, he had waited right outside, smiling to himself as visitors were evacuated from the exhibition. When a large number of police cars and the fire brigade arrived, Franke threw down his cigarette and hurried to catch a train home.

LATER THAT EVENING a Gestapo officer went to a former palace of the Prussian court on Hermann-Göring-Strasse, the road that ran from the Brandenburg Gate along the Tiergarten to the Potsdamer Platz. Renovated at a cost of more than 3 million marks by 160 workmen, this villa was Goebbels's official residence—one of his many homes in the Reich.[7]

The officer was led through a mahogany-walled hallway by one of Goebbels's eighteen domestic staff and shown into the Reichsminister's study. The man had the unenviable task of telling the short man in the tight jacket that his prestigious exhibition had been attacked.

He told Goebbels that an incendiary device with two bottles of phosphorus carbon disulfide had "exploded" in the farmhouse and that eleven people had been taken to the hospital with "superficial wounds." The fire had been extinguished before it could spread. A special Gestapo unit had been put together to hunt down the saboteurs.

Goebbels listened quietly, but inside his anger was growing: Although his control over the Nazi press would ensure that not a word would be printed or broadcast about the attack, gossip would spread and reflect badly on him—as the owner of the exhibition and the Gauleiter of the city.

He sent the man away, telling him he expected results quickly.

# 22

## A Student in Munich

THE SUN WAS shining on the spring morning in 1942 when Sophie Scholl set out on what she saw as her new and exciting life as a student in Munich.

Leaving Ulm railway station, she watched the countryside pass by, and picked at the piece of cake that her mother had baked her. On this favorite railway journey, she loved to rest her head against the window and watch the peaks of the Bavaria hills come into view.

Not yet twenty-one, Sophie was bright and intelligent, and was fortunate in Nazi Germany to be making the eighty-kilometer journey to Munich's Ludwig Maximilian University, where the quota for female students was set at just 10 percent.

As the place where Hitler had made his reputation as an agitator and public speaker in the years after the First World War and the city where he had launched his attempted 1923 putsch to take over the regional government of Bavaria, Munich had strong links with the Nazi Party. Hitler had attended anti-Bolshevik "instruction courses" at the university in 1919; he and Goebbels had planned the persecution of the Jews at his favorite restaurant, the Osteria Bavaria; and he kept an office in the Brown House, the Nazi headquarters in Brienner Strasse. The building also stored the Blutfahne, the blood flag, which had been carried at the head of the 1923 march when the police had opened fire and was still spattered with the blood of the wounded.

It had been a difficult few months at home. During an unguarded moment in his office, Robert Scholl had vented his anger and frustration in the company of a young secretary. "This Hitler is God's scourge on mankind!" she had heard him say. "If war does not end soon, the Russians will be sitting in Berlin within two years."[1] The young woman had been given the job by Scholl, and she was grateful to him for the work. She was fond of him but such was the influence of the regime on her, she simply did not feel she could let the comments pass. She reported her boss to the Gestapo, who arrested him under the Treachery Act of 1934. Released to finish a project he was working on for the local council's finance department, Scholl still had the threat of trial and imprisonment hanging over him, and it had cast them all down.

Sophie had found solace in religion and in her friendship with the Catholic scholar Professor Carl Muth, who had become an inspiration to both her and her brother. She would be lodging with Muth for the first month of her course.

At Munich station, Sophie was met on the platform by her brother Hans and his girlfriend, Traute Lafrenz. Although she wanted to get to Muth's home, Hans was eager to take her somewhere first.

At his room in Schwabing, his friends Alexander Schmorell and Christoph Probst were waiting for them—and they were looking forward to meeting her.

HANS SCHOLL HAD known twenty-five-year-old Alexander Schmorell since the autumn of 1940, and their conversations about philosophy and theology had developed into angry tirades about the Nazis. Tall and lean, with tawny brown hair, Schmorell, who was known to all by his childhood nickname of Shurik, had been born in Russia but brought up in Munich by his German father after his mother had died. Conscripted into the army, he had been among the marching figures who had entered Austria and Czechoslovakia. When asked to swear allegiance to Hitler, Schmorell had refused and requested to be discharged from the army. That request was, of course, turned down, but his commanding officer chose not to report his defiance to the Gestapo. Schmorell, like Scholl, was now studying medicine. Tall, popular, and charming, he liked to present himself as a bohemian and artistic type—and had become Hans's best friend.

It was through Schmorell that Scholl had met Christoph Probst, a dependable and self-deprecating young man whom everyone seemed to like. Probst had grown up hating the way Nazism sought to persecute people of faith. While only a teenager, he had been devastated by the death of his father, who had taken his own life during a bout of severe depression. He remained close to his stepmother, who was Jewish, and tried to support many Jewish friends. He had been at Ludwig Maximilian University since the outbreak of war, and was now having to combine his studies with serving in the Luftwaffe and looking after his family. Married to Herta Dohrn, who shared his repulsion of the Nazis, he had two children and knew anything he did to oppose the regime put them at risk. But for Probst, the Nazi euthanasia program and the persecution of the Jews had made it impossible for right-minded people to ignore the crimes of the Nazis.

Probst had introduced Scholl and Schmorell to Willi Graf, a devoted Catholic and opponent of the regime who had been arrested back in January 1938 for his membership in an anti-Nazi youth group.

It was Graf who provided the friends with further information about what was happening to Jews and other civilians in the East. He had worked as a medical orderly in field hospitals during the invasion of Poland and Yugoslavia, and had only recently returned from the Soviet Union. The others shivered when they heard his stories from Russia and "of things so terrible" he would not have thought them possible. As he had told his family in Saarbrücken in a letter home from the front: "I wish I had not seen what I have seen."

THAT FIRST DAY with her brother's friends was everything Sophie had hoped it would be. They chatted about their favorite subjects, and made plans to go to concerts, the cinema, and restaurants. Saying good-bye to Inge and her parents in Ulm that morning, she had felt like a child; here she was a grown-up.

Quite quickly, the group also began talking about the Nazis and what could be done to show their opposition. The students told Sophie that the student union at the university was dominated by Nazi Party members, but that the wider student body could be open to discussion and might even be a fertile ground for growing opposition.

Hans also had something to confess to Sophie, though he did not know that he should: The next step that they took could put them all in danger of their lives. He and Schmorell had been agonizing over how to turn their anger into an active resistance campaign. Lafrenz and Probst had been drawn into their discussions, which went on long into the night. What form should protest take? Could they make bombs—*should* they make bombs? No, they were nonviolent, Christian; they could not take human life. In the end they had decided that—like the anonymous figures who had spread the word of Bishop von Galen—they should put their views into leaflets and send them out through the post. It seemed like a mild form of resistance, but in Nazi Germany it was a capital crime. Even as they agreed on the action to take, they knew—though only in their early twenties—that they could well be signing their own death warrants. "I always understood that I could lose my life in the event of an investigation," Schmorell said. "I ignored this all because my deep urge to combat National Socialism was strong."[2] The leaflets would be anonymous, of course, but they decided early on that they should feature the name of an organization: It would make the Nazis believe they could be dealing with a large number of dissenters. Hans Scholl chose the name randomly, the White Rose, based on a poetic ballad that he had been reading, but also as it "would sound good and would give the impression that there was an agenda."[3]

Schmorell borrowed a portable Remington typewriter from a neighbor and gave it to Hans, who began to write: "Nothing is so unworthy of a civilized nation as allowing itself to be governed without opposition by an irresponsible clique that has yielded to base instincts." He stated that "every honest German is ashamed of his government," but who could imagine the "dimensions of shame" when the "most horrible of crimes . . . reach the light of day?" Stating that the Nazi system had put "every man into a spiritual prison," he called for "passive resistance . . . before it is too late." He quoted Schiller and then Goethe, and again inspired by the Galen leaflet, he called on the recipient to "make as many copies of this leaflet as you can and distribute them."

During the period the leaflet was being written, Hans introduced Sophie to Josef Furtmeier, a friend of the architect Manfred Eickemeyer. Furtmeier, a former civil servant who had lost his job after refusing to join the Nazi Party, was—according to Traute Lafrenz—a "walking encyclopedia."[4] The Scholls nicknamed the seventy-two-year-old "the Philosopher" as they were held spellbound by his conversation late into the night. Furtmeier said the German population had to be roused into action by protest that could counter the propaganda being put out by the state.

The Scholls would leave his home filled with thoughts of making a Christian, peaceful protest against Germany's "criminal war makers," and would chat about a new international community of states that could rise up after the war and stop such horror from happening again.

At some point, in the excitement, Hans told Sophie about the White

Rose leaflet he was writing. Immediately, she wished to be involved. It must have caused Hans terrible pain to draw Sophie into the conspiracy, but knowing her as he did, he knew that she was yearning to stand up to the regime. With her devotion to God and humanity, her desperation to do what was right, she could be the emotional heart of the group.

First, she tried to obtain a duplicating machine from her boyfriend, Fritz Hartnagel—although without explaining why—but he could not help.

In the end Hans spent 32 marks on a duplicating machine, made a hundred copies of this first leaflet, and sent them out to addresses he found in the Munich telephone directory. Most of the addresses were randomly picked, but Hans also chose innkeepers because he believed they might gossip with customers.[5]

Sitting in clouds of pipe smoke, Hans Scholl and Schmorell worked together on a second leaflet, drawing on their love of philosophical discussion and on what Graf had recently told them about the war in the East: "Since the conquest of Poland three hundred thousand Jews have been murdered . . . in the most bestial way." It was a "most frightful crime against human dignity, a crime that is unparalleled in the whole of history," and it "must be the sole and first duty, the holiest duty of every German to destroy these beasts."[6] Ending with a quotation from the antiwar philosopher Lao Tzu, the White Rose again urged people to copy and distribute the leaflet.

It was early July when this leaflet arrived at the randomly chosen addresses to which it was sent. By then Hans Scholl, Alexander Schmorell, and Willi Graf had received some devastating news: They were being sent to the Soviet Union at the end of the semester. The war against the Soviet Union had being going on for a year, and the Wehrmacht had launched a major offensive to once again try to break the Red Army. It was a posting that made the blood run cold.

With weeks to go, and with Sophie's help, they went back to their work with added vigor, determined to make a difference while they still had the chance. Another student medical orderly, Jürgen Wittenstein—whose father, a First World War test pilot, had been killed before his son was born—was recruited to help with the third and fourth leaflets. These described Germany's "dictatorship of evil" and tried to stir people from their torpor.

The third leaflet claimed to hear the reader say they know about the dictatorship, so "why bring that to our attention again"? If you know, said the resisters, "why do you not bestir yourselves, why do you allow these men who are in power to rob you step by step, openly and in secret, of one domain of your rights after another, until one day nothing, nothing at all, will be left but a mechanized state system presided over by criminals and drunks?" The essay stated that "everyone is in a position to contribute to the overthrow of this system" by using "passive resistance."

"At all points we must oppose National Socialism, wherever it is open to attack . . . The military victory over Bolshevism dare not become the primary concern of the Germans. The defeat of the Nazis must unconditionally be the first order of business . . ."

For the first time more detailed suggestions on how to rebel were also made, and they went beyond passive resistance. In a section most probably written by Schmorell, sabotage was mentioned as a way to fight back—a highly provocative proposal at the height of war. Of armament plants and war industries, Nazi gatherings and rallies. At universities and laboratories. It urged people not to give to collections for the war effort, and ended with a quote from Aristotle: "The tyrant is inclined constantly to foment wars."

Written by Hans Scholl, the fourth leaflet warned against celebrating Hitler's recent successes in North Africa and Russia, as the offensive in Egypt has "ground to a halt" and the "apparent success has been purchased at the most horrible expense of human life." It painted a picture of a state in which the leaders do not "count the dead," as mourning "takes up her abode in the country cottages, and there is no one to dry the tears of the mothers." Every word that comes out of Hitler's mouth "is a lie."

Scholl depicted a Christian battle between Good and the "servants of the Antichrist": "Has God not given you the strength, the will to fight? We must attack evil where it is strongest, and it is strongest in the power of Hitler."

Suspecting that many would believe the leaflets were British propaganda, Scholl knew that it was important to stress that they were produced by Germans daring to speak out. He wanted to show that there was an alternative to "traditional German apathy." He declared that the "White Rose is not in the pay of any foreign power" and that it was "trying to achieve a renewal from within of the severely wounded German spirit." Nazism would only be broken by "military means," and the country's rebirth "must be preceded . . . by the clear recognition of all the guilt with which the German people have burdened themselves."

Hans Scholl signed off: "We will not be silent. We are your bad conscience. The White Rose will not leave you in peace!"[7]

These leaflets were copied and sent out, with probably not more than a hundred copies being made of each.[8] Wittenstein, who had edited the third and fourth leaflets of the group, bravely traveled to Berlin with some in a suitcase and left them at various points for people to pick up and read.

The group was supported now by another Ulm student, Hans Hirzel, the son of the local Lutheran minister, who made an astonishing confession to the Scholls: It had been he who had been secretly duplicating the sermons of Galen in their area.[9] He had pushed them through the mailbox at the Scholls' home as part of his campaign to mail them anonymously to people he thought would approve of them. This action had inspired Scholl. It had seemed a good, peaceful, and possible way to fight back.

But there was a doubt that ran through every member of the group: Was anybody reading what they were saying? Or was every recipient too scared of or too enthralled by Nazism to take any of it in? Were all the leaflets they sent being put in the trash unread or passed to the Gestapo, which must by now be investigating?

Hans Scholl's doubts over the effectiveness of the campaign were particularly strong. As he packed for the mobilization to Russia, he began to think that he would not bother with the campaign anymore.[10] Anxious and a little demoralized, he pinned his hopes on Kurt Huber, a forty-nine-year-old professor of philosophy and psychology at the university, who he felt might lift their spirits and provide the group with mature guidance.

Small, pale, and with a heavy limp left over from a childhood illness, Huber seemed an unlikely inspirational figure—but he was capable of holding more than two hundred students spellbound during his lectures on German philosophers. Brought up in Stuttgart by middle-class, conservative parents, he viewed the Nazis as a movement of violent and uncouth revolutionaries who were causing the unnecessary deaths of thousands of valiant German soldiers. Loathing the compliance of his colleagues who fell in with Hitler's movement for personal gain, during lectures he occasionally let fly a risky comment that did not fit into the regime's way of seeing the world. Once, on mentioning the Dutch philosopher Spinoza, he had joked: "Careful, he's a Jew! Don't let yourselves be contaminated."[11] The students had laughed nervously or pretended not to hear, and he escaped repercussions.

Sophie attended his lectures and noted that he appeared to be anti-Nazi. Perhaps he could add gravitas to their campaign.

The students invited him to one of their meetings at Schmorell's home and asked him whether he had received one of the White Rose leaflets—knowing that they had sent one to him. He said he had, but looking around the room at the Scholls, Traute Lafrenz, Probst, and Schmorell, he suddenly seemed guarded and nervous. When they tried to talk politics, he said "active resistance" to the regime was "impossible," and left soon afterwards.

On July 22, the group met Huber again, this time behind the heavy black-out curtains at the architect Eickemeyer's studio, where they raised a brandy glass to the students who were due to leave for the Soviet Union the following morning. The partygoers included many students who knew nothing of their friends' secret activities, and some even gossiped about the White Rose leaflets being obviously the work of Communists.

Fiercely anti-Communist, Huber—the only older, gray-haired guest—did not like the youngsters' excited talk about Communism. And when he heard Schmorell say that German soldiers, on witnessing the kinds of atrocities perpetrated by the Einsatzgruppen in Poland, should engage in passive resistance, too, he became angry and snapped that soldiers had to follow orders. The brief row brought him out of his shell, and when someone asked him about passive resistance, he hesitated before stating that the only way to get rid of Hitler was to assassinate him. He then talked at length about the bombings of Cologne and Hamburg, where he feared the architectural treasures of Germany—its cathedrals and museums—were being destroyed. Some of the young guests listened in awe as he described how the nation was losing its most visible emblems of German spirit.

But looking around him at the bohemian group, slouching on stools and cushions and picking at cake, he said: "We are not factory workers. We cannot take to the streets."[12]

The Scholls again did not feel they could invite him into their group, although—seeing the way he had galvanized those present with his impromptu speech—they still believed he could help them.

The following morning Sophie insisted on going along to the freight yard at the Ostbahnhof railway station to see off her brother, Schmorell, Graf, and Wittenstein, who had also been posted to Russia. Probst was leaving Munich, too, but only going as far as Innsbruck, to serve with a

Luftwaffe medic unit.[13] It was a sad farewell. The train was due to take them a long way from home, through Poland to Russia. It would be three months before they came home, if they came back at all.

Sophie stayed, watched them chat. She wondered how her mother must feel back in Ulm: Not only was Hans on his way to the Russian Front, but Werner, her youngest, barely twenty years old, was there, too.

Hans looked up at his sister. Her dark hair—now a little longer than usual—was at her shoulders; her satchel-like briefcase, bursting with books, was hooked by its handle over a spike in the fence separating her from them. Seeing that he was looking at her, she gave a big smile and he smiled back. When he looked away again, her look changed. She was engrossed in thought.

The first phase of the White Rose was over. Their minds now were filled with thoughts of where to take it next.

AT THE END of the semester Sophie Scholl returned to Ulm and the family home in the shadow of the cathedral. Coming through its door, she had a torrent of thoughts she would have liked to share but she could not: how she and Hans were at last doing something about the plague that had taken over their land.

At home, though, she felt much younger than she did at the university. There she was an independent woman, a free-thinking scholar; here, with her mother and father, she was their child again. And they desperately needed her support.

The trial of Robert Scholl for his outspoken words against Hitler had been set for the beginning of August. He appeared in the Special Court in Stuttgart—where Hans had appeared in 1938—and was sentenced to four months in prison, a sentence that was considered lenient. Scholl also lost the legal license he needed to work in financial services, and although a friend— Eugen Grimminger, who hated the Nazis—took over his business and offered Inge a job, the imprisonment left the family struggling for money.

These were lonely times for Sophie. Her father was in prison; her brothers, Hans and Werner, were in Russia; and then Fritz Hartnagel, whom she had not seen since the spring, was sent there, too. The family also received news that Ernst Reden, who had remained friends with Inge, had been killed. The news and the effect it had on her sister made Sophie step up her resistance to the war. "It's got to stop," she told her family.[14]

Soon after, a letter arrived ordering Sophie to fill in her summer with two months' labor service at a local arms factory. The work was grim, consisting of long hours among the deafening machinery. Sophie described it as "very like slavery," and indeed most of the others working the machines were captured Russian women who had been forced to work in this most dangerous of home-front industries. Sophie saved some of the money she received and went to see Hans Hirzel, the young student from Ulm who had copied the Galen sermons. She gave him money to buy a duplicating machine.

With every week that passed, there seemed to be bad news. She feared for Hartnagel, who was now at Stalingrad, and wept for Carl Muth when his home was damaged by one of the first bombing raids on Munich. Her father was eventually freed early and in good health, but she could not get over the injustice of his being humiliated and jailed in the first place. She told him she could not forgive the Nazis "who had made it happen."[15]

Hans was due back for the winter semester, which was to start at the beginning of November. She longed to see him again but worried over the "uncertainty" that "casts a shadow over all the days to come."[16] In her diary she wrote: "I ought to be overjoyed at being with him again, but there is something troubling my joy."[17]

She wondered how Russia had affected her brother, and she feared, too, the inevitable outcome of his return: that together they would renew the campaign of the White Rose.

# 23

## An Order for Gerstein

I N JUNE 1941, as the German armies pushed into the Soviet Union, a tall, lean man in the black uniform of the SS climbed the steps of a large building in the Knesebeckstrasse in Charlottenburg.

Kurt Gerstein had been in uniform for a year now, but he had never learned to be comfortable in it. The tunic sagged at his thin shoulders, his belt hung a little loose at his narrow waist, and the cap sat awkwardly on his head. But his dedication to his work and his knowledge of engineering and medicine had got him noticed by his superiors.

When he reported for duty, an orderly told him to wait, and he looked around him and wondered what his new posting had in store. This was the Institute of Hygiene, whose long corridors housed laboratories and rooms where scientists and their assistants worked in strict secrecy. There were research departments in chemistry, parasitology, bacteriology, and meteorology. Gerstein had been told he would be working in the department of water hygiene under Dr. Fritz Krantz, a mineralogist.

As he waited, Gerstein reflected on the past twelve months. He had done his basic training at Langenhorn in Hamburg, where he had befriended his instructor—a professional soldier named Sergeant Robert Weigelt—despite being a poor recruit who often reported sick and could not even march in time. Weigelt saw Gerstein as an "ultra-Christian," but he was also good-natured and loyal, and he did what was asked. Weigelt noted that his recruit's main foible was a habit of disappearing alone, but when he headed off into the town, he always brought back Weigelt a bottle of schnapps. Once the first bottle had been accepted, Gerstein realized he had an unknowing ally in the kindly sergeant from Hesse.

When the group of recruits, which included university graduates and doctors, reflecting the Nazis' desire to bring "professional talent" into the ranks of the SS, was transferred to Arnhem in Nazi-occupied Netherlands, Gerstein's trips off base continued. He had discovered that an old friend from the mining industry, a Dutch engineer named J. H. Ubbink, lived nearby.

One day Ubbink opened the door of his house to find Gerstein standing there in uniform. The Dutchman hurried his friend inside, not wanting his neighbors to see. "This doesn't mean a thing," Gerstein said, gesturing to the uniform. "The man inside it hasn't changed."

Gerstein explained his reasons for volunteering, and the two men prayed together. Ubbink was concerned about the huge risk his friend was taking.

"We Germans have got to lose this war," Gerstein told him. The effect of the words on Ubbink, a citizen of a conquered nation, were electric. "Better a hundred Versailles treaties than that the present gang of criminals should remain in power. What does it profit a nation to gain the whole world if it lose its own soul?"[1]

Ubbink went to a drawer and brought out a copy of Hermann Rausching's book *Hitler Speaks*, which contained early interviews with the Führer revealing the hatreds that consumed him. Banned in Germany, the book was an underground hit in Holland. Gerstein sat and flicked through its pages. He read Hitler's words: "This revolution of ours is the exact counterpart of the great French revolution. And no Jewish God will save the democracies from it. There is a stern time coming, I shall see to that. Only the tough and manly will endure. And the world will assume a new aspect."[2]

When he had finished, Gerstein looked at Ubbink. "It is only too true," he said.

Gerstein took a copy of the book and later posted it anonymously through the door of his friend Pastor Rehling—who for some time was too afraid to read it as he feared its delivery had been a Gestapo trick.

Back on base, Gerstein continued to appear the loyal soldier. He threw himself into his training, and reports to SS headquarters highlighted his talent for inventing new procedures for solving technical problems and noted his qualifications in medicine. Here was a man who, while perhaps not the greatest at drill, could still be a real asset to the SS.

Gerstein knew that his status in Hitler's most elite and loyal unit set him apart. It was even marked on his body: As with all members of the SS, his blood group had been tattooed under his left armpit so that he would be guaranteed preferential treatment in any hospital in the Reich.

But all the while his mind was elsewhere. When Gerstein met up with another friend, he told him that it was unpleasant to be "misread" as a Nazi by others, but that he was "obliged to congratulate himself" on his "camouflage."[3] He still only hinted at his double life in letters to his wife, Elfriede—who remained in Tübingen throughout his service—telling her that he often thought of "Nietzsche's well-known phrase that I've so frequently quoted to you."

Elfriede remembered the phrase, of course, but she wondered what on earth her husband meant. The words from Nietzsche were "Live dangerously!"

THE SS REPORTS on Gerstein's skills had eventually reached Berlin, and he was sent to take a course at the School of Decontamination at Oranienburg, just north of the capital. Then had come the posting to the Institute of Hygiene.

His new boss, Dr. Krantz, was no more impressed with Gerstein's unsoldierly appearance than the NCOs at SS training school had been. "Do for God's sake try and smarten yourself up," was one of the first things he said to him, and it would become an order he would often repeat. But he was impressed with Gerstein's knowledge and work ethic.

Over the next few months they worked on tests on the chemical and bacterial content of various water supplies, and traveled extensively to test the drinking water at army bases and prisons. In one police prison Gerstein dropped his cigarettes near some prisoners and left them. Krantz was convinced it was a deliberate act but did not challenge his assistant. He told colleagues the man was being of enormous help to him.

The institute's chief was a tall, thin man with tight lips and a voracious appetite for work. Professor Joachim Mrugowsky was thirty-six, devoted to Himmler, and a man always on the lookout for any scheme that would tackle the problems presented to the Third Reich. In the halls of the institute he appeared the ultimate capable civil servant—open to ideas, keeping an eye out for talented colleagues—but he was in fact a ruthless Nazi who had already played a role in some of the regime's atrocities. Back in the spring of 1939 he had been called to Buchenwald concentration camp to advise on a typhus epidemic. His order was swift and ruthless: Kill off the most hopeless cases and preserve medical supplies for those who could be treated.[4]

Now, though, as the German army moved through Russia and Ukraine, putting captured Red Army soldiers and the civilian population into work camps, typhus had again become a problem. Mrugowsky was told there were ten thousand cases in the Wehrmacht, and he had to deal with it as a "frontline priority."

Mrugowsky put the reports from the Eastern Front on Gerstein's desk and asked for his thoughts. Reading through, Gerstein saw immediately that disease was being spread not just through dirty water but through clothes and cooking utensils as well. The solution would be to find a way of decontaminating these items in battlefield conditions, he told the chief. Mrugowsky—under pressure from Himmler—asked if he could do it, and Gerstein said he could but would need to put together a small team. Mrugowsky had his secretary draw up all the necessary paperwork and, in addition, give Gerstein special travel documents, safe-conduct passes, and access to official cars. Gerstein brought in his old training sergeant, Weigelt, to support him, together with a Luftwaffe meteorologist named Armin Peters and a pharmacist, Friedrich Geissert. Soon after he joined, Geissert, who spoke French, was dispatched to Paris to talk to people at the Pasteur Institute on Gerstein's behalf about typhus vaccines.

Working day and night, Gerstein developed a high-pressure steam device for delousing uniforms, blankets, and underclothes that destroyed not only the lice but also their excrement. He then invented a mobile filter unit to kill bugs in drinking water. The two devices were demonstrated for the army, which approved both and rushed them into mass production in factories in Munich and Celle.

Mrugowsky took the credit from the high command, but also knew he needed Gerstein to continue with the work he was doing. When, in November 1941, one of the judges who had excluded Gerstein from the Nazi Party saw him in SS uniform and reported him to SS high command, urgent inquiries were made at the institute, but the complaint was quickly dismissed by Mrugowsky.

Gerstein and his team now found themselves traveling to all corners of France and Germany. They built and delivered disinfection trucks for troops and a pump to repel mosquitoes in army hospitals. They advised on sanitation when sewer and water pipes were destroyed during heavy raids by the RAF on Bremen and Hamburg. They traveled at will on the passes supplied by Mrugowsky.

But Gerstein was already seeing and hearing evidence of the crimes that he had gone into the SS to identify. He had visited the concentration camps to inspect water supplies and seen the conditions in which prisoners were working, and very early in January 1942 he was consulted on experiments being carried out by a colleague, Major Dr. Erwin Ding—who both distrusted and loathed Gerstein because of his closeness to Mrugowsky—to test the effectiveness and safety of various typhus vaccines. A report on the tests stated that people at Buchenwald had been given the various treatments and that five had died. Tests were continuing in block 46.[5]

A few days later Gerstein visited a soldier friend who had been wounded at the front. The friend said that once he let down his guard, Gerstein seemed to have "stretched his nerves to the limit" and appeared to be a "bundle . . . of hate, fear, and despair." Gerstein told the friend that what he had seen in the SS was draining the life out of him. "He was so appalled by the satanic practices of the Nazis that their eventual victory did not seem to him impossible," said the friend later.[6]

Gerstein was staring into abyss. He was about to disappear into it.

THE SNOW WAS falling in Berlin on the morning of January 20, 1942, when a series of black cars swept through the gates of the SD villa at Am Grossen Wannsee 56–58, in a suburb southwest of Berlin. Some fifteen senior officials of the Reich had been invited to the villa that morning, and they greeted each other warmly as they flapped the snow off their uniforms with their gloves.

The villa offered a most relaxed atmosphere in which to do business, and as they took their places around the large table, army orderlies inquired after their orders for drinks.

Two out of three attending had a university degree, and over half had the title doctor, mainly in law. Only two were over fifty.[7] The man who had arranged the meeting, Reinhard Heydrich, the chief of the SD and the Security Police and Himmler's right-hand man, was thirty-seven.

The previous summer Heydrich had been tasked by Reichsmarschall Hermann Göring to "make all the necessary preparations to organize the complete solution of the Jewish question within the German sphere of influence in Europe." The task had fallen to Heydrich as it had been he who had formed the Reich Central Office for Jewish Emigration in Berlin soon after Kristallnacht.[8]

While Jews were already being summarily executed in the East, Heydrich calmly provided tables and reports to establish clarity on the policy.[9] Jews who were fit to work should be made to "work their way eastwards constructing roads," the conference agreed, and "doubtless the large majority will be eliminated by natural causes." Those who remained alive would be those most likely to resist, the administrators of death agreed, and they "will have to be dealt with appropriately, because otherwise, by natural selection, they would form the germ cell of a new Jewish revival."

Germany and the Czech protectorate must be "cleared" first and then occupied Europe would be swept from west to east. All Jewish people should be brought to transit ghettos before being transported onwards by train.

The minutes recorded much discussion of "evacuation to the east," although Adolf Eichmann, of the RSHA, the Reich Security Main Office, later stated the real language in the room was far more open about killing.[10]

With the logistics broadly agreed upon, the meeting drew to a close. The men stood, stretched their legs, and, sipping cognac, asked after each other's families and looked through the villa's large windows at the snow settling on the icy water of the lake outside.

HORST DICKTEN KNOCKED on the door and entered Kurt Gerstein's office in the Institute of Hygiene.

Dickten was a former frontline soldier who had been wounded and was now marked unfit for active service. He had joined Gerstein's staff as an assistant, and while he enjoyed working for him, he had to admit Gerstein was an eccentric boss: He would combine work trips with walks around antique shops in Brussels and art galleries in Paris and would bring back gifts for work colleagues. Sometimes he raised eyebrows with his practical jokes, too: A favorite was wearing a clothes brush in his revolver holster.

But Dickten was also aware that Gerstein was covering up a distaste for the regime that bordered on something far stronger. The two men would never speak about it at work, but they had talked when they were on the road and realized it was a distaste that they both shared. Gerstein made Dickten both smile and worry when he told him that every evening when he got home to his apartment on Bülowstrasse, he would unbutton his SS officer's tunic and tune his radio to the BBC.

On that morning early in 1942, though, Dickten found his boss sitting at his desk with his face as white as a sheet. Waving his friend to take a seat, Gerstein pushed across the piece of paper that he had been reading. The subject heading was the first thing Dickten saw: "Solution of the Jewish Problem." He scanned through. It was about the installation of "necessary" buildings and appliances in an occupied territory in the East. The same words that had caught Gerstein's eye and made his blood run cold now did the same to Dickten: "for the gassing of the Jews."

The regime's rabid hatred of Jewish people was not a shock—it was deeply engrained in German society—but what this document was describing in Gerstein's eyes was an extension to the euthanasia program, and this time not for the criminally insane or chronically ill but for fit and healthy people just because they were Jewish.

Gerstein and Dickten wondered what it all could mean and went across to the Unter den Linden to see friends in the SS Office of Economy and Administration, from where the concentration camps were run. Gerstein's department was funded from this office, and he brought back from Paris presents for some people there, but if any of them knew about extermination camps, they said little and looked back strangely when questioned. "We were in the heart of hell," Dickten said later. "Any curiosity was suspect."[11]

ON JUNE 8, 1942, a man in civilian clothes presented himself at Kurt Gerstein's office and introduced himself as Major Rolf Günther, of the Reich Security Main Office. Gerstein knew instantly that he worked for Eichmann.

He explained that Gerstein was being given a top secret mission that he could not even discuss with his colleagues. He was to procure 572 pounds of liquid prussic acid and take it to an undisclosed location by truck. Only the driver would know the location.

When Gerstein asked politely why he had been chosen, he was told it was because he was the SS's leading decontamination expert. More detailed written instructions would be given within twenty-four hours.

These arrived as Günther had said, and Gerstein reread the sheet of paper a number of times. It was marked "Top Secret" and had a red border all around its outside edge. Gerstein's instructions were plain: He was to order the quantity of Zyklon B, a variant of hydrocyanic or prussic acid that released deadly fumes on contact with the air. Only one firm, Deutsche Gesellschaft für Schädlingsbekämpfung (German Corporation for Pest Control), which was known in the trade as Degesch, or one of its subsidiaries could supply this chemical.[12] When he had made the arrangements, transport would be laid out for him. Again, no location was given.

On receiving the letter Gerstein left his office and traveled out to Dahlem, near the Grunewald, to St. Anne's Church, Pastor Niemöller's old parish. It was a terrible risk as the church and its new pastor, Herbert Mochalsky, were under suspicion by the Gestapo for holding services in the tradition of the now-banned Confessing Church.

St. Anne's held a daily service, and Gerstein sat at the back; all the same Mochalsky saw the new man and feared he was the Gestapo. As Gerstein listened, he became more and more convinced that he had been right to come. The sermon that day was constructed around the Fifth Commandment— "Thou shalt not kill."

When the fifty or so parishioners had left, the stranger approached Mochalsky and grabbed his arm. "Providence must have guided my footsteps," he said. "Something terrible has happened to me."

Gerstein then showed the terrified pastor the written order. Mochalsky saw the words "Top Secret" and looked away, but Gerstein read it out.

"This consignment is intended to kill thousands of people. You know what I mean? The sort of people who are labelled sub-human."

Gerstein was distraught. He talked about a relative having been murdered in the euthanasia program, about why he joined the SS, and about suicide. If he killed himself, two people who had supported him in the SS would die, too, he claimed.

And he kept looking at the order. "A consignment of prussic acid."

"Herr Pastor," Gerstein pleaded, "what am I to do? What am I to do?"

AT THE BEGINNING of August 1942 an army truck and a gleaming black staff car arrived in Kolin, a town a little over thirty miles from Prague that since medieval times had been home to German settlers, Slavs, and a large Jewish population. Set in a region of hilly forests, the town was overshadowed by the chimneys of the potash plant. Owned by a subsidiary of the Degesch company, it had become dedicated to the production of the Zyklon B gas.

While the containers of gas were being loaded onto the truck, Kurt Gerstein walked among some of the employees of the factory. Most, it seemed, believed the gas was being used to kill vermin and parasites. Without saying so directly, Gerstein asked questions of the gas's effectiveness, which gave them enough information to understand that it was now being used on human beings. Gerstein hoped that word would get out.

Very quickly the small, deadly convoy was on the road again. Seated with Gerstein in the back of the car was SS Lieutenant-Colonel Dr. Wilhelm Pfannenstiel, an urbane and highly intelligent professor of hygiene from the University of Marburg who was carrying out an inspection of the camps. While the professor talked about his large family and the driver took them onwards into Poland, Kurt Gerstein's inner turmoil ate at his conscious. Did the professor know what was going on? He had to. How could he sit and talk happily, as if on a family outing to the countryside? And was he—Gerstein—any better? Everyone in the car had their hands dirty. They were all playing a part in a terrible crime.

At the next stop, Gerstein had an idea. Going to the back of the truck, he inspected the cargo and pretended to become alarmed. "One of the containers is leaking," he told the others, none of whom could smell or detect anything wrong. But they knew that he was the expert and no one wanted to risk being too close to this deadly chemical. Gerstein "identified" the ruptured canister, and it was taken to the side of the road and buried.

It was a small victory, but in the context of what Gerstein feared was happening, did it mean anything? He was soon to get an idea of the scale and horror of what the Nazis had unleashed in the East.

KURT GERSTEIN'S ZYKLON B party arrived at the SS barracks in Lublin on August 17, 1942. The barracks, named after the SS's first leader, Julius Schreck, who had died of meningitis in 1936, were occupied by only a small group of men, and it was from here that Operation Reinhard was being organized.

The local SS police chief, Brigadier-General Odilo Globocnik, welcomed the party and proceeded to introduce them to the details of Reinhard. The operation was named in honor of Reinhard Heydrich, who, less than five months after presiding over the orders for the murder of the Jews at Wannsee, had himself been killed in Prague by Czech resisters trained by the British Special Operations Executive.

Everything they were being told, said Globocnik—a tall man with swept-back hair and a slightly bulbous nose—was in the strictest secrecy. Two men had already been shot for talking about the project outside the barracks. Official documents on Reinhard described the "transfer" of Jews, but here in Poland, Globocnik was developing the phenomenon of the death camp, the creation of an industry based on the mass extermination of a race of people.

Gerstein knew that gas vans, in which the exhausts had been directed into the rear cabin to asphyxiate those carried inside, had been used in East Prussia during 1940 to kill "euthanasia" victims, but Globocnik said that stationary killing centers had been installed at Auschwitz, at first to kill Russian prisoners of war.

In this region, Globocnik boasted, he was creating a network of death camps. He had begun by forcing Polish laborers to build a camp at Belzec, which he thought might be used to gas all the Jews from the Lublin area. Belzec had now been joined by camps at Sobibor and Treblinka. Gradually, Globocnik's goal had developed into the liquidation of all Polish Jews.[13] Mass-killing operations had started at Belzec that spring and in Auschwitz during the summer.

At Belzec, Sobibor, Treblinka—and a fourth Polish camp, Chelmno— the plan was to kill every Jew within a few hours of arrival.[14]

Globocnik announced he was taking Gerstein and Pfannenstiel on a tour, and they drove ninety miles to the southwest into the birch woods and sparsely populated countryside of Galicia. They came to the small village of Belzec, a cluster of wooden houses and a tall church tower, and drove on as hens and chickens scattered from the roadside. A short distance on to the south, nestled against the side of a wooded slope, was a group of huts and a gate marked "Belzec. Special Establishment of the Waffen SS." To one side of the camp, a branch of the Lublin-Lvov railway came to an end behind a line of thick conifers, which concealed it from the outside world. A single lookout tower with a machine gun and searchlight watched over all.

Gerstein took in the series of buildings. A small railway station. A large shed labeled "Cloakroom" in which there was a collecting office with the sign "Objects of value." A "hairdressing salon" with seats for a hundred people. Then an alleyway between thick rolls of barbed wire leading to the Bade und Inhalationsräume, the "bathing and inhalation rooms."

Globocnik explained that the commandant, Christian Wirth—the policeman who had put Hitler's T4 euthanasia program into such deadly practice—would not be available until tomorrow. A sergeant-major who had worked with Wirth on T4 would show them around.[15] They walked to the Bade und Inhalationsräume and saw that on each side of the steps to the entrance were two large flowerpots filled with geraniums. Over the door was the inscription "Hackenholt Foundation," and above it a Star of David. Inside was a long, unlit concrete corridor. Off the corridor were the windowless gas chambers.[16]

On the journey there, Globocnik had been clear with Gerstein as to what was expected of him. "We need you to improve the service of our gas chambers," he told him, explaining they functioned off an engine exhaust.[17] "What is wanted is a more toxic gas that works faster."

It was hot and sunny that first day in Belzec, and to Gerstein the smell around the buildings was "pestilential." There were flies everywhere.

There were no prisoners at the camp that day and no train arrived. But the air was heavy with murder. Gerstein was found a billet in the village that night and promised a demonstration of Operation Reinhard the following day.

# 24

## Belzec

A BRIGHT AUGUST morning. The sun rose above the broad plains of Galicia, an area of central Eastern Europe that over the centuries had known many masters. From beyond the trees came the creak of metal wheels on a train line as a steam locomotive labored to bring the forty-five trucks it had shunted from Lvov to a rest.

Kurt Gerstein and the SS chemist Pfannenstiel watched as many of the two hundred Ukrainians used by the SS to run the camp stood waiting for the wheels to come to a halt.

By the simple building that had been made up to look like a rustic railway station, a small number of Jewish musicians played marching songs, as instructed.

Beside them was Christian Wirth, a smiling figure with a Hitler mustache and an immaculate SS uniform. As he waited, he tapped his riding crop against the side of his leg, a sign perhaps of a little apprehension: He wanted everything to go well in front of this expert from Berlin, Gerstein, as he had a point to prove. Wirth believed the fumes from the engine they had attached to the death chambers were the most efficient way to kill—after all, the system had worked perfectly well for him through his time with T4—but his former subordinate Rudolf Höss, now in command at Auschwitz, argued for the use of Zyklon B.

Eichmann and Günther, who had arranged Gerstein's visit, favored Höss, and Wirth was eager to prove them wrong.

The middle managers of death were as keen to appear as efficient to their superiors as those from any industry.

There is one-upmanship even in genocide.

* * *

AT FIRST, AS the wooden doors of the train trucks were slid open, all went well for Wirth. For five months the routine had been the same. Everyone at the camp knew their roles.

On the train the people stood still and silent until, on a German command, the Ukrainian guards stepped forward, leather whips cracking.

"Out! Out! Everybody out! Quickly!"

Men, women, and children jumped down. Whips cracked at their feet and across their shoulders. They looked around, wondering where they were. It was a place without pity, they could see, but it was somewhere. Perhaps there would be a prison. A prison, you could cope with. There was always the hope that you might one day be free.

Bags and bundles were thrown down from the trucks. Old suitcases. Then more people came out. It seemed endless. Somebody muttered that there were six thousand on the train, although almost a quarter were dead inside the dark corners of the cars.[1]

A loudspeaker broke across the shouts, cries, and sobs. "Ihr geht jetzt baden, nachher werdet Ihr zur Arbeit geschickt!" "You are going to take a bath now, afterwards you will be sent to work."[2]

Work! Work would be a relief, no matter how arduous. Work was life!

And then: "Everyone without exception is to undress entirely. Spectacles and false teeth are to be removed. Clothes to be piled in a heap. Objects of value to be handed in at the office."

At these words, Gerstein immediately saw a growing agony on many of the faces. They knew what this meant. There was to be no voucher or receipt for the valuables. No return.

On the fence, a sign in Polish repeated the instructions and added: "One must go completely naked to the showers."[3]

Women with babies, children, the elderly stripped—frightened, embarrassed, painfully vulnerable. They were barefoot, too, having to use their cold, tired fingers to tie their shoes together in pairs. Perhaps Gerstein remembered Hitler's words from the banned Rauschning book he had been reading: "Nature is cruel: therefore we are also entitled to be cruel."

The women and girls were taken to the "hairdressing salon," and their heads were shaved.

Then they were hurried through the channel in the barbed wire, the Ukrainians waving their rifles at their bare backs.

As the column reached the Bade und Inhalationsräume, a large SS man stepped forward, his belt sitting on his fat stomach. He addressed the naked group in a calm, fatherly manner.

"Don't worry! You aren't going to be hurt!"

At each stage a new level of cynical cruelty . . .

"All you have to do is take a deep breath. It strengthens the lungs—a precaution against disease!"

There were questions from the bravest. "What's going to happen to us?"

The fatherly SS man smiled. "The men will have to work, building roads and houses," he said. "But not the women! If they want to they can do the housework and the cooking. Now, come on!"

They moved up the stairway and through the door, under the Star of David and the "Hackenholt Foundation" sign.

There were prayers now.

Those in front hesitated, but the guards kept pushing the others forward and the leaders were propelled onwards into the rooms.

As one woman of about forty came up the steps, she turned on the three men who were silently watching. She looked into Gerstein's eyes and cursed her murderers. Wirth swung at her with his whip, and she was pushed inside.

Gerstein, witness and criminal, said nothing. What should he say? He could not enter the chamber with them, no more than in that moment he could stop this. But his very presence condemned him. He prayed silently to himself, pressed himself into a corner. He looked away, too ashamed to be the last face seen by fellow human beings in such distress.

But there was no escape. The pain and guilt were enough to make him wish he was dying, too.

The guards packed their victims in tightly. Wirth said there were hundreds inside. The guards pressed more in. The SS and their helpers had to use their shoulders to force shut the heavy doors. Bars were slammed down and the lights switched off. That brought more screams. The prayers and cries could still be heard for some time. And the shouts of anger and hatred, too. But the people were forced together so tightly, unable to move, that their energies for crying out soon sapped.

"Hackenholt!" The cry echoed across the camp. Gerstein watched an SS sergeant run up. He was the man in charge of the truck whose exhausts were fed into the chambers to choke the victims. Hackenholt! Gerstein looked at the sign above the door: "Hackenholt Foundation." A kind of joke.[4]

The others from the train who could not fit into the gas chamber still stood in the camp, all naked. Gerstein looked across at them and someone said: "The same in winter."

Without thinking, Gerstein replied: "Yes, but they could catch their death of cold."

"Yes, exactly what they are here for!" came the reply.

Hackenholt tried to start the engine from which the carbon dioxide would cough and belch and kill the people inside. It failed to start, and failed to start again. Wirth stamped back and forth, talking anxiously to Hackenholt. He tried to act firm, but inside he was losing it. Why the screwup today when the man from Berlin was here! He'd report back not only to Globocnik but to Himmler himself! Wirth thought only of his embarrassment while the hundreds inside suffered unimaginable agony.

Minutes turned into an hour. In his anger Wirth whacked the Ukrainian who was helping Hackenholt fix the engine across the face with his riding crop. Just for someone to take it out on.

A stopwatch ticked—part of Gerstein's instruction to judge the most efficient method for committing industrial-scale murder.

From inside, the cries returned: "Help us! Please help us!"

Pfannenstiel put his face to a peephole in one of the chamber doors. People stacked together so close they could not even shrink to the floor. Pfannenstiel was an educated man, a professor, but he viewed this obscene tableau of human suffering dispassionately.

The engine finally started. Two hours and forty-nine minutes had passed, according to the stopwatch.

With the engine, the lights came on in the chambers and the observers pressed their eyes to the peephole. The chambers began to fill with smoke.

After thirty-two minutes all were dead. Wirth asked Gerstein what he thought. Perhaps he could not speak.

Later Gerstein described the scene that followed: "From the other side men from the work command open the wooden doors. They have been promised—even Jews—freedom, and some one-thousandth of all valuables found, for their terrible service. Like basalt pillars the dead stand inside, pressed together in the chambers. In any event there was no space to

Arvid and Mildred Harnack, who developed an anti-Nazi organization in Berlin and passed Hitler's secrets to the Americans and Russians.

Luftwaffe intelligence officer Harro Schulze-Boysen, who told the Soviet Union that Hitler was about to attack, and his wife, Libertas, an aristocrat who worked for a Nazi film unit and secretly collected evidence of Nazi atrocities.

*Unless otherwise noted, photographs are provided courtesy of the German Resistance Memorial Center.*

Greta Lorke, a distinguished academic and friend of the Harnacks who recruited writers, filmmakers, and poets to work against the regime.

Michigan-born John Sieg, a former journalist who worked on the German railways and helped unite working-class and academic resisters in Berlin, and his Polish wife, Sophie Wloszczynski, who supported his work.

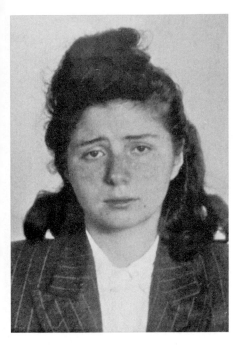

The distressed face of Liane Berkowitz, a determined opponent of the Nazi regime, as photographed by the Gestapo upon her arrest. Liane was nineteen years old at the time and was pregnant.

Electrician Herbert Baum, who became an inspiring leader of German Jewish resistance and planned sabotage in Berlin.

A group of young men out for a run. Among them are Felix Heymann (*far left*), who took part in all the major activities of the Herbert Baum group, and Baum himself, who is lying on the ground to the right.

Wild times for some of the youngsters who refused to conform to Nazism, including Herbert Baum (*hanging onto the truck on the right*), who was older than many of his friends, and Herbert Budzislawski (*laughing in the middle at the back*). Budzislawski told his Gestapo interrogators that fighting back was the only way "to live in Germany as a human being."

Hans Oster, of the Abwehr. His hatred of the Nazis ensured that he became one of the regime's most consistent opponents.

Hans von Dohnanyi, a childhood friend of Arvid Harnack and Dietrich Bonhoeffer. As an Abwehr officer he opened a secret file on Hitler's crimes and worked with Oster to rescue Jews.

*Top left*: Admiral Wilhelm Canaris, the head of the Abwehr, allowed Oster, Dohnanyi, and others to build an anti-Hitler conspiracy inside German military intelligence.

*Top right*: Pastor Dietrich Bonhoeffer was a leading German theologian and Dohnanyi's brother-in-law who worked with the Abwehr as it sought to make peace with the Allies.

*Left*: General Ludwig Beck, a former chief of staff of the German armed forces, was a staunch critic of the Nazis and a leader of the resistance.

*Top left*: Major Friedrich Heinz was a former Nazi who was persuaded by Oster to switch his allegiances and agreed to lead an assassination squad against Hitler.

*Top right*: Colonel Claus von Stauffenberg had suffered terrible injuries in battle but led the July 20 bomb attack on Hitler.

*Right*: Colonel Henning von Tresckow was at the heart of the resistance. A principled and inspirational officer, he was a driving force behind wartime efforts to kill Hitler.

Colonel Claus von Stauffenberg and his friend and fellow Valkyrie conspirator Colonel Albrecht Mertz von Quirnheim.

Alexander Schmorell, of the White Rose, had refused to swear the army's oath of allegiance to Hitler before he joined up with the Scholls.

Hans Scholl; his sister, Sophie; and Christoph Probst, key members of the White Rose resistance group in Munich.

*White Rose Foundation*

Willi Graf described the atrocities in Poland and the Soviet Union to his friends in the White Rose.

Professor Kurt Huber, whose conscience made him support the students of the White Rose. *Wolfgang Huber*

Fritz Kolbe, an unassuming and hardworking diplomat in the German Foreign Office who despised the Nazis and became one of the United States' most efficient spies inside the Third Reich. *From the author's collection*

Allen Dulles ran the Office of Strategic Services in Switzerland, monitoring the German resistance and running Fritz Kolbe as an agent.

*From the author's collection*

Ordered to supply concentration camps with poison gas, SS officer Kurt Gerstein tried to warn the Allies about the Holocaust.

Staff at Belzec, the extermination camp where Kurt Gerstein first witnessed the full horror of the Holocaust. Gerstein saw Lorenz Hackenholt, the man third from the right in the black gloves, start the engine used to produce the lethal gas.

*From the author's collection*

Falk Harnack, Arvid Harnack's brother, who made contact with the White Rose and hoped to unite the various elements of German resistance.

Walter Schellenberg headed the SD (the Sicherheitsdienst), the counter-intelligence agency of the SS, and was both a spymaster and a spy catcher.

Luftwaffe judge advocate Manfred Roeder, who prosecuted the Harnack and Schulze-Boysen groups and investigated the anti-Nazis of the Abwehr.    *From the author's collection*

Roland Freisler, the ruthless judge of the People's Court, who presided over the trials of the White Rose and many other resisters.    *Bundesarchiv*

The Bendler Block today. It was from here in the office of German high command that Stauffenberg and the others coordinated Operation Valkyrie on July 20.

*Above*: The courtyard of the Bendler Block, where key conspirators, includir Stauffenberg, were summarily executed

*Left*: The memorial plaque on a wall in the courtyard of the Bendler Block.

HIER STARBEN
FÜR
DEUTSCHLAND
AM 20 JULI 1944

GENERALOBERST LUDWIG BECK
GENERAL DER INFANTERIE FRIEDRICH OLBRICHT
OBERST CLAUS GRAF SCHENK VON STAUFFENBERG
OBERST ALBRECHT RITTER MERTZ VON QUIRNHEIM
OBERLEUTNANT WERNER VON HAEFTEN

The home of the Bonhoeffer family in Charlottenburg, Berlin, where Dietrich Bonhoeffer planned anti-Nazi activities with his friends. He was arrested here in April 1943.

*Above*: Inside the execution shed at Plötzensee prison. Against the far wall is the wooden beam lined with metal hooks from which many resisters were hanged.

*Right*: The brick shed in the outer yard of Plötzensee prison in which many members of the anti-Nazi resistance were executed.

*All photos on this page courtesy of the author*

*Above*: Munich University today. Hans and Sophie Scholl entered the building through the doors beneath the center arches on the day they threw leaflets into the Lichthof.

*Right*: The Lichthof, or atrium, inside Munich University. Sophie Scholl threw the leaflets from the balustrade, just below the clock.

*All photos on this page courtesy of the author*

*Above*: The view from the balustrade looking down into the atrium.

*Left*: The house in Franz Joseph Strasse, Munich, in which Hans and Sophie Scholl had rooms. From here they planned the activities of the White Rose.

The memorial plaque on the house in Franz Joseph Strasse.

SOPHIE UND HANS
SCHOLL
DIE UNTER DEM ZEICHEN
DER „WEISSEN ROSE"
AKTIVEN WIDERSTAND
GEGEN DAS DRITTE REICH
GELEISTET HABEN WOHN-
TEN VON JUNI 1942 BIS
ZU IHRER HINRICHTUNG
AM 22· FEBRUAR 1943
HIER IM RÜCKGEBÄUDE

The names of the Herbert Baum group listed on a memorial in the Lustgarten, outside Berlin Cathedral.

fall down or even bend forward. Even in death one can still tell the families. They still hold hands, tensed in death, so that one can barely tear them apart in order to empty the chamber for the next batch. The corpses are thrown out, wet from sweat and urine, soiled by excrement, menstrual blood on their legs. Children's corpses fly through the air. There is no time. The riding crops of the Ukrainians lash down on the work commands. Two dozen dentists open mouths with hooks and look for gold. Gold to the left, without gold to the right. Other dentists break gold teeth and crowns out of jaws with pliers and hammers."[5]

Because of the engine failure, Wirth was behind schedule. He shouted at his men to hurry. Whips cracked. "Schnell! Schnell!"

But even in a rush, every part of the dead was probed and searched for hidden gold, diamonds, and other valuables. Wirth picked up a large metal box and carried it to Gerstein. "Lift this can full of gold teeth!" he challenged him with a laugh. "That is only from yesterday and the day before yesterday! You won't believe what we find in gold and diamonds every day."

The bodies were taken from the chambers and thrown into large pits dug in the ground. The dead from the train already had been put in the pit. There was shouting and a lashing of whips on the slave camp workers: Someone had forgotten to check these bodies for valuables. People jumped in now, started the search. Black clouds of flies swirled.

In one pile of belongings two gold coins caught the sun. Both Wirth and Gerstein saw them. With a smile, Wirth leaned down, picked them up, and stuffed them hastily into his pocket.[6]

WIRTH WAS AGITATED after the problem with the engine, knowing that Gerstein's job was to assess the work at Belzec—not to judge its humanity but its efficiency.

The issue with the engine had not happened before, he told Gerstein, and he asked him not to propose any changes to Berlin.

Another train was coming later. More of the same. Gerstein could see nothing he could do to stop it. But he salved his conscience by making a decision on the Zyklon B. They would not use it. The consignment he had brought appeared to be contaminated anyway, he lied.

On the way back to Lublin, the car and truck stopped and Gerstein supervised the burial of the Zyklon B.

* * *

THE FOLLOWING DAY the inspection continued. Treblinka was a much larger camp to the northeast of Warsaw. A month earlier the Nazis had begun to clear the Jews from the Warsaw ghetto. This was the most ambitious "clearance" operation to date. There were half a million Jews in the ghetto.

But it was only forty miles from the ghetto to the gates of Treblinka, and in a month almost 67,000 had been brought to the gas chambers and murdered upon their arrival.[7] With every deportation a precise timetable had been devised. Train loaded and dispatched. Arrived, unloaded, cleaned, returned empty to Warsaw. Repeat. Repeat. Repeat.

When Gerstein visited, three gas chambers were in use in Treblinka.[8] Wirth was once again his guide. The weight of work from the transports from Warsaw was beginning to take its toll. A sorting yard was covered with piles of clothing, shoes, and suitcases left by murdered Jews.

In the officers' mess, Wirth treated Pfannenstiel and Gerstein to a "Gothic banquet." Himmler had ordered that the visitors be spared nothing—meat, butter, alcohol. Someone raised a glass to the "humanity" of those running the camps. Within a few months Wirth himself would receive a promotion.

Outside the trains kept coming. Wirth was happy that Gerstein would report back favorably to Berlin. In truth, Treblinka had started to collapse under the chaos of clearing the ghetto, whose inmates were far from willing to accept their horrendous fate.

A week after Gerstein's visit a courageous young man from the town of Kielce, whose name does not appear to have been recorded, was stopped from giving his mother a final farewell embrace. He produced a knife and stabbed the Ukrainian guard standing between them.

In instant retribution the train was unloaded and everyone was machine-gunned.[9]

THERE WAS NO hiding place. Kurt Gerstein now knew exactly what was going on in the death camps of Poland. Despite dumping the Zyklon B containers, he had failed to save any lives. How could he disrupt such an industry of death?

The next day, while Pfannenstiel continued his tour, a car took Gerstein straight from Treblinka to Warsaw, where he caught the night train to

Berlin. He wandered to the sleeping car, searching for a bed, but it was full. There was another man in the corridor without a bed, too. A conductor told him he was a Swedish diplomat.

The man eyed him suspiciously, wondering if the SS man was following him.

At a station in a town an hour west of Warsaw, the train paused and the two men stepped onto the platform and took out cigarettes. Gerstein did not have a match and the other man passed across his box. It had the words "Swedish Consulate" on it. The words seemed to transfix the SS man. Lighting his cigarette, he said: "I want to talk to you. May I come and see you in Berlin?"

The Swedish diplomat—Baron Goran von Otter—might have been more suspicious now of a trap, but the sweat on Gerstein's forehead, the tears in his eyes, persuaded him. "Yesterday I saw something appalling." Gerstein was weeping now.

In hushed tones, Otter asked him what he meant. But Gerstein was sobbing, unable to say anything for the moment but "Etwas Furchtbares . . . Etwas Furchtbares . . ." "Something appalling . . ."

"Is it to do with the Jews?"

The train whistle blew, and the two men went back on board. They sat on the floor at the end of the corridor, where Gerstein slowly brought himself under control and passed Otter his identification papers and his orders. In the poor light of the blacked-out train, Otter slowly took in what they said. For hours the two men talked, Gerstein describing all that he had seen and begging Otter to tell his government. He gave Otter the names of the men running the camps and explained how he had come to be in the SS.

Gerstein's voice became loud, pleading, and Otter urged him to hush as someone might overhear. While Sweden was neutral, there were still many dangers, and Otter was actually returning from visiting a compatriot in a Warsaw jail. The man had been arrested by the Gestapo after having contact with the Polish resistance.[10]

The Swede was completely convinced of Gerstein's sincerity. He seemed brokenhearted. Otter again and again promised that he would speak to someone, but Gerstein went on. With each day thousands were dying, he said.

"If you tell the Allies then they can drop millions of leaflets all over

Germany so that the people will know what is happening and they'll rise up against Hitler."

Gerstein still wept as he spoke.[11]

AFTER RETURNING FROM Belzec and Treblinka, Kurt Gerstein spoke to anybody he trusted about what he had seen.

His colleague Horst Dickten had taken a room in Gerstein's apartment and received a call from Gerstein to pick him up from the railway station. At first Dickten could not find him as he had taken himself to a dark corner. He was still trembling, as he had been with Otter on the train. He staggered as he walked, and Dickten had to help him to his car. Back at the apartment he slumped onto the bed.

"You're ill," Dickten said. "I'll call Dr. Nissen."

Gerstein shook his head and began to cry. His housekeeper, Leokadia Hinz, a woman in her late fifties of Slavic origin, brought him hot, sweet tea. He sat up and refused to have the curtains opened. Dickten took his pulse and found that his heart was racing.

"It's not on my own account," Gerstein said, his voice weak. "Leave me alone now."

He slept until late in the afternoon, when he asked Dickten to read the Bible to him.

After a while Dickten could see that Gerstein's mind was elsewhere. He paused, and in the silence of the darkened room, the SS man said: "What pardon can there possibly be for men like that?"

Soon after, Gerstein appeared like the ancient mariner to tell his horror story to old friends. Late one night he knocked at the door of Otto Dibelius, the Protestant bishop who had officiated at Gerstein's wedding. The words came pouring out of him and he refused to sit down. He was tormented by a woman's voice from inside the gas chamber, he said. "Help us! Help us! Help us!"[12]

Gerstein visited his old friend Pastor Kurt Rehling and told the story of the camps while he sat in the man's kitchen in Hagen. Rehling was struck by the strange juxtaposition of Gerstein's story of the state crimes and the SS death's head emblem on his cap on the table in front of him. "You must realise that all this is a state secret," Gerstein said, his voice trembling. "Anyone who divulges it, and anyone who listens, is risking death. You and I are now both in danger of our lives."

Rehling leaned forward and urged his friend to "shout out the truth." "I must proclaim it from the pulpit!" the pastor said.

"No," Gerstein said, throwing up his hands. "Not a newspaper would report it. There would simply be a news item the next day saying that a respected Protestant pastor had had to be hurriedly removed to a mental hospital. And there you'd be forced to give me away, and my friends as well, and we wouldn't be able to help anyone."

Gerstein's assessment was probably right, of course, but how much of his fear about speaking out was moral cowardice? That question agonized him.

"Perhaps we ought to be thinking less of our chances of success and more of our moral duty," Rehling told him.

Gerstein told him he was carrying cyanide in a ring, as he was afraid of endangering others. "If I'm caught I shall use it to make sure I don't betray my friends. Under torture a man will say anything."

GERSTEIN WAITED PATIENTLY for news from the Swedish embassy. Otter must have got the news out by now, but there had been nothing on the BBC and no leaflets had been dropped by the RAF.

In desperation and aware that foreign embassies in Berlin were watched by the Gestapo, Gerstein decided to make contact with Otter. In civilian clothes he spent hours waiting near the Swedish embassy, keeping to side streets nearby and not directly outside. Otter recognized him immediately.

After their meeting on the train, Otter had taken Gerstein seriously. He had made discreet checks on the SS man with Dr. Otto Dibelius, a friend of Niemöller's who had been a leading figure in the Confessing Church. Then, satisfied that Gerstein was a genuine anti-Nazi despite his role in the Waffen-SS, Otter had made a full report to the Swedish government. The report had been met with a sense of disbelief, and for fear of aggravating their relationship with Hitler, it would not be forwarded to London until after the war ended. Sweden did, though, leave open its borders for Jews seeking to escape.

Gerstein also contacted the Swiss legation in Berlin. The Swiss—surrounded as they were by the forces of fascism—were afraid of antagonizing Hitler. They were also reluctant to accept Jewish refugees. The German Red Cross had been taken over by the Nazis—and Gerstein would later report its president, Ernst-Robert Grawitz, to the Allies for being a key figure in the concentration camp movement.[13]

Later, Gerstein contacted his Dutch friend Ubbink, the engineer who had given him his copy of Rauschning's *Hitler Speaks*, and asked him to get a message to the Dutch resistance. Ubbink spoke to an underground leader who did not believe Gerstein's story and decided not to tell London.

The papal nuncio in Berlin was Archbishop Cesare Orsenigo. The pope's representative in Germany had sought not to interfere in the running of Hitler's state, and preached a policy of "compromise and conciliation" with the Third Reich. He was unlikely to help, although Gerstein did not know that. For Gerstein the pope offered a voice that could not be ignored by the world and that, even during war, might affect the attitudes of Adolf Hitler.

Gerstein made no appointment with the nuncio, fearing a request would be refused. Instead he turned up one day and in uniform. Gerstein told an official why he wanted to see Orsenigo, but the man appeared uninterested. "Are you a soldier?" the man asked. Gerstein explained who he was. After consulting with Orsenigo, the officials had Gerstein removed from the building.[14]

When Gerstein got home to his apartment, he slumped into a chair, smoking and drinking brandy. His face was so pale that Dickten asked him if someone had "given him away."

"It's worse than that," Gerstein told him. "I've lost my last hope."

IN AUGUST 1942, word did reach the United States of the extermination of the Jews and of the use of prussic acid in Belzec, via the World Jewish Congress. In addition, Jan Karski, a member of the Polish resistance, managed to escape to London with details of Operation Reinhard, and was seen by Foreign Secretary Anthony Eden and later in Washington by Roosevelt. On December 17, 1942, the Allies put out their first official statement of the war denouncing the Nazi killing of Jews.[15] "Those responsible for these crimes shall not escape punishment," the Allies declared.

At Christmas 1942 Pope Pius XII referred to "persons condemned to death solely for reasons of nationality or race," without referring specifically to Jews. By this time Gerstein had made one final effort with the Catholic Church, having secured a meeting with an assistant to Bishop Konrad Preysing, of Berlin, who was a significant opponent of the Nazis. The assistant had promised to pass the message on to the bishop and the pope. Gerstein never found out if this promise was kept.

Despite the condemnation from the Allies, there had been no plan to target the German people with pamphlets explaining what was going on in the concentration camps and no mention of a way in which to rescue the Jewish people of occupied Europe.

KURT GERSTEIN HAD joined the Waffen-SS to investigate the crimes of the euthanasia program and to bear witness.

Meaningful efforts to tell foreign governments and the pope appeared to have failed. The strain was destroying him, and he found himself pleading with friends to pass on his message. "Helmut," he told a friend, Helmut Franz, "you must tell people."

There were also elements of resignation setting in. He had once hoped to get an old friend from his Bible Circle days to join in and support him in his work at the Institute of Hygiene. He had hoped Herbert Eickhoff might bear witness, too. The SS had turned down Eickhoff's application.

After Treblinka, he visited Eickhoff and talked about what he had seen. "He was full of shame and fury and horror," Eickhoff said later.

Thinking about how Eickhoff had failed to come to work with him, Gerstein said: "Thank God! I can never tell you how thankful I am that you didn't get into the Institute of Hygiene."

Another old friend asked, how was it possible for a Christian and a man of honor to stand and watch the horrors he had seen?

"The machine has been set in motion, and I can't stop it," Gerstein told him. "It's something to have seen it with my own eyes, so that someday I can testify to it."

At work Gerstein became short-tempered and angry. On Christmas Eve the Institute of Hygiene held a staff party during which Gerstein stormed off. After a long search Dickten eventually found him and took him to an institute doctor who lived on the edge of the city. Gerstein disappeared again and was found in the woods nearby. He was standing with his back against a tree with a pistol in his hand. He was trapped between the need to escape the horror he had seen—which kept repeating itself over and over in his head—and the desire to stay alive to tell the tale. Remember everything, forget nothing, he told himself. But the remembering was a pain almost too difficult to endure.

The doctor reported everything to the chief, Mrugowsky, who callously resolved to push Gerstein deeper and deeper in his work. Gerstein was sent to Ravensbrück and Buchenwald to inspect the camps and report back, and then was asked to prepare further consignments of gas for Auschwitz, the immense extermination center where more than a million would die, and for Oranienburg. Each time Gerstein kept his own name on the paperwork so he could keep control of the delivery and if possible sabotage it. He included instructions that these deliveries were to be used for "disinfection purposes" only and not for the gas chambers. He told a female friend, Alexandra Bälz, who was anti-Nazi: "All I can do is to get rid of the prussic acid before it reaches its destination, or render it useless. But how many times will I get away with it?"[16]

On one delivery to Globocnik, Gerstein took control of the delivery truck while his escort slept and ran the vehicle off the road. Slightly injured, he told the other man that the containers were now dangerous and would need to be buried at the roadside.[17] He later told his wife the truth and said that while burying the acid he had splashed the sleeve of his tunic and had to take it off as quickly as possible.[18]

These actions were his attempt to interfere in the process of mass murder, but Gerstein knew they did nothing to hold back the tide. There were other deliveries, more gas. The chambers went on killing.[19]

IG Farben owned 42.5 percent of Degesch, the company with the monopoly for making Zyklon B. The period since the Wannsee conference had been good for business. IG's dividends on its Degesch investment for the years 1942, 1943, and 1944 were double those of 1940 and 1941.[20]

# 25

## The Hunted

WITH GOEBBELS DEMANDING constant updates on the investigation into the firebombing of his *Soviet Paradise* exhibition in the heart of Berlin, a huge number of officers were now questioning Jews, "trouble-makers," and factory workers.

Many had heard the reckless Joachim Franke boast about his role in the resistance against Hitler, and in inquiries, his name came up more than once. Four days after the attack, agents went to the AEG factory in Oberschöneweide on the outskirts of the city and arrested the thirty-seven-year-old in the machine shop where he worked as an engineer.

Taken to Gestapo headquarters, Franke took a cigarette from his interrogator and—perhaps hoping for leniency or with a sense of bragging bravado—he began to name those who had helped him.

As officers listened, they sent a team to Siemens, where Herbert Baum, Marianne Cohn, Gerhard Meyer, and Heinz Rotholz were arrested.

In another part of the building Heinz Joachim heard about the arrests and waited anxiously for the Gestapo to come for him, but they did not.

Instead, they went to the Kaiser Wilhelm Institute and arrested Werner Steinbrink in the very laboratory where he had mixed the chemicals for the incendiary devices.

The Gestapo units then spent the next twenty-four hours sweeping up Franke's friends: Karl Kunger, the typesetter George Vötter and his wife Charlotte, Hilde Jadamowitz and Hans Mannaberg, and Franke's wife, Erika. Back at AEG again, they brought in Franke's workmates Walter Bernecker and Artur Illgen, who had painted anti-Hitler slogans on walls around Berlin. Irene Walther and the translator Suzanne Wesse were arrested at their homes.[1]

On May 23, staff at the Jewish kindergarten on Jerusalemer Strasse opened the door to the Gestapo. They had come to take Sala Rosenbaum away. The school's director, Debra Bahnmüller, a Jew married to an Aryan, telephoned Martin Kochmann and told him not to go home. Aware that the line might be tapped, she told him that his wife was ill and he should go to a house in Auguststrasse. Rushing to the address, he found Frau Bahnmüller and his friend Jacob Berger waiting for him. Berger agreed to go to Kochmann's flat to get him some money and clothes. He also took away a box of illegal books. The Gestapo did not appear to be watching.

Kochmann went to warn Charlotte Paech—an old friend of the Baums' who worked as a nurse and was a committed antifascist—and her partner, Richard Holzer, on Zechliner Strasse. Warnings were then passed to Heinz Birnbaum and Felix Heymann. At midnight on May 24, two days after the first arrests, the five of them and Heinz Joachim met at Alexanderplatz. All had been involved in antifascist activities for as long as they could remember, and the area around the huge railway station was where many of them had met to discuss politics. Then, it had been almost like a game; now, they were the hunted.

Huddled in the shadows, whispering and smoking heavily, they tried to work out their next move. What evidence did the Gestapo have against the Baums, Kochmann's wife, Sala, Birnbaum's girlfriend, Irene, and the others? What could they do to help their friends?

Birnbaum mentioned the cache of materials in the basement of Baum's building on Stralauer Strasse. There were all the items they had used for the leaflets and pamphlets—the duplicating machine, paper, and ink. Paint, too. Then there were some of the carpets they had taken in the fake Gestapo raid, and a pistol that Alfred Eisenstädter had left when he escaped Germany. There was enough there to hang Baum and Cohn, and maybe the others, and perhaps lead the Gestapo to them as well.

Late the next night Kochmann, Heymann, and Birnbaum walked quickly to Baum's house and crept into the cellar. There they packed everything into sacks and dragged them three hundred yards to the Waisenbrücke, which crossed the Spree at Rolandufer. Waiting near the blacked-out wrought iron lampposts on the nineteenth-century bridge were Richard Holzer, Heinz Joachim, and Hella Hirsch.

Walking down the steps to the riverbank in the shadow of the bridge, they dropped the pistol, duplicating machine, paper, and flyers into the water. Some money was split, and Holzer took some cartons of cigarettes.

Heymann, Kochmann, and Birnbaum each took a suitcase with some of the carpets from the theft. They were valuable and might still be sold to get funds to support them on the run. Heymann took his suitcase to a friend's house and asked him to store it for him, while Kochmann checked his into a luggage storage area at the Gesundbrunnen train station in Wedding.

Kochmann then traveled to see a friend of the French-speaking Suzanne Wesse among the foreign workers at a factory in Spandau and bought a Belgian identity card in the name of Alfons Buys. He spent the night at Charlotte Paech's flat.

The next morning he borrowed Richard Holzer's bicycle and rode to the nearest train station. Storing the bike on the train, he traveled to Potsdam. From there he cycled sixty miles to Brandenburg and took another train bound for Hanover. He was almost halfway there when he was challenged by a railway policeman and could not produce a work-leave pass. Arrested and sent to Magdeburg, he was told he would be sent back to Berlin.

The police had him, but they still believed he was a Belgian worker named Buys.

KOCHMANN'S WIFE, SALA Rosenbaum, was in a cell in the Polizeipräsidium Berlin on Alexanderstrasse, an imposing four-story building alongside the railway station. A prisoner of the Gestapo, she had been given no food since her arrest and was not allowed to sleep. Aware that she was worried about her husband, two agents stood outside and discussed him in loud voices.

"Thank God the Jew Kochmann is dead," one said.

"Good riddance," said another.[2]

Exhausted, Rosenbaum went into deep despair. With her long history in Jewish and left-wing youth groups, she knew as many names as Baum. She had, in many ways, been a coleader of his group. Determined not to give away her friends, she decided on drastic action.

The next time the door opened she was ready. She raced out of the darkness of her cell, shoved past the guard, and threw herself over the banister and down a stairwell.

AFTER DUMPING THE gun in the river at the Waisenbrücke, Heinz Birnbaum had gone to Harry Cühn's house on Lietzenburger Strasse, close to the scene of the fake Gestapo robbery.

Knowing that, whatever his friends said in their interrogation, the alarm would be raised because he had failed to turn up at work, he took a chance to contact Ellen Lewinsky, the woman who had helped him smuggle the detonator out of the factory they worked in.

He was waiting for her in the darkened staircase of her apartment building when she came home. She said the Gestapo had been to the factory looking for him, and so, although there had been no news in the press about the attack, she had assumed it had gone ahead. She had also assumed he had escaped to France as planned. He said he still planned to but needed her help.

"I still have papers in the apartment—on the bookcase," he said quickly. "They have to be taken out. Will you do it?"

Once again the nineteen-year-old agreed to help her friend. He made her memorize an address to which she should go afterwards.

"With a little luck we'll see each other again." He smiled, and ran down the stairs.

Lewinsky was taking a terrible risk. Birnbaum was high on the Gestapo's wanted list. There was every chance his home could be watched.

She knocked at his house and, when the landlady answered, told her she needed to take away some of Heinz's possessions. She knew straightaway the police were not there as the landlady said, "Is he in trouble?"

"I think so," Lewinsky said.

"Quick, come in."

Lewinsky grabbed the items and stuffed them into a shopping bag. Removing her yellow star, she took the U-Bahn to the address Birnbaum had given her and knocked on the door. It was opened by a man she did not know.

"I was told to give you this," she said.

"I know. Thank you very much."[3]

The door closed quickly on her, and she hurried away. She never saw her friend Heinz Birnbaum again.

CHARLOTTE PAECH HAD been destined to go into nursing. As a child, she had suffered from rickets and tuberculosis but had not received the greatest of care. She had vowed that she would study medicine and be sure she did better for others. By seventeen she had left home, living in nursing quarters and mixing with Herbert Baum, Marianne Cohn, and Sala Rosenbaum.

But she had never met Joachim Franke and had avoided any association with the arson attack, so when the roundups came, she was able to continue her job at the Jewish hospital on Exerzier Strasse unmolested. She was about to finish a shift there when the Gestapo appeared with a prisoner on a stretcher. Paech recognized the unconscious figure immediately: It was Sala Rosenbaum.

Although the Gestapo gave the nurses no explanation of what had happened, Rosenbaum's suicide attempt at the police station had been thwarted by some netting stretched across the stairwell. It had partially broken her fall, but she had still suffered terrible injuries, including a broken spine and fractured skull. As the Gestapo had no knowledge of a connection between the two women, Paech was able to tend to Rosenbaum when she regained consciousness. She was able to whisper to Paech that the group had been betrayed by Joachim Franke. A rumor had spread that Franke had been an informer for the Gestapo—although this has never been proven. "Everyone's been arrested," Rosenbaum whispered, in agony on every word she spoke. "I don't know what's happened to Martin."

With the Gestapo on guard on the ward, there was nothing Paech could do for her friend but keep her as comfortable as possible. With her injuries there would be no chance of escape.

SALA ROSENBAUM'S HUSBAND, Martin Kochmann, had been brought back to Alexanderplatz and was now in the same police station where she had tried to take her own life.

Held in a large locked hall packed with foreign prisoners, Kochmann sat quietly, shrugging his shoulders when people spoke, wondering how he could persuade the police that he was the Belgian worker he claimed to be. He looked at the grimy, tired group around him and wondered what their crimes had been. Just being foreign, he supposed. Then he thought about Sala and his friends. They had been in Gestapo hands for days now. It was too horrible to imagine what might be happening to them. Richard Holzer's words came back to him, his fears about the Nazi reaction to the arson attack. Reprisals, he'd talked about. It was too horrible to think about, and he was too tired.

He folded his jacket for a pillow and tried to sleep on the hard wooden bench.

THE GESTAPO REPORTED the arrests to Goebbels, who, six days after the arson attack, referred in his diary to this "club of saboteurs and assassins"—a mix of "Jews, half-Jews and Aryans."[4] He added later: "Now I'll accomplish my war against the Jews of Berlin. I've ordered the preparation of a list of Jewish hostages . . . Ten Jews in a detention camp or under the ground are better than one of them who is free."

Then, on May 27, news reached Berlin that Reinhard Heydrich had been gravely injured in the attack by Czechs in Prague. The Nazi hierarchy immediately linked this audacious attack on one of the most senior figures in the Reich with the arson in the center of Berlin. The remaining Jews in Berlin represented "an invitation to assassinations," Goebbels wrote. "I don't want to be shot in the belly by some 22-year-old Ostjude like one of those types who are among the perpetrators of the attack against the anti-Soviet exhibition."[5]

Revenge would be swift. Five hundred Jewish men were rounded up, and half were sent to either the SS barracks at Lichterfelde or Sachsenhausen concentration camp, where they were immediately shot. Another 250 were imprisoned in the same camp or sent to Auschwitz. None are known to have returned. The families of 154 of the men were shipped to Theresienstadt, a ghetto in Czechoslovakia that for many was only a disease-ridden stop on the way to Auschwitz.

On May 28, the director of the Jewish hospital called all of his staff together and told them gravely that five hundred of their community had been arrested in response to the arson attack.

Charlotte Paech left the meeting and went back to tend to her friend Sala Rosenbaum. She could not bring herself to tell her of the wrath being brought down on Berlin's Jews.

THE MASS EXECUTIONS and deportations had not included any of those involved in the attack, some of whom remained on the run.

Twenty-one-year-old Heinz Birnbaum's days of freedom were coming to an end, though. While hiding at the home of Harry Cühn, he received a message to say that Werner Steinbrink wanted to meet him at the Kaiser Wilhelm Institute. Unknown to Birnbaum, Steinbrink had been in custody for well over a week. The message had been sent by a Gestapo informer. When Birnbaum went to the grand building in Dahlem, the Gestapo was waiting.

Others among the group were staying free by using the false identity cards the group had bought and stored, and by sheltering in a small network of illegally rented flats that Baum had kept as safe houses.

Heinz Joachim and Marianne Prager, who had now been married nine months, were hiding in a summer cottage in Petershagen that had been rented with false papers by Gerhard Meyer's wife, Hanni. Hanni had been inconsolable since Gerhard's arrest but had been talked out of going underground by her family, who said going on the run would look like an admission of guilt. Consequently, when the Gestapo came for Hanni Meyer on June 3, she had nowhere to hide.

A search of Meyer's home by the Gestapo led to discovery of the Petershagen cottage. On June 9, Heinz and Marianne—who still dreamed one day of seeing the little sister she had said good-bye to on the Kindertransport—were arrested.

FELIX HEYMANN AND his girlfriend, Hella Hirsch, seemed to have beaten the odds. Posing as two French workers, they were staying in a Baum group flat in Fredersdorf. Hirsch's teenage sister, Alice, who had been trying to make some money as a cleaner, was in another of the group's rooms in Glienicke but would later move in with them.

For days Heymann and Hirsch barely dared to leave their flat, but they had no money and little food. Heymann sneaked out and asked friends for work. A Hungarian friend helped him a little, and one evening in their hiding place, Heymann and Hirsch decided to get married. The wedding was held in secret with barely a witness. Hella, who was twenty years old, told a friend that they wanted to do it in case their lives were cut short.

During the second week in June the newly married couple began to wonder if the arrests were over. Hungry and isolated, they decided to return to their jobs at the IG Farben factory, where they were forced laborers. They were greeted with a wedding gift from their coworkers and settled back into their shifts. But the special Gestapo team tasked with tracking down the saboteurs was still on the case, and on July 8 Heymann wandered into the building where he lived and was warned by the landlady that the police were looking for him. Unable to warn Hella or her sister, Alice, he went to see an old non-Jewish friend named Wolfgang Knabe, who worked on the railways at Wedding. The friend agreed to put him up for a few days.

At the factory, two Gestapo men handcuffed Hella Hirsch and took her to Alt Moabit, a nineteenth-century prison that the Nazis used as a detention center for political prisoners. Hella's sister was brought in the same day, as was Harry Cühn's fiancée, Edith Fraenkel.

A week later Lothar Salinger, Helmut Neumann, and Siegbert and Lotte Rotholz were arrested. The Rotholzes were suffering from scarlet fever and had to be dragged from their beds. Hildegard Loewy was arrested at home in front of her mother. As the Gestapo burst into her home, she kissed a photograph of her boyfriend, who was living nearby, and hid it between the pages of a book.

THE GESTAPO CELLS were now full, and the prosecutor at the Sondergericht—National Socialist Special Court—prepared his case for trial. The question of guilt for the Baum group would be a foregone conclusion, but how many would face the death penalty?

Herbert Baum had already suffered the wrath of Himmler's secret police. Identified very quickly as the ringleader, Baum could expect little mercy from the Gestapo, and he received none. He was seen only once after his arrest, when officers took him to the Siemens factory where he had worked. He had already been beaten, and his face was a bloody pulp.[6] The macabre parade around the site was staged in the hope that other associates would give themselves away, perhaps by trying to bolt. Nobody did. The Gestapo turned on Baum and asked him to identify his coconspirators. He said nothing.[7]

The Gestapo kept no record of its interrogation of Herbert Baum, but it appears to have reserved its most severe methods for him. Gestapo torture was less common on German prisoners than on those in the occupied territories, but Baum—the man who had humiliated the Nazi elite—was both a Communist and a Jew. Special permission was generally required for "intensified interrogation" but not, according to rules laid down by Heydrich in 1941, when applied to "Communist or Marxist functionaries, Jehovah's Witnesses and saboteurs."[8] Anything up to twenty-five strokes with a bamboo cane was permissible on any prisoner, but Baum could expect far worse: being plunged into a cold bath until he could barely breathe; having electrical wires attached to his hands and genitals; suffering a device based on a garlic press applied to his testicles; being hung from the ceiling by his hands.[9] On June 11, 1942, after three weeks in custody, Baum died. Most likely the torture went too far, although as in all such cases the Gestapo recorded his death as a suicide. The day after his death, Gestapo chief Heinrich Müller changed the rules on intensified interrogation "for simplicity's sake" so it could be used in cases where a prisoner had "important facts concerning hostility to the state and nation" but was unwilling to reveal them.[10]

Herbert Baum, who had led one of the most significant groups of resisters in Germany, a group that united women and men, Jews and non-Jews, died in the darkness of a Gestapo cell. He was thirty. His friends now faced the charade that presented itself as Nazi justice.

THE FIRST TRIAL of the Baum group took place at the Sondergericht V in Berlin on July 16 and included the core members who had been arrested early on. All were accused of high treason. Sala Rosenbaum—unable to walk after breaking her back in her suicide attempt—had to be carried into court on a stretcher.

She was sentenced to death.

As were Baum's wife, Marianne Cohn; Sala's best friend, Suzanne Wesse, whose language skills had helped the group make contacts with foreign workers; Hilde Jadamowitz; Heinz Joachim; Hans Mannaberg; Gerhard Meyer, who had married his fiancée, Hanni, only seven months earlier; Werner Steinbrink; and Irene Walther.

Joachim Franke, who many of his co-accused considered their betrayer, was also in the dock and was also sentenced to death. If there had been any agreement with the Gestapo, it had not saved him.

SALA ROSENBAUM'S HUSBAND, Martin Kochmann, was in custody, but the Germans still believed he was a Belgian worker. He spent six weeks in the detention hall at Alexanderplatz before he was given a hearing in front of a judge.

Presenting his papers as "Alfons Buys," Kochmann said he was the son of a German woman who had become homesick and wanted to return to Belgium. He said he was a good worker and not a troublemaker. Inquiries were made at the factory in Spandau at which Buys supposedly worked, and a foreman was brought to the court by a police officer. The man, who was Dutch, was asked by the court if he recognized Buys. Kochmann's heart sank: He knew his charade must be over. But the Dutchman nodded and said, "Yes, this is Buys." The judge thanked the man and turned Buys over into the Dutchman's supervision to return to the forced-labor factory. The pair got as far as the S-Bahn station without a word and then Kochmann said: "It would be a shame for you to waste your money on a fare for me."[11]

The Dutchman smiled, waved good-bye, and hopped on the train back to Spandau.

Wondering who else might be still at large, Kochmann headed straight back to the flat owned by the nurse Charlotte Paech on Soldiner Strasse. He found that her partner, Richard Holzer, had used his Hungarian passport to escape to Hungary and that she was hoping to follow him. However, for the moment, Paech was going through her own agonies, not related to her Baum group work but to an incident that had happened earlier that year. A Jewish woman had needed an abortion as her Aryan husband had threated to divorce her. Separation would have put her and her other children in danger of arrest. Paech had allowed her kitchen to be used for the procedure. It had gone ahead successfully, but the doctor had been denounced. He, the woman, and her children were sent to a concentration camp. Paech was arrested and received a one-month prison sentence that had been deferred due to her hospital work. Now she was waiting for the court to contact her to say the sentence had to be served.

Paech's ex-husband, Gustav, a former trade unionist, agreed to help his former wife. The couple had separated after his descent into alcoholism following a period in Gestapo detention for leading a railway strike. He still loved her; she was fond of him. Gustav agreed to look after her flat and their daughter, Eva—who, now aged nine, had been born a few months after Hitler came to power—and to keep stalling the court and prison authorities over her sentence.

Paech was worried that her ex-husband might get into trouble, but she was desperate and agreed to his plan. She and Kochmann went into hiding, first in the center of Berlin and then in the farming town of Kummersdorf, about twenty miles south of the city. On August 18, eager to see her daughter, she returned to Berlin and called with a friend. There was terrible news: The prison authorities had lost patience with Gustav, and the Gestapo had arrested him. No one knew where little Eva was, and, in hiding, Paech had no way of finding out.

Out of her mind with worry, she wandered down the street near her flat, too afraid to knock on the door to speak to a neighbor.

As she walked, she saw Jewish friends gathering around a poster edged with a thick red line. When everyone had moved on, taking care not to be seen, she took a look and felt her legs buckle.

It was the announcement that ten people—those tried on July 16—had been executed at Plötzensee. She turned away, stunned, and staggered down the street.

PLÖTZENSEE PRISON, WHERE so many of the Third Reich's enemies of state met their end, stood on a large expanse of land covering the size of about thirty soccer fields, where fashionable Charlottenburg met the working-class area of Wedding.

Dating from the nineteenth century, the prison had become—since 1933—a facility for pretrial confinement for persons arraigned on political charges. Most were due to come before the Nazi regime's Special Courts or the People's Court, but it was also a place of execution. The war years had seen an increase in the numbers of political suspects awaiting execution and foreign forced laborers who had fallen foul of the regime. From 1890 to 1932, there were thirty-six people executed at Plötzensee; between 1933 and 1945, there were 2,891.[12] About half of those executed were Germans, most of whom had been sentenced to death for acts of resistance against the state.

From the air, the main building of the prison, known as House III, resembled a large cross. It was here that condemned prisoners were brought immediately before their sentence was to be carried out. The special cells on the ground floor where the condemned would be shackled had become known as the "house of the dead." Their final steps would then take them outside through a small courtyard and to the execution shed, where, for women, the Fallbeil, or guillotine—deemed to be a more humane form of execution—was waiting. The redbrick building they would pass included a chapel, an infirmary, and dormitories for prison staff.

The first ten to die from the Baum group had faced the guillotine. On August 18 they came through House III one by one. In a corridor they were allowed a final cigarette together. One of them offered one to Joachim Franke, who, eyes filled with tears, said, "You do this for me, now?"[13]

In the execution shed waited Ernst Reindel, a stocky man in his early forties who wore dark trousers, a top hat, and tails. One of Nazi Germany's three state executioners, Reindel had been proficient in carrying out the state's will with an axe until the numbers of deaths had become such that the guillotine was preferable.

Reindel dispatched the ten condemned in thirty-seven minutes, between 5:00 and 5:37 a.m. Prison officials noted that he and his three helpers had shown remarkable efficiency, especially when they took into account the fact that Sala Rosenbaum had been unable to walk and had to be wheeled into the chamber. Paralyzed from the neck down, Rosenbaum had been unable to position herself under the blade, and so the men had had to lift her into place.

The executioners at Plötzensee received a 60-Reichsmark bonus for each execution. The families of the dead were invoiced for expenses. The public prosecutors charged 1.50 Reichsmarks for each day in custody in the prison, 300 Reichsmarks for the execution, and 12 pfennigs to cover the cost of posting the invoice.

KEY MEMBERS OF Baum's group remained on the run. Felix Heymann was hopping between different friends' homes in Berlin and in the countryside nearby. He spent two weeks of July in a hayloft, and August and September sleeping on friends' floors. Every person who gave him shelter, and there were at least half a dozen, was risking their life.

Charlotte Paech had returned to the countryside around Kummersdorf after the shock of finding that her friends had been executed, her ex-husband arrested, and her young daughter missing. Sitting in a field one August afternoon, she saw a German in Luftwaffe uniform approach her across a field. Knowing there was a base nearby, she hoped the man was just being social and that appeared to be the case.[14] He asked to sit with her, shared some food, and chatted about trivial things. Before he left, he asked if he could see her again, but she said she was returning to Berlin the following day.

Paech traveled to Berlin to look after her friend Rita Meyer, who had a fever. Rita's husband, Herbert, was also ill, and they were also now harboring Martin Kochmann.

One day there was a heavy banging on the door and everyone thought their time had come. Rita answered while the others hid, daring not to breathe. After a few moments she closed the door and came back into the room. The tension was broken by dark humor: The Gestapo had been looking for the Jews who lived next door, and had seemed quite unaware that they were calling at a house harboring two wanted fugitives.

But a Gestapo game was afoot, designed to use the last of those on the run to incriminate others. Paech's ex-husband, Gustav, had been beaten and tortured, and had revealed the names of friends, incriminating himself and others. He had since been sent to Sachsenhausen.

On October 7, the Gestapo decided they had given the others enough rope. They banged on the door of the Meyers' flat again—and this time it was for real. Trapped, Charlotte Paech asked to be allowed to use the bathroom.

As she was about to shut the door, a Gestapo man grabbed her purse from her hand and shook it open: A dose of poison from the hospital fell out. He turned on Paech, beating her to the floor before a colleague dragged her out and threw her into a van alongside the Meyers.

Kochmann had been out when they called but returned later, unaware of the danger. He knocked and was let in by the Gestapo. He had been on the run for more than three months, but now his freedom was ended.

LESS THAN A week after the arrests at the Meyers' flat, the Gestapo finally caught up with Felix Heymann, who had been skipping from friend to friend. Like Paech he tried to kill himself on arrest and almost succeeded—cutting his throat with a razor blade. He was taken to the Jewish hospital, and his life was saved by nursing staff under Gestapo supervision.

On the floor occupied by the Gestapo at the Alexanderplatz Polizeipräsidium, Charlotte Paech was put in an office to await interrogation. She tensed as she heard heavy boots in the corridor, and the door swung open. In came the "Luftwaffe" man she had met in the field. He was Gestapo, and they had been following her the whole time, hoping she would give away Richard Holzer—now in Hungary—or others. The man who had flirted with her turned out to be a brutal and sadistic Nazi. In an interrogation that lasted through the night, he broke her jaw. He told her that they already knew everything so she might as well speak. She refused. She was given no bread or water, and allowed no sleep. The torture was repeated the following night, and again, and again. In the end, instead of making continual denials, she fell completely silent.

After three weeks they stopped coming to her cell block to take her away for questioning.

The second trial of the Baum group took place in December 1942. Harry Cühn, the black marketeer whose fiancée, Edith Fraenkel, was among the accused, had arranged a worthy defense attorney for them—something not normally seen in a Nazi courtroom.

Heinz Birnbaum and Heinz Rotholz had both been tortured in the weeks before the trial but had given nothing away.

When he appeared before the court, Birnbaum had just turned twenty-two, and in many ways he was still a child at heart. He had never learned to cook for himself, preferred chocolate to any other kind of food, and called everyone either "girl" or "buddy" from behind his boyish grin.[15] But he had stayed in Berlin when his mother had left because even as a young teenager he had been committed to fighting Hitler, and he showed maturity and commitment when he faced the judge in the Special Court. "We are here not as political fighters," he said. "We have been condemned as Jews."[16]

The defense attorney, a First World War veteran named Masius, managed to successfully argue that three of the accused should receive prison terms: Lotte Rotholz, eight years; Edith Fraenkel, five years; Alice Hirsch, aged just nineteen, three years. He also launched an appeal when the others—for the "protection of the people and Reich"—were condemned to death.

The condemned were Birnbaum, whose lover, Irene Walther, had already been executed; Hella Hirsch, Alice's older sister, who had married Felix Heymann while on the run; Marianne Prager, whose sister had escaped on the Kindertransport; Hildegard Loewy, who despite only having one arm had tried to escape out of a window of the jail;[17] Hanni Meyer, whose husband, Gerhard, had already been executed; Helmuth Neumann, a friend of Joachim Franke's; Heinz Rotholz; Lotte's husband, Siegbert Rotholz; and Lothar Salinger.

The court had heard statements of remarkable courage from them all. Heinz Rotholz stated: "I knew about the preparations of the sabotage action against the 'Soviet Paradise.' Had the comrades not excluded me from the act because of my Jewish appearance, I would have gone to the exhibit and taken part."

Lotte Rotholz told the Gestapo: "One must utilize every opportunity to fight against the present regime. One thing was clear to me: as a Jew I must not lag behind . . . My ties were and remain with Baum."[18]

Music-loving Marianne Prager wrote in her last letter to her mother and father: "Think of the songs we all sang together—all is fine! Live well, my beloved parents!"[19]

All spent the winter in Plötzensee prison. Ellen Lewinsky, the friend of Birnbaum who had smuggled a detonator out of the factory for him, received a note from him saying he was freezing in his cell. She knitted a sweater and gloves, and they were smuggled in to him.

On March 4, 1943, Wilhelm Röttger readied himself for a long day at work with a series of cigarettes. Another of the main three Nazi executioners, the chain-smoker was two days short of his forty-ninth birthday. Working bare-chested, he prepared the guillotine with efficiency, allowed the prison pastor to say his last prayer with the condemned, and then carried out his work.

When the blade had fallen, he turned to the representative of the court who was present and stated formally: "Herr Staatsanwalt, das Urteil ist Vollstreckt." "Mr. Prosecutor, the verdict is enforced."[20]

He said it ten times that day as Birnbaum and the others from the second trial were executed.

The bodies of Hella Hirsch and Marianne Prager were among those supplied to the University of Berlin's Institute of Anatomy, where Dr. Hermann Stieve had become one of the most influential specialists in his field despite the fact that many of the bodies with which he was supplied during the Nazi era were headless.

# 26

# Hitler's Bloodhound

MANFRED ROEDER WAS the forty-two-year-old son of a district judge from Kiel whose boyish looks belied a cold, unfeeling, and abusive personality. Holding the position Oberkriegsgerichtsrat—a judge advocate with a colonel's rank—Roeder was a rising star, handling the most difficult cases, and a protégé of Hermann Göring. A teenage soldier during the First World War, he had worked in the district court before joining the military judiciary.

His obsession was with the preservation of government authority, a cause for which he would bully, trick, and sarcastically bait defendants. Canny in court, he was also a clever detective who would pursue his quarry to the end. He was to be the chief investigator and prosecutor in the Berlin Rote Kapelle case.

Göring personally picked Roeder. The Luftwaffe chief felt humiliated by the case. He had been a mentor to Schulze-Boysen and an admirer of his wife. Determined to make them pay, he traveled to Vinnitsa in Ukraine on his command train to find Roeder, who was working as a chief legal officer for Luftwaffe Air Fleet 4. The area stank of death: The Einsatzgruppen were carrying out their orders to murder every Ukrainian Jew. Roeder's role as a lawyer in the area was not to stop or investigate such murders; he was there to prosecute soldiers who did not carry out their orders.

Roeder saw immediately what the Rote Kapelle case could do for his career. Göring's anger showed how the scandal had struck at the heart of the regime, involving not Jews like the Baum group but people considered the highly educated Berlin elite. The fact that it had been decided the trials would be heard in the Reich Court-Martial, the highest military court, and not the People's Court was both an honor and an opportunity. For the first time in Nazi legal history, the sentences of the court would be passed to Hitler for his review and his confirmation.[1]

In November 1942, Roeder received more than thirty volumes of Gestapo reports, which he took several weeks to work through and summarize in an indictment, in which he dismissed the group as "Communist fanatics, disoriented introverts . . . and disillusioned bourgeois."[2]

As he worked, the brave soldiers of the German Sixth Army got hammered at Stalingrad.

Roeder recognized that to satisfy the regime and the nation, it would be necessary to not just convict these people; they must be humiliated, too. The only mistake he could make would be to show leniency.

BURIED UNDER PAPERWORK, Roeder put the files on Harro Schulze-Boysen, Arvid Harnack, and Adam Kuckhoff to one side.

All three had confessed under torture to passing secrets to the Soviets. That was high treason and meant the death penalty. There was also some evidence that early on Harnack and Kuckhoff had received financial expenses from the Soviets—and so therefore they could be portrayed as traitors for hire. Roeder made a note that he would describe these as the "wages of treachery" in court. The case was sealed. Harnack's brother, Falk, and his friend Egmont Zechlin were making appeals on his behalf, but they would come to nothing.

The Gestapo report was deliberately prurient, seeking to paint the group as debased and depraved, an aberration in Nazi society. To policeman Strübing, the men were libertines and the women seductresses, thus removing any sense of gallantry from their actions. Libertas Schulze-Boysen and Mildred Fish-Harnack were depicted both as lesbian lovers and man-hungry nymphomaniacs. The strangely puritanical Roeder found evidence of Libertas's affairs and the fact that she had posed naked as an artists' model for the Schumachers to be sickening and more evidence of depraved lives. Erika von Brockdorff was dismissed as having been a "bar girl" when she was young—although in fact she had been briefly a model and later a stenographer in the civil service—and was portrayed as being such a sexual predator that during her questioning two Gestapo men had to be present at all times. Warming to the theme, by the time the case came to court, Roeder claimed that Brockdorff had had "intimate relations with four Soviet agents in a single night."[3]

By December he had chosen seventy-six people to stand trial. The rest were released.

* * *

WITZLEBENSTRASSE 4–10 IN the Charlottenburg district of Berlin was a four-story building with heavy copper entrance doors, above which was carved into the stone a crowned Prussian eagle grasping a snake in its talons. Beneath the bird, the bold word "REICHSKRIEGSGERICHT" was chiseled into the stonework. The main courtroom was high-ceilinged, with a long desk behind which the judges sat. Looking down on the head judge was a large bust of Adolf Hitler. Throughout the war the judges had passed sentence, most usually as it was the highest military court, on those claiming to be conscientious objectors or accused of desertion.

Early on the icy cold morning of Tuesday, December 15, 1942, a green police van arrived in the courtyard of the Reichskriegsgericht and out shuffled the group that Roeder had marked as the thirteen main defendants in the case. They included Arvid and Mildred Harnack, Harro and Libertas Schulze-Boysen, Kurt and Elisabeth Schumacher, Hans Coppi, and Horst Heilmann. Colonel Gehrts—the psychic-believing divorcé who had been tricked by Schulze-Boysen—was among them but was taken to another courtroom to be dealt with separately. His lawyer planned to argue a case of "weak character" and diminished responsibility.

As the prisoners were led out of the sealed areas of the van, they exchanged looks. They had not seen each other since their arrests and had been allowed no visitors. Harnack saw the state that his wife was in and felt his heart break. The previous night he had written what he knew must be his last letter to her. "Despite everything, I look back gladly on my life," he had written. "The darkness was outweighed by the light . . . Our intense work meant that life was not easy for us, and the danger of being overwhelmed not slight. Nonetheless, we remained living human beings."[4]

Upstairs an official attached a placard on the courtroom door. It read: "Prozess unter Ausschluss der Oeffentlichkeit"—"Secret Trial, Public not admitted." Soldiers with fixed bayonets on their rifles stood guard outside the door and in the corridor leading down the steps to the cells. Inside the courtroom two defense lawyers sat at tables. Each had thick files containing copies of the indictments prepared by Chief Prosecutor Roeder, but the defendants had not been permitted to see the paperwork outlining the evidence or the charges, and their family members were not allowed to attend.

A Gestapo commissar sat at another table, preparing to make notes of any evidence from the accused that might enable them to track down further resisters.

Shortly before nine o'clock, with the first snow of the day beginning to fall outside the room's window, an official led in the accused. He motioned them to sit on wooden chairs facing the horseshoe table where the judges would sit. The silence in the room stretched until the door opened behind the judges' dais. Everyone in the court snapped to attention and gave the Hitler salute except the defendants.

The five judges—a vice admiral, two generals, and two members of the Reich Court-Martial's permanent judicial staff—sat down. Prosecutor Roeder was the last to enter the room and take his place at the table.

Ignoring the defendants, Roeder rose to his feet and told the judges he had personally prepared the indictments within the frame of the Reich's laws. Each contained evidence obtained after questioning within the permitted legal limits. Each of the accused had volunteered to sign his or her recorded evidence without duress. The prosecution had witnesses available, he said, from the Gestapo and the criminal police, who could give evidence, if necessary, of searching the homes and offices of the accused and discovering the evidence that justified the charges. The prosecution case was founded on the acquisition of state secrets that were fully listed in the indictments, including where they had been stolen from and recovered.

Roeder turned to the defendants. One by one he called out their names and read out the charges they faced. Each stepped forward in turn to learn they were accused of high treason against the state. Espionage at a time of war. "Providing military strength to the enemy." Roeder then again turned to the judges and reminded them that each charge carried a death sentence.

Throughout the proceedings that followed, the defense counsel neither criticized Roeder as he harangued and interrupted the defendants, nor complained to the court that some of the prisoners had been tortured. The prisoners, though, spoke for themselves: telling Roeder they had not been motivated by money or sex, as he alleged, but by common decency and hatred for the regime. Harnack said that he felt "morally bound" to act. The Gestapo official at the back of the court, noting each defendant's impassioned speeches against the Third Reich, dismissed them all as "political fanatics."[5] The regime, unable to accept that high-born Germans such as these could hate Hitler so much, was already building up its distorted myth of the group as obsessive, warped Stalinists.

Although family members were denied access to the trial, word did sneak out. When Schulze-Boysen's younger brother was told that the court had heard that the Luftwaffe officer had "never honestly served the National Socialist state," he took it not with a sense of shame but pride.[6]

Mildred Fish-Harnack alone received some sympathy from the judges. The president of the court, Alexander Kraell, who was in fact ambivalent toward the Nazis, declared that Frau Harnack as "a foreigner, an American, who had come to Germany in 1929 . . . could hardly be expected to understand Germany's political development or her husband's views about them."[7]

On December 19, the judges handed down their verdicts. The men were all sentenced to death, as were Libertas Schulze-Boysen and Elisabeth Schumacher. Mildred Fish-Harnack, who it was argued had "acted more out of loyalty to her husband than of her own volition," was sentenced to six years' imprisonment, and Erika von Brockdorff to ten.[8]

It was now for Roeder to report to Göring. When the Reichsmarschall heard the word "imprisonment," he exploded with rage. He had been "commissioned by the Führer . . . to cauterize this abscess," he shouted. "The Führer would never agree to this!"[9]

The files were sent to Hitler and Field Marshal Keitel, who confirmed the death sentences. The verdicts on the two women who had been spared death came back without signature or comment. There would have to be a retrial in front of a new judge.

Roeder worked into the night to set about firming up his case against the two women. They must not escape death.

DEATH FOR THE members of the Harnack and Schulze-Boysen group must come with dishonor. In the hierarchy of capital punishment the firing squad was considered to have some dignity and was reserved for military men. The guillotine was quick and considered kind. It was a death for young people and women.

Hanging had no dignity at all. It was for spies and partisans. It degraded the person and the acts they had committed.

But Plötzensee had no gallows, so as Berlin prepared for Christmas, laborers installed a long steel beam in the execution shed and fit eight meat hooks along its length. Roeder sought to deny the prisoners a priest, but the prison chaplain, a Protestant pastor named Harald Poelchau, learned of the executions and visited each in turn.

Throughout the afternoon the prisoners wrote their last letters home. Harnack, comforted by the fact that he had seen his wife escape the death penalty, told his family: "I would have liked to see you all one more time. Unfortunately, that is not possible. But my thoughts are with you all."

Harro Schulze-Boysen wrote that with people dying "all over the world" in the war, "one extinguished life does not matter very much." He had done what he had done "in accordance with my head, my heart, and my convictions."

His wife wrote to her mother: "If I may ask one thing of you, tell everyone about me. Our death must be a beacon." She said the agony of her unwitting betrayal of her friends to the police secretary Gertrud Breiter had now passed, as her friends had forgiven her and "we go to our end with a sense of fellowship only possible when facing death."[10]

As she listened to the noise of the guards working their way along the condemned cells, Libertas added: "So, my love, the hours strike: first Harro goes and I think of him. Then Horst goes, and I think of him. And Elisabeth will think of me."[11]

And so it went.

One by one, in the darkness of a cold evening three days before Christmas, the lights went on in the cells. It was seven o'clock. They came to Harro Schulze-Boysen first. Handcuffed, led alone to the execution shed, where Roeder waited, smart and upright in his dress uniform, a sword hanging from his hip.

A curtain separated each of the meat hooks. Schulze-Boysen was still hanging when Harnack was brought in. He walked to the space beneath the noose, his body upright and calm. The hangman stood on a stool. Harnack was lifted up and a noose was placed over his head. The stool was kicked away.

Then Kurt Schumacher; then John Graudenz, the former *New York Times* writer, who had helped Jews escape deportation.

At eight o'clock came those to be executed by guillotine.

Horst Heilmann, the nineteen-year-old friend who had tried to warn Harro Schulze-Boysen. Hans Coppi, whose wife was pregnant with their first child and was awaiting trial. Kurt Schulze, a GRU radio operator who had tried to help Coppi fix his radio.

Libertas Schulze-Boysen turned to the executioner, her voice a croak, and said: "Let me keep my young life."

A moment later there was only Elisabeth Schumacher to think of Libertas.

Then she, too, was gone.

THROUGHOUT THE NEXT day, Libertas Schulze-Boysen's mother, Thora Eulenberg, searched for her daughter. She tried Alexanderplatz, Prinz-Albrecht-Strasse, the Lehrter Strasse prison. At each office she waited until a Gestapo officer or guard told her they had no idea where her daughter was and sent her onwards.

All knew, of course. It was just that there was a dark humor in sending the woman on. She even had a Christmas parcel under her arm for the girl!

Still in the dark, she tried to contact Göring himself. She knew the Reichsmarschall, had played piano for him—surely he could help. He did not answer her calls.

Throughout Christmas she waited and hoped. Like the other families, she had to believe her loved one was still alive. Only when the court offices reopened in the new year did she learn that her daughter had been dead since December 22.

By that time the courts were ready to add to the grim list of the condemned.

ARVID HARNACK'S BROTHER, Falk, went to see Roeder to request the return of Arvid's body and to ask if Mildred's prison sentence could be commuted.

"They are both lost," Roeder told him brusquely, and then leaned forward: "What is your attitude, anyway, toward the National Socialist state?"

Falk Harnack paused, but avoided the question. "What do you mean, 'Mildred is lost'? The highest German court has just sentenced her to six years' prison. The sentence cannot be changed. It can only be lightened by an appeal for mercy."

Roeder stood and, indicating the conversation was over, waved his hand and said, "On the orders of the Führer there will be a retrial."[12]

\* \* \*

THE RETRIAL OF Mildred Fish-Harnack and Erika von Brockdorff took place on January 12, 1943, in front of Judge Karl Schmauser, who knew exactly what was expected of him. Even if he had not had the weight of the Führer's gaze over his shoulder, the grim news from Stalingrad convinced him that there was only one option for a court in the case of "Soviet spies."

Mildred read and reread her last letter from Arvid until the paper was worn and faded. She went through Christmas believing she was starting a prison sentence. Early in the new year, she was told about the retrial. As the guards came to take her from her cell, she took the letter from inside her dress and passed it to her cellmate, asking her to keep it safe. The woman, a young Communist named Gertrud Lichtenstein, was so touched that she safeguarded the letter even when the Nazis put her on a train to Ravensbrück.

No record of the retrial was kept, but Schmauser accepted Roeder's claim that Fish-Harnack was far from a simple accomplice to her husband: She was part of the same treasonous conspiracy as those who had already gone to the gallows.

Again, Roeder put Brockdorff's sexuality at the heart of his case. Schmauser listened intently to the more salacious claims, and Brockdorff found the hearing so ridiculous that she laughed. Schmauser told her angrily, "To me this case is too serious for laughter. You will have the smile taken off your face in the end."

Brockdorff looked defiant. "And even on the scaffold I'll laugh in your face!" she told him.[13]

When Schmauser concluded that the only permissible sentence for the two women was death, the defiant Brockdorff told him, "This new trial has robbed me of the last thing I had left: my belief that there is justice in Germany."[14]

Colonel Gehrts was sentenced to death, too, after Roeder presented a medical report that showed he was fully responsible for his actions.

And the very next day Roeder brought in a new set of defendants, people who had helped in the printing and distribution of antifascist leaflets, including nineteen-year-old Liane Berkowitz, who was six months pregnant, and Cato Bontjes van Beek, whose other crimes had included giving cigarettes and food to French prisoners of war and helping Jews. Roeder argued that all had provided "aid and comfort to the enemy," and the court showed no mercy. Hitler and Keitel personally insisted that Berkowitz and Bontjes van Beek be executed.

Before the month was out, Hilde Coppi, Karl Behrens, the dentist Helmut Himpel and his fiancée Maria Terwiel, and Adam Kuckhoff had come before the court and been sentenced to death. Hilde Coppi had just given birth to a child in prison. Her execution would be delayed for only as long as she nursed it.

MILDRED FISH-HARNACK HAD always felt a part of Germany, but not the Germany of Adolf Hitler.

On the evening of February 16, 1943, the bolt on the door of the death cell in Plötzensee prison slid back and the prison chaplain, Pastor Poelchau, entered. She smiled weakly to see him again: The Protestant pastor had sat with Mildred late into the previous night, praying and talking. He had been the first to tell her that her husband had been executed several weeks earlier but that he had been brave to the end.

Dressed in his vestments, he held an English Bible in his hand. Mildred Fish-Harnack stood to greet him, but he gestured for her to sit. She was thin, and when she coughed, her body was wracked in pain. Malnutrition and tuberculosis. Although she was only forty years old, her blonde hair had turned white. She told him she had spent her last hours translating some lines of Goethe into English. "No being can to nothing fall / The everlasting lives in all."

He gave her a photograph of her family, which a friend had asked him to smuggle in. He watched in pain as she kissed the face of her mother over and over, and held it to her lips.

Poelchau put his hand on her arm to steady her as she read from the Bible he had brought her: "Though I speak with the tongues of men and of angels, and have not charity, I am become as sounding brass, or a tinkling cymbal."

She did not pause as someone entered the cell. "Rejoiceth not in iniquity, but rejoiceth in the truth."

The stone-faced man who had entered the cell motioned for Mildred to open her mouth as he searched for gold fillings and exchanged her shoes for wooden clogs. Using shears, he cut her hair, baring her neck for the guillotine's blade.

Then, as he handcuffed her hands behind her back, Mildred turned to Pastor Poelchau and said: "Und ich habe Deutschland so sehr geliebt"— "And I loved Germany so much."

Held between two guards, Mildred was led down the corridor, across a courtyard, and into the execution chamber. The room where Arvid had died.

She did not look at the table behind which sat the representatives of the state—the lawyer and the prison governor who were that day's bureaucrats of death—or at the man in the long black coat, white gloves, and tall black hat.

She heard the words read to her, "Prisoner, you are sentenced to death for helping to prepare high treason, showing favour to the enemy, and espionage. The military court has sentenced you to death by guillotine," but said nothing.

The governor nodded to the man in the tall hat: "Executioner, carry out the sentence."

He pulled back the black curtain to reveal the execution chamber. Beneath the steel beam, built especially for the meat hooks, was a brass-and-wood guillotine. At three minutes to seven, the light glinted on the falling blade.

Mildred Fish-Harnack was the first and only American woman executed on the order of Hitler.

When the Gestapo made a final inventory of her possessions, they found among them the boat ticket that her husband had bought her before the war had broken out. She had left it unused, out of her love for him and for Germany.

IN ALL, FORTY-FIVE people connected to the Rote Kapelle trials in Germany were sentenced to death, including nineteen women. They had helped Jews, distributed leaflets, organized clandestine meetings, translated foreign broadcasts for the German public. The Harnacks had provided secrets to the Americans, and with the Schulze-Boysens and the Kuckhoffs had given key military intelligence to the Soviets. They had been prepared to do anything to help any nation that fought against the criminal regime running Germany.

The last to die went to the gallows on August 5, 1943. Two were mothers who had recently given birth.

Liane Berkowitz's daughter had been taken away from her as soon as she was born, but Liane had decided to name her baby Irene, and the young woman went to the gallows wondering what had happened to her. Mercifully, she never learned that little Irene died as part of the Nazis' euthanasia program.[15] Berkowitz died on the guillotine with Hilde Coppi, whose baby son, born in prison and named Hans after his father, had also been taken away but would survive.

Also marched to the execution shed that day were Adam Kuckhoff, Maria Terwiel, and Cato Bontjes van Beek. There were three-minute intervals between each death. Like the others, they went to their end not knowing if their acts of opposition had made any difference at all: It must have felt they had not. Bontjes van Beek wrote poignantly to her mother: "There is no great glory attached to involvement in this business."[16]

The women's bodies were delivered to Dr. Stieve, the anatomist at the University of Berlin who had dissected the bodies of some of the women in the Baum group. The orgy of executions had now led him into new research about the impact of terror on the female reproductive organs and the menstrual cycle. He had been monitoring and examining the women since they had been told of the date of their executions, and was delivered their corpses within ten minutes of death so that he could promptly remove organs for examination.

Earlier in the year he had received Mildred Fish-Harnack's body, but he had recognized her, and feeling unable to perform the dissection, he had the body cremated and the ashes returned to the family.

IN THE MEANTIME, the wrath of Nazi "justice" toward the Herbert Baum group also went on. Others were executed during the spring and summer of 1943, including the typesetter George Vötter and Artur Illgen, who had painted anti-Nazi slogans on public buildings, while Rita Meyer, who had sheltered Martin Kochmann and Charlotte Paech, was sent to Auschwitz. She would survive; her five-year-old daughter, Barbara, would not. Her husband, Herbert, had been tortured in front of her by the Gestapo. He died after being submerged in a bath of cold water.[17]

Martin Kochmann, Felix Heymann, and Herbert Budzislawski, who had been arrested only because he was a longtime friend of Baum's, were tried on June 29, 1943. Kochmann and Heymann were described as "dangerous threats to the security of the Reich." While there was little evidence against Budzislawski other than the fact that he was a Communist and a Jew, he was found guilty—effectively by association. He had shown great courage in his interrogations, however, telling the Gestapo that a Jew was compelled to fight "injustice in Germany" as it was the only way to "live in Germany as a human being."[18]

On the night of September 7, 1943, dozens of prisoners were lined up outside their cells in Plötzensee and marched in groups of eight to the execution chamber, where Reindel waited. It was like a scene from hell: An air raid was under way, and part of the prison had been hit. Dark corridors were lit up by the glow of flames. The heavy walls of the prison shook.

There was no electric light in the killing room as a bomb had knocked out a generator. Reindel worked by candlelight, and he worked fast.

A noose was put around the neck of the condemned. He or she was then lifted up by Reindel's assistants, and Reindel would take the loop and hang it on a hook "as one would hang a dress." As he worked, a clerk drew a small cross next to the name of each of the dead.

Kochmann was number thirty-two that night. Heymann, thirty-three. Budzislawski, thirty-four.

In all, Reindel executed 186 people as the candlelight flickered.[19] Afterwards he slept during the day and came back to execute more than sixty others over the coming nights.

THE NURSE CHARLOTTE Paech had been due to die that night.

After being beaten and tortured by the Gestapo, she had stopped saying a word. Her story then became a comedy of macabre errors. The Gestapo had uncovered the fact that, along with most of the others, she had been committed to anti-Nazi action since before Hitler came to power. She was sent to a brutal forced-labor camp, and then tortured again. Still, despite cuts, bruises, lack of food, and a broken jaw, she gave them nothing.

Then one day while at Lehrter Strasse prison she was told she was being indicted for high treason—a charge that would inevitably carry the death penalty—and she would appear in court on June 29 with Kochmann, Heymann, and Budzislawski.

However, a completely separate Gestapo investigation had uncovered the fact that she had been using bogus food coupons to obtain food for three others. While in custody in Berlin she was tried in her absence 120 miles away in Leipzig and sentenced to eighteen months in jail. The Baum investigation team told Leipzig she could not be sent to jail there as she was facing a much more serious trial in Berlin.

However, the transportation orders had already been processed and a bailiff dispatched to Lehrter Strasse to personally deliver her by train to Leipzig. Upon her arrival at Leipzig-Kleinmeusdorf prison, the bailiff was told that the prisoner could not be admitted because the jail was for Aryan prisoners only. The man took Paech to a detention center, ready to be sent back to Berlin. While there, she fell ill with scarlet fever and was put in quarantine.

She was still there when Kochmann and the others were tried. The senior prosecutor in Berlin showed surprise to find she was not in the dock.

She was eventually sent back to Berlin on July 16, once again handcuffed to a private policeman. On arrival she was told she had been sentenced to death—another verdict in her absence. However, the officer at the detention center said it was not clear if the death sentence could yet be considered official as no formal date of execution had been sent on from the court.

Paech was put in a cell with five other Jewish women. Over the next few nights, three of them were taken away and executed, but no one came for her.

The regime that worked so tirelessly in pursuit of inflicting pain and judicial murder had forgotten to process her death sentence.

ONE OF THE key members of the Harnack group found herself in a similarly surreal judicial limbo.

Greta Lorke, Mildred Fish-Harnack's old friend from their student days in Wisconsin, sat alone in the women's prison at Charlottenburg. One day in August, Pastor Poelchau called at her cell and sat for a moment before speaking. "Now, they are all dead," he said at last, his voice quiet. "Your husband, and the girls. All of them."

But Lorke remained. When she was called back to court, she heard that her death sentence had been revoked and that she had been sentenced to ten years in prison, where she was to join a production line making gas masks.

At her last court appearance, she could see that the wind had gone out of the sails of the Rote Kapelle prosecution. The Nazi justice system had lost interest in her.

And she could see why. Manfred Roeder was no longer anywhere to be seen. He had been given far bigger fish to fry. Roeder was by now trying to bring down Admiral Canaris and the Abwehr.

Meanwhile, events in southern Germany had brought another branch of the German underground resistance into the open.

# 27

## White Rose: The Harnack Connection

THE SUMMER POSTING to the Russian Front had hardened Hans Scholl's resolve to increase the activities of the White Rose.

The troop train had paused in Warsaw, allowing them to sip on vodka in a bar before walking through streets "surrounded by misery."[1] Scholl later told Traute Lafrenz that they had seen the Warsaw ghetto, where perhaps half a million Jews were starving in run-down houses, cut off from the outside world. Traveling on, they had eventually reached the Soviet Union and the ruins of Vyazma, a town that had been destroyed by German aircraft ten months earlier.[2] From there it had been a short march to Gzhatsk, eighty miles due west of Moscow, right at the front of the German advance. At night Scholl would watch the muzzle flashes of the Russian artillery and then wait for the shells to hit the town around him. Willi Graf said the ruins of its tall houses rose "spookily in the moonlight." For Alexander Schmorell, who had been born in Russia and spoke the language fluently, the pain of seeing the country destroyed was heartfelt.

Schmorell and Scholl spoke to local people and to patients in the field hospital and began to hear firsthand about the atrocities committed under the guise of Hitler's war on Bolshevism. Schmorell shared folk tales and folk songs from his youth to win over suspicious peasant farmers and argued with fellow soldiers who dismissed them as Slavs and "Asiatic inferiors." He risked a court-martial when he saw a German guard beating a Russian prisoner and pushed the soldier away.

Schmorell vowed that when he left Russia, he would never wipe the Russian mud off his boots, and that he would return one day.

Hans Scholl read Dostoyevsky and Tolstoy by candlelight in his bunker, and scoffed at the Nazi idea that these giants of literature must come from the ignorant hordes of Asiatic Russia. The friendly moments he shared with local Russians only made him sink further into a kind of depression. War, he thought, was "the most unimaginative of all human activities."[3] Those quiet moments of reflection, though, were few and far between. The hospital was busy, the wards lined with the maimed and dying. "I have no music in me anymore," Scholl wrote after one long shift. "Now all I hear are groans and screams of people in torment."[4]

However, among the death and misery, Hans did find a sense of hope. Many of the soldiers at the front were showing signs of dissent. Much of it was just the usual grumblings of the Landser, the German infantryman, of the kind one might hear in any army, but it revealed to him that he and his friends were not alone in their complete disillusionment with the Nazi hierarchy. One favorite joke among the men was imagining that Hitler had decided to visit the front in Russia to raise their morale. On visiting a group of men huddled in a bunker, the Führer asked, "And, you, soldier, what would be your final wish if a Russian shell landed right near you?" "Only," replied the soldier, "that my Führer was standing beside me."[5]

Soldiers along the front knew, of course, that such "defeatism" was likely to end in front of a firing squad. While he was in Gzhatsk, Scholl heard the story of a company commander who had been heard to brand the Nazi leaders as "criminals." The young man's Iron Cross, awarded for bravery in battle, did nothing to prevent him from being put against a post and shot.[6]

Despite this, Scholl took risks, too, when his natural humanity simply overcame any fear he might have. Once, while walking to the rear of the front line, he spotted a group of Russian women being made to carry and break rocks to help repair a road. Among them was a sickly young Jewish girl, with a Star of David stitched into her ragged clothing. As he watched, he realized she could barely swing the heavy pick she was gripping in her calloused hands. Reaching into his pocket, he brought out his iron ration, a mixture of chocolate, dried fruit, and nuts, and handed it to her. She saw only the uniform and not the kindness in his face, and threw the gift down at his feet. Unperturbed, he picked it up and dusted it down. How could he show her that he meant only kindness? He walked to the edge of the road and plucked a small flower, which he then laid with the food at the girl's feet. "I only wanted to give you some pleasure," he said and quickly walked away, realizing she might overcome her pride and fear if he did not watch her. When he was at a distance, he turned quickly and his heart swelled. The ration had been picked up and shoved into her pocket and the flower was in her hair. This moment of human connection stayed with him until word came that the medical company was being returned to Germany.

The young men marched back to Vyazma, where they were deloused and assembled at the station. Graf managed to buy a samóvar before the journey, and the cattle car that took them out of Russia was filled with the smell of hot tea. Through the ragged holes in the wooden sides of the train, they watched the countryside roll by, and occasionally caught sight of a peasant with a cart trundling along a rough road. Graf spoke for them all when he said he was worried about what would happen to the Russians they had met.

When they stretched their legs during a stop at the Polish border, these sentiments were fresh in their minds. Close to the station a group of Russian prisoners was being roughly herded into a barbed-wire enclosure. The men dragged their feet through exhaustion and starvation; their tattered clothes hung off them. Scholl, Schmorell, and Graf wandered over, holding out cigarettes for them to take. Schmorell exchanged a few words with them, but the soldiers on guard turned on the medics. There was an angry argument, which threatened to spill over into violence, but then the train whistle blew and there were shouts from the station. The medics ran back, still exchanging insults with their fellow soldiers.

The soldier medics did not take a walk in Warsaw on the way back; they stayed on the train. They had seen enough. Jürgen Wittenstein, who was returning on the train, too, said Russia had left them feeling a mix of "shock, horror, and rage."[7]

TWO DAYS AFTER Hans and Sophie met up again in Munich in November 1942, the Allies landed tens of thousands of troops in Morocco and Algeria, areas of French North Africa controlled by the Hitler-supporting Vichy regime. The invasion—code-named Operation Torch—took pressure off the British soldiers fighting Rommel in Egypt and allowed the Allies to take naval control of the southwest Mediterranean. The invasion would also make possible an assault on southern Europe. For Roosevelt, Torch was a turning point in the war.

The Scholls had opposed the war throughout—even during the German successes of 1939 and 1940—and now the tide looked to be turning in

North Africa and Russia. As they listened to the German radio broadcasts, which tried to disguise or downplay any downturn in the Wehrmacht's fortunes, they remained as resolute as ever in their beliefs that the German people had to fight against the Nazis and strike them "the most telling blows."[8] Hans told his sister that no matter how much Goebbels's radio broadcasts exalted the spirit and morale of the German soldiers in Russia, he had seen for himself that many of them were exhausted and worn down by the horrors of the war in the East.

On the surface the Scholls returned to "normal" student life. The rather privileged way in which the trainee doctors were treated meant that Hans and his friends returned from the front to enjoy all the benefits of university life again. They attended lectures, as if they had only been at home for the holidays, and he, Schmorell, and Graf resumed their membership of the Bach Choral Society. Hans and Sophie now each had a room at Franz-Joseph-Strasse 13, in the fashionable suburb of Schwabing, where the landlady was largely absent, having taken to the country to avoid the by now regular terror of the air raids. Hans, who had split from Traute Lafrenz, started a relationship with an art student, Gisela Schertling, who became friendly with the group but was a devoted National Socialist and so was never told anything about their real political feelings or their work. Lafrenz continued to work with the White Rose, who now met most nights at the Scholls' lodgings to discuss how next to proceed.

They all heard and discussed the foreign radio reports about the arrests of the "spies and traitors" of the Rote Kapelle. They had been shocked to hear that there were senior people in the civil service and in the Luftwaffe— right in the heart of Hitler's Berlin—who were resisting the regime. It meant that they were not alone, and that there was resistance high up in the government itself. All now agreed with Hans Scholl that the way forward was to find out if there were other groups, and to create a network of resistance across the major cities of Germany. Such moves would put them in greater danger: the more people they tried to contact, the greater the risk of exposure through denunciation or contact with somebody already on a Gestapo watch list. But this consideration was put to one side, and the discussion turned to how they would find people away from their immediate circle in Munich.

The breakthrough came quickly, through Lilo Ramdohr, an artist friend of Schmorell's. Ramdohr had met Falk Harnack through his work as a director with the National Theater in Weimar, and they were now in a relationship and planned to get engaged to be married.[9] Falk, she told them, had been a student in Munich in 1933 and had clashed with supporters of the brownshirts on the streets. He had even distributed anti-Hitler leaflets, she said, and had been among a group of students calling for a university strike in 1938. She could set up a meeting.

THIS LINK THROUGH Lilo Ramdohr to Falk Harnack seemed a stroke of luck, but when she told them that Harnack was stationed with an infantry company in Chemnitz, they grew anxious. The train journey to the city close to the Czech border would be subject to checks and controls. Two soldiers traveling so close to the border and reluctant—because of association with Arvid Harnack, who was under arrest in Berlin—to give the name of the man they were meeting could be charged with desertion. They also wanted to carry copies of the first four White Rose leaflets so they could show Harnack the kind of work they had been doing.

The risks were great, but the dream of expanding their resistance was too powerful. Hans and Schmorell headed to Chemnitz and found Harnack in a quiet inn named Sächsischer Hof.[10] Harnack, in his late twenties and so a little bit older than the others, led the conversation. They talked all day, first in the downstairs tavern and later in a private room upstairs. With the door locked, Falk Harnack spread out the four White Rose leaflets on a small table and studied them. They were typed out, single-spaced, on cheap duplicating paper. Falk read the rage that came out of them and shivered at the dangers the members of the group faced for writing and mailing out these leaflets.

But he had criticisms of the young group's writing: It was too academic, he said. Too intellectual. The words and phrasing were from the worlds of literature and philosophy, not the simple messages that would speak to the masses. Hans Scholl and his friend took the criticism well: They knew it made sense. After all, they were all middle-class, intellectual, and from comfortable backgrounds. Schmorell's father was wealthy and lived in a large villa in the Munich suburb of Harlaching. Christoph Probst came from a rich merchant family, and he lived as a private scholar who was not only learning medicine but also funding his own research into Eastern religions. Graf's father was a wine wholesaler and the owner of a large banqueting hall.

Falk shared his own beliefs with them: that despite the arrests of his brother and sister-in-law, the resistance had to develop a broad antifascist consensus in every city across Germany. People who had been enemies during the days of the Weimar Republic—from the Communists on the left to the conservatives and army on the right, with the Social Democrats and the liberals in the middle—must all come together as one to bring down Hitler.

And then he told them something that shocked and inspired them: a secret cabal of generals had built up a resistance network that planned the seemingly impossible—the assassination of Adolf Hitler and the complete overthrow of his regime.

INSPIRED BY THEIR meeting with Falk Harnack, the White Rose sought to expand its membership and activities.

Scholl and Schmorell made another journey, this time to Stuttgart, to see Eugen Grimminger, the friend who had taken over Robert Scholl's business when he had been jailed. Hans Scholl knew he could trust the fifty-year-old accountant. Married to a Jewish woman named Jenny, Grimminger had helped a number of Jews escape Germany in 1938 and 1939. He had lost his prewar job in the civil service because of his marriage to a Volljüdin, and the Nazis considered him "politically unreliable," but for the moment they left him alone.

Grimminger was anxious about what the two students might want to talk about and suggested they walk where they might not be overheard. In the end they stopped and sat on a loading bay of a bus and tram company. The younger men lit pipes as they talked, and from behind the smoke Hans Scholl took a deep breath and told Grimminger about the White Rose, the leaflets written so far, and those that could be yet to come. We are looking to unite resistance across Germany, Scholl told him, and yes, it does exist. He asked Grimminger about his friends in the industrial community around Stuttgart, and the accountant told him there were murmurs of dissent among some. Scholl seemed to suggest that a coup could take place and oust Hitler from the chancellery. The suggestion at once terrified and excited Grimminger. But what do you need from me? Grimminger asked.

The answer was money. To expand operations, buy new supplies, and travel, the little group of the White Rose needed more funds. Grimminger sighed and walked back and forth. He admired these young people and clearly saw the spirit of his friend Robert in his son Hans. Germany needed young people like this, now more than ever. But to fund their operation would be taking a leap that simply petrified him, not for his own sake but for his family's. Any money he handed over would be an act of treason. He could not take that risk. It would be a death warrant for his Jewish wife and her family, and probably for him, too. The conversation became heated, with Grimminger angry about being asked to involve himself so deeply— although his temper was more likely a disguise for the frustration he felt for not appearing to help. He apologized to Scholl, they shook hands, and the two students left empty-handed.

But all the way home Grimminger's conscience played on him. If people like him did not help the young people, who would? They had taken a tremendous risk in contacting him, and were going to continue putting their lives on the line. Their goal was to make a better life for everyone, especially Germany's Jews. He slowly changed his mind, wrote a check for 500 marks, and sent it to Hans Scholl. He did not ask for repayment: It was a gift. A gift to do good. It was an act of generosity that would cost Grimminger far more than money.

Back in Munich, the architect Manfred Eickemeyer pledged money, too, handing over 200 marks in cash, and Willi Graf had saved up 50 marks, which he put into a kitty overseen by the group's treasurer, Sophie.

Deciding that the group's first outlay should be on a bigger and faster duplicating machine, Traute Lafrenz took the train to Vienna, where her uncle owned an office-supply company. He told her the war had made it difficult to source supplies for individuals, but he promised to try to get her something by the spring—which seemed a long time to wait for the impatient twenty-three-year-old. Not to be disappointed, she went to see her aunt Mimi, who had connections with the University of Vienna, and asked her to deliver some leaflets to trusted members of the student body.

After returning to Germany, Lafrenz headed north to her native Hamburg, where she had many left-wing friends, having studied in a liberal arts school and later at the university. Nazism had never really dominated in Hamburg, a busy port with a large international influence. A movement of working-class teenage rebellion, known as the Edelweiss Pirates, had been active in the city, and the Gestapo reported on a strong "swing movement" among upper-middle-class kids. The regime sought to clamp down on these American-influenced musical gatherings as it believed the will to shun Nazi-approved music of the völkisch in favor of Benny Goodman and Louis Armstrong led to rebellion of other sorts.[11]

In Hamburg, through former classmates Heinz Kucharski and Greta Rothe, Lafrenz found a loosely connected group of students and intellectuals who were eager to learn about the work of the White Rose in Munich.[12] They numbered about fifty—many more than the White Rose—but lacked cohesion. They met in bookstores and carefully selected coffeehouses and debated what to do. The chemistry students among them discussed stealing nitroglycerin, which could be used to blow up a railway bridge used regularly by German troop trains or even Gestapo headquarters. Their ambitions had been great, but only now were they congregating around a leader: a former soldier named Hans Leipelt, who had served with distinction in Poland and won a bravery medal for the destruction of a tank. Despite his courage, Leipelt had been dishonorably dismissed from the army when it was discovered that his mother was half-Jewish.[13] Leipelt—who wore round steel-rimmed glasses and had a shock of unruly dark hair— was inspired by the copy of the White Rose's third leaflet that Traute Lafrenz had brought with her. He resolved to make his group the northern branch of the White Rose.

Willi Graf also traveled extensively in the period around Christmas 1942, having volunteered to use the winter holiday to gain support from his own contacts. Packing a bag full of leaflets and a duplicating machine, he went to visit friends at the University of Bonn—where he had previously studied—and later people he knew from school in Saarbrücken. Showing astonishing bravery, he then traveled on to Cologne, Ulm, and Freiburg, where he discovered a small core of resisters on the faculty led by Heinz Bollinger in the philosophy department and his brother Willi, a medic at the local military hospital. Graf gave them the duplicating machine and a pile of White Rose leaflets, and in return Willi Bollinger said he knew how to copy military passes and army train tickets if they required any. He also showed Graf the cache of guns he had been quietly storing away.[14] At each stop Graf sought out people he felt might help the resistance movement. Almost everywhere he met fear and suspicion. Old friends just could not believe what he was asking of them, while others felt it was more honorable to help their nation win the war first and then change the leadership. Many, though, were filled with respect for his courage and resolve: "He was one of those young people who have always found it impossible to remain indifferent in the face of injustice," one friend said later.

It was lonely work, but the quiet and stoic Graf carried it out with care and without drawing attention to himself. In the end he recruited only four people: the Bollingers, Helmut Bauer, and Rudi Alt.

In Ulm, Sophie worked with Hans Hirzel—the son of the minister at the Martin Luther Church—and two of his friends, Franz Josef Müller and Heinrich Guter, to mail out more leaflets. They found a hiding place behind the organ of Hirzel's father's church in which to sit and talk as they wrote the addresses on the envelopes.[15]

IN MUNICH, HANS and Sophie Scholl found solace from the stresses of their underground activities in a bookshop hidden in the shadows of the twin domes of the Frauenkirche. Josef Söhngen's bookshop was as peaceful and eccentric as its owner, and the Scholls loved them both. Söhngen did little to hide his feelings about the Nazis and the concentration camps from his loyal customers, and he listened with horror to Hans's stories from Russia. He saw the young man as tense but determined, and in his apartment above the shop they would talk about politics in more detail. One night, Hans Scholl came in, sat down, and said he needed to "recover his balance." He explained about his little network and his hopes to expand it.

Söhngen said he had a friend named Giovanni Stepanov, an art historian, who had links with the Italian antifascist movement. The bookshop owner often arranged talks for the Italian in Munich, and he could introduce Scholl to him. It seemed like an opportunity to expand, but unfortunately the next time Stepanov came to the city Hans was visiting Ulm.

Scholl did, however, finally succeed in recruiting the group's oldest member, Kurt Huber, the professor with the ability to inspire during his lectures. Huber had remained friends with Scholl despite his concerns about the effectiveness of passive resistance. He cared deeply for the university students, seeing them as the future of a better Germany, and Hans was one of a small group that he invited home for coffee and cake. They would sit with Huber's wife nearby and his young children, Birgit and Wolf, playing in another room.

In silence Huber listened to Scholl's descriptions of atrocities in Russia, and one day when Scholl brought Willi Graf along, the two men admitted to being involved with the White Rose leaflets. Huber was alarmed but said he doubted whether the leaflets would have any effect at all on the Nazis. Scholl admitted he had his doubts, too, but repeated the sentiments expressed in the fourth leaflet, that bringing down Nazism had to take priority over everything, including opposing Communism. He also told Huber about the resistance groups in the army. The professor was shocked but heartened: He respected the army a great deal and believed they were the only section of society that could offer truly meaningful resistance.

Scholl said he wanted to write more leaflets, with better appeals to the people, and he asked for Huber's help in preparing them.

Despite his reservations, Huber agreed to become involved. "In a state where the free expression of public opinion is throttled," he said, "a dissident must necessarily turn to illegal methods."[16]

AS 1943 BEGAN, Hans Scholl was excited about the circle of people he had brought together. "All the energy one expends comes flowing back," he told his friend Otl Aicher.[17]

Hans and Schmorell now wrote separate drafts for the group's fifth leaflet. They were working against the backdrop of bad news from the front. German soldiers were encircled by the Red Army at Stalingrad, and the Russians were calling on them to surrender; Panzer armies were in retreat; the Allies were threatening to take Tripoli. The students tried to incorporate all this into their new "Call to All Germans."

When the writing was done, the group came together in Hans's room, with Kurt Huber invited to decide between the two versions. Scholl and Schmorell read Huber their work, while Graf and Sophie looked on: two students reading theses to a professor, but these were not term papers; they were tracts that could get them killed.

Huber did not like Schmorell's: It had a "Communist ring" to it and was too pro-Soviet. Scholl's, he said, was more tightly critical of Hitler's regime. At this point Huber felt deeply that "since the Führer assumed the high command and dismissed our most competent generals, the striking power of the German army has been catastrophically weakened."[18] Huber also objected to the plan to publish the fifth leaflet not under the banner of the White Rose but as "Leaflets of the Resistance Movement in Germany." Huber said it felt heavy and clunky, while "White Rose" had implied purity and courage; the students disagreed. They believed the new name fit in with their new knowledge of a wider resistance network and would give the impression that this German phase of resistance was part of a Europe-wide movement.

This time the appeal to Germans was shorter, punchier, without the lengthy Biblical and philosophical quotations of the previous four. Hans had taken the advice given by Falk Harnack to talk more directly to "the masses." "The war is approaching its destined end," it began, ". . . in the East the armies are constantly in retreat and invasion is imminent in the West. Mobilization in the United States has not yet reached its climax, but already exceeds anything that the world has ever seen. It has become a mathematical certainty that Hitler is leading the German people into the abyss." The phrase "mathematical certainty" was a clever play on a phrase often used by the Führer.

The reader was told emphatically, "Hitler cannot win the war; he can only prolong it," and was again urged to turn away from Nazism and to think about how history would view the German people: "Are we forever to be a nation which is hated and rejected by all mankind? No."

A significant element of Schmorell's text appears to have survived Huber's intervention, with the text being adapted after he left.[19] "Do not believe the National Socialist propaganda which has driven the fear of Bolshevism into your bones. Do not believe that Germany's welfare is linked to the victory of National Socialism for good or ill . . . The workers must be liberated from their condition of downtrodden slavery under National Socialism."

Hans Scholl ended with a statement of wishes that drew on the conversations he and Sophie had had with Josef Furtmeier, "the Philosopher," about an international community of states protecting the world from war. "Freedom of speech, freedom of religion, protection of the individual citizen against the arbitrary actions of authoritarian states—these are the foundations of the New Europe."[20]

WHILE THE FIFTH leaflet was in production an event took place in Munich that was unprecedented in the history of Nazi Germany: a spontaneous student revolt that saw fistfights and a march through the streets. The White Rose felt they had helped create an atmosphere in which the protest took place, although it was ultimately sparked by a clumsy speech from the highest-ranking local Nazi official.

The protest would mark a key moment in the chain of events that would bring the wrath of the regime down upon the young students.

The SS leader Heinrich Himmler himself had created the concept of Lebensborn—the Spring of Life—and a chain of nursing homes where "racially pure" babies could be born. German women were told it was their duty and an honor to provide babies for the Reich and were encouraged to become pregnant by SS officers whether or not they were married to each other. Himmler was said to have been delighted by the sons of the Reich whom Nazi mothers had called Heinrich after him.[21]

A keen proponent of the idea that women should be providing babies for the Third Reich as a priority over all other aspects of their lives was Paul Giesler, the forty-seven-year-old Gauleiter of Munich and Upper Bavaria.

With his high forehead and middle-aged paunch, out of uniform Giesler looked like a middle manager in a provincial bank. In it he struck fear into those under him. An enthusiastic Nazi who had been an SA leader since 1924, he looked forward to delivering a key speech to mark the 470th anniversary of the founding of the university. The location for the event was the main auditorium of the Deutsches Museum, a science and technology center on an island in the Isar River, in the center of Munich. The students were ordered to attend, although the Scholls and Schmorell ignored this, having pledged never to attend a Nazi-sponsored event. The main hall was reserved for SS officers and male members of the staff, while female students were made to stand on a balcony. Traute Lafrenz and Gisela Schertling, who had very different views on Nazi ideology, were among those who heard Giesler speak. He had chosen to be provocative, viewing students as draft dodgers, "twisted intellectuals," and "falsely clever minds," who knew nothing about "real life." There were murmurings of discontent and a stony silence when he roared: "Real life is transmitted to us only by Adolf Hitler, with his light, joyful and life-affirming teachings!"[22]

With a disdainful eye he then turned his attention to the female students, who, he said, instead of reading books should be using their "healthy bodies" to provide the Reich with a baby a year. "And for those women students not pretty enough to catch a man," he leered, "I'd be happy to lend them one of my adjutants. And I promise you that would be a glorious experience!"

As he spoke these words, twenty women tried to leave the balcony in protest but were arrested by brown-shirted students. Male students rushed to their aid, and fights broke out. Giesler spoke on, but his words were drowned out by shouts, people stamping their feet, and chairs screeching on the floor as students and SS men struggled and fought at the back of the auditorium and in the lobby.

Some female students ran out and were arrested. Angry male students got into fights with university brownshirts and members of the SS. The female students who had been arrested were released in the confusion and called people together in groups. They burst out of the doors, crossed the bridge off the little island, and headed north along the bank of the Isar. As they marched, they linked arms and sang. For the people outside the art museum with its permanent Nazi exhibition of "Great German Art," the sight of the young marchers was a complete shock. No one had seen voices raised in protest—an angry group of people marching in dissent—for almost ten years.

And although the police broke up the march as it walked between the historic buildings of Ludwigstrasse, the protest had already become a major topic of conversation across the city. Sophie told her friends there was a direct link between their leaflets and the unrest. Their message was getting through!

The march gave the White Rose fresh hope, and they threw themselves into work to disseminate the fifth leaflet in much greater quantities. This time they went a lot further than before, producing between eight thousand and ten thousand copies, all printed in the artist's studio belonging to Manfred Eickemeyer, who was away but had left Hans the key. They worked through the night, continuing during air raids, only stopping the duplicating machine when someone passed close by outside on Leopoldstrasse. It was hard work as the machine had to be cranked by hand, the copies appearing one by one. Sophie and Traute Lafrenz traveled across the city, buying special mimeograph paper, stamps, and envelopes in various locations, aware that a bulk buy would attract attention. They disguised their missions as fun shopping trips, sometimes grabbing a bite to eat in a favorite restaurant, the Deutscher Kaiser on Wilhelmstrasse or an Italian restaurant, the Bodega, in Schwabing. The tension of one trip was broken when Sophie saw a dray horse and rushed to pat its neck. "There, there, old boy," she said, "everything'll be all right." The moment made Lafrenz smile.[23]

The work to get this huge batch of leaflets out to the public was dangerous and exhausting. Every member of the gang was involved. In Munich they left them in telephone kiosks, the entrances and stairways of apartment blocks, and beer halls, and mailed some from dozens of mailboxes.

They also wanted to get away from the city and took huge risks by carrying suitcases filled with leaflets on the train. Each member always traveled alone and placed the case in the overhead rack of a different compartment, to distance himself or herself from the "criminal" material. Graf's contact Willi Bollinger helped with counterfeit travel passes.

Scholl followed this routine on a journey to Salzburg, where he left the station and found mailboxes in quiet streets and posted 150 leaflets. Schmorell carried a case filled with 1,400 leaflets to Linz and Vienna. To confuse the authorities, he mailed 400 from Vienna to Frankfurt, 200 from Linz, and the rest from Salzburg. Graf traveled in uniform but without a pass—thus putting himself at risk of arrest for desertion—to Cologne and Bonn.

Sophie's journeys took her to Augsburg, Ulm, and Stuttgart, and in all she mailed close to a thousand leaflets.[24] In Ulm she was helped again by Hirzel, Müller, and Guter, and also could not resist showing her father one of the leaflets.

He looked at it admiringly but then suddenly said, "Sophie, I hope you two haven't anything to do with this?"

Sophie looked indignant and lied. "How can you even suspect that?" she said.

With the group feeling exhilarated at this period of intense activity, Christoph Probst, whose wife was expecting their third child, had a terrible sense of foreboding. He warned his friends that they were still in the jaws of a ruthless state: With their success, the danger was increasing. The young idealists of the White Rose had demanded attention for their message: They were now getting it.

In the oppressive corridors of the Munich Gestapo a special squad was being formed with one mission: to hunt them down.

# 28

## Swift Arrests Demanded

ROBERT MOHR, A dark-haired man in his midforties, prided himself on what he considered his fairness, his skills in getting a confession from criminals, and his ability at remaining calm under pressure. "Unflappable" was how colleagues described him.

And he was guessing he would need all of those qualities now, as he hurried down a corridor in Munich's redbrick Wittelsbach Palace, a former royal building but now the headquarters of the city's Gestapo. Mohr had been summoned to the office of the head of his department, Schäfer, and he found him angry and nervous. In his hand was a sheet of paper that he quickly passed to Mohr as if it were toxic.

As Mohr read it, he realized it was a kind of poison. A poison against the state. A winner of an Iron Cross, 2nd class, during the First World War, Mohr had been a detective since 1919, switching to the political police in 1938, and he thought he had seen it all. But he had never seen anything like the "Call to All Germans," which he now held in his hand. As far as he knew, nobody had ever dared to spread such treasonous material.

The agitated Schäfer told him that hundreds of these filthy leaflets had been collected in Munich, from park benches, telephone booths, and cinemas, and that they were creating "great disturbance at the highest levels of the Party and the State."[1] He swallowed hard when he said the Munich Gestapo had been instructed to find the culprits without delay, and that meant that Mohr had to clear his desk of all other work and concentrate only on this.

"Swift arrests are demanded!" Schäfer said. "Arrests expected! Understood?"

Mohr nodded with the resigned look of a policeman of more than twenty years' standing when being barked at by somebody promoted above his skills to the level of Oberregierungsrat—upper administrative official.

Mohr returned to his office and began work immediately. It was a police formality to rule on the content of the leaflet. The Gestapo conclusion that it was "hostile to the state in the highest degree" was of no surprise, but where had it come from and how much of this literature was there?

Mohr sent men out to shops to try to find out where the paper and envelopes had been purchased, and to warn local post offices to contact them immediately if someone came in asking for large quantities of stamps. He telephoned other Gestapo offices and found that copies of the same leaflets had been found in Stuttgart, Vienna, Ulm, Frankfurt, and Augsburg. Stuttgart officers told him the ones reported there had been posted in Vienna. The Frankfurt Gestapo reported envelopes postmarked Salzburg. What he was discovering shocked Mohr: The situation was far worse than even the terrified Schäfer feared.

From a criminal policeman's perspective, it was an intriguing and complicated crime, but with so many leaflets and envelopes he knew there would be clues. That gave him hope. But as a political policeman, he had fears, too: What sort of effect was this resistance propaganda having on the wider population?

MOHR'S MEN QUICKLY found copies of another four leaflets. All were undated, but Gestapo reports on where and when they had been received gave Mohr an idea of the order in which they had been written and posted. These others were longer and claimed to come from the "Weisse Rose" as opposed to the "Widerstandsbewegung in Deutschland," but he suspected the person behind them was actually the same. But who was the author, and was there more than one?

Mohr engaged the help of Professor Richard Harder, a language expert, who began by analyzing the first White Rose leaflet. He immediately picked up on the fact that the writer had been deeply influenced by Christian ideals and was most probably a young romantic rather than an embittered loner. He would be part of a group but not a violent resistance organization, Harder declared. There had been a call for passive resistance, but without explanation of what form it should take. The second leaflet seemed more polemic than the first and showed knowledge of the war in Poland, but offered no further clue as to its author. Studying all five as a whole, Harder said the author had an academic or theological background, but it was not yet possible to say whether the leaflets originated in Munich, in one of the other cities where they had appeared, or from somewhere else in the Reich.

However, while the pressure on Mohr was about to increase, he would also receive a significant clue.

THE IMPACT OF the defeat at Stalingrad on the Nazis and on the German nation was devastating.

Saturday, January 30, 1943, was to be a special occasion for the Nazis, marking ten years of the regime. The day before, General von Paulus—surrounded and in a hopeless situation in the Russian city—telegraphed Hitler his congratulations. Hitler responded by promoting him to field marshal and reminding him that no German field marshal had ever surrendered. That Saturday Hitler had chosen not to speak at a party event, and instead Göring's voice was heard across the nation. Even in a thousand years every German will speak of Stalingrad with "religious awe," he claimed.

The nation was being prepared for heroic death and defeat, but the extent of the horror would still fill its people with shock. In the frozen ruins and trenches of Stalingrad, Paulus and more than ninety thousand German soldiers were laying down their arms.

Germany awoke on February 3 to slow marches being played over the radio. Then a voice finally announced that the battle was over. "The sacrifice of the 6th Army was not in vain," chimed the state broadcaster. "As the bulwark of the historic European mission it has broken the assault of six Soviet armies for several weeks . . ." The German soldiers and their officers had "fought shoulder to shoulder to the last bullet. They died so that Germany may live."[2]

There was a slow roll of drums and then a recording of the soldiers' song "Ich hatt' einen Kameraden," and three minutes' silence. Three days of national mourning were to follow.

Gestapo reports from Bavaria noted that morale among the population was lower than at any time during the war so far.[3] A population that had been kept in the dark about previous setbacks and had been fed positive versions of other defeats was left confused and frightened. Perhaps the war would not be won after all.

Everyone knew someone who was grieving over a loved one lost in Russia. Sophie Scholl fretted for days over the fate of Fritz Hartnagel, with whom she had had little contact for months but eventually found out he had escaped Stalingrad, alive but suffering the agonies of severe frostbite.

As the day closed on that first day of national mourning, Hans Scholl and Alex Schmorell decided to take an extraordinary risk. Without consulting Sophie or the others, they sneaked out into the darkened streets with paint and brushes, and wrote "Freedom" and "Down with Hitler" on the walls of apartment blocks, state buildings, and the university. At each location one would paint while the other stood watch, with a loaded pistol in his pocket. When there was time, they added to their words a white swastika crossed through with a smear of red paint.

The following day, as students arrived for their lectures, they found Russian women laborers struggling to wash the paint from the front of the university building. As Traute Lafrenz watched, she saw Hans Scholl smile and then head on inside. He had not stopped to watch this spectacle as everyone else had, and she immediately suspected he was behind it. Sophie suspected her brother, too, and later confronted him in his room: "You did that, didn't you?" Hans nodded and laughed.

"Take me with you next time!" Sophie urged him.

Over the next couple of weeks, Hans, Schmorell, and sometimes Willi Graf headed out through the city after midnight with pots of paint. They even obtained a heavy black tar, which was harder to clean off. Once, the three of them headed down Ludwigstrasse to a memorial to those wounded or killed during the 1923 putsch. On this sacred spot for the Nazi Party, they smeared "Down with Hitler!" in thick paint. It was audacious and foolish.

Christoph Probst met up with Hans and agreed to write a new leaflet, but he warned that the graffiti campaign was putting them in great danger.

Probst was right to be cautious. Reading the reports in his office in Wittelsbach Palace, Robert Mohr began to form the opinion that the graffiti vandals might also be the authors of the White Rose leaflets. While this did not yet help him identify them, it did allow him to concentrate his investigation on Munich.

Students had protested against Giesler, he noted, and his language expert had suggested there could be an academic background to this "White Rose." The university had also been targeted by the graffiti artists.

Mohr contacted informers at the university and told them to be alert for any suspicious activity around the campus.

\* \* \*

KURT HUBER FELT the pain of the Stalingrad defeat deeply. He agonized over the fate of the heroic German soldiers, who had endured frostbite and shelling, sacrificing their lives in a hell far from home; they had been let down by the Nazi regime. Words rushed through his head as he tried to sleep. He was so angry that he could not rest.

A few days after Paulus's surrender, Huber's wife, Clara, awoke to find that he was not in bed. In fact, she was not sure that he had come to bed at all. Going downstairs, she found him in his study, hunched over the typewriter. She sensed that he did not want to show her what he was writing, but looking over his shoulder, she read the words: "Fellow fighters in the Resistance! Shaken and broken, our people behold the loss of the men of Stalingrad. Three hundred and thirty thousand German men have been senselessly and irresponsibly driven to death and destruction by the inspired strategy of our World War One Private First Class. Führer, we thank you!"

Clara felt her blood run cold. She begged her husband to destroy what he was writing. How could he do this with their two children asleep in a room upstairs? He pushed her away gently. The less she knew, the better.

By the time he had finished, Huber had covered the whole page. Addressing "fellow students," he told them that Hitler and his comrades had "debased and twisted those beautiful German words" of "Freiheit und Ehre"—freedom and honor.

"Der Tag der Abrechnung ist gekommen," he wrote. "The day of reckoning has come." He carefully underlined these words. "The reckoning of German youth with the most abominable tyrant our people have ever been forced to endure."

He then turned to recent local events. "The lewd jokes of the Gauleiters insult the honour of the women students. German women students at the university in Munich have given a dignified reply to the besmirching of their honour, and German students have defended the women in the universities and have stood by them. That is the beginning of the struggle for our free self-determination . . . The name of Germany is dishonoured for all time if German youth does not finally rise up . . . Women students! Men students! . . . The German people look to us! The dead of Stalingrad implore us to take action."

* * *

ON FEBRUARY 8, Falk Harnack came to Munich on leave to see his fiancée, Lilo Ramdohr. That afternoon they both visited Hans Scholl's room with Schmorell. Falk smiled at the fact that even the messy interior of the flat, with its piled books and manuscripts and Impressionist prints tacked on the walls, seemed to reject the formal organization of society demanded by the Nazis. However, he was also concerned that the group looked tired and that they had half-written essays for new leaflets lying about the place. It was the kind of carelessness that could cost you your life in the Third Reich. Schmorell tidied up but proudly told him that the leaflets had made an impact in Munich.

Scholl handed Harnack the fifth leaflet, "Call to All Germans," and the visitor read it through. He was impressed—it was a genuine political leaflet, he said—but he still questioned the effectiveness of the campaign. If you want to be a true part of change, you need to link up with the main network of resistance in Berlin, he said. Hans Scholl was buoyed—the White Rose was being taken seriously.

The next day, the entire group—apart from Probst, whose wife was ill in the hospital after giving birth to their third child, and Sophie, who was in Ulm—met at the Franz-Joseph-Strasse flat. The building had run out of heating oil, and the room was freezing cold. The group stayed wrapped up in heavy coats and mufflers.

It was the first time Kurt Huber had met Falk Harnack, and he did not like him. But all listened as Harnack informed them about the state of the German resistance movement. He did not talk about his brother's death or the loss of that group. Instead, he told them that a full-scale rebellion was possible at any time. All elements of the resistance movement had to agree to a broad coalition from left and right. It would be agreed that only three political parties would be allowed in post-Nazi Germany—Marxist, Christian, and Liberal—and that there would be state control of financial institutions and industry. To Huber, this was a "Bolshevik" vision, and he told Harnack that he could not work with him. The students disagreed, and defended the visitor from Berlin.

Not wanting to cause further arguments among the group, Falk Harnack left. Before going, he confirmed with the students that they were invited to a meeting of the resistance in Berlin. They should be outside the

Kaiser Wilhelm Memorial Church at 6 p.m. on February 25. The students shook hands with him and said one of them would be there for sure.

Although Harnack had gone, the atmosphere in the unheated room remained tense.

Huber had brought along the leaflet that he had written himself—the sixth leaflet of the group. He sat while Scholl, Schmorell, and Graf read through what he had written. It was uncomfortable and slightly demeaning for the older professor to be judged by young undergraduates.

They all agreed it was great but took issue with a line demanding that students should "support our glorious Wehrmacht." They felt the army was fighting the war for Hitler so one could not support the army without supporting the war. There was nothing glorious about the war, they said. As serving soldiers, they felt they had the right to overrule Huber. He reacted angrily, and said the leaflet should be published in full or not at all. The young men held firm.

Huber got up, told them his relationship with the White Rose was over, and stormed out of the room.

He was to never see Hans Scholl again, but with his brief foray into resistance work he had sealed his own fate.

FOR TEN DAYS in early February, Sophie Scholl had been at home in Ulm, helping out her mother and father. Her father, she told Fritz Hartnagel in a letter, "is so happy when I come and seems so surprised when I leave," while her mother busied herself with a "thousand small chores." Her parents' love, she said, "is something wonderful," one of the "most beautiful things that has ever been given to me."

She left home and returned to Munich on February 11. There she found Hans distracted and exhausted, from long nights making documents and writing graffiti and from the sheer tension of his secret life.

The argument with Huber had upset him, and although the older man had insisted they destroy the leaflet he had written, Hans had decided to use it—without the line about the "glorious Wehrmacht." He, Schmorell, and Graf had already run off between 1,500 and 3,000 copies of Huber's leaflet, and now Sophie joined them as they addressed and put them into envelopes. Hans then made a trip to a local post office and bought 1,200 8-pfennig stamps. When he left, a clerk reported the purchase to the Gestapo. Sophie later mailed out the leaflets.

Christoph Probst, who a few days earlier had agreed to write the next leaflet, now brought a handwritten version to Hans. It was perhaps the most ambitious essay yet and was designed to be printed and distributed to frontline troops. Claiming Hitler was a "military charlatan," it called for a cease-fire and negotiations with the Allies as a way of finding an "honorable end to the war," and proposed a new international order under the sponsorship of Franklin D. Roosevelt.

Hans Scholl took the draft and put it in his pocket. Probst's leaflet would never be printed or circulated, but its consequences would be great.

Late on the night of Tuesday, February 15, Scholl turned up at the home of the bookseller Josef Söhngen and showed him the leaflet written by Huber. It was their call to fellow students, Scholl explained, adding that he planned to place copies outside lecture halls in the university later that week. Söhngen was horrified. It was far too dangerous, he told his friend.

Hans said he was aware of the dangers, but it had to be done.

It was after midnight and they were tired, but as they shook hands Söhngen had the awful feeling that his young friend was saying a final good-bye.[4]

HANS SCHOLL HAD secretly become obsessed with the idea that the Gestapo had him under surveillance, and although it did not, there was a legitimate reason for his fear.

Back in November, the Scholls' friend in Ulm, Hans Hirzel, had been trying to recruit new members for the group when he had been horrified to find out that one of the people he had spoken to was a Gestapo informer. Hirzel returned to the young man and explained that it was all a joke and he had been making it up. The informer seemed convinced.

But because during the chat Hirzel had mentioned Hans Scholl's name, he contacted Scholl and told him to be prepared for trouble. Between them they arranged a code. If there was trouble from the Ulm Gestapo, Hirzel would ring Scholl and tell him that a book named *Machtstaat und Utopie* (*The Absolute State and Utopia*) was out of print.

On February 17, a Gestapo agent arrived at Hirzel's home in Ulm and took him in for questioning. A rumor had reached them that he had been bragging to friends about his resistance activities. Hirzel realized that this denunciation might have come from the man he had met before Christmas, but also that they appeared to have little evidence. Hirzel told them it was all just stories and that he was sorry. Finding it hard to believe that the local minister's son could be a member of the resistance, the Gestapo let him go.

Hirzel rushed to the Scholl home, determined to warn Hans, whom he admired and respected. Only Inge was at home, but she contacted her friend Otl Aicher, who was staying at Carl Muth's home on the outskirts of Munich. Aicher contacted Scholl to say that he had an important message for him.

Scholl told Aicher to be at his place in Franz-Joseph-Strasse the following morning. He had something to do first thing, but he would be home by eleven.

At eleven the next morning the only people at the address where Hans and Sophie lived were agents of the Gestapo.

# 29

# Long Live Freedom

THURSDAY, FEBRUARY 18, was a beautiful early spring day in Munich. A day to shed scarves and hats, a day for the German public to feel as if they had at last seen off another winter of war. The sky was a perfect blue, the sun shining bright.

Sophie Scholl decided to skip her first two classes that morning, including one with Kurt Huber. Moving between her room and Hans's in the otherwise empty house, the two siblings prepared themselves for the day. On a table were two neat stacks of leaflets—about 1,500 to 1,800 in all. These they placed in a large suitcase, which Hans would carry, and Sophie's smaller red briefcase. Sophie pulled on a warm overcoat and at half past ten closed the door to their apartment. They planned to head to Eickemeyer's studio later on: Sophie had his key, and Hans was carrying Probst's handwritten leaflet in the inside pocket of his jacket.

Sophie was particularly pleased with Huber's "fellow students" leaflet, and she chatted away to Hans on the twenty-minute walk to the university. As they arrived, they bumped into Willi Graf and Traute Lafrenz, who were on their way to a neurology lecture in another building and so could not stop to talk. They all quickly agreed to meet later. As they hurried off to catch a streetcar, Traute turned to Willi and asked why Hans was carrying such a large suitcase into lectures. Traute said she had a strange feeling, but Willi just shrugged.

The Lichthof, the building's large inner courtyard with its great glass-domed ceiling, was empty. The doors were closed on the lecture halls, which were packed with students.

In the center of the Lichthof were two marble statues from the mid-nineteenth century. The Scholls started here, working separately to place bundles of leaflets around the feet of the statues and at the base of the pillars in the hall. Then, moving quickly but trying not to make too much noise on the stone flooring, they moved up the stairs to the second and third floors, leaving leaflets in piles outside the lecture halls and on the windowsills, and on the stairways themselves.

Hans placed a bundle of leaflets on a balustrade under one of the arched ceilings overlooking the open space of the foyer.

Sophie looked at the leaflets. In an instant she thought about the effect they were having. How previously their words had inspired the female students to stand up to Nazi control, how the young men had supported them. She saw the words in Huber's latest appeal: "Students! The German people look to us!"

And without thinking, she stepped forward and with her hand swept the bundle out into the void. It was a dramatic, liberating flourish—a moment of wild energy and freedom—which saw the white paper flutter down like leaves.

But it was also a terrible mistake that ensured there would be no escape from the building.

At that moment, the doors of the lecture theaters opened and the students began bustling out. They saw the paper fluttering down and reached out to see what it was. And they heard the shouts, too—of fifty-six-year-old university handyman Jakob Schmid, who while doing his rounds through the Lichthof had seen the paper being launched from the balustrade. Instinctively, he shouted and began running up the stairs, affronted that someone could be littering one of the spaces for which he was responsible.

"Stop!" he shouted, racing up the short staircases.[1]

Sophie heard him and rushed into an empty room, quickly hiding the key to Eickemeyer's studio. Coming out again, she joined Hans and they began to rush away. Just then Schmid appeared, saw the suitcases and more papers scattered nearby, and grabbed at Hans. "You're under arrest!" Schmid told him.

Hans turned on him. "That's absurd," he said. "You can't arrest somebody at the university!"[2]

But Schmid was dogged, and the true nature of the Scholls' actions was dawning on him. Sophie, her little red bag in her hand, shrugged and admitted she had thrown the papers into the Lichthof.[3] Schmid marched the two students to the office of the building superintendent, Scheidhammer, who had already ordered that the doors to the university be closed and that nobody be allowed to leave. Another university official, named Hefner, picked up the phone and rang the Gestapo. The call was put through to Mohr's secretary.

Within moments Mohr was rushing to the university with a team of agents. Over the last few days he had faced uncomfortable questions from Berlin after Schäfer had informed him that the search so far had been unsuccessful. They had confirmed the use of the same typewriter for the leaflets and had told innkeepers and hoteliers to be on the lookout for the "violent criminal" behind the dissent. A reward of 1,000 Reichsmarks had been posted, advertised in several newspapers, and it had brought in seven suspects, six of whom had already been dismissed.[4] Mohr did not think the seventh had anything to do with the campaign either.

But if this was the breakthrough in the investigation that the call from the university suggested, then Berlin would be delighted.

BY THE TIME Mohr and his men had reached the university, the Scholls were being held in the office of the university rector, Professor Walter Wüst. A loyal Nazi, he held the rank of colonel in the SS and prided himself on his expertise in the new Nazi-approved subject for study: "Aryan Culture."

Although the Scholls had an anxious thirty-minute wait before Mohr arrived, he was surprised to find them looking calm and almost relaxed. He demanded to see their identity papers and found them to be in order. Looking them over and asking a few personal questions, he realized they were a brother and sister from a middle-class family, well educated and hardly "hot-heads." His sense of snobbery made him suspect the janitor was wrong. These two kids could not be part of a revolutionary movement calling itself the "Resistance Movement in Germany."

Turning to Sophie, he said, "Why were you carrying a suitcase?"

"I was going home to Ulm for a few days."

Mohr looked at the large suitcase on the desk and eased open the lid.

"But why is it empty?"

"I was going home to bring fresh clothes back with me."

Mohr nodded. The answer seemed plausible. There was a pause. He was waiting for something.

Then two of his men came in, having meticulously picked up all the leaflets from the Lichthof. All watched as the men neatly collected the papers in bundles and began stacking them into the empty case. They fit perfectly.

Mohr sighed; perhaps his instinct was wrong. He looked at the two again. They were both still calm, especially the girl. She did not even bat an eyelid when he told his men to take them straight to Gestapo headquarters.

As the police turned to talk to each other, Hans slid out the handwritten leaflet from his inside pocket and began to tear it apart under his seat. The two Gestapo men spotted him, wrenched the pieces from his hands, and gave them to Mohr. Scholl had twisted and torn it, but Mohr could easily see what it was: another of those attacks on the government and its armies: "Will all Germans be sacrificed to the forces of hatred and destruction?"

Mohr asked Scholl why he had tried to destroy it. Scholl said it had been given to him by a student he did not know. He had not read it but was afraid it might incriminate him.

The Gestapo officer looked again at the note. It was handwritten, unlike the others. It might well have been just a note handed out. Scholl could be telling the truth; he'd find out later.

Anyway, the handwriting was a fresh clue. He wondered whose it was.

THE STUDENTS AND staff of the university were still being held in the building, with some of Mohr's men moving among them asking if they had seen anything. Kurt Huber—whose 10 a.m. lecture Sophie had been due to attend—was among them. He had seen a copy of the leaflet that the Scholls had thrown about the place and had realized it featured his words. His blood had run cold.

The Scholls were handcuffed and led out through the building. A Gestapo agent named Achter had a grip on Hans's arm, but as Scholl passed through the crowd, he suddenly turned and shouted, "Tell him I won't be coming home this evening!"

Achter reached out and grabbed a figure from the crowd. He was sure that Scholl had been trying to pass a message to him. The man turned out to be an army lieutenant named Karl von Metternich, who was home on leave and angrily denied knowing Scholl. Metternich's room at a local hotel was searched and he was placed under house arrest, but nothing was found to link him to Scholl.[5]

In fact, Scholl had shouted his warning because he had seen Gisela

Schertling in the crowd and he had hoped she would alert Alex Schmorell. But as Hans and Sophie Scholl were bundled into the back of the green Gestapo van, Schmorell had in fact seen it all. He was standing in the crowd, watching events unfold and horrified for his friends.[6]

Turning away, he rushed to take a streetcar to Willi Graf's home on Mandlstrasse. The blood was pounding in his head. The students had talked about what would happen if one was arrested. They had a plan; they had just always hoped they would never have to use it.

Arriving at Graf's, he found that he was out and so left a cryptic message that he knew he would understand. It meant that they should meet the next day at the Starnberger Bahnhof, a quiet wing of the central station, serving mainly regional train services heading into the Bavarian Alps.

Terrified to walk the streets—perhaps the Gestapo even had his description—he went to Lilo Ramdohr's home and hid away there.

WILLI GRAF WAS at the university clinic all day and heard nothing about the arrests. He did not arrive home until just before midnight. Throughout the evening everybody had been talking about what was going on in Berlin, where the propaganda minister had been giving a major speech at Berlin Sportpalast that was being broadcast to the nation. Graf was not interested in what Goebbels had to say.

When he opened the door to his room on the second floor, Gestapo agents were already inside. He and his sister, Anneliese, were arrested and taken to Wittelsbach Palace.[7]

GOEBBELS'S SPEECH IN Berlin that day would become known to all Germans as the "Total War" speech. Addressing fifteen thousand party faithful in an arena festooned with garlands and swastika flags, Goebbels made it clear that these nurses, armament workers, scientists, Eastern Front veterans, and teachers represented the nation listening on their wireless sets. "I see thousands of German women," he said. "The youth is here, as are the aged. No class, no occupation, no age remain uninvited."[8] While Hitler brooded over the defeat at Stalingrad in the Wolf's Lair, his headquarters in the forests of East Prussia, Goebbels was determined to galvanize the nation.

He asked the crowd if they were prepared to "follow the Führer through thick and thin," to put up "with even the heaviest personal burdens," and to work "sixteen hours a day . . . to give your utmost for victory." And each time this eager Nazi crowd, which he claimed represented the nation, shouted back: "Ja!"

"I ask you do you want total war? If necessary, do you want war more total and radical than anything that we can imagine today?"

"Ja!"

"Do you agree that everyone who goes against the war effort in any way should pay for it with his head?"

The crowd came to its feet and applauded, drowning out the speaker. Shouts began of "Führer command, we follow!"

The seeds were sown for a war that would only end with their own nation's destruction. And on the way the state would murder anyone who tried to stop the madness.

Looking around the arena, Goebbels held out his hands, and the crowd hushed a little to hear him.

"You have given me your answers! You have told our enemies what they needed to hear!" He drew breath and called out from behind the lectern one of his favorite quotations, from the soldier-poet Theodor Körner: "Das Volk steht auf, der Sturm bricht los!" "Now let the nation rise, let the storm break!"[9]

The applause and cries of support came at him like a wave. It was a "veritable tumult of frenetic feeling," Goebbels later confided to his diary.[10] "It could not have gone better."[11]

GOEBBELS HAD SPOKEN for hours. He said later he had sweated so much in his double-breasted jacket that he had lost seven pounds in weight during the speech.[12] But for many Germans it had been a drone. Some had listened to it in the background; others had not listened to it at all. Most realized it was propaganda, a form of lying, even if they did not know how much was true and what was made up. They suspected, of course, that those present were among the keenest supporters of the regime, but they could not know, for instance, that gramophone recordings of ovations and cheers had been blasted into the arena to supplement the crowd and to provide them appropriate cues for their apparent hysteria.[13]

Putting the bombast aside, though, there was a general sense that, from this position in the war, what Goebbels was saying was essentially correct: If they wanted to fight on, it would require the "total war" that the baying crowd had agreed to.

The speech was playing in Wittelsbach Palace, the headquarters of the Munich Gestapo, although Sophie and Hans Scholl did not hear it or Goebbels's call for those who harmed Germany's war effort to "lose their heads."

Sophie was checked in at reception by Else Gebel, a prisoner who was allowed to do light clerical duties as part of her Nazi "reeducation." Gebel took her name, address, and family details, signed in her belongings, and searched her. Sophie was then fingerprinted and photographed. Her brother went through the same procedure. They would be allowed no lawyer or visitors, they were both told.

Sophie was taken to a cell that she would be sharing with Gebel herself. Gebel told her she was serving sixteen months for being a courier with a Communist resistance network. "If you have a leaflet on you destroy it now," Gebel told her.

Robert Mohr decided to carry out Sophie's interrogation, while a colleague, Anton Mahler, would question Hans, with the support of other agents. The interrogations were carried out in adjacent rooms, and when Sophie said she was worried that they were beating Hans, Mohr opened the door to show that they were not.

Throughout the afternoon Sophie was questioned about her father's political views and why she opposed National Socialism. She said that when she was a teenager she had found the "political meetings" of the League of German Girls to be "boring" and felt that they were "incorrect from a pedagogical point of view." She told Mohr that the arrests of her and her siblings during the crackdown on the d.j. in 1937 were "completely unjustified."[14]

She then bravely told Mohr what she felt was the "most important reason for my antipathy to the movement."

"I perceive the intellectual freedom of people to be limited in such a manner as contradicts everything inside of me," she said. "I would like to state that I personally would like to have nothing to do with National Socialism."[15]

Mohr asked her about the events earlier that day at the Lichthof. Sophie said she had arranged to meet her friend Gisela Schertling—who she was clear did not share her views as she had been brought up a National Socialist—at her own apartment at noon, but had changed her mind and decided to go home to Ulm by train. She was at the university to tell Schertling—who was at Huber's Introduction to Philosophy lecture—that she would not be there if she called around. In the building they had seen leaflets lying around, and her brother had picked one up, laughed, and stuffed it in his pocket. She had taken him up to the third floor to show him where she sometimes attended lectures, and while there she had seen the pile of leaflets on the balustrade and had given them a shove so they "fluttered to the ground."

Sophie looked calmly at Mohr and added: "I now realize that what I did was a stupid mistake, which I now regret but cannot change."[16]

After several hours, Sophie was returned to her cell, where she was given a hot bowl of soup, a piece of bread, and some coffee.

Mohr sat at his desk with his chin on his hands and again those doubts began to surface. The young woman seemed so convincing, so calm; perhaps she was telling the truth.

Those doubts disappeared when his men returned from the Scholls' rooms at Franz-Joseph-Strasse 13 with the results of their search.

THE GESTAPO HAD pulled the two rooms apart, and it had been worth it.

They came away with a large quantity of 8-pfennig stamps, a typewriter, envelopes, letters, and a notebook in Sophie's handwriting.

There were bonuses for the Gestapo men, too. As they searched, there were two rings on the doorbell. First, Gisela Schertling called, fresh from seeing Hans's arrest and looking for Schmorell. Then Inge's friend Otl Aicher arrived with his message from Hirzel in Ulm—the one he had promised to deliver, warning Hans that he might be in danger. Both Aicher and Schertling were taken into custody, and the Gestapo sealed the building.

The items from the search were placed on Mohr's desk and he began to go through them. Sophie's notebook appeared to be a ledger of accounts— items bought against money received or saved. But there was something else: a list of addresses in Augsburg and Munich. He had found the mailing list of the White Rose. Mohr was shocked: He had been prepared to believe the young woman was innocent.

He reached for the letters and flicked through them. One of them caught his eye. He looked on his desk for the scraps of paper that Hans Scholl had tried to dispose of in the rector's office and held them and the letter together. There was little doubt: They were written in the same hand.

The name on the letter was Christoph Probst.

* * *

GISELA SCHERTLING HAD by now been interviewed, and had named Schmorell as someone who was with Hans "all the time" and had mentioned other friends—Huber, Söhngen, and Muth.

Schertling was in no doubt that Hans and his sister had taken the leaflets to the university.[17]

AICHER WAS RELEASED after only a short time in custody and took an express train to Ulm to tell the Scholl family about the arrests. Traute Lafrenz arrived at the family home for the same reason.

Robert Scholl made inquiries with the Gestapo and was told they would be given no information about the arrests and they could not visit their children.

HANS AND SOPHIE Scholl were interrogated throughout the night, and Sophie was confronted with the list of items found in her room. She stuck to her version of events. But next door her brother was struggling.

After several hours of questioning from Anton Mahler in which the agent seemed to be trying to use Hans's answers to incriminate his sister, Schmorell, and Schertling, Hans Scholl broke.

For months Scholl had shown the most amazing reserve and courage. He had seen the horrors of Russia and what his nation was doing in the East; he had organized clandestine meetings and graffiti attacks in the street and made train rides carrying the leaflets of the White Rose, knowing that at any checkpoint he could be arrested and captured. And he knew that with every risk he took, he was in danger of bringing his dearly loved sister down with him.

He told Mahler he was "ready to tell the whole truth."[18] But he would not blame others and took the entire responsibility on himself: He had written the leaflets and bought the duplicator, he said. The leaflet in his pocket had been written by his friend Christoph Probst, but he had asked him to write down his thoughts and had never told him about the leafleting campaign. "All other persons with the exception of Probst are in my opinion not guilty," he said. "I believed that this inner duty was greater than the oath that I had sworn as a soldier. I knew what I took upon myself and I was prepared to lose my life by so doing."[19]

\*   \*   \*

HANS SCHOLL'S CONFESSION came at 4 a.m.[20] Mahler quickly informed his boss, Mohr, and he confronted Sophie, who immediately claimed shared responsibility with her brother. She said they had come up with the idea of the leaflet campaign together the previous summer.

"We were convinced that Germany had lost the war and that every life that is sacrificed for this lost cause is sacrificed in vain," she told Mohr. "I would also like to tell the truth about the events in the University of Munich this morning. I hereby confess that my brother and I brought these leaflets into the university in the suitcase that was confiscated upon our apprehension. We also scattered the leaflets. In my estimation, there were about 1500–1800 leaflets entitled 'Fellow Students!' and about 50 entitled 'Call to All Germans.'"[21] In her exhaustion she also admitted Schmorell might have helped in the distribution of some of the leaflets. She was finally allowed back to her cell at 8 a.m. The second interrogation had lasted more than ten hours.

Mohr had all he needed on the siblings. He also had enough to arrest Schmorell and Probst.

THE GESTAPO CHECKED with the Bergmannschule, where the army medical students were trained, and found that Alex Schmorell had missed a roll call. A "Wanted!" posted was published with a reward of 1,000 marks for information leading to his arrest.

Lilo Ramdohr had stayed at arm's length from the White Rose, but her relationship with Falk Harnack meant she might eventually be implicated. She acquired a Bulgarian passport in the name of Nikolai Nikolaeff for Schmorell. Schmorell took the photograph out of his student identification card and pasted it into the passport. They came up with a plan for him to escape through mountain passes and over the border into Switzerland.

Ramdohr went with Schmorell to the Starnberger Bahnhof, where he was hoping to keep his appointment with Willi Graf. Neither could have had any idea that Graf had been arrested overnight.

Schmorell went inside and looked around. Gestapo agents in their familiar long leather coats and slouch hats appeared to be everywhere. Everybody's papers were being closely checked.

Schmorell and Ramdohr walked quickly away.

\* \* \*

CHRISTOPH PROBST WAS with his unit on a Luftwaffe base near Innsbruck. Friday was pay day and he was on the way over to see the cashier.

Probst's wife, Herta, was still in the hospital following the birth of their third child, and he was eager to get to Munich for the weekend to see Michael, Vincent, and little Katja.

The cashier gave him a sideways glance and said his pay was not here. He was to report to his superior. If Probst sensed a problem, there was little he could do. When he reached the officer's door, he knocked and was called in. Once inside, he heard the door close behind him.

Two Gestapo men stepped either side of him, and one opened Probst's suitcase, which was on the officer's desk.

"Take off your uniform and put on civilian clothes," they told him. "You're under arrest."

AFTER THE FALLOUT from his speech, Paul Giesler apologized to the student body of the university for his remarks. But the apology was given begrudgingly, and privately the Nazi official was seething at the humiliation he had suffered at the hands of the students. The unprecedented protest that followed had embarrassed him in Berlin.

The White Rose leaflets had increased his anger.

Then on the morning of Friday, February 19, he was brought the news he had been waiting for from the Gestapo: a list of five names with an additional possible suspect. He read down the list: Scholl, Hans Fritz, medical student; Scholl, Sophia Magdalena, student of natural sciences and philosophy; Schmorell, Alexander, medical student; Probst, Christoph, student company, Luftwaffe; Graf, Willi, medical student; Graf, Anneliese, philosophy student.[22] Schmorell was the oldest, he noted. Just twenty-five. He seethed as he read the note on the motive for their actions: a belief that "students and the intelligentsia should purge the National Socialist system from the people."[23]

The traitors were in custody, and he wanted action taken quickly. He sent a telex direct to Martin Bormann, Hitler's private secretary, regarding this group's "highly treasonous activity" and requesting a "quick trial" as the crimes had led to "severe unrest among the civilian population in southern Germany." He said this could only be done if the male accused—all members of the armed forces—were not punished by an army tribunal but were tried with the women in the People's Court.[24]

At 5 p.m. that afternoon Bormann responded, having ordered Field Marshal Keitel to discharge Scholl, Graf, Schmorell, and Probst from armed service. All could be tried in the People's Court.

Delighted, Giesler told his staff that the trial must take place that Monday—February 22—and "that the execution take place immediately following."[25] He requested from Berlin the permission to hang the members of the White Rose in Marienplatz, close to a column commemorating the end of Swedish occupation during the Thirty Years' War, or—better still— outside the university as a warning to its students.[26] But Heinrich Himmler stepped in to warn that public executions could encourage further demonstrations. There would be executions and they would be swift, he said, but carried out in secret.

Even before the court session had opened, the verdict and sentence had been decided.

MOHR FELT HIS case against the Scholls was solid, but he needed more on Graf and Probst, so he brought Sophie back to the interrogation room.

Despite her predicament—she knew by now that her confession would most likely lead to her execution—Sophie remained firm. She said Willi Graf was not actively involved in the leafleting campaign, Anneliese was "apolitical," and "as far as I know, [Probst] had absolutely nothing to do with the writing, production, and dissemination of the leaflets."

Mohr sighed. It was by now the early hours of Saturday. He was tired; she must be exhausted. But he could see he would get no more from Sophie Scholl.

Before closing the interrogation, he held her gaze and asked if she had not now come to the conclusion that her conduct must be "viewed as a crime against the common good . . . especially in this phase of the war." Then he leaned forward and added plainly: "And that this conduct and action must be met with the most severe sentence possible?"

Sophie shook her head firmly.

"From my point of view, I must answer no," she said. "Now, as before, I believe I have done the best that I could for my nation. I therefore do not regret my conduct. I wish to take upon myself the consequences of my actions."[27]

Mohr stood up and the officer taking the notes packed up. As Sophie Scholl was being led to the door, Mohr tried to explain to her the National Socialist's "worldview," why it mattered, and what Hitler had accomplished.

Sophie stopped and looked at him. "You are wrong," she said. "I would do it all over again—because I'm not wrong. You have the wrong worldview."[28]

CHRISTOPH PROBST CAME into the interrogation room not knowing who else from the group was under arrest. He had had no contact with anyone else and did not even know about the events at the university.

He took full responsibility for the handwritten leaflet found in Hans Scholl's pocket and tried to protect Sophie: She was "just a girl" under the influence of her brother. Probst appealed for mercy, saying he was suffering from depression and had a sick wife and three children.

But once he was back in his cell, a file was prepared for the People's Court. Hans Scholl, Sophie Scholl, and Christoph Probst were all charged with high treason.

THE CHARGE WAS read to each in turn in their cells. The trial, they were told, would take place the following day.

Sophie turned her face away from her cellmate, Else Gebel, and looked at the sunlight pouring in through the cell window. "Such a beautiful sunny day," she said, "and I have to go . . ." But then she straightened and turned back to the other woman. "But how many are dying on the battlefields? How many young lives full of hope? What difference does my death make if our actions alert people?"

Mohr visited the cells and encouraged them each to write short letters home. They all thanked their parents and apologized for the pain they were causing. Probst told his "mother, sister, wife, and children that I live only for you," and that "nothing is too difficult for us to endure."

In her letter home, Sophie stressed that her religious faith remained strong and that she hoped people would see that what they had done was right.

Mohr took the letters, but they were never sent. The Gestapo still feared the conspiracy might be much larger and believed the publication of the letters might inspire others. They were later destroyed.

Sophie Scholl knelt by her prison bed and prayed before trying to sleep. The lights in all three condemned cells remained on all night.

*    *    *

IN THE DREAM the sun was shining and the sky was a perfect blue. A woman was carrying a child up a slope to a church. Sophie Scholl could see that the woman was herself and that the child was dressed in a long white christening dress.

The slope got steeper, but Sophie held the child tightly and her stride was sure and determined.

Then suddenly a hole began to open up in the ground, and she placed the child on the ground beyond it before she herself plunged into the dark abyss that had opened up beneath her feet.

It was seven in the morning on Monday, February 22, 1943. The last day of Sophie's short life.

Sitting on her bed, she told the dream to her cellmate, Else Gebel, who listened intently, and then asked, "But what does it mean?"

Sophie leaned forward. "The child is our idea," she said. "In spite of all obstacles, it will prevail. We were permitted to be pioneers, though we must die early for its sake."[29]

In his cell Hans Scholl used the short stub of a pencil to scratch out a single sentence from Goethe on the wall. It was a favorite saying of his father's, and it gave Hans much-needed strength: "Hold out in defiance of all despotism."

Sophie Scholl traveled to the Palace of Justice, a huge building covering several city blocks, in a separate police car from her brother and Probst. Inside all three were seated in the dock flanked by uniformed armed guards with bayonets fixed on their rifles. The People's Court was presided over by a president and two professional judges assisted by two legal representatives of the SS and SA. There were no witnesses for the defense, and the public was banned from entering the courtroom.

At 10 a.m. the president of the court had not arrived—his express train from Berlin had been delayed—so the court discussed some basic legal issues. The accused cast their eyes around the room. They were without friends. Most of the seats were taken by people in brown and black uniforms. Even their defense counsel, who would speak for them, considered them enemies of the state.

Then the door behind the judges' bench swung open and in strode a man in blood-red robes and a red cap. Everyone except the defendants jumped to their feet, raised their arm, and shouted, "Heil Hitler!"

Roland Freisler was one of the most terrifying and demented figures in a regime full of individuals capable of the most monstrous acts. Freisler was a forty-nine-year-old lawyer who had been a prisoner of war during the First World War and had studied the law in Jena. He had been a member of the Nazi Party since 1925, and Hitler had personally appointed him the president of the People's Court six months earlier. In the People's Court only his word and opinion mattered, and the accused who came before him were all traitors to the state and social parasites. As they spoke in their defense, he would scream and shout at them, or pretend not to be listening. The embodiment of hatred, he turned his court into a theater of horror, a charade of justice.

Reich Prosecutor Weyersberg opened proceedings by outlining the case, and the accused were asked to confirm their identities. They were then asked to explain their parts in the leafleting campaign. As they tried to tell their stories, Freisler became increasingly angry, and when the evidence was brought in—the leaflets themselves, a duplicating machine, and paint used in the graffiti campaign—he began screaming at them.

Only Sophie showed no signs of intimidation. "Somebody had to make a start," she shouted at him. And then to the courtroom: "What we said and wrote are what many people are thinking. They just don't dare say it aloud!"[30]

Freisler had instructed that nothing the defendants said should be recorded in the trial transcript, but a young lawyer named Leo Samberger was so impressed with them that he noted what he could in his notebook. The official record states only that "the accused explained their side of the matter."[31]

The prosecutor concluded his case by demanding the death penalty for all three accused. The defense counsel then asked for a "just sentence" for Hans Scholl, a "mild punishment" for Sophie Scholl, and a "mild punishment" for Probst, the young father of three.[32]

The trial clerk recorded that the accused were "granted the last word," but did not record it when Sophie told Freisler: "You know the war is lost. Why don't you have the courage to face it?"

Probst said he had done what he had in the interests of the country and to spare Germany further bloodshed. Spectators in the court shouted insults and abuse at him—describing him as a traitor to the dead of Stalingrad—and Freisler insulted him over the idea expressed in his handwritten leaflet that Roosevelt should lead a community of nations after the war. The name of the US president sent Freisler into a screeching rage. Hans Scholl tried to speak on his friend's behalf but was shouted down.

The judge stood up and announced an adjournment for a working lunch, during which he and his fellow judges would consider their verdicts. The accused remained in the courtroom, watching the university janitor Jakob Schmid take congratulations from the Nazi figures in the public seats. Schmid, who had attended to give evidence, had not been required to take the stand because of the accused's confessions. He had received a 3,000-mark reward for his capture of the Scholls.

Robert and Magdelena Scholl were not allowed into the court and were sitting outside. Someone passed them a message that the judge was considering his verdicts. They took comfort in the presence of their younger son, Werner, who was at their side, having just returned on leave from the Russian Front, and his friend Jürgen Wittenstein.

"Will they have to die?" Magdelena asked Wittenstein.

He tried not to nod but could not hide the truth. "If I had just one tank I'd get them out," he told her, clenching his fists. "Then I'd blow up the court and take them to the border!"[33]

There was a flurry of activity in the courtroom as people headed back to their seats. The judges were returning. In the confusion Robert Scholl sneaked into the room and whispered loudly into the ear of the defense lawyer named Klein. "Go to the president of the court and tell him that the father is here and he wants to defend his children!"

Klein hesitated, but Scholl insisted and Klein made his way to the judges' bench. As he listened, Freisler screeched and pointed his finger at Robert Scholl. "Remove that man from my court!" he screamed.

Guards grabbed Robert Scholl's arms and began dragging him to the door. "There is a higher court before which we must all stand!" he shouted, freeing a hand to point at Freisler. Then, gesturing to the accused, he added: "They will go down in history!"

The guards shoved Scholl through the door and held it closed. Freisler read his verdict from handwritten notes, speaking so quickly everyone struggled to hear what he was saying. "In the name of the German people! . . . During a time of war, the accused have called for the downfall of the Reich in leaflets . . . They have aided and abetted the enemies of the

Reich and demoralized its armed forces . . . Any other sentence would erode public support for the war . . . The accused are sentenced to death!"[34]

The Nazi officials in the court murmured their approval but looked to the dock as Hans Scholl shouted at the judge: "Today you will hang us, but soon you will be standing where I stand now!"[35]

As the courtroom emptied, Werner Scholl walked in, no one questioning the man in uniform. He found his brother and sister being handcuffed, and his eyes welled up with tears. Hans and Sophie each gave him a hug and held him tight until the guards told them it was time to move. "Stay strong!" Hans told him. "No compromises."[36]

And then he was gone.


THE FIRST WHITE Rose trial closed at 12:45 p.m.[37]

The accused were driven quickly to Stadelheim prison, a large building on the edge of the Perlach Forest to the south of the city. Adolf Hitler had served a short jail sentence there in 1922, and in 1934, Ernst Röhm had been shot by firing squad in cell number 70 on the Führer's orders.

As the three were escorted to single cells, Leo Samberger—the friendly lawyer who had watched the trial—took Robert Scholl to the state attorney's office to enter a clemency plea. There they were told it would be best if they hurried to the prison to see their children.

At the prison the Scholls were allowed to meet first Hans and then Sophie in a small visiting room. Sitting in a striped prison uniform, Hans looked tired but resolute. "I have no hatred," he said, holding his parents' hands. "I have put everything—everything—behind me."

Robert Scholl repeated his words from court. "You'll go down in history," he said. "There is such a thing as justice—in spite of all this."[38] Then, fighting back the tears, he added: "I'm proud of you both."[39]

Hans asked them to send his love to his friends, and then tears came to his eyes. He composed himself, shook his parents by the hand, and left.

A female warden then brought Sophie in. She was dressed in her own jacket, blouse, and skirt, and she greeted her mother and father with a smile.

Her mother offered her some sweets, which she took. "I didn't have any lunch," she explained.[40]

Her mother gripped her hands, not wanting to let go. She searched her daughter's face for pain or fear, but saw only a sense of triumph.[41] "Sophie," she said, "to think you will never come through the door again."

Sophie sighed. "Oh, what do these few short years matter, Mother?" she said. Then she looked at both parents, knowing there must be pride as well as anguish. "We took all the blame for everything," she said. "That is bound to matter in time to come."

"Remember Jesus," Magdelena said.

"Yes. But you, too."[42]

The meeting was over and Sophie stood to leave. She smiled and showed her parents no sadness. Only afterwards, when Mohr looked in on her in the reception cell, did she have tears in her eyes. "I've just said goodbye to my parents," she said. "I'm sure you understand."

BEGINNING AT 4 P.M. Sophie, Hans, and Christoph were brought in turn to the prison office, where Reich Prosecutor Weyersberg was waiting.

As they stood before him, he said there would be no clemency and the death sentence would be carried out at 5 p.m. It was barely three hours since their trial had ended—and until that moment they'd had no idea how little time they had to live. Probst's wife was still in the hospital and so he had no opportunity to say good-bye to her or his children. They would not know of his fate until later.

The prison chaplain, Karl Alt, visited the accused in their cells. Both the Scholls read aloud Psalm 90: "Teach us to consider that we must die, so that we may be wise."

Alt spoke the words of John's Gospel to them: "Greater love hath no man than this, that a man lay down his life for his friends."

Probst converted to Catholicism in prison, receiving his first Holy Communion and the last rites. "In a few minutes we will meet eternity," he said.

Sophie was taken from her cell first and led across a courtyard to a small building. Inside an anteroom a Nazi official sat at a table and asked her to confirm her name. "Sophia Magdalena Scholl," she said proudly.

"For high treason and aiding and abetting the enemy, the court has sentenced you to death by guillotine," he told her.

The guillotine inside the death chamber consisted of a wooden bench on which the victim would lie and a tall upright wooden frame down which the blade would run. It stood behind a black curtain, and at its side was Johann

Reichhart, who, with his black hat, white gloves, and bow tie, looked a little like a vaudeville magician.[43] Since 1924 he had been the official executioner for the Bavarian State Ministry of Justice, having succeeded his uncle in the role. He was a busy man. At this stage in the war, the father of three had requested a special dispensation from the police to break the speed limit so that he could get to his many appointments on time, although the authorities had turned down the request.[44]

Two male prison guards walked Sophie to the guillotine. Reichhart used these men to hold the condemned steady. Sophie's head was moved in place and Reichhart released the blade.

Forty-eight seconds had passed since she had left her cell.

The prison doctor, Koch, pronounced her dead, and the clerk recorded that she had been "calm and collected."

Sophie's body and head were transferred quickly to a coffin, and Hans was brought in.[45]

As he was placed in the apparatus of death, the twenty-four-year-old shouted, "Long live freedom!" The clerk carefully recorded that fifty-two seconds had passed since he had left his cell.[46]

Christoph Probst came in as calm as the Scholls. He seemed to have found an inner peace. Forty-two seconds passed from the moment he left his cell to his death.[47] Reichhart maintained that the more swiftly the sentence could be carried out, the more humane he would feel he had been to the condemned.

Back in the main building of the prison, while one official typed up a special notice announcing the executions of three outsiders—Einzelgänger— who had "shamelessly committed offenses against the armed security of the nation and the will to fight of the German Volk," another moved from cell to cell collecting their belongings.

In Sophie's cell, lying on the bed she had neatly made, was her copy of her indictment for high treason.

On the back she had written, in a steady hand, a single word: "Freiheit." Freedom.

# 30

## On the Run

ALEX SCHMORELL WAS on the run and desperate for help. He took a train to Innsbruck on that Saturday after the Scholls' arrest, but a contact arranged by Lilo Ramdohr failed to meet him at the station.

Hunted, alone, and with very little money, he headed into Mittenwald, a town in the shadow of the Bavarian Alps that he knew well from skiing trips. He had a Russian friend there, a coachman who worked at a castle that had been converted into a health resort. The friend agreed to hide him. As they walked through the town, they were stopped by a police patrol. Schmorell took out the bogus Bulgarian passport, which Ramdohr had bought for him on the black market, and handed it over. It had not been scrutinized before.

The policemen looked at the photograph, questioned Schmorell, but then waved them on.

But the relief was short-lived. Someone in the town had already recognized Schmorell and gone to the police. Word reached Schmorell's friend—whom Alex would later protect by telling the Gestapo he had been sleeping in haystacks—and Schmorell headed into the mountains.

While the weather that month in southern Germany was mild, the Alpine slopes were still no place for a man without adequate boots and warm clothing, and whose food supplies were running low. Sitting on a rock with the white-tipped peaks around him, Schmorell decided to return to Munich.

He arrived back in the city on the night of February 24 and planned to visit a former girlfriend. When he arrived at her street, the air raid alarm sounded and the RAF began to pound the city.

Hurrying down into the shelter in the building's basement, he saw his friend and tried to signal to her, waving her to come to the entrance so that they could speak.

He immediately knew he had made a mistake. His friend was pregnant, terrified by the bombs, and horrified to see him. He had no idea that the manhunt for him had included posters and notices in the newspapers. Suddenly everyone in the shelter seemed to be looking at him. People turned on the pregnant woman, and she had little choice but to be honest and confirm who Schmorell was. A man in a uniform of a railway worker stepped forward and grabbed at his arm. "You're under arrest!"

Schmorell broke free and ran into the street, but alerted by the shouts, a number of soldiers caught him and wrestled him to the ground.[1] Within moments a messenger was running through the burning streets to get the Gestapo.

During interrogation the Gestapo realized Schmorell had no idea that the others had been executed. Schmorell, seeking to protect his friends, whom he believed still alive, took full responsibility for the White Rose campaign. In his courage and loyalty, he condemned himself.

THE DAY AFTER Schmorell's arrest Falk Harnack was busy in Berlin on resistance business. At four in the afternoon, he visited Dietrich Bonhoeffer and his brother Klaus at the latter's flat. Falk had met them after visiting Arvid before his execution. He had immediately liked the pastor. Bonhoeffer had a warm face; he inspired you. As another of his friends once remarked, "When he walked into a room you could no longer be a coward."

Although Bonhoeffer had shared Oster and Dohnanyi's names with Falk Harnack, he was keen to link the Abwehr and government opposition to younger civilian opponents of the regime. He had been delighted when Falk had told him about the students in Munich and the work they were doing to inspire others. Unaware of the White Rose arrests, Falk said he was off to meet one of them.

Two hours later Falk Harnack hurried to the meeting point by the Kaiser Wilhelm Memorial Church in western Berlin. There was no sign of Hans Scholl.

Always security conscious, Falk left and returned an hour later. He waited for twenty minutes but dared not wait any longer.

He walked off. He did not know what had happened, but he feared the worst.

Two days later, back on his base at Chemnitz, he received a letter from Lilo Ramdohr. It said simply: "Our friends on the front have fallen."

Falk Harnack sank down on his bed. If he had survived association with his brother's group, he knew he would not get away from the dragnet bringing down the student resistance. He was half right.

WILLI GRAF, HIS sister, Anneliese, and Gisela Schertling were already in custody. Traute Lafrenz and a student friend named Katharina Schüddekopf soon joined them. Then the Ulm Gestapo swooped down on the Lutheran minister's son Hans Hirzel and his sister, Susanne, and their friends Franz Josef Müller and Heinrich Guter. Eugen Grimminger, who had written a check to support the Scholls' activities, was arrested in Stuttgart, and Graf's contact Heinz Bollinger in Freiburg.

Kurt Huber's wife, Clara, was in the country with their son, on a regular trip to barter with farmers for food. One morning as Huber slept at home, there was a rapping on the door and his twelve-year-old daughter, Birgit, opened it to have three Gestapo agents push past her into the house.

Kurt Huber was still in bed when they burst into his bedroom and arrested him.[2]

IT WAS ROUTINE to arrest the families of political prisoners in the Third Reich. All of the accused knew that their loved ones would be subject to the concept of Sippenhaft—clan arrest.

After learning of Hans's and Sophie's executions via the newspaper, the Scholl family was devastated. Elisabeth had been waiting for a bus when she picked up a newspaper and saw the front-page headline describing her brother's and sister's beheadings. "I wished there and then that I was insane so I did not have to comprehend this," she said later. "I was just four days away from my own 23rd birthday and I felt that my entire world had been destroyed."[3]

Then the Ulm Gestapo came and took them all away. Magdalena Scholl and Inge were held until the end of July 1943. Elisabeth was also eventually released. Werner was allowed to return to his unit. But their father, Robert Scholl, was sentenced to two years in prison.

The second White Rose trial took place on April 19, again before a screeching Roland Freisler. There were fourteen defendants and the hearing lasted a full fourteen hours. Again, there was little attempt at legal balance: Kurt Huber's lawyer suddenly jumped up during the reading of a White Rose leaflet, saluted Freisler with a "Heil Hitler!" and said he could no longer listen to these insults against the Führer and so would withdraw as the professor's representative.[4]

It was after ten at night when Freisler gave his verdicts. Huber, Willi Graf, and Alex Schmorell—who had all been charged with high treason—were to be executed.

Eugen Grimminger, "who gave money to a traitor who aided and abetted the enemy," was sentenced to ten years in prison. More devastating still, as Grimminger had feared, the case had brought his Jewish wife to the attention of the authorities. Once in custody, he could no longer protect her. Jenny Grimminger was transported to Auschwitz, where she later died. Her sister, Senta, and her family was also rounded up. They died in Riga.[5]

The rest also received jail sentences: Heinz Bollinger and Helmut Bauer, both recruited by Graf, seven years each; Hans Hirzel and Franz Josef Müller, "immature boys seduced by enemies of the State" who had "supported treasonous leaflet propaganda against National Socialism," five years each; and Heinrich Guter, eighteen months for having knowledge of "propagandistic intentions" but failing to report them. Gisela Schertling, Katharina Schüddekopf, and Traute Lafrenz were guilty of the same offense as Guter, but "since they are girls" they received one year in jail, and Susanne Hirzel, who was guilty of "inexcusable naivete" for disseminating leaflets without knowing what they contained, received six months.[6] The gender-based comments in the verdicts against the women were carefully designed to insult and belittle the female students at the university, who had dared to rise up against the Gauleiter's speech.[7]

There was a surprise for the final defendant, though. Falk Harnack, who had been arrested in Chemnitz, was told that while he "had knowledge of treasonous activities" and did not report them, his case was subject to "such special circumstances that it is impossible to punish him for this omission." The special circumstances, it appeared, were that Falk was the "only remaining son" of a distinguished family.

Freisler told him that he was "therefore acquitted."

It seemed a most uncharacteristic act of generosity, but of course it was nothing of the sort: The Gestapo saw that the Harnack connections to Arvid and his group and to the White Rose had been much more than a coincidence. Which other traitors did he know?

Falk Harnack was released in the hope that he would lead the Gestapo to a wider network of resistance.

A PLEA FOR clemency for Alex Schmorell was considered and immediately dismissed by Reichsführer Himmler. Execution was "just punishment" for his "reprehensible deeds," which were "largely attributable to his Russian bloodline," Himmler stated.

"As thousands of valuable German people put their lives on the line for the Fatherland, it would be irresponsible to set aside the death sentence in this case," the Reichsführer stated.[8]

In his cell in Stadelheim, Schmorell came to accept his fate. "I'm going with the awareness that I followed my deepest convictions and the truth," he wrote to his parents. "This allows me to meet my hour of death with a conscience at peace."[9]

Like his friends, he had a strong Christian faith. He told his lawyer, Siegfried Diesinger, who continued to support Alex after the trial, that he felt he had "fulfilled my life's mission."

Kurt Huber had more to do. He spent his time in the condemned cell writing a book on the philosopher Gottfried Leibniz, which he hoped would provide some income for his family after his death. In a last letter home he thanked his wife and children for making his life rich and beautiful.[10] At his trial Huber had stated: "The basic demand for true national community has been destroyed by the systematic undermining of trust among fellow humans. There is no more terrible judgement on a nation than the admission, we must all make, that no-one feels safe from his neighbour, that even a father does not feel safe from his own sons anymore."[11]

Schmorell and Huber were executed on July 13, 1943, although Willi Graf still waited. His journey to the Rhineland and the Saar to drum up support for the White Rose still intrigued the Gestapo. The detective Robert Mohr was convinced he could make Graf incriminate others further, but he could not. Graf continued to protect those who were still in custody, saying that Willi Bollinger had refused to take part in the leaflet campaign. Graf said Bollinger told him: "I will not sacrifice myself for something like that!"[12]

He had been in solitary confinement for eight months when the executioner's room was prepared for him. In his last letter home Graf said: "On this day I'm leaving this life and entering eternity. What hurts me most of all is that I am causing such pain to those of you who go on living . . . I ask you, Father and Mother, from the bottom of my heart, to forgive me for the anguish and the disappointment I've brought you . . . Hold each other and stand together with love and trust."[13]

THE AMERICAN PUBLIC first learned of the White Rose resistance movement on April 18, 1943, almost two months after Sophie and Hans Scholl and Christoph Probst were executed. The *New York Times* reported that there had been a "student revolt" following Gauleiter Giesler's speech at the university and that a "woman, brother and another soldier" had been beheaded for "issuing anti-Nazi tracts."

The newspaper report had been wired by a correspondent in Stockholm and was based on an article in the Swedish magazine *Veckojounalen*. Somehow the news had reached Sweden, although the names were at first garbled—Sophie was listed as "Maria Scholl" and Probst's first name was given as "Adrian"—but were later corrected. A copy of Huber's leaflet was paraphrased in the article. "The war was condemned and German youths were urged to establish a new Europe," the *New York Times* reported.

Elements of the trial were also reported. Hans Scholl was said to have replied to an allegation that he was a Communist—the familiar Nazi slur for any dissenter—with the line "I am not a Communist; I am a German."[14]

When Schmorell, Huber, and Graf were executed, the *New York Times* paid a full tribute to all six. "An animal brought up in a sty may be expected to behave like a pig," it stated. "But these Munich students, few or many, representative or otherwise, rose gloriously out of the mud, protesting in the name of principles which Hitler thought he had killed forever. In years to come we, too, may honor Sergeant Hans Scholl, Sophia Scholl, Christophe Probst, Alexander Schmorell, Karl Huber and William Graf, slain in Munich for a cause that is also ours."[15] Willi Graf's sentence of death had, at that stage, not been carried out, but such was the fog created by the Nazi justice system that people might assume that it had.

The Swedish source for the reporting of the White Rose leaflet was either a crewman who had brought it from the docks at Hamburg, where the northern group was active, or Helmut James Graf von Moltke. Moltke had traveled to Oslo in March 1943 and brought a number of the White Rose leaflets, which he passed to the Norwegian bishop Eivind Berggrav, whom he and

Bonhoeffer had previously met.[16] The leaflets were translated into Norwegian and printed in resistance newspapers there before being sent to England.[17]

The US Air Force dropped a huge number of the White Rose's sixth leaflet, which had been reprinted by the Office of Strategic Services, over German cities.[18] The Gestapo was so angry that they summoned Clara Huber to their Munich headquarters in the Wittelsbach Palace to shout at her. She came away filled with pride.[19]

The leaflet airdrop showed that serious interest was now being taken in the German resistance by the Americans.

# 31

## Mr. Douglas and Mr. Wood

THE HOUSE AT Herrengasse 23 in the old quarter of Bern was quint-essentially Swiss. Under its red-tiled roof and behind its dark shutters, it seemed wonderfully neutral, an anonymous haven of bourgeois contentment. Reached with a short walk along the cobbles from the cathedral and the Aare River, it attracted little attention, much like its owner. His height was the only thing that threatened to give him away; that and the fact that, as he often wore a bow tie, neighbors had wondered if he might be English. Otherwise, his corduroy and tweed clothes and his thick glasses suggested an academic background, a professor, perhaps, at the university. But what academic removes the bulb from the streetlight outside his front door to help conceal the faces of his visitors?[1]

In fact, the Swiss foreign police, the Fremdenpolizei, set up especially to monitor visitors for any violations of Swiss neutrality, had a thick file on Allen Dulles. He had been in Bern twenty-five years previously as a young foreign service officer collecting intelligence on Germany and the Austro-Hungarian Empire. Between the wars he had worked for the US State Department but had given it up to be a Wall Street lawyer. It was then that he had met William J. Donovan, the hugely charismatic Irish American who, in 1941, had created the OSS on Roosevelt's orders. The papers that the Fremdenpolizei had received on forty-nine-year-old Dulles stated that he was the special assistant for legal affairs to the US ambassador to Switzerland. In fact, he was running an OSS office with express orders to "establish and maintain contacts with underground anti-Nazi movements in Germany."[2]

Switzerland was in a key location at the heart of Europe, surrounded since November 1942 by Nazi Germany, fascist Italy, and occupied France. Dulles had been one of the last outsiders to get in, arriving in Bern on November 8, the day Allied forces invaded North Africa. After the invasion, the Germans had immediately moved their forces into the southern Vichy zone of France, sealing the Swiss off from the outside world. Early in the war Switzerland had been a target for invasion itself, but it suited Hitler to have a relatively stable economy on his border with whom his government could exchange gold for currency with which it could continue to wage war.

Very soon, the wily, well-connected Dulles had begun to receive visitors: the psychoanalyst Carl Jung, who agreed to provide psychological analyses of the Nazi leaders; Willem Visser 't Hooft, the Dutch head of the Geneva-based World Council of Churches, who told Dulles all about Bonhoeffer and the information he had received from him; and Adam von Trott, of the Kreisau Circle, who first visited in January 1943. "Support us or we will be tempted to turn to the Soviets," Trott pleaded. Dulles told him that Roosevelt and Churchill were demanding "unconditional surrender" and there was nothing more he could say. "To stop short of total military victory, to allow Germany any doubt of its total defeat, would have been unthinkable on our part," he said.[3]

After Trott left, Dulles took a walk to a favorite café and brooded over a meal: He personally felt the Allies should be doing more to encourage the German opposition.

His view was strengthened the day after meeting Trott when another messenger arrived from Germany: Oster's close associate Hans Bernd Gisevius, who, although listed officially as the German vice-consul in Zurich, was now the Abwehr's main operator in Switzerland. Gisevius introduced himself as a friend of Visser 't Hooft and of Hjalmar Schacht, the former Reichsbank president, whom 1938 coup leaders had seen as a possible leader of Germany. The lumbering, poorly sighted Gisevius had been escorted to Herrengasse by one of Dulles's unofficial agents, who walked the German along a riverside terrace in the dark and into the house via a virtually concealed basement doorway. Although conscious that Gisevius's visit might be a trap, Dulles hoped it was a genuine contact from Admiral Canaris. He noted in his file on the German resistance that Gisevius was one of the admiral's "lieutenants." He added: "Am trying to keep closely informed concerning this organisation [the Abwehr] especially as antagonism between it and Gestapo reported."[4]

Gisevius had to be cautious at first, too, and struggled to hide his nerves. Dulles told him to "Call me Allen" and, smiling, joked that he would call the six-foot-five-inch-tall German "Tiny." Dulles said that he could see Gisevius was carrying a terrible burden and he hoped that he could help. Relaxing a little, Gisevius outlined the extent of the opposition and claimed that an attempt would soon be made on Hitler's life. After that first meeting Dulles sent a telegram to OSS Washington: "Axis nationals and those of Axis controlled countries are trying to communicate with us as a result of the Russian offensive [Stalingrad], which is deeply affecting public opinion . . . [Gisevius] said that it is very important that encouragement be offered to the effect that negotiation with the United Nations for a durable peace could be instituted if the Nazi leaders were eliminated by the group resisting them."[5]

Meetings between the two men now became a regular occurrence, with Dulles quickly beginning to trust Gisevius. One evening the Abwehr man brought him fragments of cable traffic that the Germans had intercepted, revealing that they had broken the State Department code used by the US legation. Dulles then strengthened the American's encryption systems.

When Gisevius revealed he was writing a book, Dulles offered him the help of Mary Bancroft, a former freelance journalist who analyzed the German press for the OSS. She worked with Gisevius on the manuscript, drawing out of him more and more information about life in Germany, the Abwehr, and the German resistance.[6] Gisevius was happy to talk. He began to tell Dulles the names of generals and politicians in the opposition, and on realizing the extent of the conspiracy, Dulles told Bancroft to stay absolutely silent about Gisevius; otherwise "five thousand people will be dead."[7]

The British were skeptical of Gisevius, having never got over the humiliation of Schellenberg's Venlo operation, in which they had lost two agents and a Dutch officer, and so was the US War Department in Washington.

Donovan telegrammed Dulles in April to say that he had been told to inform him that "all news from Bern these days is being discounted 100 per cent by the War Department," as it saw the city as "an ideal location for plants, tendentious intelligence and peace feelers." Donovan, though, said he knew Dulles could "distinguish good intelligence from bad," and he stressed his faith in his man in Bern.

Dulles, in turn, was determined to keep faith with any Germans trying to rid their nation of Hitler.

* * *

THROUGH AUSTRIAN CONTACTS, Dulles learned of a new Nazi "terror weapon." Kurt Grimm, a portly and very wealthy expert in international law, and Franz Josef Messner, a businessman whose rubber company had offices around the world, were both Austrian-born but secretly vehemently anti-Nazi. Through their extensive contacts in German industry, they discovered that German scientists were working on a "flying contraption perhaps in the form of an aerial torpedo" and that Hitler had ordered them to have it ready by the beginning of winter 1943.[8]

Gisevius agreed to find out more and in May reported back that the scientists were developing two weapons: the V-1 "buzzbomb" and the larger, higher-flying V-2 rocket. Hitler had predicted that once the V-weapons were in operation, "London would be levelled to the ground by the end of 1943."[9] The work was being carried out on a peninsula on the North Sea coast called Peenemünde. Dulles's intelligence was reported to Washington and London, which had also received reports about this highly secret underground installation.

On August 17, six hundred British bombers pounded the site, setting the rocket program back months. The first V-1's did not get used until June 13, 1944, too late to thwart the D-Day landings; the first V-2 hit London more than two months later.

GISEVIUS HAD CONTACTED Dulles on the orders of Canaris himself. The Allied demand for the unconditional surrender of Nazi Germany had spurred the admiral into action: He saw before him the total destruction of Germany unless he could reach out to the Allies and find a way to peace. Throughout 1943 he sent out envoys, including two who had been appealing to the Allies as a matter of conscience from the very beginning.

Trott and Moltke, of the Kreisau Circle, had never been put off by the continual rebuffs. Now, with the support of the Abwehr, they traveled separately to Turkey in the summer of 1943 to make contact with German Foreign Ministry officials there who were in touch with agents of the OSS. Moltke first offered himself to the OSS as someone who could be brought to England to negotiate and then suggested he could arrange that a senior German general staff officer should secretly visit London "to arrange with the Western Allies to open up the German Western Front."[10] He was proposing conspiracy on a grand scale that would dwarf Oster's betrayal of the plans for the Western Offensive in 1940.

In November 1943, Moltke again traveled to Turkey and was introduced to the American military attaché Major General R. G. Tindall, but the American was suspicious and only probed Moltke for military information.

Soon after, Donovan received a letter written on the paper of the German embassy in Ankara and signed by Dr. Paul Leverkuehn, who had been well-known in Washington before the war. It stated that the German opposition could not guarantee that the entire Western Front would remain inactive in the event of an Allied invasion of France, but it did have sufficient influence with Wehrmacht and Luftwaffe commanders to ensure that countermeasures to repel the invasion might be delayed. If this delay could be achieved, then the Allies should agree to negotiate with the opposition after a coup had gone ahead.

Donovan discovered that German economist Karl Brandt, now a professor at Stanford University, California, was in New York on business and sent members of his staff to bring Brandt to his office in Rockefeller Center. Donovan told him that what he was about to show him had to be treated in the utmost confidence. Brandt—who regularly advised Donovan on the anti-Nazi movement in Germany—nodded, and studied the letter carefully. It was genuine, he said, as he knew of these conspirators in Germany, and was sure Donovan must be well informed about them.

Straight after the meeting, Donovan gave the letter and a summation of Brandt's opinion on it to his assistant, Emmy Rado, and, assigning her an armed guard, sent her to the White House. Rado was told to tell Roosevelt that in Donovan's opinion, based on Brandt's advice, the offer from the German resistance should be accepted. Roosevelt read the documents with interest but told Donovan that he would never negotiate with these "East German Junkers."[11]

But Dulles in Bern was by now running an agent who would change that view.

ON THE NIGHT of August 18, hours after learning of the success of the Peenemünde raid, Dulles sat in the back of his chauffeur-driven Citroën as it crossed the winding River Aare and navigated the backstreets of the Kirchenfeld district of Bern. A church clock sounded midnight as they drove.

Leaning back in the seat, his pipe clutched between his teeth, Dulles pondered the meeting ahead. Earlier that day he had been sitting at his desk in his official office in Dufourstrasse when there had been an urgent knock at the door. The man who entered was young and handsome, with an elegantly thin mustache. Gerry Mayer was a German specialist with the Office of War Information, but he worked closely with Dulles, who had a great admiration for him and valued his views on the European political scene. Mayer was a little out of breath from taking the stairs two at a time and seemed to be excited about the sheaf of papers that he held in his hand. He explained that a German named Dr. Kocherthaler had arrived in his office and presented him with the documents that he laid on Dulles's desk.

The OSS man flicked through them. They were diplomatic cables, each signed by a German ambassador or by Ribbentrop himself. One described plans for a network of pro-Nazi agents in French North Africa; another, from Franz von Papen, the ambassador in Turkey, discussed Britain's use of agents in Ankara. It was a treasure trove.

Mayer said that Kocherthaler's source was a dedicated anti-Nazi from the German foreign service who was at that moment in Bern. "This man is willing, indeed eager, to provide this kind of material to you," Kocherthaler had told him.[12]

Dulles knew that the man might be a plant, either being used by the Germans to expose Dulles as a spy to the Swiss or to break the American code when Dulles had to relay the content of the cables to Washington. But he also knew that there was a third possibility: that the visitor to Bern was telling the truth.

Back in 1917, when based in Bern for the first time, Dulles had been leaving the legation early on a Friday afternoon to play tennis with a girlfriend when the telephone had rung. Dulles had answered it and found that the caller was Lenin, whom Dulles knew led a bunch of ragged revolutionaries based in Zurich. Lenin was ranting, impatient, and insistent that he talk to someone. Dulles told him to call back Monday and put the phone down. Instead of calling back, Lenin headed to Petrograd to take control of the Russian Revolution. Dulles never forgot his mistake and shared the story with others in the most self-deprecating way. The moral, he told them, was simple: Never refuse to listen to someone, no matter how improbable their tale.[13]

And so he had asked Mayer to arrange a meeting with the mystery man at Mayer's flat just after midnight.

\* \* \*

THE MAN WHO waited for Dulles was short, stocky, and bald but for a ring of blond hair that circled his head. He was nervous, pacing the floor and talking excitedly. Dulles could see why the local British intelligence officer had sent him away, assuming immediately that he was a rather inadequate Nazi spy.

But remembering Lenin, Dulles tried to look beyond the man's furtiveness. As he listened to the German speak, he decided that he could see in his eyes what he thought to be an "honest determination."[14]

Then the man took a large brown envelope from his inside jacket pocket and laid it on the table. Dulles could see a red wax seal with a swastika, but the envelope was already open. The man reached inside and carefully removed a stack of tissue-thin pieces of paper—mimeographed copies of telegraph traffic between the German Foreign Ministry in Wilhelmstrasse and embassies around the world and various military command units. Dulles, who had been introduced to the man as "Mr. Douglas," took the documents and began to look through them. There was a cable on German troop morale on the Eastern Front, an assessment of sabotage attacks by the French resistance, and minutes—sometimes in the man's spidery handwriting—of conferences with Ribbentrop.

Realizing that Dulles was obviously the senior man in the room, the visitor laid out a piece of paper on the table and began to draw a sketch, which he knew would please him.

Dulles asked him what it was. The man said it was a map of Hitler's Wolf's Lair headquarters at Rastenburg.

"Here is Hitler's bombproof hideout situated underground. Here is Ribbentrop's train. There are the railroad sidings where Himmler and Göring set up quarters . . ."[15]

Dulles took the map, studied it, and then leaned back in his chair. In his basic German, he asked the man to tell him who he was and why he was bringing all of this material to the Americans.

Mayer brought them something to drink, and the man began to tell his story.

HIS NAME WAS Fritz Kolbe. He was forty-three and the son of a Berlin saddle maker who had always told him to "do good" and "never fear the future."[16]

A man of energy and a working-class determination to better himself, he had started his working life on the German railways, becoming the country's youngest stationmaster, but he longed for a career in the diplomatic service. After studying at night school, he got a university place, and later passed his foreign service examinations. In 1925 he joined the consular service in Madrid. His chiefs in Berlin were delighted with his work: He carried out his duties reliably and without fuss. Colleagues saw him as a little eccentric, and when the Nazis came to power, his refusal to join the party was dismissed as characteristic of his quirkiness. In fact, he loathed the Nazis and their anti-Semitism. "For me," he told a Jewish friend, "between an Aryan and a Jew, the only difference is that one of them eats kosher food and the other one doesn't."[17] During a posting to South Africa he forged passports for Jewish friends to ensure they could disappear as refugees and went through his own personal turmoil: His first wife, Anita, died young, leaving him with a son, Peter, whom—reasoning he could not look after him alone—he placed with a foster family. A brief second marriage to a Swiss woman collapsed within months after she threatened to report his anti-Hitler views to the German authorities.

When the war began, Kolbe was recalled to Berlin and began the daily routine of turning up for work at one of the Foreign Ministry's grand entrances at Wilhelmstrasse 76 and maintaining an image as an efficient minor official. He turned down one promotion as it would have put his nonmembership of the party under a spotlight. But danger was always present: A senior official challenged his boss as to who was that man who "doesn't even give the Hitler salute when we come in," and Kolbe was given a warning.

To let off steam, he met old hiking friends for games of chess at the Café Kottler in the Schöneberg neighborhood or went for runs in the Grunewald. His friends—Walter Girgner, who owned a factory making clothes, a police captain named Kurt Arndt, and a Siemens engineer named Kurt Weinhold—all shared his hatred of the Nazis, but as Hitler's armies moved into France, Holland, and Belgium, they asked what could be done to change anything. "Speaking for myself, I can no longer tolerate these lies," Kolbe whispered loudly.[18]

At home that night, writing with his left hand and wearing gloves, Kolbe began to write notes in block capitals: "What is pessimism? Not winning the war and maintaining Nazi power. What is optimism? Losing the war and seeing the Nazis go."

Like so many others, Kolbe's path to resistance had begun in the simple act—with potential deadly risk—of writing anonymous leaflets and mailing them or leaving them in public places. His friends soon began to help.

THE SKETCH OF Hitler's Wolf's Lair that Kolbe had drawn for Dulles was done from memory.

Promoted to work for Karl Ritter—Ribbentrop's liaison with the German military high command—Kolbe became the man whose job it was to sift through military and embassy reports to decide which needed first Ritter's and then Ribbentrop's attention. He had made a ten-day trip to Rastenburg in September 1941 to personally hand-deliver Ritter's mail, and overheard a discussion in which a senior army officer reported the execution of prisoners of war in the East. Once back in Berlin, he told friends that Germany was carrying out a "war of extermination" in Russia and that he could no longer be any part of it.

Through a new friendship with the surgeon Ferdinand Sauerbruch, he became a member of the highbrow discussion group the Wednesday Club, whose members included Ludwig Beck and a Catholic scholar named Georg Schreiber. Kolbe and Schreiber discussed Clemens von Galen's sermons on the T4 euthanasia program, and Schreiber whispered that Sauerbruch had heard that seventy thousand people had been "eliminated" under the policy. "Old people, the tubercular, the war wounded, and others deemed Lebensunwerte Menschen, unworthy to live," he said.

Kolbe was pale. "Tell me, how can I continue to serve this regime?" he asked the prelate. "I want to leave this country, but that is not possible . . . If I stay, am I morally tainted by my status as an official?"

Schreiber looked Kolbe in the eye. "If you are in this post, it's because God willed it for one reason or another."

Like Kurt Gerstein, Kolbe resolved to stay in Germany—and use his position of trust in the Nazi regime to work against it from within.

ONE NIGHT EARLY in 1943, while sweating out a bombing raid in the huge air raid shelter beneath the luxurious Hotel Adlon, close to the Brandenburg Gate, Kolbe came to a decision: He would find a way to contact the British and tell them everything he knew about the German war effort. The only way he could save Germany was by making Hitler lose the war.

Kolbe had already tentatively tried to contact Donald Heath—the

Harnacks' contact at the US embassy—before he had been withdrawn from Berlin two years earlier, but when no response had come back, he had become frightened and shrunk away. Now he had a new and, he felt, safer plan. He had become friends with Maria von Heimerdinger, the prim and proper daughter of a Prussian aristocrat, who as assistant chief of the Foreign Office's courier section helped choose diplomats for foreign trips and postings. Heimerdinger was cultured and refined, and Kolbe sensed a disdain for the vulgar Nazis and an admiration for his own conviction not to give the Hitler salute. Afraid to approach her in the office, he sat with her during another air raid and talked about having business interests in Switzerland. He wondered casually whether she would be able to assign him as a courier to Bern. While he was not a romantic figure, Heimerdinger was charmed by him and said she would see what she could do. It would be nice to escape the bombing for at least a few days, she said, and he smiled.

FRITZ KOLBE HAD left Berlin from the Anhalter Bahnhof on the evening of Sunday, August 15. He was carrying a leather briefcase containing the diplomatic mail for the German legation in Bern, his diplomatic passport, and his orders. If he walked a little stiffly, it was because he had gone to his office, pulled down his pants, taken two envelopes containing top secret documents from his safe, and strapped one around each of his thighs with string.

When the train reached the Swiss border at Basel, the passengers all had to get off at the "German station," where both customs officers and Gestapo spies made their checks. But Kolbe's papers were in order and there were no body searches. He carried on to the Swiss platform and took a train to Bern. Having been turned down by the British, he had come to the Americans.

ALLEN DULLES'S PIPE smoke filled the room by the time Kolbe finished his story. The American now leaned forward, tapping the pipe on the table, and asked Kolbe if he wanted money.

The German said he wanted nothing more than expenses so he could buy presents for Heimerdinger to maintain her friendship, and then he repeated his hatred of the Nazis. "It is not enough to clench one's fist and hide it in one's pocket," Kolbe said. "The fist must be used to strike."[19]

The two men agreed to meet later in the week, before Kolbe returned to

Germany, and the German went off into the night. Dulles and Mayer spent the next few hours going through the documents and working out which items to prioritize for their next report to Washington. Dulles had already begun to trust Kolbe, believing him not to have the devious intelligence or effortless duplicity of a spy; he seemed to be more the heartfelt, if slightly naive, idealist. The two men opened a file on Kolbe, which could be shared with the British, who could assist in confirming the German was who he said he was.[20] The file was opened under Dulles's new code name for Kolbe: George Wood.[21]

Back in his room at the Terminus Hotel in a square outside the railway station, Kolbe could not sleep. He had crossed a line. The Nazis would call him a traitor, the Americans a spy. He saw himself as a patriot whose duty it was "to fight such a government . . . and shorten the war."[22]

Taking off his shoes, tie, and jacket, he sat at the small table in his room and began to write his last will and testament, which he planned to leave in Bern for "Mr. Douglas" to look after.

# 32

## The Brandy Bomb

WITH HIS PENCHANT for Teutonic mythology, Hitler cast himself in the model of the wolf—strong, cunning, ruthless, a lord of the forest. Delighted that the name "Adolf" comes from the Old German word "Adelwolf," meaning "noble wolf," he encouraged the children of friends to call him "Onkel Wolf," and with his own almost childlike excitement he referred to this nickname, which he had chosen for himself, in the code names for his military headquarters.

During the Battle of France in 1940, he had occupied concrete bunkers just inside the Belgian border, which he called Wolfsschlucht, Wolf's Gorge.[1] His most eastern headquarters was located in a pine forest in Ukraine and was known as Werwolf. A collection of wooden huts and concrete bunkers, it was built by Ukrainian and Russian prisoners whom Hitler had shot to maintain its secrecy.

However, his most favored base by far was the one built in a thick forest in East Prussia and known as the Wolfsschanze, the Wolf's Lair, the complex that Kolbe had sketched for Dulles.

The Wolfsschanze was constructed by forced labor as Hitler prepared for Operation Barbarossa. He had first stayed there on June 23, 1941, and it had become his most-used home. Although it was built at a time he felt might see his greatest triumph, its thick concrete came to symbolize his sullen mood after Stalingrad. There were ten bunkers, some with concrete roofs seven feet thick, and various barracks buildings for the Führer's guard. The complex was surrounded by concrete pillboxes, minefields, and electrified barbed wire, as well as a gloomy forest that was freezing in the winter and infested by midges during the summer months. Hitler's bunker was inside a central "safe zone" known as Security Zone One. Here he could walk with his young Alsatian, listen to records, and spend evenings delivering monologues to his staff. There was a second complex for the Wehrmacht operations staff and an army headquarters, where Brauchitsch and Halder were based. On the railroad track nearby stood a special train on which Göring—designated by Hitler as his successor in the event of his death—spent much of his time.

The Wolfsschanze was heavily guarded and situated in one of the remotest parts of the Reich, so getting access to Hitler would now be one of the most difficult problems to overcome for Colonel Henning von Tresckow, who had vowed to kill Hitler in a bomb attack. Since the summer of 1941— with the exceptions of short visits to Berlin and his private home on the Obersalzberg—Hitler had made the Wolfsschanze his permanent headquarters. Officers below the rank of general were seldom in his company, and all had to remove their guns.

Hitler rarely ventured out. He never visited field hospitals to comfort the war wounded or walked among the bombed-out streets of a city to show solidarity with the German people. The suffering of his people seemed as remote to him as the agony of those in the concentration camps.

But with great skill Tresckow now designed a way to draw him into visiting Kluge's headquarters at Smolensk.

Hitler was planning an attack across a narrow area of the Eastern Front in which Erich von Manstein's army group would push forward in the south and Kluge's in the north before closing together in a pincer and capturing a large number of Soviet troops. Hitler, who had become fixated on the war in the East, felt the attack—code-named Citadel—would give the German army the initiative through the spring and summer of 1943.

Tresckow contacted Hitler's aide-de-camp, Rudolf Schmundt, an old classmate of his, and quietly told him that Kluge and others at Army Group Center command were against Citadel and a visit from the Führer could restore confidence and harmony. Impatient with both Kluge and Manstein, Hitler jumped at the chance to put his "weak" generals in their place. Tresckow was heartened further when he learned that Himmler was planning to visit, too—his death would weaken the SS and give the coup a great chance of success.

After discussing with Georg von Boeselager the use of his cavalry unit in a machine gun attack on Hitler and Himmler, Tresckow eventually decided that a bomb would be most effective. Tresckow's plan was simple: to have the British plastic explosives, provided by Dohnanyi of the Abwehr, planted on Hitler's plane when he left. The plane bomb could look enough like an accident or enemy attack to cause doubt among Hitler's supporters and allow extra time for a coup, led by Oster and the others in Berlin, to take place.

On March 7, Canaris flew to Smolensk for a general intelligence conference. He brought with him Oster, Lahousen, Gersdorff, and Dohnanyi, who met with Tresckow and were told the details of his plan, which he code-named Operation Flash. It was set for March 13, he told them. Oster and Dohnanyi assured him that everything in Berlin was prepared for the coup.[2]

On March 13, as Tresckow and Fabian von Schlabrendorff awaited Hitler's arrival at the airfield, Kluge pulled Tresckow aside. Himmler was not coming, he said. To kill Hitler now would cause a civil war, with Himmler turning the SS against the army, and would just pave the way for another Nazi despot. "For heaven's sake, don't do anything today," he snapped and walked off.[3]

At that moment, out of a gray sky came the sound of a small fleet of aircraft. Tresckow had a decision to make, and he quickly decided that Hitler's death mattered above all other considerations.

He nodded to Schlabrendorff, who was already on an open telephone line to the conspirators in Berlin. "Operation Flash is ready," Schlabrendorff told the Abwehr's captain, Ludwig Gehre.

"The ignition can be switched on," came the reply. Berlin was prepared.

Schlabrendorff returned to Tresckow's side to watch the planes approach. To their dismay they saw that the group included two identical Focke-Wulf Fw 200 Condors with a fighter escort. If they were to plant a bomb while the planes were on the ground, they would need to know which aircraft Hitler would be leaving in.

As the planes taxied, a cold wind blew across the airfield and onto the neck of Captain Georg von Boeselager, standing at the head of a line of men from his cavalry unit. For an instant, as the pilot dropped the throttle and the propellers came slowly to a stop, he wondered whether he and his men might get a clear shot at Hitler when he stepped onto the tarmac.

Just then a fleet of SS motorcycle troops roared onto the airfield, and Boeselager—who the day before had been in action against partisans—gave up on his thoughts of shooting Hitler. The door opened and Hitler came down the steps. Seeing that Himmler was not there, Boeselager questioned Tresckow. Don't worry, Tresckow told him, the bomb plan would go ahead as it could look like an accident. This day would not end with Hitler alive, he said.

Hitler was rushed to Kluge's headquarters, his car flanked by the SS motorbikes. The two men met in a conference room. Tresckow was among those ordered to join them; like the others he surrendered his gun at the door. Tresckow was shocked to see that Hitler was ashen-faced, that his left hand shook, and that his speech was slow and hesitant.

Afterwards, Tresckow took Schlabrendorff aside. In his eyes there was a fleeting moment of doubt, from being so close to the others in Hitler's entourage whom he knew would die with the Führer. "Should we really do it?" he asked.

"Yes," replied Schlabrendorff. "We must."

The two men then sat down to lunch with Hitler and members of his group and indulged in light conversation. To Tresckow's right was Lieutenant-Colonel Heinz Brandt, who was in Hitler's party and would be accompanying him on the same aircraft to the Wolf's Lair. Tresckow casually asked him if he would mind taking two bottles of brandy to his friend General Helmuth Stieff, who was at Rastenburg. They were a payment for a lost wager. Brandt laughed and happily agreed.

Back at the airport Tresckow took the package from Schlabrendorff and handed it to Brandt. "The brandy," he said. "For Stieff." Brandt took the gift and placed it in the cargo hold. Hitler's aircraft was fitted with an armor-plated central section, in which the Führer traveled, but the bomb was big enough to blow the aircraft out of the sky.

The bomb in the package had been prepared by Philipp von Boeselager. A few moments earlier Schlabrendorff had opened it and pressed a small button on the device. This released a corrosive chemical that slowly began to eat through a wire holding back a spring. An hour later the spring would cause a striker to hit the bomb's detonator and set off the explosion.

As Hitler's aircraft lifted off the tarmac and banked away toward Vinnitsa, Tresckow looked at Schlabrendorff. Neither man spoke. Schlabrendorff turned and lifted a telephone. Eventually getting through to Gehre again, he told him Flash had been "sparked." Then he and Tresckow returned to headquarters and waited for news of the explosion.

For two hours they heard nothing and then the telephone rang: Hitler had landed safely in East Prussia.

The disappointment was quickly overtaken by panic. If the bomb had not gone off, it had now become evidence of an assassination plot. If it was found, Tresckow and Schlabrendorff were dead.

The two men remained calm, though. While Schlabrendorff contacted the conspirators in Berlin to confirm the assassination attempt had failed, Tresckow picked up the telephone and, calling Rastenburg, asked Brandt if he had managed to deliver the brandy to Stieff. When Brandt apologized, saying he had not yet had the time, Tresckow said that was not a problem as he had given him the wrong package. Would he please hold on to it? His aide-de-camp was due to visit Rastenburg on a regularly scheduled mail plane the next day and would exchange them.

Schlabrendorff tried to remain calm as he arrived at Rastenburg—perhaps the bomb had been discovered and he would be arrested straight-away. He found Brandt, who laughed at the mix-up and handed the bomb over to Schlabrendorff with a jerk of the hand that made the visitor wince. Schlabrendorff gave Brandt a genuine gift for Stieff.

Schlabrendorff got quickly back into his car and was driven to the neighboring railway junction of Korschen, where a siding provided over-night accommodation for visitors. Once on his train, he locked the door of his sleeper car and carefully slit open the package with a razor blade. The spring had been released and the detonator cap struck, but it had not ig-nited the explosive. Schlabrendorff suspected that the explosive had failed because the bomb had been stored in the hold of the aircraft and had be-come too cold.

TRESCKOW IMMEDIATELY PUT a second assassination plot into op-eration.

Hitler was due to attend a special event at the Zeughaus on Unter den Linden on March 21—Heldengedenktag, Heroes' Memorial Day. He would be accompanied by Himmler and Göring.

Pride of place at the event would be given to Soviet weaponry that had been captured by Army Group Center. Tresckow had to nominate an offi-cer from the army group to escort Hitler around the exhibition, explaining the weaponry on display.

He chose his coconspirator Colonel Rudolf-Christoph von Gersdorff, his official liaison man with the Abwehr. A thirty-seven-year-old immac-ulately turned-out officer from the Silesian nobility, Gersdorff had grown increasingly disillusioned with the war since the death of his wife the previous year.

Walking on the banks of the Dnieper, Tresckow turned to Gersdorff and said, "Isn't it dreadful? Here we are, two officers of the German General Staff, discussing how best to murder our commander-in-chief." Seeing Gersdorff's anxiety, he added, "It must be done. This is our only chance . . . Hitler must be cut down like a rabid dog."

To his absolute credit Gersdorff did not hesitate. The next day he flew to Berlin.

The Zeughaus was a grand baroque building, close to the Lustgarten, which had been used as an arsenal since the late seventeenth century.[4] Gersdorff had been there before, but when he visited the day before the event, the enormity of his role as assassin sank in.

However, he was determined to see the plan through. As he listened to his guide explain where he would meet Hitler, where to stand when he was talking to him, and the route the Führer would take around the exhibition, Gersdorff secretly sized up the opportunities for planting a bomb. Hitler would be on the move, so even if security were not so tight, it would be hard to leave a bomb on a timer designed to explode at the exact time he went past. In addition, the building was lined with guards. The lectern where Hitler was due to speak appeared to be watched at all times, and the room was busy with workmen laying out rows of chairs.

It gradually dawned on Gersdorff what would be required for the assassination attempt to work: "It became clear to me that an attack was only possible if I were to carry the explosives about my person, and blow myself up as close to Hitler as was possible," he said later. The plot had become a suicide mission.

That evening Gersdorff went to the Eden Hotel and received the bombs from Schlabrendorff. Gersdorff knew he was spending his last night on earth, but he remained absolutely steadfast. Back in his room he realized he had only ten-minute fuses, but as Hitler's visit was due to last half an hour, he would have plenty of time. Everything prepared, he turned off the light but could not sleep.

Arriving at the Zeughaus the next day, he was told the event would be delayed for about an hour. Gersdorff tried to calm his breathing as he waited and watched the other members of the Nazi high command arrive. Göring strode in dressed in a white uniform and wearing red leather riding boots. The Reichsmarschall, who was still assumed to be Hitler's successor, had become a grotesque figure, a slave to his sloth, vanity, and love of luxury. His face was made up, and he carried a bejeweled baton. Himmler followed in his black uniform, his eyes cold behind his silver-rimmed glasses; then came the weak-willed head of the army, Wilhelm Keitel, who was so keen always to do the Führer's bidding the conspirators called him "the Nodding Ass," and the equally sycophantic Karl Dönitz, chief of the navy, who still believed Hitler had been "Heaven-sent" for the German people.

Gersdorff trembled. If he held his nerve, he could wipe out the entire rotten clique running Germany.

Then at last, at 1 p.m., Hitler arrived in an open-top Mercedes to the sounds of Bruckner's Seventh Symphony. He gave a short hesitant speech from the lectern and began his tour. Gersdorff, standing close by, reached into the pockets of his greatcoat and pressed the buttons on the two bombs. In ten minutes they would explode. Ten minutes in which Gersdorff had to walk around, awaiting not only the Führer's death but also his own. It was a torturous, selfless, and exceptionally brave act. As he tried to interest Hitler in the Russian weaponry on display, the acid burned through the wires on the devices in his pocket.

WAITING OUT IN the western suburbs, Dietrich Bonhoeffer and Hans von Dohnanyi were at the home of their friend Rüdiger Schleicher, next door to the Bonhoeffers' house on Marienburger Allee. Like Dohnanyi, Schleicher was a top lawyer. He was married to Bonhoeffer's sister Ursula, and they were all together to rehearse for a surprise musical performance they were planning a week later to celebrate the seventy-fifth birthday of Bonhoeffer's father, Karl.

Bonhoeffer played piano, Dohnanyi sang, and Schleicher played violin; all three were aware of the Gersdorff plot, as were Christine and Ursula.

Dohnanyi, who had a driver and a car waiting outside ready to rush him into the center of the city when the coup began, kept an anxious eye on the clock and waited for the telephone to ring.

His wife studied the way he bit his lip nervously. "It must go off at any moment," she whispered to her sister.[5]

\* \* \*

AT THE ZEUGHAUS, Hitler appeared not to be listening to the descriptions given by Gersdorff and others of the Soviet artillery pieces. Göring tried to enthuse him, but Hitler's gaze remained vacant. Suddenly, he turned on his heel and led his entourage through a side door back onto Unter den Linden. He had cut his half-hour visit down to just a few minutes and was now making his way slowly along a line of almost three hundred wounded soldiers.

Gersdorff was aghast but could not follow without raising the suspicion of Hitler's SS bodyguard. Not only had he missed his chance, but his coat was laden with explosives that were about to go off. He walked quickly to the restroom and locked the door. Carefully removing each bomb, he slowly separated the detonator from the explosives—the only way to deactivate them.

It was only afterwards, as he rushed for a drink in a nearby club, that he realized that he could not stop his hands from shaking.[6]

THAT NIGHT HITLER made his first speech to the German people since the defeat at Stalingrad, although, on a day dedicated to the fallen, he made no direct reference to the battle. The omission and the poor delivery of the speech—the once great orator spoke quickly and in a monotone—shocked many of the German public who had supported him.

A rumor spread that the real Führer had suffered a nervous breakdown after Stalingrad and was being kept under house arrest on the Obersalzberg. The man on the radio was an imposter.

The shine of the early victories, the making Germany great again, had dulled. War had worn down enthusiasm for hate-filled rants about Bolshevism and World Jewry. The Allies were demanding Germany's complete capitulation, but the Nazis were determined for Germany to fight on.

For the German people there was no way out, no end in sight.

They were unaware what part destiny had played that last week in ensuring their future remained tied to that of Adolf Hitler.

It was a cold, bright spring morning in Berlin the day after the event at the Zeughaus. Oster and Dohnanyi walked in the Tiergarten, among the greens and browns of the trees, the sound of the traffic somehow reassuringly consistent on the Charlottenburger Chaussee.

It was good to be free to talk here, although their mood was subdued. When they had met Tresckow a fortnight earlier at Smolensk, he had described the difficulties of trying to reach Hitler now that he had withdrawn so far into his shell. And to the Abwehr conspirators, who had once dreamed of seizing Hitler in the Reich Chancellery, the Führer seemed very remote indeed: completely untouchable to anyone in their sphere of influence in Berlin.

In fact, although they still wondered whether they could play a part in the hunt, it was their own scent that had now been picked up by the dogs.

Wilhelm Schmidhuber, the courier in Oster and Dohnanyi's operation to smuggle Jews into Switzerland, was in the hands of the Gestapo and was ready to talk.

The Gestapo assigned one of its finest investigators to the case. SS Second Lieutenant Franz Sonderegger was a forty-four-year-old career policeman whose work on political crime predated the rise of the Nazis. He had a nose for when a suspect was telling the truth and knew that questions to ask to make them reveal more than they cared to. But he did not need to be particularly wily with Schmidhuber.

At his very first interrogation on January 10, 1943, Wilhelm Schmidhuber told him that there were extensive links between the Abwehr and the Vatican; that there was a "treasonable association" between Beck, Goerdeler, and Dohnanyi; and that there was a "generals' clique" that opposed Hitler. Sonderegger knew that he was on the brink of a political sensation. He kept probing, and Schmidhuber kept talking.

He confirmed that there had been peace talks with the British using the Vatican as a go-between and that the Abwehr had opened a new channel of communication with the Allies via Switzerland and Sweden. The plan used the Protestant churches and was led by Pastor Bonhoeffer, he said.

Over the following interrogations, he spilled the beans on Operation 7— Dohnanyi's successful mission to obtain false papers for German Jews and have them moved across the border into Switzerland. Schmidhuber suggested the whole operation had been about rescuing Jews and that the official mission brief, to spread Nazi propaganda, was just a cover. Dohnanyi had sent Schmidhuber across the border with $100,000 for the escapees, he stated.

Dohnanyi, Schmidhuber told Sonderegger, was an old-fashioned conservative who regretted the "destruction of almost every civilized value on the European continent." He believed a collapse of the fighting fronts would lead to the end of the regime, and was therefore giving thought to a "stand-by government that can bring the fronts to a standstill."

Sonderegger had the files on all the people mentioned by Schmidhuber sent to his office, and filled in dates, names, connections, and theories on an evidence board. He also ordered that Dohnanyi's mail and telephone calls be monitored.

After several weeks he put together a sixty-five-page full report for his chief, Heinrich Müller, who was known to all as Gestapo Müller. The report concluded that the whole Abwehr conspiracy was led by Admiral Canaris himself.

Müller put the file on Reichsführer Himmler's desk and told Sonderegger to await further instruction.

When it came, it shocked Sonderegger to the core: The file was returned to his office with Himmler's handwriting on the front page. He had written: "Kindly leave Canaris alone!"[7]

HIMMLER HAD A strange relationship with Canaris. He saw the admiral as Canaris would have liked to be seen—as a master spy with a nose for espionage. There was much he would overlook to maintain Canaris's skills and the use of the Abwehr, which, although troubled, was still important to Germany's war effort. Himmler reckoned on maintaining the admiral's help while also working to bring the Abwehr into his SS empire.

In addition, Himmler knew that—in spite of his position at the head of the SS and Gestapo—there were those who saw him as a natural heir to Hitler, and he even had his spies make inquiries as to what peace terms the Allies would seek if Hitler were dead. If Canaris was making overtures to the Allies, then, the ever-pragmatic Himmler reckoned, he could actually benefit from them.

Because Schmidhuber and his co-accused, Heinz Ickrath, held Luftwaffe ranks, their file was sent to the military investigators at the Reichskriegsgericht, the Reich Court-Martial department, or RKG, which took it over. No action should be taken on Canaris, they were told, but Himmler required regular updates on progress against the others. The file remained a political hot potato, with officers unsure which way to take the investigation without getting themselves into trouble with the Gestapo or even Himmler himself. Even Field Marshal Wilhelm Keitel, Hitler's closest military adviser, seemed "genuinely scared to death" when told about the file and refused to tell the Führer about it.[8]

It would require someone with keen investigative skills, a fearless sense of his own power, and a ruthless hatred of the Reich's enemies to take this difficult case further.

It was then that someone thought of Manfred Roeder, the man who had sent the members of the Rote Kapelle to the guillotine.

# 33

## The "Z Grau" File

WITH THE ROTE Kapelle trials complete and the conspirators either dead or awaiting execution, Manfred Roeder's stock was riding high. He had been the natural choice to take on the Abwehr investigation.

Taking over the file on April 3, 1943—two weeks after Gersdorff was foiled at the Zeughaus—he concurred immediately with the Gestapo officer Sonderegger's conclusions that there was a major Canaris-led conspiracy. An inquiry such as this would need to be handled delicately, but its potential impact on an individual's career was staggering. Roeder was delighted.

While not a member of the Gestapo, Roeder had built up a strong working relationship with it during the Rote Kapelle case, and he immediately requested—and was granted—the use of Sonderegger to partner him in the new investigation.

Roeder told Sonderegger he intended to waste no time. Together they reviewed a transcript of one of Sonderegger's interviews with Schmidhuber in which the businessman had described a meeting with Hans Bernd Gisevius, the Abwehr's man in Switzerland, who was angry with Canaris as he felt he was making life hard for Gisevius when he should be "looking out for himself." According to Schmidhuber, the disgruntled agent had confided to him that Canaris had given military secrets about the German offensive in the East the previous summer to the Russians and had been aware that Oster had told the Dutch about the attack in the West in 1940.[1] If this small reference in a long transcript were true, Roeder told his colleague, then they were looking at a prosecution for high treason. The Abwehr, Roeder felt, was full of "weak" people, and they were "going to clean the whole place out."[2]

The two men drew up plans for a series of raids to take place on April 5. They started at Abwehr headquarters, with Roeder cannily proceeding—

given the political sensitivities of the case—in a quiet and unobtrusive manner. He and Sonderegger arrived at 10 a.m. and presented their paperwork authorizing the raid. Roeder, in his Luftwaffe uniform, did all the talking, while Sonderegger, in civilian clothes, stood back and observed.

An orderly escorted them immediately to Canaris's office, where Roeder stated they planned to arrest Dohnanyi and search his room. Canaris politely asked on what grounds, and was told that Dohnanyi was suspected of corruption, abuse of authority, and numerous currency offenses. There were suspicions of treasonable activities, he added ominously, with his taller henchman watching the admiral's reaction carefully.

Canaris appeared lost for words. Although he had known that investigations had been taking place into some of his staff, he appeared shocked now that the reality of it had hit him: A police search was being carried out in the heart of German military intelligence. Perhaps he considered whether to complain to Keitel, blustering at the outrage of it all, the impudence, the security risk, but instead he stood slowly and said he would witness the arrest and search.

The three men walked down the corridor to Oster's office, where Canaris explained that Dohnanyi was to be arrested. Oster, who was wearing a civilian suit, turned on Roeder: "Then kindly arrest me too, because Herr von Dohnanyi has done nothing I don't know about," he said.[3]

Canaris told him to shut up, and all four walked through the communicating door to Dohnanyi's office. Roeder arrested Dohnanyi and told him his room was going to be searched. Sonderegger remained just inside Oster's office, almost unnoticed but watching everything.

Dohnanyi and Oster exchanged anxious glances. Like others who had dared oppose the regime, they had feared this moment, but were they prepared for it? For the last few weeks Oster's energies had been consumed by planning for the coup that would have followed Hitler's death in the aircraft bomb or at Gersdorff's hands at the arsenal. Canaris had urged Oster to check that Dohnanyi—who had a lawyer's obsession for keeping files that he thought would be key legal documents in his fight against Hitler—had destroyed his records, but he knew he had not followed up on the order vehemently enough. Dohnanyi knew that there were documents in his green safe that could form a charge of conspiracy against him, and he tried to conceal his horror when Roeder asked to see its contents. At first, he claimed to have mislaid the key, but as Roeder persisted, he "found" it.

Roeder opened the safe and placed file after file on Dohnanyi's desk. Most were either genuine intelligence files or could be explained away as such: travel expenses claimed by political informants, foreign currency forms, and reports on the Jewish refugees smuggled out of the country, which Dohnanyi believed had the watertight cover story that they were being used to spread word that international press reports of atrocities against the Jews were untrue.

But then Roeder lifted out a folder that was marked "Z grau" on the front, and Dohnanyi tried to innocently flick through and remove three pages. Roeder saw him and told him to replace them before continuing his search.

Oster stood in front of the desk and, with his hand behind his back, removed the same pieces of paper and tucked them inside his jacket. Sonderegger watched it all from the doorway, then, stepping into the room, held out his hand and had Oster hand over the pages.

Roeder demanded Canaris order Oster to leave, and he did. Roeder then took a moment to look at the three pages that the Abwehr men were keen to hide. All three contained short typed reports. One outlined—without names—a conspiracy of people within the military and church groups who had agreed to overthrow National Socialism. The second was a proposal for a post-Hitler Germany in which the country was divided into a northern and southern state. Both, Roeder could see, were basic agreements of policy by opponents of the regime.

But it was as he read the third document that his face could not disguise a smile of satisfaction: "For a considerable time now, a small circle of prominent clerics in the German Protestant Church have been debating how the Protestant Church can help in this war to bring about a just and lasting peace and construct a social system based on Christian foundations . . . It is possible that the Pope enunciated his basic peace aims in his last two Christmas messages that the British and American (as well as the Dutch, Norwegian and French) Protestant Churches are already devoting very keen consideration to these same questions . . . It appears extremely important and desirable that a German Protestant cleric should be enabled, not only to hold discussions on the subject with representatives of the Catholic Church in Rome, but also to familiarize himself with the relevant activities of the worldwide Protestant Churches in Geneva or Stockholm."

Roeder realized that with Sonderegger's file he might now have enough to hang not only Dohnanyi, and perhaps Oster and Canaris, but also Bonhoeffer and Josef Müller.

Sonderegger called the Gestapo in Munich to have Müller arrested, while Roeder arranged for Dohnanyi to be taken into custody.

The pair then headed to Sakrow on the outskirts of the city to search Dohnanyi's home and to arrest his wife, Christine. They would then head on to find Bonhoeffer.

Wanting to keep the whole operation to themselves, they had no time to waste: they had a busy day ahead.

DIETRICH BONHOEFFER HAD spent the morning writing in his study at his parents' home. At lunchtime, he came downstairs and tried to telephone his sister. The receiver at the Dohnanyi home was lifted almost immediately and a man's voice asked sharply who was ringing. Bonhoeffer quickly replaced the receiver. Christine von Dohnanyi was not answering her own telephone; a stranger was. Bonhoeffer knew immediately that the person he had spoken to must be a Gestapo agent and that the state police were searching the Dohnanyis' home.

Bonhoeffer went back to his study and destroyed some documents, leaving others—which had been prepared to throw the Gestapo off the scent—on his desk. He then went next door to the house that his other sister, Ursula, shared with her husband, Rüdiger Schleicher, and told her that the Gestapo would almost certainly soon arrest him. He ate with Ursula and waited. The Gestapo arrived at the Bonhoeffer home at four in the afternoon and sent his father to fetch him. Bonhoeffer found the two men upstairs in his study, carefully leafing through his books and writing. One introduced himself as Judge Advocate Manfred Roeder and his colleague as a detective named Franz Sonderegger; he said Bonhoeffer was requested to accompany them to the police station.

Bonhoeffer looked closely at Roeder. The Rote Kapelle case had not been reported, but he knew through the family that this was the man who had sent his cousin Arvid Harnack to the gallows. Now here Roeder was for him. Reaching onto a table, Bonhoeffer picked up a Bible and asked if he could bring it with him. Roeder said he could.

The two men led Bonhoeffer downstairs and down the short path to the white picket gate. A black Mercedes sat waiting at the curb. Bonhoeffer got in the back. As the car moved off, he looked out at the family home. He would never see it again.

*    *    *

ON HIS RETURN to his office after a highly successful day, Manfred Roeder had one last task before he rested and came back refreshed and prepared for the interrogations of his prisoners.

Contacting Keitel's office directly, he filed a complaint of negligence against Hans Oster. Within ten days Oster was dismissed from the Abwehr, and although still permitted to wear uniform as an officer in the Reserve Army, he was required to remain at his Berlin or Dresden home. His movements were kept under tight observation by Gestapo men seconded to Roeder. Canaris, suspecting correctly that he himself would be Roeder's prize catch, did nothing to protect his former chief of staff.

On hearing what had happened at Abwehr headquarters, Ulrich von Hassell noted that the central conspirators had "completely compromised" themselves. He feared now that "nothing will be achieved."[4]

ROEDER TOOK BONHOEFFER to Tegel, a military prison in an area of forest and lakes on the northwestern edge of Berlin. On being processed, the pastor asked a guard why he had been arrested. "You'll find that out soon enough," the man told him.

At first, the guards treated Bonhoeffer badly, with the same cruelty and scorn meted out to the other prisoners. Bread was thrown into his cell as if he were an animal being fed at a zoo, and the blanket on the bed smelled so badly that he preferred to shiver in the cold. He was placed in an isolation cell in the top floor, denied visitors, letters, newspapers, or cigarettes. The guards were not allowed to speak to him, even when they opened the door to take away the bucket that he used as a toilet. He was to be treated as one of the prison's most serious cases, sharing a wing with men who had been condemned to death. The cries of one kept him awake at night.

However, the attitude of the prison authorities soon changed. The guards at Tegel were not Gestapo staff but professional soldiers who were deemed to be too old or unfit for active service, and when word went around that Bonhoeffer's mother was a close cousin of Paul von Hase, the military commander in Berlin, they were profoundly impressed. Few wanted to be seen treating someone who called Hase "my uncle" with anything less than respect. Bonhoeffer was moved to the third floor, into a cell with views across the prison yard to the pine trees of the Jungfernheide, which for centuries had been used as royal hunting grounds. His new cell had a plank bed and a bench along the length of one seven-foot-long wall. When one guard started to clean his cell for him every day, Bonhoeffer's embarrassment at being treated differently than the other prisoners grew, and when he was offered larger rations, he refused—knowing that if he got more, someone else might get less.

A second reason attitudes to Bonhoeffer changed was due to Roeder and Sonderegger, who reasoned that if the pastor was allowed visitors and letters, he might give himself and others away. Roeder was confused about Operation 7, and he could not believe that highly educated men such as Dohnanyi, Bonhoeffer, and the others had been primarily interested in the fate of a small number of Jews. There had to be more to the money-laundering scheme than what they had so far uncovered. The more relaxed Bonhoeffer became and the more connection he had with others, Roeder reasoned, the more opportunities there might be for him to reveal some details of the treasonable activities that Schmidhuber had alleged. He believed the pious pastor might be the weak link in the chain. Roeder allowed Bonhoeffer to have his Bible, books, and writing paper, and encouraged him to write to his family and friends.

Roeder followed the same plan with Dohnanyi, who had been taken to the Wehrmacht officers' prison on the Lehrter Strasse. He was told he would be allowed to write to Bonhoeffer. Dohnanyi assumed that Roeder would read any correspondence and saw the letter as an opportunity to present his own version of events to the Gestapo. Confident that his own legal expertise and cunning would put him at an advantage against Roeder, Dohnanyi reasoned that the most important strategy he could follow would be to protect Bonhoeffer from the investigators. He reckoned the conspirators must be continuing their plans to overthrow the Nazis, and so, if he could keep the Gestapo off the scent, he and Bonhoeffer might survive until the new regime took over. Dohnanyi's letter to Bonhoeffer was warm and personal, subtly noting that "you can't imagine how unhappy I am to be the reason why you . . . suffer like this."[5]

Bonhoeffer understood: Dohnanyi wanted him to deny knowledge of anything incriminating. He chose to act the well-meaning pastor who found the world of military intelligence into which he had been recruited far too worldly and confusing. "I am the last person to deny that I might have made mistakes in work so strange, so new and so complicated as that of the Abwehr . . ." he said. His work for the Abwehr, he claimed, had been a way of "rehabilitating" himself in the eyes of the state, which had doubted his loyalty and that of all those associated with the Confessing Church. Hadn't the SS newspaper *Das Schwarze Korps* dismissed members of the church as "treasonable action in clerical garb"?

Bonhoeffer pretended to be flustered by the interrogations. "I often find it hard to follow the speed of your questions, probably because I am not used to them . . ." he told Roeder.[6]

Roeder's investigation was watched closely by many in the Nazi high command. Not only was Himmler always weighing whether to move against the Abwehr, there also was a feeling that a prosecution of senior members of the Abwehr would taint the Wehrmacht, in the way Roeder's exposure of Harro Schulze-Boysen had cast a slur on the Luftwaffe.

Roeder continued to tread carefully. His initial inquiries concentrated on whether the Abwehr should have enabled Bonhoeffer to be excused from military service and continue work relating to the church, his involvement in the travel arrangements for the Jewish people who had traveled abroad, and his own trips abroad. Bonhoeffer successfully argued that he was simply working for the Abwehr as part of his devotion to the state. Before his arrest, it had been agreed with the others that he would defer the details of the operations to them; he was just doing what he was asked, without seeing the wider picture. "It was my brother-in-law who suggested to me that with my church connections, I should enter the service of the Abwehr. Despite considerable inner scruples, I took advantage of his offer because it provided me with the war work that I had wanted ever since the beginning of hostilities, even making use of my ability as a theologian."[7]

When his initial inquiries stalled, Roeder contacted Bonhoeffer's fiancée, Maria von Wedemeyer, and told her she was invited to visit him.

Bonhoeffer had met Wedemeyer at her family's Pomeranian family estate, an idyllic setting among picturesque lakes and tall forests. She was half his age and, despite her privileged background, dreamed of an independent life studying mathematics. Her family was also devoutly Christian and vehemently anti-Nazi. Tresckow was her uncle and Fabian von Schlabrendorff her father's cousin. During her courtship with Bonhoeffer, both her father and brother were killed in action on the Eastern Front. Perhaps conscious that he himself was not in the military, Bonhoeffer had discussed his opposition to the regime with her, saying that there "must also be people able to fight from conviction alone . . . perhaps even by working against the regime." Maria felt it was "very responsible of him to seek out the genuinely right course of action."[8]

Although only nineteen, she had listened when Bonhoeffer explained how his conviction deepened. When word had reached him that, in despair, at the height of the deportation of Berlin's Jews, Hugo Distler—a distinguished young composer of organ music—had killed himself with "Bible and cross in hand," Bonhoeffer told Maria: "The life together, toward which through God's goodness we hope to move, is like a tree that must grow from deep roots silent and hidden, strong and free."[9]

Wedemeyer's family, who had known so much grief, respected Bonhoeffer but feared how close he was to conspiracy. They worried for her. She had picked a dangerous time to fall in love. When Roeder contacted her, they were frightened. But Wedemeyer hid her fear. Several months had passed since Bonhoeffer had been arrested and, of course, Wedemeyer was desperate to see him. They had planned to get married as soon as they were able, and both still hoped that day would come.

Keen to outmaneuver Bonhoeffer, Roeder did not tell him that Wedemeyer was coming. Bonhoeffer was taken to a strange room and made to wait. After an anxious few minutes, the door opened and Roeder announced that he had a surprise. When Wedemeyer was brought in by the arm, Bonhoeffer was visibly shaken. His first thought was that Roeder had arrested her to try to get him to confess. Bonhoeffer fell silent, showing his own fear and adding to Wedemeyer's discomfort. Roeder stayed in the room throughout, smiling when the pair held hands across the table.

But Roeder underestimated Wedemeyer's intelligence and independence of spirit. She asked little and did nothing to force Bonhoeffer into making difficult explanations in the investigator's presence, instead chatting about her hopes for the wedding and the furniture her grandmother in Stettin had promised them for their new home. She joked about her wish that he himself could be the pastor performing at his own wedding. When a guard took Bonhoeffer away by one door and Roeder led her by the arm to another, she pulled free and ran to the pastor to give him a warm embrace.

Roeder uncovered no evidence of treason in Bonhoeffer's actions, but charged the pastor with avoiding military service—although the prosecutor recognized that Bonhoeffer's presence on the exemption list was for others, including Dohnanyi, Oster, and perhaps Canaris, to justify.

Bonhoeffer became optimistic that he was over the worst, but also was adamant that his actions—always disguised in his letters—had been honorable. He wrote to his friend Eberhard Bethge that, looking back to 1939, when he had rejected the chance to stay in the United States, he found that he did not regret "for a moment" coming back or "any of the consequences."

"I knew quite well what I was doing, and I acted with a clear conscience..." he wrote. He regarded his prison sentence as "being involved in the fate of Germany in which I was determined to share."[10]

With a letter to his fiancée, Maria von Wedemeyer, he enclosed a poem with the words "While all the powers of good aid and attend us / boldly we'll face the future, come what may."

ROEDER HAD PUT aside the third document he had seized from Dohnanyi's office at first, hoping further investigations would establish who had written it. Both he and Sonderegger agreed that the contents of it were evidence of a conspiracy by members of the Abwehr to negotiate with the Allies— through the Vatican—the political shape of Germany after the Nazi government had been overthrown.

But when they sat across the interrogation table from Dohnanyi, the thin, bespectacled Abwehr lawyer said he understood exactly why they thought that—that was exactly what the document was meant to look like. It was actually a coded memo, he said, and he freely admitted that he had written it with the help of Bonhoeffer. It actually meant the opposite of what it seemed to imply. It constituted covert instructions to Bonhoeffer to approach the Vatican and probe for whatever information he could get on the Allies' intentions toward Germany after the war. It was simply part of an intelligence-gathering operation and had been approved by Oster.

Dohnanyi seemed to have persuaded Roeder and Sonderegger, but when they approached Oster, he did not tell the same story. He said he had no knowledge of the document and also contradicted Bonhoeffer's evidence about his being dispatched abroad as an Abwehr agent.

Then, having had to submit his questions in advance to his chief at the RKG, Roeder was allowed to question Canaris himself. The admiral seemed weak and dejected. He denied using Bonhoeffer as an agent or having an intelligence department in any way associated with ecclesiastical affairs. He then refused to answer any other questions. Although he had not yet been officially accused of anything, it was Canaris's head that Roeder most prized.

Roeder then searched Abwehr files. He could find no record of Bonhoeffer being listed in its agents' card index and no copies of any agent reports being filed by the pastor. Was this evidence of a man helping his brother-in-law evade military service—a serious enough offense in wartime—or was it indicative of something even worse?

But Roeder knew he still had no definite evidence on which to risk his career on a prosecution of what Schmidhuber had termed the "generals' clique."

DOHNANYI SAW A way out. He was well-known for his poor ability with money and his constant need to meet the demands of his own spending.

On facing the questions on Bonhoeffer's military exemption, he encouraged Roeder to steer the interrogation in the direction of a number of wealthy friends who had also been exempted from military service on Dohnanyi's recommendation. These friends had gifted Dohnanyi money or helped him obtain funds in other ways. Schmidhuber himself had assisted Dohnanyi with letters of credit, while a broker who also employed Dohnanyi as a legal adviser had arranged a loan at a vastly reduced rate of interest with which the Dohnanyis had bought their home.

Buoyed by the news that Roeder had released his wife from custody, Dohnanyi believed that if he could keep Roeder's interest in an investigation into what could effectively be seen as bribes, he might escape the noose.

BUT STILL INTENT on breaking the grand conspiracy, Roeder turned his attention to Josef Müller.

The Gestapo had been suspicious about the staunchly Catholic Müller's relationship with the Vatican for three years, and Roeder believed he must know a great deal about the third document's reference to "discussions" with Rome.

Bonhoeffer had met Roeder with a feigned naïveté about the intelligence work he had been asked to carry out, while Dohnanyi had sought to confuse him with a mix of courtroom argument and the doublespeak of the intelligence world.

The broad-shouldered, barrel-chested Müller simply refused to budge from a position of sure-footed obstinacy.

"Well, are we both agreed," Roeder began slyly at their first encounter, "that Germany would be inconceivable without the Party?"

"Yes, certainly, Colonel!" Müller responded, apparently sincere in his blind obedience to the state. He then went on, at length, to list his many friends in the SS.

Agreeing only with Roeder's repeated attacks on any conspiracy against the state and denying everything else, Müller caused his interrogator to quickly descend into personal insults and abuse. Müller took it, as he knew then that he had won.

And later, when the Gestapo used the very worst of its "legal" and illegal torture methods on Joe the Ox, he still refused to give anything or anyone away.

GISEVIUS'S INTERVIEW WITH the investigator also descended into a stand-up row after Gisevius vehemently denied telling Schmidhuber that Canaris and Oster had given military secrets to the Russians and Dutch. Soon after, Gisevius disappeared back over the border to his Abwehr office in Switzerland, and he told Allen Dulles and the American journalist Mary Bancroft, with whom he was secretly writing his book, that he would only return when he received the signal that a strike was about to be made on Hitler.[11]

When Canaris heard about the row with Gisevius, he complained about Roeder's attitude and approach to his men. But powerful friends, sympathetic with the anti-Nazi Abwehr men, including the senior Reich Court-Martial counsel Judge Karl Sack, advised Canaris not to make too much of a fuss for two reasons: First, they believed the whole investigation might well just peter out, and second, if Roeder were taken off the case, all investigations into the Abwehr might be handed over to the Gestapo.

By now, it seemed the troubled Abwehr had virtually ceased to function as an intelligence organization, and when British and US forces landed in Sicily on July 10, 1943, the Judge Advocate General Rudolf Lehmann and Roeder's chief, Alexander Kraell—who were both loyal to Canaris—decided on an audacious plan. With Germany's ally Italy facing collapse, the two men managed to persuade Keitel that the investigation was a distraction, that there appeared to be no prospect of getting to the bottom of it, and there was no possibility of a conviction for treason. All political aspects of the investigation should cease.

The proposal was submitted at just the right moment: as news came in on July 25 that Mussolini had been removed from power and the pressure of the war increased. But Lehmann and Kraell were still amazed when Keitel agreed to it without hesitation and, thanking Roeder for his hard work, ordered him to remove the "burden" of his investigation from the Abwehr.

Privately livid, Roeder obediently agreed. There was little else he could do: Himmler had approved Keitel's decision. Roeder produced a list of charges devoid of political content. Schmidhuber, Ickrath, and Dohnanyi were charged with currency offenses and malfeasance, while Dohnanyi was also accused of "undermining the war effort." Oster was accused of complicity, released from active service, and put under observation by the Gestapo; Bonhoeffer was charged with evading military service.

Roeder walked away from the case disappointed but with a promotion to soothe his anger.

Canaris had escaped, although Keitel saw to it that more of his old allies—such as Lahousen—were also removed from their posts. Beck asked Canaris to send Gisevius to Rome to brief the pope, through Father Leiber, that the German opposition had suffered a blow but had not been neutralized completely.

HAVING ESCAPED ROEDER'S investigation, Canaris went back to work with his energy apparently renewed. He had played his cards close to his chest, not putting himself at risk by attempting to defend others if he knew his lies could be disproved, and refusing to answer questions that he had not needed to. But with the war at a crucial stage, he was about to take a risk that would bring him back to the attention of his enemies.

Only days after Roeder's political investigation was shelved, Keitel instructed him to go to Venice and liaise with the head of Italian military intelligence, General Cesare Amè. Keitel vitally needed confirmation from Amè that Italian fascists would fight on at Germany's side under the new leader, Pietro Badoglio. The Germans were already moving three divisions into Italy in case Badoglio defected to the Allies.

Canaris and Amè met among the Gothic columns, artwork, and antique furniture of the luxurious Hotel Danieli, and the German immediately sensed that, despite reassuring words, Amè knew his new government was looking for a way out of the war. Without letting on that he knew the Italians were lying, he agreed with Amè on a communiqué to send to Hitler describing the Italians' determination to fight on.

The words agreed upon, Canaris suggested a breath of air, and the pair walked along the Palazzo Dandolo with their aides some distance behind.

"Heartiest congratulations," Canaris said when he was sure they were out of earshot. Amè turned to him, not understanding, but the admiral went on: "Congratulations on your July 25. We could use one too. Germany's one dream is to get rid of Hitler."

As wily as Canaris, Amè quickly assessed the situation. He decided that trusting the German might be worth the risk.

Telling Canaris he was counting on his discretion, he said, "All we're doing today is trying to gain time. An armistice [with the Allies] will be offered very shortly, but it's essential that Italy isn't paralysed by a harsh and immediate Nazi occupation."

"There is only one way of achieving that," said Canaris, believing that Italy's end might hasten Hitler's. "Prevent the Wehrmacht from reinforcing its troops in Italy by every possible means. To put it in a nutshell, try and let as few German soldiers into Italy as you can."

Amè hesitated. The admiral was saying far more than he had expected. Perhaps it was a trap after all. He started to turn away. But Canaris held his arm softly. "My dear General Amè," he said, "you can rest assured that I shall say nothing of this in Berlin. On the contrary, I shall strongly emphasize that Italy intends to fight on at our side."

Canaris watched two young Italian soldiers pass by, then continued, his voice more urgent: "It's impossible for you to hold out longer than a month. You must withdraw from the fray, you don't have any choice. But remember: Allow as few German soldiers across the Brenner as you possibly can."[12]

Canaris returned to Berlin and took his next risk. He reported in the strongest terms his belief that Italy would stay in the war on the German side and that there was no need to transfer German forces in anticipation of an Italian collapse.

A copy of Canaris's written report reached Walter Schellenberg at the SD, who had been keeping a file on the Abwehr's failings since before Heydrich had left for Prague. Schellenberg and his chief, SS Lieutenant-General Ernst Kaltenbrunner, shared the same ambition: to create a single German secret service under SS control. Himmler had so far demurred over the request.

Thirty-three-year-old Schellenberg was an instinctive spy. The product of a middle-class household—his father had owned a business making pianos until the firm went bankrupt during Germany's interwar economic collapse—he had dreamed of the life of a diplomat, traveling the world and hearing and sharing international gossip. While he attended Bonn University, two of his professors had asked him to write secret reports on fellow students for the SS. It was a role that he greatly enjoyed, and it proved his passport into the ranks of the SD. Charming and quick-thinking, he combined daring and skill with intelligence and caution. Grand adventures like the capture of the two British agents at Venlo had made him a favorite of Himmler.

Schellenberg was an old friend and admirer of Canaris. They enjoyed riding horses together. But as well as being ambitious, Schellenberg was a deeply mistrustful man, and believing what Canaris was saying about Italy was a lie, he sent his own agents to Rome. They made discreet investigations at first, then—uncovering Amè's homosexual relationship with his chauffeur—forced the Italian to admit what was really going on and Canaris's part in it. Schellenberg reported to Himmler, who asked for the SD file to be left with him. Himmler was again intrigued more than alarmed by Canaris's possible links to the Allies and held the file on his desk.

The Italian capitulation on September 3 did not lead to an uprising against Hitler as Canaris optimistically had hoped. The war in Italy settled into one of bloody attrition.

And Schellenberg, scenting blood back in Berlin, learned of another way in which the Abwehr was being exposed to scandal.

ABWEHR AGENT MAJOR Otto Kiep was a regular visitor at the home of Hanna Solf, widow of the Weimar Republic's ambassador to Japan, Dr. Wilhelm Solf. An experienced diplomat, he had known Solf for many years, but the visits were not social. Fifty-six-year-old Solf was a committed anti-Nazi who sheltered Jews, liaised with friends in the Kreisau Circle, and created her own group in Berlin. Middle-aged or retired, the members of the Solf Circle discussed ideas rather than planned coups, but their beliefs ran counter to the regime, and they met so they could talk freely in a relaxed atmosphere without fear of being denounced.

The group included Solf's daughter, Countess Ballestrem; Countess Hannah von Bredow, a granddaughter of Bismarck's; and Karl Ludwig Freiherr von und zu Guttenberg, who had published a subtly antifascist Catholic magazine called Weisse Blätter (White Pages), for which both Klaus Bonhoeffer and Ulrich von Hassell regularly wrote articles. Although wartime paper shortages had put the magazine out of business, Guttenberg remained friends with former advisers Carl Goerdeler and Ludwig Beck, and knew of their plans for a post-Hitler government.

On September 10, 1943, the Solf Circle met for tea and conversation at the home of Elisabeth von Thadden, a longtime member of the group who ran a school for girls near Heidelberg. Thadden had invited, for the first time, a Swiss doctor named Paul Reckzeh from the Charité Hospital in Berlin. Reckzeh was a very pleasant man with stories of Switzerland, where many of the group had spent time on vacation. He appeared to share their own hatred of the Nazis, and on hearing the group knew many anti-Nazi Germans who had fled to his country, he offered to take letters from the group members to them when he went back to Switzerland. Thadden was among those who were delighted with the offer, handing Reckzeh a letter for a German friend working with the World Council of Churches.

The group of friends broke up and went their separate ways, having enjoyed a lovely evening. In the darkness, Reckzeh was happier than most. A Gestapo spy, he had uncovered a den of what he saw as semitreasonous discussion. When he reported to his chiefs, it was decided to keep the group under observation. Telephone lines were tapped and Reckzeh continued to attend the meetings. Each event brought fresh evidence against the group, including Major Kiep, and letters sent for friends in Switzerland made it no farther than Gestapo headquarters.

Then, early in the new year, Captain Ludwig Gehre, of the Abwehr, learned about Reckzeh from a Gestapo contact and warned his friend Helmuth James Graf von Moltke, whom he knew to be friends with Solf. Moltke warned Solf and Kiep, but telephone calls between the group were intercepted by the Gestapo, who swooped in to arrest Solf and her friends on January 12. A week later, after agents reviewed a transcript of a telephone call made by Moltke himself, he, too, was arrested.

The operation again turned unwanted attention on the Abwehr. Not only had Kiep been arrested, but Gehre, too—his warning to Moltke having been discovered.

This time Canaris would not escape his enemies.[13]

NEWS OF THE Abwehr connection to the Solf Circle reached Schellenberg just as details of another Abwehr failing were being added to his file.

In Italy, aircraft reconnaissance had reported a large buildup of Allied shipping in Naples harbor, and military commanders had asked the Abwehr for an assessment as to whether an amphibious operation was being planned. Canaris investigated and gave them a personal assurance that it was not. When on January 22 three hundred Allied landing craft struck the beaches at Anzio, fifty miles behind the German lines, an investigation into the intelligence failure naturally centered on the Abwehr.

Schellenberg added to his file complaints from Ribbentrop about Abwehr sabotage operations in Argentina and Spain interfering with the work of his foreign service, and the defection of an Abwehr officer, Erich Vermehren—a close friend of Adam von Trott's—in Turkey to the British. Exaggerating Vermehren's importance, Schellenberg wrote a report that Kaltenbrunner used to brief Hitler.

The Führer stewed in anger over Canaris. Himmler sensed the admiral's days were over. Having vacillated between stepping in hard to take over the Abwehr and standing back to see where its approaches to the Allies took it, Himmler now had his senior officer at Hitler's headquarters, Brigadier-General Hermann Fegelein, casually suggest that the Führer allow the Reichsführer-SS to take over the "whole works" as a single, unified intelligence service. The answer provided a simple solution for Hitler. With a wave of his hand it was to be done, and he could think of something else.

Canaris was removed from his post and ordered to remain at the thirteenth-century Burg Lauenstein, a castle in the mountainous Frankenwald where the Abwehr's forgery department was based. Staff there had been told that the admiral had freedom to move around the winding corridors of the building and walk his two dachshunds on the grounds, but he would have restricted contact with the outside world. It was house arrest, albeit in grand surroundings.

Meanwhile, in a meeting on Himmler's special train, *Heinrich*, the Reichsführer plotted the complete takeover of the military intelligence service with Kaltenbrunner, Schellenberg, and Gestapo Müller and the expansion of the empire of the SS.

A few weeks later Schellenberg visited Burg Lauenstein to explain that the Abwehr had been dismantled. Schellenberg might have not sought the personal humiliation of his old friend, but it appeared to be an unintended consequence of his triumph in a battle of wits.

# 34

## Unmasking Cicero

LATE ON THE night of October 7, 1943, Gerry Mayer drove a dark Citroën quickly through the streets of Bern. Turning into a side street, he pulled over to pick up a short man whose face was concealed by a hat and turned-up collar. After a few minutes he dropped the man next to a riverside pathway and watched him disappear up an alley.

The man opened a gate into a rear garden, pushed through overgrown shrubbery, and tapped at a door. It was opened quickly—he was expected—and he was ushered into a ground-floor living room where a glass of brandy was pushed into his hand and Allen Dulles's pipe smoke filled the air.

Fritz Kolbe was back in Switzerland, and he had brought more of Hitler's secrets.

THE THOUGHTFUL NEW Yorker prodded at the open fire as Kolbe began to talk. First, the German wanted to tell him his adventures. The bombing over Berlin was very heavy, he said. Whole streets in Charlottenburg, where he lived, and in Steglitz and Lankwitz had been flattened. It was horrible to see. And the day before he had left the city, he had been cycling down the Unter den Linden to his office when the sirens had begun to wail. Just as he was turning left into Wilhelmstrasse, an armed warden had blown a whistle, made him stop, and demanded to see his pass. Kolbe showed him a document that allowed him to be out after curfew, and just at that moment, a bomb landed farther down the street, blowing both men to the ground. Staggering back to his feet, Kolbe looked at the crater in the road, roughly where he would have been had the warden not challenged him. Reaching into his pocket, he produced a Havana cigar he had bought in Switzerland and offered it to the warden. The two men laughed with relief, and Kolbe went on his way.

Fräulein von Heimerdinger had been pleased with the chocolates and gifts he had brought back from Bern, too, and had been delighted to arrange this next trip for him. This time, though, he had made one change, he told Dulles. Having got hold of an official Foreign Ministry swastika stamp, he had hidden his booty in plain sight. He placed the official envelope that he carried for the Reich inside another larger envelope along with the two hundred documents he carried unofficially for the Americans. He then used his stolen stamp to seal the large envelope, making the whole package a "diplomatic" one that would not be opened by any snoop on the train or at the customs posts. He had separated the packages as soon as he got into Switzerland, burned the large spare envelope in the toilet, and flushed away the ashes.

Kolbe now handed the documents to Dulles and Mayer, who had parked his car farther down the street and watched for a while to see if the visitor had attracted any attention.

At their first meeting Dulles had allowed little to show on his face, but now as he flicked through, it was hard to conceal his interest. He saw immediately that there was information that required not just confirmation but urgent action as well. There was a cable that revealed that the German legation in Dublin was about to begin broadcasting on a clandestine radio details of Allied shipping movements, which would be passed to U-boat packs operating in the Atlantic.[1] Another cable from the German embassy in Buenos Aires reported the impending departure of a large convoy that would soon be leaving the United States for Britain. Dulles contacted Washington within hours and had the convoy's schedule altered.[2]

Mayer found an alarming document that revealed that the Germans and pro-Nazi French officials had created a list of Frenchmen known to be fighting with Charles de Gaulle, and they were considering arresting or even executing their relatives.[3]

On each of the next few nights, Kolbe sneaked out of the Hotel Jura, was picked up by Mayer, and met with Dulles. The American was particularly fascinated by the continuing development of the German opposition, although he made no mention of Gisevius, Trott, and Moltke's missions. One night Kolbe produced a map of Berlin and suggested fresh bombing targets. "This particular Telefunken plant produces precision instruments for the Luftwaffe," he said, marking the location with a dark circle. "In the

Lichterfelde district is the enlarged SS barracks, home to the Leibstandarte SS—Hitler's personal guard!"[4]

One night, on returning to the Jura, Kolbe began to suspect that the hotel manager was a Gestapo plant. Deciding he needed to create a cover for himself, Kolbe made a lewd joke and in the offices of the German legation during the daytime he dropped hints about the "pretty Swiss women." One night, before seeing Dulles, he went to the Café Colombine, a notorious brothel, and the next day he went to see a medical specialist in venereal diseases. When the clinic presented him with a bill, instead of destroying the ordinarily rather embarrassing document, he stashed it carefully in his pocket. It could be preserved as an alibi for his nocturnal behavior. When the short, bald, straitlaced Kolbe sheepishly hinted to Dulles the lengths he had gone to cover his visits, the American could not help but smile. He was warming to the German: He might not be the dashing spy of popular fiction, but "George Wood" was becoming one of the most efficient the Americans had known.

Before letting Kolbe return to Germany, Dulles agreed on a number of ways that the two could communicate, including a correspondence of phony love letters and postcards between Kolbe and an address in Bern where one of the German's anti-Nazi Jewish friends lived.

The quantity of material in Kolbe's documents was such that Dulles drafted in several US airmen, whose aircraft had made forced landings in Switzerland, to help transmit their contents to Washington. Soon after, another route for communication was opened when the Mediterranean island of Corsica was liberated, and Dulles ordered that the George Wood material be microfilmed. Through a liaison with the French resistance, Dulles arranged with the engineer of the Geneva-to-Lyons train to install a secret compartment over the firebox in his cab. If the locomotive was searched, the engineer could flick a lever and his incriminating cargo would be tipped into the flames. If all went well, the engineer would pass the documents to a colleague in Lyons, who would take them by bicycle to Marseilles, from where smugglers would take them to Corsica and a waiting American plane.

By the time that was set up, Kolbe was back in Berlin and about to expose a Nazi spy who was threatening to uncover the Allies' invasion plans for the liberation of France.

* * *

ELYESA BAZNA WAS an Albanian who been brought up in Istanbul during World War I and the often brutal occupation of the city by British, Italian, and American forces. Over the years he had tried many occupations, from gunrunner to taxi driver to fireman. A thief, a womanizer, and an opportunist, Bazna found work in the diplomatic community of Ankara, thanks to his skill with languages in general and French in particular, the lingua franca of the diplomats of the time. Having been fired by a German businessman who found him reading his mail, Bazna got a job with a British embassy official, who later recommended him to Sir Hughe Knatchbull-Hugessen, the British ambassador in Turkey.

In October 1943, within a month of becoming Knatchbull-Hugessen's valet, Bazna copied the key to his safe and began regularly photographing its contents. One dark evening late in the month, he walked to the city's Atatürk Boulevard and, after double-checking he was not being followed, slipped into the German embassy. He was seen by Ludwig Moyzisch, a Viennese former journalist whose official title was commercial attaché but who was in fact the station chief of the SD. Bazna had practiced for the moment and launched into a story of his hatred for the British, of how they had killed his father and how he wanted to see them lose the war.[5] He had documents, he said, of "exceptional quality." He would give them two rolls of film for 20,000 pounds, with subsequent rolls of film costing 15,000 each. The Germans had two days to think about it; otherwise he would give them to the Soviets.

Moyzisch and the German ambassador, Franz von Papen, who wanted to pay the money, reported to Ribbentrop in Berlin, who handed the file to the spy chief Walter Schellenberg. Schellenberg was suspicious but intrigued. He liked the bravado of the mysterious contact, and he trusted Moyzisch. He ordered a courier plane to fly to Ankara with the money.[6]

The first deal done, Moyzisch developed the two rolls of film. They included copies of secret correspondence between the British embassy in Ankara and the Foreign Office in London; the ambassador's private notes on conversations and negotiations between Britain and Turkey, and Britain and Russia; a complete list of materials shipped from the United States to the Soviet Union under the lend-lease program; and a provisional report on a recent conference of the foreign ministers of Britain, America, and the USSR.[7]

Papen was overjoyed. He believed the spy could help him either persuade neutral Turkey to join the Axis or at least stop it from allowing the
Allies to use its territory for operations in the Balkans. When Schellenberg
saw the documents, he realized that the agent could be used to perhaps
greater purpose: With the supposedly secret correspondence in SD hands,
its code breakers could crack the British code.

It was agreed to back Bazna, and because "his documents spoke so elo-
quently," he was to be named after the Roman writer Cicero.[8]

But Cicero would be an expensive asset, and as the Germans prepared
to budget 200,000 pounds for the operation, it was agreed to split the burden between Schellenberg's office and the Foreign Office. Under the agreement, copies of all of the Cicero documents would go both to the SD and
the Foreign Office.

And as Fritz Kolbe was in charge of handling which documents and
reports were read each day by Ribbentrop, everything Cicero sold to the
Germans passed across his desk.

THE BRITISH KNEW nothing about Cicero. Knatchbull-Hugessen went to
his room each night, handing his suit to his trusted valet and slipping into
bed beside his wife, who always took a sleeping pill.

Effortlessly and discreetly going about his work like the faithful servant he appeared to be, Bazna would wait until the fifty-seven-year-old
Englishman was sound asleep, open his safe, and take the documents to a
quiet corner of the house. There he set up a light and clicked away with his
Leica camera. When Knatchbull-Hugessen awoke, the safe was as normal
and his trousers had been neatly pressed.

Although Bazna did not read English himself, he could see that much
was top secret, would please Berlin, and would keep making him rich. If he
had been able to read the documents, he would have seen that he was operating at a crucial time in the war, and that reports on many diplomatic
events were passing through Cairo. That November, Churchill, Roosevelt,
and China's Chiang Kai-shek flew to Cairo to discuss future policy in the
Pacific, and soon after the British and American leaders flew on to Tehran
to discuss Poland's future with Stalin and, significantly, make a commitment to the Soviet dictator that they would invade France in the coming
year. As time went on, the word "OVERLORD" was discovered stamped
on some of Cicero's documents. Schellenberg realized it was the code word

for the invasion and demanded he be told each time the word was detected in Allied radio communications.[9] If Cicero kept producing documents at this rate and of this quality, the spy chief hoped he could provide him with the date and location of the Allied second front.

And then, just after Christmas, Fritz Kolbe—Dulles's agent George Wood—boarded a train from Berlin, which was diverted and delayed by air raids, but eventually delivered him back to Switzerland.

NOBODY ELSE IN the Foreign Ministry had wanted the courier trip to Bern, as it meant missing the Christmas holiday with their families. These were precious times to spend with your loved ones. The German newspapers were filled with black-bordered death notices, which, Kolbe noted, had once regularly featured the phrase "Für Führer und Vaterland" or the even more personal "Er fiel für seinen Führer," "He died for his Führer," but now rarely did.[10]

Heimerdinger approached Kolbe and apologized for this being the third time in a few months that she had asked him, but would he mind? No, of course, he wouldn't.

Over the course of a few nights between Christmas and New Year's, Kolbe went through the documents and his own verbal reports with Dulles, as the American sat at his chair in front of the open fire, festive decorations hanging from the wall, and Mayer translated some of the more difficult passages of German.

There were details of a Junkers factory in Dessau, where the Luftwaffe's first jet aircraft, the Messerschmitt 262, was being assembled, and details of V-1 rocket construction sites in Belgium and France.[11] There was information about atrocities against populations of occupied countries and diplomatic cables between Germany and Spain and Portugal.

Dulles was by now convinced of Kolbe's honesty and told Donovan: "I now firmly believe in the good faith of Wood and I am ready to stake my reputation on the fact that these documents are genuine."[12] These were bold words at the height of a war in which misinformation and double agents were being deployed extensively, but Dulles trusted his gut, and Donovan did, too.

Colleagues in Washington and London, though, remained cautious and this very nearly caused a deadly and disastrous delay in acting on one document that Dulles had highlighted as being a "blockbuster."

Several communications between Papen and Ribbentrop had referred to the existence of an agent named Cicero. Dulles flagged the first one, sent from the German embassy in Ankara to Berlin on November 4, in particular: "A number of [official British] documents have come to us from a new walk-in," Papen crowed, adding that he had charged Moyzisch with the man's "further exploitation" and was sending the SD officer to Berlin "to make a personal report." For the sake of security only a very few people in the embassy knew of the source, he said, adding: "In future communications I shall designate this source 'Cicero'; request that questions about him be sent eyes-only to the ambassador."[13]

The Allied intelligence services were shocked when they grasped the contents of Dulles's report, which he also delivered to the British SIS in Switzerland. The source appeared to be in the British embassy, he told them.[14] After first asking Dulles to get more information from Kolbe, the SIS eventually agreed to send two detectives to Ankara. Dulles asked that their inquiries be discreet so as to avoid any suspicion falling back on his own agent.

Bazna was questioned but faked such stupidity and nervousness that it seemed impossible that he could be a spy. But the investigation persisted, with the OSS using its own source inside the German embassy, a secretary named Cornelia Kapp who wished to immigrate to the United States, to try to uncover Cicero.

Feeling the net closing on him, and having obtained 300,000 pounds from the Germans, Bazna calmly handed in his notice at the British embassy, worked the remaining weeks of his employment, and disappeared.[15]

In Berlin, the well of information on Operation Overlord, which Schellenberg had hoped Cicero might provide, dried up.

FRITZ KOLBE TRAVELED back to Germany as 1943 turned into 1944. Part of him wondered what the new year would bring, but mainly his thoughts were consumed by the next few hours.

Making these trips to Bern, with illicit material in his case, had a huge strain on him. He was pale and drawn, his eyes tired from the nights briefing Dulles, and as he looked out the window, there was nothing to comfort him. There was such a contrast between the cold Christmas streets of Bern and the Germany he now passed through. Bombed-out towns, tired faces standing on each platform.

And as the minutes ticked down to his arrival at Potsdam—the track at the Anhalter Bahnhof having been destroyed—the fear began to rise. In his nightmares he had pictured the scene over and over: his stepping off the train to be greeted by the Gestapo, dragged to a waiting car, and rushed to who knew where. Even in the freezing train, the thought made his hands and forehead sweat.

But back in the city, the Gestapo was not waiting. Instead there was the usual struggle to get transport home, the queue for food in the shop, and, everywhere, the pile of rubble that the city had become.

The RAF had been pounding Berlin in a sustained campaign for more than six weeks, with hundreds of heavy bombers coming over in waves. The buildings around Alexanderplatz, Oranienburger Tor, and Reinickendorf were ruins. Streets burned, burst pipes spewed water and sewage, buildings collapsed as people scurried by. Seven elephants at the zoo had been burned alive. Twenty-one people died in a stampede when they tried to push into a public shelter as sticks of bombs fell in a street nearby.[16] They were among the thousands who had died, and word passed slowly to friends and relatives: Most telephones were dead, too.

As Kolbe walked wearily through the burning streets of Charlottenburg, he had to hold a handkerchief over his mouth, such was the choking effect of the smoke.

Darkness filled the air, so he could not tell if the sun was out.[17]

# 35

## Enter Stauffenberg

GERMANY WAS LOSING the war. The summer offensive at Kursk had failed, and the Red Army was counterattacking. Italy had been cut loose from the Third Reich. And as Fritz Kolbe had witnessed as he walked through the capital, the RAF had begun its Battle for Berlin.

While the Reich had begun to collapse, though, the fortunes of the German opposition had fared little better. The military resisters had suffered a miserable few months. The investigation into the Abwehr group had left the conspirators without an effective leader in Berlin. Canaris—even now he had begun to send out his peace emissaries—had never been a leader, only an enabler, but Oster's loss to the conspirators was great. He was respected and well-known, with contacts in all branches of the armed services, as well as in the civil service and the political class that proposed to form the government that would replace the Nazis. Since before the war had even started, he had been the driving force for the anti-Nazi opposition. Now everything seemed to rest on Henning von Tresckow, who since the summer of 1941 had been stuck on the Eastern Front.

While Tresckow did not have Oster's position or influence, he did have his energy and determination, and frustrated by the failure of the March plots, he determined to spend as much time as he could in Berlin. He took leave in May and July, and spent it planning for his attempt on Hitler, and from August to October he worked at the army personnel department. With Oster gone, he had to make new alliances and friendships in an atmosphere of high suspicion, where senior officers naturally played their cards close to their chest and were reluctant to commit to a dangerous conspiracy.

Tresckow was effectively reconstructing the conspiracy, and it would take time—although he himself admitted that he felt time was something that Germany had little of. He told Goerdeler that he believed that during 1944 the Red Army would be on the verge of sweeping into East Prussia.

The first key contact Tresckow secured was Colonel Helmuth Stieff on the army general staff. The two men had known each other for some time. Stieff had been the apparent recipient of the "brandy" Tresckow and Schlabrendorff had sent on Hitler's airplane. During a visit to Berlin, Stieff told Tresckow that he accepted that Hitler had to be killed. Having been introduced to Beck, Stieff agreed that the conspiracy needed the support of a high-ranking frontline commander and that he would take on the role of sounding out Kluge of Army Group Center. Stieff managed to get Kluge to agree to come to Berlin to meet Tresckow, Beck, and Goerdeler. He asked Goerdeler for his assessment of what could be achieved through negotiations with the British and the French to make peace in the West. Goerdeler, always optimistic, said Germany's war on Britain had forced Churchill to side with Russia. Peace must be made with Britain, he said. The military men then had a private discussion without Goerdeler, whom they knew to be against assassination. When Goerdeler was asked back into the room, Kluge told him Hitler would never be accepted by the Allies as a negotiator and he must be removed by force. Goerdeler argued and said that instead Hitler must be made to see reason. Kluge was dismissive. He said firmly that Goerdeler should leave something like this to the army, although the meeting broke up on friendly terms.

Kluge appeared to be bringing military power and urgency to the coup. However, on returning to the front, his car was attacked and he was wounded. Tresckow, though, pressed on. He knew time was short and he was still lacking the two key elements: an assassination plan that would this time succeed and a man with the conviction to see it through.

Tresckow pressed General Friedrich Olbricht, who had held senior military posts around Germany, for support. A deeply religious man, Olbricht viewed the actions of the Nazis as a disgrace to Germany. In his role as deputy commander of the Reserve Army, he was in a high position in Bendlerstrasse in Berlin, where the complex of buildings included the Ministry of War and the high command of the army.

As he walked the immense corridors of the huge concrete structure, an idea began to form in Olbricht's mind. Since December 1941, the Reserve Army had had in place a plan in which it could mobilize large numbers of reserve officers and troops in the event of a major counteroffensive by the

Red Army. On use of the code words "Valkyrie" and "Rheingold," large numbers of cadets, soldiers on the sick list, and reservists in industrial jobs could be mobilized efficiently. Friedrich Fromm, the commander in chief of the Reserve Army, had had the plan revised a number of times, and during the summer of 1943, the Valkyrie plan had become one in which a large number of reserves could be rapidly assembled to deal with major internal disturbances caused by an uprising of foreign laborers, an enemy paratroop landing, or even the death of Hitler himself. It now represented the construction of a new Home Army, turning new recruits, training units, and soldiers on courses into combat groups. As it allowed for the rushed, emergency mobilization of troops, Olbricht began to wonder if the plan could be used for a coup itself.

He showed the official Valkyrie plan to Tresckow and explained his thoughts. If a legitimate plan could be put in place for martial law, and distributed to training bases and barracks organized by the Reserve Army as a way of securing Nazi power, this could be subverted by coup planners as a way of actually seizing power themselves.

Tresckow immediately saw the potential of mobilizing forces across Germany with such swiftness that the Nazi hierarchy could be removed before most of the army knew exactly what was happening. The apparent security operation would in fact be a putsch.

Valkyrie would be cunning and daring. Tresckow began to rework it to include not only the assassination of Hitler but the killings of Himmler, Göring, and Ribbentrop at their headquarters in East Prussia. If Hitler himself could be killed by the conspirators, then the 18th Artillery Division of Army Group Center would descend on the Nazi elite, believing it was acting to crush a coup led by treacherous elements of the SS. With luck the army could be used to take command of the leading Nazi apparatus of powers before the junior officers started asking questions.

But organizing a coup that demanded such administrative skill, as well as courage and daring, required support. Tresckow needed a man who shared his commitment to help see it through. He already had the man in mind.

TWO WEEKS AFTER Hitler escaped Gersdorff's secret suicide mission at the Zeughaus in Berlin, the man who was now to become central to the conspirators' plans to kill Hitler was standing in a heavy Horch jeep as it moved slowly along a column of trucks and tanks through a mountain pass on the Tunisian coast near Gafsa.

Claus von Stauffenberg was the son of the marshal to the court of the last king of Württemberg. He was a sportsman, a poet, and a man of strong Roman Catholic convictions who had grown up in the idyllic surroundings of Greifenstein Castle to the north of Munich and been educated in the liberal atmosphere of Stuttgart, where he excelled in Latin, Greek, and philosophy.

Soldiering had been in his genes, and after graduating from the War Academy in Berlin, he had joined the general staff in 1938 as a quartermaster officer in General Erich Hoepner's 1st Light Division, which had been renamed the 6th Panzer Division shortly after the outbreak of war. He had served in combat positions in all of Hitler's major campaigns, from the Sudetenland to Poland, France, and Tunisia. The poet was a man of action.

But he was also a fair-minded Christian who believed in justice and discipline. During Operation Barbarossa, he had been appalled by the atrocities committed by the SS and SD in the name of Hitler's "racial annihilation war." The mass murder of the Jews in Russia disgusted him. He condemned the use of forced labor, the murder of Soviet commissars, and the mistreatment of Russian prisoners of war, which had led to thousands of deaths. During the first months of the Soviet campaign he had asked a like-minded colleague to collect everything that implicated the SS. In Russia, he had become friendly with Tresckow, although they had at first argued over the war—until spring 1942, Stauffenberg had thought it could be won—and he was not stationed close enough to him to yet become a part of the resistance.

In May 1942, Stauffenberg's attitude against the Nazis had hardened further when colleagues brought him reports of the massacre of Ukrainian Jews by the SS.

By September 1942, now seeing Hitler as a kind of Antichrist, he had declared to people that he himself was prepared to kill Hitler and had become so outspoken that he had been transferred to the 10th Panzer Division in North Africa as its senior staff officer. Friends in Russia had said the posting was for his own safety.

Still filled with hatred for the Nazis, he was now busy organizing the withdrawal of a convoy along a mountain road, and when a squadron of American fighter-bombers spotted it, the German vehicles were badly exposed. As explosions rocked the dusty hillside above him and vehicles were set alight, Stauffenberg remained on his feet, urging the convoy on. There was nowhere to hide; they had to keep moving.

When one of the aircraft came in on a strafing run, he jumped down from the jeep and covered his head with his hands. Bullets raked along the roadway and into the vehicle, peppering it with holes and cutting in two a junior officer who had been at Stauffenberg's side. As the aircraft moved away, a medic rushed to Stauffenberg, fearing he was dead. His face was covered with blood—he had lost his left eye—and his right hand was a bloody stump. There were shrapnel wounds all down his back and legs. They rushed him to a nearby field hospital but assumed he would be dead before sunset. Surgeons removed what remained of his right hand and two of the fingers on his left. After a few weeks he was transferred back to Germany, where he underwent further operations and had his sight restored to his right eye. He refused to give in to his injuries, and even with only three fingers remaining he would push away anyone wanting to help him get dressed or to tie his shoelaces. Despite his horrific injuries, his determination to do something about the Nazis was undiminished. He told a friend, the son of his surgeon, Ferdinand Sauerbruch: "I could never look the wives and children of the fallen in the eye if I did not do something to stop this senseless slaughter."[1]

Tresckow knew Stauffenberg from Russia, and he was well aware of his feelings toward the Nazis. There was nothing, for the moment, that suggested to him that Stauffenberg might be a potential assassin—his injuries were too severe—but he knew he could help in the planning. Tresckow arranged for Beck and Olbricht to meet Stauffenberg at Sauerbruch's home, and they were much impressed. "Stauffenberg!" Olbricht, who was reluctant to run the coup himself, said afterwards. "He's the man we need!"

When Stauffenberg was discharged from the hospital, Olbricht gave him a post as chief of staff in the Reserve Army in Berlin. Tresckow immediately sought him out and told him about Valkyrie, explaining that no coup could be successful without the death of Hitler.

For Stauffenberg the coup was entirely legitimate. He saw the army as both the most conservative institution in Germany and one of the most deeply rooted in the people. He also understood that to make peace Germany would have to abandon all its territorial claims, even the ones that Goerdeler and Hassell had once supported, such as the cessation of the Sudetenland. "Since the generals have so far done nothing," Stauffenberg said, "the colonels must now go into action!"[2]

Stauffenberg believed he had been spared from death in Tunisia for a purpose, and was energized by his meeting with Tresckow. The time had come to save Germany, he told his wife, Nina. In Berlin, thanks to his brother Berthold, he met up with his cousin Peter Graf Yorck and was introduced to the Kreisau Circle, quickly becoming a close friend of Trott's. Trott's contacts abroad and knowledge of international affairs led him to become Stauffenberg's foreign affairs adviser, discussing how a post-Nazi Germany might forge new relationships with other nations.

Tresckow watched Stauffenberg's building of relationships with interest and admiration. With Oster unavailable and Beck suffering ill health, Stauffenberg was the man of action in Berlin who could change the course of the war and rescue Germany from the annihilation that would come if it followed total war to its inevitable conclusion.

TRESCKOW AND STAUFFENBERG dared not correspond by telephone or post, and they could not be seen together. They met in the Grunewald, being sure they were not followed, and set up fold-out desks and chairs on which to work.

They were helped by three women whom they trusted completely: Tresckow's wife, Erika; her childhood friend forty-year-old Margarete von Oven, a secretary at the Bendler Block, the headquarters of the army high command; and Ehrengard Gräfin von der Schulenburg, a secretary at an office overseeing the military districts of Germany. Together they typed the orders for the army declaring a state of emergency and proclamations to be made to the general public after the coup. These condemned the behaviors of party officials and explained how the army was acting to save the country from catastrophe. The three women worked on typewriters that they then hid, and all wore gloves so as not to leave fingerprints on the paper. The most dangerous moments came when they had to carry the illegal documents from the Grunewald back to their offices, where they were stashed in safes pending the need to issue them. The key proclamations were hidden by Stauffenberg and his older brother Berthold. Draft orders that were revised on discussion with Beck, Goerdeler, or Olbricht also had to be carefully destroyed. On one occasion Nina von Stauffenberg carried a rucksack full of documents to the family country home in Bamberg and burned them on the grounds.

In October 1943, Tresckow and Stauffenberg had Olbricht sign an order that would significantly reinforce Valkyrie—and so their coup—by making units of the field army located in the "Home Forces area" at the time of the operation also subject to the operation. This meant experienced soldiers who were reforming units or recuperating would be available to the coup. Major Hans-Ulrich von Oertzen, a fellow conspirator who had served with Tresckow in Russia but was now attached to the Home Army, helped draft the orders. Field Marshal von Witzleben, who would take command of the Wehrmacht, signed the orders proclaiming a state of emergency.

Stauffenberg also drew into the plan a concentration of soldiers around Berlin and, importantly, ensured that agencies outside the Wehrmacht—including the SS, Waffen-SS, and party members—were not informed of the Valkyrie plan. Valkyrie looked perfect, both as the defensive measure it officially was and as a framework for a coup. If conditions were right, Fromm could mobilize military units across Germany to take control of key areas.

BUT TRESCKOW AND Stauffenberg had three major problems to overcome. The mobilization of the Reserve Army would need to come from Olbricht's boss, Colonel-General Friedrich Fromm, a large, cautious man who believed in the army's central position in German society, disliked Hitler, but would not commit completely to the coup. While not opposing it, he would seek to hold himself back and see who came out victorious—the regime or the conspirators—and then back the winner. Olbricht had a simple, if not perfect, solution: If Fromm did not participate in the coup, he would have him arrested and issue the Valkyrie orders himself.

The second problem did not seem so easy to solve. In fact, Tresckow realized it could not be dealt with in advance at all. The coup depended on the blind obedience of officers and soldiers given very difficult orders in what would be a most shocking time: the death of the Führer. What impact would the questioning attitude of a suspicious officer have? What if commanders in the Reserve Army who were supportive of the coup were on one of their frequent tours of inspection when the order came in? What if Goebbels rallied support in Berlin? The answers would remain unknowns for the conspirators, although they realized the more convincing the motivations for the initiation of Valkyrie, the greater the chance of their success.

That brought them to the third and most fundamental problem: To be sure they could spread the story of a putsch by the SS effectively and swiftly, and show the army that events were at their most extreme, they needed to be certain that Hitler was dead. That meant finding a person with access to Hitler who would go through with killing him.

However, Tresckow's time in Berlin was coming to end. On being told that he was taking over a regiment on the Eastern Front, not only away from Berlin but also away from Army Group Center's headquarters, from where he had coordinated his resistance, he told Stauffenberg that the future of the coup now would be largely in his hands.

As Tresckow headed east, Stauffenberg set about recruiting an assassin.

STAUFFENBERG WOULD HAVE volunteered for the role himself. However, for the moment, his injuries still troubled him and, crucially, his position gave him no access whatsoever to Hitler.

The first two people he asked turned him down, including Tresckow's contact on the general staff, Colonel Helmuth Stieff, who, after profound consideration, said he felt unable to carry out the killing. A friend then introduced Stauffenberg to a young infantry captain named Axel von dem Bussche. A tall, blond, heroic man—the perfect Aryan specimen—Bussche, like so many of the others, had been deeply affected by witnessing atrocities in the East, particularly the massacre of thousands of Jews at gunpoint in Dubno in western Ukraine. Having watched the shootings by the Ukrainian SS, Bussche had suffered a kind of breakdown in which he had blamed himself for being there and not doing anything—although there was little he could have done. Like Gerstein at Belzec, he agonized over whether he should have lain down and allowed himself to be killed, too, but got through this personal crisis by resolving to do something about the Nazis.

With Stieff's help, Bussche was able to visit the Wolfsschanze and formulate a plan. Hitler carried out regular inspections of new uniforms meant for the front, and Bussche—a war hero with the Iron Cross, 1st class, and a number of other decorations—could be detailed to model the new greatcoat for the Führer. Bussche would carry a kilo of explosives and a four-and-a-half-second fuse from a stick grenade inside the coat and detonate it when Hitler came near.

However, a few days before the demonstration was due to take place, the train carrying the uniforms was hit in an air raid and the event was postponed.

Bussche was then transferred back to active service. In January 1944, he was badly injured in battle, losing a leg and spending a long time in the hospital. His part in the conspiracy was over.

His friend Lieutenant Ewald von Kleist—son of conservative landowner Ewald von Kleist-Schmenzin, a vehemently anti-Nazi friend of Oster's—volunteered to take Bussche's place, but the demonstration of uniforms never took place and the plan was abandoned.

Then Tresckow contacted Stauffenberg and said he believed he had found the man and the opportunity to kill Hitler.

EBERHARD VON BREITENBUCH was a handsome cavalry captain with dark eyes and hair slicked back in the style of the time. At the beginning of the war he had been an aide to Witzleben, a longtime member of the anti-Hitler movement, and his own antipathy to Hitler had become well-known.

Because of his views, Tresckow had him transferred to Army Group Center, where he had become aide first to Kluge and then to Field Marshal Ernst Busch. Tresckow had hoped that through a drip feed of his views Breitenbuch might influence them both to believe Hitler must go. In the litany of horror that was the war in the East, Breitenbuch had witnessed what he viewed as the corruption of the German army. Unable to forget the summary executions of partisans he had witnessed in the Bialowieza Forest in eastern Poland, he told Tresckow that if the chance came he would be prepared to try to kill Hitler.

On March 9, 1944, Breitenbuch asked Tresckow and Major von Oertzen, who had returned to Russia with Tresckow, to meet him in his office. When they arrived, he told them he was due to accompany Busch on a visit to Hitler at Berchtesgaden in two days' times. Tresckow immediately asked him if he was willing to take explosives with him—this was the chance, Tresckow explained, to stop the thousands of casualties on the front and the deaths of the women and children in the air raids. Although taken aback that in two days he might kill Hitler, Breitenbuch steadied his nerves. He rejected the bomb, saying he was afraid he might make a mistake in trying to set it off or that it might be too conspicuous. Instead, he said, he would prefer to use a pistol. Tresckow nodded. "Aim only for the head and neck," he said. Then, shaking the young man's hand, Tresckow said the chance to end the war rested with him.

Busch and Breitenbuch were met at the airfield in Salzburg by Hitler's chauffeur in the Führer's supercharged Mercedes and driven briskly into the mountains. Tresckow, who in the time available had gone ahead without reference to Goerdeler and Beck, contacted Berlin to give a "preliminary warning" that there could be news from the Berghof.

Before heading to Berchtesgaden, Breitenbuch solemnly posted his watch and wedding ring to his wife. She remained in his mind as he sat in the anteroom in the Berghof, waiting to be ushered in with a number of other officers for his meeting with Hitler in the house's great hall. One of Hitler's staff walked along the group and took their caps, belts, and sidearms.

But they were not searched, and Breitenbuch had a loaded 7.65 mm Browning in his pocket.

Breitenbuch's heart was in his mouth. As he listened to the others talking, he realized that within a few minutes Hitler would be dead and he would be, too. Göring passed through and made a bad joke. The others laughed; Breitenbuch found he could not.

Suddenly the doors to Hitler's office were opened and everyone stood up. An SS bodyguard directed everyone forward. Breitenbuch was at the back of the group, moving slowly. His legs seemed weak; his hands were sweating. Although at the back of the group, he could see Hitler in the room ahead, with Göring, Keitel, and Goebbels. He fingered the pistol, cocked and loaded in his pocket. A few more minutes . . . The stony faces in the black uniforms to his left and right seemed to lock their eyes on him.

Then one stepped forward and put a hand in front of his chest. Junior aides would not be allowed into this meeting, the guard said. Breitenbuch's unwitting commander argued for him, although Breitenbuch himself could not speak, his mouth was so dry. The guard was adamant.

Breitenbuch turned away and stood on the terrace with another officer barred from the conference. Breitenbuch felt lost in the mountains that surrounded him. He almost felt like he would fall into the valley below. The other man saw the sweat on his forehead and asked if he was all right. Breitenbuch's hands were shaking so much he suggested he go to the hospital in Berchtesgaden to be checked out.

"It's nothing," Breitenbuch said at last. "I'll be better soon."

On hearing of the plot's failure, Tresckow almost began to believe in Hitler's personal invincibility. Everything he had tried had failed, and now Hitler was retreating further and further into his sealed cage, where the conspirators simply could not get at him. Tresckow had no time to wallow, though; all around him German soldiers were dying. He was fighting for his own life and the lives of his men. On every front the German armies were collapsing. Early in June, Rome fell to the Americans; then immediately afterwards came the D-Day landings in Normandy.

# 36

## Valkyrie

THE GERMAN HIGH command had believed the invasion could come at any point within range of the Allied air bases in southern England: anywhere from the coast of Holland to Cherbourg on the tip of the Cotentin Peninsula in France. But defenses had been most effectively strengthened in the areas of the Pas de Calais and the beaches of Normandy. The man in charge of pushing the invaders back into the sea was Field Marshal Erwin Rommel, the "Desert Fox," who, since the days of his North African victories, was by far the most popular of all German commanders with soldiers and the public.

But Ludwig Beck believed the German army in France could be ordered not to block the Allies, to leave the way open and allow anti-Nazi leaders to request favorable peace terms with the British and Americans. It was an audacious suggestion and would only have any possible hope of success if it had Rommel's support.

Rommel had only recently been approached by the conspirators. He had a key opponent to Hitler on his staff, Dr. Hans Speidel, who, despite having previously been sanctioned for disobeying the Führer's orders, had achieved the rank of lieutenant-general. The Desert Fox was also influenced by Dr. Karl Strölin, who, as mayor of Stuttgart, had played a major role in rounding up Jews in the city but had later turned against the regime. Strölin introduced Rommel to Goerdeler, and Goerdeler introduced him to Beck. On May 15, 1944, Rommel met the key conspirator Stülpnagel and discussed the role of Western armies in the event of a coup against Hitler. Only the arrest of Hitler was discussed, and not his assassination.[1] The meeting had been a positive one from the conspirators' point of view, certainly to the extent that they did not see Rommel standing in their way.

In Berlin, after D-Day, during an emergency meeting in Stauffenberg's flat at Tristanstrasse 8, Wannsee, a core group of the conspirators—which included Olbricht's chief of staff Albrecht Mertz von Quirnheim, Fritz-Dietlof Graf von der Schulenburg, Berthold von Stauffenberg, and Adam von Trott—discussed switching the coup to the West, in combination with Beck's plan to allow the Allied armies through without putting up a defense. Goerdeler and Gisevius had sent messages backing the plan, but Stauffenberg and the others felt it took too much out of their hands. First, it depended on the Allies' willingness to negotiate. Second, it took away their efforts to restore Germany's honor by ridding their nation of Hitler themselves.

Rommel discussed with Gerd von Rundstedt and Stülpnagel the prospect of beginning armistice negotiations with the Allies, although he was pessimistic. Rommel believed the Normandy defense would collapse quickly anyway, so an offer to the Allies by the German army that it would stand aside would not seem that appealing: The Germans, he felt, had little to bargain with.

However, on July 15, Rommel dictated a bold message to Hitler, saying he had one "last chance" to avoid disaster.[2] The message was still on his desk when the very next day Rommel—the only man with the charisma to carry the German army with him and bring off Beck's plan—was badly hurt in an air attack. The coup in the West was abandoned, and the "last chance" message that Rommel had dictated for Hitler was passed to Kluge, the new commander in chief in the West. Although he told General von Falkenhausen he agreed with its contents, he decided it should not be sent.[3]

But by now Stauffenberg had himself gained access to Hitler—and could get close enough to kill him.

ON JUNE 7, 1944, General Fromm, chief of staff to the commander of the Reserve Army, took Stauffenberg to a special briefing at Hitler's headquarters at Berchtesgaden. Stauffenberg had no explosives or gun, and was introduced by Fromm as a brilliant staff officer. Noting his injuries, Hitler greeted him warmly, holding his maimed left hand in his. Here was an army officer Hitler felt he could respect.

Then, in front of Göring, Keitel, Himmler, and Speer, the Führer asked him to outline the plan for Operation Valkyrie, the official version designed to hold Germany together in the event of an invasion or uprising.

The landings in France had renewed the senior Nazis' interest in homeland security issues. Stauffenberg spoke clearly and his voice did not waver, despite the fact that all those to whom he spoke would be killed when the coup was put into operation. Hitler approved the plan.

Back in Berlin the deeply Christian Stauffenberg told his wife that the atmosphere in the room had been fetid and that all, apart from Speer, were clearly "psychopaths." In his office in the Bendler Block he read the reports from the West and East, and told a friend: "Now it is not the Führer or the country or my wife and four children which are at stake," he said. "It is the entire German people."[4]

Fromm had been impressed with Stauffenberg, and on July 1, 1944, he promoted him to full colonel and made him his chief of staff. In this new role he would be required to supervise the training and supply of units across Germany for service at the front. Most significant, he would report to Hitler personally. There was no longer any need for him to search for an assassin: Stauffenberg could kill Hitler himself. He confided immediately to his cousin Peter Graf Yorck von Wartenburg that he was prepared to do it.

On learning that Stauffenberg had not only got Hitler to sign the Valkyrie orders but now had personal access to the Führer as well, Tresckow sent him a message: "The assassination attempt must take place at whatever cost. Even if it does not succeed we must still act. For it is no longer a question of whether it had a practical purpose; what counts is the fact that in the eyes of the world and of history the German resistance dared to act. Compared with that nothing else is important."[5]

FROMM'S REASONS FOR promoting Stauffenberg were unclear.

Hitler had been impressed with Stauffenberg's briefing and that reflected well on Fromm. But Fromm knew Stauffenberg's feelings for the regime, and on taking his office, Stauffenberg told him he intended to use his position to launch a coup d'état.

Fromm had told the conspirator Wolf-Heinrich Graf von Helldorf, Berlin's police chief, that it would be best if Hitler killed himself, but he never committed to the coup.

His comment to Stauffenberg that he should not "forget that chap Keitel when you make your putsch"—he hated Keitel—indicated that he prioritized his own benefits over those of Germany's. He was, as Ulrich von Hassell said dismissively, an "opportunist."

All the same, his acceptance of Stauffenberg persuaded some that he was on board. Allen Dulles reported to Washington from Bern that a courier from Gisevius had informed him that Fromm had joined the conspiracy.[6]

ON JULY 6, Stauffenberg was at the Berghof again, accompanying Fromm for a two-hour meeting with Hitler about the creation of new divisions for the Eastern Front. This time he carried explosives in a suitcase, which Speer joked innocently was looking "remarkably plump." Stauffenberg smiled. He was a busy staff officer with a lot of paperwork to carry. The conversation moved on.

Stauffenberg still hoped an assassin could plant the bomb and escape. He took his contact on Hitler's staff, Colonel Stieff, aside and asked if he could plant the bomb at an event being held in Schloss Klessheim, Hitler's favorite Austrian palace, near Salzburg. Stieff refused. He was Stauffenberg's only other conspirator with access to Hitler. Without Stieff, he had to be prepared go it alone. "The man who has the courage to do something must do it in the knowledge that he will go down in German history as a traitor," Stauffenberg admitted to friends. "If he does not do it, however, he will be a traitor to his own conscience."

On July 11, Stauffenberg was back at the Berghof, with the bomb once again in his briefcase. This time, determined to make the attack himself, he had placed a plane on readiness at Salzburg airport in order to fly him to Berlin after he had left. On arrival at Hitler's private residence he was told by Stieff that Himmler would not be there. "Good God, ought one then not still do it?" Stauffenberg asked.

Stieff was against killing Hitler without Himmler, as were many of the conspirators, knowing that if the SS chief survived the first stage of the coup, he would turn the machinery of his SS and Gestapo against them. Making an excuse, Stauffenberg left the room to telephone General Beck and Field Marshal von Witzleben. In code, he told them that Himmler was not there—should he go ahead and kill Hitler? The senior officers told him that they could not leave Himmler alive to put down the coup. Stauffenberg sweated it out and afterwards met Stieff and General Erich Fellgiebel, head of communications at army high command, for lunch. They ate in silence.

When Goerdeler heard that the officers had not gone ahead, he said angrily, "They'll never do it!"[7] Fellow political conservative Canaris shared Goerdeler's skepticism, although his animosity to the plan was based on a dislike of what he saw as Stauffenberg's socialist principles and idealism. He particularly disliked Stauffenberg's plan for a broad new political movement including people from a range of backgrounds, including Communists.

With the battle raging in Normandy, and full army divisions being captured in the East as the Russians took Minsk and pushed on into Lithuania, Poland, and Romania, the Hitler conferences became regular briefings. On July 15, Stauffenberg was summoned to the Wolfsschanze, Hitler's Wolf's Lair, in East Prussia, where Hitler had flown to the previous day. Hitler planned a series of three meetings to take place throughout the afternoon. Increasingly frustrated, although morally conflicted by the knowledge that his bomb was bound to kill unintended victims, Stauffenberg was determined that this was the day on which to act.

He was rushed into the first meeting without the chance to start the timer on the bomb. Himmler was again not present. After twenty minutes the meeting broke up and Stauffenberg phoned Beck and Olbricht in Bendlerstrasse to find out if he should go ahead. Albrecht Mertz von Quirnheim answered and relayed the conversation back and forth.

As he waited, the men on the other end of the line debated and made phone calls to other conspirators. The tension for Stauffenberg must have been almost unbearable.

Finally they had a decision. Again they told him to delay.

Stauffenberg, who had been carrying a briefcase with a British bomb for more than two weeks, had had enough.

He spoke quietly to Mertz. "Ali, you know that in the last resort it is only a matter between you and me . . ."

Mertz hesitated, aware of the other men's eyes on him, although they could not hear what was being said.

"What do you say?" Stauffenberg said.

Mertz turned his face away from the others. He and Olbricht had taken a risk that morning and ordered an alert to the guard battalion and the army schools near Berlin. It was the preparations for Valkyrie.

"Do it!" Mertz said.

Stauffenberg returned to the briefing room to find that the second short meeting had broken up. He had missed it. As he had to speak at the third briefing, other officers came to him to discuss his presentation, and he knew that he would have no chance to set the bomb: a process that involved crushing a time pencil with a pair of pliers that had been especially adapted for the use of a man with only three fingers.

Again making an excuse, Stauffenberg rang Olbricht again and told him to abandon the coup. Olbricht panicked and had to drive around the army garrisons in Berlin, telling them to stand down.

The next time Valkyrie was triggered, the coup must go ahead—but the order must not be given until Stauffenberg confirmed Hitler was dead.

IN BERLIN, THE pressure was growing on the conspirators.

Field Marshal Wilhelm Keitel was extremely suspicious of Olbricht's actions on July 15 and was only just persuaded by Olbricht's claim that it had been a practice alarm drill. It would be an excuse that he could not get away with again.

Time was running out. Stauffenberg learned that a Gestapo warrant had been issued for Carl Goerdeler's arrest, and the former mayor of Leipzig went into hiding on a friend's country estate. He sat by the radio awaiting news of the putsch. At his side was the list of names that he had proposed as members of the cabinet of the new provisional government under his chancellorship.

Socialist conspirators Julius Leber—who had spent many years in a concentration camp during the 1930s—and Adolf Reichwein, who were both earmarked to hold positions in the conspirators' post-Nazi government and were key contacts of Moltke and Yorck, were also arrested after meeting with the Communist underground of Bernhard Bästlein, which had been infiltrated by the Gestapo.[8] Word reached Stauffenberg, who was known to both men, that they were being tortured: At any moment they could give him away. Stauffenberg's nerves were at a breaking point. At every meeting he attended he risked betrayal and summary execution, and all the while he planned to go ahead with an act that would shock his nation. He was irritable, tired, struggling to maintain the facade of the upright, efficient staff officer. His surgeon, Ferdinand Sauerbruch, actually advised him that his health was too poor to be involved in the coup at all.

For Stauffenberg, the time had come to act before everything collapsed. He told friends this time he would act whether or not Himmler was present.

\* \* \*

ON JULY 19, Stauffenberg was told he was required to be at the Wolf's Lair for a one o'clock conference the following day. This time he requested to take his adjutant, Lieutenant Werner von Haeften.

A friend of Bonhoeffer's, Haeften had actually discussed his own ideas for killing Hitler with the pastor and, having been wounded on the Eastern Front, had been transferred to Stauffenberg's staff with Olbricht's help. He had been unable to attend the conference on July 15. If he had, perhaps events might have turned out differently, as he would have been able to help Stauffenberg set the bomb.

Now he and Haeften knew their time had come. Stauffenberg told him that this would be his final attempt on Hitler's life.

Needing to breathe and think, Stauffenberg visited his friend Adam von Trott zu Solz at his flat in Rheinbabenallee and then asked his driver to stop outside a Catholic chapel that he knew well. It was very late, but the priest could see the concern on his face and welcomed him inside. They spoke in hushed tones for a few moments, Stauffenberg saying he had an important question to ask. "Father, can the Church grant absolution to a murderer who has taken the life of a tyrant?" he said. The priest breathed deeply and took a moment to answer. Only the pope could grant absolution in such a case, he said, but he would look into it further. Stauffenberg nodded and shook his hand, knowing he would never hear the answer he wished to hear.

When he returned home, he could not sleep, so he stayed up with Berthold to read new poems by their other brother, Alexander.

They rose at five o'clock the following morning, and Stauffenberg packed his bags. He placed a clean shirt inside his briefcase, laid two bombs on top, and then folded the rest of the shirt over them. Berthold accompanied him to Rangsdorf airfield, where Haeften was waiting. The Stauffenberg brothers bid each other farewell, Claus telling his brother that his wife and children were staying in a country house in Württemberg. "I leave them in your hands," he said.[9]

Stauffenberg's conversation with the priest appeared still on his mind, but he had come to his own conclusion. Even without the promise of absolution, he knew what he had to do. As they walked to the airplane, he turned to Haeften and said, "Fate has offered us this opportunity, and I would not refuse it for anything in the world. I have searched my conscience, before God and before myself. This man is evil incarnate."

Haeften knew the torment he had been through over the killing as he had been through it himself.

The Junkers Ju52 carrying the two men arrived at the airfield at Rastenburg at 10:15 a.m. A car took them the four miles to the Wolf's Lair. The roadway was dappled by the July sunshine coming through the thick green forest. Inside Hitler's compound Stauffenberg had the chance to enjoy a midmorning breakfast while sitting beneath an oak tree.

Stauffenberg was then ushered into a preliminary briefing at which Keitel informed everyone that the conference had been brought forward to 12:30 p.m. as Hitler had a meeting with Mussolini later. The conference would take place in a briefing room at the end of a long, single-story block made of wood and fiberglass, with a reinforced concrete roof resting on brick piers. Stieff and Stauffenberg had hoped the conference would take place in its usual location, Keitel's underground bunker, where the blast would be contained and deadlier, but the bunker was deemed too unpleasant in the heat.

A few moments before it was due to begin, Stauffenberg asked Keitel's adjutant, Major Ernst John von Freyend, if there was somewhere he could freshen up and change his shirt. It was a hot day, and Stauffenberg was a man with obvious injuries and physical difficulties: Freyend was immediately sympathetic and showed him to his own quarters. Haeften, who would assist him to dress, went with him. He had the briefcase with him.

Once they were inside the toilet in Freyend's quarters, Stauffenberg began priming the timer on the first one-kilogram bomb. The timers could be unpredictable in the heat of summer, but Stauffenberg estimated it would go off within half an hour.

Tension was high in headquarters with the bad news from Normandy: The Americans were in Saint-Lô, and the British had taken Caen.

Outside the conference room, Keitel was impatient and asked where Stauffenberg was. As he spoke, a call came through for Stauffenberg from General Fellgiebel, head of communications at army high command, who was awaiting word to block telephone and teleprinter communications in and out of the Wolf's Lair once Hitler was dead. Freyend took the call and, knowing Keitel was angry, sent Sergeant-Major Werner Vogel to tell

Stauffenberg that Fellgiebel had called and that he should hurry up to get to the conference.

Vogel found Stauffenberg and Haeften working with an object that they then pushed into a briefcase. Stauffenberg told him gruffly that he was on his way. Freyend appeared and called out: "Stauffenberg, come along, please!"[10]

Stauffenberg and Haeften now had no time to set the other timer, and Vogel was standing in the door. As Stauffenberg left the room, Haeften quickly stuffed the second bomb into his own case. Had it been in Stauffenberg's—even without the timer—it would have been detonated with the first bomb and caused an explosion twice the size.[11]

The conference had already begun when Stauffenberg arrived. Leaving his belt and hat in an anteroom, he went inside. Hitler looked up, recognized Stauffenberg, and shook his hand.

The room was about thirty feet by twelve and was dominated by a heavy oak table around which about twenty-five people were seated. Hitler sat in the middle on the long side of the table nearest the door. He faced the windows, open because of the heat and beyond which one could see the trees and grounds of the compound and the surrounding forest, but his head was down, his eyes moving on the maps that were spread out along the tabletop as Major-General Adolf Heusinger briefed him on German positions on the Eastern Front. Stauffenberg was due to speak later on which elements of the Reserve Army could be brought into action to block the Soviets in Poland and East Prussia.

Because of hearing difficulties left over from his injuries, Stauffenberg had requested a seat at the table close to Hitler. Room was found for him to Hitler's right but toward the end of the table. Freyend, who had carried in his briefcase for him, placed it at his feet. The heavy table was built on thick plinths rather than legs, and one of the plinths was between the bomb and Hitler, but they were barely a few strides apart.

There was no Göring or Himmler, but there was also no going back. The bomb was primed.

The conferences were not quiet like a church service. People hurried in and out all of the time, carrying papers, rushing to the telephone. After just a few moments, Stauffenberg stood and said he needed to make a call. Some looked up, but most took no notice. He left his cap on the table; he would be back in a moment.

A bomb now ticked just a few feet from Hitler—as close as Georg Elser's had almost six years previously. Many had died in the intervening years in the name of Hitler's rampant nationalism and racial war.

But this time he would not be leaving the room before the bomb went off.

ACROSS GERMANY AND beyond the conspirators were ready for word from Stauffenberg. Orders had been prepared and were ready to be telexed to various military units as part of the Operation Valkyrie policy. They contained details of the imposition of martial law; lists of people who were to be arrested, including the commandants and guards of all the concentration camps; and orders regarding closing down telecommunications and radio outlets. Three speeches had been written to be delivered over the radio. Two would be directed at the armed forces and would be delivered by General Beck and Field Marshal von Witzleben. The third was addressed to the German people and would be given by Goerdeler. In Paris, General Carl Heinrich von Stülpnagel, the military governor of France, would arrange for the troops under his command to arrest all Gestapo and SS officers.

OUTSIDE THE CONFERENCE room Stauffenberg told Freyend he needed to make the return call to Fellgiebel. Freyend nodded and returned to Hitler's briefing.

Out in the passage, the telephone operator, Sergeant-Major Arthur Adam, put through the call and then turned back into his office. Stauffenberg paused until he had gone and then replaced the receiver and walked swiftly outside, following the path to the Wehrmacht adjutants' building, where Haeften and Fellgiebel were waiting. Haeften had already ordered a car for them.

IN THE CONFERENCE room Heusinger broke off to get extra information from Stauffenberg on reserve forces that could be mobilized to Poland. When he realized Stauffenberg was not there, he apologized to the Führer, and said he would get the information on the colonel's return. Freyend said he had had to respond to an earlier phone call.

Hitler seemed not to hear. Absentmindedly he turned his head back to the map that Heusinger now wished to draw his attention to. He leaned forward, his chin in his hand. It was 12:42.

At that moment the bomb went off.

*  *  *

THE EXPLOSION DESTROYED one of the walls of the briefing room and blew out all of its windows. The oak table Hitler had been leaning on shattered, and wooden beams dropped down from the ceiling. The room was filled with paper, pieces of the plaster ceiling, and sections of broken partition wall. Smoke hung in the air, and some of the wood beams were on fire. The grass outside was littered with splinters of wood and burned paper.

Colonel Brandt, the man who had been Tresckow's unwitting messenger with the brandy bomb, had been sitting near the bomb and had his left foot blown off. Schmundt, who had previously given Tresckow information about Hitler's movements, had lost an eye and a leg. General Korten, who had taken Stauffenberg's seat after he had left, had been disemboweled by the explosion. All three would soon die.

In a corner of the room, the stenographer, Heinrich Berger, lay on the floor, his body surrounded by a lake of his own blood. Both his legs had been blown off. As others tried to help him, he died.

Around the room bodies lay still while others stumbled, concussed, deafened, partially blinded, and stepped over broken furniture. Everyone's clothes had been burned; skin was blackened and bruised.

In shock but having avoided serious injury, Keitel moved through the debris and dust, searching for his Führer.

REMARKABLY, THE EXPLOSION—while heard around the compound— did not at first raise suspicion.

Weapons were constantly being fired in the area, and flak teams practiced their drills. The explosion might have been an animal stepping on one of the mines that surrounded the perimeter.

The driver who had picked them up earlier, Erich Kretz, was waiting. He pointed out to Stauffenberg that he had forgotten his cap and belt, but the officer snapped back that it did not matter. As they moved off, they could see smoke rising from the area of the briefing hut and scraps of paper swirling in the air.

Stauffenberg easily bluffed his way past the sentries at Guard Post 1, but by the time the car reached the outer perimeter the alarm had been raised. Stauffenberg had to telephone an officer he knew who was prepared to authorize his passage. The officer had no idea of the true nature of the explosion and had no reason to connect it to Stauffenberg.

Once through, Stauffenberg told the driver to hurry to the airfield. He and Haeften now needed to be in Berlin to ensure the coup's success.

As the eight-cylinder Horch accelerated along the East Prussian forest road, Haeften took the second unused explosive from his bag and hurled it into the undergrowth. Both men exchanged glances, afraid to speak because of the driver.

By 1:15 p.m. they were airborne and heading for the capital. Certain Hitler was dead, they hoped the men in Berlin had swung into action.

IN THE WRECKAGE of the briefing room Keitel saw Hitler stumbling toward the door. As he walked, he beat at flames on his trousers and rubbed at singed hairs on the back of his head. Keitel reached out and embraced him. "My Führer, you are alive, you are alive!" he cried, and tears began to roll down his face.

Hitler did not speak. His uniform jacket was torn, and his trousers and long underwear were in shreds, but he did not appear to have any serious injuries. He was led to his bunker, where his doctor, Theodor Morell, examined him. Both arms were hurt. He could barely lift his right, and the left was covered with bruises. There were cuts on his face, and his eardrums had burst. More than one hundred wood splinters were removed from his legs. As the doctor worked, Hitler complained that his new trousers had been ruined. He later had them packaged up and sent to his fiancée, Eva Braun, in Berchtesgaden to show how he had cheated death.

When his devoted valet rushed in, Hitler smiled grimly. "Linge," he said, "someone has tried to kill me."

As Morell worked on him, Hitler began to think once again about how Providence had spared him, just as it had with Elser. He gestured to his tattered clothing with a sense of pride. "I am invulnerable, I am immortal," he said, repeating the words over and over again with a growing euphoria.[12]

HIMMLER AND GÖRING were summoned to Hitler's bunker, and an urgent discussion began as to who had carried out the attack.

Hitler had at first been willing to believe that the bomb had been left by forced laborers who were reinforcing the buildings to protect the compound from air raids. This was the theory then transmitted to Goebbels and Speer, who were seated in the study of the propaganda minister's palatial home at Hermann-Göring-Strasse in Berlin. Goebbels shouted at Speer about his use of foreign workers, and then the two men carried on about their business. Goebbels then, apparently unconcerned, took his afternoon nap.

At the Wolf's Lair, though, the finger of suspicion quickly moved away from the foreign workers when Stauffenberg's name was mentioned. The telephone operator, Sergeant-Major Adam, had first suggested the officer and been shouted down. But determined, and alerted by the fact that Stauffenberg had left his cap and belt, he went to Bormann, who listened with interest as Adam breathlessly explained his suspicions.

Bormann investigated and praised Adam's intelligence. The zealous sergeant-major was later rewarded with a promotion, a reward of 20,000 marks, and a house in Berlin.

Bormann told Hitler that Stauffenberg had come to the meeting late, had left early, and had now disappeared.

Hitler raged. The army! The weak-willed, useless army officers who had lost so many battles and betrayed Germany were now trying to kill him. His vengeance would be swift and complete. All under suspicion must die.

# 37

## Valkyrie Unravels

THE SUN WAS beating down in Berlin. Shoppers rushed into the U-Bahn or leaped on a tram. It was a Thursday, a good chance to get ahead of others and search the largely empty shelves of the shops before the weekend. Conversations about shortages of potatoes and vegetables were as common as those about the fighting in Normandy. As yet there was no hint of what had happened in East Prussia or what was about to start in the city.

The heat added to the sense of stress in the Bendler Block, the army headquarters that had become the nerve center of the coup. By 1:30 p.m. the coup leaders had been told an attack had been made and that they should carry on. But the messages that had reached General Olbricht and Lieutenant-General Fritz Thiele, Fellgiebel's communication chief in the city, had been vague and confusing. "Something fearful has happened, the Führer's alive," Fellgiebel's own telephone message had said.[1]

The conspirators did not know if the bomb had gone off, if Stauffenberg had postponed again, or if he had been discovered. If the "fearful" thing that had happened was Stauffenberg's death, then there seemed to be no reason to launch the coup and put them all in danger for nothing. Without confirmation of Hitler's death, Fromm would not launch Valkyrie, and Olbricht decided they must wait.

On arrival at Tempelhof, Haeften rang ahead and announced that Hitler was dead. His words were passed down the corridors of the block. The atmosphere was electric—a strange mixture of fear, tension, and excitement. But when Haeften and Stauffenberg arrived there at around 4 p.m., they were told that only some of the Valkyrie orders had been issued. Stauffenberg's friend Colonel Mertz von Quirnheim had issued the order

for mobilizations "against an uprising" to all regional military commanders. He acted against both Olbricht's and Fromm's wishes.

Stauffenberg headed to his office on the third floor, where his brother
Berthold, Schulenburg, and Lieutenant Ewald von Kleist were waiting.
"He's dead," Stauffenberg said before the others had the chance to say a
word. "I saw how he was carried out."

Stauffenberg and Haeften went to Olbricht's office. Stauffenberg said,
"The explosion was as if the hut had been hit by a six-inch shell. It's hardly
possible that anyone could be alive."

On seeing Stauffenberg and after relentless pushing from Mertz, Olbricht agreed to take the remaining Valkyrie orders from his safe and present them to Fromm for his signature. Olbricht told Fromm that Hitler was
dead, but Fromm was not convinced.

Telephone lines to the Wolf's Lair had now been opened again, and
Fromm managed to get through to Keitel, who told him categorically that
the Führer had suffered only minor injuries.

Olbricht summoned Stauffenberg, who told Fromm that he knew Hitler was dead.

"That's impossible," Fromm said. "Keitel has assured me to the contrary."

Stauffenberg said Keitel was lying and that in any case Mertz von
Quirnheim had issued the orders for Valkyrie. Fromm banged his fist on
the table, summoned Mertz, and told him he was under arrest.

Stauffenberg stepped between them and told Fromm that it was he who
was under arrest. Fromm rushed at Stauffenberg and tried to hit him, but
Kleist and Haeften drew their pistols and Kleist pressed his firmly into
Fromm's stomach.

Fromm was pushed into an anteroom, where the telephone was discon-
nected and the door locked. He was given a supply of sandwiches and wine.

Olbricht was now determined to act. There was no going back. Returning
to his office, he worked with Mertz and his duty officer, Captain Friedrich
Klausing, to present the teleprint messages for dispatch. At 4:30 p.m. Klausing
gave the first to the signal traffic officer, who glanced down at it and read the
words: "The Führer, Adolf Hitler, is dead . . ."

The officer's face showed a moment of shock, and then duty took over.
Four female teleprinter operators went to work. It would take hours to send
the messages.

"An unscrupulous clique of combat-shy party leaders has attempted, by exploiting this situation, to take our hard-pressed combat troops in the rear and seize power for their own ends . . ."

There was a state of emergency. Witzleben was now in supreme command of the armed forces . . .

Then a second message quickly followed, ordering the military protection of radio stations, telegraph offices, and main exchanges. Gauleiters, police commissioners, and SS and Gestapo commanders were to be removed from their posts and held in confinement until further notice . . .

As the orders were received over the following couple of hours in barracks across Germany, officers reacted with confusion. Hitler was dead. Could it be true? Arrest SS and Gestapo commanders? To many it seemed unthinkable.

Committed, although his health was failing, Beck moved through the Bendler Block, telling staff he had taken over command of the state and that Witzleben was commander in chief of the army. Hoepner, who had been dismissed by Hitler two years earlier, arrived in civilian clothes, opened a suitcase, and began to dress again in the uniform of a colonel-general. He took over Fromm's role as head of the Reserve Army, although it was to be a short-lived command. Olbricht explained the doubts about the news from Rastenburg, but Beck said they owed it to the German people to keep on, no matter what the doubts about Hitler's death.

Olbricht called Bonhoeffer's uncle Lieutenant-General Paul von Hase, the military commander of Berlin, who ordered Major Otto Remer, a thirty-two-year-old fanatical Nazi and a holder of the Knight's Cross for gallantry, to seal off the government quarter of the city with his Grossdeutschland guard battalion. Hase was a man of civilized sensibility, perhaps unsuited to a coup. His order to seal the area should have specifically required the immediate arrest of Goebbels and other senior officials. It left room for doubt.

Remer, believing he was acting in the name of the official Operation Valkyrie and helping to put down an anti-Hitler coup by members of the SS and the party, went off to do his duty. At 6:30 p.m. his troops surrounded Goebbels's residence and barbed-wire barricades were unfolded in the street. People watched in surprise, then hurried home. As rumors spread about a coup, people wondered whose side the soldiers in the street were on.

Speer arrived at Goebbels's city villa moments before Remer's men and was told by a now fully alert Goebbels that a full-scale military putsch was under way and that he had been unable to contact Himmler. After watching through a gap in the curtains as Remer's troops lined up, rifles at the ready, Goebbels went into his bedroom, opened a drawer, and took out a box of cyanide pills, which he then placed in his pocket. For the moment even the most powerful people in Berlin did not know how this day would end.

But important elements of the coup had not been executed. Declaring martial law in their capital city and arresting their own uniformed countrymen required a level of ruthlessness that the men in Berlin had not shown. There had been no planning for the possibility that for some time during the afternoon the coup leaders in Berlin might be unsure if Hitler was dead: It had been felt that any kind of contingency for failure would frighten off the waverers in key positions who were desperately needed for the coup to succeed. Now those same waverers were distancing themselves from events, not convinced by the early rumors that Hitler had died.

And senior dissenters were smelling a rat and turning up at the Bendler Block. General Joachim von Kortzfleisch, commander of the Berlin military district, was first. When told he could not see Fromm, he refused to issue the Valkyrie order, saying this was a coup and he would have no part in it. He rushed down the corridor, shouting: "The Führer is not dead! The Führer is not dead!" Kleist caught up with him and held him at gunpoint.

Kortzfleisch's men had been required to occupy the most important party buildings and SS offices. One of his officers eventually issued the order, but for some time no troops were available to carry it out. As time passed, Kortzfleisch's failure to return from Bendlerstrasse began to cause confusion and then suspicion among his officers.

Tanks from Armored School II in Krampnitz had begun to move slowly by road toward the center of Berlin, but the unit's regular commanding officer, a conspirator, was on inspection duty, so the officer in charge that day was Colonel Wolfgang Glaesemer, who supported the regime. Concerned and suspicious, Glaesemer drove on ahead to Bendlerstrasse. On meeting Olbricht, he realized what was happening and accused him of stabbing Germany in the back. Glaesemer was locked in a room but managed to escape and return to his unit. He ordered his tanks back to the barracks.

Tresckow's fears during the planning stage for the problems he could not solve in advance were being realized: Officers were not always following orders, and people whom the coup relied upon were sometimes not at their posts. There had been no practical and secure way of informing everyone when the putsch would be launched.

Major Remer's Grossdeutschland guard battalion had the cordon of the government quarter complete, but it had been decided in Hase's office that it would be inappropriate to have Remer arrest Goebbels: The Reichsminister was the honorary colonel of the battalion, and it would put Remer in an embarrassing position. No one had been tasked to arrest Goebbels and his telephone had not been cut off. Watching the activity in the street, the propaganda minister quickly realized that not only was state radio still broadcasting, but the coup leaders had made no effort to broadcast their own messages to the nation. This was not how he would have staged a coup.

Among Remer's men was a reserve officer, Lieutenant Hans Hagen, who as a staff writer on *Das Reich* knew Goebbels well. Standing on duty on Wilhelmplatz, Hagen began to suspect that something was wrong and sneaked off to speak directly to Goebbels, who confirmed his fears that a putsch was under way and that the soldiers outside were either traitors or acting under traitorous orders. Hagen told Goebbels that Remer was a loyal Nazi who had obviously been duped into acting as he had. Goebbels sent Hagen outside to talk to Remer. Hagen told Remer what was really happening and said he must talk to Goebbels or risk being executed for treason. Remer hesitated: He did not know whom to believe. Perhaps Goebbels himself was part of the coup? A mistake either way could cost him his head. Hagen pleaded again, saying it was Hase's order he had to disregard. Still unsure and carrying a cocked revolver in his hand, Remer agreed to come inside and hear what Goebbels had to say.

Goebbels held Remer in a stare and asked him if he was a true National Socialist.

"Yes," Remer said. "Very much so." Then, keen to uncover the conspiracy, he dared ask the propaganda minister, "Are you a National Socialist? Are you faithful to the Führer?"

"I am," Goebbels said. "I give you my word of honor."

Goebbels told him that the assassination attempt was part of a military and political insurrection, but Remer remained shocked and confused. He had received orders from his military commander only a short time ago, which Goebbels claimed were based on a lie. But Hase had told him the plotters included senior members of the party: Was Goebbels one of them?

Goebbels stepped from behind his desk and asked Remer if he remembered his personal oath to the Führer. Yes, Remer told him, but the Führer is dead.

"The Führer is alive!" Goebbels told him. "I spoke with him only a few minutes ago."

Goebbels leaned closer to the major, who still held the gun at his side. "Would you like to speak to him?"

Goebbels had an adjutant arrange a call through to Rastenburg on his "Führer line."

Remer took the telephone receiver, and after a moment he heard a weak but familiar voice, which asked if he realized who he was speaking to.

Goebbels watched the effect on Remer as he suddenly came smartly to attention. "Jawohl, mein Führer!"

Hitler spoke slowly and deliberately, his voice rising in tone as he went on. "Do you hear me? So I'm alive! The attempt has failed. A tiny clique of ambitious officers wanted to do away with me. But now we have the 'saboteurs of the front' and we'll make short shrift of this plague! You are commissioned by me with the task of immediately restoring calm and security in the Reich capital, if necessary by force. You are under my personal command for this purpose until the Reichsführer-SS arrives in the Reich capital!"

"Jawohl, my Führer! As you order, my Führer!"[2]

The line went dead. Remer's face was flushed, first with shock, then excitement as he realized he had gone from being an unwitting traitor destined to be shot to a hero of the hour with command of troops across the city. The hour in which Nazi Germany would be saved was his.

Goebbels, of course, saw the hour as his own, but smiled to see that the officer had now become a most powerful ally. Remer remained at attention as Goebbels addressed him, explaining that the young major now outranked Hase and was in military control of Berlin. Goebbels told him he wanted to address Remer's men and asked the major to have them assembled in the garden.

Goebbels's speech won over Remer's troops. They and others in positions around government buildings in Berlin began to follow new orders to hunt down the conspirators at Bendlerstrasse and to block main approach routes to the city so that they could explain to units arriving for Valkyrie what was really happening.

In the meantime, the wily Canaris—who had been allowed to move back to his Berlin home and had avoided contact with the putschists—had already sensed which way the wind was blowing and sought to extricate himself from suspicion. Judge Karl Sack had come to his house to tell him what was happening and not to give up hope, but the admiral told him all was already lost. When the judge left, Canaris went to his new office in Potsdam—where he had been allowed to run a small department analyzing German trade agreements—and sent a telegram to East Prussia congratulating Hitler on his miraculous escape. Canaris was the first opponent of the regime to jump ship.

And now the public started to hear the official version of events. Goebbels ordered a radio broadcast stating that Hitler had survived an attack on his life and was well enough to be back at work. He ordered that the message be repeated over and over. Broadcasting House had never been in the hands of the conspirators. By the time Hase had the troops available to take it, they were no longer following him—they were taking orders from Remer, who set up an army and SS guard on the building loyal to the Nazi regime.

As radios crackled out the message, the plan began to slip from the putschists' hands. Although they sent out orders stating that the radio was lying, too much doubt had now set in.

IN PARIS, THOUGH, General Carl Heinrich von Stülpnagel had acted decisively. On receiving the Valkyrie order from Beck at 6 p.m., he ordered the arrest and disarming of the SS and SD contingent in the city. The operation would start at 11 p.m. so as to avoid the spectacle of the French population witnessing Germans fighting among themselves.

Beck asked, "What about Kluge?"

The field marshal, whom Tresckow had consistently tried to bring into the conspiracy, had replaced the despairing Rundstedt as supreme commander in the West three weeks after the Allied invasion and, since Rommel was injured, also now controlled Rommel's armies.[3]

After recovering from his own injuries suffered in the East, Kluge had taken the role after a personal meeting with Hitler, from which he had emerged with his belief in National Socialism apparently rejuvenated. He was a man who took his opinions from the last person he had spoken to. The impassioned pleas from Tresckow he had listened to over and over on the Eastern Front were long forgotten, and when Tresckow had sent Georg von Boeselager to see him early in July, Kluge said he would be at Beck's disposal only if Hitler was dead; he would promise no more.

Kluge had been given no warning that the coup would be attempted that day, and he returned from a visit to the Normandy front to his headquarters at La Roche Guyon, forty miles northwest of Paris, to find wild confusion and an anxious, urging Beck on the telephone line.

Beck told him Hitler was dead and they needed his support. "Herr Kluge," Beck went on, "the fate of Germany is at stake!"

Kluge said he would think about it and call back. He then managed to get through to Stieff in the Wolf's Lair. In the rarefied and frightening atmosphere of the Wolfsschanze, Stieff had realized the coup was failing and he was on the wrong side. In a bid to save himself he told Kluge with faked joy: "The Führer is perfectly well and in excellent spirits!"

Kluge turned to his chief of staff, General Günther Blumentritt, and said, "It's just a bungled assassination attempt!"

He ordered Stülpnagel to come to La Roche Guyon immediately, and looking at the clock, he wondered what kind of mess the conspirators had got him into.

Stauffenberg remained steadfast: When an SS major-general came with two other officers to arrest him, he instead had them placed under arrest. Yorck and Gerstenmaier, the theologian, met at the Bendlerstrasse to find out how the coup was progressing across Berlin. Carrying both a pistol and a Bible in his pocket, Gerstenmaier said he had a sense that the conspirators were being too gentle with their opponents. They were dealing with Nazis, he said. There would need to be shooting. Gisevius—who had returned from Switzerland to support the coup—agreed and said a unit should be sent to Prinz-Albrecht-Strasse and the Propaganda Ministry to shoot Gestapo Müller and Goebbels out of hand. "We've got to have some corpses now," he said. Wolf-Heinrich Graf von Helldorf contacted the Bendler Block to ask why Hase had not requested his men to support the arrests of the party officials.

Stauffenberg had gone from one telephone call to another, trying to cajole regional commanders into supporting the action—lying to Hitler loyalists, appealing to potential resisters—but almost at the same time that the Valkyrie orders were arriving by teleprinter, the commanders were receiving telephone calls from Keitel and his staff stating they should be ignored. "The Führer is alive and in good health . . . Orders from Fromm, Witzleben, and Hoepner not to be executed."

The slow speed at which the Valkyrie orders had been delivered and the radio broadcasts stating Hitler was alive robbed the coup of its impetus. Faced with the prospect of committing to a failing coup and sacrificing their lives, most commanders held back or sided with the regime: What was the point of dying for nothing? they reasoned.

By midevening it was apparent that the coup was failing. Witzleben declared it all "a fine mess" and, saying it was now too late for the coup's troops to occupy Berlin, got up and left for home.

Dr. Otto John, Klaus Bonhoeffer's friend from the Lufthansa legal team and an adviser to the coup, called at Bendlerstrasse to see if he could help. When there appeared to be nothing for him to do, he told Haeften he would ring at eight the following morning.

"Perhaps we shall all have been hanged by then," Haeften told him.[4]

John was one of the last to leave before the countercoup began.

SHORTLY AFTER 8 P.M. General von Stülpnagel—the commander in chief in France—arrived at Kluge's headquarters outside Paris with Lieutenant-Colonel Cäsar von Hofacker, who had been Stauffenberg and Beck's liaison man with Stülpnagel.

Kluge listened to Hofacker's summation of events and described it as a "bungled affair." Stülpnagel and Hofacker appealed to Kluge for his support, and he refused.

"The attempt has failed," Kluge told him. "It's all over."

"Herr Field Marshal," Stülpnagel said, "I thought you were acquainted with the plans. Something must be done."

"Nothing more can be done!" Kluge told him. "The Führer is still alive."

"But you knew all about it," Stülpnagel said.

"No, I had no idea," Kluge said.

The two conspirators looked at him angrily, and for a moment it looked as if they might come to blows.

Then Kluge waved his hand and invited them to come into the next room for dinner.

They sat with other members of Kluge's staff, but the tension was unbearable. Asking Kluge for a word in private, Stülpnagel told him about the orders to arrest the SS and SD in Paris.

Kluge flew into a rage. Stülpnagel had gone over his head. "This is intolerable!" he shouted.[5]

Blumentritt telephoned Stülpnagel's chief of staff, Colonel Hans-Otfried von Linstow, who said the orders could not be stopped as they were already being carried out.

In fact, the Wehrmacht operation in the French capital went smoothly. Around 1,200 men were arrested and taken to the Wehrmacht prison at Fresnes and the old Fort de l'Est in Saint-Denis without a shot being fired. The SS chief, on being told he was being arrested because of an SS coup, simply said, "There must be some misunderstanding," but went along quietly. The SD chief was apprehended in a nightclub.

In the darkness outside Kluge's headquarters, the field marshal ordered Stülpnagel to return to Paris, release the imprisoned men, and then consider himself suspended from duty.

Leaning close so he could not be overheard, Kluge added: "It would be best for you if you put on civilian clothes and disappear."

Stülpnagel, who was a proud military man, loyal to Beck, and had been committed to the opposition since the coup plans of 1938, said for him that was not an option.

Back in the city Linstow believed all was going well until, sometime after 10 p.m., Stauffenberg called him from Berlin to say it was all over. "My executioners are hammering at the door," he said.[6]

A SMALL GROUP of men from the General Army Office sat in a room in the Bendlerstrasse discussing the radio messages that Hitler was alive and a new announcement that Himmler had taken over the Reserve Army.

The men had been asked by Olbricht to form a guard at the entrance to the building, and they were awaiting weapons. As they discussed what was going on, they decided they did not want to become a part of a coup; they must demand to see Fromm.

The weapons arrived: submachine guns, pistols, and hand grenades. The group armed themselves and, led by Lieutenant-Colonel Franz Herber, headed off through the corridors of the huge building, going from room to room, pointing their weapons at people and demanding to know: Were they "For or against Hitler?"[7]

They took over the building's telephone exchange and, on reaching the corridor of the senior staff offices, stormed Olbricht's room, demanding to see Fromm.

As Olbricht argued with them, shots were fired in the corridor. Herber headed through the door, and Klausing shot at him. Herber fired back.

Stauffenberg clamped his pistol to his side with the stump of his right arm, cocked it with the three fingers of his left hand, and fired at one of Herber's men.

Stauffenberg was struck in the shoulder. Clutching his wound, he half slumped to the ground. Resignedly, in pain and exhaustion, he removed the eye patch from his left eye socket.

The brief gun battle over, the men went to Fromm's office, where Haeften was burning papers on the floor. Fromm was brought from his apartment rooms, and realizing that if he acted quickly he might save his own skin, he told the conspirators he was putting them under arrest for high treason. When he demanded their weapons, Beck requested to keep his for "private use."

"Do so at once," Fromm said curtly, denying him the chance to leave the room.

Beck put the gun to his head, but the sixty-four-year-old general, who had fought bravely in the First World War and disliked the Nazis from the beginning, was hesitant. He had been ill before this dreadful moment, his voice and body weak. Now he could barely lift the gun. He fired, but the shot only grazed his temple.

Hoepner and Olbricht sat at Olbricht's desk and wrote their last statements and letters.

Beck, still refusing to hand over his gun, tried a second suicide attempt and fell to the floor, still alive but in agony.

Fromm was told that a unit of Remer's troops had entered the courtyard of the building and that Himmler had been appointed head of the Reserve Army. Himmler was, in fact, on his way to Berlin with the Führer's orders ringing in his ears: "Shoot anyone who resists, no matter who!"[8]

Fromm had to act quickly and get rid of any witnesses to his own treachery.

He announced that he had held a court-martial in the name of the Führer and had condemned Olbricht, Mertz von Quirnheim, and Haeften to death. He condemned Stauffenberg, too, but refused to mention his name, referring to him only as "this colonel whose name I will no longer mention."

Fromm turned to one of the Hitler loyalists in the room. "Take a few men and execute this sentence downstairs in the yard at once!" he ordered.

Stauffenberg tried to argue on behalf of Mertz and Haeften, saying they had acted on his orders and should be spared. On his pleading, Fromm agreed only that another man—the Panzer general Hoepner—be spared for now and sent to Lehrter Strasse prison. Elsewhere in the building, Berthold von Stauffenberg, Fritz-Dietlof Graf von der Schulenburg, Peter Graf Yorck von Wartenburg, who would have become state secretary to the Foreign Office had the coup succeeded, and Eugen Gerstenmaier, a theologian who like Bonhoeffer had opposed the "German Christians," were among those being detained. Only Gerstenmaier would escape execution.[9]

Stauffenberg, Olbricht, Mertz, and Haeften were marched swiftly from the room. As Fromm made to follow, he glanced down at the dying Beck and summoned an NCO into the room. The man stood over the stricken former chief of the general staff and shot him dead.

The four condemned men were escorted downstairs and into one of the quadrangular courtyards of the War Ministry. It was about midnight, and the scene was lit by the headlights of an armored car. A firing squad of ten men was hastily assembled, all ordinary soldiers who had no real understanding of the events that had brought them all to this place.

Olbricht was first. Made to stand in the pool of light on a pile of building sand left over from construction work, he said nothing. There was no ceremony. The officer of the Grossdeutschland guard battalion called aim and fire, and Olbricht was shot dead.

Stauffenberg was brought forward, but as the firing squad took aim, Haeften rushed in front of his friend and took the hail of bullets.

Stunned, Stauffenberg was placed again on the sand. Looking from Haeften's body to the line of men aiming their rifles at him, he called out: "Es lebe das heilige Deutschland!" "Long live sacred Germany!"[10]

The shots rang out. The soldiers might have wondered what he meant, but they had no time to think. Mertz von Quirnheim was pushed forward and shot.

Their four bodies, and Beck's, were thrown into the back of a truck and taken away to be buried.

Fromm sent a junior officer to dispatch a telegram stating that the coup had been suppressed and the ringleaders executed. He then spoke to the soldiers in the courtyard, explaining that on this special day Hitler's life had once again been saved by Providence.

"Sieg Heil! Sieg Heil! Sieg Heil!"

THE PARIS SS and SD men were released in the early hours, with very little apparent animosity. The military commandant of Paris, who had been in on the coup, went for a drink with the head of the SS, whom hours earlier he had had locked up.

Kluge cabled Keitel to say he had thwarted the coup in France.

AT MIDNIGHT A radio microphone was set up in the "teahouse" of the lair of the bloodied wolf now intent on vengeance. It had taken some time to ensure that Hitler's speech could be broadcast to all German stations simultaneously and be recorded to be replayed.

He was addressing the German people, he told them, first, "so that you can hear my voice and know that I am unhurt and in good health.

"Secondly, so that you can hear the details of a crime for which there can be few comparisons in German history. A tiny clique of ambitious, unscrupulous, and criminal and stupid officers hatched a plot to eliminate me and, along with me, to exterminate the staff of the German High Command."

His survival, he said, was "another sign from Providence that I must continue my work and so I shall carry on with it." He had escaped with only a very few minor grazes, bruises, and burns, he told them.

"At a time when the German armies are engaged in a very tough struggle, a very small group . . . thought they could stab us in the back just like in November 1918. But this time they have made a very big mistake . . .

"The circle represented by these usurpers is extremely small. It has nothing to do with the German Wehrmacht . . . It is a very small clique of criminal elements, which will now be mercilessly exterminated . . ."

THE MORNING AFTER the failed bomb plot, Tresckow sat with his adjutant, Schlabrendorff, in an office in the Second Army barracks in Ostrov, 250 miles away from Berlin.

Outside, the Polish dawn was breaking with a blue sky; it looked like it might be a beautiful day. In the distance they could hear the boom of artillery.

Both men were broken by the news from Germany. Tresckow said the "whole world will vilify us now," but he was "still firmly convinced that we did the right thing."

He spoke slowly: "I consider Hitler to be the arch-enemy not only of Germany but of the world. When, in a few hours, I appear before the judgement-seat of God, in order to give an account of what I have done and left undone, I believe I can with good conscience justify what I did in the fight against Hitler. If God promised Abraham that he would not destroy Sodom if only ten righteous men could be found there, then I hope that for our sakes God will not destroy Germany. None of us can complain about our own deaths. A person's moral integrity only begins at the point where he is prepared to die for his convictions."[11]

He told Schlabrendorff that he hoped to save his family from suspicion by disguising his death as a partisan attack. Schlabrendorff tried to talk him out of it, but Tresckow was determined. They shook hands and Tresckow headed outside.

Waiting at his car was Eberhard von Breitenbuch, the man who had dared to try to kill Hitler at the Berghof. He had sought Tresckow out to console him on Stauffenberg's failed attack. He found him calm and relaxed.

Tresckow asked Breitenbuch if he could accompany him to the front, but the younger officer said he was on an assignment for General Walter Model, for whom he was now working as a liaison officer.

Tresckow patted him on the shoulder. "That's too bad," he said. "I would have liked you to witness my death . . ."

"But you're not going to . . ."

"Yes, I am. I don't want to let our enemies have the satisfaction of taking my life as well. We will see each other in a better world."[12]

Driving to the front, Tresckow walked into the forest and fired off a few shots as if in a gun battle. He then primed a grenade and held it under his chin.

A Wehrmacht report noted that he had "died a hero's death fighting in the front line," and his remains were brought back to the family estate of Wartenberg, where they were buried with military honors.

But the Gestapo was not persuaded, and his wife, Erika, who had helped type up the Valkyrie orders, was arrested soon afterwards. To complete their vengeance, they had Tresckow's body exhumed and taken to Sachsenhausen, where it was incinerated.

Similar revenge was taken on the bodies of Beck, Olbricht, Stauffenberg, Mertz, and Haeften, which had been buried in Matthäikirche cemetery in the hours after their execution. The following day Himmler ordered the SS to Schöneberg to have them dug up, their uniforms stripped of their medals, and the bodies burned. No record was to be kept of where the ashes were scattered.

By then the Nazi police and legal system had turned its full attention to the Führer's demand for vengeance.

# 38

## Sonderkommission 20 Juli

FOR HITLER, THE conspiracy provided clear proof that army leaders had deliberately sabotaged Germany's military campaigns.

He had always been suspicious of his generals, impatient with their "weak," cautious attitude before the war, angry at their failures or hesitancy during it. The bomb plot convinced him that they had been wrecking his work. "Now I know why all my great plans in Russia had to fail in recent years," he ranted. "It was all treason!" For Hitler the traitorous generals' presence was like a "blood poisoning," undermining the morale of the German people. "These most base creatures to have worn the soldier's uniform in the whole of history . . ." he shouted. "This rabble which has preserved itself from bygone times, must be got rid of and driven out!"[1] When the names of aristocrats such as Peter Graf Yorck von Wartenburg and Ulrich von Hassell were read to him, Hitler sneered: "We wiped out the class struggle on the Left, but unfortunately forgot to finish off the class struggle on the Right."

After Fromm had sought to cover his tracks with the swift executions of key conspirators at the Bendler Block, the arrival of Remer, Kaltenbrunner, and SS Major Otto Skorzeny ended the summary executions and sought to restore order. On arrival in Berlin, Himmler ordered that no further independent action be taken and immediately appointed Gestapo Müller to head the Sonderkommission 20 Juli. The unit brought together four hundred Gestapo and SS investigators, including Sonderegger, who had pursued the Abwehr case with Roeder, and SS Colonel Walter Huppenkothen, who had served as a Gestapo liaison officer to Einsatzgruppen in Poland and as a Gestapo commander in Kraków and Lublin, where a large number of Jews had been murdered. Huppenkothen added a further element of ruthlessness to the proceedings by creating a special torture squad under SS Major Kurt Stawitzki.

The net was cast wide. Six hundred people were arrested within days, but no records were kept of all those detained—or indeed all those executed.[2] Even the slightest suspicion of sympathy for the coup was grounds for arrest, and the families of the conspirators were to be locked up, too. Stauffenberg's wife, Nina, was pregnant with the couple's fifth child at the time of the assassination attempt and gave birth in prison. Her other four children, who were aged between three and ten, were taken to an orphanage and given a different surname.

Many, like Tresckow, succeeded in cheating the hangman's noose. Major Hans-Ulrich von Oertzen, interrogated at the Berlin military district headquarters on the Hohenzollerndamm, hid two rifle grenades in sand buckets in a corridor on the way to the restrooms. After being arrested, he asked to use the toilet, snatched one of the grenades, held it to his head, and detonated it. Severely wounded but not dead, he crawled to the other bucket, found the other grenade, and detonated it inside his mouth.

Rommel, when threatened with a public trial and the arrest of his family, took poison—as did Kluge.

Meanwhile, in the Great Hall of the Berlin Supreme Court, the People's Court sat in judgment of the conspirators. Hitler told Roland Freisler, the maniacally angry, shouting judge who had tried the members of the White Rose: "I want them to be hanged, strung up like butchered cattle."[3] Freisler needed no encouragement: He was more incensed than ever by the attempt on the Führer's life. With a bust of Hitler behind him and huge swastika flags streaming down the walls, he spat his hatred at the accused, shouted over them, yelled that they were traitors and murderers. Sentences had been decided before each "trial" began: When Trott was listed for trial, it was noted that he would be "condemned to death at the next session of the People's Court."[4]

Despite Freisler's ranting, a few of the accused managed to speak. Ewald von Kleist-Schmenzin said treason against Hitler had been a "command from God," while Werner von Haeften's brother, Hans-Bernd, told the astonished Freisler that Hitler would go down in history as a "great perpetrator of evil." Both were hanged at Plötzensee.[5]

Ludwig Beck's friend Fritz Dietlof Graf von der Schulenburg, who had shared his vision of a united, federal, and peaceful Europe with his friends in the Kreisau Circle, refused to be flustered by Freisler, who referred to him as "Scoundrel Schulenburg." When Freisler accidentally called him

"Count Schulenburg" by mistake, the aristocrat laughed and said, "Scoundrel Schulenburg, if you please!" When Freisler sentenced him to death, Schulenburg said, "We resolved to take this deed upon ourselves in order to save Germany from indescribable misery. I realize that I shall be hanged for my part in it, but I do not regret what I did and only hope that someone else will succeed in luckier circumstances."

Only the three hundred specially chosen spectators in the court got to hear their words. Goebbels ordered that reporters were not permitted to publish anything from the speeches of the accused.

Yorck von Wartenburg, of the Kreisau Circle, was among the first of the two hundred people executed after Valkyrie to die. In a last note to his wife from his prison cell, he wrote: "They can take the uniform from us, but not the spirit in which we acted." Those to follow him to the gallows included Generals Erich Hoepner, Erwin von Witzleben, and Erich Fellgiebel; Colonel Stieff; and the conspirators in Paris, Stülpnagel, Hofacker, and Linstow.

The trials continued until the final weeks of the war. The senior policeman Arthur Nebe had faked his own suicide, dyed his hair, and gone into hiding with the help of friends. Arrested in January 1945, he was hanged in March.[6] Fromm was shot on March 12. Carl Goerdeler, who had also been arrested while on the run, was executed on February 2, 1945. In his last letter, he wrote: "I ask the world to accept our martyrdom as penance for the German people."

The scene at Plötzensee was truly macabre. Denied the last rites or pastoral care, and wearing rough prison clothes and wooden shoes, the condemned were marched into the execution room, where ropes were swiftly passed around their necks. Their bodies were then lifted and each rope placed over a hook. Making them hang rather than drop from a gallows prolonged their suffering as it could take several minutes to die. The executioners—fortified by cognac—were advised to leave them hanging there for twenty minutes to be sure.

Both the executioners and the hanging men cast huge shadows on the whitewashed walls as the room was being lit for film cameras that whirred throughout.

Goebbels had had the film crew cover the trial and executions. During the trial, the film's director, Hans Hinkel, had to ask Freisler not to shout so loudly as he was distorting the sound. Hinkel's edited version of the court proceedings was given the title *Action X—Traitors before the People's Court* and ran for three and a half hours. When it came time to view the executions— twenty minutes of silent film—Goebbels closed his eyes. Only short excerpts of the trial footage were ever shown to the public.

Hitler eventually had the film locked away, but it was stolen and turned up in Switzerland before the end of the war. The foreign press division of the Propaganda Ministry reported to Goebbels that when it was viewed there on March 5, 1945, "the audience got a frightful impression."[7]

THE GESTAPO'S ROUTE back to the Abwehr conspirators began when Gestapo Müller was astonished to hear a suggestion that Colonel Georg Hansen—Schellenberg's right-hand man—had confirmed to Haeften in advance of the coup that he would help the conspirators occupy Gestapo headquarters if he was asked. Müller found it impossible to believe that Hansen was a traitor, but under interrogation, the colonel confessed. After being tortured, he began to name names and stated he believed that Canaris was the "spiritual instigator of the revolutionary movement" and that the admiral had made an important personal contribution by "maintaining the requisite contacts abroad."[8]

Müller informed Schellenberg, who was astonished. Schellenberg's professional rivalry with Canaris did not stop him from liking and respecting him. He found it hard to believe he could be a leader of the anti-Nazi movement, and there was nothing in Canaris's behavior on July 20 to raise suspicion. However, Schellenberg agreed that he should be the one to arrest the admiral.

Schellenberg left his driver at his car and knocked on Canaris's door alone. Although the admiral had guests, the SD man reckoned Canaris must have seen him coming, as the little admiral himself opened the door and not his servant.

Stepping calmly aside to let his visitor past, Canaris said, "Somehow I felt that it would be you."[9]

Schellenberg explained that Hansen had led them to him, and Canaris nodded. Canaris's guests left, leaving their half-finished coffee cups on the table, and Schellenberg said he should pack a bag and come with him.

As Canaris paused, the SD officer added more softly: "If the Herr Admiral wishes to make other arrangements, then I beg him to consider me at his disposal. I shall wait in this room for an hour and during that time you may do whatever you wish. My report will say that you went to your bedroom in order to change."

Canaris smiled. "No, dear Schellenberg," he said, "flight is out of the question for me. And I won't kill myself either."

Schellenberg waited while Canaris packed his bag. When at last he came downstairs, he said, "Well, then, let's go."[10]

COUP INVESTIGATOR COLONEL Huppenkothen knew all about the Abwehr investigation from Sonderegger. On hearing of Canaris's arrest, the two men revisited the old file—which had been largely abandoned on Keitel's orders a year earlier. Sonderegger believed the case had been covered up, despite all of his hard work. With the influential Huppenkothen's help he now saw a chance to see the investigation through.

Knowing that on July 20 Canaris had been either at home, entertaining neighbors and with his servant present, or in his office—from where he had sent the evening telegram to Hitler—Sonderegger turned his attention to Oster, whose name had come up during the interrogations of the bomb-plot conspirators.

Through what Sonderegger saw as old-fashioned detective work, he set about establishing Oster's whereabouts on the day of the bomb plot. Oster had told investigators he was at his manor house in the countryside near Leipzig, but Sonderegger uncovered a food ration card that showed Oster had in fact been at his Berlin apartment at Bayerischer Platz that day. A document found at Olbricht's office showed that Oster had been listed as a liaison with the military districts after the coup. Sonderegger was convinced he had come to Berlin to await his moment to play a central role in a post-Hitler Germany.

He had Oster arrested in Leipzig and brought to the dungeon cells at Prinz-Albrecht-Strasse, where he was manacled day and night and placed on one-third rations. Huppenkothen and Sonderegger both took part in his interrogation, one being probing but sympathetic, the other threatening and angry. Oster played the role of an old-fashioned career officer, uncertain of politics, a reactionary who had not understood the Nazi revolution. He confessed to nothing but was happy to talk.

Schellenberg had taken Canaris to a prison in Fürstenberg an der Havel, where a number of senior officers were being kept. But with total power vested in the commission, Sonderegger had him transferred to the

Gestapo cells. He then requested the handing over from the army prison of two of Oster's key contacts: Hans von Dohnanyi and Josef Müller. Both men—like Bonhoeffer—had faced no trial after Roeder's investigation but had remained in custody.[11] All the key Abwehr conspirators—apart from Bonhoeffer—were now in Gestapo custody, held in small, dark cells behind heavy steel doors. They were allowed no visitors and no contact with other prisoners.

Josef Müller was tortured but refused to speak. Hans von Dohnanyi had been injured in a bombing raid on the Lehrter Strasse prison and had suffered a stroke that had left him partially paralyzed. Knowing the Gestapo was coming for him, he had persuaded his wife, Christine, to smuggle in food infected with a diphtheria bacteria so that he could infect himself with it. In too much pain to speak, and unable to walk or control his bowels, Dohnanyi avoided giving anything away to his interrogators. Sonderegger sneaked in a doctor, but Huppenkothen was livid and sent Dohnanyi to Sachsenhausen. "Let him croak on his own shit!" he told Sonderegger angrily.[12]

Gestapo Muller interrogated Canaris, but the admiral appeared to have an answer to every charge and could rightly claim no involvement in the Stauffenberg plot.

However, the Gestapo produced a star witness, Alexander von Pfuhlstein, now a major-general and a former army divisional commander whom Oster had cautiously approached a couple of years earlier to join the coup. Pfuhlstein told the Gestapo about a partly coded but highly incriminating conversation in which Oster had spoken about "reorganizing the leadership of the armed forces." Asked by Sonderegger why he had not reported it at the time, Pfuhlstein said he felt he had not enough proof of treasonous activity to be believed.[13]

Taking Pfuhlstein's evidence to Oster, Sonderegger managed to gain the admission that discussions had taken place in 1942 about a reorganization of the army "if necessary against the Führer's wishes" and that these measures had later been developed by him and Dohnanyi into a plan to include "the party, the police, the administration, the working class, and, finally, the army." Oster admitted that Olbricht had also become involved and that Canaris was aware of the plan.

Sonderegger realized that through a mixture of detective work, threats, sleep and food deprivation, and Gestapo torture, he had what effectively amounted to a complete admission that there had been an Abwehr plan to depose Hitler as commander of the army and leader of Germany.

Confronted with Oster's testimony, Canaris was strident: "I was never in doubt that any change of government during the war would not only be construed as a stab in the back but would disrupt the home front," he told Sonderegger. "I was also convinced that neither our Western enemies nor the Russians would accept an offer of peace, which they would automatically regard as a sign of weakness. Were they actually to accept one in the first instance they would do so only for show, in order to submit a ruthless demand for unconditional surrender thereafter. It would be 1918 all over again, but in a far worse form."[14]

Oster, he said, had come up with many dreams and schemes as part of his intelligence work, but he—Canaris—had been unimpressed and had dismissed many of them.

Sonderegger then had Pfuhlstein and Oster confront Canaris in the interrogation room. The conversation descended into a shouting match in which Pfuhlstein accused the admiral of being a defeatist and Canaris shouted at Oster that he had never been involved in a conspiracy against the regime.

The men were taken back to their cells. Sonderegger was convinced of both Canaris's and Oster's guilt, but he was determined to break the defenses of these two great intelligence men.

Like many detectives on a major case he felt it in his bones that somewhere in the files or among the disgruntled employees of the Abwehr, the key bit of evidence he so craved was just waiting to be discovered.

IT CAME OUT of the blue and from an unlikely source.

Kurt Kerstenhan had been an Abwehr driver. A self-centered grumbler and agitator, he had no intention of being drawn into an investigation into treason in which he had played no part. As the personal driver for Werner Schrader, an Abwehr officer involved in the procurement of Stauffenberg's explosives who had committed suicide after the bomb plot, Kerstenhan knew he was a witness on Sonderegger's list.

He scratched his head to think if there was a morsel of helpful intelligence that he might give the detective that would bring him under the protection—rather than the suspicion—of the Gestapo. He had been involved in no anti-Hitler discussions or plans for the coup, but something had always troubled him. On September 21, he turned up at Gestapo headquarters and asked for Sonderegger.

This might be nothing, he told the Gestapo detective, but in 1942 he had helped drive two carloads of documents from Abwehr headquarters to a building with the word "Seehandlung" over the entrance. Then later the same group of men had returned to the building and moved the documents to Camp Zeppelin, a security zone inside the army training center at Zossen, on the southern outskirts of Berlin, to which the Abwehr had moved its headquarters to escape the air raids.

The detective was intrigued. Who was in charge of the operation? Sonderegger asked. Schrader and Friedrich Heinz, he was told.

Sonderegger quickly discovered that the distinctive "Seehandlung" inscription belonged to the Prussian State Bank, where Heinz's stepbrother was manager. Sonderegger issued a warrant for Heinz's arrest, but tipped off, the man whom Oster had chosen to kill Hitler if the 1938 coup had gone ahead went on the run.

Sonderegger asked Kerstenhan if he would recognize the bunker at Camp Zeppelin to which he delivered the files. The driver said he would.

The detective sensed he was onto something, but he could have never imagined what: Hidden in one of the 130 safes at Camp Zeppelin were Oster and the conspirators' complete files. It was enough to hang everyone who had so far escaped the wrath of Hitler.

All Sonderegger had to do now was find the right safe.

BY THE SUMMER of 1944, untried but unreleased, Dietrich Bonhoeffer had been detailed to work in the sick bay of Tegel military prison, where the radio was kept on to comfort patients.

It was there he listened to the broadcasts describing the failure of the plot and the subsequent arrests and executions, and he began to fear for his family. Early in August he heard that his mother's cousin Lieutenant-General Paul von Hase had been tried and executed on the same day. On August 23, his fiancée, Maria von Wedemeyer, visited him. The strain was showing on her face, and although she had moved in with Dietrich's parents to be nearer to him, she was struggling to sleep and suffering from headaches brought on by stress and worry. Bonhoeffer held her hands and told her not to lose heart.

Bonhoeffer was secretly wondering how long it would be before the Gestapo came for him, and he began to plan his escape from Tegel.

As yet nothing had been found that would link Bonhoeffer to the July 20 plot, and he was still able to talk with guards and move about the prison as part of his work comforting the sick.

Among the prison guards who had befriended Bonhoeffer was a Corporal Knoblauch, a deeply Christian working-class soldier from north Berlin.[15] Bonhoeffer provided Knoblauch with spiritual guidance, as he had to many guards and prisoners, and they now discussed a plan that would see Bonhoeffer escape and Knoblauch go into hiding. He wanted nothing more to do with his job in the prison.

Bonhoeffer told his sister Ursula during a visit that she needed to get a workingman's overalls in his size, together with food coupons and money, and deliver them to Knoblauch's house. Knoblauch, he said, was confident that in this guise he would be able to walk out next to the guard, as there were many workmen coming and going to fix air raid damage. The difficulty would be finding somewhere to hide and getting to Switzerland.

On Sunday, September 24, Ursula and her husband, Rüdiger Schleicher, drove—with their daughter Renate in the back of the car—to the address Dietrich had given them and gave a package to Knoblauch. The family told the guard they were desperately looking for somewhere he and Dietrich would be able to hide that was not associated with the family.

Almost a week went by, and the following Saturday everything changed. Klaus Bonhoeffer was driving home when he saw a Gestapo car parked outside his house. Turning away, he drove to the home of his sister Ursula and, suddenly distraught, said he was considering taking his own life to save his wife and children from trouble. Ursula talked him out of it.[16]

Then, Paul von Hase's wife, Margarete, arrived at the house. Heartbroken since the death of her husband, the mother of four was looking to Ursula and Rüdiger for support. She had just been released from prison, and all her other friends had turned her away.

Finally, as Ursula tried to comfort both her brother and aunt, Corporal Knoblauch knocked at the door. Taking Ursula and Rüdiger aside, he wondered if they could get Bonhoeffer a false passport and a flight to Sweden. The pastor had told him he knew people there. The couple explained that the plan might be in trouble as Klaus believed the Gestapo was after him. Knoblauch left quickly, saying he would tell Dietrich.

Sitting in his cell, Bonhoeffer realized that to escape now would bring down certain hell on his family. All would no doubt be arrested, and Maria, too.

On Monday, Knoblauch returned to Ursula's house to find out that the Gestapo had already taken Klaus away. He told Ursula that, fearing for his family, Bonhoeffer had given up any hope of escape.

A couple of days later Rüdiger Schleicher was arrested, and then, on October 8, Bonhoeffer was moved from Tegel to the dark, windowless, underground cells of the Gestapo prison at Prinz-Albrecht-Strasse.

In the days that he had planned and then rejected the idea of escape, the true nature of his opposition to the regime had finally come to the surface.

CAMP ZEPPELIN HAD revealed its secrets to Sonderegger.

After the Abwehr driver Kerstenhan had identified the bunker, Sonderegger had gone in search of the key to the safe. Both were missing, he was told. Unwilling to do anything that might damage the contents of the safe, Sonderegger contacted its manufacturers in Dortmund and had them send a locksmith, who opened it easily. Inside were cardboard boxes, files, and folders, which the detective removed and scanned through.

He was astounded. The conspirators seemed to have recorded everything. The files revealed not only details of the July 20 plot but also anti-Hitler plots going back to 1938. There were files on the Blomberg-Fritsch affair and on Josef Müller's peace meetings with the Vatican; files on Bonhoeffer's trips abroad and messages to Britain; draft postcoup speeches by Beck; notebooks belonging to Dohnanyi; three pages on the implementation of a coup d'état written by Oster; assessments of the composition of a new government with signed amendments by Oster, Groscurth, Gisevius, and Heinz; and carbon copies of twenty pages from what appeared to be Admiral Canaris's diaries. The files went on and on.

Although a member of the Gestapo, Sonderegger was a detective at heart. Even he had doubts about the future of the Hitler regime. As he sat in the bunker, he felt elation at what he had uncovered but a sense of shock, too. He knew that every man who had contributed to these files had signed his own death warrant.

He reported to Huppenkothen that what had been uncovered necessitated a complete rethinking of the Gestapo's assessment of the anti-Nazi movement. They had previously understood that it originated during late

1941 and early 1942 in dissatisfaction with Hitler's military strategy and the brutal war in the East. But the majority of the documents in the safe dated from 1938, 1939, and 1940, and so the actions and attitudes of people like Oster and Beck had not been based on the worsening military situation at all: They were a deep-set opposition to what Hitler stood for even during the early successes in Poland and France.

The files also contained names, Sonderegger went on, whom the Gestapo had previously hardly considered: Generals Thomas and Halder; the head of the criminal police, Nebe; Field Marshal von Brauchitsch; the Abwehr's Lieutenant Commander Liedig; and many more. Huppenkothen listened in astonishment and then—telling his office staff that he was not to be disturbed—sat down to read the files for himself. It took him several days to gain even a superficial knowledge of what they contained.

When Gestapo Müller heard about the contents of the Zossen safe, he told Huppenkothen that he was to discuss them with no one—and that even a report to the board of the July 20 Commission must be delayed. Everything surrounding the discovery was to be considered "Geheime Reichssache—Ministersache"—the highest Reich security classification. While they discussed how to tell the Führer that generals and others had been conspiring against him for longer than he had believed, Kaltenbrunner reported to Hitler's secretary and closest confidant, Martin Bormann, flatly that: "It now emerges from confiscated material found in an Abwehr safe that plans were already afoot in earlier years to effect a change of government by military means."[17]

It fell to Huppenkothen to prepare the Führervorlage, the briefing for Hitler. It ran to 160 pages and included a report, an analysis, and two appendices of photocopies of the most important documents. Hitler read it alone, and even in his anger and paranoia—and his obsessive belief that these betrayals, not his own actions, had brought about Germany's defeats—he recognized that the scale of the conspiracy, its length, and the positions of those involved had to be dealt with privately. His vengeance against the July 20 conspirators had been swift and public. A second high-ranking wave of arrests would make it look like the opposition was broad and strong. He ordered that inquiries must continue in the strictest secrecy; that he would require a full report once the interrogations were complete; and that the cases must not be dealt with in the People's Court, from where word might leak out.

Huppenkothen and Sonderegger continued their investigations. Goerdeler and Karl Sack, judge advocate general of the army, who had been earmarked by Goerdeler to be justice minister in the new Germany, were questioned about the Zossen file, as was Bonhoeffer. The lives of his family hung upon his answers, Bonhoeffer was told. However, he continued to present himself as merely an emissary of the Confessing Church and as someone doing work for the Abwehr—the purpose of which he did not always fully understand.

Eventually, in a bid to spare his family further inquiry, he admitted only to being an enemy of National Socialism, a stance he took through Christian convictions, he said. One day in the washroom he met Tresckow's cousin and coconspirator Fabian von Schlabrendorff, who was also a cousin of Maria von Wedemeyer. The connection gave Bonhoeffer heart. Schlabrendorff—despite having suffered a heart attack after his interrogators forced metal spikes under his fingernails and into his bare legs—had also so far managed to fend off all the accusations put to him by the Gestapo.

However, on being confronted with the contents of the Zossen safe, Oster confessed all. After so many years living in the shadows, it was a relief to put it all in the open: defend his patriotism and proudly declare his opposition to Nazism. "The game is lost, the dice have fallen," he told Sonderegger. "Yes, from the beginning I had no other intention in my mind but to overthrow Adolf Hitler and his criminal regime."[18]

His former chief, Canaris, though, continued to fight. Feigning exasperation, he told his inquisitors that he had gone along with elements of the conspiracy so that he could track it and intervene when necessary. This, he said, was his duty as the head of the intelligence service. Even Josef Müller's visits to the Vatican were intelligence-gathering operations, he said—couldn't they see that?

When Huppenkothen became angry, so did Canaris—affronted that he should be accused of having betrayed his country. They tried to humiliate him, making him scrub the floors of the dungeon block; he would not give in.

But back in his cell, away from their taunts and prying gaze, he sometimes felt overcome by a terror that made him sick to his stomach. He was holding on to a terrible secret: one that he could do nothing about. The Zossen file was not the only cache of incriminating documents held at the military base. The loose pages of his diaries were only a tiny part of his record of military and political affairs. The complete diaries—running to five thick black ring folders—were in another safe at Camp Zeppelin. Only Canaris himself knew of their whereabouts, but without any knowledge of what was going on at the Zossen base, the admiral lived in daily fear of their discovery.

SUSPECTING THAT DOHNANYI believed he had escaped him by making himself appear even sicker than he was, Huppenkothen could not resist the opportunity to gloat over Sonderegger's Zossen discovery.

On October 5 he strode into the sick bay at Sachsenhausen, stood over Dohnanyi's bed, and, with a sneer of satisfaction on his face, reached into his attaché case.

Removing a document, he placed it on Dohnanyi's bed. "There!" he said. "At last we've got the evidence against you we've been looking for, for two years."

Dohnanyi glanced at it but pretended not to be interested. "Oh, have you?" he said. "Where did you find it?"

"Zossen."

It was a page from Dohnanyi's Chronicle of Shame containing evidence of Nazi crimes against humanity. He had kept it and other files because he believed one day it would form the basis of a trial of Adolf Hitler. And because it would reveal to those who came after that even in the heart of this darkness, there had been kept alive a spirit of the other Germany: self-sacrificing, heroic, humanitarian.

Dohnanyi tried to wipe his eyes behind his spectacles. He wanted to hide his feelings, but he knew the look on his face gave him away.

It was hard not to feel that the Nazis had won.

# 39

## Götterdämmerung

O N JANUARY 30, 1945, the Red Army crossed the Oder and sparked an enormous stampede, as millions of Germans fled west. Thousands were driven toward Berlin, where the streets were littered with barricades created from the bricks of destroyed buildings and from the furniture of dead neighbors. Teenagers and old men were hurriedly recruited into the Volkssturm and told to fight to their deaths against the battle-hardened troops and heavy tanks closing in on their home from the East. Bombers pounded the city day and night.

On February 3, the city suffered its heaviest daylight raid yet. Nearly a thousand bombers of the US Eighth Air Force came over in waves. During two hours of hell, blocks of houses and public buildings were turned to rubble. The streets around Alexanderplatz were a mass of ruins; among stacks of gray bricks lay the shredded clothes and limbs of the dead. Even after the planes had left, the air was thick with smoke and dust that blocked out the sun. Figures shuffled along in shock, carrying small items, all that was left of their homes.

In Prinz-Albrecht-Strasse the Gestapo headquarters were set ablaze. The prisoners crammed in the air raid shelter under the courtyard—known as the Himmler-Bunker—watched anxiously as the concrete roof seemed to shake and crack, but it held firm. In the shelters it seemed one could hear every bomb whistle down and feel each explosion. Schlabrendorff shared a glance with Bonhoeffer, who appeared calm and returned the look with a reassuring smile.

A day earlier, although Bonhoeffer could not have known it, his brother Klaus and brother-in-law Rüdiger Schleicher had been sentenced to death. Schlabrendorff was waiting to be taken to the People's Court for sentencing as soon as the raid was over.

Hiding from the explosions in a subway station nearby was Dr. Rolf Schleicher, who had come to appeal his brother's death sentence. Dr. Schleicher was desperate to continue on: Although he knew Freisler's court could not be sitting in such a raid, he also knew how swiftly Nazi "justice" worked. The sooner he made his plea, the better.

Finally, when the bombing ceased, the wardens let him and the others out into the streets. Reaching the People's Court, he saw that it had been badly damaged in the raid and part of the building was ablaze. There were shouts for a doctor, and Schleicher—a senior doctor at a hospital in Stuttgart—made himself known and climbed over the rubble and into a courtyard to where a small group was huddled around one man lying on the ground, his head covered in blood. Schleicher could tell immediately from the anxious looks of the group that the man was someone of importance. As he stepped forward, he could also tell that he was dead.

One of the group urged him to check. Schleicher knelt down, searched for a pulse, and found none.

But he continued to look down into the thin, sharp features, which he now recognized. He could barely believe it. It was Roland Freisler, Hitler's hanging judge, who a day earlier had sentenced his brother to death and to whom he had traveled to make the appeal for clemency.

An officer of the court demanded Schleicher write a death certificate, but he refused until he could see Otto Thierack, the minister of justice. Although he had presided over a system in which appeals for clemency were summarily dismissed and executions carried out in haste, Thierack— a thick-set man with a large, bald domed head and a deep dueling scar on his cheek—was intrigued by the coincidence that Schleicher had tended to the man he had come to see and agreed to delay Rüdiger's execution. (The sentence would not be changed, though, and on April 23, with the Red Army inside the city limits of Berlin, and having been tricked into thinking they were being released, Rüdiger Schleicher and Klaus Bonhoeffer were each shot in the nape of the neck on a field near the Lehrter Strasse prison.)

February 4 was Dietrich Bonhoeffer's thirty-ninth birthday. His parents had been unable to visit him because of unexploded bombs in the street near the prison, but they had managed to get a parcel containing a volume of Plutarch's writings to him. They hoped that when the ruins from the street had been cleared, the Gestapo would let them see their son.

However, three days later, with water, light, and heating no longer available at the damaged building on Prinz-Albrecht-Strasse, the Gestapo decided to move certain key prisoners away from the Berlin raids. Perhaps, some of them reasoned, they were to be used as bargaining chips with the Allies.

Two vans were brought into the courtyard, and the prisoners were marched down from their cells. In a healthy society they would have been men of standing; in Nazi Germany they were enemies of the state, prisoners in rags. All now shuffled forward, blinking in the first daylight they had seen for weeks, in some cases months.

Into the first van stepped Dr. Kurt von Schuschnigg, the former chancellor of Austria; Dr. Hjalmar Schacht, the former head of the Reichsbank, who had been part of Oster's 1938 plot; Admiral Canaris; General Hans Oster; Judge Sack; General Halder; General Thomas; and Captain Theodor Strünck, who had been one of Oster's contacts with Allen Dulles. The van was bound for Flossenbürg, a small concentration camp in Bavaria where the staff had distinguished themselves among the camp network by becoming experts in using prisoners for various medical experiments.

The second van contained a similarly illustrious group. Among those taking a seat on the benches inside were General von Falkenhausen, whom the diplomat Hassell had brought into the conspiracy; Franz Liedig, Oster's friend, who had conspired with him in 1938 to kill Hitler and who had been with him the night he had given the secrets of the Western Offensive to the Dutch; and Captain Ludwig Gehre, who had tried to escape the Gestapo dragnet after the July 20 bomb plot by entering a suicide pact with his wife. Having shot her dead, he turned the gun on himself and blew out an eye. Hideously wounded, he was arrested and tortured.

Also destined for the second van, and handcuffed together, were Josef "the Ox" Müller, the man who had taken Oster's messages of peace to the pope and who despite extreme torture had given away none of his friends, and Dietrich Bonhoeffer. They helped each other into the back of the van.

This group was destined for Buchenwald, a camp in a beech forest where tens of thousands had died, having been worked to death, starved, and beaten to keep an armaments factory nearby operating twenty-four hours a day through the height of Hitler's war. Conditions there had been part of Dohnanyi's file of Nazi shame that he had shared with Oster and Bonhoeffer.

\* \* \*

THE FIRST GESTAPO van reached Flossenbürg that evening, driving through the gates and between the lines of barbed wire and watchtowers that had marked the end of hope for so many.

Sonderegger jumped down from the cab of the truck and, with only a glance toward the lines of huts in which the enemies of the dying Reich struggled for life, climbed the steps to the commandant's office. In his hand Sonderegger carried a list of prisoners and Gestapo instructions as to how they should be confined: permanently shackled but fed well enough to maintain good enough health to be interrogated.

Flossenbürg's commandant, SS Lieutenant-Colonel Max Kögl, who had been a senior officer in the concentration camp network for eight years—managing murder at Dachau and Ravensbrück, the gas chambers of Majdanek—nodded. The orders would be followed to the letter, he assured his visitor.

AT BUCHENWALD, THE "prisoners of honor" found themselves not in the main camp but in the prison cellar of a high building that housed the camp staff. As with the new arrivals at Flossenbürg, they would be provided with more food than regular prisoners: soup at midday and bread and marmalade in the evening.

Bonhoeffer shared a cell with Friedrich von Rabenau, a general whose strong Christian faith had pitted him—like Bonhoeffer and Gerstein— against the Nazification of the church. Rabenau had acted as a liaison between Beck and Goerdeler as they had planned the political future of Germany after the coup. Bonhoeffer and Rabenau chatted about theology and played chess with a set given to them by another prisoner, Captain Sigismund Payne Best, one of the British intelligence officers captured by Schellenberg's men at Venlo back in 1939.

In another cell was another member of the conspiracy who, although cleared by the People's Court, had still been returned to prison. Colonel Horst von Petersdorff, a fifty-two-year-old who had won bravery medals in both world wars, was now dreadfully sick, having been buried in rubble during the Berlin raid on February 3. The other prisoners worried for him—and for Gehre and Müller, who were also both seriously ill, having been weakened by violent interrogation—but they could hear the thunder of the artillery and began to believe liberation might be close.

Late in the evening of Tuesday, April 3, the sixteen prisoners in the cellar were told to gather their things and were marched up the steps to where a battered green van waited for them. The guards pushed them into the back and locked the doors. The van was built for half as many passengers, so there was no room to move or stretch their legs. As they waited, the air raid siren sounded and the guards disappeared into a shelter. When they returned, the engine was started and the van moved off. The prisoners quickly discovered that their agony included not only a lack of space and a fear of where they were being taken, but also the fact that the van was fueled by a wood burner at the front that belched smoke into the back. When the engine was idling, and for the first few minutes after it moved off, the passengers choked on the smoke. They traveled through the night at fifteen miles an hour, with nothing to eat or drink and no light. In the morning the passengers had to complain angrily to be allowed out into the fields to relieve themselves.

After thirteen hours on the road they arrived at Weiden, a small town in northern Bavaria, which they knew to be near Flossenbürg. The guards stopped at the local police station and when they came back told the prisoners that they had inquired if the camp could take them but had been told it was too full. One of the passengers whispered to Bonhoeffer that that must mean they were not marked for death: If they were, the lack of space at Flossenbürg would not have mattered, as they would have just admitted them and executed them.

Bonhoeffer looked around the dark, smoky, cramped van and wondered if in the confusion of a collapsing Germany this small, disheveled group of the apparently condemned might somehow escape the bureaucracy of death.

CONFINED IN A stone building in Flossenbürg known as "the Bunker," Canaris, Oster, and the other special prisoners were beginning to wonder the same thing. Each was handcuffed, and their ankle shackles were attached by chains to the wall, but even in this predicament they dared hope.

Rumors of the war reached them in snippets: The Allies had crossed the Rhine, the Americans were swinging toward Bavaria, the Russians were threatening Berlin.

Canaris had begun to communicate with the prisoner in the next cell by a simple code using taps on the wall for different letters. The former spy chief's neighbor was a Danish cavalry captain and member of his country's military intelligence service, Hans Mathiesen Lunding, who had been in his cell for almost a year. Lunding noted that Canaris remained remarkably upbeat, believing that he would survive until the Allies liberated the camp.

The admiral could not know that in Berlin the Gestapo had—by good fortune—uncovered the final piece of evidence against him and the Oster conspiracy.

As German forces prepared for a last-ditch battle to propel the Russians from the outskirts of the capital, Camp Zeppelin at Zossen became a major new base for infantry staff. Nazi loyalist General Walter Buhle arrived at the camp looking for new offices. In the search he found a safe filled with several black ring binders, each containing hundreds of pages of Canaris's diaries and private thoughts on the Nazi hierarchy and the war.

Buhle, of course, knew all about Canaris's fall from grace, and he had no sympathy for the "traitors": He had been in the Wolf's Lair conference and had been seriously wounded by Stauffenberg's bomb. He immediately contacted SS Colonel Johann Rattenhuber, the man in charge of Hitler's personal security, who had the binders delivered at once to the Führerbunker, the air raid shelter of the Reich Chancellery in which Hitler had been living for almost four months.

On reading it, Hitler turned to Rattenhuber and Kaltenbrunner, and spat out a list of names: Canaris. Oster. Sack. Bonhoeffer.

Standing, with his hands gripped as if around an enemy's neck, he stared into Rattenhuber's eyes and wailed: "Destroy the conspirators!"

Kaltenbrunner, a lawyer, disliked straightforward killing. He had no problem with liquidating the men, but it should be done in what he saw as a judicial manner. It was hypocrisy, as he knew there would be no fair trial, no defense, no appeal, but to satisfy his legal mind he turned it over to Huppenkothen. Kill them—but after a trial, came the order.

Huppenkothen took up the challenge swiftly and with enthusiasm. He already had the paperwork for the indictment—the contents of his report to the Führer after the discovery of the Zossen file. He called for a car in a mood of high excitement. At last these high-placed traitors would get what they should have got years ago. As the Reich imploded all around him, he set out on his quest to finish the Abwehr business.

At Sachsenhausen, he had Dohnanyi brought into an annex to the camp headquarters. The former lawyer, who had once dreamed of bringing Hitler to justice, was almost completely paralyzed by the effects of his stroke and disease, and he was carried into the makeshift court on a stretcher. He listened as the charges of high treason were read out and Huppenkothen outlined the contents of his notes against Hitler, plans for the Operation 7 rescue of the Jews, and his preparations for the coup. There was no hope for the accused. Dohnanyi was sentenced to death by hanging.

Without drawing breath, Huppenkothen set about the details of the next trial. He looked again at a written order from Gestapo Müller: Oster, Canaris, Bonhoeffer, and Sack were to be sentenced to death.

Swift inquiries revealed that some of the men were at Flossenbürg, but some were not. A group including Bonhoeffer had left Buchenwald, his office was told, but had not arrived at Flossenbürg.

Another telephone call revealed that the group had called at the police station in Weiden but been turned away.

At Weiden, the police officer who answered the telephone was given an earful of abuse by the caller from Berlin and told to find the green van and the prisoners on the list.

HAVING BEEN TURNED away from Flossenbürg, the guards driving the smoky green van from Buchenwald appeared confused as to what to do next, but they headed south out of town, dark smoke filling the early-afternoon sky. A few miles into the countryside a police car came up quickly from behind, overtaking the van and waving for it to stop. The rear doors were suddenly flung open and three names were shouted: "Liedig! Müller! Bonhoeffer!"

Bonhoeffer was deep in the huddle of bodies, next to the partition with the cab. Liedig and Müller got out, and Gehre—a friend of Müller's who did not want to be separated from him—followed. The police officers did not hang around to check; they dragged the three men to the car and drove off.

No one said anything as the van carried on with its journey. They had no idea whether the three had been taken off to be killed or to be saved. The flame-fired engine chugged onwards, and when it next stopped, the guards invited the passengers to get out and to wash their faces at a water pump outside a farmhouse. A woman emerged from the farmhouse and gave them all milk and rye bread.

After the break they traveled on to Regensburg, where their guards introduced them at the prison as "very important people."

"Oh," said one of the warders, unimpressed, "some more aristocrats. Well, put them with the other lot on the second floor."[1]

Bonhoeffer and the others slept five to a cell and the next morning queued in a long corridor for the washroom with the other prisoners, whom they found were all Sippenhäftlinge, the relations of those condemned for the July 20 plot, including General Halder's wife; Ulrich von Hassell's daughter, who had had her two children—aged two and four—taken away from her; and Goerdeler's wife, who had been arrested at their home in Leipzig. She talked to Bonhoeffer about her husband's execution—at Plötzensee on February 2—and the pastor did his best to provide her with comfort.

But the stay at Regensburg was short for the prisoners from Buchenwald, and that evening the guard who had driven the smoky green van turned up and announced it was time to leave. The van headed southeast, along the Danube, but suddenly lurched in the road, causing the driver to slam on the brake. The steering column was broken. The guards looked in each direction along the isolated road. There were no cars and no buildings in sight. They told the prisoners that they might have to spend the night in the van. They tried to make themselves comfortable but got little sleep. It started to rain, and the drops battered on the roof like drumbeats. The next morning one of the guards waved down a motorcycle and got a lift back into Regensburg. When he reappeared, he was followed by a strange and worrying sight: a large civilian bus with upholstered seats carrying a squad of men with machine guns who announced that they were from the SD. They waved the prisoners into the bus and, leaving the Buchenwald guards at the side of the road, sped along the Danube, looking for a place to cross. The bridge at Straubing had been bombed by the Allies, but German soldiers had laid a pontoon bridge farther on. The bus swung across the bridge and headed northeast into a landscape of lush green meadows, hillside pine forests, and red-roofed houses.

The prisoners watched the beautiful countryside pass, their armed guards reflected in the windows, and again wondered what their destination held for them.

Then the journey got stranger still. The driver, seeing something on the roadside up ahead, laughed and shouted to one of the soldiers. The bus pulled up, the doors opened, and in jumped a group of young women who had been flagging down a lift. Laughing and flirting with the armed men, they asked about the dirty group of passengers at the back. One of the SD men smiled and said they were making a propaganda film. The prisoners heard and wondered if it was a joke to impress the women or if it could be the truth.

After the passengers got off again, there was silence until the bus reached Schönberg, a pretty and, until recently, quiet village, whose population had been swollen by refugees arriving from the East. The school had become a prison, and because of the van's breakdown, some of the political prisoners who had been at Regensburg had arrived there before the bus. There was no food, but the most "important" prisoners were given small but comfortable beds in what had been an infirmary for girls. Despite the hunger in their bellies they slept well, and the next day, a villager brought them bread and some potato salad, which they carefully shared.

Bonhoeffer sat on his bed and looked out toward the Bavarian Forest, which covered the low mountains that rose along the Czech border. From here its trees were as beautiful as a painting, but he knew that inside the forest could be as dark as a fairy tale.

HAVING ARRIVED AT Flossenbürg, Huppenkothen demanded to see the accused. It was then the guards realized with horror that Bonhoeffer could not be found.

The guards reexamined the occupant of each cell. Fabian von Schlabrendorff was accused of being Bonhoeffer and protested that he was not. When Müller and Liedig turned up, both were accused of being Bonhoeffer.

It slowly dawned on the guards that the pastor was not there. The police who had stopped the van had not brought Bonhoeffer as instructed. Word went out to the Gestapo, who telephoned around frantically and finally tracked down the whereabouts of the prisoners who had been in the van.

Two agents were told to get to the school at Schönberg, find Bonhoeffer, and bring him in.

SUNDAY, APRIL 8. As the sun shone through the upstairs windows of the building, one of the prisoners asked Bonhoeffer if he would lead a small service. At first, knowing that many were Catholic, he refused, saying that he did not wish to impose on their faith. But all encouraged him, saying it would mean a lot to them—even an atheist said it would make his day. Bonhoeffer read some verses and spoke about the spirit of their imprisonment and the ways in which they could take strength from it.

He was still speaking when the door opened and two grim-faced men in civilian clothes stepped into the room. Everyone knew immediately that they were the Gestapo.

"Prisoner Bonhoeffer," one of them said. "Get ready to come with us."

The room went cold. Everyone knew what the words "Come with us" meant.

They gathered around Bonhoeffer and all shook hands. The pastor handed one of Goerdeler's sons the volume of Plutarch that his family had given him two months earlier for his thirty-ninth birthday and asked him to return it to them.

He asked the Englishman Best to remember him to Bishop Bell. "Tell him that for me this is the end but also the beginning," he said as he shook Best's hand. "With him [Bell] I believe in the principle of our Universal Christian brotherhood which rises above all national interests, and that our victory is certain."[2]

Then, flanked by the two Gestapo men, he was gone.

IT TOOK ABOUT three hours for the Gestapo men to drive north to Flossenbürg and deliver Bonhoeffer to Huppenkothen.

The commandant Kögl had laid out a courtroom in the headquarters building, and in an adjoining office he and Huppenkothen discussed the process to come. They were joined by SS Judge Otto Thorbeck, from Nuremberg, who had arrived in Weiden by train but had to cycle the last twelve miles to the camp on a borrowed bicycle.

Showing them Gestapo Müller's order, Huppenkothen explained that the convictions and sentences were preordained. Thorbeck and Kögl showed no surprise; in fact Kögl wondered why they were bothering with the pretense of the trials.[3]

With all the accused in the camp, the proceedings could begin. SS guards escorted Oster—his ankles still shackled together—into the courtroom first. It was 4 p.m.

Huppenkothen lifted the file in front of him and read the indictment. Oster, like Dohnanyi, was accused of high treason. He had worked against the National Socialist government since 1938, the prosecutor told him, and had made treasonous approaches to the Allies via the Vatican. As he had in his later Gestapo interrogations, Oster proudly admitted it all. He knew he had no chance of survival in this camp of horror. Even if the Allies were at the gates, he felt sure the SS would execute him. Thorbeck passed the death sentence. It would be carried out at dawn, he said.

After a short break for the court staff to have a drink and a bite to eat, Canaris was brought in. The indictment was the same as Oster's. Huppenkothen told him he had used his offices and power to conceal Oster's subversive group.

Once again, Canaris—although his head must have told him all was lost—bit back. He had played along with the conspiracy in order to expose it, he claimed.

Thorbeck interrupted his testimony and recalled Oster. The two friends faced each other in unimaginable circumstances. Oster knew immediately that Canaris, still trying to maintain dignity in a gray suit and tie, was fighting back. But he could not do the same. They started to argue. "Of course, you supported us," Oster insisted.

"I did it for show," Canaris cried desperately, looking from Oster to Thorbeck and back. "Don't you understand?"

"No," Oster said. "That's not true. I can only say what I know. I'm not a rogue."

In the silence that followed, Thorbeck asked Canaris if Oster was falsely incriminating him.

There was a pause, a sigh. "No," Canaris said quietly, the fight finally gone from him.[4]

The two former friends were taken back to their cells. There would be no other words between them.

Thorbeck sat into the night and sentenced Sack, Gehre, and Bonhoeffer to death. Gehre had been arrested by the Gestapo during the crackdown on the Kreisau Circle but he had later escaped from custody, thus incurring the wrath of "Gestapo" Müller. Marked for death for some months, his name had been added to the list of people to face the court martial.

In his cell the Dane Lunding heard the shackled men going to their trials and later the slow, sad shuffle back.

At 10 p.m. there was a tapping on his wall. "My time is up. Was not a traitor. Did my duty as a German. If you survive remember me to my wife."[5]

THE STONE CELL block was roused before dawn on April 9, 1945, by the barking of dogs and the shouting of the guards as they mustered for roll call at 5:30. The corridor was suddenly illuminated by arc lamps.

A wooden wall projected from the roof of the building at its western end, and hooks and nooses had been fixed to the supporting beams. A guard went along placing a small wooden stepladder beneath each noose.

The prisoners—each in their prison clothes—were dragged from their cells at 6 a.m. and made to strip. Bonhoeffer knelt on the cold stone of the building's washroom cell to say a prayer.

The camp doctor, SS Major Hermann Fischer, watched as the men were led to the end of the corridor and made to stand as the verdict of the court was read out to each in turn.

Then, one by one, they were herded outside to the gallows. Canaris, Oster, Bonhoeffer, Sack, Gehre.

Huppenkothen watched as they each climbed the few wooden steps and the noose was placed over their heads.

Then the steps were kicked away.

Fischer was standing close to Bonhoeffer as he prepared for his turn, a prayer once again on his lips, his face remarkably calm. The doctor later recalled: "In the almost fifty years that I worked as a doctor, I have hardly ever seen a man die so entirely submissive to the will of God."[6]

As the bodies were being gathered up, Huppenkothen rang Sachsenhausen. He needed to confirm for his records that the execution of Hans von Dohnanyi had been carried out at the same time. The commandant told him that it had.

Satisfied, Huppenkothen replaced the receiver. His final task for Nazi Germany had been completed to his and the regime's total satisfaction.

IN HIS CELL at Flossenbürg, Lunding strained to hear what was happening and noticed the prisoners never came back. After the dogs stopped barking, he was finally brought some food.

The guard told him Canaris was dead, and the Dane asked if the Germans always treated their officers that way.

"He wasn't an officer," came the reply. "He was a traitor."[7]

INSTEAD OF BEING taken to the crematorium, the bodies of the men were carried to an open area near the spot where they had been hanged. They were stacked in a pile and burned.

In his cell, Müller detected the smell of burning flesh and rushed to the window. Specks of dust seemed to dance in the air and some tumbled through the bars.

A few fell on the back of Müller's hand, where he gripped the window ledge. They were pieces of skin—his friends' skin.

Joe the Ox—who had risked his life for peace and survived some of the most hideous Gestapo torture—slowly slid to the cold floor of the cell and wept.

TWO WEEKS LATER, soldiers of the US Army arrived at Flossenbürg and found that the guards had largely cleared it out, leaving behind 1,600 who had been too sick to walk. Thousands of others had been force-marched to Dachau, with many dying or being murdered on the way. Josef Müller, Liedig, Schlabrendorff, Schacht, Halder, Falkenhausen, Schuschnigg, and Thomas were among those who survived. Liberated on April 15, they were driven to safety in the back of a US Army truck.

SPRINGTIME IN THE Institute of Hygiene in Berlin had brought with it the fear of a future after Germany had lost the war. Documents were burned; crimes erased.[8]

Kurt Gerstein watched it all. A depressed and solitary figure, he had become quick to anger with friends, and told them he hated Germany. "I'm one of the most unhappy men on God's earth," he said.[9]

But while the horror he had witnessed had helped turn the hair under his SS cap white, he was still working in the heart of the Nazi killing machine, still in his black SS lieutenant's uniform, still being driven in a dark chauffeur-driven car.

When Gerstein again sought out Pastor Mochalsky at Dahlem, the priest found him to be "ravaged by fear and anguish. He was sick, in the psychological as well as physical sense of the word. Above all, he lived in constant fear of the SS."[10]

Nothing could give him comfort from the desperation he felt at being unable to stop the carnage. In the silence of his apartment on Bülowstrasse, his double game had brought him to the brink of a nervous collapse. In the ruins of Berlin, the God of wrath he had always believed in had shown Himself to be real. What did God think of him? Would He see the purity of his motives?

Late in March 1945, Gerstein abandoned his post in Berlin, dressed in civilian clothes, and visited his wife and three young children in Tübingen for what was to be the last time. He still hoped that he might be able to survive and tell his story directly to the advancing Allies; he still believed the only thing that could give meaning to his existence would be for him to bear witness. "People will hear about me," he told Elfriede. "You can be sure of that! You will be astounded to learn all the things I have done . . ." He leaned down and kissed her. "In three or four weeks, I shall be back again."[11]

She never saw him again.

He left the house—afraid that the Gestapo might be after him—and went into hiding with various friends. In the middle of April, while hiding with a family named Straub in Metzingen, he learned that an SS unit was nearby. He left the house and drove toward the Allies.

A few weeks earlier, an old friend, Helmut Franz, had asked him how he would convince Allied troops that he was not a war criminal. Gerstein said people in the resistance knew who he was and there were many who could vouch for his "personal integrity." Franz remembered: "He went so far as to believe that, as a direct witness of the worst crimes of the Nazis, the important role of informing the German people devolved upon him. He felt he was on the threshold of a vital stage in his life, with many positive tasks to perform."[12]

If he could get through the lines, Gerstein believed, he would be okay. On April 22, he borrowed a motorcycle, sped through the front line, and surrendered to French forces in the town of Reutlingen, to the south of Stuttgart, where the military commandant believed him to be a genuine anti-Nazi. The commandant—who was busy still fighting a war—sent him westward to Rottweil, where he was put up in the Hotel Mohren and ordered to check in with the French police every day. On April 26, he began to write his report about what he had seen at the death camps, first in stilted, handwritten French and then in German. He typed up both versions on a typewriter borrowed from a local pastor.

Gerstein tried to give his report to the French authorities but found that they were not interested in receiving it.[13] The French wanted only to know what he could tell them about possible SS "Werewolves," members of a last-ditch resistance force already suspected of killing a soldier in Reutlingen.

At the beginning of May, two Allied servicemen, British intelligence officer Major Derek Evans, and an American chemist, Colonel John W. Haught, wandered into the lounge of the hotel. These were the first British and American personnel he had seen, and he told them he wanted to speak to them about the concentration camps. He gave them his French report along with some invoices for Zyklon B, a letter written to him by Degesch, and a list of his anti-Nazi friends and acquaintances.[14] He also showed them an anti-Nazi religious pamphlet he had written before the war, and said he served in the SS as an undercover agent for the Confessing Church.

The two men took Gerstein seriously—part of their brief was to find out about German development of combat gases—and reported the meeting to their superiors, adding: "Dr Gerstein fled from the Nazis only three weeks ago. He is evidently still affected by his experiences and has difficulty in talking about them. But he is anxious that the guilty parties be brought to trial for their crimes and states that he is prepared to act as a witness . . . There is reason to consider whether Dr Gerstein should not be protected against the local Nazis."

Gerstein felt he was being listened to, and wrote to his wife with a copy of his report and with instructions that, if she had any problems, she should take it and the warrants for his arrest before the war to the military governor. He told her that he was to appear at the International Court of Justice as a "material witness against the war criminals."[15] Shortly afterwards a broadcast from Radio Lyon quoted a German source named Kurt Gerstein as describing the extermination of prisoners by gas in concentration camps.

French army intelligence took him to Paris, where he was questioned about SS activities in France. John Haught said the French did not ask him about Poland.

On July 5, Gerstein was put into the Cherche-Midi military prison, where, five days later, he was told he was being investigated as a war criminal. The cells were windowless and had no lighting or heating. It was alive with bugs and lice, and the food was poor. The guards referred to the German prisoners as *chiens*, dogs.

In his cell Gerstein began a letter to his Dutch friend J. H. Ubbink, asking him to write down a few things about him, a reference. "One never knows how useful a thing of that kind may yet turn out to be . . . It isn't that people don't believe me, but my situation was a rather special case."

He congratulated Ubbink on the liberation of his country from "our brood of vipers and criminals," and added: "Ask your people if, now at least, they believe what went on in Belzec, etc." The letter was never sent.

Now Gerstein was confronted with the charge that the French planned to bring: that "he issued orders on and after February 1942 leading to the killing of an immense number of human beings in . . . gas chambers . . ."

Gerstein was being accused of being a leading proponent of the gas chamber. A list of war criminals was prepared for investigators in London, names based on Gerstein's evidence—Eichmann, Günther, Pfannenstiel, Wirth, Hackenholt—only Gerstein's name was among them, too. The list was reported in *France-Soir*. Among those with whom he shared a cell block was Karl Buck, charged with being commandant of two concentration camps in Alsace—but the two barely spoke. Gerstein said only a few words to his guards, too. "I've nothing to reproach myself with—nothing!" he said. But he appeared completely broken.

Unknown to Gerstein, Baron von Otter, the Swedish diplomat he had met on the Polish train, wrote to his counterpart in London, urging him to help a German named Gerstein.[16] The London man began inquiries, but it was too late.

On the afternoon of July 25, 1945, Kurt Gerstein, who had been moved into solitary confinement a few days earlier, was found hanging in his cell. He had torn a strip from his thin blanket, looped one end around his neck, and tied the other around the bars of a ventilator grille. The prison doctor certified "death by self-strangulation."

The idea of suicide had been no stranger to Gerstein. He had considered it many times before. Now, though, all the risks he had taken had come to nothing. In the eyes of those he had sought to alert to the Holocaust, he was just another war criminal.

On August 3, Gerstein's body was buried in the Thiais cemetery in Paris by the French authorities. The coffin was too small for his six-foot-one-inch frame, so his head was tucked down to the side. His name was spelled wrong on his grave, "Gastein." His family was not informed of his suicide for three years.[17]

Four days after Gerstein's body was interred without ceremony, the Swedish embassy in London handed the British Foreign Office Baron von Otter's request that the former SS officer be protected. Gerstein had given the Swedish legation in Berlin valuable information on the concentration camp at Belzec, it stated.

Even if in the chaos of postwar London there had been someone to help, it was too late for Kurt Gerstein.

And too late for the many Jews of Belzec.

EVER SINCE BONHOEFFER had been moved from the Gestapo headquarters, Maria von Wedemeyer had been searching for him. Hearing he might be at Flossenbürg, and showing tremendous courage, she had actually turned up at the camp with a parcel of warm clothing and asked to see him. She had been turned away.

She turned twenty-one the day the Americans liberated Flossenbürg, but there was no good news for her birthday. It would be several weeks before she and the Bonhoeffer family learned of his fate. By then Hitler was dead, the war in Europe was over, and Germany was counting the cost of twelve years of Nazi terror. For the relatives of the resisters there would be difficult times ahead, as their loved ones faced accusations of betrayal, but it was to the spirit of the honorable dead that they would look as they sought to rebuild their nation.

On July 27 a special memorial service was held for Bonhoeffer. Organized by Bishop Bell, it took place at Holy Trinity Brompton Church in South Kensington, London. Broadcast on the BBC and in Germany, it featured British and German speakers, including Franz Hildebrandt, whom Dohnanyi and Bonhoeffer had helped escape Germany before the war. Coming while the war in the Pacific against Hitler's ally Japan still went on, it was a remarkable act of reconciliation in the spirit of what many in the opposition to Hitler hoped Europe might come to represent after the war.

In Berlin, Maria and Bonhoeffer's parents—coming to terms with not just Dietrich's and Klaus's deaths but those of their sons-in-law Rüdiger Schleicher and Hans von Dohnanyi, too—listened in silence to the broadcast.[18]

Afterwards, the radio silent, they comforted themselves with one of Dietrich's favorite sayings: "No battle is lost until it has been given up for lost."[19]

IN THE CHAOS of war's end there were few left to mourn those who had stood up to the Nazis. But there were the children, those whose parents had been taken from them, those who would spend a lifetime learning about the fathers and mothers they had lost.

More than three hundred relatives of the July 20 plotters had been arrested under the Nazi Sippenhaft law, which allowed for the detention without trial of the accused's immediate and sometimes distant relatives.[20] Many were children, whom the Nazis sought to cleanse of their "tainted" bloodlines.

In Bad Sachsa, a spa town in central Germany, the Nazis created an SS "children's village," where conspirators' children could be "reprogrammed" and offered for adoption to SS families. The children were given new surnames and were forbidden to talk about their families.

However, as the country imploded, the Nazis never got the chance to go through with the adoption plan, and many were returned to relatives.[21]

Other children, though, were marked for execution. At Easter 1945 the Nazis started the process of transferring them to Buchenwald by taking them as far as the local railway station at Nordhausen. But the truck had to turn back due to a heavy Allied air raid.

Among those on board were four of Claus von Stauffenberg's children.

Word about the village had spread among the families of the freed children, and on being released from prison herself, Stauffenberg's aunt Countess Alexandrine von Üxküll-Gyllenband was determined to find those who were still being held.

Alexandrine was resourceful and well connected, having worked for the Red Cross during the First World War. Volunteering with the organization once again, she gained the help of a sympathetic French army officer and drove to Bad Sachsa. There she found not only Claus's children but his brother Berthold's, too.

Revealing to a local businessman what had been going on in the village, she was able to persuade him to lend her a bus. The Stauffenberg children and others then climbed on board.

As the bus headed west to the French zone, the children looked out the windows at the ruins of their country.

# Afterword

REDEMPTION FOR THE German nation was a powerful motivation for many who stood up to Hitler. "We shall need very many of us just people if there is to be anything left of us that can still bear a name before God and the world," Theodor Haecker, who inspired the young people of the White Rose, wrote in his diary.[1]

In refusing to be dehumanized and crushed as individuals, they sought to prove to themselves and to others that not all of the nation had submitted. They were keeping alive the part of the country they loved in their own actions. And to the civilized world today, their actions still matter, as they shine a message to us: Decency and honor can be maintained, and the instinct for human solidarity will survive even in the most fascistic of regimes. When power and violence attempt to crush all into conformity, there will always be those who cannot be suppressed.

One must remember that the resisters operated in a society where the machinery of propaganda ensured that there was only condemnation of their actions and no reporting at all of the concentration camps or atrocities. There was no public, vocal opposition behind which a campaign could be built. Anyone whose conscience dictated that they must oppose Hitler had to overcome the fact that their neighbors saw only one picture of the Nazi state. The regime ran a perfect campaign of fake news, of which to question and oppose was a betrayal of the nation and the fighting soldier.

As Falk Harnack wrote in 1963, there is "a fundamental, worldwide difference between high treason and espionage committed in a democratic state and in a bestial dictatorship . . . where all opposition to the government is brutally suppressed . . . Hitler's dictatorship had at its disposal limitless power; it had extraordinary means of support. Only the most extreme measures had any real chance of success. The resistance acted from moral duty. Above all, the people had to be torn from the criminal path that Hitler's leadership had trodden, and a national catastrophe had to be avoided. That was the opinion both of the right as well as the left resistance."[2]

There is no greater measure of the challenges that the German opposition to the Third Reich faced than the immense personal cost that they paid for their courage.

THE HARNACKS, THE Bonhoeffers, and many other resisters such as Justus Delbrück need not have stayed in Germany during the Nazi era. They all had opportunities to leave before the war clouds came. The chemist Max Delbrück did leave and settled in the United States. He later won a Nobel Prize but always felt a sense of uneasiness about his decision to go. Those who stayed and resisted deserved the greater credit, he decided.[3] That credit was not always forthcoming.

The world had been tipped on its head by the war. In Germany the widows and children of Gestapo and SS men were considered patriots. Old army groups still met and sang Nazi songs, while meanwhile the widows and children of the conspirators were shunned, denied pensions, and denounced as traitors.

In December 1946, a war crimes unit of the United States Army of Occupation in Germany reported on its investigation into the death of Mildred Fish-Harnack. It found: "[She] was in fact deeply involved in underground activities aimed to overthrow the government of Germany; that the trial (although secret) was conducted before five judges of the highest state military court and that this court, in view of the activities in which had been engaged, was justified in imposing the sentence which was imposed."[4] The fact that the court had sat twice in order to get the right result for Hitler was not taken into account. Nazi law had been upheld by the American lawyers.

There was no doubt that the reputation of the Harnacks had been tarnished by the Red Orchestra's links to Russia. American investigators relied on captured Gestapo records to make their judgments—but the Gestapo had had no inkling of the Harnacks' connection to the United States and had investigated and prosecuted the group as a Soviet spy ring, embellishing its connections to Moscow.

Inside Germany they were spies of a foreign power, therefore traitors, not idealist patriots. To the Americans, they were first and foremost Soviet agents. During the Cold War, judgments were particularly harsh, but as the journalist Margret Boveri, who knew the Harnacks and many of their friends, has noted: "Judgements change with the passage of time and reflect the varying constellations of political and ideological power." For her, the group around the Harnacks and Schulze-Boysens should be remembered as "the intellectual heirs of the French Revolution, the bearers of its ideals of progress, democratic egalitarianism and, of course, the concomitant equality of the sexes."[5] For Freya von Moltke, widow of Helmuth von Moltke and herself a member of the Kreisau Circle: "They were people who wanted to do something, who couldn't put up with nothing being done. To write off all the Red Orchestra people as Communists misses the truth."[6]

As Mildred suggested on the way to the scaffold, it was for her love of Germany and the freedom of human beings that she had acted. She loved America, admired President Roosevelt, and hated the effect the worldwide Depression had had on working people. In recent years Mildred's name is finally being remembered, with the author Shareen Blair Brysac having done much to rehabilitate her image. September 16—her birthday—is now Mildred Harnack Day in Wisconsin. Children in public schools spend the day discussing her courage and her legacy.

THE SAME COLD War tensions that had seen the image of the Harnacks and the others dragged through the mud played a part in protecting some of the officials of Nazi justice.

In the fourth leaflet printed by the White Rose, Hans Scholl had urged that none of the "scoundrels in this regime" should go free at the end of the war, with their "abominable crimes" forgotten as they "rally to another flag and then act as if nothing had happened."[7]

He might have been writing about Manfred Roeder, who early in May 1945 was taken into American custody and was quickly passed to the Counterintelligence Corps (CIC). With focus turning to what the Bolsheviks would do now that Hitler was dead, Roeder explained that he was an expert in rooting out Soviet spies. A British intelligence investigation into the Harnack/Schulze-Boysen group had concluded that they were anti-Nazi rather than Moscow agents, but Roeder embellished the links between the group and Trepper's Rote Kapelle, and he intrigued the CIC. The Harnacks' work for the Americans was not considered. When Nuremberg prosecutors submitted files for his prosecution, the CIC took Roeder into custody and out of the grasp of the war trials.

Roeder shared the protection of the CIC with Walter Huppenkothen, whose hands were bloodied from service with the Einsatzgruppen and from his pursuit to the death of Bonhoeffer, Canaris, and Oster. A Nuremberg lawyer wrote to the CIC saying it was "hard to believe" it could protect "two such notorious, unscrupulous opportunistic Nazis."[8] However, Roeder and Huppenkothen promised the CIC they could identify dozens of German Communists, and they played on American intelligence fears that many members of the Rote Kapelle may have survived and would continue to operate a postwar spy network in Western Europe.

By 1948 the CIC realized it had "exploited [Roeder] to the fullest extent" and that the Rote Kapelle had ceased to exist. However, by then, CIC involvement appeared to have wrecked the Nuremberg lawyers' chances of prosecuting either Roeder or Huppenkothen. Both were released.

Roeder became a political figure on the postwar German far right and used his public voice to further besmirch the image of the German resistance, attacking not only those who had died but also Greta Lorke, by then living in East Germany with a job as a senior civil servant, and Helmut Roloff, who had become a well-known concert pianist.

He died in 1971, still unrepentant and still boasting about his CIA friends. He had never stood trial.

Huppenkothen did come before a court in West Germany but was controversially acquitted of murder. In 1955 he was convicted of violating procedures in the executions of Canaris and the others and sentenced to seven years in prison.

THE GESTAPO DEAL with the People's Court over Falk Harnack—to overlook his involvement with the White Rose in the hope he would inadvertently lead them to other anti-Nazi conspirators—yielded nothing.

After his release the army transferred Harnack from Chemnitz to Greece, where the army was fighting a guerrilla war with partisans. Through local villagers Harnack made contact with members of the Greek resistance and indicated that he was working in opposition to his own forces.

On December 20, 1943, Harnack's commanding officer received an order from Himmler requiring that the army deliver him to the SS. Himmler was getting nothing from the court deal.

Falk Harnack was told that he was being returned to Chemnitz and was accompanied to the airstrip by a lieutenant with whom he was friendly.

With his luggage already on the aircraft, Falk realized something was wrong.

"Is it bad or good?" he asked the lieutenant.

"Not good," came the reply.[9]

Both Harnack and the lieutenant knew that if he got on the plane he would be flying to his death. The officer agreed to let Harnack escape, and he headed into Athens, still in German uniform. He eventually reached a partisan group that agreed to let him fight with them.

After the war he wrote and directed films, including *Der 20. Juli* about the July 20 bomb plot.

When Harnack discovered Roeder's telephone number in Frankfurt am Main, he regularly rang him in the middle of the night to berate him.

Some of the Berlin Rote Kapelle survived. Günther Weisenborn served a prison sentence but returned to his career as a writer. In 1955 he collaborated with Falk Harnack on *Der 20. Juli*.

On being released from a prison in Waldheim, near Dresden, Greta Lorke walked for days through a Germany of broken bridges, bombed buildings, and field-strewn corpses to get back to Berlin. Once there she found her parents and her son, Ule, and then searched for Hans, the son of Hans and Hilde Coppi, who had both been executed. He had survived, and Lorke became his godmother. Lorke also took in Erika von Brockdorff's young daughter, Saskia.

Lorke was feted at first in East Germany, as the Communists tried to claim the German Rote Kapelle as their own, but she found herself trapped between the unrealistic Soviet depiction of her friends and the debate about its "treasonous" activities in the West, which had been inflamed by a book by Roeder.

With sadness, she confided in Hans Coppi—the orphaned baby who went on to be an engineer and historian of the Rote Kapelle—that her time in Wisconsin had been the "happiest time in her life."[10]

AFTER THE WAR, Anatoli Gourevitch, the Soviet agent whose mission to contact Harro Schulze-Boysen in Berlin had been tracked by the Gestapo, was flown to Moscow, where he admitted having cooperated with the Germans after his arrest. Sentenced to twenty years in a gulag, he was released in 1955 under an amnesty to Soviet citizens who "assisted the foreign invaders in the Great Patriotic War in 1941–1945."

Alexander Korotkov, who recruited Arvid Harnack in Berlin, later became head of the KGB in the Russian zone of the devastated and Allied-occupied city. He died in 1961 of a heart attack while playing tennis.

THE COURAGEOUS STUDENTS in Hamburg were inspired rather than discouraged by the executions in Munich, and quickly began reprinting the White Rose leaflets.

Student Hans Leipelt had been thrown out of Hamburg University because he was half-Jewish and had moved to Munich, where a chemistry professor named Heinrich Otto Wieland was refusing to turn away Jewish students.[11] With the support of Jürgen Wittenstein, he collected money to help Kurt Huber's family. Clara Huber received the money anonymously through a priest and never knew where it came from.

Leipelt teamed up with his new girlfriend, Marie-Luise Jahn, and began reprinting the sixth White Rose leaflet, which had been written by Huber. At the top of the page they put a new heading: "And their spirit lives on, despite all!"[12] Both were arrested in October 1943, and the Gestapo also brought in Leipelt's Jewish mother, Katharina, a doctor of science who had supported the Hamburg group's activities. A year passed before Leipelt and Jahn were tried. He was sentenced to death; she was given twelve years in jail.

Leipelt, who had never met the Scholls, was executed in the same death chamber at Stadelheim on January 29, 1945. Katharina Leipelt died a few weeks before her son. She took her own life while in prison, as did her friend Elisabeth Lange.[13]

The Hamburg group also included Dr. Curt Ledien, who was hanged on April 23, 1945, and Gretl Mrosek, philosophy student Reinhold Meyer, and medical students Frederick Geussenhainer and Greta Rothe, who all died in custody in a swathe of Nazi retribution in the final days of the war.

Inge Scholl described the Nazis' determination to keep killing resistance fighters in the last few weeks of the war: "Their revenge against people who as individuals had dared to attack the essential idea of the regime was to pull their opponents down to death along with themselves."

Heinz Kucharski, who had led the Hamburg group after Leipelt went to Munich, had been condemned to die, too. He was being transported to the execution site when he made a daring and successful escape from a train and ran free into the night.

\* \* \*

TRAUTE LAFRENZ, WHO had been a key member of the White Rose in Munich and had helped support the group in Hamburg, was rearrested after the clampdown in the north. She spent more than a year in various prisons before being freed in April 1945 when American soldiers liberated Bayreuth. After the war she moved to the United States.

Robert Scholl was also released from jail when Germany was liberated. He went on to become mayor of Ulm before his death in 1973. His wife, Magdalena, died in 1945, her heart broken: She lost not only Hans and Sophie in the war, but also Werner, who was killed on the Eastern Front in 1944.

Elisabeth Scholl became close to Sophie's boyfriend, Fritz Hartnagel, after the executions. They later married and settled in Stuttgart.

Inge Scholl married Otl Aicher in 1952, and she worked tirelessly to keep alive the spirit and memory of the White Rose. She was supported by the families of Willi Graf, Kurt Huber, Alex Schmorell, Christoph Probst, and many others.

Sophie Scholl has almost two hundred schools named in her honor across Germany. She and Hans were voted among the top five greatest Germans in a poll by a television network in 2003. The square outside the main building at Ludwig Maximilian University is named in their honor.

FOR ORGANIZING THE rescue of thirteen Jewish people in Operation 7, Hans von Dohnanyi was recognized as one of the Righteous Among the Nations at a special ceremony in Berlin in 2003, which was attended by his three children.[14]

WHAT DOES KURT Gerstein's dual role in the resistance and the Holocaust reveal to us today? The enormity of the killing dwarfs his actions. Around 1.1 million people were murdered in Auschwitz alone—and one million of those died for no other reason than that they were Jewish. They came from all over Europe and died with Polish political prisoners, Gypsies, Russian prisoners of war, Jehovah's Witnesses, homosexuals, and others deemed enemies of the state.[15] An estimated 1.4 million were killed in the three Operation Reinhard camps, Sobibor, Treblinka, and Belzec, where Gerstein had first witnessed the horror behind the "final solution to the Jewish question."[16]

We are all characters of contradiction, but the contradictions in Gerstein's life were immense. He was both rigidly Christian and a joker, a product of convention and a rebel. Somewhere in that personality was a man who saw the rigidity of Nazi evil and had to subvert it. As a child he had written criticisms of his homework on the class blackboard for his schoolteacher to see; as a young adult he stood up in the front row of a Hitler Youth theater production to criticize its anti-Christian message; as an SS officer he wore a clothes brush in his gun holster; and when confronted by the Holocaust, he pretended the murderous gas canisters were damaged. His story comes from the heart of a horror story, so real we can barely believe it. Because of that, it must be instructive.

In a letter to his father in March 1944, Gerstein said, "[A man] must never exonerate himself to himself before his conscience and before the higher order of things to which he is subject by saying, 'that is not my business, I can do nothing to change things.'"

His father always misunderstood Gerstein's coded way of talking and told him only that, as a soldier, he must follow orders: The "responsibility is with the man who gives the orders, not the one who carries them out."[17]

In his reply, his last letter to his father, Kurt Gerstein said, "Whenever I have received orders of such a nature, I have either never carried them out or I have used a diversion to prevent them from being executed."

But is that enough? There was no doubt he was a witness, but also surely a participator. In August 1950, Gerstein's name was put before the denazification court in Tübingen—the court having been convened as Gerstein would need to be rehabilitated in order for his wife to receive a war widow's pension. Pastor Martin Niemöller, head of the Confessing Church, spoke up for him and described Gerstein as "certainly rather a peculiar saint, but a man of absolute purity and straight as a die."[18] He added: "He was prepared to sacrifice, and indeed did sacrifice, his honour, his family and his life."[19]

The court noted that Gerstein "represented the type of man who, by virtue of his deepest convictions, disavowed the Nazi regime, even hated it inwardly, but collaborated with it in order to combat it from within and to prevent worse things happening."

It acknowledged his efforts to divert Zyklon B from its use in the Holocaust by marking containers as "disinfectant only," but noted that "the possibility cannot be excluded that in this he did not entirely succeed." It also accepted that he "rendered useless two shipments of prussic acid" and that these were "acts of resistance which ... placed him in very great jeopardy."

But despite his great effort and best intentions, he was "not sufficiently important or influential to stop this machine ... The machine was stronger than he was. In the end, he realized this and manifestly suffered greatly from his consciousness of the fact."[20]

It concluded: "The court is of the opinion that the accused did not exhaust all the possibilities open to him and that he could have found other ways and means of holding aloof from the operation ... After all his previous experience, it must have been absolutely clear to him that he, as an individual, was in no position to prevent these extermination measures or, by rendering useless trifling quantities of the prussic acid supplied, to save the lives of even some of the persons concerned.

"Accordingly . . . the court has not included the accused among the main criminals but has placed him among the 'tainted.'"[21]

Saul Friedländer, who spent the war hidden in a Catholic boarding school in France and later discovered that his parents had been murdered in Auschwitz, has written: "The Tübingen Court did not deny that Gerstein had carried out acts of resistance; it condemned him, in effect, for the uselessness of his efforts. He is punished, in a way, for not having behaved like the great majority of 'good' Germans and waited quietly until all the Jews were dead; paradoxically, the 'innocence' of such Germans is contrasted with the 'guilt' of a man who was obliged in some degree to accommodate to the crime in order to resist it . . . Is such a resistance therefore less or more 'guilty' of the crime than the passive spectator who tolerates it without moving against it?"

What more could Gerstein have done to restrain the criminals of the Third Reich? In practice, probably nothing. The killing did not depend on him. Should he have escaped, or even committed suicide? Or was he right to stay and bear witness? After all, what is not in doubt was that Gerstein's was no cell-block conversion: He had been clear all along to friends and religious mentors that he was joining the Waffen-SS to expose its crimes. One can question his wisdom—his sanity even—but not his initial intent.

Yes, there is something in the Biblical saying that "He that toucheth pitch shall be defiled therewith," and Gerstein was defiled, but he was also the one who saw the horror and knew that it was wrong. Had there been many more Gersteins—each trying to get the message out, each destroying gas canisters—they would have been acknowledged as heroes. But there was only him. His actions were carried out in loneliness; the reaction to his warnings increased his isolation; he died alone.

Fifteen years after the Tübingen judgment, the premier of the province of Baden-Württemberg, Kurt Kiesinger, overturned the guilty verdict. Gerstein was declared not guilty. "Gerstein resisted National Socialist despotism with all his strength and suffered consequent disadvantage," Mr. Kiesinger stated. Baron von Otter had been among those who had given evidence for Gerstein.

But perhaps the binary option of a guilty or innocent verdict presents parameters too simplistic by which to judge a case as complex as Gerstein's. Writing about Gerstein adds another layer of complication to an abomination that words struggle to describe. In any case, how can we make sense of the Holocaust?

THE FRIENDS OF Herbert Baum represented one of the most significant civilian German resistance groups, and they paid a high price for standing up to tyranny.

Even those in the group who escaped the executioner did not survive the war. Alice Hirsch, Lotte Rotholz, and Edith Fraenkel, who had received prison sentences, were later sent to Auschwitz, where they were murdered.

But those who had stayed out of Gestapo hands survived—largely due to the courage of others.

Ellen Compart was protected by a Christian named Willi May and his Jewish wife, Gerda, who showed remarkable courage in obtaining a duplicate set of her own identity papers for Compart to use. It was an astonishing act that saw Gerda talk herself out of Gestapo suspicion—one of those heroes that history rarely has the opportunity to record.

Ursula Ehrlich also survived in hiding in Berlin, as did Harry Cühn. Rita Meyer survived Auschwitz and Ravensbrück.[22]

CHARLOTTE PAECH ALSO survived. When the court that had sentenced fellow members of the Baum group to death failed to process her warrant for execution, she disappeared into a detention center and sat out her sentence. The authorities then realized she was a nurse and sent her to the deportation center that they had set up in the pathology department of the Jewish hospital in Wedding, where she had worked for fourteen years. It was good to be working in a familiar building and helping patients again—even though the circumstances were dire. Many of the inmates at the makeshift prison were only there as they had contracted typhus and were deemed too weak to be transported.

One day Paech was called to the warden's office, where the secretary informed her that the Gestapo suspected there was a "loose end" in her file and they were reopening her case. Paech did not know why she was still alive, but feared now that the Gestapo would come for her.

The three-story building, which dated from the start of the First World War, was surrounded by a wall that had been partially destroyed in an air raid. Guards had put up a fence, and Paech learned they were due to erect another. She reckoned she could climb or squeeze through one but would never have the time to get over the second fence, which was due to be erected on a Monday morning.

Sunday afternoon patrols were carried out not by the Germans but by a Jewish Gestapo informant who was deeply unpopular with inmates. Paech decided that she would try to escape while he was on duty: Getting him into trouble might be a bonus.

During an exercise period Paech approached the man and told him she had permission to walk outside the fence from one of the Gestapo men. They argued, but the man gave in because he knew that Paech was considered a good nurse and model prisoner by the Gestapo.

Once beyond the wall she walked up and down a few times and realized the prisoners were trying to distract the guard. She slipped through a gap in the broken wall and into the street.[23]

After all she had been through, she was free again. The streets of Wedding looked bombed out, frightening, hostile, but also wonderful.

Never recaptured, she later married Richard Holzer, the man who had warned against the consequences of the Baum arson attack and who had spent the remainder of the war in Hungary.[24] She died in September 1980.[25]

THE YOUTHFUL COMMITMENT and courage of the Baum group is inspiring. Most were aged between ten and thirteen when Hitler came to power and were in their very early twenties at the time of the *Soviet Paradise* arson attack. Charlotte Paech earned the nickname "Grandma" from the group as she was thirty-two at the time.[26]

These young people maintained their resistance to the regime while living with intense persecution and with the trials of life in Nazi Germany: not only the deportations of friends and relatives but also personal trage- dies such as that suffered by Harry Cühn and Edith Fraenkel, whose baby died, aged just six months, at the height of their resistance activity.[27] Oth- ers in the group had children at home whose lives were put in danger by their courage. Suzanne Wesse's daughter, Katherina, was just five when her mother was executed.

Hella Hirsch, who had worked as a forced laborer for IG Farben in Ber- lin, was executed two days before her twenty-second birthday. She had been admired by friends as being wise and serious beyond her years. They remembered her saying, "Progress in history seems to come about only through human suffering. Terrible events have to happen and great de- struction has to take place for the Phoenix to rise from the ashes. In our situation only a complete German defeat could lead to a new beginning, but we might be vanquished and wiped out in the process."[28]

Today, there are two monuments to the Baum group in Berlin: at the western entrance to the Weissensee Jewish cemetery and at the Lustgarten.[29]

FRITZ KOLBE ESCAPED Berlin in the middle of March 1945 in an official Foreign Office Mercedes that kept breaking down. It took him more than two weeks to reach Bern. After five days in the city, his visa ran out and his bosses were expecting him back, even though the Soviets were closing in on the German capital. But Kolbe had no intention of returning. The man who had done so much to bring down the criminals who ran his country was finally seeing the endgame he desired play out. But it left him without a nation, without a home.

Fritz Kolbe became a "stowaway," living under the protection of his spymaster, Allen Dulles.

But there was little reward for him after the war, even though Eisen- hower called him "one of the most valuable agents we had" and he had passed 2,600 documents to the Americans.

He tried to get a job in the Foreign Ministry of the new Germany, but there were remnants of the Nazi regime still in place. Kolbe was seen as a traitor. Eventually he found work as a subscriptions manager for a presti- gious monthly magazine that, among things, gave voice to the people who had resisted Hitler. It was in this magazine that surviving conspirators of the July 20 plot first told their stories.

Kolbe and Dulles remained friends. When Dulles received the Medal of Merit from President Truman in 1946, much of the work cited in the honor had come from intelligence brought to him by Kolbe. Dulles went on to become director of the CIA, the intelligence organization that grew out of the wartime OSS.

When Fritz Kolbe died in 1971, there were twelve people at his funeral in Bonn. Two were unknown to the family and the rest of the congregation. They laid a wreath and left quietly.

The wreath had been laid on behalf of the CIA.

DONALD HEATH, THE diplomat and spy who had worked with Arvid Harnack in Berlin, never forgot Arvid or Mildred.

In 1947 he traveled to Berlin and tracked down Falk Harnack to ask about their deaths. Falk told him what he understood had happened, and the American listened in absolute silence. When Falk finished, Heath got up and went into the garden alone. Falk realized he was crying.

Heath went on to enjoy a forty-year career in the US Foreign Service. In the early 1950s he was the first US ambassador to the newly independent countries in Indochina—Vietnam, Cambodia, and Laos. He died in 1981, aged eighty-seven.[30]

OF THE PEOPLE on the Gestapo vans that took the Canaris and Oster groups to Flossenbürg and Buchenwald, Schacht, Schuschnigg, Liedig, and Generals Halder, Falkenhausen, and Thomas would survive the war, although Thomas died in Allied captivity soon after. The Abwehr officer Captain Theodor Strünck was executed the same day as Canaris and the others.

On April 15, 1945, two weeks before the Americans liberated the camp, Georg Elser was shot in the back of the neck by an SS man and his body burned. Elser's hometown of Königsbronn now features a memorial and permanent exhibition to him.

Tried at the People's Court, Fabian von Schlabrendorff, the former lawyer and Tresckow's right-hand man, revealed details of his torture, which he successfully argued made his testimony inadmissible. Escaping a death sentence, Schlabrendorff survived incarceration in Flossenbürg and Dachau.

Despite having been tortured to the extent that he had suffered a heart attack, Schlabrendorff refused to name names and saved the lives of many others, including three of Hitler's would-be assassins. Because of his courage Axel von dem Bussche, Rudolf-Christoph von Gersdorff, and Eberhard von Breitenbuch survived the war. Gersdorff, who had planned to blow himself and Hitler up in the Zeughaus attack, in fact won the Knight's Cross in France a little over a year later.

Bussche, Gersdorff, and Breitenbuch had all entered into assassination attempts in which they, too, would have died. As they showed such selfless courage, it is a failure of history that their names are not more widely remembered.

Philipp von Boeselager, who when he died in 2008 was the longest surviving of the July 20 conspirators, also owed his life to Schlabrendorff. When asked by the Gestapo about Boeselager and his brother Georg, Schlabrendorff had looked shocked. "The Boeselager brothers? No, they're excellent soldiers, completely loyal. They had nothing to do with it. You're wasting your time."[31] Georg, who had been prepared to shoot Hitler when he landed in his plane on the Eastern Front, was killed in combat in East Prussia late in August 1944.

Ulrich von Hassell had been arrested prior to the July 20 coup. In the wake of the bomb plot, he was among the many from the wider conspiracy who were executed. He died on September 8, 1944, at Plötzensee prison. Carl Goerdeler was executed at the same location on February 2, 1945.

ACCORDING TO THE German Resistance Memorial Center, 104 official death sentences were handed down in relation to the July 20 plot.[32] Countless others committed suicide or died in prison. Most of the condemned were executed in the brick execution shed at Plötzensee, where almost 2,900 death sentences passed by the People's Court, the Special Courts, and the Reich Court-Martial were carried out during the Nazi reign of terror. More than half were German-born.[33]

The July 20 plot failed in its immediate aim, of course, which was to kill Hitler and topple his government, but as historian Hans Mommsen has noted: "The importance of this plot did not lie in its immediate success, but in the attempt to save Germany's reputation in the world as a starting point to overcoming Nazism."[34]

In the end, though, might we still ask, was it worth it? Most resisters stood no chance of overthrowing the Hitler regime. Only the army could change the course of history, and in the end even it failed. The pages of this book are filled with people who died before their time—the executed, the persecuted, those driven to suicide by torture and the fear of betraying a friend. Those who resisted the Nazis paid a terrible physical price. Moments of mercy were rare.

But these resisters show that even in the most terrible of times there are those among us who cannot help but maintain personal integrity, a sense of the individual, and political and moral principles. The individuals who played an active part in the Holocaust were able to continue because of the tolerance and passivity of others. Doing something meant that you stood against it and maintained your humanity. Fighting back, as Baum group member Herbert Budzislawski told his Gestapo interrogators, was the only way "to live in Germany as a human being."[35]

Sophie Scholl once confided to her diary about the horror all around her and the guilt she felt for being part of a nation that had created it. "Doesn't every human being, no matter which era he lives in, always have to reckon with being accountable to God at any moment?"

To be able to stand with honor before God, she knew, one had to resist evil.

AN ACCUSATION OF treason has always hung over those who tried to bring down the Nazis from within. When a nation sinks to a moral low, it seeks to accuse those who speak out of disloyalty to its flag.

Dietrich Bonhoeffer described the dilemma that he and the others faced as having "either to hope for the defeat of their nation in order that Christian civilization might survive, or to hope for victory entailing the destruction of civilization."[36]

But the charge of treason is bogus. As bogus as Nazi justice and Roland Freisler's claim to be an honorable judge.

Nazi Germany forfeited its rights to be considered a legal state: Therefore the actions of the people in the pages of this book were resistance, not treason. They acted with tremendous courage, knowing the odds were stacked against them. They showed no personal ambition, only hopes for their nation and for humanity. Many represented the very antithesis of blinkered nationalism, knowing they were committing high treason as they sought a better outcome for all.

As Hans Oster told the Dutch officer to whom he had revealed the plans of Hitler's invasion of Western Europe: "People may well say that I am a traitor but in reality I am not. I regard myself as a better German than all those who are trotting along behind Hitler. It is both my purpose and my duty to liberate Germany, and with her the world, from this plague."[37]

Hitler had begun a vast war of conquest that Oster and others felt would ultimately result in Germany's destruction: Oster's purpose was not to destroy his country but to save it.

And in the end, while they could not save their nation, they did ensure that, as Germany sought to find itself again, it could cling to a spirit of goodness and purity: a resistance, an opposition, a White Rose.

As Henning von Tresckow, a leading spirit in the movement to remove Hitler and the man who inspired Stauffenberg, said, "We must prove to the world and to future generations that the men of the German Resistance movement dared to take the decisive step and to hazard their lives upon it. Compared with this, nothing else matters."

# AUTHOR'S NOTE

Gordon Thomas was drawn to the subject of the anti-Nazi resistance by his wife, Edith. Edith is German-born and related to one of the earliest opponents of the Nazi regime, Herbert von Bose, who was assassinated on Hitler's orders in 1934. For some time they had discussed how they might be able to bring together the stories of the various elements of German society that opposed the Nazis.

I had known Gordon Thomas for many years as a friend and had followed his career with admiration. I began working with him on his previous book, *Shadow Warriors*, helping him to complete that manuscript when he fell ill. With his good wishes, I then took on this book.

Gordon died in March 2017. On a professional level it is very sad that Gordon did not live to see this book's completion. On a personal level he is a much-missed friend.

—Greg Lewis

# ACKNOWLEDGMENTS

There are a number of people to thank: (in the UK) Edith Thomas, for her support, friendship, and work on German translations; (in Ireland) Mary Sharkey; (in Belgium) Marie Cappart, a researcher in French and Dutch; (in France) Myrfyn Jones; (in the UK) Len Mullins, Phil Nifield, Pete Nash, Will Davies, Dinah Jones, Caroline Lynch-Blosse, Peter Dennis, and my brother Mark Lewis, who is an expert at searching old bookshops for me; the staff of the many archives and museums who have helped me and are listed in the pages of the bibliography, in particular the Gedenkstätte Deutscher Widerstand (German Resistance Memorial Center) in Berlin. Professor Dr. Johannes Tuchel and Susanne Brömel deserve extra thanks for their help in sourcing photographs. Every reasonable effort has been made to identify the copyright owners of all the photographs. Any errors are accidental and will be corrected in future editions upon advice to the publisher.

Thanks also to my agent, Don Fehr, and to his assistant Heather Carr, at Trident Media Group; and to my editor, Brent Howard, and his colleagues John Parsley and Cassidy Sachs at Dutton, who got behind the project from the beginning.

As I researched this book, it struck me that Kurt Gerstein's story would be the most difficult to tell. He was both witness and participator in the Holocaust. The work of Professor Deborah E. Lipstadt and her colleagues at the Holocaust Denial on Trial website helped persuade me I had to find a way to do it. One unfortunate consequence of the internet has been the resurgence of those who wish to deny that the Holocaust ever happened. Gerstein has become a key target for those seeking to undermine the truth about the deaths of well over a million people during Operation Reinhard. True, he got some details wrong, especially when relying on information given to him by others, but as Professor Lipstadt notes: "The testimony of German perpetrators and Jewish survivors corroborates Gerstein's account on all the major points of the process and method of mass murder in the Operation Reinhard death camps of Treblinka and Belzec." Read, for instance, *Holocaust Journey* by Martin Gilbert for further witness testimonies. The idea that there were not gas chambers at Treblinka and Belzec is simply a rewriting of history and an insult to the dead. We all have a responsibility to stand up to it.

Special thanks to my wife, Moira, and children, Evan and Caoimhe, who are both under ten and just learning about World War II. As I immersed myself in the study of a regime that sought to legalize and normalize racial hatred, violence, torture, and oppression, their regular visits to my attic office served as a reminder of how beautiful life is.

Greg Lewis, UK, 2018

# BIBLIOGRAPHY

## ARCHIVES, MUSEUMS, AND WEBSITES

Bundesarchiv Berlin (formerly Berlin Document Center).

Bundesarchiv Koblenz.

Dokumentation Obersalzberg, run by the Institute for Contemporary History, Munich (www.obersalzberg.de).

Franklin D. Roosevelt Presidential Library (fdrlibrary.org).

Gedenkstätte Deutscher Widerstand (German Resistance Memorial Center), Berlin.

The Holocaust: Crimes, Heroes and Villains (auschwitz.dk).

Holocaust Denial on Trial (hdot.org).

Holocaust Education & Archive Research Team (holocaustresearchproject.org).

Jewish Women's Archive (jwa.org).

Orte jüdischen Lebens in Berlin, 1933–1945 (ojl.beuth-hochschule.de).

Seeley G. Mudd Manuscript Library, Princeton, New Jersey: Allen W. Dulles Papers.

Traces of Evil: Remaining Nazi Sites in Germany (tracesofevil.com).

United States Holocaust Memorial Museum, Washington, DC.

White Rose History: January 1933–October 1943 (whiterosehistory.com), which includes English versions of the White Rose Gestapo files for those unable to visit the Bundesarchiv.

Yad Vashem, the World Holocaust Memorial Center, Israel.

## TESTIMONIES AND DOCUMENTS

Charlotte Holzer testimony (item number 3549543), Yad Vashem. Testimony given in East Berlin, 1964.

Rita Zocher testimony (item number 3558251), Yad Vashem.

White Rose Gestapo interrogations.

White Rose execution records.

White Rose investigation files.


## BOOKS

Alvarez, David. *Spies in the Vatican.* Lawrence: University Press of Kansas, 2002.

Andreas-Friedrich, Ruth. *Berlin Underground, 1938–1945.* New York: Henry Holt & Co., 1947.

Axelrod, Toby. *Hans and Sophie Scholl.* New York: Rosen Publishing Group, 2001.

Bauer, Yehuda. *Jews for Sale?* New Haven, CT: Yale University Press, 2009.

Beevor, Antony. *The Second World War.* London: Weidenfeld & Nicolson, 2012.

Best, Captain S. Payne. *The Venlo Incident.* New York: Skyhorse Publishing, 2016.

Bethge, Eberhard. *Bonhoeffer: An Illustrated Biography.* London: HarperCollins, 1979.

Boeselager, Philipp von. *Valkyrie: The Plot to Kill Hitler.* London: Weidenfeld & Nicolson, 2009.

Bonhoeffer, Dietrich. *Dietrich Bonhoeffer: Works,* Vol. 13, *London, 1933–1935.* Edited by Keith Clements. New York: Fortress Press, 2007.

———. *A Testament to Freedom: The Essential Writings of Dietrich Bonhoeffer.* Edited by Geffrey B. Kelly and F. Burton Nelson. New York: Harper One, 1995.

Bonhoeffer, Dietrich, and Maria von Wedemeyer. *Love Letters from Cell 92: The Correspondence Between Dietrich Bonhoeffer and Maria von Wedemeyer, 1943–45.* Edited by Ruth-Alice von Bismarck and Ulrich Kabitz. New York: Abingdon Press, 1995.

Borkin, Joseph. *The Crime and Punishment of I. G. Farben.* London: André Deutsch, 1979.

Boveri, Margret. *Treason in the Twentieth Century.* London: Macdonald & Co., 1961.

Breitman, Richard. *Official Secrets: What the Nazis Planned, What the British and Americans Knew.* London: Penguin Group, 1998.

Breitman, Richard, Norman J. W. Goda, Timothy Naftali, and Robert Wolfe. *U.S. Intelligence and the Nazis.* New York: Cambridge University Press, 2005.

Brothers, Eric. *Berlin Ghetto.* Gloucestershire, UK: Spellmount, 2012.

Brysac, Shareen Blair. *Resisting Hitler: Mildred Harnack and the Red Orchestra.* New York: Oxford University Press, 2000.

Carr, William. *A History of Germany, 1815–1990.* London: Edward Arnold, 1969.

Chadwick, Owen. *Britain and the Vatican during the Second World War.* Cambridge University Press, 1986.

Chandler, Andrew. *George Bell, Bishop of Chichester.* Grand Rapids, MI: William B. Eerdmans Publishing Company, 2016.

Collier, Martin, and Philip Pedley. *Germany 1939–45*. Oxford: Heinemann, 2000.

Coppi, Hans. *Harro Schulze-Boysen—Wege in den Widerstand: Eine biographische Studie*. Koblenz: Fölbach, 1993.

Cox, John. "The Herbert Baum Groups." In *The Human Tradition in Modern Europe, 1750 to the Present*. Edited by Cora Granata and Cheryl A. Koos. Lanham, MD: Rowman & Littlefield, 2007.

Dalin, Rabbi David G. *The Myth of Hitler's Pope*. Washington, DC: Regnery Publishing, 2005.

Dallin, David J. *Soviet Espionage*. New Haven, CT: Yale University Press, 1955.

Delattre, Lucas. *Betraying Hitler*. London: Atlantic Books, 2005.

Dodd, Martha. *Through Embassy Eyes*. New York: Harcourt, Brace, 1939.

Dodd, William. *Ambassador Dodd's Diary, 1933–1938*. Edited by William E. Dodd Jr. and Martha Dodd. London: Victor Gollancz, 1941.

Dumbach, Annette, and Jud Newborn. *Sophie Scholl and the White Rose*. Oxford: Oneworld, 2007. First published in the US in 1986 as *Shattering the German Night*.

Engelmann, Bernt. *In Hitler's Germany*. London: Methuen, 1989.

Fest, Joachim C. *Hitler*. London: Weidenfeld & Nicolson, 1974.

Flannery, Henry. *Assignment to Berlin*. London: Michael Joseph Ltd., 1942.

Franz, Helmut. *Kurt Gerstein*. Zurich: ABC-Verlag, 1964.

Friedländer, Saul. *Counterfeit Nazi*. London: Weidenfeld & Nicolson, 1969.

Galante, Pierre. *Hitler Lives—and the Generals Die*. London: Sidgwick & Jackson, 1982.

Gilbert, Martin. *Atlas of the Holocaust*. London: Michael Joseph Ltd., 1982.

Gisevius, Hans Bernd. *Valkyrie: An Insider's Account of the Plot to Kill Hitler*. Boston: Da Capo Press, 2009.

Goebbels, Joseph. *Die Tagebücher von Joseph Goebbels*. Edited by Elke Fröhlich. Munich: KG Saur, 1995.

Goerlitz, Walter. *History of the German General Staff, 1657–1945*. New York: Praeger Publishers, 1953.

Gross, Leonard. *The Last Jews in Berlin*. New York: Carroll & Graf Publishers, 1992.

Haecker, Theodor. *Journal in the Night*. New York: Harvill Press, 1950.

Hanser, Richard. *A Noble Treason*. New York: G. P. Putnam's Sons, 1979.

Hassell, Ulrich von. *The Ulrich von Hassell Diaries*. Barnsley, UK: Frontline Books, 2010.

Heiber, Helmut. *Goebbels*. New York: Hawthorn Books, 1972.

Herzstein, Robert Edwin. *The War That Hitler Won*. London: Hamish Hamilton, 1978.

Hoch, Anton, and Lothar Gruchmann. *Georg Elser: Der Attentäter aus dem Volke*. Frankfurt am Main: Fischer Taschenbuch Verlag, 1980.

Hoffmann, Peter. *The History of the German Resistance, 1933–1945.* Cambridge, MA: MIT Press, 1977.

Höhne, Heinz. *Canaris.* London: Secker and Warburg, 1979.

———. *Codeword: Direktor.* New York: Ballantine Books, 1982.

Hull, David Stewart. *Film in the Third Reich.* Berkeley: University of California Press, 1969.

Joffroy, Pierre. *A Spy for God.* London: William Collins & Sons, 1971.

Kaplan, Marion. *Between Dignity and Despair: Jewish Life in Nazi Germany.* Oxford University Press, 1998.

Kershaw, Ian. *Hitler.* London: Penguin Books, 1998.

———. *Popular Opinion and Political Dissent in the Third Reich.* Oxford: Clarendon Press, 1983.

Knopp, Guido. *The SS: A Warning from History.* Stroud, UK: Sutton Publishing, 2003.

Kopleck, Maik. *Berlin 1933–1945.* Berlin: Links Christoph Verlag, 2004.

Kuckhoff, Greta. *Vom Rosenkranz zur Roten Kapelle.* Berlin: Verlag Neues Leben, 1974.

Larson, Erik. *In the Garden of Beasts.* London: Transworld, 2011.

Lifton, Robert Jay. *The Nazi Doctors.* New York: Basic Books, 1986.

MacDonogh, Giles. *A Good German: Adam von Trott zu Solz.* London: Quartet Books, 1989.

Manvell, Roger. *The Conspirators 20th July 1944.* New York: Ballantine Books, 1971.

Mark, Ber. "The Herbert Baum Group." In *They Fought Back*, edited by Yuri Suhl. New York: Crown Publishers, 1967.

McDonough, Frank. *The Gestapo.* London: Coronet, 2015.

———. *Sophie Scholl.* Stroud, UK: History Press, 2009.

Metaxas, Eric. *Bonhoeffer: Pastor, Martyr, Prophet, Spy.* Nashville: Thomas Nelson, 2010.

Moaz, Eliyahu. *A Jewish Underground in Germany.* World Zionist Organisation, 1965.

Moltke, Freya von. *Memories of Kreisau and the German Resistance.* Lincoln: University of Nebraska Press, 2003.

Mommsen, Hans. *Germans Against Hitler.* New York: IB Taurus & Co., 2003.

Moorhouse, Roger. *Berlin at War.* London: Bodley Head, 2010.

———. *Killing Hitler.* London: Vintage Books, 2007.

Müller, Ingo. *Hitler's Justice: The Courts of the Reich.* Cambridge, MA: Harvard University Press, 1992.

Murphy, David E. *What Stalin Knew.* New Haven, CT: Yale University Press, 2006.

Nelson, Anne. *Red Orchestra.* New York: Random House, 2009.

Ottaway, Susan. *Hitler's Traitors.* Barnsley, UK: Leo Cooper, 2003.

Parssinen, Terry. *The Oster Conspiracy of 1938.* London: Pimlico, 2003.

Pateman, Colin. *Beheaded by Hitler.* Stroud, UK: Fonthill, 2014.

Perrault, Giles. *The Red Orchestra.* London: Mayflower, 1970.

Persico, Joseph. *Piercing the Reich.* London: Sphere Books Ltd., 1980.

Peukert, Detlev J. K. *Inside Nazi Germany.* London: Penguin Books, 1989.

Rappaport, Doreen. *Beyond Courage.* Somerville, MA: Candlewick Press, 2012.

Rauschning, Hermann. *Hitler Speaks.* London: Thornton Butterworth, 1939.

Read, Anthony, and David Fisher. *Berlin: The Biography of a City.* London: Hutchinson, 1994.

Rees, Laurence. *Auschwitz: The Nazis & the 'Final Solution.'* London: BBC Books, 2005.

Ribbe, Wolfgang, and Wolfgang Schäche. *Die Siemensstadt.* Berlin: Geschichte und Architektur eines Industriestandortes, 1985.

Roberts, Andrew. *Hitler & Churchill: Secrets of Leadership.* London: Weidenfeld & Nicolson, 2003.

Roon, Ger van. *German Resistance to Hitler: Count von Moltke and the Kreisau Circle.* London: Van Nostrand Reinhold Company, 1971.

Roseman, Mark. *The Villa, the Lake, the Meeting.* London: Penguin Books, 2003.

Russell, William. *Berlin Embassy.* New York: E. P. Dutton, 1941.

Rychlak, Ronald J. *Hitler, the War, and the Pope.* Huntington, IN: Our Sunday Visitor, 2000.

Schellenberg, Walter. *The Memoirs of Hitler's Spymaster.* London: André Deutsch, 2006.

Scholl, Inge. *The White Rose: Munich 1942–1943.* Middletown, CT: Wesleyan University Press, 1983.

Schwab, Gerald. *The Day the Holocaust Began.* New York: Praeger, 1990.

Self, Robert. *Neville Chamberlain.* London: Routledge, 2006.

Shirer, William. *Berlin Diary.* New York: Galahad Books, 1995.

Snyder, Louis L. *Encyclopedia of the Third Reich.* Hertfordshire, UK: Wordsworth Editions, 1998.

Speer, Albert. *Inside the Third Reich.* New York: Macmillan, 1970.

Srodes, James. *Allen Dulles: Master of Spies.* Washington, DC: Regnery Publishing, 1999.

Stargardt, Nicholas. *The German War.* London: Vintage, 2015.

Stein, Harry. *Buchenwald Concentration Camp 1937–1945: A Guide to the Permanent Historical Exhibition.* Wallstein Verlag, 2004.

Steinhoff, Johannes, Peter Pechel, and Dennis Showalter. *Voices from the Third Reich.* Boston: Da Capo Press, 1994.

Taylor, Telford. *Munich: The Price of Peace.* New York: Doubleday & Company, 1979.

Vinke, Hermann. *The Short Life of Sophie Scholl.* New York: Harper & Row, 1984.

Visser 't Hooft, Willem. *Memoirs.* Geneva: WCC Publications, 1973.

Waller, John. *The Unseen War in Europe.* New York: Random House, 1996.

Weisbord, Robert G., and Wallace P. Sillanpoa. *The Chief Rabbi, the Pope, and the Holocaust*. Livingston, NJ: Transaction Publishers, 1992.

Werth, Alexander. *Russia at War, 1941–1945*. London: Pan, 1964.

Wiemers, Gerald, ed. *Ein Stück Wirklichkeit mehr. Zum 25. Jahrestag der Ermordung von Adam Kuckhoff*. East Berlin: Deutsche Akademie der Künste zu Berlin, 1968.

Wind, Renate. *A Spoke in the Wheel: The Life of Dietrich Bonhoeffer*. London: SCM Press, 1991.

## MAGAZINE AND NEWSPAPER ARTICLES

Bradsher, Greg. "A Time to Act." *Prologue* (US National Archives), Spring 2002.

"Doctor W. E. Dodd Dies." *New York Times*, February 10, 1940.

"Donald R. Heath, 87; Served as a U.S. Envoy." *New York Times*, October 17, 1981.

Eley, Geoff. "Hitler's Silent Majority? Conformity and Resistance Under the Third Reich (Part One)." *Michigan Quarterly Review*, Spring 2003.

Hall, Allan. "Nazis slaughtered my brother and sister with a guillotine." *Daily Mail*, January 18, 2014.

"It Happened Here: The Venlo Incident." *After the Battle* 11 (1976).

Jones, Nigel. "Claus von Stauffenberg: the true story behind the film Valkyrie, starring Tom Cruise." *Telegraph*, August 17, 2008. www.telegraph.co.uk/culture /film/3558716/Claus-von-Stauffenberg-the-true-story-behind-the-film -Valkyrie-starring-Tom-Cruise.html.

"Le dossier Gerstein." *Le Monde juif*, 1964.

McDowell, Edwin. "Donald S. Klopfer dies at 84; co-founder of Random House." *New York Times*, May 31, 1986.

"Nations farther apart than ever, says ex-envoy Dodd." *Los Angeles Times*, December 23, 1937.

vanden Heuvel, Katrina. "Grand Illusions." *Vanity Fair*, August 1991.

## TELEVISION DOCUMENTARIES

*History File Nazi Germany: Opposition to Hitler* (BBC, 2000).

*Wisconsin's Nazi Resistance: The Mildred Fish-Harnack Story* (WPT, 2011).

*The Red Orchestra* (Stefan Roloff, When 6 is 9 Productions, 2003).

## ONLINE ARTICLES

"American Nazi organization rally at Madison Square Garden, 1939." Rare Historical Photos, February 19, 2014. rarehistoricalphotos.com/american-nazi-organi zation-rally-madison-square-garden-1939/.

Appelbaum, Barbara. "Ellen and Erich Arndt." Rochester Holocaust Survivors Archive. www.rochesterholocaustsurvivors.org/individual%20Resource%20Folders /Arndt%20Erich%20and%20Ellen/Arndt%20Eric%20and%20Ellen.html.

Harrison, Jonathan, Roberto Muehlenkamp, Jason Myers, Sergey Romanov, and Nicholas Terry. "Belzec, Sobibor, Treblinka: Holocaust Denial and Operation Reinhard. A Critique of the Falsehoods of Mattogno, Graf and Kues." Holocaust Controversies, December 2011. holocaustcontroversies.blogspot.co.uk /2011/12/belzec-sobibor-treblinka-holocaust.html.

Marcuse, Harold. "George Jürgen Wittenstein: A Resistant German's Journey from Beilstein Castle to Santa Barbara." UC Santa Barbara, updated September 27, 2015. www.history.ucsb.edu/faculty/marcuse/projects/whiterose/George Wittenstein.htm.

Smilovitsky, Leonid. "Ilya Ehrenburg on the Holocaust in Belarus." Belarus SIG, October 2002. First published in *East European Jewish Affairs* (London), Summer-Winter 1999. www.jewishgen.org/Belarus/newsletters/misc/IlyaEhren burg/index.html.

"The Soviet Famine of 1931–33: Politically Motivated or Ecological Disaster?" UCLA Asia Pacific Center, May 5, 2003. www.international.ucla.edu/asia /article/3838.

## BOOKLETS

Deutschkron, Inge. *We Survived: Berlin Jews Underground.* Berlin: Gedenkstätte Deutscher Widerstand, 2015.

*The White Rose, Exhibition on the Student Resistance Against Hitler.* Munich: Weisse Rose Stiftung, 2006.

# NOTES

The opening quote, "There are times when madness reigns / And then it is the best who hang," is taken from Albrecht Haushofer's *Moabit Sonnets*. Incarcerated in Berlin's Moabit prison after the July 20 bomb plot, Haushofer, who had known many members of the resistance, from people in the Kreisau Circle to Arvid Harnack and Harro Schulze-Boysen, wrote a series of poems later published as *Moabit Sonnets*. Haushofer was executed by the Nazis a few days before the end of the war in Europe. The poem from which the epigraph is taken is featured on the website Dokumentation Obersalzberg (obersalzberg .de/en/exhibition/widerstand/), which is run by the Institute for Contemporary History, Munich. The lines were translated by Frank Gillard.

## INTRODUCTION

1. Anne Nelson, *Red Orchestra* (New York: Random House, 2009).
2. Terry Parssinen, *The Oster Conspiracy of 1938* (London: Pimlico, 2003).
3. Eric Metaxas, *Bonhoeffer: Pastor, Martyr, Prophet, Spy* (Nashville: Thomas Nelson, 2010).
4. Albert Speer, *Inside the Third Reich* (New York: Macmillan, 1970).

## CHAPTER 1: Meetings in Madison

1. Shareen Blair Brysac, *Resisting Hitler: Mildred Harnack and the Red Orchestra* (New York: Oxford University Press, 2000).
2. Ibid.
3. Margret Boveri, *Treason in the Twentieth Century* (London: Macdonald & Co., 1961).
4. Harnack later wrote on his work résumé that Commons had "decisively influenced me." Brysac, *Resisting Hitler*.
5. Brysac, *Resisting Hitler*.
6. Mildred Fish-Harnack to Bob Fish, November 6, 1931, Clara Leiser Collection. Brysac, *Resisting Hitler*.
7. Mildred Fish-Harnack to Georgina Fish, October 18, 1930. Brysac, *Resisting Hitler*.

8. In the summer of 1929, approximately nine hundred thousand were out of work in Germany. By December 1930, it was three million; by July 1931, it was five and a half million; and by the beginning of 1932, more than six million. William Carr, *A History of Germany, 1815–1990* (London: Edward Arnold, 1969).

9. Franz Josef Müller, a member of the German resistance and later the director of the White Rose Foundation in Munich, stated: "A German communist is not exactly the same as a Russian communist. It's very different. How communistic is a German communist? Or a French communist? You cannot compare them with Stalinists. The old German communists were idealists. In the GDR, after they got money, that was something else. But after '33, most of the German resisters who were killed were communists." Brysac, *Resisting Hitler*.

10. Some believe that the famine was a deliberate act of genocide by Stalin to quell Ukrainian nationalism. Stephen Wheatcroft, professor of history, University of Melbourne, Australia, carried out a major study of the causes of the famine and the number of people who died. Speaking to the Center for European and Eurasian Studies at UCLA in May 2003, he stated the famine of 1931–1933 was caused neither "entirely" by design nor by accident. He argued that the famine was an accidental consequence of ill-conceived policies, and that Ukraine suffered inordinately for demographic reasons. UCLA reported, "On the basis of substantial analysis of Soviet registration documents and mortality statistics, Wheatcroft concluded that the estimates of the human losses have been grossly exaggerated. In his view, the number of deaths due to the famine should be more accurately reported at around 4.5 million. A number, he was careful to point out, which represents a horrendous human tragedy. But a tragedy at 4.5 million people is not any greater tragedy if the number is inflated to 7 million or more." "The Soviet Famine of 1931–33: Politically Motivated or Ecological Disaster?" UCLA Asia Pacific Center, May 5, 2003, international.ucla.edu/asia/article/3838.

11. Brysac, *Resisting Hitler*.

## CHAPTER 2: Enemies of the People

1. Ian Kershaw, *Hitler* (London: Penguin Books, 1998).
2. Martin Collier and Philip Pedley, *Germany 1939–45* (Oxford: Heinemann, 2000).
3. Kershaw, *Hitler*.
4. Brysac, *Resisting Hitler*.
5. Nelson, *Red Orchestra*.
6. Roger Moorhouse, *Berlin at War* (London: Bodley Head, 2010).
7. Susan Ottaway, *Hitler's Traitors* (Barnsley, UK: Leo Cooper, 2003).
8. In testimony at the Nuremberg war trials, General Franz Halder said that Göring had told him: "The only one who really knows about the Reichstag fire is me, because I set it on fire." Frank McDonough, *The Gestapo* (London: Coronet, 2015).
9. Ottaway, *Hitler's Traitors*.
10. Kershaw, *Hitler*.
11. McDonough, *The Gestapo*.
12. Heine's words are now part of a memorial on Bebelplatz, off the Unter den Linden, in Berlin, Germany. The quote is from his play *Almansor*, written between 1821 and 1822, and referred originally to the burning of the Koran in Granada during the 1500s.
13. Kershaw, *Hitler*.

14. Ian Kershaw, *Popular Opinion and Political Dissent in the Third Reich* (Oxford: Clarendon Press, 1983).
15. According to a decree issued by Göring on July 6, 1934, and ratified by Hitler on July 20.

## CHAPTER 3: The American Embassy

1. William Dodd, *Ambassador Dodd's Diary, 1933–1938*, eds. William E. Dodd Jr. and Martha Dodd (London: Victor Gollancz, 1941).
2. "Doctor W. E. Dodd Dies," *New York Times*, February 10, 1940.
3. Erik Larson, *In the Garden of Beasts* (London: Transworld, 2011).
4. The site of the future permanent home for the US embassy at Pariser Platz, right next to the Brandenburg Gate, had been damaged by fire in 1931 and was not yet in use.
5. David Stewart Hull, *Film in the Third Reich* (Berkeley: University of California Press, 1969).
6. Anthony Read and David Fisher, *Berlin: The Biography of a City* (London: Hutchinson, 1994).
7. Martha Dodd, *Through Embassy Eyes* (New York: Harcourt, Brace, 1939).
8. Ibid.
9. Katrina vanden Heuvel, "Grand Illusions," *Vanity Fair*, August 1991.
10. Diary entry dated July 28, 1933. *Ambassador Dodd's Diary*.
11. Larson, *In the Garden of Beasts*.
12. McDonough, *The Gestapo*.
13. Diary entry dated July 5, 1934. *Ambassador Dodd's Diary*.
14. Boveri, *Treason in the Twentieth Century*.
15. Brysac, *Resisting Hitler*.
16. Larson, *In the Garden of Beasts*.
17. Brysac, *Resisting Hitler*.
18. Larson, *In the Garden of Beasts*. The name is sometimes written as "Vinogradov."
19. Brysac, *Resisting Hitler*.
20. Edwin McDowell, "Donald S. Klopfer dies at 84; co-founder of Random House," *New York Times*, May 31, 1986.
21. The translation was published in 1936.
22. Kershaw, *Hitler*.
23. An impediment to Milch's career in the Nazi hierarchy might have been the fact that his mother was Jewish. Göring—who was keen to keep his friend—had her sign a legal affidavit stating that Milch was his father's illegitimate offspring and not her son at all. Milch eventually rose to be a general field marshal of the Luftwaffe. Louis L. Snyder, *Encyclopedia of the Third Reich* (Hertfordshire, UK: Wordsworth Editions, 1998).
24. Individuals in Germany did monitor and report on this rearmament program. Plötzensee Memorial Center tells the story of Berlin-born Communist Liselotte Herrmann, who had been expelled from the University of Berlin by the Nazis. Through Communist friends who had also gone underground, she learned about the production of armaments in the Dornier plant in Friedrichshafen and about the construction of an underground munitions factory near Celle—information she passed on to a member of the German Communist Party who was in exile in Switzerland. Arrested in December 1935, Herrmann spent nineteen months awaiting

trial before being sentenced to death for "treason and acts preparatory to high treason" in 1937. She was executed in June 1938, along with three friends who had helped her—Stefan Lovasz, Josef Steidle, and Artur Göritz. Herrmann's young son was left to be brought up by his grandparents.

25. See Kershaw's *Hitler* for an excellent analysis of how Hitler's standing was "transcending purely party interest."
26. Brysac, *Resisting Hitler*.
27. Larson, *In the Garden of Beasts*.

## CHAPTER 4: The Battle for German Youth

1. Inge Scholl, *The White Rose: Munich 1942–1943* (Middletown, CT: Wesleyan University Press, 1983).
2. Annette Dumbach and Jud Newborn, *Sophie Scholl and the White Rose* (Oxford: Oneworld, 2007.)
3. Eric Brothers, *Berlin Ghetto* (Gloucestershire, UK: Spellmount, 2012).
4. "Cohn" is sometimes spelled "Cohen."
5. Leonard Gross, *The Last Jews in Berlin* (New York: Carroll & Graf Publishers, 1992).
6. Brothers, *Berlin Ghetto*.
7. John Cox, "The Herbert Baum Groups," in *The Human Tradition in Modern Europe, 1750 to the Present*, eds. Cora Granata and Cheryl A. Koos (Lanham, MD: Rowman & Littlefield, 2007).
8. Testimony of Herbert Ansbach. Quoted in Brothers, *Berlin Ghetto*.
9. Cox, "The Herbert Baum Groups."
10. Brothers, *Berlin Ghetto*.
11. Detlev J. K. Peukert, *Inside Nazi Germany* (London: Penguin Books, 1989).
12. Ibid.
13. Frank McDonough, *Sophie Scholl* (Stroud, UK: History Press, 2009).
14. Brothers, *Berlin Ghetto*.
15. Richard Hanser, *A Noble Treason* (New York: G. P. Putnam's Sons, 1979).
16. Reden was found guilty of having a homosexual relationship with a teenager and was given a three-month prison sentence.
17. McDonough, *Sophie Scholl*.
18. Ibid.

## CHAPTER 5: The Moscow Connection

1. Harnack's Moscow file recorded that Hirschfeld had tried to persuade Harnack that by "going underground, he could achieve far more in the struggle against Hitler." Brysac, *Resisting Hitler*.
2. *The Ulrich von Hassell Diaries* (Barnsley, UK: Frontline Books, 2010).
3. Brysac, *Resisting Hitler*.
4. William Dodd to Douglas MacArthur, August 27, 1934. Larson, *In the Garden of Beasts*.
5. Brysac, *Resisting Hitler*.
6. Ibid.
7. Ibid.
8. The German American Bund's popularity peaked around a rally that it held in Madison Square Garden in February 1939 and that it claimed was attended by

more than twenty thousand supporters. Dressed in his own brand of Nazi uniform, leader Fritz Julius Kuhn addressed the crowd from a stage decked with a massive portrait of George Washington—whom he considered "the first Fascist"—as well as swastikas and American flags. He attacked President Roosevelt for being part of a Bolshevik-Jewish conspiracy, dismissing him as "Frank D. Rosenfeld" and calling the New Deal "the Jew Deal." Following the rally, fights broke out among Kuhn's followers and protesters. Kuhn was later jailed for tax evasion and embezzlement, and the bund disintegrated following the attack on Pearl Harbor.

9. William C. Bullitt to Franklin D. Roosevelt, December 7, 1936. Larson, *In the Garden of Beasts*.
10. Diary entry dated June 4, 1937. *Ambassador Dodd's Diary*.
11. Diary entry dated June 5, 1937. *Ambassador Dodd's Diary*.
12. Larson, *In the Garden of Beasts*.
13. Diary entry dated August 11, 1937. *Ambassador Dodd's Diary*.
14. "Nations farther apart than ever, says ex-envoy Dodd," *Los Angeles Times*, December 23, 1937. William E. Dodd, the ambassador so affected by the horror and oppression of Nazi Germany, never recovered from the strain of his posting to Berlin and died in February 1940.
15. Martha Dodd never completely cut her ties to the Soviet Union. In 1956, after being accused of being a spy, she fled the United States. The charges were later dropped, but she chose to remain in exile in Prague.
16. Martha's lover Boris Winogradov, who was by now based in Warsaw, was also called home. He was tried on the same charges as Bessonov and executed.
17. Brysac, *Resisting Hitler*.

## CHAPTER 6: Hans Oster

1. Kershaw, *Hitler*.
2. Joachim C. Fest, *Hitler* (London: Weidenfeld & Nicolson, 1974).
3. Ibid.
4. Roger Moorhouse, *Killing Hitler* (London: Vintage Books, 2007).
5. Heinz Höhne, *Canaris* (London: Secker and Warburg, 1979).
6. Joseph Persico, *Piercing the Reich* (London: Sphere Books Ltd., 1980).
7. Höhne, *Canaris*.
8. Metaxas, *Bonhoeffer*.
9. Moorhouse, *Killing Hitler*.
10. Peter Hoffmann, *The History of the German Resistance, 1933–1945* (Cambridge, MA: MIT Press, 1977).
11. Parssinen, *The Oster Conspiracy*.
12. Ibid.
13. Telford Taylor, *Munich: The Price of Peace* (New York: Doubleday & Company, 1979).
14. Parssinen, *The Oster Conspiracy*.
15. Hoffmann, *The History of the German Resistance*.
16. Ibid.
17. Parssinen, *The Oster Conspiracy*.
18. Ibid.
19. Ibid.
20. Ibid.
21. Roger Manvell, *The Conspirators 20th July 1944* (New York: Ballantine Books, 1971).

22. Parssinen, *The Oster Conspiracy*.
23. Taylor, *Munich*.
24. Ibid.
25. Ibid.
26. Oster had also sent his friend Lieutenant-Colonel Hans Böhm-Tettelbach, a retired army officer, to London, but his contacts were not well enough connected to make any impact on the cabinet.
27. Taylor, *Munich*.
28. Ibid.
29. The literal translation is "I have fallen from heaven," and the phrase is used to express astonishment. It was a favorite phrase of Hitler's.

## CHAPTER 7: Munich

1. Public Record Office, London, cabinet paper ref: PRO CAB 23/95/32–61. Quoted in Parssinen, *The Oster Conspiracy*.
2. Robert Self, *Neville Chamberlain* (London: Routledge, 2006).
3. Chamberlain's letter to his sister Ida, written a few days later, and quoted in Taylor, *Munich*.
4. Taylor, *Munich*.
5. Parssinen, *The Oster Conspiracy*.
6. Taylor, *Munich*.
7. Parssinen, *The Oster Conspiracy*.
8. Metaxas, *Bonhoeffer*.
9. Parssinen, *The Oster Conspiracy*.
10. Taylor, *Munich*.
11. Public Record Office, London, cabinet paper ref: PRO CAB 23/95/234–45. Quoted in Parssinen, *The Oster Conspiracy*.
12. Parssinen, *The Oster Conspiracy*.
13. Nicholas Stargardt, *The German War* (London: Vintage, 2015).
14. Diary entry dated September 26, 1938. William Shirer, *Berlin Diary* (New York: Galahad Books, 1995).
15. Diary entry dated September 27, 1938. Shirer, *Berlin Diary*.
16. Taylor, *Munich*.
17. Hans Bernd Gisevius, *Valkyrie: An Insider's Account of the Plot to Kill Hitler* (Boston: Da Capo Press, 2009).

## CHAPTER 8: America's Spy

1. Larson, *In the Garden of Beasts*. Wilson's posting to Berlin was a short one: He was withdrawn by Roosevelt after Kristallnacht.
2. Nelson, *Red Orchestra*.
3. Donald Heath to Henry Morgenthau, May 2, 1939, Morgenthau papers, Franklin D. Roosevelt Presidential Library, Hyde Park.
4. Nelson, *Red Orchestra*.
5. Giles MacDonogh, *A Good German: Adam von Trott zu Solz* (London: Quartet Books, 1989).
6. Report by George Kennan. Nelson, *Red Orchestra*.
7. Nelson, *Red Orchestra*.

8. Quoted in Nelson, *Red Orchestra*.

9. Donald Heath to Henry Morgenthau, May 2, 1939, Morgenthau papers, Franklin D. Roosevelt Presidential Library, Hyde Park.

## CHAPTER 9: Kristallnacht

1. Kershaw, *Hitler*.
2. Ibid.
3. Gerald Schwab, *The Day the Holocaust Began* (New York: Praeger, 1990).
4. Traces of Evil (tracesofevil.com).
5. Hanser, *A Noble Treason*.
6. I. Scholl, *The White Rose*.
7. Brothers, *Berlin Ghetto*.
8. Cox, "The Herbert Baum Groups."
9. *Dietrich Bonhoeffer Works, Vol. 13, London, 1933–1935*, ed. Keith Clements (New York: Fortress Press, 2007).
10. Metaxas, *Bonhoeffer*.
11. Many decades after his death in 1958, an allegation was made that Bell had abused a young girl during the 1940s and 1950s. The police concluded that there was sufficient evidence to have arrested Bell had he been alive, and in 2015 compensation was paid to the victim. Bell's supporters waged a furious campaign on his behalf, as he was a man of such high reputation. The victim noted: "Because he did good things, they automatically assume that he couldn't do anything wrong, which was rather hurtful because a lot of men who have done good things have also done very evil things." The way the Church of England handled the case was the subject of review by a leading barrister at the time this book was being prepared.
12. Doreen Rappaport, *Beyond Courage* (Somerville, MA: Candlewick Press, 2012).
13. Brothers, *Berlin Ghetto*.

## CHAPTER 10: A Summer Ends in War

1. Dietrich Bonhoeffer, *A Testament to Freedom: The Essential Writings of Dietrich Bonhoeffer*, eds. Geffrey B. Kelly and F. Burton Nelson (New York: Harper One, 1995).
2. Kershaw, *Hitler*.
3. Ibid.
4. Diary entry dated March 15, 1939. Shirer, *Berlin Diary*.
5. The words of French foreign minister Georges Bonnet. Quoted in Taylor, *Munich*.
6. Kershaw, *Hitler*.
7. The words were spoken by diplomat Ernst von Weizsäcker to G. A. Astakhov, the Soviet chargé d'affaires in Berlin, on May 30, 1939. Quoted in Alexander Werth, *Russia at War, 1941–1945* (London: Pan, 1964).
8. Antony Beevor, *The Second World War* (London: Weidenfeld & Nicolson, 2012).
9. Bonhoeffer, *A Testament to Freedom*.
10. Willem Visser 't Hooft, *Memoirs* (Geneva: WCC Publications, 1973).
11. Kershaw, *Hitler*.
12. Sophie Scholl to Fritz Hartnagel, September 5, 1939.
13. Beevor, *The Second World War*.
14. Diary entry dated October 15, 1939. Shirer, *Berlin Diary*.

15. Ruth Andreas-Friedrich, *Berlin Underground, 1938–1945* (New York: Henry Holt & Co., 1947).
16. William Russell, *Berlin Embassy* (New York: E. P. Dutton, 1941).
17. Sophie Scholl to Fritz Hartnagel, October 5, 1939.
18. Fest, *Hitler*.
19. Höhne, *Canaris*.
20. Ibid.
21. Ibid.
22. David Alvarez, *Spies in the Vatican* (Lawrence: University Press of Kansas, 2002).
23. Diary entry dated February 14–17, 1940. *The Ulrich von Hassell Diaries*.
24. Special note dated February 23, 1940. *The Ulrich von Hassell Diaries*.
25. Parssinen, *The Oster Conspiracy*.

## CHAPTER 11: Crossing the Rubicon

1. Gisevius, *Valkyrie: An Insider's Account*.
2. Parssinen, *The Oster Conspiracy*.
3. Moorhouse, *Killing Hitler*.
4. "It Happened Here: The Venlo Incident," *After the Battle* 11 (1976).
5. Stevens and Best were imprisoned in concentration camps but survived the war.
6. Moorhouse, *Killing Hitler*.
7. "The Venlo Incident," *After the Battle*.
8. *Völkischer Beobachter*, November 10, 1939.
9. Hoffmann, *The History of the German Resistance*.
10. Moorhouse, *Killing Hitler*. Erich Kordt remained an anti-Nazi but, after 1941, took no further part in any coup attempts, having been transferred to the German embassy in Tokyo.
11. Owen Chadwick, *Britain and the Vatican during the Second World War* (Cambridge University Press, 1986).
12. Chadwick, *Britain and the Vatican*.
13. The spy was actually a man named Kurtna. Chadwick, *Britain and the Vatican*.
14. Chadwick, *Britain and the Vatican*.
15. Ibid.
16. Höhne, *Canaris*.
17. Alvarez, *Spies in the Vatican*.
18. Höhne, *Canaris*.
19. Hoffmann, *The History of the German Resistance*.
20. At the time of Dunkirk the conspirators began to fear that if the Germans invaded Britain, the Nazis would uncover the plot from British records. Müller contacted Leiber at the Vatican and asked him to tell the British to destroy documents relating to the German resistance. Osborne did pass on this message. Investigations by the author Owen Chadwick were inconclusive as to the action the British took, although he found evidence to suggest certain items had been destroyed.
21. Höhne, *Canaris*.

## CHAPTER 12: The Luftwaffe Officer

1. Heinz Höhne, *Codeword: Direktor* (New York: Ballantine Books, 1982).
2. Ibid.

3. Brysac, *Resisting Hitler.*
4. Gisela von Pöllnitz died of tuberculosis in Switzerland in September 1939, days after World War II broke out.
5. Mexico was the only other nation to provide formal support for Spain's Republican Army, sending an estimated $2 million in aid, as well as arms, supplies, and a small number of aircraft.
6. David J. Dallin, *Soviet Espionage* (New Haven, CT: Yale University Press, 1955).
7. Nelson, *Red Orchestra.*
8. Werner Dissel did remain strong. During the war he joined the Wehrmacht and continued to provide Schulze-Boysen with information. He escaped arrest. After the war he became a well-known actor in Germany, featured in more than a hundred film and television productions. He died in 2003. Internet Movie Database (imdb.com).
9. Nelson, *Red Orchestra.*
10. Ibid.
11. Brysac, *Resisting Hitler.*

## CHAPTER 13: God's Witness

1. Guido Knopp, *The SS: A Warning from History* (Stroud, UK: Sutton Publishing, 2003).
2. Saul Friedländer, *Counterfeit Nazi* (London: Weidenfeld & Nicolson, 1969).
3. United States Holocaust Memorial Museum.
4. Friedländer, *Counterfeit Nazi.*
5. Helmut Franz, *Kurt Gerstein* (Zurich: ABC-Verlag, 1964).
6. Friedländer, *Counterfeit Nazi.*
7. Franz, *Kurt Gerstein.*
8. Report by Hitler Youth member August Hoppe to his local leader Kurt Thomas. Quoted in Friedländer, *Counterfeit Nazi.*
9. Friedländer, *Counterfeit Nazi.*
10. Ibid.
11. Pierre Joffroy, *A Spy for God* (London: William Collins & Sons, 1971).
12. Kurt Gerstein to the Supreme Court of the Nazi Party, January 25, 1937. Bundesarchiv.
13. Joffroy, *A Spy for God.*
14. Ludwig Gerstein to the Supreme Court of the Nazi Party, September 9, 1938. Bundesarchiv.
15. Kurt Gerstein to Ludwig Gerstein, November 26, 1938.
16. Joffroy, *A Spy for God.*
17. Eisenach employment office to the Wintershall company, September 18, 1940. Friedländer, *Counterfeit Nazi.*
18. Kershaw, *Hitler.*
19. Metaxas, *Bonhoeffer.*
20. Renate Wind, *A Spoke in the Wheel: The Life of Dietrich Bonhoeffer* (London: SCM Press, 1991).

## CHAPTER 14: Corsican Delivers

1. Stargardt, *The German War.*
2. The first figures refer to a raid on the night of October 7–8, 1940, which brought the highest death toll in Berlin of the war so far. Eight of the dead had been buried

when an air raid shelter collapsed. The workers died on the night of November 14–15. Moorhouse, *Berlin at War.*

3. Brysac, *Resisting Hitler.*
4. Ibid.
5. David E. Murphy, *What Stalin Knew* (New Haven, CT: Yale University Press, 2006).
6. Brysac, *Resisting Hitler.*
7. Greta Kuckhoff, *Vom Rosenkranz zur Roten Kapelle* (Berlin: Verlag Neues Leben, 1974).
8. Nelson, *Red Orchestra.*

## CHAPTER 15: Life Unworthy of Life

1. The quote was recalled by Hans Lammers and appears in Robert Jay Lifton, *The Nazi Doctors* (New York: Basic Books, 1986).
2. Lifton, *The Nazi Doctors.*
3. Ibid.
4. Joffroy, *A Spy for God.*
5. Lifton, *The Nazi Doctors.*
6. Ibid.
7. Ibid.
8. Ibid.
9. When the covert operation was exposed by Galen and others, Hitler said he was closing T4 down, although it in fact continued alongside the horrors of the Holocaust. It is estimated that the number killed throughout the full span of T4 was around two hundred thousand.
10. Hanser, *A Noble Treason.*
11. Ottaway, *Hitler's Traitors.*
12. Philipp von Boeselager, *Valkyrie: The Plot to Kill Hitler* (London: Weidenfeld & Nicolson, 2009).
13. Hanser, *A Noble Treason.*
14. Ottaway, *Hitler's Traitors.*
15. Hanser, *A Noble Treason.*
16. I. Scholl, *The White Rose.*
17. Sophie Scholl to Fritz Hartnagel, May 29, 1940.
18. Sophie Scholl to Fritz Hartnagel, September 23, 1940.
19. Hermann Vinke, *The Short Life of Sophie Scholl* (New York: Harper & Row, 1984).
20. Moorhouse, *Berlin at War.*
21. Henry Flannery, *Assignment to Berlin* (London: Michael Joseph Ltd., 1942).
22. Sophie Scholl to Lisa Remppis, August 11, 1941.
23. Sophie Scholl to Hans Scholl, June 23, 1941.
24. Hanser, *A Noble Treason.*
25. McDonough, *Sophie Scholl.*
26. Hanser, *A Noble Treason.*
27. Ibid.
28. Ibid.
29. The words are from his diary, *Journal in the Night,* and are quoted in Dumbach and Newborn, *Sophie Scholl and the White Rose.*
30. Hanser, *A Noble Treason.*

31. Ibid.
32. Joffroy, *A Spy for God.*
33. Ibid.
34. Friedländer, *Counterfeit Nazi.*
35. Joffroy, *A Spy for God.*
36. Ibid.
37. Friedländer, *Counterfeit Nazi.*

## CHAPTER 16: Dangerous to Know

1. Jewish Women's Archive.
2. Cox, "The Herbert Baum Groups."
3. Barbara Appelbaum, "Ellen and Erich Arndt," Rochester Holocaust Survivors Archive.
4. Jewish Women's Archive.
5. Brothers, *Berlin Ghetto.*
6. Gross, *The Last Jews in Berlin.*
7. Ber Mark, "The Herbert Baum Group," in *They Fought Back*, ed. Yuri Suhl (New York: Crown Publishers, 1967).
8. Marion Kaplan, *Between Dignity and Despair: Jewish Life in Nazi Germany* (Oxford University Press, 1998).
9. Holocaust Memorial Center, Farmington Hills, MI (holocaustcenter.org).
10. Based on a study by Wolfgang Benz, Center for Anti-Semitism Studies, Berlin, as described by Peter Schneider, "Saving Konrad Latte," *New York Times Magazine*, February 13, 2000.
11. Brothers, *Berlin Ghetto.*
12. Bernt Engelmann, *In Hitler's Germany* (London: Methuen, 1989).
13. Brothers, *Berlin Ghetto.*

## CHAPTER 17: Operation 7

1. Bonhoeffer crossed the Swiss border on February 24, 1941.
2. Wind, *A Spoke in the Wheel.*
3. Sir Frank Roberts quoted in Andrew Roberts, *Hitler & Churchill: Secrets of Leadership* (London: Weidenfeld & Nicolson, 2003).
4. Metaxas, *Bonhoeffer.*
5. Andrew Chandler, *George Bell, Bishop of Chichester* (Grand Rapids, MI: William B. Eerdmans Publishing Company, 2016).
6. Now in modern-day Poland.
7. Ger van Roon, *German Resistance to Hitler: Count von Moltke and the Kreisau Circle* (London: Van Nostrand Reinhold Company, 1971).
8. Metaxas, *Bonhoeffer.*
9. Roon, *German Resistance to Hitler.*
10. Metaxas, *Bonhoeffer.*
11. Yehuda Bauer, *Jews for Sale?* (New Haven, CT: Yale University Press, 2009).
12. The operation is sometimes called V7.
13. Some sources give this figure as fifteen, but we have used the number recorded by Yad Vashem.

## CHAPTER 18: Tresckow

1. Moorhouse, *Killing Hitler*.
2. Boeselager, *Valkyrie: The Plot to Kill Hitler*.
3. Borisov is now known by its Belorussian name, Barysaw.
4. Leonid Smilovitsky, "Ilya Ehrenburg on the Holocaust in Belarus," Belarus SIG, October 2002. First published in *East European Jewish Affairs* (London), Summer–Winter 1999. jewishgen.org/Belarus/newsletters/misc/IlyaEhrenburg/index .html.
5. Hoffmann, in *The History of the German Resistance*, reports that not all senior army officers agreed: Colonel-General Busch, of Army Group North, heard about the murder of Jews in Kovno and dismissed them as "political matters which don't interest us, or rather they interest us but we shouldn't do anything. These things don't concern us."
6. Gisevius, *Valkyrie: An Insider's Account*.
7. Moorhouse, *Killing Hitler*.
8. Boeselager, *Valkyrie: The Plot to Kill Hitler*.

## CHAPTER 19: Questions for the Abwehr

1. Höhne, *Canaris*.
2. Ibid.

## CHAPTER 20: Rote Kapelle

1. Höhne, *Codeword: Direktor*.
2. Ibid.
3. Brysac, *Resisting Hitler*.
4. Liane's is one of the heartbreaking photographs that is today on display at the Plötzensee Memorial Center.
5. Nelson, *Red Orchestra*.

## CHAPTER 21: Fire in Berlin

1. Brothers, *Berlin Ghetto*.
2. Ibid.
3. Ibid.
4. Ibid.
5. *Das Reich*, May 17, 1942; Helmut Heiber, *Goebbels* (New York: Hawthorn Books, 1972).
6. Appelbaum, "Ellen and Erich Arndt."
7. Heiber, *Goebbels*.

## CHAPTER 22: A Student in Munich

1. Hanser, *A Noble Treason*.
2. Interrogation of Alexander Schmorell, February 26, 1943.
3. Fourth interrogation of Hans Scholl, February 20, 1943.
4. Interrogation of Traute Lafrenz, February 26, 1943.

5. Fourth interrogation of Hans Scholl, February 20, 1943.
6. Ottaway, *Hitler's Traitors.*
7. Ibid.
8. Fourth interrogation of Hans Scholl, February 20, 1943.
9. Hanser, *A Noble Treason.*
10. Fourth interrogation of Hans Scholl, February 20, 1943.
11. Dumbach and Newborn, *Sophie Scholl and the White Rose.*
12. Hanser, *A Noble Treason.*
13. Dumbach and Newborn, *Sophie Scholl and the White Rose.*
14. Hanser, *A Noble Treason.*
15. McDonough, *Sophie Scholl.*
16. Sophie Scholl to Fritz Hartnagel, November 7, 1942.
17. McDonough, *Sophie Scholl.*

## CHAPTER 23: An Order for Gerstein

1. Joffroy, *A Spy for God.*
2. Hermann Rauschning, *Hitler Speaks* (London: Thornton Butterworth, 1939). After the war the book was adjudged to have been, at least in part, made up—but it had served a propaganda purpose during the war.
3. Franz, *Kurt Gerstein.*
4. Joffroy, *A Spy for God.*
5. Ibid.
6. Franz, *Kurt Gerstein.*
7. Mark Roseman, *The Villa, the Lake, the Meeting* (London: Penguin Books, 2003).
8. Ibid.
9. A stenotypist took the minutes in shorthand, but these were later lost or destroyed. Details on the conference are based on notes taken by Adolf Eichmann.
10. Roseman, *The Villa, the Lake, the Meeting.*
11. Joffroy, *A Spy for God.*
12. Joseph Borkin, *The Crime and Punishment of I. G. Farben* (London: André Deutsch, 1979).
13. Kershaw, *Hitler.*
14. Martin Gilbert, *Atlas of the Holocaust* (London: Michael Joseph Ltd, 1982).
15. This was Josef Oberhauser, who was imprisoned for eight years by the Soviets after the war. He was later tried in the West and in 1965 was found guilty of being an accessory to three hundred thousand murders. Jailed for four and a half years, he served just half of his sentence. He died in 1979. He was the only person ever successfully convicted of crimes committed at Belzec.
16. Gerstein's memories are based on two reports that he wrote in French (a handwritten and typed-up version) on April 26, 1945, and a third version typed in German on May 4, 1945. All were prepared while in Allied custody.
17. Recent research suggests that although Gerstein referred to this as a diesel engine exhaust, it most likely ran off gasoline. According to the Holocaust Denial on Trial website, Rudolf Reder, one of only two Jewish survivors from Belzec, made a statement in 1944 to the Central Commission for Investigation of German Crimes in Poland. The website states: "He described the engine as a 'motor pedzony benzyna [gasoline-powered motor].' Reder also said that he carried 4 to 5 cans of petrol (gas) (kanistry benzyny) every day to the motor room of the gas chambers. Reder

used the Polish word for gasoline (benzyny/benzyna) not diesel, which is 'olej napedowy.'"

## CHAPTER 24: Belzec

1. Henri Roques, "The 'Confessions' of Kurt Gerstein," Institute for Historical Review, 1989, pp. 40–43. archive.org/stream/TheConfessionsofKurtGerstein/Confessions_of_Kurt_Gerstein_djvu.txt.
2. Testimony of prisoner Rudolf Reder, Holocaust Denial on Trial.
3. United States Holocaust Memorial Museum.
4. Lorenz Hackenholt was another veteran of the T4 program. He disappeared at the end of the war and was declared legally dead, although a man who served with him claimed he survived and lived under a false identity. His name is sometimes misspelled "Heckenholt."
5. Roques, "Confessions."
6. In his deposition (August 7, 1946) to the Nuremberg trials, former SS judge Konrad Morgen described a depot at Lublin where Wirth stored the items he had taken from his victims. It included a "huge pile of watches" and a "great many precious things." Morgen noted: "I have never in my life seen so much money, particularly foreign money, currency from all over the world. On top of all this there was gold melted down into ingots, great bars." See Joffroy, *A Spy for God*.
7. Gilbert, *Atlas of the Holocaust*.
8. Gerstein reported that there were eight, but some of these did not become operational until five weeks after his visit. He almost certainly was told about the new facility and confused it in his report. One can only imagine the state of his mind when he saw what was happening in the death camps and later, too, when he was writing the report. His inconsistency has been pounced upon by Holocaust deniers. As Holocaust Denial on Trial has noted, his "confusion does not negate his consistent description of the overall gas chamber buildings and the mass murder at Belzec and Treblinka."
9. Gilbert, *Atlas of the Holocaust*.
10. Friedländer, *Counterfeit Nazi*.
11. Louis Bülow, "Gerstein," The Holocaust: Crimes, Heroes and Villains, auschwitz.dk /gerstein.htm. Historian and Holocaust survivor Saul Friedländer also confirmed this meeting by uncovering a letter from the Swedish Ministry of Affairs to the Jewish Documentation Center in Paris, dated November 10, 1949.
12. Joffroy, *A Spy for God*.
13. Roques, "Confessions." In April 1942 the GRC had told the International Committee of the Red Cross (ICRC) in Geneva that it would not communicate any information on "non-Aryan" detainees, and asked it to refrain from asking questions about them. Failure to pursue this further remains a matter of regret for the ICRC to this day.
14. In his report Gerstein stated: "I tried to report to the Papal Nuncio in Berlin. There I was asked if I am a soldier. Then any further conversation with me was refused and I was asked to leave the embassy of His Holiness." Horst Dickten told Pierre Joffroy in 1968 that Gerstein had been clear to him that he had seen Cesare Orsenigo *in person* and that Orsenigo had driven him away, although this was disputed by the Catholic Church.
15. Richard Breitman, *Official Secrets: What the Nazis Planned, What the British and Americans Knew* (London: Penguin Group, 1998).

16. Friedländer, *Counterfeit Nazi*.
17. Armin Peters and Pastor Kurt Rehling quoted in Joffroy, *A Spy for God*.
18. Deposition by Elfriede Gerstein for the trial of Adolf Eichmann, February 16, 1961.
19. Based on what he had seen and the boasts of Odilo Globocnik, Gerstein had mistakenly estimated the total numbers being killed as in excess of twenty million.
20. Borkin, *The Crime and Punishment of I. G. Farben*.

## CHAPTER 25: The Hunted

1. Wesse's husband, Richard, was also arrested but later released. He became part of the forced-labor workforce at Siemens.
2. Brothers, *Berlin Ghetto*.
3. Ibid.
4. *Die Tagebücher von Joseph Goebbels,* ed. Elke Fröhlich (Munich: KG Saur, 1995).
5. Ibid.
6. Mark, "The Herbert Baum Group."
7. Ibid.
8. Hoffmann, *The History of the German Resistance*.
9. McDonough, *The Gestapo*.
10. Hoffmann, *The History of the German Resistance*.
11. Brothers, *Berlin Ghetto*.
12. Plötzensee Memorial Center.
13. Rita Zocher testimony (item number 3558251), Yad Vashem, the World Holocaust Memorial Center, Israel. Rita was an old friend of the Baum group who had hosted many of the discussion evenings at which early resistance was planned.
14. The Kummersdorf base was actually a weapons-testing establishment where rockets and tanks had been developed, and where some research for the Nazis' atomic weapons program was carried out.
15. Brothers, *Berlin Ghetto*.
16. Ibid.
17. Mark, "The Herbert Baum Group."
18. Ibid.
19. Rappaport, *Beyond Courage*.
20. Colin Pateman, *Beheaded by Hitler* (Stroud: UK Fonthill, 2014).

## CHAPTER 26: Hitler's Bloodhound

1. Höhne, *Codeword: Direktor*.
2. Brysac, *Resisting Hitler*.
3. Ibid.
4. Ibid.
5. Höhne, *Codeword: Direktor*.
6. Nelson, *Red Orchestra*.
7. Brysac, *Resisting Hitler*.
8. Höhne, *Codeword: Direktor*.
9. Ibid.
10. Ibid.
11. Brysac, *Resisting Hitler*.
12. Recollection of Falk Harnack. Quoted in Brysac, *Resisting Hitler*.

13. Höhne, *Codeword: Direktor.*
14. Brysac, *Resisting Hitler.*
15. Gedenkstätte Deutscher Widerstand.
16. Höhne, *Codeword: Direktor.*
17. Vötter, Illgen, and another friend of Joachim Franke's, Werner Schaumann, were executed on May 11, 1943. They had been betrayed by their friend. Eric Brothers suggests Franke may have turned them in in order to save his wife, Erika, who escaped execution. He might also have betrayed two others as part of the same deal with the Gestapo: Walter Bernecker, who died in Gestapo custody before he could be tried, and Karl Kunger, who was executed on June 18, 1943.
18. Cox, "The Herbert Baum Groups."
19. Plötzensee Memorial Center.

## CHAPTER 27: White Rose: The Harnack Connection

1. Graf, quoted in Hanser, *A Noble Treason.*
2. Werth, *Russia at War.*
3. Hanser, *A Noble Treason.*
4. Ibid.
5. Ibid.
6. The man's name was Michael Kitzelmann. According to Richard Hanser, the words that got him shot were "If these criminals should win, then I would have no wish to live any longer."
7. Toby Axelrod, *Hans and Sophie Scholl* (New York: Rosen Publishing Group, 2001).
8. Third leaflet of the White Rose.
9. In his last letter to his family before his execution, Arvid Harnack had talked of his "special joy" at the news that Falk and Lilo planned to get engaged, and he left a signet ring, which had belonged to his father, to her. Brysac, *Resisting Hitler.*
10. The Gestapo indictment of Harnack, dated April 8, 1943, said the Chemnitz meeting between Harnack, Scholl, and Schmorell took place "around January 1943." However, extensive research by the White Rose History website has shown this to be incorrect. The meeting took place during November 1942.
11. Peukert quotes a Hitler Youth report from February 1940 in which five hundred to six hundred people were seen to attend a swing festival featuring singing "in broken English," "jitterbugging," and boys "dancing together."
12. Hanser, *A Noble Treason.*
13. Ibid.
14. The Bollingers are sometimes listed as twins, although they were not. Heinz was born in 1916, while Willi was born in 1919.
15. Dumbach and Newborn, *Sophie Scholl and the White Rose.*
16. Hanser, *A Noble Treason.*
17. Hans Scholl to Otl Aicher, January 12, 1943.
18. First interrogation of Kurt Huber, February 27, 1943.
19. In Huber's initial interrogation by the Gestapo on February 27, 1943, he stated that after he left the meeting, he "then heard nothing further about that draft, not even whether the draft had been used as a leaflet. A lot later, Scholl told me that in his opinion, a new leaflet they had written had not met with much success. He did not, however, tell me about the text of the leaflet."

20. Hanser has written that this concluding paragraph has "the ring of a passage from the United Nations Charter, two and a half years before the charter's existence."
21. Ottaway, *Hitler's Traitors.*
22. Dumbach and Newborn, *Sophie Scholl and the White Rose.*
23. Hanser, *A Noble Treason.*
24. The best estimate is that she posted 250 to local people in Augsburg and up to 700 in several postboxes in Stuttgart.

## CHAPTER 28: Swift Arrests Demanded

1. Dumbach and Newborn, *Sophie Scholl and the White Rose.*
2. Stargardt, *The German War.*
3. Dumbach and Newborn, *Sophie Scholl and the White Rose.*
4. McDonough, *Sophie Scholl.*

## CHAPTER 29: Long Live Freedom

1. Jakob Schmid's statement to the Gestapo, February 18, 1943.
2. Ibid.
3. Ibid.
4. Schäfer's report to Reich Security, Berlin, February 11, 1943.
5. Gestapo agent Achter's report, February 18, 1943. Metternich was released later that day.
6. Dumbach and Newborn, *Sophie Scholl and the White Rose.*
7. Fourth interrogation of Willi Graf, February 26, 1943.
8. Moorhouse, *Berlin at War.*
9. Stargardt, *The German War.*
10. Heiber, *Goebbels.*
11. *Die Tagebücher von Joseph Goebbels.*
12. Heiber, *Goebbels.*
13. Moorhouse, *Berlin at War.*
14. Record of Sophie Scholl's first interview, February 18, 1943.
15. Ibid.
16. Ibid.
17. First interrogation of Gisela Schertling, February 18, 1943.
18. Second interrogation of Hans Scholl, February 18, 1943.
19. Ibid.
20. McDonough, *Sophie Scholl.*
21. Second interrogation of Sophie Scholl, February 19, 1943.
22. Anneliese Graf had been arrested purely in association with her brother. She never stood trial but worked hard after the war to tell the story of the White Rose.
23. Gestapo "list of suspects," February 19, 1943.
24. Giesler memorandum to Martin Bormann, February 19, 1943.
25. According to a note added to the Bormann memo on Giesler's behalf.
26. Dumbach and Newborn, *Sophie Scholl and the White Rose.*
27. Third interrogation of Sophie Scholl, February 20, 1942.
28. Quoted in Dumbach and Newborn, *Sophie Scholl and the White Rose*, and based on the postwar recollections of Else Gebel.
29. I. Scholl, *The White Rose.*

30. Ibid.
31. Handwritten trial transcript, February 22, 1943.
32. Ibid.
33. I. Scholl, *The White Rose.*
34. Handwritten trial transcript, February 22, 1943.
35. Words remembered by Robert Mohr, who was in the courtroom. McDonough, *Sophie Scholl.*
36. Dumbach and Newborn, *Sophie Scholl and the White Rose.*
37. Handwritten trial transcript, February 22, 1943.
38. I. Scholl, *The White Rose.*
39. McDonough, *Sophie Scholl.*
40. I. Scholl, *The White Rose.*
41. Ibid.
42. Ibid.
43. Reichhart's name is sometimes spelled "Reichart." We have used the spelling in the execution records.
44. Reichhart carried out 3,165 executions in total. After the war he executed a number of Nazi war criminals on behalf of the Americans at Landsberg prison. He died peacefully in 1972.
45. Execution record, Sophie Scholl, February 22, 1943.
46. Execution record, Hans Scholl, February 22, 1943.
47. Execution record, Christoph Probst, February 22, 1943.

## CHAPTER 30: On the Run

1. Second interrogation of Alexander Schmorell, February 26, 1943.
2. Dumbach and Newborn, *Sophie Scholl and the White Rose.*
3. Allan Hall, "Nazis slaughtered my brother and sister with a guillotine," *Daily Mail,* January 18, 2014.
4. Dumbach and Newborn, *Sophie Scholl and the White Rose.*
5. *The White Rose, Exhibition on the Student Resistance Against Hitler* (Munich: Weisse Rose Stiftung, 2006).
6. At a later trial, the Munich bookstore owner Josef Söhngen was convicted of failing to report treasonous activity and was sentenced to six months in jail. Manfred Eickemeyer, whose studio had been used as a base for some White Rose activities, persuaded the judge he had been in his Poland office the whole time, and was acquitted.
7. White Rose History: January 1933–October 1943 (whiterosehistory.com). Sentencing remarks taken from the verdict of the second White Rose trial.
8. Himmler was responding to a clemency petition by members of Schmorell's brother-in-law's family. He replied on April 11, 1943, and although he refers to the death sentence, this had not yet been decided by the court. Another indication that the court proceedings were a sham.
9. Dumbach and Newborn, *Sophie Scholl and the White Rose.*
10. Ibid.
11. *The White Rose, Exhibition on the Student Resistance Against Hitler.*
12. Seventh interrogation of Willi Graf, March 2, 1943.
13. Dumbach and Newborn, *Sophie Scholl and the White Rose.*
14. *New York Times*, April 18, 1943.

15. Names written as they appeared in the *New York Times*, August 2, 1943.
16. Gedenkstätte Deutscher Widerstand.
17. Roon, *German Resistance to Hitler*.
18. The Gedenkstätte Deutscher Widerstand estimates that "several million" of the leaflets were dropped, all with the headings "A German leaflet" and "Manifesto of Munich Students."
19. Dumbach and Newborn, *Sophie Scholl and the White Rose*.

## CHAPTER 31: Mr. Douglas and Mr. Wood

1. Greg Bradsher, "A Time to Act," *Prologue* (US National Archives), Spring 2002.
2. Lucas Delattre, *Betraying Hitler* (London: Atlantic Books, 2005).
3. Hoffmann, *The History of the German Resistance*.
4. James Srodes, *Allen Dulles: Master of Spies* (Washington, DC: Regnery Publishing, 1999).
5. Telegram from Allen W. Dulles to OSS Washington, sent January 13, 1943, receipt acknowledged January 16 (NA, RG 226, Entry 134, Box 307).
6. Bancroft and Gisevius worked for almost a year on the manuscript. It was later published as *To the Bitter End*.
7. Persico, *Piercing the Reich*.
8. Dulles's notes quoted in Srodes, *Allen Dulles*.
9. Persico, *Piercing the Reich*.
10. Höhne, *Canaris*.
11. Hoffmann, *The History of the German Resistance*.
12. Persico, *Piercing the Reich*.
13. Srodes, *Allen Dulles*.
14. Delattre, *Betraying Hitler*.
15. Ibid.
16. Ibid.
17. Ibid.
18. Ibid.
19. Persico, *Piercing the Reich*.
20. Stung by Dulles's scoop, the British Secret Intelligence Service continued to insist that Kolbe was a Nazi agent. It took some time for them to admit that through their breaking of the German code they had confirmed Kolbe's information as authentic. A memo prepared for General Donovan on October 12, 1943, stated: "Both the material and the source had stood the test and are thought to be of great value." Quoted in John Waller, *The Unseen War in Europe* (New York: Random House, 1996).
21. The name appears to have been randomly chosen, although former lawyer Dulles might have used it in reference to a celebrated nineteenth-century New York lawyer of the same name.
22. Delattre, *Betraying Hitler*.

## CHAPTER 32: The Brandy Bomb

1. When the war turned and the Allies invaded France, Hitler opened another headquarters near Soissons and called it Wolfsschlucht II, but he used it only once.
2. Hoffmann, *The History of the German Resistance*.

3. Moorhouse, *Killing Hitler.*
4. It still stands and now houses the German Historical Museum.
5. Wind, *A Spoke in the Wheel.*
6. Gersdorff was one of a tiny number of conspirators to survive the war. He later said his attempts to rejoin the West German army after the war were blocked by officers who did not want a "traitor" in their midst. He died in 1980, aged seventy-four.
7. Höhne, *Canaris.*
8. Ibid.

## CHAPTER 33: The "Z Grau" File

1. Höhne, *Canaris.*
2. Ibid.
3. Ibid.
4. *The Ulrich von Hassell Diaries.*
5. Metaxas, *Bonhoeffer.*
6. Ibid.
7. Ibid.
8. Dietrich Bonhoeffer and Maria von Wedemeyer, *Love Letters from Cell 92: The Correspondence Between Dietrich Bonhoeffer and Maria von Wedemeyer, 1943–45,* eds. Ruth-Alice von Bismarck and Ulrich Kabitz (New York: Abingdon Press, 1995).
9. Bonhoeffer and Wedemeyer, *Love Letters from Cell 92.*
10. Dietrich Bonhoeffer to Eberhard Bethge, December 22, 1943. Eberhard Bethge, *Bonhoeffer: An Illustrated Biography* (London: Harper Collins, 1979).
11. Persico, *Piercing the Reich.*
12. Höhne, *Canaris.*
13. All those arrested as part of the Gestapo's operation against the Solf Circle were executed, with the exception of Hanna Solf and her daughter, Countess Ballestrem, whose death sentences were deferred after an appeal by the Japanese ambassador to Germany. (The late Dr. Solf was still fondly remembered by the Japanese government.) By the end of the war mother and daughter had spent time in Moabit prison, Ravensbrück, and Sachsenhausen. Hannah Solf died in 1954, aged sixty-six. Her daughter died a year later, aged forty-six.

## CHAPTER 34: Unmasking Cicero

1. Srodes, *Allen Dulles.*
2. Persico, *Piercing the Reich.*
3. Srodes, *Allen Dulles.*
4. Delattre, *Betraying Hitler.*
5. Bazna's father had not been killed by the British. He had died peacefully in bed.
6. Walter Schellenberg, *The Memoirs of Hitler's Spymaster* (London: André Deutsch, 2006).
7. Schellenberg, *The Memoirs of Hitler's Spymaster.*
8. Ibid.
9. Ibid.
10. In September 1944 the Nazi authorities became so perturbed by the number of death notices containing subtle criticisms of the regime that they abolished

personalized messages and only the words "Für Führer, Volk und Reich"—"For Führer, People and Empire"—could be used. Moorhouse, *Berlin at War.*

11. Srodes, *Allen Dulles.*
12. Dulles telegram sent December 29, 1943. Waller, *The Unseen War in Europe.*
13. Srodes, *Allen Dulles.*
14. Delattre, *Betraying Hitler.*
15. After the war he tried to buy a hotel with the notes that the Germans had paid him, only to discover it was fake money produced during a counterfeit operation.
16. Moorhouse, *Berlin at War.*
17. Moorhouse quotes Berlin resident Hans Liebig: "You can hardly breathe in the city for smoke. When the sun came out on Wednesday, you just couldn't see it. We had to have a light on all day as the sky was a dirty yellow. You can't imagine it unless you have experienced it for yourself."

## CHAPTER 35: Enter Stauffenberg

1. Hoffmann, *The History of the German Resistance.*
2. Moorhouse, *Killing Hitler.*

## CHAPTER 36: Valkyrie

1. Walter Goerlitz, *History of the German General Staff, 1657–1945* (New York: Praeger Publishers, 1953).
2. Hoffmann, *The History of the German Resistance.*
3. Ibid.
4. Ibid.
5. Hans Mommsen, *Germans Against Hitler* (New York: IB Taurus & Co., 2003).
6. Telegram received 0:58 a.m., July 14, 1944 (NA, RG 226, Entry 146).
7. Metaxas, *Bonhoeffer.*
8. Leber was hanged in January 1945; Reichwein was executed in October 1944.
9. Pierre Galante, *Hitler Lives—and the Generals Die* (London: Sidgwick & Jackson, 1982).
10. Hoffmann, *The History of the German Resistance.*
11. It is impossible to be sure where the actual explosives used in the Stauffenberg bomb came from. A great number of conspirators had been involved in procuring explosives, including Philipp von Boeselager, Schlabrendorff, Gersdorff, and Werner Schrader, but Peter Hoffmann believes the July 20 bomb might actually have been newly developed German plastic explosives made by WASAG Chemicals and procured for the conspiracy by Arthur Nebe, director of the Reich Criminal Police Office.
12. Moorhouse, *Killing Hitler.*

## CHAPTER 37: Valkyrie Unravels

1. Hoffmann, *The History of the German Resistance.*
2. Kershaw, *Hitler.*
3. Rundstedt had incurred the wrath of Hitler and Keitel soon after D-Day when he replied, on being asked on the telephone from East Prussia what they should do now the invasion was here: "End the war, what else can you do?"

4. Hoffmann, *The History of the German Resistance.*
5. Ibid.
6. Ibid.
7. Evidence of Luftwaffe officer Friedrich Georgi. Quoted in Johannes Steinhoff, Peter Pechel, and Dennis Showalter, *Voices from the Third Reich* (Boston: Da Capo Press, 1994).
8. Höhne, *Canaris.*
9. Berthold von Stauffenberg and Fritz-Dietlof Graf von der Schulenburg were executed on August 10, 1944. Yorck von Wartenburg was executed in September 1944. Gerstenmaier was jailed and later released by the Allies. After the war he became a West German politician.
10. Sometimes, as in Walter Goerlitz's book *History of the German General Staff*, translated as "Long live free Germany!"
11. Mommsen, *Germans Against Hitler.*
12. Boeselager, *Valkyrie: The Plot to Kill Hitler.*

## CHAPTER 38: Sonderkommission 20 Juli

1. Kershaw, *Hitler.*
2. A figure as high as seven thousand is sometimes given for the number of arrests following the plot, but these include a Gestapo crackdown on ex-parliamentary deputies and officials of old political parties that was planned before July 20.
3. Fest, *Hitler.*
4. Hoffmann, *The History of the German Resistance.*
5. Kleist-Schmenzin, who was arrested the day after the bomb plot, was not tried until February 1945. He was executed on April 9, 1945. Hans-Bernd von Haeften was hanged at Plötzensee on August 15, 1944.
6. Nebe's part in the conspiracy had been motivated not by compassion or ideology, but by a belief that with the war all but lost, it was better to be a part of the resistance. A virulent anti-Semite, he had been an enthusiastic Nazi, linked to Einsatzgruppen killings and the murders of prisoners of war who had taken part in the "Great Escape" from Stalag Luft III.
7. Heiber, *Goebbels.*
8. From Kaltenbrunner's report to Bormann, November 29, 1944. Quoted in Höhne, *Canaris.*
9. Schellenberg, *The Memoirs of Hitler's Spymaster.*
10. Ibid.
11. Only Schmidhuber and Ickrath had officially been sentenced after Roeder's inquiry, having received four years and two years respectively for currency offenses and tax evasion.
12. Höhne, *Canaris.*
13. Pfuhlstein survived the war and later said that he only told the Gestapo what they already knew.
14. Höhne, *Canaris.*
15. The corporal's name is spelled "Knoblock" by some sources.
16. Tragically, that conversation became a source of deep regret for Ursula when much later she heard how Klaus had been tortured before his execution.
17. Höhne, *Canaris.*
18. Parssinen, *The Oster Conspiracy.*

# CHAPTER 39: Gotterdämmerung

1. Captain S. Payne Best, *The Venlo Incident* (New York: Skyhorse Publishing, 2016).
2. Bethge, *Bonhoeffer: An Illustrated Biography.*
3. Kögl went on the run after the war but was quickly captured. He committed suicide while in custody. Huppenkothen and Thorbeck were eventually tried in 1955 for their parts in the sham trials of Canaris and the others. They received seven and four years' penal servitude respectively. The only record of the Flossenbürg trials comes from their own recollections of events given at their trials.
4. Höhne, *Canaris.*
5. Ibid.
6. Metaxas, *Bonhoeffer.*
7. Höhne, *Canaris.*
8. After the war Mrugowsky was convicted of crimes against humanity and was executed on June 2, 1948. Pfannenstiel was captured by the Americans but released through lack of evidence.
9. Joffroy, *A Spy for God.*
10. "Le dossier Gerstein," *Le Monde juif,* 1964.
11. Elfriede Gerstein deposition, February 1961.
12. Franz, *Kurt Gerstein.*
13. Deposition by John W. Haught, January 30, 1961, Archives of the Israeli Police. Friedländer, *Counterfeit Nazi.*
14. It was the copy of his report that Gerstein had given to Major Evans that eventually reached the International Military Tribunal in Nuremberg. Some who have questioned details of the Holocaust have stated that the report was rejected by the court. It was in fact read into the record—by British deputy chief prosecutor Sir David Maxwell Fyfe—on the afternoon of January 30, 1946. It was "verified . . . and accepted." It was registered as document PS-1553.
15. Kurt Gerstein to Elfriede Gerstein, May 26, 1945. Friedländer, *Counterfeit Nazi.*
16. Joffroy, *A Spy for God.*
17. The section of the cemetery in which Gerstein was buried was later flattened, and no record remains of the exact location of his grave.
18. Maria von Wedemeyer moved to the United States after the war and followed her dream of becoming a mathematician. She went on to head a department at Honeywell in Boston. She died of cancer in 1977, aged fifty-three. *New York Times,* November 17, 1977.
19. Bonhoeffer and Wedemeyer, *Love Letters from Cell 92.*
20. Gedenkstätte Deutscher Widerstand.
21. Tresckow's two young daughters, Uta and Adelheid, were among those who survived. His two sons fought at the front. One, Mark, was killed in action near the end of the war, aged just seventeen. Gedenkstätte Deutscher Widerstand.

# AFTERWORD

1. Theodor Haecker, *Journal in the Night* (New York: Harvill Press, 1950).
2. A letter from the Falk Harnack Collection, Gedenkstätte Deutscher Widerstand.
3. Brysac, *Resisting Hitler.*
4. Ibid.
5. Boveri, *Treason in the Twentieth Century.*

6. Nelson, *Red Orchestra.*

7. Ottaway, *Hitler's Traitors.*

8. Breitman, *Official Secrets.*

9. Nelson, *Red Orchestra.*

10. Ibid.

11. Professor Wieland showed great courage in speaking up for Leipelt during his trial. As he took the dock as a witness for the defense, he refused to give the Nazi salute as demanded by the court. *The White Rose, Exhibition on the Student Resistance Against Hitler.*

12. Ottaway, *Hitler's Traitors.*

13. I. Scholl, *The White Rose.*

14. Yad Vashem.

15. Laurence Rees, *Auschwitz: The Nazis & the 'Final Solution'* (London: BBC Books, 2005).

16. Jonathan Harrison, Roberto Muehlenkamp, Jason Myers, Sergey Romanov, and Nicholas Terry, "Belzec, Sobibor, Treblinka: Holocaust Denial and Operation Reinhard. A Critique of the Falsehoods of Mattogno, Graf and Kues," Holocaust Controversies, December 2011, holocaustcontroversies.blogspot.co.uk/2011/12/belzec-sobibor-treblinka-holocaust.html.

17. Friedländer, *Counterfeit Nazi.*

18. Ibid.

19. Ottaway, *Hitler's Traitors.*

20. Friedländer, *Counterfeit Nazi.*

21. Verdict of the Tübingen denazification court, August 17, 1950.

22. Jewish Women's Archive.

23. Charlotte Holzer testimony (item number 3549543), Yad Vashem. Testimony given in East Berlin, 1964.

24. In Hungary Holzer had been used as forced labor by the authorities, who fortunately discovered nothing about his links to the resistance in Berlin. He was captured by the Soviets at the end of the war but managed to prove his identity as a Jewish antifascist and returned to Germany. Jewish Women's Archive.

25. Jewish Women's Archive.

26. Ibid.

27. Ibid.

28. Remembered by Ellen Compart, who worked with Hella at IG Farben. Taken from her deposition, quoted in Brothers, *Berlin Ghetto.*

29. The Baum group can be seen as one of the most powerful examples of German Jewish resistance, but others warrant mention. Werner Witebski, Max Zimmering, and Hans Dankner opposed the Nazis in Dresden and Yitzchok Gersht in Wuppertal. Resistance and dissent inside Dachau was led by Heinz Heshen and lawyer Hans Litten, who received years of mistreatment in revenge for having called Hitler as a witness in the 1931 trial of four SA men who had stabbed two workers. Litten committed suicide in 1938. Also at Dachau, Rudi Arndt helped obtain medicines and food for sick prisoners and paid with his life. In Sachsenhausen, Sala Lerner and Fried Gersht led the Jewish efforts to rebel, while in the women's camp at Ravensbrück rebellion focused on Olga Benario and Charlotte Eisenbletter, a leading member of Robert Uhrig's resistance group. We can know little of their actions, but it is fitting that their names are recorded here.

30. "Donald R. Heath, 87; Served as a U.S. Envoy," *New York Times*, October 17, 1981.

31. Boeselager, *Valkyrie: The Plot to Kill Hitler.*
32. Gedenkstätte Deutscher Widerstand.
33. Plötzensee Memorial Center.
34. Mommsen, *Germans Against Hitler.*
35. Cox, "The Herbert Baum Groups."
36. Mommsen, *Germans Against Hitler.*
37. Hoffmann, *The History of the German Resistance.*

# INDEX